GREENBERG'S PRICE GUIDE

to LIONEL TRAINS: 1945-1983

by Bruce C. Greenberg, Ph.D.

Edited by Roland LaVoie

Photographs from the Eddins Collection
and by courtesy of Frank Hare, Iron Horse Publications
and Tom McComas of TM Productions

LIONEL IS THE REGISTERED TRADEMARK OF THE LIONEL TOY CORPORATION, NEW YORK, NEW YORK. GREENBERG PUBLISHING COMPANY has no relationship with either The Lionel Toy Corporation or with Fundimensions. This book is neither authorized nor approved by the Lionel Toy Corporation or Fundimensions.

Copyright 1983

Greenberg Publishing Company
Sykesville, MD 21784
301 795-7447

Fourth Edition

Manufactured in the United States of America

All rights reserved. Reproduction in any form is strictly prohibited without the express written consent of the publisher, except for excerpts for review purposes.

Greenberg Publishing Company offers the world's largest selection of Lionel, American Flyer and other toy train publications as well as a selection of books on model and prototype railroading. To receive our current catalogue, send a stamped, self-addressed envelope marked "catalogue."

Greenberg Publishing Company sponsors the world's largest public model railroad shows. The shows feature extravagant operating model railroads for N, H0, 0, Standard and 1 Gauges as well as a huge marketplace for buying and selling nearly all model railroad equipment. The shows feature, as well, a large selection of doll house miniatures.

Shows are currently offered in New York, Philadelphia, Pittsburgh, Baltimore, and Washington, D.C. To receive our current show listing, please send a self-addressed stamped envelope marked "Train Show Schedule."

ISBN: 89778-005-1

Greenberg's Price guide to Lionel trains, 1945-1983.

    Updated ed. of: Greenberg's Price guide to Lionel trains, 1945-1982. 3rd ed. c1982.
       Includes index.z
       1. Railroads—Model. 2. Lionel Corporation.
I. LaVoie, Roland, 1943- . II. Greenberg, Linda.
III. Greenberg, Bruce C. Price guide to Lionel trains, 1945-1982. IV. Title. V. Title: Price guide to Lionel trains, 1945-1983.
TF197.G67   625.1'9   83-16343
ISBN 0-89778-005-1

INTRODUCTION

Greenberg's Price Guide for Lionel Trains, 1945-1983, fourth edition, is our most comprehensive report on the toy train marketplace. The 1983 edition records a very uneven pattern of price changes over the last four years. Many common items have not changed in price, while certain classes of items have enjoyed great popularity and have substantially increased in price. High interest rates led some investors to leave the collector marketplace and have reduced demand in general. At the present time, however, in the fall of 1983, prices are stable.

PURPOSE

The purpose of this book is to provide a comprehensive listing with current prices for Lionel locomotives, rolling stock and accessories, in 0 and 0-27 Gauges, produced from 1945 through the summer of 1983. We include those variations which have been authenticated. In a few cases we ask our readers for further information where information is missing or doubtful. Values are reported for each item where there have been reported sales.

DETERMINING VALUES

Toy train values vary for a number of reasons. First, consider the **relative knowledge** of the buyer and seller. A seller may be unaware that he has a rare variation and sell it for the price of a common piece. Another source of price variation is **short-term fluctuation** which depends on what is being offered at a given train meet on a given day. If four 773s are for sale at a small meet, we would expect that supply would outpace demand and lead to a reduction in price. A related source of variation is the **season** of the year. The train market is slower in the summer and sellers may at this time be more inclined to reduce prices if they really want to move an item. Another important source of price variation is the relative strength of the seller's **desire to sell** and the buyer's **eagerness to buy.** Clearly a seller in economic distress will be more eager to strike a bargain. A final source of variation is **the personalities** of the seller and buyer. Some sellers like to quickly turn over items and, therefore, price their items to move; others seek a higher price and will bring an item to meet after meet until they find a willing buyer.

Train values in this book are based on OBTAINED prices, rather than asking prices, along the East Coast during the summer of 1983. We have chosen East Coast prices since the greatest dollar volume in transactions appears there. The prices reported here represent a "ready sale," or a price perceived as a good value by the buyer. They may sometimes appear lower than those seen on trains at meets for two reasons. First, items that sell, often sell in the first hour of a train meet and, therefore, are no longer visible. (We have observed that a good portion of the action at most meets occurs in the first hour.) The items that do not sell in the first hour have a higher price tag and this price, although not representing the sales price, is the price observed. A related source of discrepancy is the willingness of some sellers to bargain over price.

From our studies of train prices, it appears that mail order prices for used trains are generally higher than those obtained at eastern train meets. This is appropriate considering the costs and efforts of producing and distributing a price list and packing and shipping items. Mail order items do sell at prices above those listed in this book. A final source of difference between observed prices and reported prices is region. Prices are clearly higher in the South and West where trains are less plentiful than along the East Coast.

CONDITION

For each item, we provide four categories: **Good, Very Good, Excellent and Mint.** The Train Collectors Association (TCA) defines conditions as:

FAIR Well-scratched, chipped, dented, rusted or warped

GOOD Scratches, small dents, dirty

VERY GOOD Few scratches, exceptionally clean, no dents or rust

EXCELLENT Minute scratches or nicks, no dents or rust

MINT Brand new, absolutely unmarred, all original and unused, in original box.

In the toy train field there is a great deal of concern with exterior appearance and less concern with operation. If operation is important to you, then ask the seller whether the train runs. If the seller indicates that he does not know whether the equipment operates, you should test it. Most train meets have test track provided for that purpose.

We have included MINT in this edition because of the small but important trade in pre-1970 mint items and the large volume of post-1970 sales. However there is substantial confusion in the minds of both sellers and buyers as to what constitutes "mint" condition. How do we define mint? Among very experienced train enthusiasts, a mint piece means that it is brand new, in its original box, never run, and extremely bright and clean (and the box is, too). An item may have been removed from the box and replaced in it but it should show no evidence of handling. A piece is not mint if it shows any scratches, fingerprints or evidence of discoloration. It is the nature of a market for the seller to see his item in a very positive light and to seek to obtain a mint price for an excellent piece. In contrast, a buyer will see the same item in a less favorable light and will attempt to buy a mint piece for the price of one in excellent condition. It is our responsibility to point out this difference in perspective **and** the difference in value implicit in each perspective, and to then let the buyer and seller settle or negotiate their different perspectives.

We do not show values for Fair or Restored. **Fair** items are valued substantially below Good. We have not included **Restored** because such items are not a significant portion of the market for postwar trains. As a rough guide, however, we expect that Restored items will bring prices equivalent to Good or possibly Very Good.

As we indicated, prices in this book were derived from large train meets or shows. If you have trains to sell and you sell them to a person planning to resell them, you will not obtain the prices reported in this book. Rather, you should expect to achieve about fifty percent of these prices. Basically, for your items to be of interest to a buyer who plans to resell them, he must purchase them for considerably less than the prices listed here.

We receive many inquiries as to whether or not a particular piece is a "good value." This book will help answer that question; but, there is NO substitute for experience in the marketplace. WE STRONGLY RECOMMEND THAT NOVICES DO NOT MAKE MAJOR PURCHASES WITHOUT THE ASSISTANCE OF FRIENDS WHO HAVE EXPERIENCE IN BUYING AND SELLING TRAINS. If you are buying a train and do not know who to ask about its value, look for the people running the meet or show and discuss with them your need for assistance. Usually they can refer you to an experienced collector who will be willing to examine the piece and offer his opinion.

The Lionel collector and operator have several additional sources for toy train information. First there is the companion **Greenberg's Price Guide for Lionel Trains** manufactured before World War II. It presents a comprehensive listing of Lionel 0 and 0-27 from their beginnings in 1915 through 1942, of Standard, from its beginning in 1906 through 1940 when production ceased, and of Lionel 2-7/8 gauge from 1901-1906. A new edition will be published in late 1983.

Tom McComas has written and published several handsome books on prewar and postwar Lionel trains. **Lionel: A Collector's Guide:** Volume IV, Fundimensions; V, Archives; and VI Art and Advertising. All are well written, handsomely illustrated and informative.

There are several other volumes of interest to the Lionel enthusiast. Between 1946 and 1966 Lionel issued hundreds of pages of service and instruction sheets for its dealers. These have been skillfully edited and organized into **Greenberg's Repair and Operating Manual for Lionel Trains.** This manual is the ultimate operator's guide. It helps him solve most operating problems; problems often due to design limitations. This book also discribes the development of Lionel trains. In addition we offer **Plasticville: An Illustrated Price Guide** which provides a comprehensive photographic record with current prices. These books are available directly from Greenberg Publishing Company or from your local book or hobby store.

ACKNOWLEDGEMENTS

Roland LaVoie, editor of the 1983-84 Greenberg Guide, thanks in particular **Joe Gordon** of the Toy Train Station, Feasterville, Pennsylvania, for information about 6454 and 3464 box cars, the TCA cars and the billboards and their continuing editorial encouragement. He also thanks **Lou Caponi** of Nicholas Smith Trains, Havertown, Pennsylvania, for generously sharing information about 1983 Fundimensions production and current market values.

The following people were especially helpful in creating the 1983-84 Guide: **Roger Bartelt**, for his excellent photos and textual criticism; **Steven Blotner**, for suggesting many new Postwar variations; **Louis Bohn**, for his excellent editing; **Tom Budniak**, for his detailed report on new variations; **Philip Catalano**, for his commentary and support; **Hank Degano**, for his up-to-date market reports; **Dave Ely**, for his careful manuscript reading; **David Fleming**, for his research on Lionel publications and milk cars; **Lou Goslinger** of Fundimensions, for his report on the 1983 lines; **Philip Graves**, for his excellent editing; **Ron Griesbeck**, for his assistance on steam engines and other notes; **Ralph Hutchinson**, for his notes on unusual variations; **Joe Kotil**, for his detailed notes on variations; **Ron Niedhammer**, for his detailed notes on variations, particularly steam engines and box cars; **Michael Ocilka**, for his detailed reports on flat cars and other variations; **Trip Riley**, for his excellent gondola drawings and his advice and comments; **Chris Rohlfing**, for his detailed reports on new variations; **Al Rudman** of Trackside Hobbies, for his report on the 1983 line; **Glenn Salamone**, for his report on Lionel paper; **James Sattler**, for his highly detailed reports on rare variations; **I. D. Smith**, for his superb organization of the Lionel paper chapter and his careful review of the manuscript; **Patrick Scholes**, for his assistance on steam engines; **Richard Vagner**, for his remarkable research and essay on gondolas; **David J. Weiss**, for his very careful and analytic reports on new varieties and clarifications of previous reports; **Charlie Weber**, for his detailed report on Lionel publications; **Al Weaver**, for the slides showing his billboard collection which made possible the comprehensive listing of billboards and for his other slides which helped our research process.

In addition, the following people also contributed to this book: **C. C. Boehmer, Michael Brandt, George Brewer, John Breslin, James A. Bryan, George L. Cole, David M. Dixon, L. F. Dell 'Osso, David Deitrick, Joseph Donangelo, David E. Dunn, Henry Edmunds, John Fraber, Dennis Flater, Dr. Robert Friedman, Robert Geller, D. B. Griggs, Dr. W. C. Hopper, Kent C. Jarman, Bruce Kaiser, Carl Kruelle, Richard Krapf, George Koff, James Keith, Ken Koehler, Terral Klaasen, Marvin Kerschner, Nicholas Ladd, Stanley Lapan, Terry Lemieux, Mike Lahti, Dean J. Light, Robert Lebo, Ken Landry, Richard Lord, Stephen McCabe, A. W. Morse, C. P. Marshall, Robert Mayer, Ronald Moss, Gary Mueller, Peter Nordby, Edward O'Brien, Albert F. Otten, James W. Popp, Paul Piker, Damion Pinta, Harold Powell, Robert Pendrak, Mark Rohlfing, Roy Rodd, Warren Rothschild, Jr., Larry Rohde, Ernie Rankin, Graden A. Rogers, Dr. Bernard Rubin, C. Adair Roberts, Donald Roller, Bernard Stekoll, Steve Sekely, Charles Scheltens, Brian J. Smith, Bruce Stiles, Charlie Switzer, Tony Slavianao, George Shewmake, Fred Sipple, Robert Spitzer, Steve Surratt, Roger Schreiner, Frank Schmaus, Ron Samson, Barry Smith, Francis Stem**, and **Will Sykes** (Will is 13 years old and it was his letter about billboards that provided the impetus to undertake work on that chapter).

Art K. Tom, Gerald Talley, Eugene Trentacoste, William Tompkins, Brad Thomas, George Taylor, Al Toone, Robert Ulmer, Frank Vergonet, Bobby Whitacre, Jeff Warnick, Paul Yeckel, Dick Young, and **Joseph Zydlo** also assisted us with their letters and comments. It is possible that we have inadvertently omitted contributors. If we did so, it was certainly not intended.

Projects of this magnitude are impossible without the continued assistance of fellow train enthusiasts. I am most appreciative of the continued assistance you have provided and hope that you will continue to write to myself and Roland.

The Guide was ably typeset by **Cindy Floyd** and **Karen Zandt** on our Compugraphics 1 in 7-point Century under the control of a TRS-80 Model 12 computer. The interface was manufactured by Cybertext. It was proofread by **Mary Dalton** and **Sharon Armacost**. **Janie Green**, our staff artist, put the set type in place. The cover photograph was taken by **Roger Bartelt** and the color separation was furnished by **Progressive Offset**. The book was printed by **John D. Lucas**, of Baltimore.

Finally, I would like to express my appreciation to **Roland LaVoie** for his work compiling, integrating and editing information for the 1983-84 edition. In my years as a writer, editor and publisher, I have never seen one man expend such energy, commitment and productivity as Roland has put into this edition. It gives me great confidence in the scope and accuracy of this Guide, and I trust that you will so find it.

Bruce C. Greenberg
October 19, 1983

TABLE OF CONTENTS

INTRODUCTION 3
ACKNOWLEDGEMENTS 4
TABLE OF CONTENTS 5

PART I LIONEL TRAINS: 1945 - 1969

Chapter I	Diesel and Electric Engines and Motorized Units	6
Chapter II	Steam Locomotives	32
	Mold Identification of Square Plastic Tenders by Joseph Kotil	48
Chapter III	Accessories	50
Chapter IV	Box Cars	70
Chapter V	Cabooses	93
	SP Caboose Dies, by Joseph Kotil	93
Chapter VI	Cranes and Searchlights	103
Chapter VII	Flat Cars	105
Chapter VIII	Gondolas	117
Chapter IX	Hoppers and Dump Cars	122
Chapter X	Passenger Cars	127
Chapter XI	Tank Cars	133
Chapter XII	Vat Cars	136

PART II FUNDIMENSIONS PRODUCTION: 1970 - 1983

Chapter XIII	Diesels and Electrics	137
Chapter XIV	Steam Locomotives	160
Chapter XV	Accessories	166
Chapter XVI	Hoppers	172
Chapter XVII	Box Cars, Reefers and Stock Cars	177
Chapter XVIII	Cabooses	206
Chapter XIX	Tank Cars	215
Chapter XX	Vat Cars	217
Chapter XXI	Operating Cars	218
Chapter XXII	Passenger Cars	219
Chapter XXIII	Auto Carriers	225
Chapter XXIV	Flat Cars	226
Chapter XXV	Gondolas	229
Chapter XXVI	Lionel Paper 1945-69 by I.D. Smith	232
Chapter XXVII	Lionel Billboards by I.D. Smith	238
Appendix	New York Central Gondolas by Richard Vagner	241
Index	. . . .	245

SMALL MOTORIZED UNITS

- 3360 BURRO CRANE
- 3927 Track Cleaning Car
- 68 EXECUTIVE INSPECTION CAR
- 51 NAVY YARD
- 53 Rio Grande
- 65 HANDCAR
- 55 TIE-JECTOR
- 60 Trolley
- 42 PICATINNY ARSENAL
- 57 A E C
- 50 Gang Car
- 60[A] Trolley
- 59 MINUTEMAN
- 58 GREAT NORTHERN
- 69 MAINTENANCE CAR
- 52 FIRE CAR
- 54 BALLAST TAMPER
- 41 U.S. ARMY
- 56 M St L

Chapter I
DIESEL AND ELECTRIC ENGINES AND MOTORIZED UNITS

DIESEL POWER TRUCK TYPES

Lionel diesels came with four basic motors. The study of these units shows Lionel's continuing concern with cost and quality considerations.

TYPE I MOTOR

Die-cast truck frame
Five exposed gears
Lettered: THE LIONEL CORPORATION NEW YORK
Four axle depressions
One screw
Axles not visible

TYPE II MOTOR

Built up power truck with attached side frames to suit prototype
Sheet metal bottom
Five external gears
Lettered: "LIONEL DIESEL SWITCHER, "OIL*," THE LIONEL CORPORATION NY MADE IN U.S. of AMERICA"
Four axle bearings, all visible
Two axles visible — either one or two magnetic axles
Unpainted side frames
Three position reverse
3 part pickup assembly
There are seven subcategories to Type II

TYPE II SUBCATEGORIES

Type II Subcategories	A	B	C	D	E	F	G
Oil hole with valve				X	X		X
No oil hole		X	X				
Oil hole, no valve			X			X	
One magnetized axle			X		X		X
Two magnetized axles	X		X	X	X		
Round axle bushings	X	X	X			X	X
Axle bushing with swage marks				X	X		

TYPE III MOTOR

No bottom plate
Five external gears
Exposed worm and spur gears only, worm is relatively centered between axles
No magnetraction
No axle bearings

TYPE III SUBCATEGORIES

(A) No tires, front spring mounted motor
(B) Two tires on near gear side, non-spring mounted motor, Examples: 213, 215

*It is not clear if "OIL" appears on all Type II motors, particularly Type IIA, IIB

TYPE IV MOTOR

No bottom plate
Motor has only worm and spur gears; both visible
No axle bearings, axles visible, spacers added to axle on one side
Rubber tire traction with grooved wheels to hold tire (no magnetraction)
Black motor side frames

Bold print indicates that the name appears on the side of the item. When it does not appear on the side or where its name is abbreviated, the item's popular designation, i.e., **HANDCAR,** appears in bold and its omission from the item's side is noted in the text.

Gd. V.G. Exc. Mt.

0000 ALASKA GP-7 prototype, Elliott Smith Collection NRS

41 U.S. ARMY Switcher, 1955-57, 2-4-2, gas turbine, black with white lettered "TRANSPORTATION CORPS," three position E-unit, no light. Several pieces have been reported with a red, white and blue triangle above the center window on both sides. One report says this was a post-factory addition. However, we need to learn if this variety was indeed factory produced. Reports from original owners would be very helpful. Breslin comment.
Price for usual variety 35 45 75 110

42 PICATINNY ARSENAL Switcher, 1957, 2-4-2, gas turbine, olive drab with white handrails and lettering, three position E-unit, no light.
90 150 200 275

44 U.S. ARMY Mobile Missile Launcher, 1959-62, blue with white lettering, gray missile launcher with four missiles, blue man sits at control panel, red light on roof, three position E-unit, two fixed couplers, magnetraction Type IIF motor, Type III pickups. 40 75 100 150

45 U.S. MARINES Mobile Missile Launcher, 1960-62, olive drab with white lettering, gray center unit on frame, gray launch unit, red light on roof, magnetraction Type IIF motor, Type III pickups 45 90 125 175

50 LIONEL Gang Car, 1955-64, orange body with blue bumpers, two fixed blue men, one gray rotating man, bump reverse, no light.
(A) Dummy horn in center of armature plate; V-shaped bumper bracket
15 35 45 65
(B) Same as (A) but horn on right side of armature plate 15 35 45 65
(C) Same as (B) but L-shaped bumper bracket 15 35 45 65

51 NAVY YARD Switcher, 1956-57, 2-4-2, Vulcan, light blue with white lettering, three position E-unit, no light, window struts often broken.
45 65 100 150

52 FIRE CAR 1958-61, red with white lettering, gray pump and hose reel, red light, bump reverse, man with fire nozzle turns. 80 125 150 195

53 Rio Grande Snow Plow, 1957-60, 2-4-2, Vulcan, black body and lettering, yellow cab sides, handrails and snow plow, three position E-unit, no light, one coupler, window struts often broken
(A) Lettering "Rio Grande" has letter "a" printed backwards
95 130 200 275
(B) Same as (A) but "a" printed correctly 120 170 250 350

54 BALLAST TAMPER 1958-61, 1966, yellow with black lettering, blue man in cab, one fixed coupler, shift lever for tamper action, unit is geared to half speed while tamping, two activator track clips to operate shift lever, no reverse, no light, antenna on rear easily damaged 70 100 135 180

55 TIE-JECTOR 1957-61, red with white lettering, number on side "5511", switch lever for ejector action on side, two activator track clips to operate switch lever, no reverse, one coupler on rear, no light, pulling more than one car could damage gears or cause the motor to overheat. 70 100 135 180

56 M St L MINE TRANSPORT 1958, 2-4-2, Vulcan, white cab sides and railing, red body and lettering, three position E-unit, no light, window struts often broken 150 250 300 450

57 AEC Switcher, 1959-60, 2-4-2, Vulcan, three position E-unit, no light, white body, red cab sides, window struts often broken. It is the consensus of opinion that a cream colored variety is entirely due to aging. Salamone observation **150 250 375 475**

58 GREAT NORTHERN Rotary Snowplow, 1959-61, 2-4-2, Vulcan, green body and logo, white cab, sides and handrails, snow blower rotates when moving, three position E-unit, no light, window struts often broken
(A) As described above **160 275 400 500**
(B) Unpainted green cab sides, no logo, Pauli Collection **NRS**

59 MINUTEMAN Switcher, 1962-63, 2-4-2, gas turbine, white body with blue and red lettered "U.S. AIR FORCE" "MINUTEMAN," three position E-unit, no light, black handrails **75 150 225 350**

60 LIONELVILLE Trolley, 1955-58, four-wheel Birney style, yellow plastic body with red roof, lettered "60 BLT 8-55 LIONEL," "LIONELVILLE RAPID TRANSIT" AND "SAVE TIME HAVE FARE READY". Trolly pole rotates according to direction of operation, bump reverse, interior light. Models without roof vents are believed to be earlier. Roof vents and an aluminized paper reflector on the roof underside were added to prevent roof damage due to the combination of bulb and motor heat.
(A) Two piece spring bumper, black lettering, no roof vents
40 100 150 200
(B) Two piece spring bumper, blue lettering, no roof vents, orange cast to red roof, frame has six-sided threaded bushing at attachment end of frame, Phillips head screws, trolley pole insulator has square top (part 60-41), orange motor brush holder, Rankin Collection **40 70 95 150**
(C) Same as (B), except red roof with vents, LaVoie Collection
40 70 80 135
(D) Same as (A), except red lettering, Joe Ranker Collection **NRS**
(E) Same as (A), except two motor men silhouettes rotate to show in front window according to direction car is moving **100 175 250 400**
(F) One piece bumper, blue lettering, roof vents **75 100 150 300**
(G) One piece bumper, blue lettering, no roof vents, bright red roof, frame does not have six-sided threaded bushing, slotted screws, trolley pole insulator (part 60-41) has splines on top, black motor brush holder, Rankin Collection **NRS**

65 HANDCAR 1962-66, "HANDCAR NO.65" appears embossed on side of plastic body, Friedman comment. Red pump, two vinyl men pump, one in a red and one in a blue shirt, the vinyl often causes a chemical reaction with the plastic body which damages the body where the men stand, no light, no reverse. Two different bodies are found:
TYPE I: The five-laminate rectifier is exposed and visible from the underside. It is mounted through a 3/8" x 9/16" slot in the frame end. The rectifier is numbered "G16542". The plastic body base is filled at the end center to cover the rectifier. The middle rail collector passes through a spring and a hole in the collector slide. It is soldered to the slide bottom. Griesbeck Collection.
TYPE II: The rectifier is not visible from the underside, and a stamped metal clip holds the rectifier in place. The rectifier is thin and mounts inside the frame. There is no slot. The plastic body is open at the end center. The middle rail collector slide has a vertical post through the spring to which the collector wire is attached. Griesbeck Collection.
(A) Dark yellow body **80 125 170 200**
(B) Light yellow body **90 140 180 250**

68 EXECUTIVE INSPECTION CAR 1958-61, DeSoto 1958 station wagon **without** name on side, red with cream side panel and roof, knob on roof is E-unit cutoff switch, two position E-unit, operating head and tail light
(A) Red with cream striping **75 100 130 200**
(B) All red with no striping, top knob for E-unit is a non-operating dummy, factory prototype in TCA Museum, Geller observation **NRS**
(C) Blue with cream stripe, probable pre-production prototype, Bohn observation **— — — 800**

69 MAINTENANCE CAR 1960-62, self-powered signal service car, "MAINTENANCE CAR" does not appear on side, dark gray and black body with light gray platform, blue bumpers, L-shaped bumper bracket, one blue man, sign reverses when direction reverses, "DANGER" on one side and "SAFETY FIRST" on the other **90 185 225 325**

202 UNION PACIFIC 1957, Alco A unit, 0-27, orange body with black lettering, sheet metal frame, opening where front coupler would be is closed off, dummy coupler on rear, one axle magnetraction, two position E-unit, headlight, Type IID motor, Type II pickups, no horn, no weight
13 25 30 50

204 SANTA FE 1957, Alco AA units, 0-27, Santa Fe freight paint scheme, blue body with yellow cab roof, upper stripe and lettering, red and yellow lower stripe, sheet metal frame, front and rear dummy couplers, two axle magnetraction, three position E-unit, light in both units, Type IIE motor, Type II pickup, no horn, no weight **25 37 50 95**

205 MISSOURI PACIFIC 1957-58, Alco AA units, 0-27, blue body with white lettering, sheet metal frame, front and rear dummy couplers, two axle magnetraction, three position E-unit, light in powered unit, Type IIE motor, Type II pickup, no horn, no weight **25 37 50 105**

208 SANTA FE 1958-59, Alco AA units, 0-27 Santa Fe freight paint scheme, blue body with yellow cab roof, upper stripe and lettering, red and yellow lower stripe, sheet metal frame, front and rear dummy couplers, two axle magnetraction, three position E-unit, light in powered unit, Type IIE motor, Type II pickup, horn, no weight **25 45 55 80**

209 NEW HAVEN 1958, Alco AA units, 0-27, black body with orange and white stripes and lettering, sheet metal frame, front and rear dummy couplers, two axle magnetraction, three position E-unit, light in powered unit, Type IIE motor, Type II pickup, horn, no weight **30 50 70 115**

210 The Texas Special 1958, Alco AA units, 0-27, red body and lettering with white stripe, sheet metal frame, front and rear dummy couplers, two axle magnetraction, three position E-unit, light in powered unit, Type IIE motor, Type II pickup, no horn, no weight **25 37 50 60**

211 The Texas Special 1962-66, Alco AA units, 0-27, red body and lettering with white stripe, sheet metal frame, front and rear dummy couplers, two rubber traction tires on drive wheels, weight in body, two position E-unit, light in powered unit, Type IIIB motor, Type II pickup, no horn, with weight **25 37 50 60**

212 U.S. MARINE CORP 1958-59 Alco A unit, 0-27
(A) Blue body with white stripes and lettering, sheet metal frame, opening where front coupler would be is closed off, dummy coupler on rear, one axle magnetraction, two position E-unit, light, Type IID motor, Type II pickup, no horn, no weight **16 25 35 75**
(B) Same as (A) except slightly lighter blue, much brighter white lettering and trim, no reverse unit, Type IIA motor, no tires, no magnetraction
19 30 40 85

212 SANTA FE 1964-66, Alco AA units, 0-27, Santa Fe war bonnet passenger paint scheme, silver body with red cab, nose, and stripe; yellow and black trim, black lettering, sheet metal frame, front and rear dummy couplers, two rubber traction tires on drive wheels, two position E-unit, light in powered unit, Type IIIB motor, Type III pickup, horn, with weight, E-unit lever has slot in roof, I.D. Smith observation **25 45 55 80**

213 MINNEAPOLIS & ST. LOUIS 1964, Alco AA units, 0-27, red body with white stripe and lettering, sheet metal frame, front and rear dummy couplers, two rubber traction tires on drive wheels, two position E-unit, light in powered unit, Type IIIB motor, no horn, with weight **25 37 50 70**

215 SANTA FE Alco, AB units, gray plastic body painted silver and red with black and yellow stripes and black lettering, Type IIIB motor, with weight, two-position E-unit, I.D. Smith observation **22 35 45 70**

216(A) BURLINGTON 1958, Alco A unit, 0-27, silver body with red stripes and lettering, sheet metal frame, front and rear dummy couplers, two axle magnetraction, three position E-unit, light, Type IIE motor, no horn, no weight **35 55 75 135**

216(B) MINNEAPOLIS & ST. LOUIS Uncatalogued, lighted, Alco A unit, 0-27, gray plastic body painted red, with weight, white lettering, Type IIIA motor, three position E-unit, open pilot, no front couplers **40 55 75 135**

217 BOSTON & MAINE 1959, Alco AB units, 0-27, letters B and M **only** on unit's side, black body with large blue stripe, thin white stripe at roof line, black and white lettering, sheet metal frame, front and rear dummy couplers, two axle magnetraction, three position E-unit, light in A unit, Type IIC motor, Type III pickup, no horn, no weight **30 40 60 80**

218 SANTA FE 1959-63, Alco, 0-27, Santa Fe war bonnet passenger paint scheme, silver body with red cab, nose and stripe; yellow and black trim, black lettering, sheet metal frame, front and rear couplers, two axle magnetraction, three position E-unit, light in powered unit, Type IIC motor, Type III pickup, horn, no weight

(A) Double A units (Type IIC motors)	25	35	50	65
(B) AB units	25	35	50	65
(C) B unit (dummy), used also with #220, 1961	10	15	20	30

219 MISSOURI PACIFIC Uncatalogued, c. 1959, Alco AA units, blue with white lettering, sheet metal frame, front and rear dummy couplers, two axle magnetraction, two position E-unit, light in powered unit, Type IIC motor, Type III pickup, no horn, no weight   25 37 50 75

220 SANTA FE 1961, Alco A unit, 0-27, Santa Fe war bonnet passenger paint scheme, silver body with red cab, nose and stripe, yellow and black trim, black lettering, sheet metal frame, front and rear couplers.
22 35 45 60

221 Alco A unit, 0-27, sheet metal frame, opening where front coupler would be is closed off, dummy coupler on rear, rubber traction tire on one drive wheel, two position E-unit, no light, Type IVA motor, Type III pickup, no horn, no weight

(A) **Rio Grande**, 1963-64, yellow with black stripes and lettering
18 22 30 40

(B) **U.S. MARINE CORPS**, uncatalogued, olive drab with white stripes and lettering, motor and chassis unknown   40 50 70 125

(C) **SANTA FE,** uncatalogued, olive drab with white stripes and lettering   20 30 40 55

222 Rio Grande 1962, Alco A unit, 0-27, yellow with black stripes and lettering, sheet metal frame, opening where front coupler would be is closed off, dummy coupler on rear, rubber traction tire on one drive wheel, no reverse, light, Type IVA motor, Type III pickup, no horn, no weight
12 17 25 35

223, 218C SANTA FE 1963, Alco AB units, 0-27, Santa Fe war bonnet passenger paint scheme, silver body with red cab, nose, and stripe, yellow and black trim, black lettering, A unit numbered 223; B unit numbered 218, sheet metal frame, front and rear dummy couplers, rubber traction tires on drive wheel, two position E-unit, light in A unit, horn   24 35 50 60

224 U.S. NAVY 1960, Alco AB units, 0-27, blue body with white lettering, sheet metal frame, front and rear dummy couplers, two axle magnetraction, three position E-unit, light in A unit, Type IIC motor, Type III pickup, no horn, no weight   25 37 50 60

225 CHESAPEAKE & OHIO 1960, Alco A unit, 0-27, dark blue with yellow lettering, sheet metal frame, front and rear dummy couplers, two axle magnetraction, two position E-unit, light, Type IIC motor, Type III pickup, no weight   18 30 40 75

226 BOSTON & MAINE Uncatalogued, 1960, only "BM" on sides, Alco AB units, 0-27, black body with large blue stripe, thin white stripe at roof line, black and white lettering, sheet metal frame, front and rear dummy couplers, two axle magnetraction, three position E-unit, light in A unit, Type IIC motor, Type III pickup, horn, no weight   25 37 50 70

227 CANADIAN NATIONAL Uncatalogued, 1960, Alco A unit, 0-27, green body with yellow trim and lettering, sheet metal frame, opening where front coupler would be is closed off, dummy coupler on rear, no reverse, light, Type IIIA motor, Type III pickup, no horn, made for Canadian market, with weight   30 45 80 125

228 CANADIAN NATIONAL Uncatalogued, 1960, Alco A unit, 0-27, green body with yellow trim and lettering, sheet metal frame, front and rear dummy couplers, two axle magnetraction, two position E-unit, light, Type IIC motor, Type III pickup, no horn, made for Canadian market, no weight
30 45 80 125

229 MINNEAPOLIS & ST. LOUIS 1961, Alco AB units, 0-27, red body with white stripes and lettering, sheet metal frame, front and rear dummy couplers, one axle magnetraction, two position E-unit, light in A unit, Type IIB motor, Type III pickup, horn, no weight   25 37 50 65

230 CHESAPEAKE & OHIO 1961, Alco A unit, 0-27, blue body with yellow stripe and lettering, sheet metal frame, opening where front coupler would be is closed off, dummy coupler on rear, two axle magnetraction, two position E-unit, light, Type IID motor, Type II pickup, no horn
12 17 25 40

231 Alco A unit, 1961-63, 0-27, sheet metal frame, front and rear dummy couplers, two axle magnetraction, two position E-unit, light, no horn

(A) **ROCK ISLAND**, black body with red middle stripe, white upper stripe and lettering, Type IIA motor, Type III pickup   13 20 35 65

(B) Same as (A) but without lettering and white upper stripe, motor type not known   15 22 30 65

(C) Same as (A) but without red stripe, with white upper stripe, Type IIC motor, Type III pickup   15 30 55 80

232 NEW HAVEN 1962, Alco A unit, 0-27, orange body with black stripe and black and white lettering, sheet metal frame, opening where front coupler would be is closed off, dummy coupler on rear, magnetraction, two position E-unit, light, Type IIE motor, Type II pickup, no horn, no weight
15 22 30 45

400 BALTIMORE AND OHIO 1956-58, Budd RDC passenger car, silver body with blue lettering, operating couplers at both ends, magnetraction, three position E-unit, lights, horn, single motor.   100 130 175 240

404 BALTIMORE AND OHIO 1957-58, Budd RDC baggage - mail car, silver body with blue lettering, operating couplers at both ends, magnetraction, three position E-unit, single motor, light, horn   90 130 175 275

520 Box Cab Electric, 1956-57, GE 80 ton, 0-4-2, 0-27, red body with white lettering "LIONEL LINES," sheet metal frame, single pantograph, dummy coupler on one end, operating coupler on the other end, three position E-unit, no light, no horn, check pantograph for damage. Same body used for 3535 Security Car, LaVoie observation

(A) Black pantograph   28 48 65 85
(B) Copper colored pantograph   28 48 65 85
(C) Same as (A), except re-stamped on one side to form double letter image, probable factory error, Blotner Collection   NRS

NW-2 SWITCHERS Illustrations on pages 18-19

600 MKT 1955, NW-2 Switcher, 0-27, red body with white lettering, sheet metal frame, operating couplers at both ends, one axle magnetraction, three position E-unit, no light, Type IID motor, Type II pickup, no horn.
(A) Black frame with black end rails, Type IID motor   16 30 45 70
(B) Gray frame with yellow end rails, Type IIE motor, Type II pickup*
30 50 65 90

(C) Gray frame with black end rails, Type IID motor, Type II pickup, Lower Collection   NRS

* Much easier to find on the West Coast than the East Coast.

9

205 Missouri Pacific AA
208 Santa Fe AA
209 New Haven AA
210 Texas Special AA
226 Boston & Maine AB
218 Santa Fe AA
227 Canadian National A,
221 Santa Fe A

10

ALCO DIESELS

202

212

216

221[B]

221[A]

228

230

231

232

1055

1066

2024

11

601 SEABOARD 1956, NW-2 Switcher, black and red body with red stripes and white lettering, black sheet metal frame, operating couplers at both ends, axle magnetraction, three position E-unit, light, Type IIE motor, Type II pickup, horn   35   55   70   100

602 SEABOARD 1957-58, NW-2 Switcher, 0-27, black and red body with red stripes and white lettering, sheet metal frames, dummy couplers at both ends, axle magnetraction, three position E-unit, light, Type IIE motor, Type II pickup, horn   35   55   70   100

610 ERIE 1955, NW-2 Switcher, black body, yellow lettering, operating couplers, axle magnetraction, three position E unit, light, Type IIE motor, Type II pickup, no horn.
(A) Black frame   30   50   65   95
(B) Yellow frame, Lebo Collection   NRS
(C) Same as (A), but no light, Lahti Collection 30   50   65   95
(D) Same as (B), but no light, Giroux Collection NRS
(E) Same as (A), but early production with two-axle magnetraction, no light, reportedly only a few thousand made, Yeckel observation. We do not know if this is the same as (C).   NRS

611 JERSEY CENTRAL 1957-58, NW-2 Switcher, 027, orange and blue body with blue and white lettering, sheet metal frame, one-axle magnetraction, three position E-unit, light, Type IID motor, Type II pickup, no horn
(A) Dummy couplers front and rear, Weiss Collection 35   60   75   95
(B) Dummy coupler on front, operating coupler on rear. Confirmation requested.   35   60   75   95

613 UNION PACIFIC 1958, NW-2 Switcher, 0-27, yellow with gray hood top and cab roof, red lettering, "ROAD OF THE STREAMLINERS," sheet metal frame, dummy couplers, both ends, magnetraction, three position E-unit, light, Type IIE motor, Type II pickup, no horn, bell
                                                40   75   100 135

614 ALASKA 1959-60, NW-2 Switcher, 0-27, blue body with yellow-orange lettering, yellow dynamic brake super-structure on top of motor hood, sheet metal frame, dummy couplers at both ends, one axle magnetraction, two position E-unit, light, Type IIG motor, Type II pickup, no horn, appears to be the only example of IIG motor
(A) No dynamic brake unit, Niedhammer observation   30   50   72   90
(B) With yellow dynamic brake unit atop hood   55   80 120 150

616 SANTA FE 1961-62, NW-2 Switcher, black body with black and white safety stripes front and rear, white lettering, dummy horn and bell are omitted, sheet metal frame, operating couplers at both ends, axle magnetraction, three position E-unit, light, Type IID motor, Type II pickup, horn
                                                30   40   65   85

617 SANTA FE 1963, NW-2 Switcher, black body with black and white safety stripes front and rear, white lettering, sheet metal frame, dummy couplers both ends, axle magnetraction, three position E-unit, light, Type IIE motor, Type II pickup, horn   38   65   85   120

621 JERSEY CENTRAL 1956-57, NW-2 Switcher, 0-27, blue body with orange lettering, sheet metal frame, operating couplers at both ends, one axle magnetraction, three position E-unit, no light, Type IID motor, Type II pickup, horn   32   50   70   95

622 SANTA FE 1949-50, uncatalogued as Santa Fe. Catalogued but never made as Lionel (1949) and New York Central (1950), NW-2 Switcher, first magnetraction engine, black body with white lettering, die-cast frame, coil-operated couplers at both ends, three position E-unit, light both ends, Type I motor, Type I pickup, no horn, operating bell, excellent runner, 6220 is similar except numbered for 0-27.
(A) 1949, large GM decal on cab   80 110 140 200
(B) 1950, small GM decal on lower front side of motor hood, no weight in cab   75 110 140 175
(C) 1950 late, same as (B) but weight cast in cab frame
                                                75 110 140 175
(D) "LIONEL" not "SANTA FE," catalogued but not made
                                                Not Manufactured
(E) "NEW YORK CENTRAL" not "SANTA FE," catalogued but not made
                                                Not Manufactured

623 SANTA FE 1952-54, NW-2 Switcher, 0-27, black body with white lettering, die-cast frame, coil-operating couplers at both ends, magnetraction, three position E-unit, Type I motor, Type I pickup, no horn, excellent runner
(A) Ten stanchions hold handrail to side   40   75 100 150
(B) Three stanchions hold handrail to side   35   60   85 125

624 CHESAPEAKE & OHIO 1952-54, NW-2 Switcher, 0-27, blue body with yellow stripe and lettering, die-cast frame, coil-operating couplers at both ends, magnetraction, three position E-unit, lights, at both ends, Type I pickup, no horn, excellent runner
(A) Ten stanchions hold handrail to side   40   65   90 130
(B) Three stanchions hold handrail to side   40   65   90 130

625 LEHIGH VALLEY 1957-58, GE 44 ton switcher, 0-27, red and black body with white stripe and lettering, black sheet metal frame, dummy couplers at both ends, magnetraction, three position E-unit, light, Type IID motor, Type II pickup, no horn   60   90 125 150

626 BALTIMORE AND OHIO 1959, GE 44-ton center-cab switcher, yellow lettering and frame, 027
(A) Blue body and yellow frame   60 120 175 220
(B) Lavender body and black frame, Niedhammer Collection   NRS

627 LV 1956-57, GE 44 ton switcher, 0-27, Lehigh Valley paint scheme, red body with white stripe and lettering, black sheet metal frame, operating couplers at both ends, one axle magnetraction, three position E-unit, no light, Type IID motor, Type II pickup, no horn   30   50   70   100

628 NORTHERN PACIFIC 1956-57, GE 44 ton Switcher, 0-27, black body with yellow stripe and lettering, yellow sheet metal frame, operating couplers at both ends, one axle magnetraction, three position E-unit, light, Type IID motor, Type II pickup, no horn   30   50   80   140

629 BURLINGTON 1956, GE 44 ton Switcher, 0-27, silver body with red stripe and lettering, black sheet metal frame, operating couplers at both ends, one axle magnetraction, three position E-unit, light, Type IID motor, Type II pickup, no horn. The silver finish on most pieces is not attractive. Hence a substantial premium for excellent and better.   60   90 175 220

633 SANTA FE 1962, NW-2 Switcher, 0-27, blue body with blue and yellow safety stripes and yellow lettering, sheet metal frame, dummy coupler on rear only, two position E-unit, light but no lens on light, Type IVA motor, Type III pickup, no horn   30   40   50   75

634 SANTA FE 1963, 65-66, NW-2 Switcher, 0-27, blue body with yellow lettering, sheet metal frame, plastic dummy front coupler, metal dummy rear coupler, two position E-unit, light, Type IVA motor, Type III pickup, no horn
(A) Yellow and blue safety stripes on front of motor hood and on cab, with lens   20   30   40   65
(B) Same as (A) but no safety stripes, without lens 20   30   40   65
(C) 1970, very early MPC, used old Lionel number. No safety stripes, but lens. Silver plastic bell and silver plastic brake wheel. Red end marker lights. Listed here for user's convenience.   15   20   40   50

635 UNION PACIFIC 1963, uncatalogued, NW-2 Switcher, 0-27, yellow body, red striping and trim, red "NEW 7-58," white "U.P." and "635" on front of cab, no bell, no horn, Type IVA motor, Type III pickup, light but no headlight lens, dummy couplers front and rear, weight on underside of hood, Niedhammer observation   20   35   50   75

645 UNION PACIFIC 1959, NW-2 Switcher, 0-27, black frame, yellow unpainted plastic body with red heat-stamped lettering and stripes, weight attached to hood underside, headlight with lens, two position reverse, two fixed coulers, Type IVB motor, Type III pickup.
(A) As above   20   35   50   75
(B) Heat-stamped lettering on only one side. This version was reported in our 1977 edition but subsequently dropped because questions of its collectibility arose. A subsequent report by J. Breslin indicates a second example which was obtained from Rosewood Hobbies. The questions are, therefore: Is this a collectible variation? Are there other examples in collector hands? Is this a legitimate factory error? Reader comments invited.   NRS

1055 TEXAS SPECIAL 1959-60, not shown in the consumer catalogue but listed as part of a special set "To meet the needs of the low-price mass toy market" in the 1959 and 1960 Advance Catalogues. In 1959 it was described as No. 1105 Texas Special set and in 1960 as the No. 1107 Sportsman Diesel set. In 1959, the catalogue illustration does not show some of the car numbers: unnumbered box, unnumbered plug door box, unnumbered single dome tank, 6012 gondola with two canisters and an unnumbered caboose. In 1960, it was shown with an unnumbered gondola with two canisters. 6044 AIREX box car and unnumbered caboose. We hope that our readers will verify this information. The loco is an Alco A unit, 0-27, red body with white lettering, sheet metal frame, opening where front coupler would be is closed off, dummy coupler on rear, no magnetraction or rubber tires, no reverse, Type IIIA motor, no horn, light, and weight. At this time, Lionel apparently felt that such "stripped down units", because of their low quality, did not belong in their regular line and would reflect badly on the line. Yet, paradoxically, the mass marketers could readily sell these in quantity because of their obvious low price (probably $15 or less) while trading on the Lionel Line's quality reputation. Unfortunately, consumers got what they paid for and the Lionel Line's reputation declined.
(A) Alco A unit, 0-27, red body with white lettering, sheet metal frame, opening where front coupler would be is closed off, dummy coupler on rear, no magnetraction or rubber tires, no reverse, Type IIIA motor, no horn, light with weight   12   17   25   40

1065 UNION PACIFIC 1961, uncatalogued, Alco A unit, 0-27, yellow body with red lettering and red stripe, sheet metal frame, opening where front coupler would be is closed off, dummy coupler on rear, no magnetraction, no traction tires, no reverse, Type IIIA motor, Type III pickup, no horn, with weight
(A) With light   12   17   25   35
(B) No light, I.D. Smith observation   12   17   25   35

1066 UNION PACIFIC 1964, uncatalogued, Alco A unit, 0-27, yellow body with red stripe and lettering, sheet metal frame, opening where front coupler would be is closed off, dummy coupler on rear, no magnetraction, no reverse, Type IVA motor, Type III pickup, no horn or weight   12   17   25   35

1203 BOSTON & MAINE 1972, uncatalogued, NW-2 Switcher, Fundimensions unpainted cab decorated in light blue with white lettering outside of factory, for New England Division of the Train Collectors Association; chrome plated radio wheel, bell, horn, chassis not provided; cab only. Located here in text to aid user identification, although Fundimensions' production   —   18   25   40

2023 UNION PACIFIC 1950-51, Alco AA units, 0-27, die-cast frame, coil-operated couplers on cab ends, dummy middle couplers, magnetraction, three position E-unit, light in both units, Type I motor, Type I pickup, horn, excellent runner.
(A) 1950, yellow body with gray roof and frame, red stripes and lettering   55   80   100   175
(B) 1950, same as (A) but gray nose   100   150   200   350
(C) 1951, silver body and frame with black stripes and lettering, gray roof   45   70   90   140

2024 CHESAPEAKE & OHIO 1969, Alco A unit, 0-27, blue body with yellow stripe and lettering, sheet metal frame, front and rear dummy couplers, one rubber traction tire, two position E-unit, light, Type IVB motor, Type IV pickup, no horn or weight.   15   22   30   50

2028 PENNSYLVANIA 1955, GP-7 Road Switcher, 0-27, tuscan body
(A) Yellow rubber stamped lettering, riveted railing   70   110   150   250
(B) Yellow rubber stamped lettering, welded railing, rivet holes   70   110   150   250
(C) Gold lettering, welded rails, no rivet holes   60   85   125   200
(D) Welded rails, mauve frame, Askenas Collection   NRS

2028 UNION PACIFIC 1955 GP-7, shown in Advance Catalogue, but not manufactured. The illustration on page 30 is a prototype from the La Rue Shempp Collection   NRS

2031 ROCK ISLAND 1952-54, Alco AA units, 0-27, black body with white stripe and lettering, red middle stripe, die-cast frame, coil-operated couplers on cab ends, dummy middle couplers, magnetraction, three position E-unit, light in both units, Type I motor, Type I pickup, horn, excellent runner   55   95   140   200

2032 ERIE 1952-54, Alco AA units, 0-27, black body with yellow stripes and lettering, die-cast frame, coil-operated couplers on cab ends, dummy middle couplers, magnetraction, three position E-unit, light in both units, Type I motor, Type I pickup, horn, excellent runner   55   80   100   150

2033 UNION PACIFIC 1952-54, Alco AA units, 0-27, silver body and frame with black lettering, die-cast frame, coil-operated couplers on cab ends, dummy middle couplers, magnetraction, three position E-unit, light in both units, Type I motor, Type I pickup, horn, excellent runner
(A) Smooth roof over motor   45   70   95   170
(B) Dime-sized round bump over motor   45   70   95   170

2041 ROCK ISLAND 1969, Alco AA units, 0-27, black body with white stripe and lettering, red middle stripe, sheet metal frame, front and rear dummy couplers, light, Type IIB motor, Type IIIB pickup, two position E-unit, no horn, with weight, catalogued with nose emblem but production pieces lack emblem
(A) White lettering   30   55   75   100
(B) No lettering, Degano Collection   NRS

2240 WABASH 1956, F-3 AB units, 0-27, gray and blue body with white side panels and trim, yellow heat-stamped[1] lettering, blue frame with black trucks, louvered roof vents, filled in portholes, operating coupler on front of A unit, all other couplers are dummys, magnetraction, three position E-unit, light in A unit, single vertical motor, horn   160   220   270   400

2242 NEW HAVEN 1958-59, F-3 AB units, checkerboard paint scheme, silver roof and frame, black nose, black, white, silver and red sides, lettering heat-stamped[2] on nose and sides, silver frame with black pilot and trucks, louvered roof vent, filled in portholes, operating coupler on front of A unit, all others are dummys, magnetraction, three-position E-unit, light in A unit, single vertical motor, horn, often referred to as an 0-27 engine because of its single motor, although it is shown only as a Super 0 engine in the catalogue   175   250   325   450

2243 SANTA FE 1955-57, F-3 AB units, 0-27 & 0, Santa Fe war bonnet passenger paint scheme, silver body with red cab, nose and stripe, yellow and black trim, black heat-stamped lettering, silver frame with black trucks, louvered roof vent, filled in portholes, operating coupler on front of A unit, all other couplers are dummys, magnetraction, three position E-unit, light in A unit, single vertical motor, horn, this unit is often referred to as an 0-27 engine due to its single motor and its 0-27 listing in 1955-56 but in 1957 it was catalogued in 0 gauge only   60   100   140   220

2243C Santa Fe 1955-57, F-3 B unit, came as part of 2343 and not catalogued separately; it matches 2383 AA units for which no B was made   30   50   65   85

2245 Texas Special 1954-55, F-3 AB units, 0-27, red body and pilot with white lower panel and silver frame and trucks
(A) As above   95   125   150   275
(B) Red body with black trucks and silver pilot, O'Brien Collection. Further confirmation requested.   NRS

2321 LACKAWANNA 1954-56, FM Trainmaster, gray body with yellow trim and maroon mid-stripe and lettering, side trim stripe and lettering are rubber stamped,[1] operating couplers both ends, magnetraction, three position E-unit, light both ends, twin vertical motors, horn, excellent runner,
(A) Gray roof and body   175   225   275   425
(B) Maroon roof and gray body   200   275   350   500
(C) Factory prototype shown on cover of 1954 Lionel Advance Catalogue, screens on roof vent, very elaborate paint scheme, LaRue Shempp Collection   NRS

2322 VIRGINIAN 1965-66, FM Trainmaster, operating couplers at both ends, magnetraction, three position E-unit, light at both ends, twin vertical motors, horn, excellent runner
(A) Orange yellow body with blue stripe and roof   215   275   325   475
(B) Yellow body with black stripe. Question as to existence. Confirmation requested.   NRS

2328 BURLINGTON 1955-56, GP-7 Road Switcher, 0-27, silver body with black lettering, red frame and handrails, words and emblem rubber stamped, operating couplers both ends, magnetraction, three position E-unit, light at both ends, horn   60   100   150   225

[1] Silk screened on reproduction bodies.
[2] Silk screened side lettering with nose decal on reproduction bodies.

ALCO DIESELS

219 MISSOURI PACIFIC

224 UNITED STATES NAVY

229 MINNEAPOLIS & ST LOUIS

2041 ROCK ISLAND

2041 [ROCK ISLAND] - FACTORY ERROR

2031 ROCK ISLAND

14

ALCO DIESELS

204 SANTA FE

211 The Texas Special

212 SANTA FE

213 MINNEAPOLIS & ST LOUIS

215 SANTA FE

217 BOSTON & MAINE

2329 VIRGINIAN 1958-59, GE EL-C Rectifier electric, blue body with yellow stripe, lettering, hand rail and frame, heat-stamped, single metal pantograph, operating couplers both ends, magnetraction, three position E-unit, light both ends, single vertical motor, pickup, horn, wiring easily adapted for overhead catenary operation, illustrated page 32   **135 180 280 425**

2330 PENNSYLVANIA 1950, GG-1 Electric, green with five gold stripes and red Keystone decal, 5 stripes rubber stamped,[3] twin metal pantographs, coil-operated couplers at both ends, magnetraction, three position E-unit, light at both ends, twin vertical motors, horn, wiring easily changed for overhead catenary operation, excellent runner   **225 325 450 650**

2331 VIRGINIAN 1955-58, FM Trainmaster, rubber stamped lettering and end crisscross,[1] operating couplers at both ends, magnetraction, three position E-unit, light at both ends, twin vertical motors, horn, excellent runner
(A) 1955, yellow body with black stripe and gold lettering
   300 375 450 700
(B) 1956-58, yellow body with blue stripe and yellow lettering
   275 350 425 600
(C) 1957, same as (B) but dull blue stripe   **300 375 450 700**

2332 PENNSYLVANIA 1947-49, GG-1 Electric, 5 stripes rubber stamped, twin metal pantographs, operating couplers both ends, no magnetraction, three position E-unit, light at both ends, single angle mounted motor, AC vibrator box horn, wiring easily adapted for overhead catenary operation, hard to find with stripes and lettering in good condition
(A) Very dark green (almost black) body with silver stripes, Keystone is rubber stamped   **250 325 450 625**
(B) Dark green body with gold stripes, Keystone decal   **150 200 250 350**
(C) Flat black body with gold stripes, Keystone decal   **250 350 600 900**
(D) Flat black body with silver stripes, Keystone rubber stamped
   250 375 650 1000

2333 F-3 AA units, 1948-49, screened roof vent, open portholes with lenses, grab irons on nose, ladder on cab door, coil-operated couplers on cab ends, dummy middle couplers, no magnetraction, three position E-unit, light in both units, twin horizontal motors, horn
(A) SANTA FE, Santa Fe war bonnet passenger paint scheme, silver body with red cab, nose and stripe, yellow and black trim, black heat-stamped lettering, silver frame and trucks   **90 125 150 220**
(B) **NEW YORK CENTRAL**, dark gray body with gray center stripe outlined with white trim, rubber stamped trim, heat-stamped lettering, red and white GM decal on rear side door, gray frame and trucks, this item is catalogued as #2333 but it is referred to in the service manual as #2334; since the engine number boards show 2333 we use that number   **100 150 200 285**
(C) 1948, same as (A) but rubber stamped lettering. Verification requested   **NRS**
(D) 1948, same as (B) but rubber stamped lettering   **100 150 200 300**
(E) Same as (B) but GM decal is black and white   **100 150 200 285**
(F) SANTA FE, clear body with Santa Fe nose decal and red and white GM decal, a few of these were made for display use, see page 24.   **NRS**
(G) Same as (A) but black not silver body, shown in 1948 catalogue but not made   **Not Manufactured**
(H) Same as (F), no striping on side, paste on roadname on side. Lower Collection.   **750**
(I) Same as (A), but red and white GM decals are above "BUILT BY LIONEL" at rear of cab, not on rear side doors. We would appreciate reader ownership reports so we can evaluate how common or rare this version is, Breslin Collection   **NRS**

2333C F-3B unit not made but a 2343C looks like it.   **Not Manufactured**

2334 Number listed in Service Manual for 2333(B)

2337 WABASH 1958, GP-7 Road Switcher, 0-27, blue and gray body with white stripes and lettering, black frame and handrails, heat-stamped[2] lettering, dummy couplers at both ends, magnetraction, three position E-unit, light at both ends, horn   **80 130 175 250**

2338 MILWAUKEE 1955-56, GP 7 Road Switcher, catalogued as both 0 and 0-27, black and orange body with white and/or black lettering, black frame and handrails, operating couplers at both ends, magnetraction, three-position E unit, light at each end, horn. Illustrated on page 26.

(A) Orange translucent plastic shell that is painted black, unpainted orange band goes completely around shell, decal does not adhere well to orange shell, the orange plastic of the shell is very shiny, black lettering; believed to have been made for Sears.   **500 600 850 1200**
(B) Orange translucent plastic shell that is painted black both inside and out, orange band goes as far as cab and starts again after cab, black lettering on orange band, white lettering on orange area.   **100 150 200 300**
(C) Black plastic shell painted with dull orange band that goes as far as cab and starts again after cab, black lettering on orange band, white lettering on black area.   **75 100 140 200**

2339 WABASH 1957, GP-7 Road Switcher, blue and gray body with white stripes and lettering, black frame and handrails, heat-stamped[3] lettering, operating couplers at both ends, magnetraction, three position E-unit, light at both ends   **75 130 175 250**

2340 PENNSYLVANIA 1955, GG-1, Electric, five gold stripes, red Keystone decal, stripe rubber stamped, lettering heat-stamped,[3] twin metal pantographs, coil-operated couplers at both ends, magnetraction, three position E-unit, light at both ends, twin vertical motors, horn, wiring easily changed for overhead catenary operation, excellent runner
(A) Tuscan red, special Pennsylvania paint scheme used on a few GG-1s for the "Congressional" and the "Senator,"[4] shown in the 1955 catalogue as #2340-1   **250 325 450 625**
(B) Dark green, standard Pennsylvania paint scheme for freight and passenger service, shown in the 1955 catalogue as #2340-25   **225 300 425 600**

2341 JERSEY CENTRAL 1956, FM Trainmaster, orange body with blue stripe and roof, white heat-stamped lettering, different spacing between "Jersey" and "Central" on each side, operating couplers at both ends, magnetraction, three position E-unit, light at both ends, twin vertical motors, horn, excellent runner
(A) High gloss orange, Rubin observation   **420 540 600 820**
(B) Dull orange   **300 420 510 720**

2343 SANTA FE 1950-52, F-3 AA units, Santa Fe war bonnet passenger paint scheme, silver body with red cab, nose and stripe, yellow and black trim, black heat-stamped[2] lettering, rubber stamped[2] top and side stripes, silver frame and trucks, screened roof vents, open portholes with lenses, grab irons on nose, ladder on cab door, coil-operated couplers on cab ends, dummy middle couplers, magnetraction, three position E-unit, light in both units, twin horizontal motors, horn, excellent runner   **100 125 150 250**

2343C SANTA FE 1950-55, F-3 B unit, dummy B unit, silver body with red, yellow and black trim
(A) 1950-52 screen roof vents, matches 2343   **40 65 70 100**
(B) 1953-55 louver roof vents, matches 2353   **40 65 70 100**

2344 NEW YORK CENTRAL 1950-52, F-3 AA units, dark gray body with gray center stripe outlined with white trim, rubber stamped trim with heat-stamped lettering,[2] gray frame and trucks, screened roof vents, open portholes with lenses, grab irons on nose, ladder on cab door, coil-operated couplers on cab ends, dummy middle couplers, magnetraction, three position E-unit, light in both units, twin horizontal motors, horn, excellent runner
   100 150 200 275

2344C NEW YORK CENTRAL 1950-55, F-3 B unit, dummy B unit, dark gray body with gray center stripe and white trim
(A) 1950-52 screen roof vents, matches 2344   **60 85 100 160**
(B) 1953-55 louver roof vents, matches 2354   **60 85 100 160**

2345 WESTERN PACIFIC 1952, F-3 AA units, silver and orange body with black heat-stamped lettering,[2] silver frame and trucks, screened roof vents, open portholes with lenses, grab irons on nose, ladder on cab door, coil-operated couplers on cab ends, dummy middle couplers, magnetraction, three position E-unit, light in both units, twin horizontal motors, horn, excellent runner, no B unit made. Substantial premium for fresh and bright silver paint.   **200 300 400 550**

---

[1] Silk-screened words and end crisscross, words are slightly higher on reproduction bodies.

[2] Silk screened on reproduction bodies

[3] Silk screened side lettering with nose decal on reproduction bodies

[4] Refer to **The Remarkable GG-1** by Karl Zimmermann, Quadrant Press Inc.

GG1s

2330 PENNSYLVANIA

2332 PENNSYLVANIA

2340 PENNSYLVANIA

2360[B] PENNSYLVANIA

2360[C] PENNSYLVANIA

NW-2 SWITCHERS

621 Jersey Central
601 Seaboard
611 Jersey Central
613 Union Pacific
614 Alaska

623 Santa Fe
624 Chesapeake & Ohio
6250 Seaboard
600 MKT
610 Erie

18

622 Santa Fe
634 Santa Fe
645 UNION PACIFIC
616 Santa Fe
633 Santa Fe
635 UNION PACIFIC

625 Lehigh Valley
627 Lehigh Valley
629 Burlington
626 Baltimore and Ohio
628 Northern Pacific

2346 BOSTON & MAINE 1965-67, GP-9 Road Switcher, heat-stamped lettering, operating couplers at both ends, magnetraction, three position E-unit, headlight, horn.
(A) Glossy blue body, black cab, white trim, lettering, frame and handrails
                    75 110 150 210
(B) Black body, red ends, silver and red heat-stamped lettering, black MPC frame, without GP-9 roof blister, pre-production sample made after 1970. Listed here for user convenience. Eddins Collection   **NRS**

2347 CHESAPEAKE & OHIO 1962, uncatalogued, GP-7 Road Switcher, made for Sears Roebuck, blue body with yellow heat-stamped lettering, frame and hand rails, operating couplers at both ends, magnetraction, three position E-unit, headlight, horn, very hard to find 700 900 1200 1800

2348 MINNEAPOLIS & ST. LOUIS 1958-59, GP-9 Road Switcher, red body with blue roof and white stripe, heat-stamped lettering, black frame and handrails, operating couplers at both ends, magnetraction, three position E-unit, headlight, horn   100 145 195 275

2349 NORTHERN PACIFIC 1959-60, GP-9 Road Switcher, black body with gold and red striping, heat-stamped[2] gold leaf lettering, gold frame and handrails, operating couplers at both ends, magnetraction, three position E-unit, headlight, horn
(A) Gold heat-stamped lettering, as above 105 155 210 300
(B) Gold heat-stamped 'BUILT BY LIONEL', but gold rubber stamped "NORTHERN PACIFIC" and "2349", Fleming Collection
                   105 155 210 300

General Electric EP-5 Rectifiers

2350 NEW HAVEN 1956-58, G.E. EP-5 Rectifier Electric, black plastic body with heat-stamped[3] lettering, white and orange stripes, twin metal pantographs, operating couplers at both ends, magnetraction, three position E-unit, light at both ends, single vertical motor, horn, wiring easily changed for overhead catenary operation
(A) Gray "N", orange "H", painted nose trim. Gray New Haven lettering.
                   90 160 215 275
(B) Orange "N", black "H", painted nose trim, orange New Haven lettering.
                  110 240 330 525
(C) Same as (A) but nose trim is decal 85 125 170 215
(D) Same as (B) but nose trim is decal 110 200 300 490
(E) Same as (C) but orange and white paint, stripes go completely through door   95 200 250 300

2351 MILWAUKEE ROAD 1957-58, G.E. EP-5 Rectifier Electric, yellow unpainted plastic body[4] with heat-stamped lettering, black roof and red stripe, twin metal pantographs, operating couplers at both ends, magnetraction, three position E-unit, light at both ends, single vertical motor, horn, wiring easily changed for overhead catenary operation 150 225 275 390

2352 PENNSYLVANIA 1958-59, GE. EP-5 Rectifier Electric, tuscan red or brown body with single gold stripe, heat-stamped gold leaf[2] lettering, twin metal pantographs, operating couplers, magnetraction, three position E-unit, light both ends, single vertical motor, horn, wiring easily changed for overhead catenary operation   175 225 300 425

2353 SANTA FE 1953-55, F-3 AA units, Santa Fe war bonnet passenger paint scheme, silver body with red cab, nose, and stripe, yellow and black trim, black heat-stamped[1] lettering, rubber stamped[1] top and side stripes, silver frame and trucks, louvered roof vents, open portholes with lenses, ladder on cab door, coil-operated couplers on cab ends, dummy middle couplers, magnetraction, three position E-unit, light in both units, twin horizontal motors, horn, excellent runner, for B unit see 2343C
(A) Notch cut out below coupler at bottom of pilot, 1953 production, LaVoie Collection   80 110 175 250
(B) Smooth bottom on pilot, 1954-55 production 80 110 175 250

2353C SANTA FE F-3 B unit, not made; for B unit to match 2353 see #2343C (B)   **Not Manufactured**

2354 NEW YORK CENTRAL 1953-55, F-3 AA units, dark gray body, gray center stripe outlined with white trim, rubber stamped trim with heat-stamped[1] lettering, gray frame with gray trucks, louvered roof vents, open portholes with lenses, ladder on cab door, coil-operated couplers on cab ends, dummy middle couplers, magnetraction, three position E-unit, light in both units, twin horizontal motors, horn, excellent runner 110 170 225 350

2354C NEW YORK CENTRAL F-3 B unit not made; for B unit to match 2354 see #2344C (B)   **Not Manufactured**

2355 WESTERN PACIFIC 1953, F-3 AA units, silver and orange body with black heat-stamped[1] lettering, silver frame and trucks, louvered roof vents, open portholes with lenses, ladder on cab door, coil-operated couplers on cab ends, dummy middle couplers, magnetraction, three position E-unit, light in both units, twin horizontal motors, horn, excellent runner, no B unit made. Substantial premium for fresh and bright silver paint
(A) As above   150 260 375 525
(B) Nose decal on dummy unit, Blotner Collection 150 260 375 525

2356 SOUTHERN 1954-56, F-3 AA units, green body with light gray lower stripe and yellow trim and lettering, lettering is rubber stamped,[1] black frame and trucks, louvered roof vents, open portholes with lenses, ladder on cab door, coil-operated couplers on cab ends, dummy middle couplers, magnetraction, three position E-unit, light in both units, twin horizontal motors, horn, excellent runner   155 235 315 420

2356C SOUTHERN 1954-56, F-3 B unit, dummy B unit, green body with gray lower stripe and yellow trim, matches 2356 60 75 125 180

2358 GREAT NORTHERN 1959-60, G.E. EP-5 Rectifier Electric, orange and green body with yellow stripes and lettering, lettering is heat-stamped,[1] twin metal pantographs, operating couplers at both ends, magnetraction, three position E-unit, light at both ends, single vertical motor, horn, wiring easily changed for overhead catenary operation. Original GN end decals are almost always flaking.   175 250 350 450

2359 BOSTON & MAINE 1961-62, GP-9 Road Switcher, flat blue body, black cab and white trim, lettering, frame and handrails, lettering is heat-stamped, operating couplers at both ends, magnetraction, three position E unit, headlight, horn,   80 125 150 210

2360 PENNSYLVANIA 1956-58, 1961-63, GG-1 Electric, twin metal pantographs, coil-operated couplers at both ends, magnetraction, three position E-unit, light at both ends, twin vertical motors, horn, wiring easily changed for overhead catenary operation, excellent runner
(A) 1956, tuscan body with five rubber stamped[1] gold stripes, catalogue #2360-1   50 325 420 700
(B) 1956-58, same as (A) but dark green body, catalogue #2360-25
                  200 300 390 600
(C) Tuscan body with single gold stripe heat-stamped[1] lettering and numbers   200 300 370 550
(D) Same as (C) but decal[1] lettering and numbers 200 300 370 550
(E) Same as (C) but rubber stamped lettering and numbers, probably pre-production sample   **NRS**
(F) Black body with one large gold stripe, decal lettering, rough surface on body casting shows through paint, repainted and lettered by Lionel for William Vagell   **NRS**
(G) Same as (C), but rubber stamped lettering and stripe, early production, Tom Collection   **NRS**
(H) Same as (A), but very glossy tuscan finish, two pieces known to exist, Rubin Collection   **NRS**

2363 ILLINOIS CENTRAL 1955-56, F-3 AB units, brown body with orange stripe and yellow trim, rubber stamped[1] lettering and lines, black frame, trucks, and lettering, louvered roof vents, filled in portholes, operating coupler on front of A unit, all other couplers are dummys, magnetraction, three position E-unit, light in A unit, twin vertical motors, horn, excellent runner
(A) Black lettering   195 250 350 475
(B) Brown lettering, Degano Collection 225 325 450 650

2365 CHESAPEAKE & OHIO 1962-63, GP-7 Road Switcher, blue body with yellow frame, handrails and lettering, heat-stamped[1] lettering, dummy couplers at both ends, magnetraction, three position E unit, light, no horn, no battery box fuel tank   65 90 150 200

---

[1] Silk screened on reproduction bodies

[2] Silk screened in dull gold on reproduction bodies.

[3] Reproduction bodies are painted black and have rubber stamped lettering.

[4] Reproduction bodies are painted yellow and have silk screened lettering.

G.M. F-3

2245 The Texas Special

2344 New York Central

2344C B Unit

2343C B Unit

2343 Santa Fe

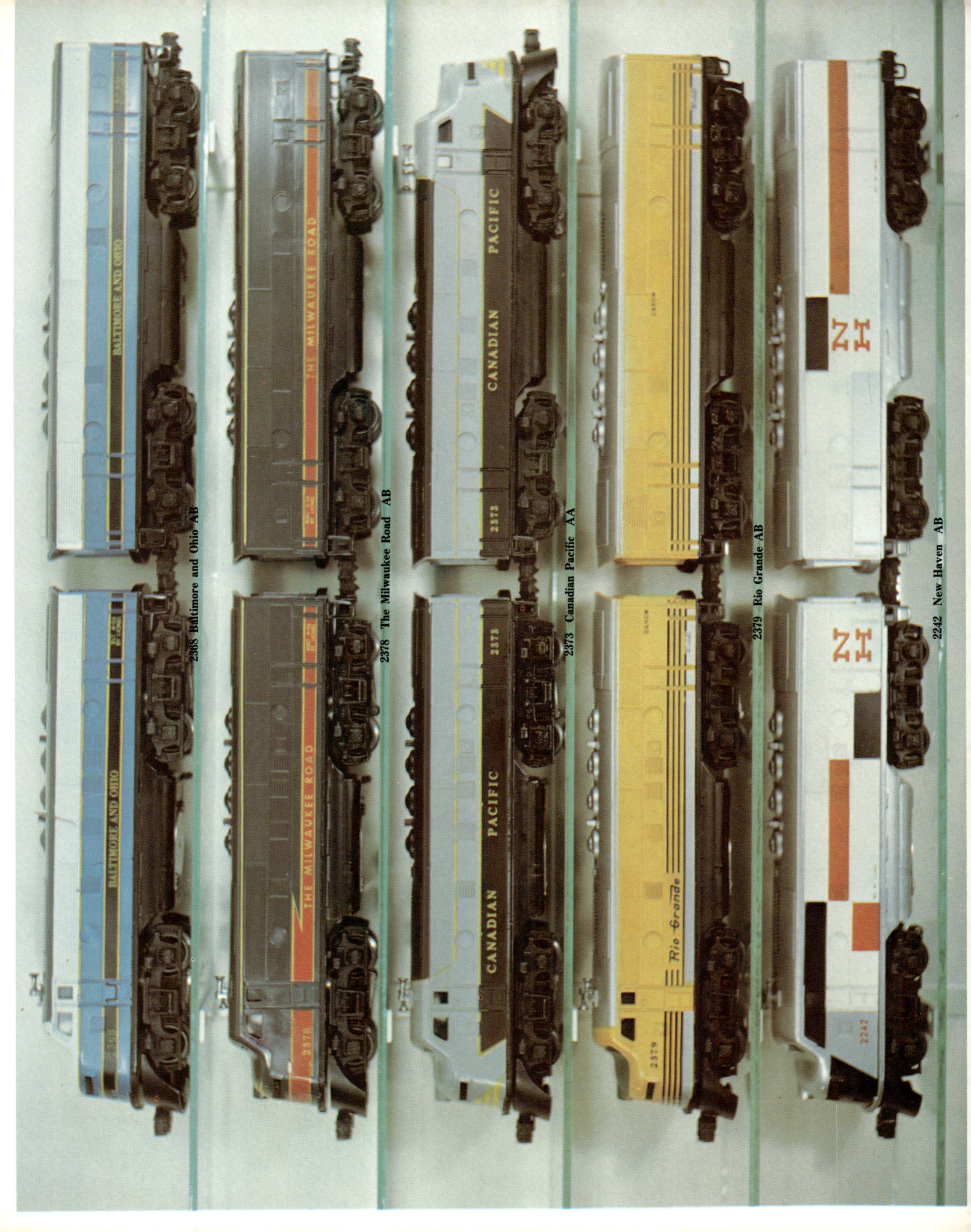

2368 Baltimore and Ohio AB
2378 The Milwaukee Road AB
2373 Canadian Pacific AA
2379 Rio Grande AB
2242 New Haven AB

CLEAR POWER
Special Display 2333 Santa Fe AA Units
Shempp Collection

2363 Illinois Central AB
2240 Wabash AB
2345 Western Pacific AA
2356 Southern AA
2356C Southern B unit

2321[A] Lackawanna FM Trainmaster

2321[B] Lackawanna FM Trainmaster

2331[A] Virginian FM Trainmaster

2331[C] Virginian FM Trainmaster

2322[A] Virginian FM Trainmaster

2341 Jersey Central FM Trainmaster

2367 WABASH 1955, F-3 AB units, gray and blue body with white side panels and trim, yellow heat-stamped lettering, blue frame, black trucks, louvered roof vents, filled in portholes, operating coupler on front of A unit, all other couplers are dummys, magnetraction, three position E-unit, light in A unit, twin vertical motors, horn, excellent runner   200   275   375   575

2368 BALTIMORE & OHIO 1956, F-3 AB units, blue unpainted plastic body[2] with white, black and yellow trim, rubber stamped lettering,[2] black frame and trucks, louvered roof vents, filled in portholes, operating coupler on front of A unit, all other couplers are dummys, magnetraction, three position E-unit, light in A unit, twin vertical motors, horn, excellent runner
 200   375   450   700

2373 CANADIAN PACIFIC 1957, F-3 AA units, gray and maroon with yellow trim and lettering, heat-stamped[1] top and sides, black frame and trucks, louvered roof vents, filled in portholes, operating couplers on cab ends, dummy middle couplers, magnetraction, three position E-unit, light in both units, twin vertical motors, horn, no B unit made, excellent runner
(A) Black frame   340   450   600   900
(B) Silver frame, Trentacoste Collection, additional reports requested   NRS

2378 MILWAUKEE ROAD 1956, F-3 AB units, gray plastic body[3] with orange lower stripe trimmed in yellow, yellow heat-stamped trim and lettering, louvered roof vents, filled in portholes, operating coupler on front of A unit, all other couplers are dummys, magnetraction, three position E-unit, light in A unit, twin vertical motors, horn, excellent runner
(A) Yellow stripe along roof line   350   475   590   875
(B) Without yellow stripe along roof line   325   450   550   825
(C) A unit without stripe, B unit with yellow stripe along roof line. This is a legitimate pair   250   375   500   600

2379 RIO GRANDE 1957-58, F-3 AB units, yellow body with silver roof and lower stripe, black trim and lettering, green panel in front of windshield, black frame and trucks, heat-stamped trim and lettering, decal nose, louvered roof vents, filled in portholes, operating coupler on front of A unit, all other couplers are dummys, magnetraction, three position E-unit, light in A unit, twin vertical motors, horn, excellent runner   305   320   370   520

2383 SANTA FE 1958-66, F-3 AA units, Santa Fe war bonnet passenger paint scheme, silver body with red cab, nose and stripe, yellow and black trim, black heat-stamped[1] lettering, rubber stamped top and side stripes, silver frame and black trucks, louvered roof vents, filled in portholes, operating couplers on cab ends, dummy middle couplers, magnetraction, three position E-unit, light in both units, twin vertical motors, horn, excellent runner, for B unit see 2243C
(A) Red cab, nose and stripe   100   130   220   325
(B) Orange red cab, nose and stripe, Lebo Collection, additional reports requested   NRS

2383C SANTA FE F-3 B unit not made, for B unit to match 2383 see 2243C
 Not Manufactured

2550 BALTIMORE AND OHIO 1957-58, Budd RDC baggage-mail car, dummy unit to match #404, silver body with blue lettering, operating couplers at both ends   110   150   200   300

2559 BALTIMORE AND OHIO 1957-58, Budd RDC passenger car, dummy unit to match #400, silver body with blue lettering, operating couplers at both ends   100   140   170   250

3360 BURRO Crane, 1956-57, self-propelled operating crane, yellow body with red lettering, dummy couplers at both ends, reverse lever on side can be operated by hand or by a track trip, a very interesting operating unit
(A) Yellow boom   40   100   150   220
(B) Yellow boom with small decal "danger"   50   110   175   240
(C) Brown cab, probable factory prototype, Bohn observation   NRS

3927 LIONEL LINES 1956-60, track cleaning car, orange body with blue lettering. Motor drives cleaning brush and does not drive wheels. Hence unit must be pulled by strong engine. A complete unit has two bottles, a brush and a wiper. Replacement brushes and wipers available. Original bottles marked "LIONEL."
(A) As described above   25   60   100   125
(B) With red running light, Kaim Collection. Additional sightings requested.   NRS
(C) Unpainted dark green plastic body, white rubber stamped lettering. The plastic pellets used in the injection mold machines are available in different colors. Lionel was consistent in using the same color pellets for its production runs. This unusual car was likely produced by the factory before its major production run, to compare alternative color schemes. Otten Collection   NRS

4810 SOUTHERN PACIFIC 1954, FM Trainmaster, black body, red stripe, preproduction prototype, Collection of La Rue Shempp, illustrated in this text; general design utilized by Fundimensions in 1979 for 8951. Illustrated on page 30   NRS

6220 SANTA FE 1949-50. Uncatalogued as SANTA FE. Catalogued but never made as LIONEL (1949) and NEW YORK CENTRAL (1950.) NW-2 Switcher, 0-27 versions of #622, first magnetraction engine, black body with white lettering, die-cast frame, coil-operated couplers at both ends, three position E-unit, light at both ends, Type I motor, Type I pickup, no horn, operating bell, excellent runner
(A) SANTA FE with large GM decal on cab, 1949, Ely observation   75   125   170   240
(B) SANTA FE with small GM decal on lower front side of motor hood, 1950, no weight in cab, Ely observation   75   125   170   240
(C) Same as (B), but weight cast in cab frame, late 1950, Ely observation   75   125   170   240
(D) LIONEL (1949) catalogued but not made   **Not Manufactured**
(E) NEW YORK CENTRAL (1950), catalogued but not made   **Not Manufactured**

6250 SEABOARD 1954-55, NW-2 Switcher, 0-27, blue and orange body with blue and white lettering, die-cast frame, coil-operated couplers at both ends, magnetraction, three position E-unit, light at both ends, Type I pickup, no horn, excellent runner
(A) 1954 SEABOARD is a decal with closely spaced lettering, Foss comment   110   135   170   250
(B) 1955, SEABOARD is rubber stamped with widely spaced lettering, Foss comment   90   120   150   230

---

[1] Silk screened on reproduction bodies

[2] Silk screened trim and lettering with decal or pressure transfer nose on reproduction bodies

[3] Reproduction bodies are painted gray with silk screened trim and lettering.

2339 Wasbash GP-7

2347 Chesapeake & Ohio GP-7

2346 Boston and Maine GP-9

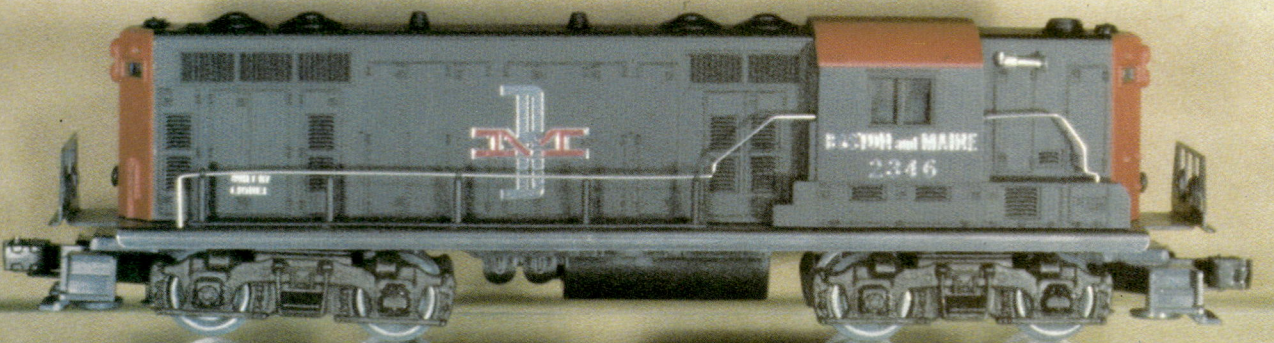

2346 Boston and Maine [Preproduction sample]

2350[B] New Haven G.E. EP-5

2365 Chesapeake & Ohio GP-7

2337 Wabash GP-7

2328 Burlington GP-7

2338 Milwaukee Road GP-7

2359 Boston and Maine GP-9

SO RARE

Four surviving factory prototypes:
2321 Lackawanna Trainmaster with screen roof vents
4810 Southern Pacific Trainmaster
2028 Union Pacific GP-7
8561 Union Pacific Caboose

Not so rare but hard to get are the 2321 maroon top Lackawanna Trainmaster and two TCA special 6464 Box Cars
Shempp Collection

2329 *Virginian Rectifier*
2358 *Great Northern*
2352 *Pennsylvania*
2351 *Milwaukee Road*
2350 *New Haven*

THE FIVE STAR GENERAL MEETS ITS HALLOWEEN BROTHER
1872 Five Star General with three passenger cars
1882 Sears Special General with two passenger cars
This brightly colored set is sometimes called the "Halloween Special."
Shempp Collection

Chapter II
STEAM LOCOMOTIVES
With the assistance of Ronald Niedhammer

                                         Gd. V.G. Exc. Mt.

221 1946-1947, 2-6-4 die-cast boiler, New York Central streamlined prototype, handrail from the pilot to the cab, very shallow stamped bell and whistles, large lens with refracting qualities, drive and connecting rods, valve gear, crosshead integral to body casting, motor with brush plate on left side and forward, casting opened up to provide room for brush holders; motor held in by screw behind smokestack and rod in front of cab, right side has large, medium and small gears, readily visible sliding shoes, blind center driver, "221" apparently rubber stamped in silver or white/silver. 221T tender marked "New York Central" with decal in black and silver, metal trucks, staple end, coil coupler, also came with 221W whistle tender. It is reported that the 1946 and 1947 castings are quite different (Ely observation). We would appreciate reader explanations of those differences.
(A) 1946 gray body, aluminum finish drivers without tires
                                30   50   65   90
(B) 1946 gray body, black finish drivers, without tires **20   30   45   65**
(C) 1947 black body, black drivers with nickel tires   **20   30   45   65**

224 1945-46, 2-6-2, black die-cast boiler; Baldwin nickel-rim disc drivers; O gauge motor with gears on left and brush plate on right; drive, connecting and eccentric rods; die cast front and rear trucks; cab detailed with two fireboxes; headlight; trim rods run from cab to pilot on both sides; nickel plated bell on bracket; motor held by screw at top rear of boiler and horizontal rod across boiler just above steam chest; rear of cab floor rounded with short drawbar. The 2466W whistle tender (or 2466 T non-whistle tender) has staple-end metal trucks and a coil coupler with sliding shoe. Two versions of the coil coupler are found: early version has open assembly and "whirly" wheels and later version has metal plate covering shoe support bracket and solid wheels. Both tenders feature metal trim, including wire guard rail which goes around the back deck. This engine was also made prewar as 224 or 224E in either black or gunmetal. It has a squared-off cab floor and a longer drawbar with ears; its tender has the older box couplers. Priced for post-war version. LaVoie comments   **35   45   60 110**

233 1961-62, 2-4-2, black plastic boiler, plastic side motor 233-100, two position reverse, smoke, light, magnetraction, 233W tender with whistle
                                           12   15   25   35

235 1962, uncatalogued, 2-4-2, black plastic boiler, two position reverse, smoke, light, magnetraction, plastic side motor 236-100
                                           14   18   28   50

236 2-4-2, black plastic boiler, white lettering, drive rod only, liquid smoke, light, plastic motor with ridged bottom, two gears visible on left side, brush holder on right side, rolled metal pick-up, magnetraction, fine cab interior detail, slopeback tender with operating coupler   **10   15   25   35**

237 1963-66, 2-4-2, black plastic boiler, drive rod only, liquid smoke unit, light, plastic motor 237-100 with ridged bottom, two gears visible on left side, brush plate holder on right side, middle rail pickups are rolled metal, rubber tire on right rear driver, fine detail inside cab, white stripe runs length of body, two position reverse unit with fiber lever through boiler top; streamlined tender lettered "LIONEL LINES," Timken trucks, ground pickup fingers on front truck, rear truck with fixed coupler, tender not numbered, see 1101 for discussion of body types   **10   15   25   35**

238 1963-64, 2-4-2, black plastic boiler, plastic side motor, Scout type two position reverse, smoke, light, rubber tires, 243W tender with whistle; see 1101 for discussion of body types
(A) Tender lettered "LIONEL LINES"   **10   20   35   50**
(B) Tender lettered "CANADIAN NATIONAL"   **NRS**

239 1964-66, 2-4-2, black die-cast body, step for bell, no bell
(A) Plastic motor with ridged bottom, two gears showing, rubber tire on right rear wheel, liquid smoke unit, 16-spoke wheels, light, fiber lever on two position reversing unit   **10   20   35   50**

(B) Better grade 0-27 metal side motor with three position reverse unit with control lever down, readily accessible brushes, loco retains slot in top for two position reverse unit, 239 (B) has a lighter stamping and a different type-face than does 239(A)   **10   20   35   50**

240 Circa 1964, 2-4-2, uncatalogued by Lionel. Came as part of Sears space set 9820 only. Black plastic boiler, plastic side motor, two-position reverse, smoke, light, rubber tires (see 1101 for full discussion of loco types). This locomotive is particularly interesting because of its set, which included a 3666 cannon car, a 6470 exploding box car, an unnumbered flat car with a green tank, a 6814 (c) rescue caboose, what appears to be a Marx - made transformer and a number of other pieces. This set, illustrated in color in the flat car section, is described in more detail under the 3666 box car listing. Set value: **300 400 600 750**

These observations are the result of the contributions of Vergonet, Bohn and Jarman. Some sets, possibly made in 1968 and numbered 11600, also came with an olive-colored range launching unit (add $100 to set values). Locomotive and tender value: **15   35   85 150**

241 1958, uncatalogued, 2-4-2, die-cast body, white stripe along loco sides, fiber lever for reverse unit between domes, 239-100 motor with ridged bottom, gears on left side, brushes on right side, liquid smoke unit, finely detailed cab interior, rubber tires. Tender with Scout side truck frames with magnetic coupler; tender cab is fastened to base with two tabs in rear and screw in front; see 1101 for discussion of boiler types and comparisons with 237 and 242   **10   13   18   30**

242 1962-66, 2-4-2, black plastic body, motor with grooved bottom, light, main rod each side, two gears visible on left side, brushes on right side, highly detailed cab interior, fiber lever for reverse unit through boiler top, stack has large hole because red gasket for smoke unit is not present. Tender with Timken trucks, one disc coupler, cab held to frame by two tabs in rear and Phillips screw in front; motor held in by slide on front and pin through cab on rear; see 1101 for a discussion of boiler types and comparisons with 237 and 241   **10   13   18   30**

243 1960, 2-4-2, black plastic body, two position reverse unit with metal lever coming through boiler top near cab, one drive rod on each side; 0-27 metal sided motor with two gears showing on left side and brush plate on right side; liquid smoke unit with bellows, highly detailed cab interior, motor held on by screw in front of reverse lever and plate in front of drivers, rubber tires, light. 243W tender, Timken trucks, disc coupler, one pickup roller for whistle and one wire for ground; see 1101 for a discussion of boiler types and comparison with 237, 241 and 242   **10   13   18   30**

244 1960-61, 2-4-2, black plastic body, bell ledge between stack and first dome, no bell, reverse lever between second dome and cab; liquid smoke with bellows, light, 0-27 247-100 motor with metal sides, two gears on left side, brushes on right side, weight under cab. Tender lettered "LIONEL LINES," Timken truck in front, arch bar truck in rear with fixed coupler, tender cab mounted by two tabs in rear, screw in front, came with either 244T or 1130T tender   **10   13   18   30**

245 1959, 2-4-2, black plastic boiler, bell ledge between stack and first dome, no bell, small molded generator unit immediately in front of cab, motor mounted by pin through boiler and mounting plate in front, weight under cab, two gears visible on left, brush holder on right, smooth bottom plastic motor No. 245-100, two position reverse unit with fiber lever, detailed cab interior. Tender with arch bar trucks, fixed coupler, see 1101 for discussion of body type   **10   13   18   30**

246 1959-61, 2-4-2, black plastic boiler, bell ledge between stack and first dome, no bell, reverse lever slot between first and second domes; single main rod on each side, light, no smoke unit, magnetraction. In late 1961, this locomotive came as part of set X-600, a special Quaker Oats promotion where-in the purchaser sent in two Quaker Oats box tops and $11.95 for the set, which included a 6406 flat car with automobile, a 6042 gondola with

221 New York Central

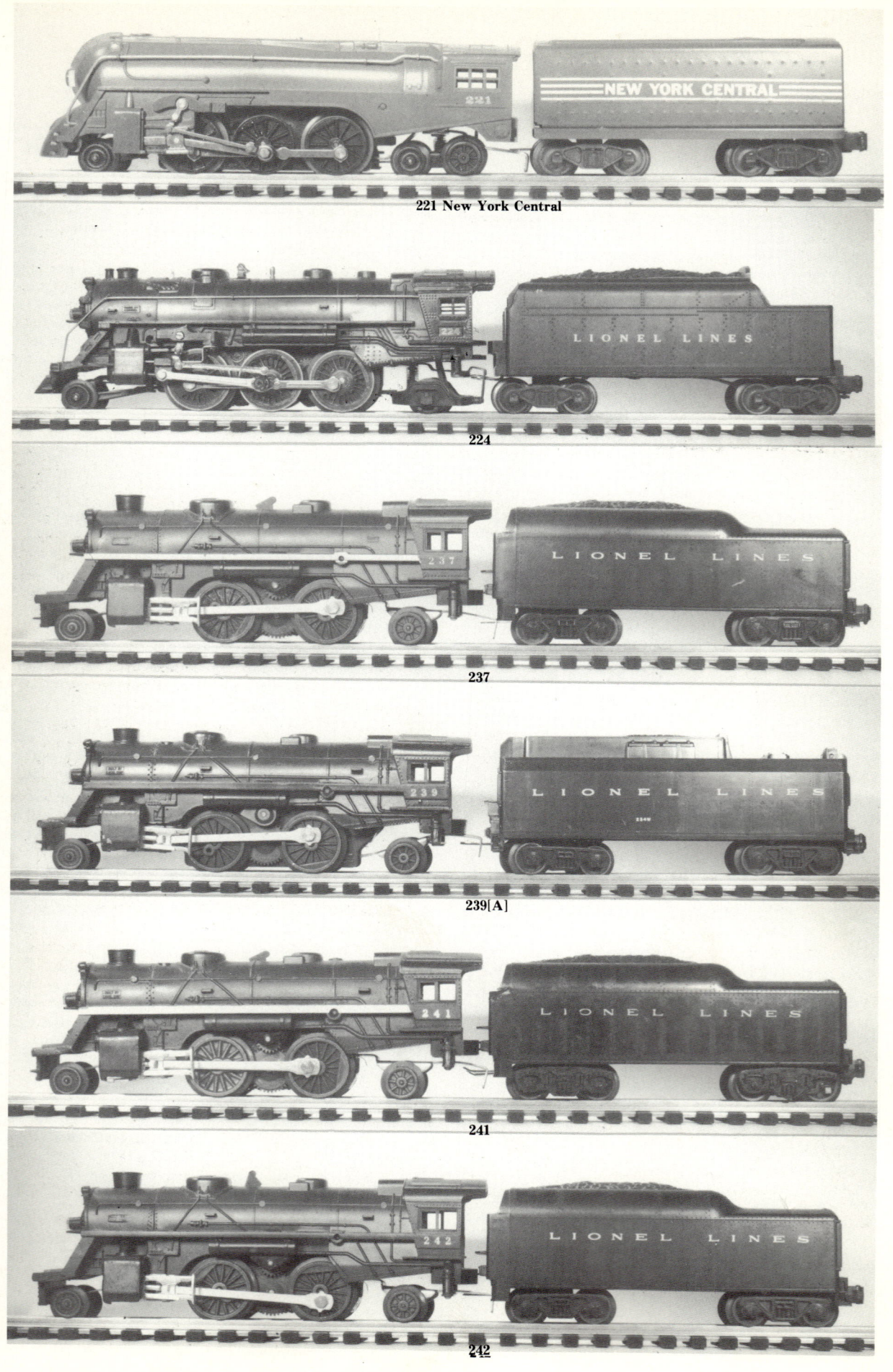

224

237

239[A]

241

242

34

canisters, a 6076 hopper car, a 6047 caboose, a 1016 transformer and track. Further details are requested concerning the cars in this set.
(A) No molded generator unit in front of cab, ridged bottom plastic motor 246-100, magnetraction, 244T or 1130T tender, tender not numbered
    10 15 20 30
(B) Molded generator unit in front of cab, smooth bottom plastic motor 246-200, no weight under cab, slopeback tender, partially open in front pilot
    10 15 20 30

247 1959-61, 2-4-2, black plastic body, blue stripe with white lettering; tender lettered "BALTIMORE & OHIO," reversing unit, motor held by screw in rear and casting mounting in front; light, liquid smoke unit with bellows. 247T tender with Timken trucks, disc coupler; cab fastened to frame by tab fasteners in rear, screw in front; see 1101 for discussion of body types
    12 18 25 40

248 1958, not catalogued, 2-4-2, black plastic boiler, 0-27 motor with metal sides, two position reverse unit
    12 18 25 40

249 1958, 2-4-2, black plastic body, bell ledge, no bell, black generator detail between reverse lever and cab, orange-red stripe with white lettering on both loco and tender. Tender lettered "PENNSYLVANIA," drive rod on each side, No. 249 0-27 motor with metal sides, brush plate on right side, two position reverse unit, metal weight underneath cab, no light in loco. 250T tender with Timken trucks, disc coupler, see 1101 for discussion of body types
    12 17 22 35

250 1957, 2-4-2, black plastic body, bell ledge, no bell, generator detail in front of cab, no reverse lever slot, orange stripes on loco and tender with white "PENNSYLVANIA" lettering; 0-27 metal side motor, three position reverse unit, lever down, weight under cab floor, light in front of loco, no lens, two gears on left side, brush plate on right side, motor held in by Phillips screw behind second dome and slot in front of motor, cab interior highly detailed. 250T tender with Timken trucks, disc coupler; see 1101 for discussion of body types
    12 17 22 35

251 Date unknown, 2-4-2, black die-cast boiler, light, two position reverse with fiber reverse lever, brushes right side, white "251" on cab beneath window, Clark Collection.
(A) Slope back tender with Timken trucks, fixed couplers.
    12 17 22 35
(B) 250T type tender, Timken trucks, fixed couplers **12 17 22 35**

637 1960, 2-6-4, catalogued as Super 0 but shares 2037 metal boiler casting, black with white lettering, smoke, magnetraction
(A) 2046W tender with whistle, lettered "LIONEL LINES," 1960
    30 40 55 75
(B) 2046W tender lettered "PENNSYLVANIA," 1961-63
    30 40 55 75

646 1954-58, 4-6-4, smoke, three position reverse unit, shares boiler casting with 2046 and 2056, boiler casting evolved from 726 casting. 2046W tender with whistle, water scoop, Timken trucks with disc couplers, two pickup rollers; with either heat-stamped or large or small rubber stamped cab numbers. This boiler casting and all other New York Central "Alco" boiler castings (726, 736, 2046 and 2056) can be found with two types of cab windows. One type has a full cross-brace which divides the window into four equal-sized small windows. The other is missing one part of the cross-brace so that there are three windows instead of four. It is often mistakenly believed that the three-window casting has a broken window support brace. Griesbeck observation.
(A) 1954, Die-cast trailing trucks, Foss Collection **60 85 120 210**
(B) 1954-58, trailing truck with plastic side frames, Foss Collection
    60 85 120 210

665 1954-59, 4-6-4, pill type smoke unit, three position reverse, magnetraction, feedwater heater in front, plastic side frame on trailing trucks, shares Santa Fe Hudson boiler casting with 685, 2055 and 2065, with either rubber stamped or heat-stamped cab numbers
(A) 6026W tender with whistle, bar-end metal trucks, magnetic tab couplers **60 85 120 210**
(B) 2046W tender **50 65 100 180**
(C) 1966, 736W tender, "PENNSYLVANIA," Hutchinson Collection **NRS**

670 1952, 6-8-6, Pennsylvania Steam Turbine shown in advance catalogue but not made **Not manufactured**

671 1946-49, 6-8-6 model of Pennsylvania S-2 Steam Turbine
(A) 1946, double worm drive, horizontal reverse unit, smoke lamp with bulb with depressed area that used Special #196 tablets, white rubber stamped number under cab window, no external E unit lever, motor labeled "ATOMIC MOTOR," slotted brush holders, jack receptacles, red Keystone on boiler front with gold lettering, shiny nickel rims on drivers, 671W tender with grab rails front and back, railing on rear deck, white "LIONEL LINES" lettering **55 100 175 250**
(B) Same as (A) but black Keystone with white lettering. **55 100 175 250**
(C) Same as (A) but red Keystone rubber stamped "6200" in silver, Griesbeck and Taylor Collections, additional observations requested **NRS**
(D) 1947, single worm drive motor, vertical reverse unit with E unit lever projecting through boiler, new smoke unit with resistance coil and bellows, white rubber stamped number under cab window, motor stamped "LIONEL PRECISION MOTOR," non-slotted brush tubes, no jack receptacles, piping detail added to boiler immediately behind air pumps, bottom plate reads "S-2 TURBO LOCOMOTIVE MADE IN THE ..." red Keystone on boiler front, 671W tender with grab rails front and back, railing on rear deck, "LIONEL LINES" lettering **50 100 175 250**
(E) 1948, similar to (C) but thin blackened steel rims on flanged drives (1st and 4th axles), bottom plate on middle rail collector reads "MADE IN THE ...," metal ballast, new streamlined, twelve wheel 2671W tender lettered "PENNSYLVANIA," tender has water scoop and plastic whistle case with whistle lying on side with opening through the water scoop, tender has back-up lights, light bracket is similar to those found on pre-war 0 Gauge cars, inside the tender is a piece of red painted plastic for the red light and clear plastic for the two side lights, coil couplers **70 115 190 300**
(F) 1948-49, 2 same as (D) but tender does not have backup lights
    40 80 130 200

NOTE: In 1972, the Train Collectors' Association produced a special boiler front designed to fit the 671, 681, 682 and 2020 S-2 turbines. This boiler front was made for the 1972 Pittsburgh convention and had special TCA stickers on the pumps and smoke box front. The casting differs from Lionel's original casting. Reader comments on the specific differences are requested. Although this is only a component, and not made by Lionel, it is closely associated with Lionel production and is located here for reader convenience.

671RR 1952, 6-8-6 Pennsylvania Turbine, see 671 for background. This locomotive is mechanically similar to 681 but does not have magnetraction due to a shortage of Alnico magnetic material for axles due to the Korean War. Loco may be marked either 671 or 671RR on cab beneath the window. Loco has one piece wheels made from sintered iron. Although the illustration of this loco shows it with a 671W tender, the correct tender is a 2046W-50. This tender has 2046W-50 stamped on the frame in silver, though its box is labeled "2046W, PRR, WITH WHISTLE". It has 4-wheel bar-end metal tracks, "PENNSYLVANIA" lettering in white, open holes at the tender rear and a marbled yellow plastic whistle housing. The loco number is rubber stamped on the loco cab, and there is a hole in the chassis between the first and second pair of drive wheels where the magnets for magnetraction would have been placed. LaVoie Collection
(A) "671" on cab **50 90 120 180**
(B) "671RR" on cab **50 90 120 180**

675 1947, 2-6-2, die-cast boiler, Pennsylvania K-4 prototype, rubber stamped cab numerals, drive, connecting and eccentric rods, smoke, light; label on cab roof underside reads "to remove the whitish smoke deposit from locomotive body, apply a little Lionel lubricant or vaseline and polish with a soft clean cloth," Baldwin disc wheels with nickel rims. 2466W or 2466WX tender with rear deck handrail, staple-end metal trucks, coil couplers, lettered "LIONEL LINES," whistle
(A) "675" on boiler front Keystone **45 80 100 180**
(B) "5690" in gold on red decal on boiler front **45 80 100 150**
(C) Similar to (B) but with new pilot with simulated knuckle coupler and lift pin; smoke stack reduced in size, 1948 **45 80 100 150**
(D) Similar to (C) but with 6466WX tender with magnetic couplers, 1949
    45 80 100 150
(E) Same as (C) but 2666T tender, Dorn comment. Additional observations requested **NRS**
(F) 1952, spoked drivers, no magnetraction, 4-wheel stamped sheet metal trailing truck, 2046 type tender, Hutchinson comment, shown in 1952 catalogue and Lionel Service Manual. Additional observations requested **NRS**

243

244

245

246[B]

246[A]

247

36

249

250

637[A]

646

665[A]

671RR

37

675

681

682

685

726[B]

726RR

681 1950-51, 6-8-6, smoke. three position reverse unit, worm drive motor, magnetraction, 6200 on decal cab front. 2671W tender stamped "PENNSYL-VANIA" in white or silver, six-wheel trucks with blind center wheels, water scoop, three holes in tender rear; 0 gauge locomotive, rubber or heat-stamped cab numerals
(A) "681" and "PENNSYLVANIA" in white   55   115   170   250
(B) 1953, same as (A) but 2046W-50 tender with four-wheel trucks. Griesbeck Collection   50   100   150   220
(C) Same as (A) but 2671WX tender with "681" and "PENNSYLVANIA" rubber stamped in silver letters, Griesbeck Collection   55   45   170   250
682 1954-55, 6-8-6, Pennsylvania S-2 Turbine prototype, similar to 681 but with lubricator linkage and white stripe on running board, 6200 on boiler front Keystone, heat-stamped "682." 2046-W-50 tender with whistle, water scoop, bar-end metal trucks, magnetic couplers, three holes on tender rear filled in, tender lettered "PENNSYLVANIA," 0 gauge locomotive
      110   175   225   325

685 1953, 4-6-4, shares Santa Fe Hudson type boiler with 665, 2055, and 2065; comments from those apply; 6026W tender has metal trucks with bar-ends, magnetic couplers, two pickup rollers and whistle, 0 gauge locomotive
(A) Early production: 2046W tender, bar-end metal trucks, magnetic couplers. Loco has embossed drive rod like 2046; later production lacks this embossing. Raised projections on crosshead guide plate where screws attach, Fleming Collection   60   100   125   175
(B) Rubber stamped 685 in silver below cab windows, 6026W tender with bar-end metal trucks, Salamone Collection   70   110   140   225
(C) Same as (B) but 685 is heat-stamped in white below cab windows, Eddins Collection   60   80   110   225

686 Uncatalogued, c.1953-54, 4-6-4. Confirmation and additional information necessary. Hutchinson comment.   **NRS**

703 1946, 4-6-4, scale Hudson, postwar version of 763, catalogued but not made, prototype exists in MPC archives, Bohn comment. **Not Manufactured**

725 1952, 2-8-4. Berkshire shown in advance catalogue but not made
      Not Manufactured

726(A) 1946, 2-8-4, Berkshire, die-cast Baldwin disc drivers with pressed on metal tires, Lionel atomic precision motor with double worm gear, boiler casting is modified prewar 226 boiler, turned handrail stanchions, two plug receptacles on brushplate to disconnect E-unit or lock E-unit in place. One receptacle locks E-unit in forward, neutral or reverse and other plug activates E-unit so that it sequentially reverses, early smoke bulb unit, nickel plated drive and connecting rods, valve gear, smoke box door swings open on hinges, flag holders, nickel plated motor side not covered by cowling as on 726(B); plate that covered the bottom of the motor extends beyond ashpan and beyond beginning of last driver, in contrast to 726(B); the plate may be removed, allowing the drive wheel axle sets to be taken out. This is a revival of the prewar "BILD-A-LOCO" motor design. Ashpan integral part of motor base casting; motor on bottom says "726 O-Gauge Locomotive, Made in U.S. of America, the Lionel Corporation, New York," compare to lettering on 726(B). When bottom plate is removed worm driving and copper wheel busings are visible, metal tires on Baldwin disc wheels, center drivers are blind, pilot truck guide plate is screwed on 726(A), and riveted on 726(B), wheels on trailing truck on 726(A) have hollow area with bridge across 726(B) concentric. Same difference for pilot truck wheels. 2426W tender has metal top cab with six-wheel trucks, plastic side frames, coil coupler with sliding shoe, handrails and longrails on front, longrails and black deck railing with six stanchions; highly desirable tender, worth at least $100; same tender came with 773, 1950 version. Second version of 1946 has different frame and motor; early model cannot be used on later frame because reinforcement was added to rear of chassis. Early locomotives which retain the original smoke bulb arrangement are considerably more scarce than the converted or later versions (Fleming comment). In addition, the casting of the early 1946 loco is open where the eccentric rod attaches to the boiler casing; in later production, this area is closed, Bratspis observation
      150   225   325   500

726(B) 1947-49, generally similar to (A) but revised boiler casting with lengthened sand domes, cotter pin type handrail stanchions, E-unit mounted vertically with lever penetrating top of boiler; plug receptacles on brush plate are eliminated; simulated coupler lift bar on front pilot, black flag holders, bottom plate reads "Made in U.S.A., the Lionel Corporation, New York," riveted metal retaining plate for pilot truck, cowling added to side of motor to hide motor, simulated springs visible from side of loco, ashpan part of bottom frame but ends at rear set of drivers, resistance coil smoke unit. Large cab metal tender, 2426W; O gauge locomotive
      155   225   275   425
726(C) 1947 only, plain pilot without simulated front coupler, otherwise like (B), has 2426W metal tender, but with cast metal whistle soundbox, loco has 671M-1 motor, Griesbeck comment   150   180   225   300

726RR 1952, 2-8-4, "RR" for Korean War issue without magnetraction, cadmium plated drive and connecting rods, valve gear, smoke unit, three position reverse unit. Tender has four-wheel metal trucks, staple-end in front, bar-end with magnetic coupler in rear, two pickup rollers, holes in tender rear filled in, whistle; less desirable tender than 2426W; O gauge locomotive
(A) As above   95   170   225   300
(B) Similar to (A) but larger "726" and no "RR" on cab, nickel-plated rods, 2046W tender, holes in rear of shell, bar-end 4-wheel trucks with magnetic couplers, Griesbeck and Fleming Collections   90   155   200   250
(C) Same as (A), but six-wheel tender with "LIONEL LINES" in small white serif lettering widely spaced on the tender side, Klaassen Collection   **NRS**

736(A) 1950-51, Berkshire, spoked style drivers without tires, die-cast trailing truck, nickel plated drive and connecting rods, valve gear, worm drive motor, three position reverse unit, magnetraction, smoke, whistle, hinged smoke box door, rubber stamped cab number; 2671W tender with six-wheel trucks, plastic truck sideframes, water scoop, coil-operated couplers, holes in rear deck; O Gauge locomotive, Griesbeck comment   95   140   240   375
736(B) 1953-54, similar to (A), but heat-stamped lettering on cab, small bracket wedge on headlight casting, collector assembly attached with two screws, die-cast trailing truck, cadmium plated rods; tender with four-wheel trucks, O Gauge locomotive, Griesbeck comment   95   175   225   350
736(C) 1955-56 similar to (B), but collector assembly attached with two screws; sheet metal trailing truck with plastic side frames; tender with four-wheel trucks, O Gauge locomotive, Griesbeck comment   95   175   225   350
736(D) 1957-60, same as (C), but collector assembly attached with one screw; 2046W tender, Griesbeck comment   95   175   225   350
736(E) 1961-66, same as (D), but 736W tender, Griesbeck comment
      95   175   225   350

746 1957-60, 4-8-4, model of Norfolk and Western J, three-position reverse unit, magnetraction, liquid smoke; 746W tender with whistle, bar-end metal trucks, magnetic coupler with tab, two roller pickups; engine and tender have red band outlined in yellow stripes, yellow lettering; "746" rubber stamped on cab, tender lettered "NORFOLK AND WESTERN", O Gauge locomotive. Short stripe tender also lettered "746W"
(A) Tender with long, full-length stripe and no 746W raised numbering, 1957 only, Rubin and Weiss observations   250   450   700   900
(B) Tender with short stripe and 746W raised numbering, 1958-60, Friedman observation   250   400   600   750

773(A) 1950, 4-6-4, scale model of New York Central J-3 Hudson. Postwar version of prewar 763 and its more detailed brother, the 700E. The 773, unlike the 763 and 700E, will run on regular O Gauge tubular curve track and offers smoke and magnetraction. Loco has plug jacks in cab for connecting three position reverse unit. Label on underside of cab states: "To remove the whitish smoke...." Catalogued as O Gauge locomotive.
(A) Has lighter stamping of "773" on cab compared with (B). Comes with very desirable 2426W tender with six wheel trucks. 1950 version has slide valve guides.   475   650   1000   1200

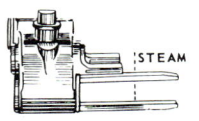

1950 Steam cylinder with slide valve guide 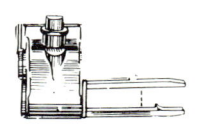   1964 cylinder without slide valve guide

(B) 1964, similar to 773(A) but with heavier heat-stamped number on cab, slide valve guides omitted from steam chest casting, steam chest not interchangeable with 773(A). "PENNSYLVANIA" tender with Timken trucks, disc coupler, two pickup rollers; "773" is more heavily stamped than on 773(A)   400   500   750   950

736[A]

746[B]   Long stripe tender

746[A]   Short stripe tender

773[A] New York Central Hudson [1950]

773[C] New York Central Hudson [1965-66]

1001

1060

1062[A]

1110

1120

1130

1654

1655

1666

2016

2018[A]

2020

2025[A]

42

(C) 1965-66, similar to (B) but with tender marked "NEW YORK CENTRAL." **400 500 750 950**

(D) Similar to (B), but has 2426W tender with plastic whistle casing, 1964-style 773 stamp, no steam chest valve guides, white marker lights on boiler front and 1950-style roller pickups. Reportedly made for Macy's in 1956. Reader comments invited. Klaassen Collection **NRS**

1001 1948, 2-4-2, first Scout loco, specially designed motor, 1001M-1 with two position reverse unit integral to motor, motor has plastic sides and smooth bottom, with two pieces of copper rolled to form pickup rollers, awnings over windows. 1001T slopeback tender with plastic top, Timken trucks, fixed coupler, galvanized base, 0-27 loco. The Lionel 1948 catalogue (page 4) shows what appears to be the same loco (note horn atop boiler front and window sunshades!). However, the catalogue shows a square tin tender rather than the slope-back tender described here. Reader comments are invited. The 1001 appears to be the first plastic boiler ever used by Lionel. This was also the first offering of the notoriously unreliable plastic-side Scout motor, which used a highly unusual engineering design for its reverse unit involving movable brush holders. Although Lionel's obvious intent was to reduce costs, this motor proved so difficult to repair that if a customer complained loudly enough, the factory or the service station would replace this motor with the conventional metal-framed motor used in the 2034. The procedure is outlined in the Lionel service manual in section LOC-1110(1951), page 1, June 1953, and section LOC-2034, page 1, August 1953. Although the plastic boiler casting for this loco was highly detailed, it did not appear again until 1959, when in obvious financial distress, Lionel brought it back. There is a Marx plastic body which is almost identical to the 1001. Was the usual role of copier and copied reversed in this instance? Reader comments invited. Bartelt comments **6 12 15 25**

1050 1959, uncatalogued 0-4-0, plastic side motor, forward only, light, side rod, 1050 slopeback tender; 0-27 loco **7 10 15 25**

1060 1960-61, 2-4-2, same boiler as 1050, no reverse, main rod only, light. This engine was not shown in the consumer catalogue, since it was intended "to meet the needs of the low priced toy train market.... for pricing and delivery information, see your wholesaler or Lionel representative." The engine came with two different tenders with at least three different sets and is illustrated in the 1961 Lionel Advance Catalogue. It has a plastic boiler with highly detailed cab interior and a curved metal piece for center rail pickup. It is classified as an 0-27 loco.

(A) 1130T tender, part of No. 1109 Huntsman Steamer set which has a 6404 flat with auto, a 3386 Bronx Zoo giraffe car and a 6047 caboose. All rolling stock has arch bar trucks and non-operating couplers. This set was offered as a Green Stamps premium set in 1960, Fleming comments. Loco and tender value: **7 10 15 30**

(B) With 1050 slope-back tender, Timken Trucks and disc coupler, part of No. 1123 Pacesetter set which included a 6406 flat with auto, a 6042 gondola with canisters and an unlettered, unnumbered caboose. Reader assistance is asked in determining the original wholesale price and the numbers printed on the boxes, Rina comments. Loco and tender value: **7 10 15 30**

(C) With 1130T tender, 3409 flat with helicopter, 6076 Lehigh Valley hopper and an unlettered, unnumbered caboose. Reader assistance is asked in determining the original wholesale price and the numbers printed on the boxes, Rina comments. Loco and tender value: **7 10 15 30**

1061 1963-64, 0-4-0; also catalogued in 1969 as a 2-4-2, black highly detailed plastic boiler, similar to 1060 and 1062, plastic side motor, rolled metal pickups, drive rod without crosshead, no reverse, no light, slope-back tender with fixed coupler lettered "LIONEL LINES". This loco was part of set 11420, which sold for $11.95 in 1963-64 (the 1969 price was not included in the catalogue). This set possesses the dubious distinction of being Lionel's least expensive set since the thirties. On the other hand, the set could be viewed as Lionel's very creative response to a difficult marketing situation. Lionel was buffeted by Marx production on one hand and race cars and space re-

1625

lated toys on the other. This set gave Lionel a chance to offer a competitive, inexpensive product. However, Lionel weakened its profit-making mechanism by such production - high quality toys at a premium price. Loco and tender value: **7 10 15 25**

1062 1963-64, 2-4-2, highly detailed plastic body, plastic side motor, rolled metal pickups, drive rod without crosshead to reduce costs, two-position reverse with lever on boiler top, rubber tire on one driver, headlight, slope-back tender lettered "LIONEL LINES," 0-27 loco. This loco is included in the No. 11430 set listed in the 1964 catalogue. Priced at $14.95, the set came with a 6176 hopper, a 6142 gondola, a 6167-125 caboose, a 6149 remote control track, a 1026 25-watt transformer and track, Winton Collection. Loco and tender values:

(A) Short headlight, drive rod without crosshead, slope-back tender, Timken trucks, fixed coupler, galvanized tender base, tender cab fastened by two tabs, contacts on tender front truck provides loco ground
 7 12 15 25

1656

(B) Long headlight, no drive rod or crosshead, large unnumbered tender, with Timken trucks, fixed coupler, contacts on tender front truck provide loco ground **7 12 15 25**

1101 1948, 2-4-2, Scout loco, die-cast boiler, sliding shoe pickups, drive rod with solid crosshead, three position reverse unit, interior cab detail, 12 rib wheels, stripped down version of 1655 powered with regular 1655-2 motor; tender with metal bottom, top; Scout trucks and coupler **7 12 15 25**

The 1101 die-cast body has a small cast bell on a small step on the boiler's left side between the smokestack and its first dome. The 1101 body design was

1665

the basis for the later 230, 240 and 250 series locos. Some of the later locos retained the step even though the bell was no longer present, i.e., 241 and 243.

The 1101 has a straight slot for the E-unit lever since the lever moves in a straight line. When the 1101 design was adopted for the 243, the slot was changed to a curved design to accommodate the movement of the two position reverse lever.

Other factors distinguish the 230, 240 and 250 series locomotives. Some have holes in the cab floor for weights (the 241 and 243), others do not. Some have thick running boards, others have thin ones. On some the reverse slot is between the first and second dome, on others between the second dome and cab.

43

2026[B]

2034

2035

2036

2037

2046

2037-500[B] Girl's Set loco with square type tender

1110 1949-52, 2-4-2, Scout with "LIONEL SCOUT" tender, die-cast boiler and cab similar to the 1101 but not interchangeable with it; Scout motor with plain plastic bottom, rounded copper pieces for pickups; drive rod with crosshead, fiber reverse lever, two position reverse; tender with metal frame and top, Scout trucks, one Scout coupler. Lord comments
(A) No hole on boiler front for smoke draft, 1949   7   12   15   25
(B) Hole in boiler front for smoke draft but no smoke unit, 1951-52
                                                        7   12   15   25

1120 1950, 2-4-2, Scout with "LIONEL SCOUT" tender, die-cast boiler, headlight, no lens, fiber reverse lever, two position reverse, plastic side motor with inaccessible brushes; rolled copper pieces for pickups; tender with metal frame and top, Scout trucks, one Scout coupler   7   10   15   25

1130 1950, 2-4-2, black plastic body similar to die-cast 2034; 2034-100 motor with three position reverse unit, short lever points down, headlight lens, main rods with guides, roller pickups which slide in and are held by a clip, large gear seen between drivers on left, brush plate on right. 1130T tender, Timken trucks, one disc coupler; 0-27 loco
(A) As described above   7   12   15   25
(B) Die-cast body instead of plastic, Niedhammer and Szabat Collections
                                                                    NRS

1615 1955-57, 0-4-0 wheel arrangement, Switcher, black die-cast body, B6 on boiler right side, red marker lights, 0-27 motor with brush plate showing on left side and two gears showing on right, operating-disc coupler in front, coupler to tender has brass spring to increase contact with tender, sliding type 0-27 pickup shoes. 1615T slope-back tender, no bell in tender, metal trucks; 0-27 loco   40   75 125 200

1882

1625 1958, 0-4-0, Switcher, black die-cast body with red marker lights, cadmium plated rods, disc-operating coupler in front, no bell, coupler to tender has spring for better contact, 0-27 plate, 0-27 motor with brush plate on left side, two gears showing on left side, B6 on boiler on right side, 1625 slope-back tender, 0-27 loco   50 100 150 250

1654 1946-47, 2-4-2, black die-cast boiler, nickel trim pipe on each boiler side, nickel bell and whistle, three position reverse unit, metal reverse lever through boiler; sliding shoe motor 1654M-1 with brush plate on left side, motor fastened to boiler in part by long pin that goes through back of boiler casting, large gear between drivers on right side, drive and connecting rods attached to solid crosshead; 0-27 loco, operates on 0-27 track but not switches or crossovers, 1654W tender with whistle(or 1654T without whistle), metal base and top staple-end metal trucks, coil coupler
                                                        8   12   20   35

1655 1948-49, 2-4-2, heavy black die-cast body with fine cab interior detail; light, drive and connecting rods, two sliding shoe pickups, improved 1655M-1 motor using double reduction gears (compare with 1654); brush plate left side, four visible gears, solid crosshead, twelve-spoked wheels, nickel bell and whistle, three position reverse, metal reverse lever through boiler near cab. 6654W metal box tender with whistle, metal trucks 8   12   20   35

1656 1948-49, 0-4-0, Switcher, black die-cast body, B6 on right side, red marker lights; light, nickel bell on bracket; 1656M-1 motor identical to 1655-1 except equipped with contact rollers rather than sliding shoes; coil-operated front coupler; two plug/jack connections from loco to tender; left plug connects loco coupler to tender, rear truck pickup shoe; center plug provides extra ground for loco through tender wheels and body. 6403 slope-back tender, staple-end metal trucks, coil coupler. Tender has bell, wire handrails and working backup light, I.D. Smith observations
(A) "LIONEL LINES" closely spaced on tender   90 150 195 280
(B) "LIONEL LINES" spaced out on tender   90 140 185 265

1665 1946, 0-4-0, Switcher, black die-cast body, red marker lights, coil-operated front coupler and wire handrails, 1662M-2 motor shared with prewar 1662 with four gears showing on left side, brush plate on right, three position reverse unit, two wires from tender plug into loco: left wire connects loco front coupler coil to tender sliding shoe, other wire provides better ground. 2403B slope-back tender with metal frame, body, bell, and metal trucks; backup light on tender, "LIONEL LINES" heat-stamped on tender, staple-end metal trucks, coil coupler, wide-spaced lettering, separate Bakelite coal pile casting and wire handrail (although illustration does not show handrail), I.D. Smith comments   95 195 250 350

Two different postwar 1666's both have the rounded cab floor but one is rubber stamped while the other has metal number plates. Bartelt photographs.

45

2055[A]

2056

2065

4671 Electronic control loco

6110

Two versions of the 2037-500 Girl's locomotive. Left has plain heat stamped lettering; right has bold fancy rubber stamped lettering. Griesbeck Collection.

1666 1946-47, 2-6-2, black die-cast loco, twelve spoked wheels with connecting rod, valve gear rod and drive rod, sliding shoe pickup, nickle tires, geared on left side and brush plate on right side, plate on bottom, "LIONEL 027," green marker lights, nickel bell on a bracket, three position reverse unit mounted between the smokestack and the first dome, limited cab interior detail consists of two firebox doors, die-cast front and rear trucks. 6654W metal box tender with whistle, staple-end metal trucks, coil coupler. Gunmetal "1666" was manufactured prior to 1945 as was "1666E." A postwar 1666 has knuckle couplers and a rounded rear cab floor. Prewar ones are square and have a long shank hook on tender

(A) No stamping on cab firebox door	25	40	55	70
(B) Silver rubber stamped X on left firebox door. X approximately 3/8 of an inch high	25	40	60	75
(C) Similar to (A) but with rubber stamped 1666 on cab	25	40	55	70
(D) Similar to (A) but with 2466WX tender with whistle, staple-end metal trucks, coil coupler	25	40	60	75
(E) Similar to (A) but with 2466T tender with staple-end metal trucks, coil coupler	25	40	55	70

1862 1959-62, 4-4-0, modeled after Civil War "General," gray boiler, red cab, green 1862T tender, 0-27 gauge, without magnetraction, two position reverse, light; lacks some boiler banding and applied piping details found on 1872, does not have smoke or whistle

(A) Gray stack	70	90	125	170
(B) Black stack	70	90	125	170

1872 1959-62, 4-4-0, modeled after Civil War "General," gray chassis and boiler, red cab and pilot, black, red and green 1872T tender with gold lettering; O Gauge, magnetraction, smoke unit, three position reverse, came with coach 1875W with whistle in set   100   195   250   300

1882 1959-62, 4-4-0, modeled after Civil War "General," uncatalogued by Lionel, sold by Sears, black boiler and smokestack, orange pilot and cab with gold lettering, does not have smoke unit or whistle

(A) Black stack, Weiss Collection	150	200	330	500
(B) Gray stack, Hutchinson Collection. Further observation requested				NRS

2016 1955-56, 2-6-4, light, does not have smoke or magnetraction, similar to 2037 with box on front pilot, three position reverse unit, "LIONEL 0-27" plate on bottom, cadmium plated drive rod and connecting rod; 6026W tender, lettered "LIONEL LINES," with whistle, bar-end metal trucks, magnetic coupler with tab, 0-27 loco   18   30   45   65

2018 1955-56, 2-6-4, box on front pilot, cadmium plated drive and connecting rods, smoke, three position reverse unit. 6026W tender and whistle, bar-end metal trucks, magnetic coupler, "LIONEL LINES" on tender side; 0-27 loco

(A) Black	20	35	50	75
(B) Blue, from Boy's Set, two known to exist				NRS

2020 1946-47, 6-8-6, model of Pennsylvania S-2 Steam Turbine. See discussion under 671. Catalogued as 0-27 but identical to 671 which was catalogued as O Gauge.

(A) 1946, double worm drive, horizontal reverse unit without external E unit lever. Since lever does not penetrate boiler, loco cab interior includes two jacks on the brush plate holder. Plugs are inserted to disconnect the E-unit or lock the E-unit in one position. Motor labeled "ATOMIC MOTOR," slotted brush holders, shiny nickle drive rims. Loco has smoke bulb, part #671-62 with bulb marked GE797, 15 watts, 12 volts. The bulb has an indentation to hold "early" smoke tablets. The bulb did not produce sufficient smoke and bulb was replaced by the resistance coil (see B). However, Lionel furnished a kit to its service stations to convert the bulb unit to resistance unit coils. Consequently, 2020(A)s will be found with resistance coil units. 2020W tender lettered "LIONEL LINES," metal trucks with staple-end on front, bar-end on rear truck with magnetic coupler. Confirmation requested. Tender has trim on rear deck and rails on both rear and front ends. Tender stamped 2020W on bottom, Shewmake Collection   45   70   100   150

(B) 1947, single worm drive motor, vertical reverse unit with E-unit lever projecting through boiler, new resistance coil type smoke unit with bellows, no plug jacks on motor brushplate, non-slotted brush tubes. 6020W tender with magnetic coupler, and plastic whistle box, Griesbeck Collection   45   70   90   140

2025 (A) 1947, 2-6-2, same as 675 (except number) but catalogued as 0-27, 5690 on boiler front. 2460WX tender with whistle, metal trucks, coil-operated coupler, railing on tender rear deck   25   35   50   80

(B) 1948-49, same as 2025(A) but pilot with simulated knuckle and lift pin. 6466WX tender with magnetic coupler   20   35   50   80

(C) 1952, 2-6-4, black steel frame, sintered iron wheels, smoke, light, no magnetraction, 6466W tender with whistle   20   35   50   80

(D) 1948, same as (B), but 2466WX tender stamped "6466WX," wire-wound coupler, staple-end trucks, Hutchinson Collection   20   35   50   80

2026 1948-49, 51-53, 2-6-2, based on 1666, feedwater heater, box added to pilot, sand dome enlarged, smoke, light, sliding shoe pickups, drive rod, connecting rod, eccentric; die-cast trailing truck, steel rimmed drivers

(A) 6466WX tender with whistle, 1948-49 . . . . 30 40 50 70
(B) 6466W or 6466T tender, rimless drivers, 2-6-4, no eccentric rod, roller pickups, stamped sheet metal trailing truck, 1951-53, I.D. Smith observation
. . . . 30 40 50 70
(C) 1952, spoked sintered metal wheels, no tires, no magnetraction because of Korean War Alnico magnetic metal shortage, 2-6-4 with four-wheel stamped sheet metal trailing truck, 2046 Type tender, shown as a 2-6-2 in 1952 catalogue, also shown in the Lionel Service Manual, Hutchinson and Bartelt observations 30 40 50 70

2029 (A) 1964-69, 2-6-4, light, smoke, rubber tires, main rod, side rod, 243W tender with whistle, available in 1967 although no catalogue was issued, 0-27 loco 13 25 40 60
(B) 1968, 2-6-4, plate on bottom reads "THE LIONEL TOY CORPORATION, Hagerstown, Maryland 21740;" the trailing truck has "Japan" embossed on it; drive rod, connecting rods, brush plate on left side, blue insulating material covers E-unit and motor field coil; gears on right side, motor has both brass and dark colored gears; motor attached by bar through back of firebox area and held in by grooves on front end; bracket holding the front truck is shiny metal, smoke unit bottom is also shiny metal; three position reverse unit, smoke. 234W Santa Fe type tender with Timken trucks and center rail pickup on both trucks, fixed coupler, whistle, "LIONEL LINES" heat-stamped in white as is 234W; from the Hagerstown set which consisted of 25000 hopper, 6014 box, 6315 tank, 6560 crane and 6130 work caboose; price for loco and tender only 15 25 40 60

2029W Loco with 1130T uncatalogued tender, "Southern Pacific," Hutchinson comment, LCCA magazine, Volume 5, #2. More information necessary
. . . . **NRS**

2034 1952, 2-4-2, die-cast body, 2034-100 motor with three position reverse unit, light, very similar to 1130 which has plastic body and Scout plastic side motor, 0-27 loco 10 15 20 30

2035 (A) 1950, 2-6-4, based on 2025 but with magnetraction, drive rod, connecting rod, eccentric rod with new crank using half-moon fitting into wheel recess, trailing truck stamped steel, sintered iron drivers. 2466W tender with whistle but without hand rails, 0-27 . . . . 20 30 45 75
(B) 1951, same as (A) but crank fastened by two projecting pins, motor has armature plates (not on 2035(A)), and has pickup rollers with fixed axles 20 30 45 75
(C) 1950, 2-6-2, uncatalogued, illustrated in November, 1950 **Model Railroader**, apparently 675-212 trailing truck. Reported by Lower and Rapp. We need additional confirmation of pieces that are known to be original with this truck arrangement. . . . . **NRS**

2036 1950, 2-6-4, similar to 2026(A) but with magnetraction, rimless drive wheels, no smoke, sheet metal trailing truck, no handrails or eccentric rod. 6466W tender without handrails, 0-27 loco 18 35 45 75

2037 1954-55, 1957-58, 2-6-4, derived from 2026 and 2036, light, smoke, magnetraction, "2037" heat-stamped in white
(A) 6026W tender, 1957 . . . . 25 35 50 100
(B) 6026 tender, 1954-55, 58-60 . . . . 25 35 50 100

2037-500 1957, 2-6-4, pink body for "Girl's Set" with blue 2037 numbers beneath the cab window, (2037-500 does not appear on cab), smoke, headlight lens, green marker lights, battery box on front pilot, nickeled simulated bell, three position reverse unit, magnetraction, drive rod and connecting rod only, brush plate on left side, gears on right side. Set includes hopper, gondola, two boxcars, caboose, and 1130T tender. Reproduction locomotives have been made which are difficult to distinguish from originals, Bohn comment. Set: 600 700 900 1500
(A) 2230T streamline tender 200 300 400 500
(B) 6026 square type tender, may be one of a kind, Degano Collection **NRS**

2046 1950-53, 4-6-4, die-cast New York Central type boiler, gears on left side, brushes on right, drive rods, connecting rods, valve gear, three-position reverse unit, magnetraction, shares casting with 646 and 2056, evolved from 726; 2046W tender with whistle, bar-end metal trucks, two pickups, magnetic coupler with tab, with or without "2046W" lettering; 0-27
(A) 1950-52, metal trailing truck 50 70 90 150
(B) 1953, plastic trailing truck 50 70 90 150

2055 1953-55, 4-6-4, die-cast Santa Fe type boiler, magnetraction, drive rod, connecting rod, valve gear, smoke unit, light, boiler front pops out, shares boiler casting with 665, 685 and 2065, 0-27.
(A) 1025W square tender, bar-end metal trucks, magnetic coupler, whistle, "LIONEL LINES" 45 70 90 150
(B) 2046W tender 45 70 90 150

2056 1952, 4-6-4, die-cast NYC type boiler, smoke, three position reverse, gears on left, brush plate on right, reversing lever slot directly in front of cab; 2046W tender has water scoop, whistle, metal trucks with bar-end, magnetic coupler, tender lettered "LIONEL LINES" in larger type than that found on tender that came with 2046, catalogued as 0-27
. . . . 45 70 90 145

2065 1954-57, 4-6-4, 4-6-4, die-cast Santa Fe type boiler with feedwater heater above boiler front, smoke, magnetraction, drive rod, connecting rod, valve gear, boiler casting on left is relatively plain. Trailer truck casting with plastic sides same as both 2065 and 2055, casting detail also shared with 665 and 685; 665 has a feedwater heater while 685 does not
(A) 2046W tender with whistle 45 70 90 140
(B) 6026W tender 45 70 90 140

2671 1968, TCA Convention tender shell only, 2046-type shell with large "TCA" in white, TCA circular logo in white, "NATIONAL CONVENTION 1968 CLEVELAND, OHIO" in white, two lines over and underscored. Versions with gold and silver lettering also exist. Quantities produced: 1,146 white, 43 gold and 11 silver-lettered, Bratspis observation. Although this chapter is devoted to locomotives with tenders we have listed this tender in this chapter since it is more easily located by our readers. Priced for white lettering . . . . — — — 75

4671 1946, 6-8-6, electronic control set, Lionel Precision motor with two jacks, decaled with black decal smaller than a dime and white lettered "ELECTRONIC CONTROL" and "L" in center, boiler front has red Keystone with gold number "6200," smoke unit. Loco numbered "671" on cab. 4671W tender with Type RU electronic control receiver affixed to frame underside, "LIONEL LINES" heat-stamped in silver, special electronic control decal, light gray with white lettered "ELECTRONIC CONTROL," tender has handrails on rear deck and rear end and handrails on tender front, wire connects loco with tender, metal trucks, staple-end, coil coupler operated by electronic control receiver; gray decal on tender matches gray button on control unit. Set consists of 4671 loco, 4671W tender, 5459 automatic dump car, X4454 Baby Ruth box car, 4357SP caboose, alternately came with 4457 Pennsylvania caboose
(A) Loco and tender only 65 100 125 175
(B) Price for set 150 180 310 425

4681 1950, 6-8-6 electronic control locomotive and tender with set. Although catalogued, this locomotive was apparently never made. This conclusion is based upon the absence of comments by readers about the omission over the last six years . . . . **NOT MANUFACTURED**

6110 1950-51, 2-4-2, black die-cast boiler, drive rod with crosshead, fiber reverse lever, two-position reverse, no light, magnetraction, 6001T tender, 0-27 loco. This Scout loco, similar to 1001, 1110 and 1120, does not use a conventional E-unit for reversing. Lionel created a very imaginative—and trouble-prone motor design which made the reversing mechanism part of the motor itself and reduced costs. This motor has a two-part field. One part is pivoted to permit it to move when attracted by the energized winding on the stationary section of the field. As the movable field pivots downward, it moves a pawl engaging the geared drums of the brush holders, causing them to rotate. The rotation changes the connections to the armature windings with respect to the field windings, and thus reverses the motor direction. The movable field and pawl stay in the low position, locking the brush holder drums as long as the field winding is energized. When the current is interrupted, the pawl spring returns the movable field and pawl to their up positions. The Scout motor includes a fiber lever which protrudes through the boiler and locks the loco in either forward or reverse, as no neutral position is possible with this design. This loco has a smoke generator, but not the usual piston and cylinder arrangement found on more expensive locos. Rather, smoke is driven up the stack by air which enters through a hole on the boiler front. Consequently, forward motion is necessary for smoke! Its magnetraction, like that of early magnetraction diesels, uses a permanent magnet fixed transversely between the rear wheels, rather than having magnetic axles carry the magnetic flux through the wheels. The magnetic circuit is completed through the sintered iron rear drivers. The tender came in a box marked 6001T and has "LIONEL LINES" in white lettering. The tender has no lettering on its bottom and Scout trucks. Although the tender shell omits the hole to the lower right of "D" in the diagram on page 48, it has one 1/4" hole, one 1/8" hole and a large rectangular opening. This engine came in set 1461S, which contained a 6002 black gondola, a 6004 box car in a box marked 6004 and a 6007 Die #3 caboose. The set sold for $19.95. These observations are compiled from the comments of Lord, Kotil and I.D. Smith. Loco and tender value 7 12 15 25

MOLD IDENTIFICATION OF SQUARE PLASTIC TENDERS
by Joseph F. Kotil
Frame Identification for Postwar Tenders

There are four versions of the 1666T-4

All molds are identified by the number 1666T-4 on the inside top of the tender.

Unlettered holes are common to all tenders

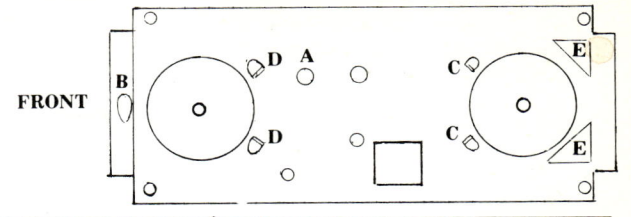

FRONT

Type I Four small holes at the front for handrails; the holes may or may not go through to the inside; all prewar and early postwar tenders are Type I. Whistle tenders have rounded corners, elongated holes punched in the front and a coal pile.	**Type I** 2466W Early		**OPTIONAL PUNCHINGS** Oval Hole B Tabs D	Punchings E
Type II Four small holes not present. The tender has a rectangular hole at the front and a hole molded in the coal pile. The coal backup web is about one-sixteenth of an inch thick.	**Type II** 2466W Late 2466WX	671W 2020W	Tabs D Hole A	Punchings E
Type III Same as Type II, but the coal backup web is thicker, about one-eighth of an inch thick. It was probably thickened to prevent it from breaking.	**Type III** 2466T 6466T	6066T	None	
Type IV Same as Type II, but one large lump of coal covers the whistle hole; this is a crude mold modification for late non-whistle tenders.	**Type IV** 6466WX Early	6020W Early	Tabs D Hole A	Punchings E
Type V Same as Type IV, but the tender has a typical coal pile over the whistle opening.	**Type V** 6466WX Late		Tabs D	Punchings E
Type VI Same as Type I, but the die for the four small holes was ground off and was used to manufacture a non-whistle tender for low-priced locomotives; it has no opening in the front.	**Type VI** 6020W Late 6466W		Tabs D Tabs C	Hole A Punchings E

49

Chapter III
ACCESSORIES

	Gd.	V.G.	Exc.	Mt.
011-11 INSULATING PINS 1940-60, for 0 gauge, white or black, each	.03	.05	.05	.05
011-43 INSULATING PINS 1961, for 0 gauge, per dozen	.40	.75	1	1.50
T011-43 INSULATING PINS 1962-66, for 0 gauge, per dozen	.50	.75	1	1.50
020X 45 DEGREE CROSSOVER 1946-59, for 0 gauge	1.50	2	4	10
020 90 DEGREE CROSSOVER 1945-61, for 0 gauge	1.50	2	4	8
T020 90 DEGREE CROSSOVER 1962, 66, 69, for 0 gauge	1.50	2	4	8
022 REMOTE CONTROL SWITCHES 1945-49, new curved control rails, new long curved rails, new auxiliary rails, new long straight rail, new location for screw holes holding bottom. For more information see Lionel Service Manual.	25	40	50	75
022LH REMOTE CONTROL SWITCH 1950-61, left hand switch for 0 gauge, with controller	10	15	25	35
022RH REMOTE CONTROL SWITCH 1950-61, right hand switch for 0 gauge, with controller	10	15	25	35
022-500 0 GAUGE ADAPTER SET 1957-61, combines Super 0 with 0 track	1	1.50	2	3
T022-5000 0 GAUGE ADAPTER SET 1962-66, combines Super 0 with 0 track	1	1.50	2	3
025 BUMPER 1946-47, 0 gauge illuminated black bumper with a piece of track, late prewar carryover, Bohn comment.	3	5	8	14
026 BUMPER 1950, Die-cast bumper with spring-loaded gray metal energy absorber, bayonet bulb socket, four wide feet, center rail pickup with notch				
(A) Red	3	5	8	14
(B) Gray	5	10	15	20
027C-1 TRACK CLIPS 1947, 1949, for 0 track, per dozen	.50	.75	1	2
30 WATER TOWER 1947-50, with operating spout				
(A) Single-walled plastic tank, solenoid makes spout move; gray die-cast base, brown plastic frame, orange tank with two binding nuts on gray roof. 6 1/8 x 10 1/8 inches high	25	45	60	90
(B) Double-walled plastic tank without place for hose connections, gray die-cast base, black metal frame, unusual variation	40	75	130	220
31 CURVED TRACK 1957-66, Super 0, 36 inch diameter	.30	.50	.60	.80
31-7 POWER BLADE CONNECTOR 1957-61, Super 0	–	–	–	.25
31-15 GROUND RAIL PIN 1957-66, Super 0, per dozen	–	–	–	.75
31-45 POWER BLADE CONNECTION 1961-66, Super 0, per dozen	–	–	–	.75
32 STRAIGHT TRACK 1957, Super O	.35	50	75	1
32-10 INSULATING PIN 1957-60, Super 0, per dozen	–	–	–	.50
32-20 POWER BLADE INSULATOR 1957-60, Super 0	–	–	–	.10
32-25 INSULATING PIN Part of 1122-500, 0-27 adapter set	–	–	–	.10
32-30 GROUND PIN Part of 922-500 0 gauge adapter set	–	–	–	.10
32-31 POWER PIN Part of 022-500 0 gauge adapter set	–	–	–	.10
32-32 INSULATING PIN Part of 022-500 0 gauge adapter set	–	–	–	.10
32-33 GROUND PIN Part of 1122-500 0-27 adapter set	–	–	–	.10

	Gd.	V.G.	Exc.	Mt.
32-34 POWER PIN Part of 1122-500 0-27 adapter set	–	–	–	.10
32-45 POWER BLADE INSULATION 1961-66, per dozen, for Super 0	–	–	–	.75
32-55 INSULATING PIN 1961-66, for Super 0, per dozen	–	–	–	.75
33 HALF CURVED TRACK 1957-66, Super 0, 4 1/2 inches	.25	.50	.85	1
34 HALF STRAIGHT TRACK 1957-66, Super 0, 5 3/4 inches	.25	.50	.75	1
35 BOULEVARD LAMP 1945-49, 6 1/8 inches high, finial top	3	4	6	10
36 OPERATING CAR REMOTE CONTROL SET 1957-66, for Super 0	1	2	4	8
37 UNCOUPLING TRACK SET 1957-66, for Super 0	1	2	4	7
38 WATER TOWER 1946-47, water put in double-walled tank; then by gravity, water flows to base, after which it is pumped by motor back up; solenoid-operated spout. Water does not come out of the spout. Die-cast tank base "No. 38," brown die-cast frame, orange tinted plastic double-walled tank with two rubber hoses subject to deterioration. Roof with metal center post for water plug in center, two binding posts for roof with rubber gaskets and speed nuts. Came with little funnel				
(A) Brown roof	50	150	225	300
(B) Red roof	60	175	250	350
38 ACCESSORY ADAPTER TRACKS 1957-61, pair, for adapting 55, 154, 497, 3360 and 3414 to Super 0	1	2	4	8
39 SUPER 0 OPERATING SET 1957	1	2	4	8
39-25 OPERATING SET 1961-66, Super 0, uncoupling and operating units	1	2	4	8
40 HOOK UP WIRE 1950-51, 1953-63, with cable reel, insulated 18 gauge wire	1	2	3	4
40-50 CABLE REEL 1960-61, 15 inches of three conductor wire	1	2	3	4
40-25 CONDUCTOR WIRE 1956-59, 15 inches of four conductor wire	1	3	4	5
41 CONTACTOR	.40	.60	.80	1
42 042 MANUAL SWITCHES 1947-59, pair for 0 gauge, change in 1950 from screw-type lamp socket to bayonet-type lamp socket	10	20	25	40
43 POWER TRACK 1959-66, 1 1/2 inch track section with ground and power terminals	1.50	2	3	4
44-80 MISSILES 1959-60, set of four for No. 44, 45, 6544 and 6844	1.50	2	3	5
45 GATEMAN 1946-49, door opens, gateman comes out with lantern, with contactor	7	12	20	30
45-N GATEMAN 1945, door opens, gateman comes out with lantern, with contactor	7	12	20	30
48 INSULATED STRAIGHT TRACK 1957-66, Super 0	.75	1	1.50	2
55-150 TIES 1957-60, 24 ties for No. 55 Tie Jector	1.50	2	3	7
56 LAMP POST 1946-49, 7 3/4 inches high	10	20	35	50
58 LAMP POST 1946-60, ivory, 7 1/2 inches high	5	7	10	18
61 GROUND LOCK ON 1957-66, Super 0	.25	.40	.50	1
62 POWER LOCK ON 1957-66, Super 0	.25	.40	.50	1
64 STREET LAMP 1945-49, 6 3/4 inches high	6	9	16	20

30(A) 　　　　30(B) 　　　　30(B)

025　026 　　　36 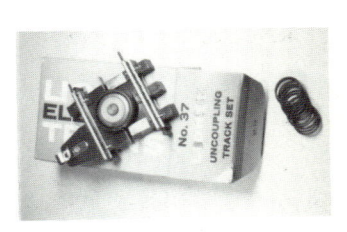　　　　37

38 　　　　38 　　　　41,153C, 145C

56 　　　70 　　71 　　75

51

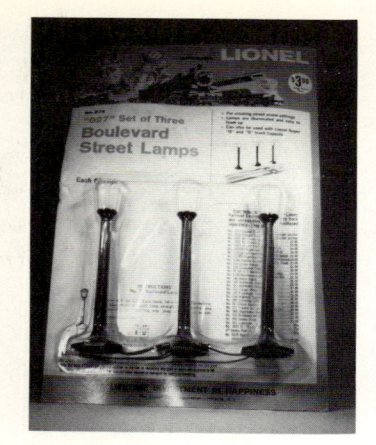

76

89

92

93

97

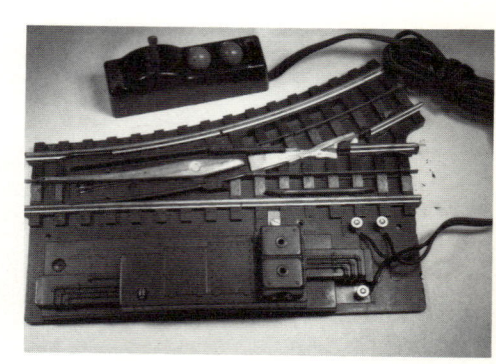

112

114

115

118

120

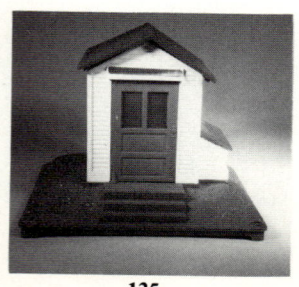

125

130

52

70 YARD LIGHT 1949-50, 4 1/2 inches high, swivel die-cast head
                                    6   20   35   50

71 LAMP POST 1949-59, die-cast 6 inches high   2   5   10   20

75 GOOSE NECK LAMPS 1961-73, set of two black lamps, each 6-1/2 inches high, base 1-3/4 x 1-1/2 inches, Young Collection. Revived by Fundimensions in 1980.   5   10   15   25

76 BOULEVARD STREET LAMPS 1955-66, 1968-69, set of three plastic light fixtures with two-pin base bulbs   2   3   4   6

88 CONTROLLER 1946-60, normally "on" button used for direction reversing   .50   .75   1   2

89 FLAGPOLE 1956-58, fabric American flag in red, white and blue with purple Lionel pennant with white lettering, white shaft, tan plastic base with four green corner plots made from sponge, 11 inches high, reissued by Fundimensions in 1983, original hard to find, Bohn comment.
                                    6   10   20   30

90 CONTROLLER, large red button embossed with "L" .25 .50 .75 1.00

91 CIRCUIT BREAKER 1957-60, electro-magnetic action, adjustable from 1 to 6 amps, 4 3/4 x 1 3/8 inches   1   2   3   5

92 CIRCUIT BREAKER CONTROLLER 1959-66, 1968-69, fixed load breaker   .50   .75   1   2

93 WATER TOWER 1946-49, aluminum finish, black spout, red base, "LIONEL TRAINS" decal with red letters outlined in black and a black line around decal edge, Lord observation   7   12   20   35

97 COAL ELEVATOR 1946-50, coal carried from tray to bunker by endless chain with buckets; switch controls bunker exit chute; yellow bunker with red metal roof, black bakelite base, aluminum colored metal frame; two binding posts on one side; three posts other side, with controller
                                    50   75   150   200

100 MULTIVOLT - DC/AC POWER PACK, 1958-66   NRS

109 TRESTLE SET Sold with set #2574 in 1961 catalogue. Pages 40 & 41, additional sightings requested, Hutchinson comment   NRS

110 TRESTLE SET 1955-69, set of 24 graduated piers   1   2   10   5

111 TRESTLE SET 1956-69, set of 10 large piers   2   3   5   7

111-100 TRESTLE PIERS 1960-63, two 4 3/4 piers   1   2   3   5

112 SUPER 0 SWITCHES 1957-66, remote control, pair with controllers   20   40   75   95

112LH SUPER 0 SWITCH 1962-66, left-hand with controller   10   20   35   45

112RH SUPER 0 SWITCH 1962-66, right-hand with controller   10   20   35   45

112-125 SUPER 0 SWITCH 1957-61, left-hand, with controller, remote control   10   20   35   45

112-150 SUPER 0 SWITCH 1957-61, right-hand, with controller, remote control   10   20   35   45

114 NEWSSTAND WITH HORN 1957-59, brown plastic base with bench on right side, yellow plastic building, gray roof, diesel horn operated by battery, battery circuit completed through controller, four connecting clips on base, bayonet-type lamp socket   20   30   50   75

115 LIONEL CITY STATION 1946-49, with automatic train control stop, red metal base, cream side with red window and door trim, red roof, lighted, three binding posts, one visible on left side, 13-5/8 inches long, 9-1/4 inches wide, 8-1/2 inches high   75   110   175   300

118 NEWSSTAND WITH WHISTLE 1958, brown plastic base with three mounting plates, building is yellow-sided with gray plastic roof, whistle unit and light inside, bench is flanked on left side by two green "sponge" bushes   20   30   50   75

119 LANDSCAPED TUNNEL 1957, 14 inches long, 10 inches wide, 8 inches high   2   3   5   7

120 90 DEGREE CROSSING 1957-66, Super 0   1   2   3   7

121 LANDSCAPED TUNNEL 1959-66, 14 inches long, 12 inches wide, 12 inches high   2   3   5   7

123 LAMP ASSORTMENT 1955-59, orange box with 48 assorted bulbs, 13-3/4 inches x 7-3/4 inches x 1-3/4 inches, with white simulated steam loco headlight beam and five oversized pictures of lamps on box cover. Box lid has "LIONEL" in white on blue field, "REPLACEMENT LAMP ASSORTMENT" in orange, and "No. 123" and "FOR MODEL TRAINS & ACCESSORIES" in blue, Salamone Collection   NRS

123-60 LAMP ASSORTMENT 1960-63, same configuration as No. 123, but larger box with 120 assorted lamps. Curiously, these lamps show less variation by type than did those in the earlier set, Salamone Collection   NRS

125 WHISTLE SHACK 1950-55, similar to 145 Gateman, but contains whistle, not lighted, dark red roof, medium red tool box top, roof, and tool box lid easily interchanged with other unit white building, red windows and door, red decal with gold lettered "LIONELVILLE" over door, frosted plastic window in door; other windows without plastic

(A) Gray base   7   10   30   50

(B) Green base   NRS

128 ANIMATED NEWSSTAND 1957-60. Newsdealer moves, newsboy turns, pup runs around hydrant, 8 1/2 inches long, 6 1/4 inches wide, 4 1/4 inches high. Green building, red roof, tan base, red hydrant. Revived by Fundimensions in 1982.   20   60   85   150

130 60 DEGREE CROSSING 1957-61, Super 0   1   2   4   8

131 CURVED TUNNEL 1959-66, 28 inches long, 14 inches wide, 12 inches high   2   3   5   10

132 PASSENGER STATION 1949-55, maroon plastic base, white building, green trim and roof, illuminated with stop feature, 6 1/2 inches high, 12 1/8 inches long, 8 1/4 inches wide, three binding clips, train stop control lever controls length of pause, base plastic is shinier than 133 base plastic
                                    11   20   30   50

133 PASSENGER STATION 1957-66, illuminated, maroon base, white building with green doors and windows, green roof, two binding clips on bottom. Similar to 132 but without train stop control   11   15   25   35

137 PASSENGER STATION 1946 catalogued but only made prewar   NRS

138 WATER TOWER 1953-57, brown plastic single-walled tank with operating spout, orange plastic roof without screw posts and without holes, differs from roofs on 30 and 38, gray plastic base, brown plastic frame, 10 1/8 inches high, base 6 1/8 x 6 1/8 inches   30   35   60   90

140 AUTOMATIC BANJO SIGNAL 1954-66, warning sign with moving arm, flashing moving arm causes light flashing, contactor 7 1/2 inches high, shown in original box   5   10   20   30

142 MANUAL SWITCHES 1957-66, Super 0, pair   10   15   20   30

142-125 LEFT-HAND SWITCH 1957-61, Super 0, manual   5   7   10   15

142-150 RIGHT-HAND SWITCH 1957-61, Super 0, manual   5   7   10   15

142LH MANUAL SWITCH 1962-66, Super 0, left-hand 5   7   10   15

142RH MANUAL SWITCH 1962-66, Super 0, right-hand   5   7   10   15

145 AUTOMATIC GATEMAN 1950-66, blue-suited watchman with flesh colored face and hands carrying lantern, emerges as train passes; lighted white plastic shed with red door, frosted plastic window material in door and window, red toolbox lid, green metal base, black die-cast base on crossing sign, white plastic crossing sign No. 309-29 with black lettering. Variations in roof color and toolbox lid covers, base 6 3/4 x 7 inches high
                                    10   15   20   30

145C CONTACTOR 1950-60   .50   .75   1   1.50

147 WHISTLE CONTROLLER 1961-66, also known as horn controller. Uses one "D" size battery   .50   .75   1   1.50

148 DWARF TRACKSIDE LIGHT 1957-60, buff colored plastic body, black lens unit, red and green bulbs, pin type bulbs, three binding clips on bottom, require 148C DPDT switch for operation, hard to find, Bohn comment
                                    15   35   50   80

150 TELEGRAPH POLE SET 1947-50, set of six brown plastic poles with metal base clips   5   10   20   30

132

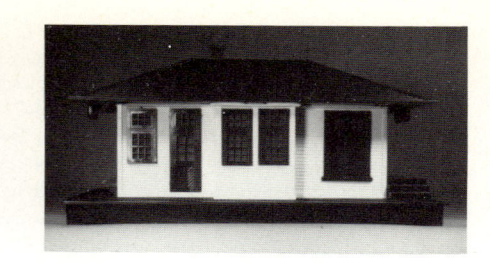

133

138

140

142-125

145

148

150

151

151

152

153

54

151 SEMAPHORE 1947-69, moving plastic blade with yellow painted tip with red and green translucent plastic inserts, black die-cast base, silver painted metal shaft, red ladder, metal bulb assembly, three binding posts on base top, with contactor   5   10   15   25

152 AUTOMATIC CROSSING GATE 1945-49, red painted die-cast base, large metal gate with black paper strip, small pedestrian gate, bayonet base bulb, two screw posts on base top, with contactor, Spitzer observation
7   10   15   30

153 AUTOMATIC BLOCK CONTROL 1945-69, two position with contactor for controlling two trains on single track, green die-cast base, aluminum shaft, orange ladder, black metal ladder holder, black die-cast lamp shell; common ground post is center post, bayonet-type bulbs, 9 inches high
6   10   15   25

153C CONTACTOR single pole, double throw   .50   1   1.50   2

154 AUTOMATIC HIGHWAY SIGNAL 1945-69, cross-buck with two alternatively flashing red bulbs, operating by 154C contactor, 8 3/4 inches high, three screw posts, black base
(A) White painted die-cast X shaped sign with black raised lettering, "STOP" in white lettering on black die-cast part, screw socket bulbs
7   10   15   20
(B) White plastic X shaped sign with white raised lettering, "STOP" in raised white lettering on black plastic, bayonet socket bulbs
7   10   15   20
(C) Same as (A), but orange painted metal base, 1950, rare, Bohn comment   **NRS**
(D) Same as (A), but metal base painted red on interior and exterior, 1950, rare, Bohn comment   **NRS**

155 BLINKING LIGHT SIGNAL WITH BELL 1955-57, similar to No. 154 but with large base containing bell. Black and white plastic base, black shaft, black plastic railroad crossing sign with white lettering, "STOP" raised white lettering, bayonet-type bulbs   6   12   20   30

Note: 155 was also used by Lionel to refer to the Prewar Station Platform

156 STATION PLATFORM 1946-51, two lights, miniature billboards, green plastic base, metal uprights, red plastic roof, 12 inches long, 3 1/4 inches wide, 5 1/8 inches high, includes four signs   5   15   25   40

157 STATION PLATFORM 1952-59, lighted with miniature billboards, maroon plastic base, black metal post, green plastic roof, 12 inches long, 5 1/8 inches high, 3 1/4 inches wide, at least 11 different signs exist, Bohn comment
(A) Campbell Soup, Switch to Rival Dog Food, Baby Ruth and Sunoco; signs can be interchanged, some are less common   6   10   20   30
(B) Same as (A) but with different signs: Dogs Prefer Rival, Airex, Baby Ruth and Sunoco   6   10   20   30

160 UNLOADING BIN 1952
(A) Short   .25   .50   1   2
(B) Long (for 3359-55 twin-bin dump car)   .25   .50   1   2

161 MAIL PICKUP SET 1961-63, the mail bag transfers from stand to car, tan plastic base contains coil, red shaft with red and white semaphore, red plastic bag holder, red plastic bag painted gray hollowed out contains a magnet. The accessory came with a second magnet which is glued to the car.
20   50   75   100

163 SINGLE TARGET BLOCK SIGNAL 1961-69, as train approaches, signal light changes from green to red automatically, can be wired to control a second train in a two train operation; contactor and wires   7   15   20   30

164 LOG LOADER 1946-50, logs unloaded from car to bin and carried to top by chain, then fall into stake-ended platform. Upon command the stakes move from a vertical to horizontal position, the logs then roll into a waiting car. Two button controller, off-on black button on left side. Orange "Unload" button on right side, 9 inches high, 11 1/4 inches wide, 10 3/4 inches long, with controller and logs, base and roof painted black, molded phenolic plastic
(A) Green metal base, yellow die-cast frame, red plastic roof
65   85   150   200
(B) Same as (A) but green roof   **NRS**

167 WHISTLE CONTROLLER 1945-46, with two buttons: one for whistle, one for direction. (Several different types have been made.)
.50   1.00   1.25   2.00

175 ROCKET LAUNCHER 1958-60, tan metal base track, boxes cover part of motor unit, white and red rocket, black plastic superstructure on gray plastic base, gray crane with gray plastic base, gray top and yellow boom, crane lowers satellite onto missile; countdown apparatus, firing button. Tower crane approximately 17 inches tall; crane with boom, cable and magnet; magnet meets magnet at end of rocket, crane lifts rocket from car or other location and locates it on missile launching platform, rocket controller launches missile; crane track fits 282R Gantry Crane   50   85   150   225

175-50 EXTRA ROCKET 1959-60, for 175   1.50   2   3   5

182 MAGNET CRANE 1946-49, winch raises and lowers block and tackle, spoked wheel control knob, differs from solid wheel of 282R, derrick revolves 360 degrees, includes one 165C controller that came with earlier prewar crane; plastic base, aluminum painted crane, black plastic cab. "LIONEL LINES" (two lines), "Lionel" in arched line, higher gray stack than on 282R; Electro-magnet has black plastic case with ridges; 282R has simple sheet metal "hat" containing magnet; "Cutler Hammer" on magnet case on 182, red metal ladder   70   90   150   200

192 OPERATING CONTROL TOWER 1959-60, illuminated control room, rotating anemometer, vibrator-powered. Does not come with radar antenna, gray plastic base, green frame, yellow tower room, green roof, orange ladders, two binding clips on bottom   75   125   185   275

193 INDUSTRIAL WATER TOWER 1953-55, gray plastic base, green shed, metal red frame, black plastic pipe, gray plastic top with red flashing light, two binding clips on bottom, 14 3/4 inches high
(A) Red metal frame   15   30   45   75
(B) Black painted metal frame, Salamone, Trentacoste and Weise Collections   **NRS**

195 FLOODLIGHT TOWER 1957-69, eight lights on one side; optional second eight lights may be affixed to other side using 195-75 extension, illustration barely shows second light on unit; tan plastic base, gray and silver plastic tower with red "LIONEL" metal and plastic eight light unit; two clips on bottom, 12 1/2 inches high
(A) As above   7   10   20   30
(B) Medium tan base embossed "199 MICROWAVE TOWER" in capitals and red rubber stamped "195 FLOOD LIGHT" Breslin Collection   **NRS**

195-75 EIGHT BULB EXTENSION 1958-60, for 195, not illustrated
2   3   6   8

196[A] SMOKE PELLETS 1946, 100 pellets in a package for bulb-type smoke unit only   —   —   —   10

196[B] SMOKE PELLETS 1947, 100 pellets in bottle for bulb-type smoke unit only   —   —   —   10

197 ROTATING RADAR ANTENNA 1958-59, plastic base; black plastic frame with orange letters, "LIONEL," orange platform, vibrator mechanism rotates radar screen. 12 inches high, base 3 x 4 1/2 inches. Antenna is missing from sample illustrated
(A) Gray base   12   25   50   75
(B) Orange base   12   35   65   100

199 MICROWAVE RELAY TOWER 1958-59, two parabolic antennae, three blinking lights, two binding clips on bottom; very dark gray plastic base, gray plastic tower, white antenna   18   40   65   95

206 ARTIFICIAL COAL 1946-68, half-pound burlap bag with red lettered "No. 206" "ARTIFICIAL COAL" "The Lionel Corporation, New York" "Made in U.S. of America"   —   —   6   8

207 ARTIFICIAL COAL Considerably smaller bag than 206, same lettering, except "Corp." rather than "Corporation"   —   —   4   7

209 BARRELS 1946-50, set of four   —   1.50   3   5

213 RAILROAD LIFT BRIDGE Shown in 1950 catalogue only; prototype made, MPC archives has crude mock-up, collector owns engineering sample, Bohn comment   **Not Manufactured**

214 PLATE GIRDER BRIDGE 1953-69, 10 x 4 1/2 inches; center sheet metal base thinner than 314, black plastic sides
(A) "LIONEL" on both sides, "BUILT BY LIONEL" in small letters in rectangular box   1.50   2   3   4
(B) "U S STEEL" on both sides instead of "LIONEL", "BUILT BY LIONEL" in small letters in rectangular box, "USS" within white-edged circle on both sides, Spitzer Collection   **NRS**

154(A)    154(B)    154

154C, OTC 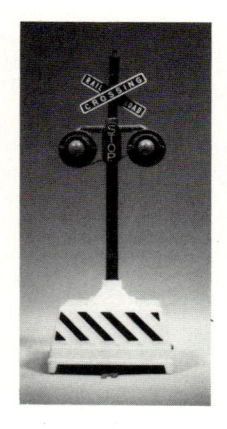   155    156

157(A) 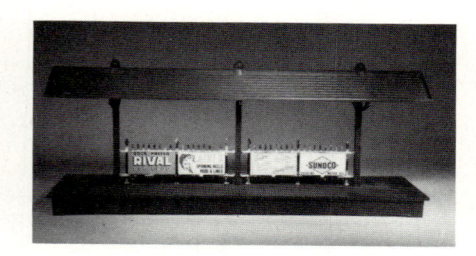   157(B)    160

161    163    164

56

252 CROSSING GATE 1950-62, black plastic base with two binding posts on underside, clip-in bulb assembly with bayonet base; plastic gate with black metal counterweights; lucite strip with two red markers; gate 9 3/4 inches long, with contactor
(A) White plastic boom   7   10   15   25
(B) Cream colored boom   7   10   15   25

253 BLOCK CONTROL SIGNAL 1956-59, 7 inches high, signal halts train automatically; tan plastic base 4 x 2 inches with black signal control box, white plastic lamp shell, pin-type bulbs, variation duration stop, level controls length of stop, three binding posts on bottom, hard to find intact with original lamp shell, Bohn comment   10   20   30   45

256 FREIGHT STATION 1950-53, maroon platform, white house with green windows, green door and roof; picket fence with billboard; lighted, two clips on bottom, 15 inches long, 5 inches wide, 5 1/2 inches high
                                                          6   12   20   30

257 FREIGHT STATION WITH DIESEL HORN 1956-57, matches 256 but with battery-powered horn and control button   12   20   35   50

260 BUMPER 1949-69, red die-cast body with spring loaded black plastic energy absorber, illuminated with bayonet bulb, spring loaded clips for outside rails
(A) Four wide feet, center rail pickup with notch   3   6   10   15
(B) Four narrow feet, center rail pickup without notch   3   6   10   15
(C) Black plastic bumper with black plastic energy absorber, center rail pickup without notch, 1968, came with Hagerstown set no. 11600, I.D. Smith observation   NRS

262 HIGHWAY CROSSING GATE 1962-69, combination flashing light and gate, black plastic base, shaft and light unit, black plastic railroad crossing sign with metal counterweight, does not have lucite strips or lenses as does 152, flashing lights have pin base   6   10   20   30

264 OPERATING FORK LIFT PLATFORM 1957-60, lift truck goes to loaded lumber car 6264, brings lumber back to platform. Includes platform with black metal base, brown deck area, white crane, orange lift truck with blue man, red flat car 6264 with timbers, platform 10 inches long, 10 5/8 inches wide, 5 1/2 inches high   50   85   140   225

282 GANTRY CRANE 1954, gray plastic crane with metal base black cab with white lettering, "LIONEL" arched, "LINES" straight across, smoke stack on cab, magnet on end of hook, cab turns clockwise or counter-clockwise, "cable" raises or lowers, magnet turns off and on, three lever controller 282C, cab sits on maroon plastic base with simulated metal plate, cab turns on maroon plastic drum. Does not come with track that fits wheels on base, however rocket launcher track is right size
(A) As above   60   90   150   275
(B) Same as (A), but red crane cab, Klaassen Collection   NRS

282R GANTRY CRANE 1956, similar to 282 in appearance and function but with changes in the mounting and gearing of the motor and a modified platform casting and platform assembly   60   90   150   275

299 CODE TRANSMITTER BEACON SET 1961-63, black transmitting kit with three binding clips and silver printed decal showing Morse Code Tower, black plastic base, gray recording unit, black top, elongated flashing bulb with unusual filament. Top is gray plastic searchlight with white scored plastic lens, metal bracket   15   25   45   75

308 RAILROAD SIGN SET 1945-49, five die-cast white enameled metal signs with black lettering   3   6   10   15

309 YARD SIGN SET 1950-59, nine plastic signs with die-cast metal bases, orange box with blue lettering, blue cardboard interior box liner with silver lettering   3   6   8   10

310 BILLBOARD 1950-68, unpainted green plastic frame with cardboard Campbell Soup advertisement, Campbell boy in red, with yellow background, red lettering; red, yellow and black soup can. This is one of probably 50 different billboard designs that Lionel made over the years; set of five frames, 1957 frames with yellow base squares, hard to find, Bohn comment
                                                          1.00   1.50   2.00   5.00

Beginning in 1950 Lionel offered a billboard assortment, the No. 310. The assortment usually consisted of five green unpainted plastic frames with an uncut sheet of eight different billboards. The billboards made through 1956 included the word "STANDARD" in black letters. Thereafter "STANDARD" was dropped from the sign. Over 50 different billboard advertisements were offered. See Chapter 27 for a listing of billboards.

313 BASCULE BRIDGE 1946-49, green bakelite bridge base, die-cast metal base underneath motor, sheet metal superstructure on bridge, red light on bridge top, pale yellow bridge tender building with orange windows and red roof, five binding posts, black metal alignment frame with permanently affixed lockon, 21 1/2 inches long, 9 1/4 inches high when bridge is level
                                                          150   200   300   425

313-82 FIBER PINS 1946-60 each   .05   .05   .05   .08

313-121 FIBER PINS 1961 per dozen   —   —   —   1.50

314 SCALE MODEL GIRDER BRIDGE 1945-50, single span, 10 inches long, heavy sheet metal plate for base, die-cast sides fastened by rivets, "LIONEL" rubber stamped in black on both sides; also lettered in small box with rounded corners "BUILT BY LIONEL"   2   5   7   10

315 TRESTLE BRIDGE 1946-47, silver painted sheet metal, illuminated with binding posts in center of span on top, 24 1/2 inches long
                                                          15   25   40   60

316 TRESTLE BRIDGE 1949, 24 x 6 1/8 inches, silver painted sheet metal
                                                          2   4   7   10

317 TRESTLE BRIDGE 1950-56, gray painted sheet metal, 24 inches by 6 1/8 inches wide   2   4   7   10

321 TRESTLE BRIDGE 1958-64, sheet metal base, gray plastic sides and top, 24 inches long, 7 inches high, 4 1/2 inches wide
                                                          5   7   10   15

332 ARCH UNDER BRIDGE 1959-66, came unassembled, gray plastic sides and black metal deck   10   20   30   40

334 OPERATING DISPATCHING BOARD 1957-60, blue attendant with white face and hands hurries across catwalk and appears to change information in illuminated slots, green board, white lines, plastic lettered material inside unit changes "information." Tan plastic base with three binding clips, clock on top and two speaker units, reverse side shows large billboard "AIREX" "REEL ROD REELS," color picture of man fishing, lower section Lionel Travel Center, 9 7/8 inches long, 4 1/8 inches wide, 7 1/2 inches high
                                                          50   100   125   175

342 CULVERT LOADER 1956-58, culvert pipes stored on sloping ramp, picked up by pincher unit and transferred to car, loaded into special gondola car 6342, length of unit is 11 1/2 x 10 x 6 inches, includes loading station with black metal base and tan plastic box-like unit; red building, dark gray roof; 6342 controller, connecting wires and culvert section; illustration shows 342 and 345 arranged for operation. Price includes car, very difficult to keep in proper adjustment, Bohn comment   50   75   125   175

345 CULVERT UNLOADING STATION 1958-59, travelling crane controlled by remote control, lowers magnet to gondola car, magnet picks up culvert section and transports it onto station, unit has black metal base, gray ramp, red tower building with gray roof, orange post on crane, black horizontal piece; 12 1/2 inches long, 9 1/2 inches wide and 7 inches high; includes gondola designed for use with 342. Culverts roll from 345 across special bridge onto 342, very difficult to keep in proper adjustment, Bohn comment
                                                          70   150   200   300

346 CULVERT UNLOADER Circa 1965-66, hand operated. Made for Sears, same as #345, except lacks motor mechanism; hand crank extends through platform top, Hutchinson observation   NRS

347 CANNON FIRING RANGE SET, circa 1962-64. Olive drab plastic battery with four cannon barrels and four silver shells. Each barrel has a firing pin which is set prior to use. A silver shell is placed in each cannon. The firing wheel is then rotated slowly, firing the shells in sequence. Came with uncatalogued Sears set. Instructions 347-10(8/64) came with unit. (We need to learn the Sears set number and its contents). Jarman Collection
                                                          50   75   100   125

348 CULVERT UNLOADER 1966-69, manual loader, with car
                                                          30   40   60   90

350 ENGINE TRANSFER TABLE 1957-60, motorized table moves train from one track to another, 17 1/2 inches long and 10 3/8 inches wide, black sheet metal with plastic tie, fastened through bottom by rails fastened through holder, control unit with three yellow buttons and one red button; yellow building with red light on top; building lifts off motor underneath; illustration shows one original and one extension unit   65   130   175   300

175    182    192

193 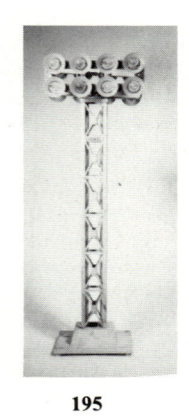   195    197    199

206, 207    214    252(A)

252(B)    253 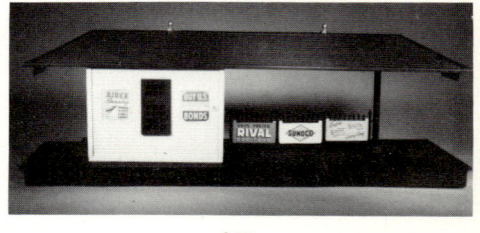   256

58

350-50 TRANSFER TABLE EXTENSION 1957-60, metal base with plastic ties, metal rails   25   40   65   90

352 ICE DEPOT 1955-57, white shed, red roof, blue man with orange arms and paddle, cubes put in end with chute that raises; chute has a cube permanently fastened at end. Another version had five cubes fastened at end, operating mechanism moves, opens car hatch, cubes come out at end with man; came with 6352-1 car, depot, cubes, station 11 3/4 inches long, 4 inches wide, 8 1/2 inches high, two binding posts. Reissued by Fundimensions in 1982.
(A) Brown plastic base   100   120   160   250
(B) Red plastic base   100   120   160   250

353 TRACK SIDE CONTROL SIGNAL 1960-61, signal changes from green to red as train passes, can be wired to control two trains; 9 inches high, tan plastic base and control box; white plastic shaft, black plastic lamp housing, black metal ladder, three control posts, three binding posts on top of base   5   10   15   20

356 OPERATING FREIGHT STATION 1952-57, maroon plastic base, white shed with green windows, door and roof, picket fence with billboard signs; two baggage men with carts run out onto platform and back into station powered by vibrator motor; one cart is orange with blue man, rubber feet for vibrator on bottom; other cart is green with blue man, two pads on bottom, bayonet light socket inside, 15 inches long, 5 inches wide, 5-1/2 inches high. Early production featured one cart with lithographed metal baggage and one without baggage. Reproduction baggage units are available. The baggage-equipped cart was discontinued early in production because the extra weight of the baggage caused erratic operation of the carts, forcing the operator to make continual voltage adjustments. Original Lionel baggage-equipped carts are probably very scarce. Bohn, Weiss and LaVoie comments
(A) As described above   30   45   70   120
(B) Same as (A), but light green unpainted plastic roof, approximately Penn Central green, Lapan Collection   NRS

362 BARREL LOADER 1952-57, barrels move up the ramp by vibrator action, gray plastic base, yellow ramp, brown plastic fence, cream colored man; 19 inches long, 4 1/8 inches wide, 4 inches high. Car not included in price, came with 6 brown-stained wood barrels   30   45   60   100

364 CONVEYOR LUMBER LOADER 1948-67, gray crackle finish, red belt conveys logs; red ladder; two green, one red spotlight lens; three blue binding posts. "LIONEL ATOMIC MOTOR," 27 7/8 inches long, 3 3/16 inches wide, 4 1/8 inches high, came with logs, controller switch   30   45   60   100

364[C] ON-OFF SWITCH 1959-64   .25   .50   1.00 1.50

365 DISPATCHING STATION 1958-59, elevated control room shows dispatchers at work, simulated radio antenna, loud speakers; 11 inches long, 5 inches wide, 6 1/2 inches high; not illustrated   35   50   75   100

375 TURNTABLE 1962-64, rotates track, powered by two D cells, black metal table rotates on 0 gauge curve rail, friction drive   50   100   145   225

390C SWITCH 1960-64, double pole, double throw switch, for HO reversing loop layouts, hard to find, Bohn comment.   .50 1.00 2.00 3.00

394 ROTARY BEACON 1949-53, light bulb heat drives beacon, bulb has dimple 11 3/4 inches high, base 5 x 5 inches
(A) Unpainted aluminum tower with black lettering   8   12   20   30
(B) Green painted steel tower   8   12   20   30
(C) Red painted steel tower   8   12   20   30

395 FLOODLIGHT TOWER 1949-56, tower with four black die-cast floodlight units, ladders, two binding clips on bottom
(A) Green painted tower. This is a common variety of the tower. However, one example has been reported by Michael Ocilka which has been rubber stamped "APR 20, 1955" on the underside of the base. We wish to know if other towers have been similarly stamped with dates and what those dates might be.   8   12   20   30
(B) Silver painted tower   8   12   20   30
(C) Yellow painted tower   8   12   20   30
(D) Unpainted aluminum tower, Keith Collection   NRS
(E) All red-painted tower with black ladder and lights, Lahti Collection NRS

397 DIESEL OPERATING COAL LOADER 1948-57, car dumps coal into large tray, tray vibrations move coal to conveyor, conveyor carries coal up and fills car; 10 1/2 inches long, 7 7/16 inches wide, 6 inches high
(A) Early model with yellow diesel cover, yard light mounted on gray die-cast metal base, red coal holding unit, two motor binding posts, wires hooked directly to lamp post   100   150   225   350
(B) Same as (A) but no yard light   90   140   200   325
(C) Later model with blue diesel motor cover and without yard lights
                                                30   40   75   125
(D) Similar to (C), but has shiny red plastic tray, later type motor and rubber coupling, Ocilka Collection   30   40   75   125

410 BILLBOARD BLINKER 1956-58, green plastic billboard unit similar to 310 but with black sheet metal base; black metal back with two binding posts; die-cast metal light unit for bayonet base bulbs, timing via metallic strip. Reissued by Fundimensions in 1982. Original very hard to find, Bohn comment.   10   15   20   30

413 COUNTDOWN CONTROL PANEL 1962, controls rocket launching, gray plastic with black lettering; red dial, countdown set lever, and start and fire buttons; on the underside are two mounting posts, through which the circuit (between the two posts) is completed by depressing the "fire" button   6   9   12   20

415 DIESEL FUELING STATION 1955-67, man comes out of building; fuel pipe moves to fueling position; gray metal base, white building with red trim and roof and gray metal base, yellow base on fueling pipe and on diesel sand tank, blue tank with white lettering, three binding posts on top side of base; 9 inches wide, 9 inches long, and almost 10 inches high   30   50   100   150

419 HELIPORT CONTROL TOWER 1952, helicopter launched by spring mechanism, red control tower with gray roof, clear windows, with spring mechanism visible inside. Yellow radar disc, yellow helicopter with black blades, white lettering on tower "LIONEL HELIPORT," not lighted, terminal base 11 x 5 x 5 1/2 inches high   75   100   135   200

443 MISSILE LAUNCHING PLATFORM 1960-62, includes platform, missile and exploding ammo dump, 11 x 12 inches   10   15   20   30

445 SWITCH TOWER 1952-57, blue towerman runs up and down stairs with red lantern, other blue towerman comes in and out of building; white building, green windows, balcony and roof; maroon plastic base; three binding clips on bottom   18   25   35   60

448 MISSILE FIRING RANGE SET 1961-63, with camouflage and exploding target range car, tan plastic base; 9 x 5 1/2 inches, gray plastic launching unit #6544-5, (launching unit also came on flat car). Small white rockets, 6448 Target Range Car with Timken trucks, two disc-operating couplers, black metal frame, white and red side, white side with red lettering, ends and roof
                                                25   35   50   75

450 SIGNAL BRIDGE 1952-58, spans two tracks, gray plastic base, black metal frame, two sets of red and green lights, inside width 7 1/2 inches, inside height 6 inches, three binding posts on each side   15   20   32   50

452 SIGNAL BRIDGE 1961-63, also known as "Overhead Gantry Signal," Signal changes from green to red as train approaches, bridge 7 3/4 inches high, gray plastic base with metal grip for fastening unit, black painted metal frame ladder, black plastic light unit, direction of light unit can be reversed   40   60   80   150

455 OIL DERRICK 1950-54, pumping motion, bulb heat causes bubbling action in tube, four aluminum oil barrels, 9 1/4 inches long, 5 1/2 inches wide and 14 1/2 inches high, orange diesel unit. Reissued by Fundimensions in 1981.
(A) Red metal base, apple green metal tower, red tower top
                                                75   100   175   250
(B) Dark green metal base and tower   NRS

456 COAL RAMP 1950-55, with operating hopper 9 1/2 inches long, not shown, gray metal ramp with red light, 35 inches long, 3 3/16 inches wide, and 6 3/16 inches high, shown with 397 Operating Coal Loader for continuous action, price for 456 with special hopper car, red coal receiving tray, steel support rods to hold tray over 397 coal loader, special controller, Bohn comments   48   60   90   150

460 PIGGYBACK TRANSPORTATION 1955-57, hand crank and lever on platform (visible in illustration) cause lift truck to move 360 degrees and cause truck platform to raise and lower, flat car and two trailers not illustrated   20   30   40   65

59

257

262

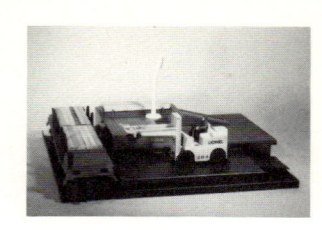

264

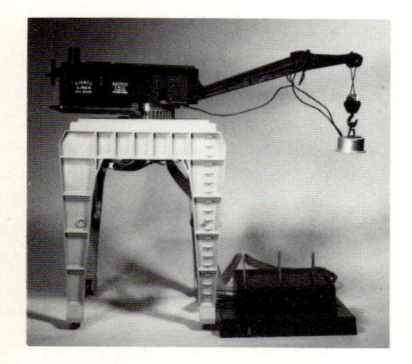

282

299

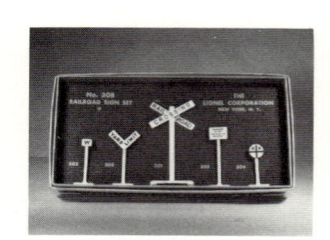

308

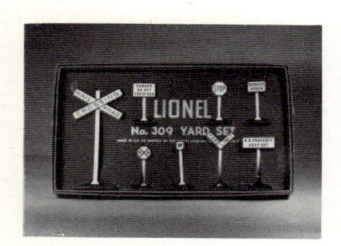

309

310

313

314

315

317

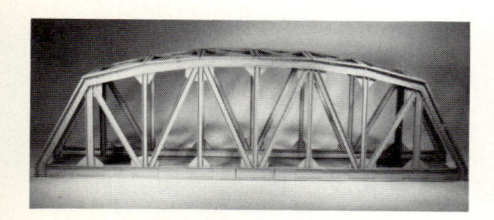

321

332

334

60

460P PIGGYBACK PLATFORM Carton lettered "PLATFORM," made for those already having a piggyback flat car with vans; red lift truck, white rubber stamped lettering "ROSS TRAILOADER," Catalano observation
20 30 40 65

461 PLATFORM WITH TRUCK AND TRAILER Red lift truck with blue man and black steering wheel, gray plastic base, white trailer with single axle and two wheels, tractor marked "MIDGE TOY, ROCKFORD, ILL. U.S.A. PATENT 2775847"
25 40 60 90

462 DERRICK PLATFORM SET 1961-62, derrick handles "radioactive" waste containers, lifts containers from car to platform, platform has three black cranks similar to those on the 6560 Crane, one crank rotates crane unit, one moves lifts, raises and lowers boom, a third raises and lowers table, plastic radioactive containers similar to those found on flat cars but without lighting assembly, 8 1/2 inches long, 11 inches wide, 1 3/4 inches high, buff plastic base, yellow crane boom
25 40 60 100

464 LUMBER MILL 1956-60, simulates the transformation of logs into dressed lumber, vibrator mechanism inside moves finished lumber, gray plastic base; white mill building with red door, gray shed, length 10 1/2 inches, width 6 inches, height 6 inches, logs, lumber, controller and mill. Reissued by Fundimensions in 1980
50 75 100 175

465 SOUND DISPATCHING STATION 1956-57, operator speaks into microphone, voice comes out of 4 inch loudspeaker in station; battery-powered, buff colored plastic base, red room, gray roof, yellow microwave tower on roof, gray microphone with left red button for train, right red button for talk, gray plastic ladder into station, also includes lock-on insulating pins, wires and four batteries, length 11 inches, width 5 inches, height 5 inches, antenna 3 inches
30 45 60 100

470 MISSILE LAUNCHING PLATFORM 1959-62, missile tilts and flies, tan plastic base, blue missile launching unit base, black cradle, white, red and blue missile, includes target car; 6470 in set; note Quonset hut type building on platform
12 17 25 35

480-25 CONVERSION COUPLER 1950-60, converts Scout coupler to remote control operation
.50 1.00 1.50 2.00

480-32 CONVERSION MAGNETIC COUPLER 1961-69, converts Scout coupler to remote control operation
.50 1.00 1.50 2.00

494 ROTARY BEACON 1954-66, red tower with vibrator-driven rotating light, 11 3/4 inches high, base 5 x 5 inches, bayonet-type bulb; two binding clips on bottom
7 12 20 30

497 COALING STATION 1953-58, bin carries coal to top of structure, coal empties into overhead storage area, released from storage area into waiting car, gray metal base, black metal posts, red metal bin, green plastic roof, with controller with one lever for up and down, other lever dumps load, 10 inches high, 6 x 9 1/2 inch base
(A) Medium green roof, as above 50 75 100 200
(B) Very dark green roof, Trentacoste Collection NRS

703-10 SPECIAL SMOKE BULB 1946, box shows 671-75 — — 3 6

760 072 TRACK 1954-57, 16 sections of 0 curved track with 72 inch diameter, each section 14 inches long (Note: reproduction track available)
15 20 35 45

909 SMOKE FLUID 1957-68, two ounces for 746, 1872, 243, etc
— — — 2

919 ARTIFICIAL GRASS 1946-64, half-pound bag of artificial grass, red lettering on bag
— — 3 5

920 SCENIC DISPLAY SET 1957-58, includes four feet of mountain paper with two tunnel portals, black and gray plastic portals with "HILLSIDE" embossed on top, "L" in circle, and 1967 in lower right, came as set of two
10 15 20 30

920-2 TUNNEL PORTALS 1958, pair of realistically molded cut stone tunnel portals
8 15 28 40

920-5 ARTIFICIAL ROCK 1958, expanded mica type mineral
50 1 2 3

920-8 LICHEN 1958, treated and colored for realistic shrubbery
50 1 2 3

925 LIONEL LUBRICANT 1946-69, large tube .50 1 2 3

926 LIONEL LUBRICANT 1955 .25 .50 1 2

926-5 INSTRUCTION BOOKLET 1946-48 .25 .50 1 2

927 LUBRICATING AND MAINTENANCE KIT 1950-53, tube of lubricant, vial of lubricating oil, can of solvent, cleaning sticks, etc 2 4 5 7

928 MAINTENANCE AND LUBRICANT KIT 1960-63, includes oil, lubricant, "Tank Clean" 2 3 4 6

943 AMMO DUMP 1959-61, target "explodes" on impact, spring loaded mechanism inside, gray metal base, green plastic body, 3 inches long, 5 inches wide, 4 inches high, four plastic parts; one each labeled "B" "A", two unlabeled ends 4 6 8 12

950 U.S. RAILROAD MAP 1958-66, by Rand McNally, full color 52 x 37 inches 3 5 7 10

Items #951 to #969 and #980 to #988 were produced for Lionel by Bachmann Bros., Inc. of Philadelphia, Pa., manufacturers of Plasticville buildings. The sets contain regular Plasticville items, although sometimes in different quantities or combinations than Bachmann Plasticville sets.
According to Dick Reddles, Bachmann Vice President, Lionel shipped its traditional orange and blue boxes to Bachmann in Philadelphia and Bachmann packed the boxes with Plasticville and shipped them back to Lionel.
To be "Mint" or "Excellent" the following items must include the Lionel box with the Lionel number

951 FARM SET 1958, 13 pieces: truck, tractor, jeep, horses, cows, harrow, plow, wagon and footbridge 3 7 20 30

952 FIGURE SET 1958, 30 pieces: people, fire plug, fire alarm box and metal boxes 3 7 15 25

953 FIGURE SET 1960-62, 32 pieces including paint brush, not illustrated 2 7 15 25

954 SWIMMING POOL AND PLAYGROUND SET 1959, 30 pieces: 12 fence pieces, 6 trees, slide, swing, teeter-totter, roundriding, bench, table with umbrella, two chairs, two chaise lounges, pool, Hemmert Collection 3 7 15 30

955 HIGHWAY SET 1958, 22 pieces; two buses, auto, seven telegraph poles, ten yellow street signs, seven green street indicators 3 7 15 30

956 STOCKYARD SET 1959, 18 pieces: corral, cows, railroad signs 3 7 15 30

957 FARM BUILDING AND ANIMAL SET 1958, 35 pieces: four farm structures, fence, gate, pump, horse, fowl and domestic animals 3 7 15 30

958 VEHICLE SET 1958, 24 pieces: three autos, two fire trucks, ambulance, bus, street signs, fire alarm box, mailbox, fire plug, traffic light 3 7 15 30

959 BARN SET 1958, 23 pieces: dairy barn, horses, fowl and domestic animals; orange and blue traditional box, not illustrated 3 7 15 30

960 BARNYARD SET 1959-61, 29 pieces: three farm buildings, dog house, tractor, truck, wagon, hoe, fowl, domestic and farm animals 3 7 15 30

961 SCHOOL SET 1959, 36 pieces: school, flagpole, two buses, street signs, fence pieces, shrubs and benches 3 7 15 30

962 TURNPIKE SET 1958, 24 pieces: interchange, stanchions, five telegraph poles, four autos, ambulance, bus and street signs 3 7 18 35

963 FRONTIER SET 1959-60, 18 pieces: cabin, windmill, fences, cows and pump 3 7 15 30

964 FACTORY SITE SET 1959, 18 pieces: factory with water tower, auto, four telegraph poles, railroad signs 3 7 18 35

965 FARM SET 1959, 36 pieces: dairy barn, three farm buildings, farm equipment, fowl, domestic and farm animals 3 7 15 30

966 FIRE HOUSE SET 1958, 45 pieces: firehouse, fire engines, alarm box, hydrant, ambulance, bus, autos, traffic light, street signs, street post, bench, mailbox, people, telegraph poles and pine trees 3 7 15 30

967 POST OFFICE SET 1958, 25 pieces: post office, mailbox, people, benches, street lights, street post, traffic lights, truck and autos 3 7 15 30

342

342, 345

345

348

350

352(A)

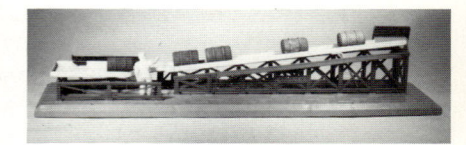

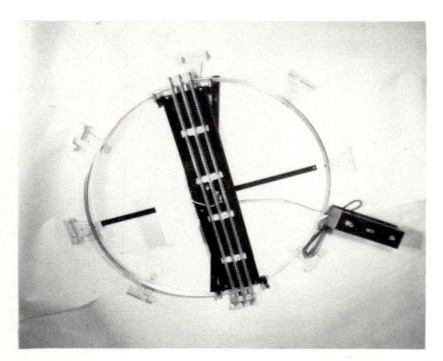

353

356

362

364

375

394(A)

62

968 TV TRANSMITTER SET 1958, 28 pieces: TV station, fence, gate, people, mailbox, fire plug, jeep, two autos and trees   7   10   20   35

969 CONSTRUCTION SET 1960, 23 pieces: house construction materials, workers and autos   10   18   30   45

Lionel Plasticville continues at 980

970 TICKET BOOTH 1958-60, 46 inches high, 22 inches wide, 11 inches deep, simulated blackboard on front, green roof with "LIONELVILLE" sign, trimmed in red, clock on roof reads 7:07; trimmed in green and red, came packed flat in carton; carton has label with "3592-1" and manufactured by United Container Corporation, Philadelphia, PA., "United for Strength"   25   37   50   75

971 LICHEN 1960-64, box with green, yellow and brown lichen, 4 1/2 ounces   2   3   4   6

972 LANDSCAPE TREE ASSORTMENT 1961-64, four evergreens, three flowering shrubs, lichen   2   3   4   6

973 COMPLETE LANDSCAPING SET 1960-64, includes 4 x 8 inch roll of grass mat, one 16 x 48 inch roll of earth, ballast and road mats   3   4   6   8

974 SCENERY SET 1962-63, 4 x 8 inch grass mat, two 3-D background mountains, bag of lichen, nine assorted trees   4   6   8   10

Lionel Plasticville continues

980 RANCH SET 1960, 14 pieces: loading pen, cattle, pigs, sheep and farm implements   3   7   15   30

981 FREIGHT YARD SET 1960, 10 pieces: loading platform with carts, switch tower, telephone poles and railroad men   3   7   15   30

982 SUBURBAN SPLIT LEVEL SET 1960, 18 pieces: split level house, pine trees, auto, ranch and fence   3   7   15   30

983 FARM SET 1960-61, 7 pieces: dairy barn, windmill, Colonial house, horse, cows and auto   10   20   35   50

984 RAILROAD SET 1961-62, 22 pieces: switch tower, telegraph poles, loading platform, figures, R.R. signs and accessories   3   7   15   30

985 FREIGHT AREA SET 1961, 32 pieces: water tower, work car, loading platform, switch tower, watchman's shanty, telegraph poles, autos, R.R. signs and accessories   7   11   18   35

986 FARM SET 1962, 20 pieces: farm house, barn and 18 domestic animals   5   11   15   32

987 TOWN SET 1962, 24 pieces: church, gas station, auto, street signs, bank and store   10   18   35   50

988 RAILROAD STRUCTURE SET 1962, 16 pieces: railroad station with freight platform, water tank, work car, hobo shacks, bench, figures, crossing gate and shanty   6   11   15   32

1008 UNCOUPLING UNIT 1957   .50   1   1   2

1008-50 UNCOUPLING TRACK SECTION 1948, Scout type   .25   .50   1   1.50

1013 CURVED TRACK 1958-69, 0-27, 9 1/2 inches long   .10   .15   .20   .40

1013-17 STEEL PINS 1946-60, 0-27, each   —   .05   .05   .05

1013-42 STEEL PINS 1961-68, per dozen   —   —   .60   .80

1018-1/2 STRAIGHT TRACK 1955-69, 0-27 gauge, 1/2 section   .10   .15   .30   .50

1018 STRAIGHT TRACK 1945-69, 0-27, 8 7/8 inches long   .10   .15   .30   .40

1019 REMOTE CONTROL TRACK SET 1946-50, for 0-27 gauge, with controller   1.50   2   5   8

1020 90 DEGREE CROSSING 1955-69, 0-27 track   1.50   2   3   6

1021 90 DEGREE CROSSING 1945-54, 0-27 track, 7 3/8 inch square   1.50   2   3   6

1022 MANUAL SWITCH 1953-69, pair, for 0-27 track   2   4   6   10

1023 45 DEGREE CROSSING 1956-69, for 0-27   1.50   2   3   6

1024 MANUAL SWITCHES 1946-52, pair 0-27,   1   2   4   10

1025 ILLUMINATED BUMPER 1946-47, with lamp and one section of 0-27 track   1   2   4   6

1045 OPERATING WATCHMAN 1946-50, large blue bakelite man with flesh colored hands and face, white flag, aluminum colored post, two binding posts on bottom
(A) Nickel warning sign with black letters   8   12   20   30
(B) Brass sign with black lettering   8   12   20   30

1047 OPERATING SWITCHMAN 1959-61, switchman waves flag as train approaches, green metal case, blue switchman with red flag, flesh colored face and hands, five railroad ties with clip holding three, blue diesel fuel tank unit on base, two binding posts, black die-cast base on rail crossing sign, white plastic sign with black letters, 4 1/2 inches high   30   50   70   125

1121 REMOTE CONTROL SWITCHES 1946-51, pair of 0-27 switches, each with two indicator lenses and rounded motor cover, single controller 1121-C-60 with two levers and four indicator light lenses, switches are 9 3/8 x 6 7/8 inches and came with either bright or satin rail finish. Units used screw-type bulbs to 1050; bayonet-type bulbs thereafter. Reliable operation, La Voie comments
(A) Flat direction indicator lenses on switches   7   10   20   30
(B) Protruding direction indicator lenses on switches, rivet location on bottom differs from (A)   7   10   20   30

1122 REMOTE CONTROL SWITCHES 1952-53, pair of 0-27 switches, each with rotating direction indicator and a single controller 1122-100 with two levers and four indicator light lenses, non-derailing design. Substantial revisions were made to the 1953 model of 1122, then a new model 1122E was introduced; see next entry
(A) Direction indicator with exposed lenses, 1952   10   15   20   40
(B) Direction indicator with recessed lenses, 1953   10   15   20   40

1122E REMOTE CONTROL SWITCHES 1953-69, pair of 0-27 switches, each with rotating direction indicator and a single controller, 1122-100 with two levers and four indicator light lenses. The shape of the switch cover was changed from that found with 1122 to accommodate the overhang of the larger 0-27 diesels. The cover has three notches, the direction indicator has recessed lenses; non-derailing rails with extra insulating break as compared with 1122(A), insulated rails inside curves rather than on outside curve rails, very reliable operation, LaVoie comment   10   15   20   40

1122LH SWITCH 1955-69, 0-27, remote control, left-hand with controller   5   9   13   18

1122RH SWITCH 1955-69, 0-27, remote control, right-hand with controller   5   9   13   18

1122-234 FIBER PINS 1958-60, 0-27 each   .03   .05   .05   .05

1122-500 0-27 GAUGE ADAPTER 1957-66, For combining 0-27 and Super 0, four ground rail pins, two insulating pins, three power rail pins   .25   .50   1   2

1640-100 PRESIDENTIAL KIT 1960, car decals, whistle stop audience, Presidential candidate   3   7   12   15

2003 TRACK "MAKE-UP" KIT FOR "027 TRACK," 1963, box has black over print: "MAKE THIS EXCITING 'LOOP-TO-LOOP' LAYOUT!" Contains eight No. 1013 curved track, two No. 1018 straight track and one No. 1023 45-degree crossover, Griesbeck Collection   **NRS**

3330-100 OPERATING SUBMARINE KIT 1960-61, kit that after assembly operates under water   5   10   15   20

3356-150 HORSE CAR CORRAL Horse moves by vibrator action, galvanized metal base; white plastic frame
(A) Green and brown interior plastic liners, black horses, came with matching car; price for corral only   10   15   20   35
(B) Same as (A) but with gray and red interior liners and white horses, price for corral only   15   20   30   40

3366-100 NINE WHITE HORSES 1959-60, extra horses for 3356   5   7   10   20

3376 GIRAFFE ACTIVATOR UNIT   2   3   4   6

3424-100 LOW BRIDGE SIGNAL SET Operated giraffe and brakeman car   2   3   4   6

3462P MILK CAR PLATFORM All metal unit
(A) Green base, white platform frame, gray steps, unpainted platform, came with milk car, price for platform only   2   3   5   10
(B) Brown base, gray steps, unpainted platform, yellow railing, came with Bosco car, price for platform only   20   28   35   50

394(B) 　　395(A) 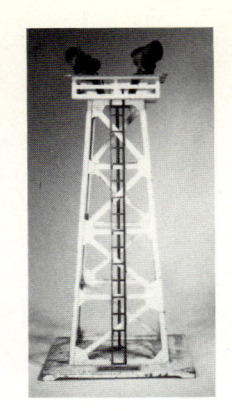　　395(B) 　　395(C)

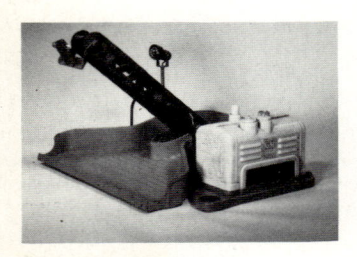

397(A) 　　397(B) 　　410

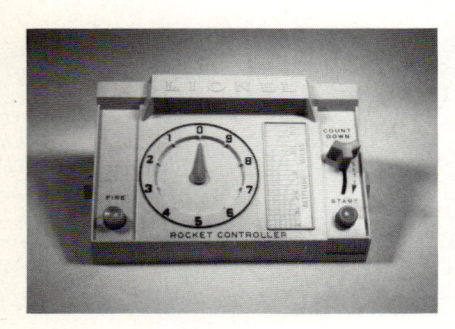

413 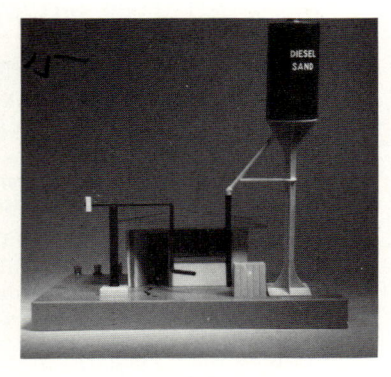　　415 　　419

445 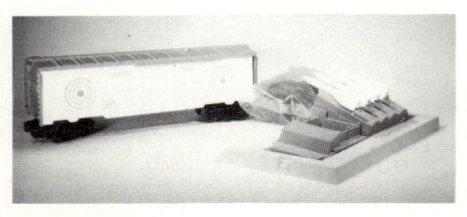　　448 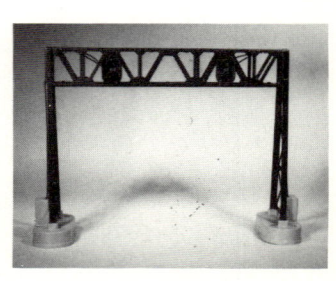　　450

64

452

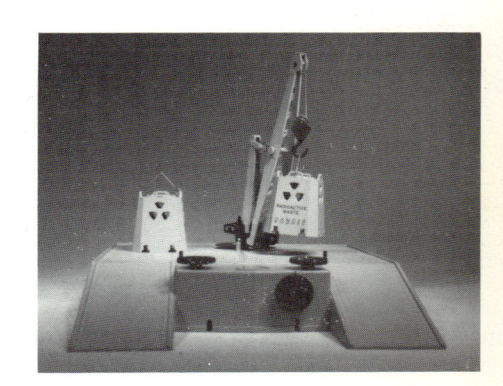

455

456

460

461

462

464

465

470

494

497

703-10

65

909

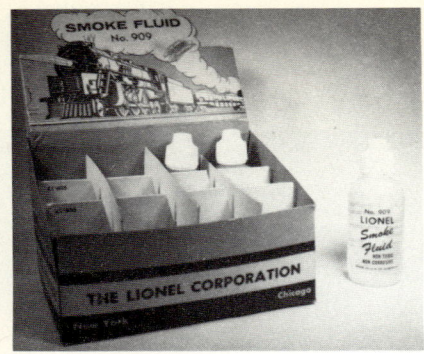

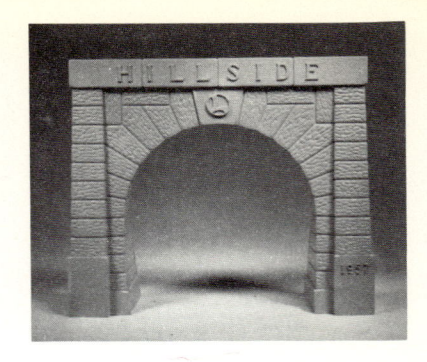

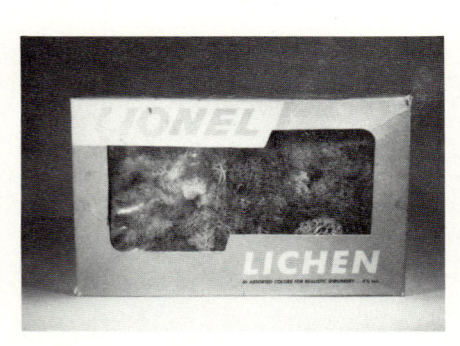

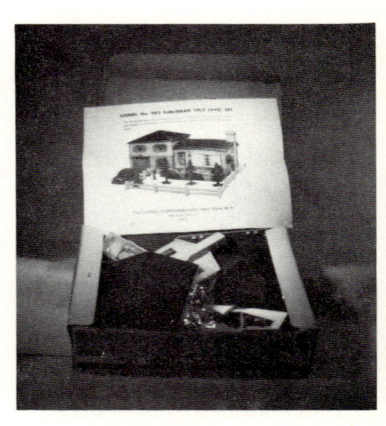

919

920

927

943

950

970

971

982

1045(A)

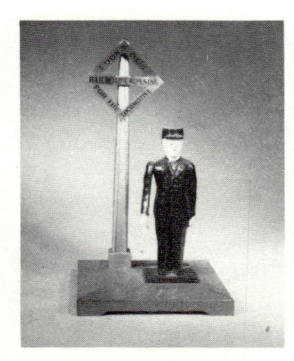

1045(B)

1047

66

3366-100, 362-78
3356-100, 3656-9

3356-150(A)

3356-150(B)

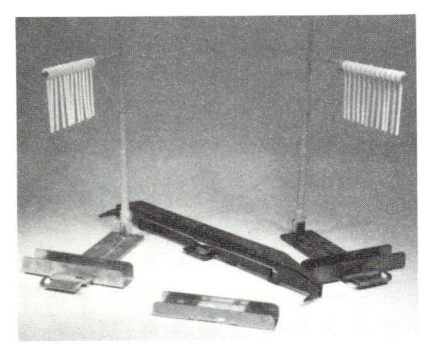

3110

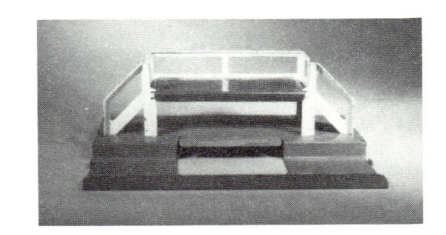

3462(A)

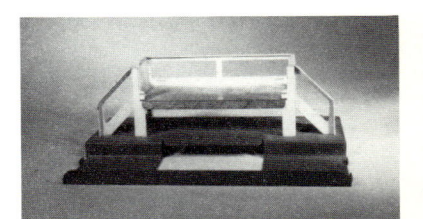

3462(B)

3530

3656(A)

3656(B)

3957-50

6418

CTC Lockon

SP Smoke Pellets

67

SPECIAL NOTE: Research of several 3462P platforms shows that this number was stamped on the bottom base of all milk car platforms. All samples observed (TOY TRAIN STATION, about 6 or 7) were from original 3472 and 3482 boxes. It's safe to conclude that 3462P is the only existing number for this platform. R.E. LaVoie

3530 SEARCHLIGHT WITH POLE AND BASE Came with blue generator car marked 3530, searchlight has red base with magnet, gray plastic housing, plastic lens, green wire and bayonet-type bulb, telegraph pole is brown unpainted plastic; black unpainted plastic base is marked "SERVICE TRANSFORMER THE LIONEL CORPORATION NEW YORK, N.Y." with aluminum metal tube, two green wires emerge from the aluminum tube, hook into the female receptacles on the box car. Price with car
    15   25   50   75

3656 STOCKYARD WITH CATTLE Cattle powered by vibrator motor march through pen into car and out, stockyard is a metal unit with plastic gates, loading ramp, came with 3656 operating cattle car, price for pen only
(A) Early version with two rubber grommets at each end, chain on right hand side (as unit faces camera), does not have decal in center, operates better than later unit   7   10   15   25
(B) Later model with metal plate on center of unit visible in illustration, binding post right side, rubber supporting pads underneath platform, platform lifts out, not permanently fastened, yellow metal frame and gate, shiny metal platform, green base with ramp for cows   5   7   12   20

3672-79 SEVEN BOSCO CANS 1960, for 3672 car   5   7   9   15

3927-50 COTTON TRACK CLEANING PADS 1957-60 .50 1 2 4

3927-75 TRACK CLEAN FLUID 1957-69, non-flammable detergent
    .50 1 2 3

5159 MAINTENANCE AND LUBRICANT KIT 1964-68 1 2 3 4

5159-50 MAINTENANCE AND LUBRICANT KIT 1969 1 2 3 4

6019 REMOTE CONTROL TRACK 1948-66, for 0-27 track, unloading and uncoupling   1 2 3 4

6029 UNCOUPLING TRACK SET 1955, 1961-63, 0-27, uncoupling only
    .25 .50 1 2

6149 REMOTE CONTROL UNCOUPLING TRACK 1964-69
    .25 .50 1 2

6418 BRIDGE sheet metal base painted black, black plastic sides with white lettered "U.S.STEEL 6418"   1 2 3 7

6650-80 MISSILE 1960, for 6650, 6823, 443 and 470 1 2 4 6

6816-100 ALLIS CHALMERS TRACTOR DOZER 1956-60
    4 6 8 15

6817-100 ALLIS CHALMERS MOTOR SCRAPER 1959-60
    4 6 8 15

6827-100 HARNISCHFEGER TRACTOR SHOVEL 1960 5 7 9 17

6828-100 HARNISCHFEGER MOBILE CONSTRUCTION CRANE 1960
    5 7 9 17

OC CURVED TRACK 1945-61, 10 7/8 inches, 0 gauge 15 25 40 70

TOC CURVED TRACK 1962-66, 1968-69, 107/8 inches, 0 gauge
    .15 .25 .40 .70

OS STRAIGHT TRACK 1945-61, 0 gauge .20 .30 .40 .70

TOS STRAIGHT TRACK 1962-69, 0 gauge .20 .30 .40 .70

1/2OC HALF SECTION CURVED TRACK 1945-66, 0 gauge
    .20 .30 .40 .70

TOC1/2 HALF SECTION STRAIGHT TRACK 1962-66, 0 gauge
    .20 .30 .40 .70

OTC LOCK ON See illustration of 154 contractor .15 .20 .30 .50

OC18 STEEL PINS 1945-59, each .02 .03 .05 .05

OC51 STEEL PINS 1961, dozen .20 .30 .50 .75

TOC51 STEEL PINS 1962-69, dozen .20 .30 .50 .75

011-11 FIBER/PINS 1946-50, each .03 .03 .05 .05

T011-43 FIBER PINS 1962-66, dozen .20 .30 .40 .60

UTC LOCKON 1945, fits 0-27, 0 and standard gauge track
    .25 .50 .75 1.25

RCS REMOTE CONTROL TRACK 1945-48, for 0 gauge, five rails, does not have electromagnet 1 2 2 3

ECU-1 ELECTRONIC CONTROL UNIT 1946 10 15 20 40

CTC LOCKON 1947-69, for 0 and 0-27 track .10 .20 .30 .40

UCS REMOTE CONTROL TRACK 1945-69, for 0 gauge
    3 5 8 15

LTC LOCKON 1950-69, with light, for 0 and 0-27 track .50 1 1.50 2

SP SMOKE PELLETS 1948-69, fifty tablets per bottle — — — 10

TRANSFORMERS

Transformers are usually bought to operate trains and related items. Hence if a transformer is not operating it has little if any value. (If a transformer is repairable, after it is repaired, it will yield the values indicated.) Several of the larger models such as the KW, V, VW, Z or ZW have some minimal value even if completely burned out - for knobs, plates and nuts. In the listing that follows, we report only Good, Excellent and Mint conditions and the value assigned assumes that the transformer is in operating condition.

1010 1961-1966, 35 watts, circuit breaker 1 1.50 3
1011 1948-1949, 25 watts 1 1.50 3
1012 1950-54, 40 watts 1 1.50 3
1015 1956-1960, 45 watts 1 1.50 3
1016 1959-1960, 35 watts 1 1.50 3
1025 1961-1969, 45 watts, circuit breaker 1 1.50 3
1026 1963-1964, 25 watts 1 1.50 3
1032 1948, 75 watts, reverse and whistle controls 9 14 18
1033 1948-1956, 90 watts, whistle control 10 15 20
1034 1948-54, 75 watts 6 9 15
1037 1946-1947, 5-17 volts, 40 watts 1 1.50 3
1041 1945-1946, 60 watts, whistle control, circuit breaker 5 7 11
1042 1947-1948, 75 watts, whistle control, circuit breaker 9 14 18
1043
(A) 1953-1957, 50 watts, black case 2 3 5
(B) 60 watts, ivory case with gold plated speed control and binding post for Girls' Set. Black base, embossed in stylized letters SA 15 20 40
1044 1957-1969, 90 watts, whistle control, direction control 10 15 20
1053 1956-1960, 60 watts, whistle control 5 8 11
1063 1960-1964, 75 watts, whistle control, circuit breaker 9 14 18
1073 1962-1966, 60 watts, circuit breaker 3 5 17
1101 1948, 25 watts 1 1.50 3
A 1947-1948, 90 watts, circuit breaker, 14-24 volts 8 10 18
KW 190 watts, operates two trains with whistle control, circuit breaker
    35 60 100
LW 1955-1966, 125 watts, green power "on light", buttons for direction and horn, circuit breaker 15 20 35
Q 1946, 75 watts, 6-24 volts, whistle control 8 12 18
R 1946-1947, two independent circuits, 110 watts, 6-24 volts 11 15 30
RW 1948-1954, 110 watts, circuit breaker, whistle control 8 15 25
SW 1961-1966, 130 watts, two train operation, whistle 18 35 50
TW 1953-1960, 175 watts, whistle control 18 40 70
V 1946-1947, 150 watts, four independent circuits 18 30 60
VW 1948-1949, 150 watts, four independent circuits 30 50 125
Z 1945-1947, 250 watts, four independent circuits, 6-25 25 50 75
ZW 1948-1949, 250 watts, four independent circuits 65 75 145
ZW 275 watts, four independent circuits. Excellent examples in great demand 70 90 160

LIONEL METAL TRUCKS

Lionel produced at least seven major types of metal trucks, each of which is described below:

I. **Metal Trucks with Early Coil Coupler, Whirly Wheels (1945).** Type I has the first postwar trucks, a remotely-operated knuckle coupler with a coil on the coupler shank and a shaft that is moved by the coil to open the knuckle. A sliding shoe contacts the special remote control uncoupling section and is mounted on a jury-rigged bracket. The bracket is readily visible on the underside of the truck. The truck side frames are fastened by a rivet swaged over resembling a "staple end." The wheels have a whirl pattern on the inside back surface and ride on thickened axles.

Bottom view of Type 1 trucks

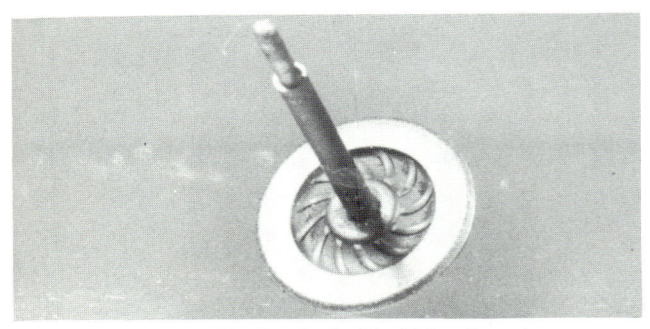

Whirly wheel with thick axle

II. **Metal Trucks with Early Coil Coupler, Regular Wheels (1945-1946).** This is similar to Type I but has wheels with regular back inside surfaces and axles of usual thickness.

III. **Metal Trucks with Late Coil Coupler (1946-1947.)** This coupler also uses an opening knuckle activated by a coil and plunger and the truck side frames have the "staple end" fastening. However the mounting bracket for the sliding shoe is integral with the metal plate that covers the bottom of the truck.

IV. **Metal Trucks with Magnetic Coupler, Staple End and No Hole on Activator Flap (introduced 1948.)** Lionel found that it could produce a highly reliable coupling action without the expense and complication of a coil plunger unit. Lionel designed a coupler that opens by pulling down a flap on the underside of the truck. To move the flap Lionel modified the remote control track and added an electromagnet to the center of that track. The electromagnet pulls the flap which is connected to the coupler by a lever arrangement so that the knuckle opens. The flap has a rivet swaged on the underside and no hole on the flap with the rivet. Type IV is a highly successful design.

V. **Metal Trucks with Magnetic Coupler, Staple End and Hole on Activator Flap (introduced circa 1950.)** This type is the same as Type IV but a hole has been added to the activator flap behind the rivet. The rivet on the flap is swagged on the truck's top surface.

Side and bottom views of two versions of the bar end truck. The left truck has a magnetic coupler, the right -- the late coil coupler

VI. **Metal Trucks with Magnetic Coupler, Bar End and Hole on activator Flap (introduced circa 1952.)** Lionel modified Type V by changing the method of fastening the side frames to the bolster with a bar fitting into the side frames. The top of the bolster is embossed.

VII. **Metal Trucks with Magnetic Coupler, Bar End Hole on Activator Flap and Tab (circa 1955.)** Lionel modified Truck Type VI by adding a tab to facilitate hand uncoupling. This design change made the trains easier for children to play with at some slight sacrifice of realism.

Side and bottom views of Type VI and Type VII

638-2361 Van Camp

1004 PRR Baby Ruth

2454 Pennsylvania

2458X Pennsylvania

2758X Pennsylvania

2954X Pennsylvania

3356[A] Santa Fe

3357 Hydraulic Platform

3366 Circus

3370 Wells Fargo

3376[A] Bronx Zoo

3376[E] Bronx Zoo

3424[B] Wabash

3428[B] U.S. Mail

3434 Poultry Dispatch

Chapter IV
BOX CARS

Gd. V.G. Exc. Mt

638-2361 VAN CAMP'S PORK & BEANS Uncatalogued, red with white and yellow lettering, coin slot, 8 1/2 inches long, non-opening door, 1962, part of set 19142, Bohn comment   7   15   20   30

1004 PRR Baby Ruth 1949-51, orange with black lettering, 8 inches long, non-opening door
(A) "Baby Ruth" in solid black lettering   2   3   4   6
(B) "Baby Ruth" in outlined black lettering   2   3   4   6

Note: 2454 appears with two different road names

2454 PENNSYLVANIA 1945-46, orange with black lettering, numbered "65400," 9 1/4 inches long
(A) 1945, orange doors, clear shell painted orange, metal trucks with early coil couplers, reported without whirly wheels, Foss and Clark Collections
   20   30   40   60
(B) 1946, brown door, metal trucks with late coil couplers, Foss Collection
   20   30   40   70

X2454 BABY RUTH 1946, orange painted orange plastic body, brown unpainted plastic doors, "Enjoy Curtiss Baby Ruth Candy" to left of door in black script, PRR logo in black to right of door, black reporting marks: EW 9-11; EH 13-0; IL 40-6; IW 9-2; IH 10-4: CU FT 3936, X2454 BUILT BY LIONEL in black below reporting marks, one large and one small hole in middle of frame, steps at corners, frame held to body by screws at corners, staple-end metal trucks, late coil couplers
(A) As above   4   8   10   15
(B) Silver painted plastic body and doors, black sans-serif lettering "Baby Ruth" to right of door, PRR logo to right of door, reporting marks below PRR logo, bar-end metal trucks with late coil couplers. Operating merchandise car with five black cubes stamped "BABY RUTH" and one red cube stamped "BABY RUTH," very rare, Roberts Collection   NRS
(C) Merchandise car, circa 1946, car throws out five plastic "Baby Ruth" cubes which resemble merchandise containers. Orange painted plastic body, black PRR logo on right side, "New 6-46" and reporting marks in black on right side, "Enjoy" in upper and lower case script and "Baby Ruth" in black outlined letters at left side of door, staple-end metal trucks, coil couplers, sliding shoes, steps, Adair Collection   NRS

2458X PENNSYLVANIA 1947, double-door automobile car, brown with white lettering, compressor assembly on underframe, metal body, continuation of prewar 2758, not illustrated   7   11   15   30

X2758 PENNSYLVANIA 1945-46, double-door automobile car, brown metal body with white lettering, compressor assembly on underframe and steps and brakewheels. A similar car was produced in 1941-42 which had automatic box couplers. Kotil reports the following variations:
(A) Staple-end trucks, whirly wheels, early coil couplers   8   12   15   30
(B) Staple-end trucks, early dish wheels   8   12   15   30
(C) Staple-end trucks, regular wheels, late coil couplers   8   12   15   30

X2954 PENNSYLVANIA Not catalogued, bakelite painted tuscan, white lettering, metal trucks, coil-operated coupler, same body as 2954, made in 1941-42. It is unlikely that this car was produced by the factory with postwar trucks. In some cases service stations and individuals removed prewar trucks and replaced them with postwar trucks.   100   200   250   350

3356 SANTA FE RAILWAY EXPRESS 1957-60 and 1964-66, operating car from horse corral set, horses move by vibrator action from car to pen and back; green car, yellow lettering, brakewheel to right of operating doors, galvanized metal bottom. Price does not include corral. For corral add $15, $20, $25, $35
(A) Lettered "BLT. 5-56," metal trucks with bar-ends, magnetic couplers with tabs   20   30   40   65
(B) No built date, Timken trucks with disc-operating couplers
   20   30   40   65

3357 HYDRAULIC PLATFORM MAINTENANCE CAR Cop and hobo move to special gray plastic on-off platform, blue plastic Type II plug door body with white lettering, Timken trucks, disc-operating couplers, price includes platform. Reissued by Fundimensions in 1982
(A) Medium blue plastic   12   17   25   40
(B) Darker blue plastic   12   17   25   40

3366 CIRCUS CAR 1959-62, operating car with nine white rubber horses and 3356-150 corral. Vibrator coils under the car, corral vibrates and miniature rubber "fingers" on base of horse causes it to move forward. (Same mechanism as found on 3356.) Unpainted ivory plastic car, 10 3/8 inches long, metal trucks with bar-ends, magnetic couplers with tabs, one black sliding shoe, red roof and catwalk. White corral with white fence, gray walkway and red inner section. As operating car faces the viewer brakewheel is on left end and "BLT BY LIONEL" appears in red, heat-stamped lettering on lower right
(A) Set   75   100   150   225
(B) Car only   40   60   80   150

3370 WESTERN & ATLANTIC 1961-64, sheriff and outlaw bob and shoot at each other, green with yellow lettering
(A) Timken trucks, disc-operating couplers   10   15   25   45
(B) Arch bar trucks, disc-operating couplers, Hutchinson Collection
   10   15   25   45

3376 BRONX ZOO 1960-69, giraffe lowers head to pass under bridge unit, action caused by special rail unit with overhead section. Timken plastic trucks with disc-operating couplers. We have also had reports of both blue and green cars with gold lettering instead of yellow, Niedhammer observation. We need to know which of the varieties listed below have this lettering. Reader comments are requested. Price for set.
(A) Blue car, white lettering, brown spotted giraffe   10   12   17   25
(B) Blue car, white lettering, solid yellow giraffe   10   12   17   25
(C) Green car, yellow lettering, solid yellow giraffe   10   12   17   25
(D) Blue car, yellow lettering, brown spotted giraffe   15   25   35   45
(E) Blue car, yellow lettering, solid yellow giraffe   15   25   35   45
(F) Green car, yellow lettering, brown-spotted yellow giraffe, Lord and Weingart Collections.   10   12   17   25
(G) Same as (A), but no lettering, Breslin Collection   NRS

3386 BRONX ZOO, 1960, shown in the 1960 Advance Catalogue as part of set no. 1109 with 1060 loco (see 1060 loco for details). Light blue body. Price includes rail/overhead unit. White lettering.
(A) Solid yellow giraffe, arch bar trucks, dummy couplers
   20   30   40   50
(B) Yellow giraffe with brown spots, Timken trucks, dummy couplers
   20   30   40   50
(C) Yellow giraffe with brown spots, arch bar trucks, dummy couplers, came with 1060 set cited above, Fleming Collection   20   30   40   50
(D) Prototype: Bongo and Bobo car, "World's Only Performing Giraffes," illustrated on page 39 in LIONEL: A Collector's Guide and History, Volume IV. Collection of Philip Mace Catalano   —   —   1000   —

3424 WABASH 1956-58, operating brakeman, Type IIB blue plastic body with white lettering, white unpainted five panel plastic door, "8-56," metal trucks with tab magnetic couplers, sliding shoe. Price includes rail trip and overhead unit
(A) White man, medium blue plastic body, blue sliding shoe
   17   25   40   60
(B) White man, lighter blue plastic body, white sliding shoe
   17   25   40   60
(C) White man, darker blue plastic body, blue sliding shoe
   22   33   50   75
(D) Man with dark blue pants, gray shirt, flesh colored skin, red cap
   22   33   50   75

71

3428 UNITED STATES MAIL 1959, operating door, Type III blue plastic body, red plastic five panel door painted red, white and blue, Timken trucks, disc-operating couplers

(A) Blue man carries gray mailbag 10 15 25 40
(B) Gray man carries blue bag 10 15 25 40
(C) Same as (A) but Type IIIB body 10 15 25 40

3434 POULTRY DISPATCH 1959-60 and 1965-66, operating sweeper, activated by remote control track, illuminated

(A) Gray plastic body painted brown with white lettering, gray man, Timken trucks, disc-operating couplers 25 30 45 75
(B) Gray plastic painted slightly darker brown, blue man with flesh colored hands, face and broom; metal trucks with magnetic tab couplers 25 30 45 75
(C) Same as (B) but gray man 25 30 45 75

3435 TRAVELING AQUARIUM 1959-62, lighted with "swimming" tropical fish; clear plastic car painted green with gold or yellow lettering; Timken trucks with disc-operating couplers and two pickup shoes. Aquarium windows appear wave-like; car interior painted black to control light reflection; vibrator motor moves continuous belt creating illusion of swimming fish. This car, rather an exotic piece, was greeted with derision by collectors at its issue, but today it is considered a highly desirable item. Reissued by Fundimensions in 1981.

(A) Large "L" with gold circle and gold lettering: "Tank No. 1", "Tank No. 2" 60 80 150 250
(B) Same as (A) but no circle around large "L" 60 80 150 250
(C) Yellow lettering, no tank designations, no circle around large "L" 40 60 80 110
(D) Similar to (C) but heavier and brighter lettering 40 60 80 110
(E) Same as (C) but no circle, no tank designation, Degano Collection 50 70 140 240

3454 PRR AUTOMATIC MERCHANDISE CAR 1946-47, car throws out six plastic "Baby Ruth" cubes which resemble merchandise containers. Reproduction cubes do not read "Baby Ruth." Aluminum paint on clear plastic with blue lettering: "New 6-46" and both "3454" and "X3454," metal trucks with staple-ends, coil couplers, sliding shoes, steps, Falter Collection 30 50 75 90

3462 AUTOMATIC REFRIGERATED MILK CAR 1947-48, operating car, man delivers milk cans, cream white paint on clear plastic with black lettering including "RT3462," staple-end metal trucks with coil couplers, sliding shoes and metal doors. The car body is attached to the base by two metal springs; remove springs to access jammed cans. This is the most popular type of operating car made by Lionel. Price includes platform and five cans. 15 20 30 40

(A) 1947, early brass base mechanism with thinner metal stock and more folding than later mechanism. The base mechanism is attached to the car frame by three and, later, four brass tabs twisted 90 degrees. The 1947 base is one inch shorter than the 1948 base, as the earlier base does not include the pivot plate found on later models. A square sheet metal plate slides out under the milkman, carrying him with it. This plate is placed within a track in the brass base under the milkman's right foot. Considerably more scarce than later versions, Fleming Collection. **NRS**
(B) 1948, later, more common mechanism with milkman attached to swinging can sweep arm. 15 20 30 40

3464 A T & S F 1949-50, 52, operating car, "X3464" on side; man appears as door opens, plunger mechanism, orange appearance, black lettering, marked "X3464" on side, metal trucks, magnetic couplers, metal or plastic doors, usually painted orange. The underlying paint varies in color. On some pieces the man is missing so that his color is unknown. The following observations are primarily owed to Joseph Kotil:

(A) Clear plastic, staple trucks, steps, blue and white man, brown metal door 6 9 12 15
(B) Same as (A) but black metal door 6 9 12 15
(C) Same as (A) but opaque blue-gray plastic, black metal door 6 9 12 15
(D) Same as (A) but blue plastic, black metal door (missing man) 6 9 12 15
(E) Marbled black plastic, staple-end trucks, no steps, blue man, black metal door 6 9 12 15
(F) Same as (E) but green plastic (missing man) 6 9 12 15
(G) Same as (E) but clear plastic (missing man) 6 9 12 15
(H) Same as (E) but clear plastic, emblem with red and yellow coloring, rare **NRS**
(I) Clear plastic, bar-end trucks, no steps, blue man, black metal door 6 9 12 15
(J) Same as (I) but black plastic door 6 9 12 15
(K) Same as (I) but orange plastic, black plastic door 6 9 12 15
(L) Orange-brown body, black metal doors. Same color as 3464XNYC, but with AT & SF lettering and numbering. Three examples known to exist, Niedhammer, Stewart and Sattler Collections **NRS**

3464X N Y C 159000 1952, operating car, "X3464" on side, man emerges as door opens, plunger mechanism, orange-brown body, white lettering "NEW 9-44" on left of black door, metal trucks with staple or bar-ends and magnetic couplers; door on operating side has single large panel, door on non-operating side has no panels

(A) Staple-end trucks, semi-gloss orange-brown, man with flesh-colored face, steps, metal doors 6 9 12 15
(B) Staple-end trucks, flatter orange-brown, all blue man, no steps, staple-end trucks, metal doors, Kotil Collection 6 9 12 15
(C) Bar-end trucks, no steps, metal doors, Kotil Collection 6 9 12 15
(D) Bar-end trucks, no steps, plastic doors, Kotil Collection 6 9 12 15

3472 AUTOMATIC REFRIGERATED MILK CAR Man delivers milk cans, "RT 3472" on side

(A) Pink and gray marble plastic body painted cream white, black lettering, short metal roof hatch, tin-plated door frame with aluminum doors, black underframe/floor with four steps; indentations on underframe for door frames; indentation visible from bottom; early operating mechanism, metal trucks with staple-ends, magnetic couplers, spring clips hold body and frame together 10 15 25 45
(B) Same as (A) but white unpainted plastic 10 15 25 45
(C) White unpainted plastic body, staple-end or bar-end trucks, magnetic couplers, long loading hatch with two simulated ice hatches and portion of catwalk; no holes in body for door frame tabs; plastic doors, base now cut out for new door assembly, four steps 10 15 25 45
(D) Same as (C) but pure white unpainted plastic body which contrasts with cream white hatch loading door and grayish white plastic doors and frame 10 15 25 45
(E) Same as (C) but grayish white body, hatch and doors, (whiter than (C)) 10 15 25 45

3474 WESTERN PACIFIC 1952-53, operating car, man appears as door opens, silver body with orange feather, metal trucks with bar-ends, magnetic couplers

(A) Medium density lettering 10 20 30 45
(B) Lighter density lettering 10 20 30 45

3482 AUTOMATIC REFRIGERATED MILK CAR 1954-55 operating car, man delivers milk cans. This is the most popular type of operating car made by Lionel. White unpainted plastic, black lettering, body fastened to frame by Phillips head screw at one end and sliding bar at other; frame base has two ridges, plastic doors, metal trucks with bar-ends and magnetic uncouplers. Price includes stand and five cans.

(A) Large numerals "3482" on upper left and small "RT 3472" on lower right 10 15 20 30
(B) Large numerals "3482" on upper left and small "RT 3482" on lower 10 15 20 30

3484 PENNSYLVANIA 1953, operating car with plunger mechanism, man appears as door opens, Type I clear plastic body painted tuscan, 1953 Type black plastic door painted tuscan, bar-end metal trucks with magnetic couplers

(A) Body and door painted tuscan-brown 10 15 25 40
(B) Body and door painted tuscan-red, appears lighter than (A) 10 15 25 40

3484-25 A.T.&S.F. 1954-57, operating car with plunger mechanism, man appears as door opens, found with Types I, IIA and IIB bodies, and 1953 and 1956 Type doors, bar-end metal trucks, magnetic tab couplers*

(A) Type I clear plastic body painted glossy or flat orange, white rubber

stamped lettering, Santa Fe herald, one-half inch long, 1954
15   20   35   45

(B) Type I clear plastic body painted flat orange, 1953 Type black plastic doors painted shiny orange, heat-stamped white lettering, Santa Fe herald 7/16 of an inch long, 1954
15   20   35   45

(C) Type IIA clear plastic body painted shiny orange, 1953 type black plastic door painted shiny orange, heat-stamped white lettering, 7/16 of an inch, Santa Fe herald
15   20   30   45

(D) Same as (C) Type IIA but heat-stamped black lettering, 7/16 of an inch long, Santa Fe herald
—   600   900   1200

(E) Type IIB red plastic body painted flat orange, 1953 Type black plastic door painted shiny orange, heat-stamped white lettering, 7/16 of an inch long, Santa Fe herald, 1956-57
15   20   35   45

(F) Type IIB orange plastic body painted brighter flat orange than (E), 1956 Type white plastic door painted shiny orange, heat-stamped white lettering, 7/16 of an inch long Santa Fe herald, 1956-57
15   20   35   45

(G) Same as (F) but door painted flat orange
15   20   35   45

(H) Type I clear plastic body painted shiny orange, 1953 Type black plastic door painted shiny orange, heat-stamped black lettering, very rare   NRS

3494-1 N Y C PACEMAKER 1955, operating car with plunger mechanism, man appears as door opens, bar-end metal trucks with magnetic couplers

(A) Type IIA red plastic body with gray painted areas, white rubber stamped lettering, with a comma under the second "s" of System
20   35   50   75

(B) Type IIB dark blue plastic body painted pastel blue, 1956 Type red plastic door painted buttercup yellow, black heat-stamped lettering, no comma under second "s" of System. See picture in prototype section for this one of a kind box car   NRS

3494-150 M.P. 1956, operating car with plunger mechanism, man appears as door opens, Type IIB gray plastic body with blue painted areas, "Eagle" on left is 5/8 of an inch long, "XME" and "Merchandise Service" on lower right, no grooves, 1956 Type yellow unpainted plastic door, bar-end metal trucks with magnetic tab couplers
25   35   50   75

3494-275 STATE OF MAINE 1956, operating car with plunger mechanism, man appears as door opens, Type IIB blue plastic body with painted white and red stripes and black heat-stamped lettering; bar-end metal trucks with magnetic couplers; letters "O", "F", "D" and "U" are placed on door sign boards. Lionel redesigned its box car door in 1956 to accommodate these letters and the new door is known as the 1956 Type door, blue plastic door painted white and red

(A) "B.A.R."is under and overscored, dark red stripes   30   40   50   75
(B) Same as (A) but medium red stripes   30   40   50   75
(C) "B.A.R." is neither under nor overscored, "3494275" is omitted
50   75   100   200
(D) Printed on only one side   NRS

3494-550 MONON 1957, operating car with plunger mechanism, blue man appears as door opens, Type IIB plastic body with white painted stripe and heat-stamped white lettering (except (C)), lettered "BLT 6-57," bar-end metal trucks with magnetic tab couplers 11 inches long, 1956 Type maroon plastic door with white painted stripe (except (C))

(A) Maroon plastic body and doors   70   100   150   250
(B) Same as (A) but missing "BLT 6-57" on one side. This is a collectible factory error. Numerous examples show the progressive fading of the "BLT 6-57" as the stamp deteriorated.   80   100   175   250
(C) Blue plastic body and orange plastic doors painted maroon with decal lettering, prototype   NRS

3494-625 SOO 1957, operating car with plunger mechanism, blue man with flesh colored face appears as door opens, Type IIB maroon plastic body painted tuscan-brown with white heat-stamped lettering, 1956 Type maroon plastic door painted tuscan-brown, bar-end metal trucks with magnetic tab couplers, 11 inches long   70   100   150   225

3530 ELECTRO MOBILE POWER or "Operating GM Generator Car," 1956-58, operating car; opening the door completes the circuit for the accompanying floodlight through the lighting pole. The pole, 3530-30, has two leads which hook into the car roof and two leads that run from the pole to the 3530-12 searchlight. The searchlight has a magnet on the bottom. Inside the car is a large plastic generator, strictly for looks (the same generator is used on the searchlight car). Fuel tanks are found under the car and appear identical to the ones on the 1047 Switchman but not on the diesels. Blue plastic car body with white and blue lettering. Popovich reports two types of pole-transformer base units. One unit has a light blue base, the other a black base, but both utility poles are brown and the riser pipes are gray. We do not know which of the following car variations came with which pole types.

(A) Orange generator, black fuel tank   15   25   35   50
(B) Gray generator, black fuel tank   15   25   35   50
(C) Same as (A) but white stripe extends through ladder to car end
15   25   38   55
(D) Orange generator, blue fuel tank, white stripe extends through ladder to car end   15   25   38   55
(E) Orange generator, blue fuel tank, short white stripe, Kotil Collection
15   25   38   55

3619 HELICOPTER RECONNAISSANCE CAR 1962-64, operating car with red helicopter, black propeller and black landing gear. The helicopter, stored inside, is launched by a spring-loaded device which is pressed to cock. The spring is released by a magnetic section of uncoupling track. Yellow or yellow-orange plastic car sides and ends with red and black lettering, Timken trucks with two disc-type couplers

(A) Yellow   17   23   45   70
(B) Yellow-orange, Degano Collection   22   28   50   100

3656 ARMOUR 1949-55, operating cattle car with cattle and corral. Cattle sometimes need prodding but move more or less continuously from corral to car and back. Orange car with white or black lettering and brown paper decal on door; metal trucks, magnetic couplers, two sliding shoes. Price includes cattle and corral. (A) and (B) are less common than (C) and (D).

(A) ARMOUR in white lettering   18   35   48   60
(B) ARMOUR in black lettering   18   45   60   100
(C) LIONEL LINES in black lettering, orange painted clear plastic, staple-end metal trucks, magnetic couplers, circa 1949-1950   14   25   30   50
(D) LIONEL LINES in white lettering, orange painted yellow-whitish opaque plastic, orange painted orange plastic double door, orange painted diecast sliding door, bar-end metal trucks, magnetic couplers, 1952-53, Kaiser Collection.   14   25   30   50

3662-1 AUTOMATIC REFRIGERATED MILK CAR 1955-60, 1964-66, operating car, man delivers late milk cans without weighted magnets. White car with brown top and doors, "L" in circle, metal trucks with magnetic tab couplers. Price includes five cans and stand.

(A) Lettered "NEW 4-55"   15   25   38   55
(B) Without built date   18   27   48   65

3665 MINUTEMAN 1961-64, operating car, fires either rocket or shells, white plastic sides, blue plastic roof that opens, Timken trucks

(A) Red, white and blue rocket with blue tip on black firing unit, two disc-couplers   12   16   30   45
(B) Green-olive drab marine cannon that fires silver painted, 1 3/4 inch long wooden shells (shells came in plastic bag inside car,) one disc coupler, one fixed coupler, Eddins Collection   15   22   35   55

3666 MINUTEMAN, circa 1964, uncatalogued by LIONEL but offered by Sears as part of set no. 3-9820. Car has operating cannon which fires gray wooden shells 1 3/4" long. The car has white plastic sides with blue lettering and a blue plastic roof which opens. It came with the following set components: (1) a 240 loco; (2) an un-numbered gray flat car with a green tank; (3) a 6470 "EXPLOSIVES" box car; (4) a 6814 (c) Rescue caboose without stretchers; (5) a no. 1249 ALLSTATE TOY TRANSFORMER with a pink top, apparently made by Marx; and (6) 10 plastic soldiers. (A jeep has been mentioned in some reports, but not all). The set box side reads as follows: SEARS SET 39820 ALLSTATE BY LIONEL/STEAM LOCOMOTIVE WITH LIGHT AND SMOKE/BOX CAR EXPLODES WHEN SHELL HITS/ROOF OF CANNON CAR OPENS AND SHELL IS FIRED AUTOMATICALLY/45 WATT TRANSFORMER WITH CIRCUIT BREAKER. Jarman, Vergonet and Bohn Collections. Price for 3666 car only.
75   125   150   200

3672 BOSCO 1959-60, operating milk car with yellow "BOSCO" milk cans; "Corn Products Co." on side, yellow sides, tuscan ends, roof door and lettering, metal trucks, magnetic couplers. Price includes platform and five cans.

(A) With Bosco decal   60   100   125   200
(B) Without Bosco decal, 1960   60   100   125   200
(C) No lettering, Bosco decal on operating box car body and frame, prototype of an operating box car   —   —   —   750

3462 Milk Car
3472 Milk Car
3484-25 A.T. & S.F.
3494-275 State of Maine
3530[D] Electro Mobile Power

3454 PRR Merchandise
3464X N.Y.C.
3484 Pennsylvania
3494-150 M.P. Eagle
3494-625 SOO

3435 Traveling Aquarium
3464 A.T. & S.F.
3474 Western Pacific
3494-1[A] NYC Pacemaker
3494-550 Monon

74

3665[B] Minuteman
3672 Bosco
6004 Baby Ruth
6014[B] Bosco PRR
6014[A] Frisco

3665[A] Minuteman
3662-1 Milk Car
4454 Baby Ruth PRR
X6014[B] Baby Ruth
6014 Frisco

3619 Helicopter Reconnaissance
3656 Armour
3854 PRR Merchandise
X6014[A] Baby Ruth
6014 Chun King

75

3854 AUTOMATIC MERCHANDISE CAR 1946-47, operating box car, tuscan with white lettering, 11 inches long, marked "3854" and "X3854," two sliding shoes on each truck; probably the rarest of all postwar freight and passenger cars, prewar car with modern trucks 150 200 250 350

4454 BABY RUTH PRR 1946, from electronic set with control receiver inside car (see Locomotive 4471), orange with black lettering, brown doors, brown electronic control decal with white lettering; metal trucks with staple-end, center rail pickups, coil-operated couplers
(A) As above 20 30 40 60
(B) Same as (A), except door has hollow interior side pin stop, rather than solid pin door stop, Hutchinson observation. 20 30 40 60

6004 BABY RUTH PRR Non-operating doors, 8 1/2 inches long
(A) Orange, Type I body with blue lettering, 1950 1 2 3 8
(B) Yellow with black lettering, 1951 2 3 5 10

X6004 BABY RUTH PRR 1951, non-operating doors, 8 1/2 inches long, Scout couplers, part of set no. 14615 (see 6110 loco for details), orange unpainted type I plastic body with blue lettering. Came in box numbered 6004. I.D. Smith observation. 2 3 5 10

6014 AIREX Uncatalogued, red Type I body with yellow lettering. NRS

X6014 BABY RUTH PRR
(A) White with black lettering, 1957 2 3 4 7
(B) Red Type I body with white lettering, 1955-56 3 4 6 8
(C) Same as (B) but lighter red with metal trucks with bar-ends and magnetic tab couplers 3 4 6 8

6014 BOSCO PRR 1958
(A) White with black lettering 15 20 30 50
(B) Orange Type I body with brown lettering 4 7 9 11
(C) Red Type I body with white lettering. Timken trucks 4 7 9 11
(D) Orange Type I body, black lettering, Kotil Collection 4 7 9 11
(E) Same as (C) but bar-end trucks, Kotil Collection 4 7 9 11
(F) Same as (D), but has raised black lettering, Blotner Collection. 4 7 9 11

6014 CAMPBELL SOUP 1969, uncatalogued, red with white lettering, question as to existence. Confirmation requested. NRS

6014 CHUN KING Uncatalogued, red Type I body with white lettering 50 75 100 150

6014 FRISCO
(A) Orange Type I body with blue lettering, 1969 2 4 6 8
(B) White Type III body with black lettering, 1964-66, 68 2 4 6 8
(C) White Type III body with very heavy black lettering, 1969 2 4 6 8
(D) White Type I body with black lettering, hole for bank, Timken trucks, one disc-operating coupler, one fixed coupler 10 15 20 30
(E) Red Type I body with white lettering 2 4 6 8
(F) Cream unpainted Type I body with black lettering, Timken trucks, two disc-operating couplers 5 6 9 12
(G) Same as (A) but Type III body, Rohlfing Collection 2 4 6 8

6014 PILLSBURY Prototype, not manufactured, Elliott Smith Collection — — — 200

6014 WIX Uncatalogued, cream white Type I body with red lettering 50 75 100 150

6014 6014 came in numerous product or road names, colors and body types. For convenience 6014s are listed alphabetically (by road or product name) with our letters. All 6014 cars have non-operating doors and are 8 1/2 inches long. The chart listing the body types follows:

6024 NABISCO SHREDDED WHEAT 1957, orange Type I body with black lettering, 8 1/2 inches long, non-opening doors 7 10 15 20

6024 RCA WHIRLPOOL 1969, uncatalogued, red Type I body with white lettering, 8 1/2 inches long, non-opening doors 30 40 55 75

X6034 Baby Ruth PRR 1953, 8 1/2 inches long, non-opening doors
(A) Orange, Type I body with black lettering 2 3 5 7
(B) Red with white lettering 2 3 5 7
(C) Same as (A) but blue lettering, Rohlfing Collection 2 3 5 7

0-27 Plug Door Box Car Types

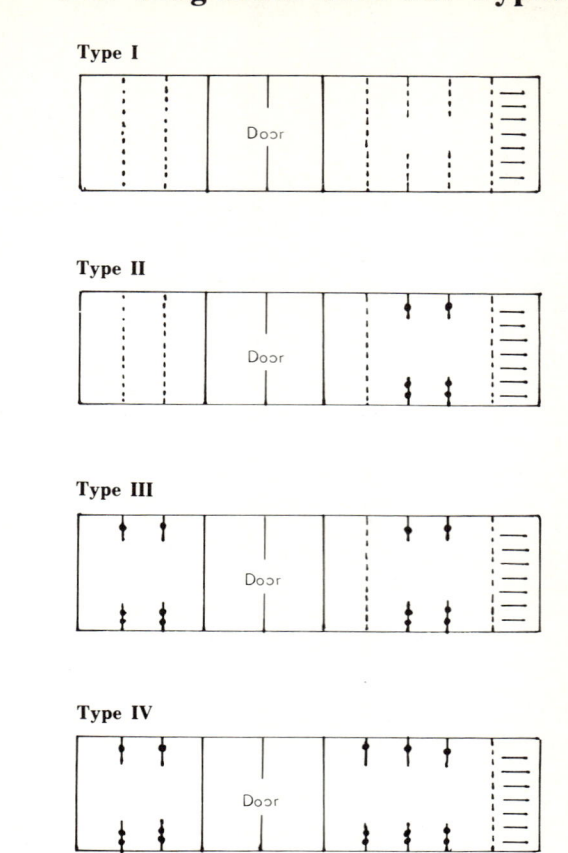

Type I

Type II

Type III

Type IV

6044 AIREX Uncatalogued, 8 1/2 inches long, non-opening doors
(A) Purple Type I body with white/bright yellow lettering — 15 22 30
(B) Medium blue Type I body with white and yellow lettering 2 4 7 9
(C) Light blue Type I body with white and yellow lettering 2 4 7 9
(D) Teal blue Type I body with white and orange lettering 40 60 80 110

6050 LIBBY'S TOMATO JUICE 1961, special Libby's promotional car, Type III body with coin slot, 8 1/2 inches long, non-opening doors, Timken trucks, fixed couplers
(A) Green stems on vegetable decal 9 13 18 25
(B) Green stems missing from decal 50 75 100 150

6050 LIONEL SAVINGS BANK 1961, coin slot, white with green, 8 1/2 inches long, non-opening doors 9 13 18 25

6050 SWIFT REFRIGERATOR 1962, coin slot, usually red with white lettering
(A) Type II body 4 7 9 15
(B) Type III body, lettering high on car 40 60 80 100
(C) White with red lettering, Gay Collection NRS
(D) Type III body, red with white lettering, white S in scroll between second and third step, Blotner Collection NRS

6352-1 PACIFIC FRUIT EXPRESS 1955-57, Union Pacific logo, "63521" on car sides, operating ice car, Type IIB unpainted orange plastic body with unpainted light brown doors, metal trucks with bar-ends and magnetic couplers. Came with ice house and five ice cubes; original cubes have bubble found in middle, reproductions do not. Price for car only. Reissued by Fundimensions in 1982.
(A) Unpainted light brown doors, four lines of medium density lettering: IL, IW, IH, CU.FT. on lower right ice house door side 25 33 40 55

76

(B) Same as (A) but heavier lettering 25 33 40 55
(C) Same as (A) but three lines of lettering: IL, IW, IH on lower right car door. For set add 30, 55, 95, 115 40 60 70 82

6356-1 N Y C 1954-55, two level stock car, 11 1/4 inches long, metal trucks, magnetic couplers, small or large lettering
(A) Flat yellow with black lettering 9 15 18 27
(B) Medium yellow with black lettering 9 15 18 27

6376 LIONEL LINES 1956-57, "CIRCUS CAR," two levels, white unpainted plastic with red lettering, 11 1/4 inches long, "BLT 4-56," red catwalk, metal trucks with bar-ends, magnetic tab couplers 15 25 35 50

6428 UNITED STATES MAIL 1960-61, "RAILWAY POST OFFICE," Type IV gray plastic body painted red, white and blue, 1956 Type deep red plastic door painted red, white and blue, heat-stamped white and black lettering, Timken trucks, disc-operating couplers
(A) Shiny red paint 9 15 20 30
(B) Flat red paint 9 15 20 30
(C) Flat red paint without lettering on one side. Examples are well known and collectible. 20 30 40 50

6434 POULTRY DISPATCH 1958-59, illuminated car showing three rows of fowl on the way to market, without a "working man." Black plastic body painted red with white lettering, gray plastic doors with black lettering, bar-end metal trucks with magnetic tab couplers 18 25 35 50

6445 FORT KNOX GOLD RESERVE 1961-63, very unusual Lionel bank modeled on the aquarium car. Clear plastic car painted silver, but with unpainted windows for viewing gold bullion inside, black lettering. Differs from the 3435 aquarium car in that there are nickel-sized circular screens at car ends, (these were open areas on aquarium car), bank slot on top.
(A) Silver painted plastic, gold bullion 40 60 75 115
(B) Gold painted plastic with silver bullion, one of a kind NRS

6448 TARGET CAR 1961-64, this car from the missile/space period is spring-loaded and designed to be shot at with a missile. When hit the car "explodes." Each car is different - one side is the "target" with two bulls' eyes, the other has "DANGER" warnings. It is quite an unusual Lionel car and is based on a modification of the Type II box car body, but rivet rows end to provide space for lettering "TARGET RANGE CAR." Ladder sections omitted on both sides to allow space for a red stripe that only appears on one side. The color of the sides and roof is unpainted plastic, with Timken trucks and two disc-operating couplers unless otherwise indicated. The car has a metal post and rubber sleeves to hold the car together. It comes with and without side slots and these slots differ in their locations - on one side they are closer to the end than on the other side
(A) Flat red sides, white roof and ends, white lettering, no slots in sides 4 6 8 15
(B) Same as (A) but slots on one side 4 6 8 15
(C) Same as (A) but shiny red sides, slots on one side 4 6 8 15
(D) Shiny red sides, ends, roof, white lettering, no side slots 4 6 8 15
(E) White sides, flat red ends and roof, white lettering 4 6 8 16
(F) White sides, shiny red roof and ends, white lettering, slots on both sides 4 6 8 16
(G) White sides, roof, ends, red lettering, slots on both sides 4 6 8 16

6454 A.T.&S.F. 1948, "63132" and "X6454" on sides, orange paint on plastic body with black lettering, brown metal doors, single panel door on one side and no panel door on other, steps, staple-end metal trucks with magnetic couplers, two small holes in frame in addition to truck mounting holes
(A) Orange painted clear plastic 10 15 20 30
(B) Orange painted black plastic, Kotil Collection 10 15 20 30
(C) Orange painted green marble plastic, Kotil Collection 10 15 20 30

6454 PENNSYLVANIA 1949-53, "65400" and "X6454" on sides, tuscan paint on clear plastic with white lettering, magnetic couplers, brown or black metal doors, Hutchinson comment. We need to know which of the varieties listed below have which doors. Reader comments invited.
(A) Slightly shinier tuscan than (B), two large and two small holes in floor in addition to truck mounting holes, staple-end trucks 8 15 20 30
(B) Slightly duller tuscan than (A), two small holes on floor, steps, staple-end trucks 8 12 15 25
(C) One large and five small frame holes, steps, staple-end trucks, Kotil Collection 8 12 15 25
(D) One large and three small frame holes, no steps, staple-end trucks, Kotil Collection 8 12 15 25
(E) Same as (D) but bar-end trucks, Kotil Collection 8 12 15 25

6454 N.Y.C. 1951, "159000" and "X6454" on sides, metal doors, steps, staple-end metal trucks with magnetic couplers, floor has two small holes plus truck mounting holes
(A) Brown paint on clear plastic with white lettering 10 15 20 27
(B) Brown-orange paint on clear plastic with white lettering 10 15 20 27
(C) Orange paint on clear plastic with black lettering, maroon doors 15 22 30 35
(D) Same as (C) but six frame holes, Kotil Collection 15 22 30 35

6454 ERIE 1949-53 "81000" and "X6454" on sides
(A) Brown with white lettering, bar-end metal trucks, no steps 10 15 20 27
(B) Slightly lighter brown than (A), staple-end metal trucks, steps 10 15 20 26
(C) Same as (A), except has black plastic doors, Hutchinson comment. NRS

6454 S P 1950-53, white lettering as follows: "SP 96743; CAPY 10000; LD LMT 12410; LT WT 44900; NEW 3-42" on left. "SOUTHERN PACIFIC LINES" in circular herald, "RXW10-5; H-13-4; EW-9-4; 1L40-6; IW9-2; IH10-6; CU FT 3713" on right. "X6454" and "BUILT BY LIONEL" on right. Staple or bar-end metal trucks, steps, Schmaus observation.
(A) Brown with white lettering, no steps, staple-end trucks 10 15 20 30
(B) Lighter brown than (A) steps 10 15 20 30
(C) Dark red, staple-end truck, Kotil Collection 20 30 40 60
(D) Dark red, bar-end truck, Kotil Collection 20 30 40 60
(E) Black painted clear plastic shell, white heat-stamped lettering, prototype. This color scheme was later used for the 6464-225, Degano Collection — — — 750
(F) Brown body and doors, smaller S P herald (rare), Niedhammer Collection NRS
(G) Dark red body and doors, smaller S P herald, Niedhammer Collection NRS

6454 BABY RUTH PRR 1948, orange body, brown metal doors with hollow door stop pin, black lettering and PRR logs, two small holes in frame, staple-end metal trucks, late coil couplers, Hutchinson observation 50 75 100 200

6024 RCA Whirlpool
6050 Lionel Savings Bank
6352-1 Pacific Fruit Express
6428 U.S. Mail
6448 Target Car

6024 Nabisco Shredded Wheat
6044 Airex
6050 Swift
6376 Lionel Circus
6445 Fort Knox Gold

6014 Wix
X6034[A] Baby Ruth PRR
6050 Libby's Tomato Juice
6356-1 NYC two level stock
6434 Poultry Dispatch

6454 BOX CARS

6454 A.T. & S.F.   6454[B] N.Y.C.

6454 Pennsylvania   6454[B] Erie

6454[C] N.Y.C.   6454[A] N.Y.C.

6454 Unpainted Body

6454 SP

LIONEL 6464 BOX CAR VARIATIONS

by Dr. Charles Weber*

Dr. Charles Weber wrote the section on 6464 box cars. His study, completed several years ago and recently updated, introduced a new level of sophistication to the study of Lionel variations. It should be noted, however, that Dr. Weber did not contribute the prices listed for the 6464 box cars. It is his strongly held conviction, that the concern with prices detracts from the essential enjoyment of toy train collecting. His willingness to contribute to this volume is most appreciated.

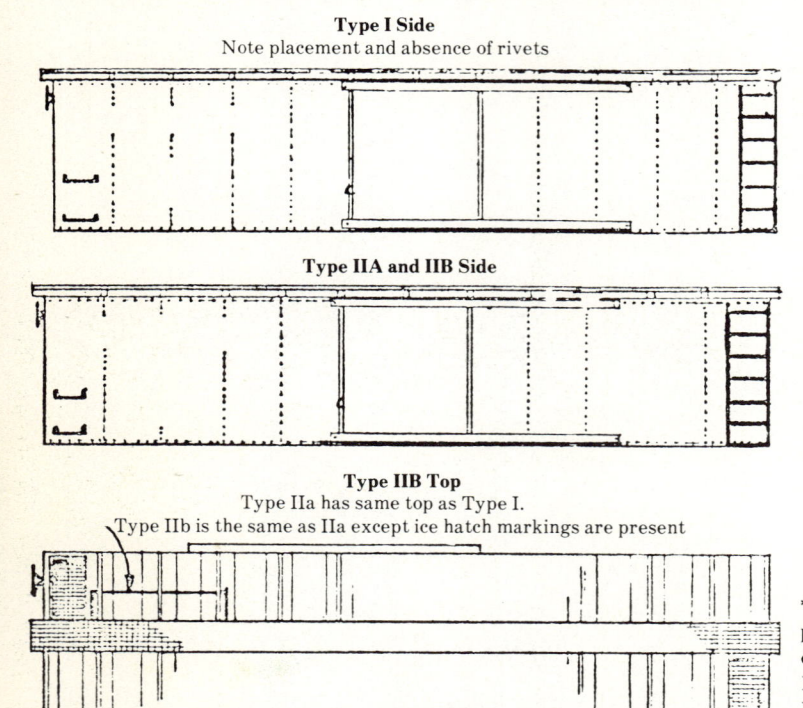

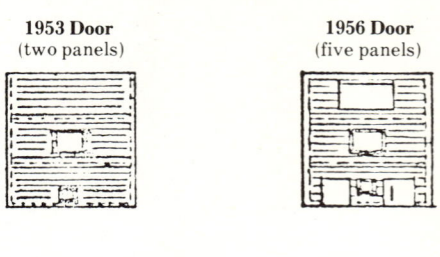

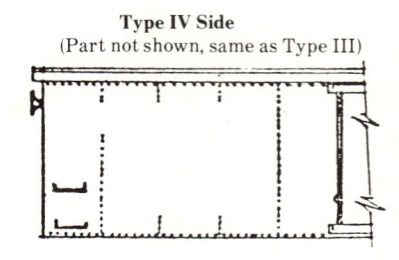

Type I Side
Note placement and absence of rivets

Type IIA and IIB Side

Type IIB Top
Type IIa has same top as Type I.
Type IIb is the same as IIa except ice hatch markings are present

1953 Door (two panels)

1956 Door (five panels)

Type IV Side
(Part not shown, same as Type III)

Drawings by Bob Fox

* Dr. Weber gratefully acknowledges the assistance of the following people without whose assistance this research could not have been carried forth: Sid Brown, Ron Niedhammer, Allan Stewart, Ernie Davis, Dick Meerly, Joe Ryan, Lee Stuhl, Joe Ranker, Elliott Smith and Bill Fryberger.

Type III Side / B Type IV Side
Type III and IV are noticeably lighter in weight and roof ribs can be seen on the inside

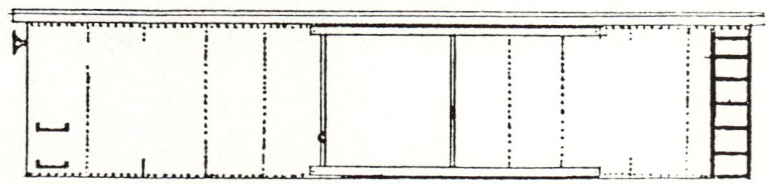

6464-1 WESTERN PACIFIC 1953-54, usually silver with blue letters, Type I body painted silver, body mold color varies, 1953-Type door, black door mold painted silver, no decals, hot press lettering, letter color varies

1 Opaque white body mold, bright blue lettering	12	18	30	50
2 Clear body mold, bright blue lettering	12	18	30	50
3 Light gray body mold, bright blue lettering	12	18	30	50
4 Black body mold, medium blue lettering	12	18	30	50
5A Clear body mold, medium blue lettering	12	18	30	50
5B Transparent blue body mold, medium blue lettering	12	18	30	50
6 Light green body mold, medium blue lettering	12	18	30	50
7 Light green body mold, dark blue lettering	12	18	30	50
8A Blue-black body mold, dark blue lettering	12	18	30	50
8B Black body mold, black lettering, one-of-a-kind				NRS
9 Clear body mold, dark blue lettering	12	18	30	50
10 Bluish-opaque body mold, red lettering, rare	500	—	1200	2000
11A Clear body mold, red lettering, rare	—	—	1200	2000
11B Clear body mold painted orange, door painted orange, white lettering, one-of-a-kind	—	—	—	2000

6464-25 GREAT NORTHERN Type I body painted glossy or flat orange, except 23B, body mold color varies, 1953-Type door, black door mold painted glossy or flat orange, no decals, except 21-23A, hot press white lettering

12 Opaque-white body, glossy orange body and door paint	10	15	20	45
13 White body, glossy orange body and door paint	10	15	20	45
14 Clear body, glossy orange body and door paint	10	15	20	45
15 Black-marble body, glossy orange body and door paint	10	15	20	45
16 Gray body, glossy orange body and door paint	10	15	20	45
17A White body, flat orange body and door paint	15	20	35	55
17B White body, glossy orange body paint, flat orange door paint	15	20	35	55
18A Clear body, flat orange body and door paint	15	20	35	55
18B Clear body, glossy orange body and door paint	15	20	35	55
19 Black body, flat orange body and door paint	15	20	35	55
20 Gray body, flat orange body and door paint	15	20	35	55
21 Clear body, flat orange body and door paint, red and green decals	100	200	250	400
22 Black body, flat orange body and door paint, red and green decals	100	200	250	400

6464-50 Minneapolis & St. Louis
6464-100 Western Pacific-b
6464-150 Missouri Pacific-b
6464-200 Pennsylvania
6464-275 State of Maine-a
6464-300 Rutland-b

6464-25 Great Northern
6464-100 Western Pacific-a
6464-150 Missouri Pacific-a
6464-75 Rock Island
6464-250 Western Pacific
6464-300 Rutland-a

6464-1 Western Pacific
6464-175 Rock Island
6464-125 New York Central
6464-150 Missouri Pacific-c
6464-225 Southern Pacific
6464-275 State of Maine-b

23A Black body, glossy orange body paint, flat orange door paint, red and green decals   100   200   250   400
23B Clear body painted tuscan, no information on door mold color, paint, decal, one-of-a-kind   —   —   1500   —

6464-50 MINNEAPOLIS & ST. LOUIS 1953-56, Type I body, painted flat or glossy tuscan, except 29B, 1953-Type door painted flat or glossy tuscan, black door mold, no decals, white hot press lettering

24 Opaque-white body, flat tuscan body and door paint   15   20   30   45
25 Clear body, flat tuscan body and door paint   15   20   30   45
26 Black body, flat tuscan body and door paint   15   20   30   45
27 White body, flat tuscan body and door paint   15   20   30   45
28 Opaque-white body, glossy tuscan body and door paint   15   20   30   45
29A Light gray body, glossy tuscan body and door paint   15   20   30   45
29B Gray body, flat tuscan over copper-colored paint, glossy, tuscan door, one-of-a-kind   NRS
30 Clear body, glossy tuscan body and door paint   15   20   30   45

6464-75 ROCK ISLAND 1953-54, 1969, Type I body, except 36A-B (Type IV), painted in shades of green or gray, mold color varies, 1953-Type door, except 36A-B (1956-Type door), door painted glossy, flat or light green, black door mold, except 36A-B (green), no decals, hot press gold lettering, except 36A-B (bright gold lettering)

31A Clear body, glossy green body and door paint   15   22   35   55
31B Same as 31A except body painted light gray   15   22   35   55
31C Same as 31A except body painted green   15   22   35   55
32 Gray body, glossy green body and door paint   15   22   35   55
33 Clear body, light flat green body paint, flat green door paint   15   22   35   55
34 Opaque-white body, flat green body and door paint   15   22   35   55
35 Gray body, medium flat green body paint, flat green door paint   15   22   35   55
36A Type IV green body, flat green body and door paint, 1956-Type green door, bright gold lettering   10   15   30   50
36B Same as 36A except light green door paint   10   15   30   50

6464-100 WESTERN PACIFIC 1954-55, Type IIA body, except 37 and 40 (Type I), opaque-white body mold (37-39) and clear body mold (40-46), orange or silver (40-46) body paint, 1953-Type door painted orange or silver (40-46), black door mold, white, gray-white or black (40-46) rubber stamped lettering, no decals

37 Type I opaque-white body, flat orange body and door paint, white lettering, blue feather numbered "1954," not 6464-100, three known copies   —   —   2000   3000
38A Type IIA opaque-white body, orange body and door paint, white lettering, lighter blue feather   100   —   25   400
38B Same as 38A except darker orange body and door paint, blue feather, large WP, small "BUILT BY LIONEL," similar to 6464-250   —   —   1000   —
39 Type IIA opaque-white body, orange body and door paint, gray-white lettering, blue feather   100   —   25   450
40 Type I clear body, silver body and door paint, black lettering, short yellow feather (18.5cm)   45   75   90   125

41-46: All have: Type IIA clear bodies, silver body and door paint, black lettering, but feather color and length vary

41 Long yellow feather (18.7cm)   30   40   70   100
42 Long yellow-orange feather, doors regular yellow   30   40   70   100
43 Short yellow feather   30   40   70   100
44 Long yellow-orange feather   30   40   70   100
45 Short yellow-orange feather   30   40   70   100
46 Yellow feather, doors yellow-orange   30   40   70   100

6464-125 NEW YORK CENTRAL 1954-56, Type IIA body except 47 (Type I), 1953-Type door, except 55, 56A, 57A and B, no decals, white lettering, except 47 and 57A (black), other characteristics vary as described

47 Type I clear body painted light yellow, white door mold painted red, black rubber stamped, one-of-a-kind   NRS
48 Clear body painted glossy gray and flat red, red unpainted door, hot press lettering, gray top row of rivets, no cedilia   20   30   40   63
49 Same as 48 except rubber stamp lettering   20   30   40   65
50 Red body painted gray, red unpainted door, hot press lettering, gray top row of rivets, no cedilia   20   30   40   65
51 Red body painted gray, red unpainted door, hot press lettering, red top row of rivets, half gray, no cedilia   20   30   40   65
52A Red-black marble body painted shiny red and glossy gray, red unpainted door, hot press lettering, gray top row of rivets, no cedilia   20   30   40   65
53A Red body painted shiny gray, white door painted shiny red, rubber stamped, red top row of rivets, no cedilia   20   30   40   65
53B Same as 53A except dull red and gray paint   20   30   40   65
54 White body painted red and glossy gray, white door painted red, rubber stamped, red top row of rivets, cedilia   20   30   40   65
55 White body painted gray and red, 1956-Type unpainted door, red door mold, rubber stamped, top row of rivets red, cedilia   20   30   40   65
56A Red body painted flat gray, 1956-Type red unpainted door, rubber stamped, top row of rivets red, cedilia   20   30   40   65
56B Red body painted flat gray and flat red, 1953-Type white door painted red, rubber stamped, half of top row of rivets red, half with cedilia   40   60   80   110
57A Red body painted gray, 1956-Type maroon door painted red, black rubber stamped lettering, red top row of rivets, cedilia   20   30   40   65
57B Red body painted glossy gray, 1956-Type white unpainted door, rubber stamped, red top row of rivets, cedilia   20   30   40   65

6464-150 MISSOURI PACIFIC Catalogued 1954-55 and 1957. This car has several interesting variations. First, the word "Eagle" comes in three sizes: large, 3/4 of an inch high, medium, 5/8 of an inch high and small, 1/2 inch high. Second, "Eagle" is found either to the left or right of the door. Third, the gray stripe on the car's side may be painted on a blue unpainted or blue painted shell, or it may be the body color itself. In the latter case, blue paint creates the gray stripe effect. Fourth, the door may or may not have a painted gray stripe.

The following characteristics apply to all Missouri Pacifics except as noted: no decals, except 58 and black and white rubber stamped lettering

59-67C: Have Type IIA bodies and 1953-Type doors

58 Type I clear body painted blue and gray, 1953-Type yellow unpainted door with gray painted stripe, decal, right 3/4 of an inch Eagle, XME, pre-production sample, reportedly one-of-a-kind   NRS
59 Navy blue body with painted gray stripe, yellow unpainted door with gray painted stripe, right 3/4 of an inch Eagle, XME   25   35   50   80
60 Same as 59 except no XME   25   35   50   80
61 Same as 59 except body painted navy blue with painted gray stripe, no XME   25   35   50   80
62 Gray body painted royal blue to create the effect of a gray stripe, yellow door with painted gray stripe, right 3/4 of an inch Eagle, XME, "3-54" on left   25   35   50   80
63 Royal blue body with painted gray stripe, yellow door with painted gray stripe, right 3/4 of an inch Eagle, no XME   25   35   50   80
64 Violet body with painted gray stripe, light yellow door with gray stripe only, right 3/4 of an inch Eagle, XME   25   35   50   80
65A Same as 64 except no XME   25   35   50   80
65B Same as 65A except faded violet body mold   25   35   50   80
66 Royal blue body with painted gray stripe, white door painted plain dark yellow, no door stripe, right 3/4 of an inch Eagle, no XME, seal on first panel   40   65   80   125
67A Royal blue body with painted gray stripe, yellow door with painted gray stripe, right 3/4 of an inch Eagle   25   35   80   80
67B Same as 67A except navy body paint and no XME   25   35   50   80
67C Same as 67A except navy body paint   25   35   50   80
68 Type IIA navy blue body with painted gray stripe, 1956-Type dark yellow door mold unpainted, no door stripe, right 3/4 of an inch Eagle, no XME   40   65   80   125
69 Type IIA white body painted royal blue and gray, 1956-Type light yellow unpainted door, no stripe, right 5/8 of an inch Eagle, XME and grooves   40   65   80   125
70 Same as 69 except dark yellow door mold   40   65   80   125
71 Type IIA white body painted royal blue and gray, 1953-Type white door with stripe, right 5/8 of an inch Eagle, XME and grooves, left "3-54"   40   65   80   125
72 Type IIA royal blue body painted gray, 1953-Type light yellow door unpainted, right 5/8 of an inch Eagle, XME and grooves   40   65   80   125

73 Type IIA navy blue body with painted gray stripe, 1953-Type yellow door unpainted, right 5/8 of an inch Eagle, XME and grooves
  40 65 80 125

74A Type IIA royal blue body with painted gray stripe, 1953-Type yellow door with gray stripe, right 5/8 of an inch Eagle, XME and grooves
  25 35 50 80

74B Same as 74A except violet body mold and MP Lines circular logo is in first panel to left of door 200 350 450 550

75 Type IIA royal blue body with painted gray stripe; 1953-Type yellow unpainted door, no stripe; right 5/8 of an inch Eagle, XME, grooves and seal on panel 30 45 75 110

76 Type IIB royal blue door with painted gray stripe, 1953-Type dark yellow door with gray stripe, right of 5/8 of an inch Eagle, XME and grooves
  30 45 75 110

77 Same as 76 except white door painted dark yellow, no stripe
  30 45 75 110

78 Type IIA light gray body painted royal blue to produce gray stripe effect, 1956-Type yellow unpainted door, no stripe, left 5/8 of an inch Eagle, XME 30 45 75 110

79 Type IIB gray body painted royal blue and gray, 1956-Type yellow unpainted door, no stripe, left 1/2 inch Eagle, XME 30 40 75 110

80 Type IIB gray body painted royal blue and gray, 1956-Type dark yellow unpainted door, no stripe, left 1/2 inch Eagle, XME 30 45 75 110

81 Type IIB gray body painted royal blue to produce gray stripe appearance, 1956-Type yellow unpainted door, no stripe, left 1/2 inch Eagle, XME
  30 45 75 110

82 Same as 81 except door has gray stripe and no XME 25 35 50 80

6464-175 ROCK ISLAND Catalogued 1954-55, Type I body, except 87 (Type IIA), silver body and door paint, 1953-Type black door, no decals, hot press lettering in various colors

83 Clear body mold, light blue lettering 25 35 60 85
84 Black body mold, medium blue lettering 25 35 60 85
85 Clear body mold, medium blue lettering 25 35 60 85
86 Opaque-white body mold, black lettering — — — 750
87 Type IIA gray body, medium blue lettering NRS

6464-200 PENNSYLVANIA Catalogued 1954-55, most characteristics vary but all are without decals and have white hot press lettering

88 Type I clear body painted tuscan brown, 1953-Type black door painted tuscan brown 30 45 75 105

89 Same as 88 except body and door painted glossy tuscan red
  30 45 70 105

90 Type I opaque-white body painted tuscan red, 1953-Type black door painted tuscan red 30 45 70 105

91 Type IIA clear body painted tuscan red, 1953-Type black door painted tuscan red 30 45 75 105

92 Same as 91 except opaque-white body mold 30 45 75 105

93A Type IV body, tuscan brown and 1956-Type tuscan brown door painted tuscan brown, no "New 5-53" designation 20 30 45 75

93B Same as 93A except door mold and paint are tuscan red
  20 30 45 75

94 Type IV tuscan brown body, 1956-Type tuscan brown door painted tuscan brown, with "New 5-53" built date NRS

6464-225 SOUTHERN PACIFIC Catalogued 1954-56, Type IIA body except 95 (Type I), flat black (95-97) or glossy black (98A-99) or black (100) paint body, all with 1953-Type black door molds, no decals, red, white and yellow rubber stamped lettering

95 Type I black body painted flat black, black painted door, one of three NRS

96 Opaque-white body painted flat black, flat black painted door
  15 30 45 70

97 Same as 96 except black body mold 15 30 45 70

98A Black body painted glossy black, flat black painted door, lighter stamping 15 30 45 70

98B Opaque white body painted glossy black, flat black painted door
  195 — 340 400

99 Red body painted glossy black, doors painted silver then glossy black
  15 30 45 70

100 Black body painted black with silver roof, black painted doors NRS

6464-250 WESTERN PACIFIC Catalogued 1966-67, Type IV orange body mold, 1956-Type gray door mold, no decals, white rubber stamped lettering

101 Light orange body paint, dark orange door paint, medium blue feather
  15 30 40 60

102 Orange body and door paint, light blue feather 15 30 40 60
103 Same as 102 except medium blue feather 15 30 40 60
104 Same as 102 except dark blue (purple-blue) feather 15 30 40 60

6464-275 STATE OF MAINE Catalogued 1955, 1957-59, 1956-Type door, no decals, white and black lettering, characteristics vary considerably but are identified by groups when possible

106A - 111C have Type IIA bodies and grooves and are rubber stamped

106A White body painted red and navy blue, red unpainted door
  30 60 90 150

106B Same as 106A except royal blue body 30 60 90 150

107 White body and door molds; red and navy blue body and door paint
  21 37 55 75

108A White body and door molds, red and royal blue body and door paint
  21 37 55 75

108B Same as 108A except blue body mold 21 37 55 75

109 Navy blue body painted red and white, white door painted red and navy blue 15 30 40 60

110 Same as 109 except red and royal blue door paint 15 30 40 60

111A Royal blue body painted red, white and royal blue, white door painted red and light royal blue 15 30 40 60

111B Same as 111A except red and dark royal blue door paint
  15 30 40 60

111C Royal blue body painted red, white and navy blue, white door painted red and royal blue 15 30 40 60

112A Type IIB body, royal blue body and door, red and white body and door paint, no grooves, white hot press, black rubber stamped 15 30 40 60

112B Same as 112A except lettered BAR only, on No. 6464 NRS

113 Type IIB blue-violet body painted red and white, royal blue door painted red and white, no grooves, white hot press, black rubber stamped
  15 30 40 60

114-120B have Type III bodies, no grooves, hot press white and rubber stamped black lettering

114 Royal blue body and door molds, red, white and navy blue body paint, red and white door paint 15 30 40 60

115 Navy blue body and door molds, red, white and light blue body paint, red and white door paint 15 30 40 60

116 Royal blue body and door molds, red, white and light blue body paint, red and white door paint 15 30 40 60

117 Royal blue body painted red, white and light blue, navy blue door painted red and white 15 30 40 60

118 Royal blue body and door molds, red, white and light blue body paint, red, white and royal blue door paint 15 30 40 60

119 Royal blue body and door molds, red and white body and door paint
  15 30 40 60

120A Marble (red, white and black) body painted red, white and light blue; light whitish-blue door painted red, white and lighter blue
  15 30 40 60

120B Same as 120A except red, white and royal blue body paint and navy door mold 15 30 40 60

6464-300 RUTLAND Catalogued 1955-56; yellow door molds; no decals; 1955 cars have rubber stamped lettering; 1956 cars are hot pressed.
NOTE: Some Rutlands have shown up with repainted doors because of the high Rutland prices. Three ways to distinguish a Rutland with a repainted door from one that has not been repainted are:
(A) Green paint on door bottom should match the body's paint perfectly
(B) Where colors abut there should be some irregularity (i.e., beading, blurring or barely palpable ridge).
(C) On the bottom half of the back of the doors there should be a faint green, mist-like speckle caused by paint backspray.

122-128B have Type IIA bodies; 1953-Type doors except 127 (1956-Type door)

121 Yellow body and door molds; dark green body paint; door unpainted; dark green and yellow-orange rubber stamped lettering; "R" on left
  15 35 55 75

6464-375 Central of Georgia
6464-425 New Haven-b
6464-500 Timken
6464-525 Minneapolis & St. Louis
6464-725 New Haven-a
6464-900 New York Central

6464-350 Missouri, Kansas & Texas
6464-425 New Haven-a
6464-475 Boston & Maine
6464-515 Missouri, Kansas & Texas
6464-700 Santa Fe
6464-825 Alaska

6464-325 Baltimore & Ohio Sentinel
6464-400 Baltimore & Ohio Timesaver
6464-450 Great Northern
6464-510 New York Central
6464-650 Denver & Rio Grande
6464-725 New Haven-b

LEHIGH VALLEY
LIONEL LINES
2037
Pacemaker
FREIGHT SERVICE
M-K-T

122 Yellow body and door molds; very glossy dark green body paint; door unpainted; dark green and yellow-orange rubber stamped lettering; "R" on left **15 30 40 60**
123 Yellow body and door molds; dark green body paint; "split door" has dark green bottom; dark green and yellow-orange rubber stamped lettering; "R" on left **150 200 300 450**
124 Gray body painted dark green and yellow; door unpainted; dark green and yellow-orange rubber stamped lettering; "R" on left **15 30 40 60**
125 Clear and white marble body painted dark green and yellow; unpainted door; dark green and yellow rubber stamped lettering; "R" on left **15 30 40 60**
126 Yellow body and door molds; dark green body paint; unpainted door; light green and yellow rubber stamped lettering; "R" on left **15 30 40 60**
127 Yellow body and door molds; dark green body paint; 1956-Type unpainted door; light green and yellow hot pressed lettering; "R" on right **12 25 35 70**
128A Yellow body and door molds; super glossy dark green body paint; door unpainted; dark green and yellow rubber stamped lettering; "R" on left; solid shield herald **— — 1000 1200**
128B Same as 128A except dark green paint on body and bottom of "split door" **— — 1750 —**
129-131B Type IIB body; light green and yellow hot pressed lettering; "R" on right
129 Yellow body and door molds; dark green body paint; 1956-Type unpainted door **12 25 35 70**
130A Yellow body and door molds; flat green body paint; 1956-Type unpainted door **12 25 35 70**
130B Same as 130A except "split door" with dark green bottom **150 225 300 475**
131A Blue body; 1953-Type door; dark green and flat yellow body and door paint **150 225 300 475**
131B Same as 131A except yellow marble body mold **150 225 300 475**
131C IIA Type body, brown paint; 1953-Type door with gold lettering; one of three **NRS**

6464-325 B&O Sentinel Catalogued in 1956 only; IIB gray body painted aqua-blue and silver; 1956-Type gray door painted aqua-blue and silver; yellow, green and silver decals; navy blue and silver hot pressed lettering **80 130 200 275**

6464-350 MKT [KATY] Catalogued in 1956 only; IIB Type body; 1956-Type door; no decals; hot press white lettering except 137 (black lettering)
133 Maroon body painted tuscan red; dark cherry red unpainted doors **60 90 130 175**
134 Maroon body painted tuscan brown; dark cherry red doors painted tuscan brown; doors and sides almost match **60 90 130 175**
135 Maroon body painted tuscan brown; maroon unpainted doors **60 90 130 175**
136 Tuscan red unpainted body; dark cherry red unpainted doors **60 90 130 175**
137 Girl's Set pink body, white door paint (?); black lettering; one-of-a-kind **NRS**
138 Maroon unpainted body; dark cherry unpainted doors **65 85 135 175**
139A Shiny maroon unpainted body; maroon unpainted doors **65 85 135 175**
139B Same as 139A except flat maroon body and door molds **65 85 135 175**
140 Maroon (?) unpainted body, black unpainted door **65 85 135 175**

6464-375 CENTRAL OF GEORGIA Catalogued 1956-57 and 1966-67; 1956-Type gray door painted silver; yellow and red decals except 149A; hot press lettering
141-145B have Type IIB body molds and Blt. 3-56 dates
141 Maroon body; silver painted roof and oval; maroon and white lettering **20 35 55 85**
142 Same as 141 except mottled oval **20 35 55 85**
143 Duller maroon body; silver painted roof and gray oval; maroon and white lettering **20 35 55 85**
144 Maroon body; silver painted roof and gray oval; red and white lettering **20 35 55 85**
145A Bright maroon body; silver painted roof and gray oval; red and white lettering **20 35 55 85**
145B Same as 145A except maroon and white lettering **20 35 55 85**
146-149B Type IV body mold; silver roof and gray oval
146 Darker maroon body; red and white lettering; no built date **20 35 55 85**
147 Same as 146 except maroon and white lettering **20 35 55 85**
148 Gray body mold; red painted body; red and white lettering; with "BLT 3-56" **— — 2500 3000**
149A Maroon body; maroon and white lettering; no built date or decal **200 300 400 550**
149B Same as 149A except has "BLT 3-56" **200 300 400 550**

6464-400 B&O TIMESAVER 1956-57, 1969, 1956-Type door; hot press lettering; other characteristics vary as described
150A - 156A have Type IIB body molds; orange, black and white decals; blue and white lettering except 152B (black and white lettering)
150A Navy blue body and door molds, orange and silver body paint; orange painted door stripe; "BLT5-54" **15 30 45 75**
150B Same as 150A except light navy blue body mold **15 30 45 75**
151 Light navy blue body painted orange and silver; royal blue door with painted orange stripe,"BLT5-54" **15 30 45 75**
152A Royal blue body painted orange and silver; royal blue door with painted orange stripe; "BLT 5-54" **15 30 45 75**
152B Same as 152A except black and white lettering **15 30 45 75**
153 Dark blue body and door molds; orange and silver body paint; orange door stripe; "BLT2-56" **25 50 85 130**
154 Same as 153 except navy blue body and door molds **25 50 85 130**
155 Same as 153 except royal blue body and door molds **25 50 85 130**
156A Blue (?) body with orange stripe; blue (?) door with brown-orange stripe,"BLT 2-54," unpainted roof **NRS**
156B Same as 156A except medium blue body and door molds; door stripe (?); no mention of unpainted roof; black and white lettering **25 50 85 130**
156C No body or door mold color or paint information; only that "BLT 5-54" on one side and "BLT 2-56" on other **NRS**
157 - 162 have Type IV medium bright blue body and door molds and no built date
157 Body painted lighter blue, dull orange and silver; door painted lighter blue with bright orange; black and white lettering; dull point **10 15 30 45**
158 Same as 157 except dull orange door paint and sharp point **10 15 30 45**
159 Lighter blue, bright orange and silver body paint; lighter blue and dull orange door paint; black and white lettering; sharp point **10 15 30 45**
160 Same as 159 except dull point **10 15 30 45**
161 Dark blue; bright orange and silver body paint; lighter blue and bright orange door paint; blue and white lettering; sharp point **10 15 30 45**
162 Same as 161 except dull point **10 15 30 45**
163 Yellow body painted light yellow and white; yellow door painted light yellow and white; blue or black and white lettering; no information as to decals or lettering application; no built date; 1969 "Timken" colored paint; one-of-a-kind **— — 1200 —**

6464-425 NEW HAVEN Catalogued 1956-58; black body paint, except 164B (glossy black); 1956-Type unpainted door, except 168 (orange); no decals; white hot pressed lettering; with full seriph except for 164A and 164B (partial seriph)
164A - 170 have Type IIB black body molds, except 169 (gray);
164A Light orange door mold; partial seriph **10 20 30 45**
164B Glossy black body paint; light orange door mold; partial seriph **10 20 30 45**
165 Dark orange door mold **8 15 25 37**
166 Light orange door mold **8 15 25 37**
167 Dark orange door mold **8 15 25 37**
168 Black door with orange paint **8 15 25 37**
169 Gray body painted black; light orange door mold **8 15 25 37**
170 Black unpainted door **8 15 25 37**
171-175 have Type III black painted bodies; and unpainted doors
171 Gray body mold and dark orange door molds **8 15 25 37**

86

172 Black body mold; light orange door mold	8	15	25	37
173 Marble body mold; light orange door mold	8	15	25	37
174 Same as 173 except dark orange door mold	8	15	25	37
175 Same as 173 but orange (?) door mold	8	15	25	37

6464-450 GREAT NORTHERN Catalogued 1956-57 and 1966-67; 1956-Type door; except 182 (1953-Type); red, white and black decals, except 183 (without black); yellow and olive hot press lettering

176 Type IIB dark olive body painted dark olive, orange and dark yellow; dark olive door painted dark olive, orange and light yellow; "BLT 1-56"	15	30	50	80
177 Same as 176 except door painted dark olive and orange only, does not have yellow lines	25	50	75	100
178 Type III blue body painted dark olive, orange and dark yellow; light olive door painted light olive, orange and light yellow; "BLT 1-56"	30	55	85	125
179 Type IV light olive body painted light olive, light orange and light yellow; light olive door painted light olive, light orange and light yellow; no built date	15	30	42	70
180 Same as 179 except dark orange body and door paint	15	30	40	70
181 Type IV light olive body painted light olive, orange and light yellow; light olive unpainted door no built date	15	30	40	70
182 Type IV light olive body painted light olive and (?); 1953-Type black door painted flat orange; no built date	15	30	45	70
183 Type IV light olive body painted light olive, orange and light yellow; light olive door painted light olive, orange and light yellow; red decal only; no built date	15	30	45	75

6464-475 BOSTON & MAINE Catalogued 1957-60 and 1967-68; 1956-Type black unpainted except 194-195B (see text descriptions); no decals; black and white hot pressed lettering

184 Type IIB medium blue unpainted body; "BLT2-57"	10	20	25	40
185 Same as 184 except lighter blue body mold	10	20	25	40
186 Type III black body painted flat blue; "BLT 2-57"	10	20	25	40
187A Type III unpainted light blue body; "BLT2-57"	10	20	25	40
187B Same as 187A except marble body mold	10	20	25	40
187C Type III marble body mold painted medium blue; no built information	10	20	25	40
187D Type III light green body painted medium blue; "BLT 2-57"	10	20	25	40
187E Same as 187D except very light blue body paint	10	20	25	40
187F Type III marble body painted light blue; "2-57" date	10	20	25	40
188 Type IV dark blue body painted blue-purple; "BLT 2-57"	8	15	20	32
189 Type IV unpainted light blue body mold; "BLT 2-57"	8	15	20	32
190 Same as 189 except no built date	8	15	20	32
191 Type IV unpainted medium blue body mold; "BLT 2-57"	8	15	20	32
192A Type IV gray body painted darker blue; "BLT 2-57"	8	15	20	32
192B Same as 192A except light blue body mold	8	15	20	32
193 Type IV gray body painted darker blue	8	15	20	32
194 Same as 193 except white unpainted door mold; no built date; unblackened door runner rivets	8	15	20	32
195A Type IV yellow body painted darker blue; white door painted black; no built date; unblackened door runner rivets	8	15	20	32
195B Same as 195A except light blue body paint	8	15	20	32
196 Type IV gray body painted blue-green; color similar to #2346 GP-9 diesel	8	15	20	32

6464-500 TIMKEN Catalogued 1957-58 and 1969; 1956-Type door; hot press lettering

197 - 205 Type IIB body; charcoal lettering; except 204 (shades of black); orange, black and white decal, except 204 (yellow)

197 Yellow body and door molds painted white	12	24	40	65
198 Same as 197 except door painted golden yellow and white	12	25	40	65
199 Same as 197 except door painted yellow and white	12	25	40	65
200 Yellow body painted white; white door painted yellow and white	12	25	40	65
201 Yellow body and door molds painted yellow and white	12	25	40	65
202 Yellow-orange body and door molds painted white	20	35	50	70
203 Orange-tinted body painted white; yellow door painted white	12	25	35	65
204 Dark blue body painted yellow and white; yellow door painted white; all decal lettering in shades of black; #6464-000	12	25	35	65
205 Light gray body painted yellow and white; yellow door painted white	12	25	35	65
206 Type III yellow body painted white; yellow door painted white; orange, black and white decal; charcoal lettering	12	25	35	65
207 Same as 206 except orange-tinted door body	12	25	35	65

208 - 212B have Type IV yellow body and door molds; orange, black and white decals; charcoal lettering, except 210 - 212 B (see text) and no built dates

208 Darker yellow and white body paint; lighter yellow and white door paint	12	25	35	55
209 Lighter yellow and white body paint; darker yellow and white door paint	12	25	35	55
210 Darker yellow and white body and door paint; glossy black lettering	12	25	35	55
211 Darker yellow and white body paint; lighter yellow and white door paint	12	25	35	55
212A Darker-yellow and white body and door paint	12	25	35	55
212B Yellow body paint; red hot press lettering	—	—	1200	—
212C Green body paint; white hot press lettering	—	—	750	—
212D Green body paint; gold hot press lettering	—	—	750	—
212E Same as 212D except red lettering	—	—	850	—

NOTE: Box cars 213A - 215 were made by MPC in 1970 for Glen Uhl. The cars carried a unique identification, "BLT 1-71 BY LIONEL MPC." These cars are listed here because of their 6464-500 numbers. All yellow cars came with metal trucks as did 200 of the orange cars. It is reported that 500 yellow and 1,300 orange cars were manufactured.

213A Blank number boards, yellow body painted yellow; yellow door painted yellow; light orange, black and gray decals; glossy black lettering	15	30	40	75
213B Same as 213A except light yellow body and door paint	15	30	40	76
214A Blank number boards, orange body and door molds painted orange; light orange, black and gray decals; glossy black lettering; plastic trucks	15	30	40	80
214B Same as 214A except metal trucks	15	30	40	80
215 "9200" number boards; orange body painted orange; orange door painted orange (?); glossy black (?) lettering; fifty made, plastic trucks	70	100	200	250

6464-510 NEW YORK CENTRAL PACEMAKER Catalogued 1957-58; light green-blue body paint; 1956-Type dark yellow door mold painted light flat yellow; no decals; black hot press lettering, from Girl's Train, no cedilia or built date

216A Type IIB royal blue body mold	100	150	300	380
216B Same as 216A except gray body mold	100	150	350	425
216C Type IIA royal blue body				NRS

6464-515 KATY Type IIB dark yellow body painted light flat yellow; except 218B and C; 1956-Type navy blue door painted light green-blue, except 218B and C; no decals; dark brown-charcoal hot pressed lettering, except 218B and C, from Girl's Train set

217 As above	100	150	250	400
218A Overstamped with 6464-150 lettering				NRS
218B Tan body paint; sky blue door paint; beige lettering	—	—	1500	—
218C Light yellow body paint; sky blue door paint	110	—	285	325

6464-525 MINNEAPOLIS & ST. LOUIS 1956-Type door, except 221 and 222 (1953-Type); no decals; white hot press lettering

219 Type IIB unpainted red body and door molds	10	20	25	40
220 Type IIB red body and door molds painted flat red	10	20	25	40
221 Type IIB red door painted red; 1953-Type white door painted red; doors and body paint match	10	20	25	40
222 Type IIB red body painted flat red, 1953-Type unpainted red door	10	20	25	40

PROTOTYPE AND RARE 6464 BOX CARS

- 3494-1[B] NYC
- 6464 W.P.
- 6464-375 Central of Georgia
- M. Steinthal
- 6464-650 Denver & Rio Grande
- 3494-1[A] NYC
- 6464 W.P.
- 6464-375 Central of Georgia
- 6464[F] Hathaway Denver
- 6464-650 Denver & Rio Grande
- 6464[T] NYC
- 6464[E] Clemco
- 6464 Parker Kalon
- 6464 Western Pacific
- 6464-825 Alaska [258A]

PROTOTYPE AND RARE 6464 BOX CARS

- 6464[U] Pillsbury
- 6464[K] Tidewater
- 6464[N] DSSA
- 6464[Q] Burlington
- 6352-1[D] PFE
- 6464[C] Hotpoint
- 6464[J] Cookie Box
- 6464[M] Wabash
- 6464[P] Louisville & Nashville
- 6464[S] NYC
- 6464[B] Hotpoint
- 6464[I] M & SL
- 6464[L] Norfolk Southern
- 6464[O] Louisville & Nashville
- 6464[R] Great Northern

223 Type III gray body painted red; red door painted red
  10 20 25 40
224 Same as 223 except black body mold 10 20 25 40
225 Same as 223 except marble body mold 10 20 25 40
226 Type IV gray body painted red; red unpainted doors 10 20 25 40
227 Same as 226 except maroon door mold painted red on outside only
  10 20 25 40
229A Type IV gray body painted red; black unpainted door
  10 20 25 40
229B Type IV gray body painted maroon; unpainted white door mold; color similar to 6464-375   —   —   750

6464-650 DENVER & RIO GRANDE WESTERN Catalogued 1957-58 and 1966-67, usually found with silver painted band on lower side and lower door and silver painted roof. A black stripe usually separates the yellow and silver areas. The car has yellow painted body and doors with silver painted bands across the body and doors and a silver painted roof. The car also comes with an unpainted yellow body, but with silver painted bands and a silver roof. Rare variations include cars without silver painted roofs. The following items have 1956-Type yellow doors, except 239B; no decals and black hot press lettering

230 Type IIB light orange-tinted body, with silver painted side band and roof; unpainted yellow door with silver painted band; built date
  22 40 60 85
231 Type IIB yellow body with silver painted side band and roof; yellow unpainted door with silver painted door band 22 40 60 85
232 Type IIB light yellow body painted yellow with silver side band and roof; yellow unpainted door with silver painted band 22 40 60 80
233 Same as 232 but without black stripe on door separating yellow and silver areas 25 50 75 100
234 Type IIB light yellow body with silver painted side band and roof; unpainted yellow door with silver painted door band; no black door stripe or built date **NRS**
235 Type IIB yellow body painted light buttery yellow with silver painted side band only; yellow doors painted light buttery yellow with silver painted door band; built date **NRS**
236 Type IIB yellow unpainted body with silver painted side bands only; yellow unpainted doors with silver bands; built date **NRS**
237 Type IV unpainted yellow body with silver painted side bands and roof; yellow unpainted doors with silver painted bands; no built date
  20 30 40 60
238 Type IV lighter yellow body with silver painted side bands only, no silver paint on roof; yellow unpainted doors with silver painted bands; no built date **NRS**
239A Same as 238 but yellow body **NRS**
239B Type IV gray body with yellow painted body including roof and with silver painted side bands; gray door painted yellow with gray painted band; built date   —   500   750   1000

6464-700 A.T. & S.F. Catalogued 1961 and 1967; Type IV gray body, except 240 (Type III); 1956-Type gray door mold, except 240 (red door mold); no decals; white hot pressed lettering, except 243 (see text)
240 Type III body with red paint; red unpainted door mold
  300 450 600 —
241A Red body and door paint 18 32 65 80
241B Same as 241A except medium red body paint 18 32 65 80
242 Medium red body paint; silver door paint 18 32 65 80
243 Medium red body paint; red door paint; "FORD" lettering rubber stamped on right **NRS**
244 Lighter red body and door paint 18 32 55 80

6464-725 NEW HAVEN Catalogued 1962-68 and 1969 and 6464-735; Type IV gray body mold, except 247C (black); 1956-Type unpainted door; no decals; hot pressed lettering
245A Lightest orange body paint; black door mold; black shiny lettering
  8 15 20 35
245B Same as 245A except lighter orange body paint; black not shiny lettering 8 15 20 35
246A Lighter orange body paint; black door mold, dull black lettering
  8 15 20 35
246B Medium orange body paint; black door mold; high gloss black lettering (shinier than 245) 8 15 20 35
247A Medium orange body paint; black door mold; glossy black lettering
  8 15 20 35
247B Black body paint; orange door mold; white lettering
  11 22 40 70
247C Black body painted black; orange door painted orange; white lettering; Type VII trucks; McCormack Collection **NRS**

6464-825 ALASKAN Catalogued 1959-60; 1956-Type door; no decals; hot pressed lettering
248 - 252 have Type III bodies
248 Gray body painted dark blue and yellow, gray doors painted blue; doors slightly lighter blue than body, yellow and orange lettering
  70 90 120 170
249 Same as 248 but dark yellow and orange lettering 70 90 120 170
250 Dark blue body painted with yellow stripes; dark blue unpainted doors; yellow and orange lettering, doors and body match 70 90 120 170
251 Dark blue body painted dark blue and yellow; gray doors painted dark blue; yellow and orange lettering 70 90 120 170
252 Royal blue body painted dark flat blue and yellow; white doors painted glossy dark blue; yellow and orange lettering 50 75 100 140
253 Type III body, black unpainted door mold, other information unknown
  NRS
254 Type IV body, yellow unpainted door mold, other information unknown
  NRS
255 Type IV royal blue body painted dark blue and yellow; dark blue doors painted dark blue, light yellow and orange lettering; doors and body match
  80 110 150 200
256 Type IV gray body painted dark blue and yellow; gray doors painted dark blue; yellow and light orange lettering 80 110 150 200
257 Type IV royal blue body painted dark blue and yellow; white door painted dark blue; yellow and orange lettering; doors and body match
  80 110 150 200
258A Type IV light gray body painted dark blue and yellow; white door painted dark blue; yellow and orange lettering 80 110 150 200
258B Type IV light gray body painted dark blue and yellow; white unpainted door; white lettering   —   —   1200   —

6464-900 NEW YORK CENTRAL Catalogued 1960-67; Type IV gray body, except 259 (Type III black body); 1956-Type door; no decals; red, black and white hot pressed lettering
259 Type III black body painted light jade green; gray door painted light jade green; thinner red lettering **NRS**
260 Light jade green painted body and door; gray door mold; thinner red lettering 15 25 40 70
261 Dark jade green body and door paint; gray door mold; thicker red lettering 15 25 40 70
262A Light jade green body paint; black unpainted door mold, thicker red lettering 15 25 40 70
262B Same as 262A except gray door mold 15 25 40 70

6464-1965 TCA SPECIAL (Pittsburgh) Uncatalogued but made in 1965 for TCA National Convention; Type IV gray body painted blue; 1956-Type gray door, except 265 (black door); blue door paint, except 265 (unpainted); no decals; white hot pressed lettering. 800 Produced.
263 #6464-1965 on bottom   —   —   250   300
264 #6464-1965X on bottom. Only 74 produced.   —   —   275   325
265 Unpainted black door; no number on bottom **NRS**
266 On bottom, "Presented to Joe Ranker" **NRS**

6464-TCA SPECIALS In 1967, as they had in other years, TCA asked Lionel to make their special convention car. Lionel was unable to do so, and TCA therefore purchased a number of 6464 series box cars and specially labeled them for the conventions. Each car was rubber stamped "12th T.C.A. NATIONAL CONVENTION BALTIMORE MD. JUNE - 1967" on the bottom. They were also rubber stamped with sequential numbers on the bottom. In addition, an extra brass door was supplied with each car. The brass doors were silk-screened in blue "TRAIN COLLECTORS ASSOCIATION ORGANIZED 1954 INCORPORATED 1957" and showed a railroad crossing signal lettered "NATIONAL CONVENTION BALT MD JUNE 67." It is believed that several hundred convention cars were distributed. It is reported, but not verified, that brass door reproductions have been made and that cars have been rubber stamped to appear as if they were 1967 Convention cars. The following is a sampling of convention cars:

267A 6464-250 WESTERN PACIFIC Type IV light orange body painted dark orange, 1956-Type gray door painted dark orange; no decals; white heat pressed lettering, stamped 547 — — — 275

267B Similar to 267A but stamped "548"; dark blue feather — — — 275

267C Similar to 267A but stamped "178;" unblackened rivets — — — 275

268 6464-375 CENTRAL of GEORGIA Type IV maroon body painted with silver oval, 1956-Type gray door painted silver; yellow and red decals; white and red heat pressed lettering; no built date, rubber stamped "411" — — — 275

269 6464-450 GREAT NORTHERN Type IV light olive body painted light olive, 1956-Type olive door painted light olive, orange and yellow, red, white and black decals, yellow heat pressed lettering, rubber stamped "228" or "254" — — — 275

270 6464-475 BOSTON & MAINE Type IV dark blue unpainted body, 1956-Type black unpainted door, no decals, black heat pressed lettering, "BLT 2-57," rubber stamped "580" NRS

271 6464-525 MINNEAPOLIS & ST. LOUIS Type IV gray body painted red, 1956-Type red unpainted doors, no decals, white heat pressed lettering, "BLT 6-57," rubber stamped "588" NRS

272 6464-650 DENVER & RIO GRANDE WESTERN Type IV yellow unpainted body with silver painted band and roof, 1956-Type yellow unpainted door with silver painted band, no decals, black heat pressed lettering, rubber stamped "387" or "483" — — — 275

273 6464-700 A.T. & S.F. Type IV gray body painted red, 1956-Type gray door painted red, no decals, white heat pressed lettering, rubber stamped "220" or "360" — — — 275

274 6464-735 NEW HAVEN Type IV body, 1956-Type door, no decals, black heat pressed lettering, other details unknown NRS

275 6464-900 NEW YORK CENTRAL Type IV body, 1956-Type door, no decals, white, black and red heat pressed lettering, other details unknown NRS

276 6464-000 BOSTON & MAINE Type IV body, 1956-Type door, black lettering, specially numbered "6464-000" rather than 6464-475, other details unknown, one-of-a-kind NRS

6464-1970 TCA SPECIAL [Chicago] Uncatalogued but made in 1970, TCA National Convention car, Type V yellow body painted slightly darker yellow, 1956-Type red door mold, no decals, white hot pressed lettering, 1,100 produced

277 Unpainted door — — 90 110
278 Red door paint — — 90 110

6464-1971 TCA SPECIAL [Disneyland] Uncatalogued but made in 1971, TCA National Convention car, 1,500 produced

279 Type VII white body painted white, 1956-Type dark orange-yellow door painted yellow, no decals, red, black and blue hot pressed lettering — — 160 200

6468-1 BALTIMORE & OHIO 1955, double-door automobile car, Type A body,* white heat stamped lettering

(A) Tuscan brown painted black plastic body and doors 75 110 150 250
(B) Shiny blue painted black plastic body and doors 9 12 18 30
(C) Shiny blue painted clear plastic body, shiny blue painted black plastic door 9 12 18 30
(D) Flat blue painted clear plastic body, flat blue painted black plastic door 9 12 18 30
(E) Shiny blue painted off-white opaque body, Kotil Collection 9 12 18 30
(F) Flat blue painted off-white opaque body, Kotil Collection 9 12 18 30

6468-25 NEW HAVEN 1956-58, double-door automobile car, Type B orange unpainted plastic body,* black plastic door, bar-end metal trucks, magnetic couplers, "BLT 3-56"

(A) Full serif lettering with large black N and large white H 8 13 17 30
(B) Same as (A)but N missing serifs at top on right 8 13 17 30
(C) Same as (A) but brown painted doors, magnetic tab couplers 20 30 50 80
(D) Full serif lettering with large white N and large black H 70 110 140 190
(E) Same as (D), but half serif lettering, Blotner Collection 70 110 140 190

6470 EXPLOSIVES 1959-60, Type III red plastic body** with white lettering, Timken trucks with disc-operating couplers, spring-loaded car that explodes when hit by a missile

(A) Red 2 3 5 15
(B) Orange-red 2 3 5 15

6472 REFRIGERATOR 1950, white unpainted plastic, black lettering, "4-50," "RT 6472," plastic doors, spring clips hold body to frame, magnetic couplers

(A) Staple-end metal trucks 5 7 10 18
(B) Bar-end metal trucks 5 7 10 18

6473 HORSE TRANSPORT CAR 1962-64, unpainted dark yellow body, heads bob as car rolls

(A) Heavily stamped maroon-brown lettering 5 7 10 18
(B) Lightly stamped maroon-brown lettering 5 7 10 18
(C) Lightly stamped red lettering 5 7 10 18
(D) Lighter yellow body, red lettering, Popovich Collection NRS

6480 EXPLOSIVES Type III body,** white lettering

(A) Flat red roof, ends and sides, side grooves, Timken trucks 2 3 5 18
(B) Shiny red roof, ends and sides, side grooves, Timken trucks 2 3 5 18
(C) Flat red roof, ends and sides, no side grooves, arch bar trucks 2 3 5 18
(D) Shiny red roof, ends and sides, side grooves on both sides, arch bar trucks 2 3 5 18

6482 REFRIGERATOR 1957, white unpainted plastic car, non-operating versions of 3482, black "L" in double circle, "EW 9-11 EH 8-10 IL 29-6 IW 8-4 IH 7-5 CU.FT. 1834 RT 6482," opening doors with springs, body held to frame by frame tab at one end and Phillips head screw at other, four non-operating ice hatches on roof, no brakewheels, sheet metal floor with two lengthwise ribs protruding outward for almost two-thirds of car length but no holes for mechanism, Timken trucks, disc-operating couplers, Popovich and Jackson Collections 10 18 25 35

6530 FIRE FIGHTING INSTRUCTION CAR 1960-61, white lettering and doors, Timken trucks with disc-operating couplers. The car came without firefighting instructions!

(A) Unpainted red plastic body 10 20 35 50
(B) Black plastic body — — 750 —

6556 KATY M-K-T, 1958, stock car, red plastic body painted red, white lettering, white doors, two-level stock car, bar-end metal trucks, magnetic tab couplers. Came in only one set, no. 2513W, Super O, with 2329 Virginian. This is the most scarce stock car. Lord Collection 60 90 120 170

6572 RAILWAY EXPRESS, 1958-59, refrigerator, red and white express decal, instrument panel on side with sliding cover, flat brown spring inside door guide shuts door. This car and its close match, 6672, come with plug doors, as did their prototype. The plug door fits into the car body side so that when it is shut, it fits flush with the side, unlike the overlapping doors found with most box cars. The plug door seals the interior more effectively. Griggs observations.

(A) Blue plastic roof and green plastic sides painted dark green with dull gold lettering, bar-end metal trucks, magnetic tab couplers 25 35 50 80
(B) Gray plastic painted light green, shiny gold lettering, bar-end metal trucks, magnetic tab couplers 15 22 30 50
(C) Circa 1964, gray plastic body painted light green, dull gold lettering, Timken trucks, disc-operating couplers 10 15 25 40

* There are two types of automobile bodies:
Type A does not have an ice hatch, as on 6352-1.
Type B has a faint line across the roof nearer brakewheel end, as on 6352-1.
** A modification of a Type III body: rivet rows are short to leave "TARGET RANGE CAR" lettering on No. 6448.

(D) Green plastic roof and sides painted light green, dull gold lettering, Timken trucks, magnetic tab couplers   12 18 25 40
(E) Dark green plastic roof and green plastic sides painted flat dark green, dull gold lettering, 2400 series passenger trucks   25 35 55 77
(F) Same as (D), but shiny gold lettering similar to that found on (B), Fleming Collection   15 22 30 50

6646 LIONEL LINES 1957, stock car, plastic body, black "L" in circle, 9 inches long
(A) Orange painted clear plastic body   3 10 15 25
(B) Orange unpainted plastic body, Kotil Collection   3 8 10 20

6656 LIONEL LINES 1949-55, stock car, black lettering, 9 inches long
(A) Bright yellow, 1949, large black "L" in circle above car number, "LIONEL LINES CAPY. 80000" in black, one brakewheel, metal door guides, staple-end metal trucks, magnetic couplers, Warnick Collection.   3 5 10 14
(B) Same as (A), but orange body and bar-end metal trucks, Warnick Collection.   3 5 10 14
(C) Bright yellow body, "ARMOUR" decal, black "L" in circle, "6656," brown decal, yellow lettering, red star, staple-end trucks, magnetic couplers, two oval holes on base, Brooks Collection   25 50 75 100

6672 SANTA FE 1954-56, refrigerator car, white body with brown roof, instrument panel on side with sliding aluminum cover, brown spring inside door guide shuts doors, bar-end metal trucks, magnetic tab couplers, Griggs observations.
(A) Black lettering with Lionel "L" in circle   15 20 35 55
(B) Same as (A) but without "L" and circle   20 30 40 65
(C) Same as (A) but blue lettering   12 18 25 35
(D) Same as (C) but three lines of data to right of door   15 20 30 50

PROTOTYPE BOX CARS

These cars, from the collection of Elliott Smith, are now in the collection of Bill Eddins.

6464[A] PARKER KALON Type IIB* unpainted gray plastic body, 1956 Type unpainted black plastic door, decal lettering, "6464(B)" does not appear on car   — — 400 —

6464[B] 0000 HOTPOINT Type III white plastic body painted yellow and black, 1956-Type red plastic door painted yellow, black decal lettering, different designs on each side, "6464(B)" does not appear on car   **NRS**

6464[C] 0000 HOTPOINT Type IIB gray plastic body painted red and white, 1956-Type yellow plastic door painted red, black decal lettering, different designs on each side, "6464(C)" does not appear on the car   — — 1500 —

6464[D] PARKER KALON Type IIB black plastic body painted white, 1956-Type unpainted orange plastic door, decal lettering, "GENUINE PK SELF TAPPING SCREWS," "6464(A)" does not appear on the car, reportedly shown at 1964 Toy Fair, Parker Kalon was a Lionel subsidiary   **NRS**

6464[E] CLEMCO AERO PRODUCTS INC Type IV gray plastic body painted red, 1956-Type gray plastic door painted red, paper label loosely fastened on car, "6464(E)" does not appear on the car, reportedly shown at 1964 Toy Fair, Clemco was a Lionel subsidiary   **NRS**

6464[F] HATHAWAY DENVER Type IV gray plastic body painted red then blue, 1956-Type gray plastic door painted red then blue, paper label loosely fastened on car, "6464(F)" does not appear on the car, reportedly shown at 1964 Toy Fair, Hathaway Denver was a Lionel subsidiary   **NRS**

6464[G] M. STEINTHAL & Co Type IV opaque plastic body painted red then white, 1956-Type opaque plastic door painted white, paper label loosely fastened on car, "6464(G)" does not appear on the car, reportedly shown at 1964 Toy Fair, M. Steinthal was a Lionel subsidiary   **NRS**

6464[H] NO LETTERING Type IIB bright blue unpainted plastic body, 1953-Type black unpainted plastic door   **NRS**

6464[I] 0000 M & SL Type I clear plastic body painted green, 1953-Type black plastic door painted green, yellow decal lettering, Louis Knapp Collection   **NRS**

6464[J] 0000 [XP476] D & R G W COOKIE BOX Type HB blue plastic body painted shiny gloss white, 1956-Type blue plastic door painted shiny gloss white, black and red decal lettering, body screws and two tabs painted white   **NRS**

6464[K] 6464-0000 [XP 572] TIDEWATER SOUTHERN Type IIB blue plastic body painted brown, 1956 blue plastic door painted brown, yellow decal lettering   **NRS**

6464[L] 0000000 [XP540] NORFOLK SOUTHERN Type IIB blue plastic body painted light brown, 1956-Type blue plastic door painted light brown, white decal lettering   **NRS**

6464[M] 0000000[XP 521] WABASH Type IIB gray plastic body painted tuscan, 1956-Type gray plastic door painted tuscan, white decal lettering   **NRS**

6464[N] 0000000 [XP527] DULUTH, SOUTH SHORE AND ATLANTIC Type IIB gray plastic painted red and black, 1956-Type blue plastic door painted red, white decal lettering, marked "XP476" on underframe   **NRS**

6464[O] 0000000 [XP571] LOUISVILLE & NASHVILLE Type IIB gray plastic body painted red, 1956-Type yellow plastic door painted red, white decal, underframe marked "XP570"   **NRS**

6464[P] 0000000 XP709] LOUISVILLE & NASHVILLE Type III gray plastic body painted blue, 1953-Type red plastic door painted blue, yellow decal lettering   **NRS**

6464[Q] 0000 BURLINGTON Type III blue plastic body painted red, 1956-Type gray plastic door painted red, white decals   **NRS**

6464[R] 0000 GREAT NORTHERN Type IV gray plastic body painted green, 1956-Type gray plastic door painted green, white and red decal lettering   **NRS**

6464[S] 0000 [XP670] NYC Type I black plastic body painted chocolate brown with double automobile doors, gray plastic doors painted chocolate brown, white decals   **NRS**

6464[T] 0000 [XP534] NYC [NYMX] Type I reefer, white plastic body painted yellow with black stripe, red plastic roof painted aluminum, red plastic door with yellow paint and black stripe, white and black decal   **NRS**

* Type IIB refers to a 6464 body type.

Chapter V
CABOOSES

Note: Middle row cabooses have been modified with stacks, ladders and tool boxes.

In this chapter, we list cabooses by catalogue number. Usually the catalogue number appears on the car's sides. The exceptions almost always involve a suffix. For example, one caboose is catalogued as a 6017-100; the 100 is the suffix, but it only has the number 6017 on its sides. In the text for this item, we explain that only 6017 is found on the car's sides. Any item whose catalogue number does not correspond to the number on the car's sides is identified.

Prior to 1970 Lionel made five basic caboose body types: the Southern Pacific (SP), work caboose, Pennsylvania C-5, Pennsylvania N5C and the bay window caboose. Each came with various add-ons, including lights, operating couplers at both ends, window inserts, smoke stacks, tool boxes, etc. The Southern Pacific (SP) was by far the most popular style and the majority of Lionel's cabooses were based on the SP prototype.

In the first edition of the postwar Lionel Price Guide, two basic SP molds were identified: Type I and Type II. Since that time, further analysis by Joseph Kotil has uncovered significant new information about these cabooses. As a consequence, the information on caboose types has been expanded in the following manner. Type I is subdivided into Dies 1, 1A, 2, 2A, 3, 3A, 3B and 3C. Mold Type II is now called Die 4. Type I cabooses in this section have been reclassified as being Die 1 through Die 3C, whenever possible.

SP CABOOSE DIES BY JOSEPH KOTIL

The major elements of caboose construction as they relate to die identification are listed below as are the definitions of Dies 1 through 4.

A. Window Frames, Front and Rear Cupola Windows
1. No window frames Dies 1, 1A, 2, 2A, 3, 3A, 3B and 3C
2. Window frames Die 4

B. Step Construction
1. Thin, early type Dies 1, 1A, 2, 2A, 3, 3A, 3B and 3C
2. Thick, later type Die 4

C. Reinforced Stack Plug Opening
1. Present Dies 1, 1A, 2, 2A, 3C and 4
2. Not present Dies 3, 3A, and 3B

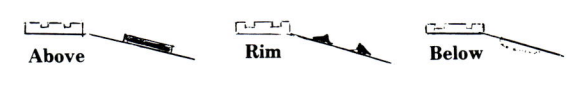

FIGURE 1

D. Stack Plug [where no stack]
1. Above — plug raised parallel to roof slope Die 3
2. Rim — rim raised parallel to catwalk with recessed center Dies 1, 1A, 2 and 2A
3. Below — plug below roof line, parallel to catwalk Die 4

E. Vertical Rivets Below Side Windows 3 and 4
1. 8 rivets Dies 1, 2, 3, 3A, 3B and 4
2. 4 rivets Dies 1A, 2A, 3C and 4

F. Ladder Slot
1. Present Dies 1, 2 and 4
2. Not present Dies 3, 3A, 3B and 3C

G. Wedges along Catwalk, Roof Panel 4
1. Present   Dies 3B and 3C
2. Not present   Dies 1, 1A, 2, 2A, 3, 3A and 4

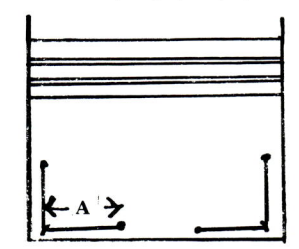

Low cupola railing
A equals 3/16 long
A equals 11/32 short

FIGURE 2

H. Cupola Roof Railings
1. High roof railings   Dies 1, 1A, 2 and 2A
2. Low, short roof railings (11/32")   Die 3
3. Low, long roof railings (3/16")   Die 3A, 3B and 3C
4. Curved roof railings   Die 4

Space between grab iron and rivet 2

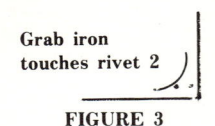

Grab iron touches rivet 2

Grab iron touches rivet 3

FIGURE 3

I. Grab Rail at Corner
1. Grab rail touches rivet 2   Dies 1 and 1A
2. Grab rail clears rivet 2   Dies 2 and 2A
3. Grab rail touches rivet 3   Die 4

J. Extra Rivet Between Door Rivet Row and Roof Rivet Row, at End
1. No extra rivet   Dies 1, 1A, 2 and 2A
2. Extra rivet   Dies 3, 3A, 3B, 3C, 3D and 4

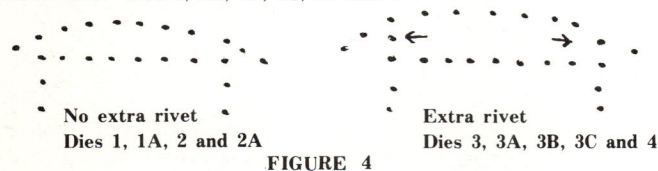

No extra rivet
Dies 1, 1A, 2 and 2A

Extra rivet
Dies 3, 3A, 3B, 3C and 4

FIGURE 4

K. Three Extra Rivets on Panel 2
(Rivets and lines faintly seen reveal repair of damaged die on panels 1 and 2)
1. No damage and repair   Dies 1, 1A, 2, 2A, 2B and 4
2. Damaged and repaired   Dies 3, 3A, 3B and 3C

L. Catwalk Overhang Supports
1. No supports   Dies 1, 1A, 2, 2A, 3, 3A, 3B and 3C
2. Supports   Die 4

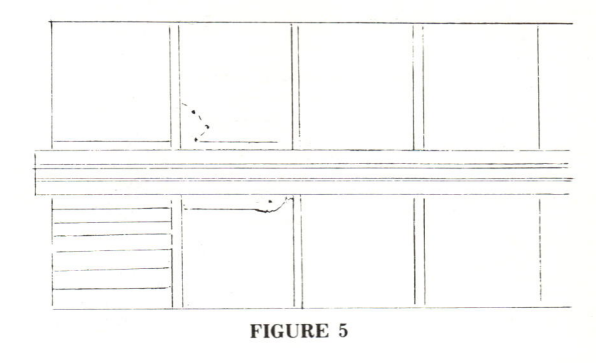

FIGURE 5

SP DIE CHARACTERISTICS

	Die 1	Die 2	Die 3	Die 4
A.	No window frame on front and rear cupola windows	No window frame	No window frame	Window frame
B.	Thin steps	Thin steps	Thin steps	Thick steps
C.	Reinforced stack opening	Reinforced stack opening	Stack opening not reinforced	Reinforced stack opening
D.	Rim-type stack plug	Rim-type stack plug	Raised plug	Lower plug
E.	8 rivets below windows 3 and 4	8 rivets below windows 3 and 4	8 rivets below window 3 and 4	4 rivets below windows 3 and 4
F.	Ladder slots	Ladder slots	No ladder slots	Ladder slots
G.	No wedges by catwalk	No wedges by catwalk	No wedges by catwalk	No wedges by catwalk
H.	High cupola roof detail	High cupola roof detail	Low cupola roof detail	Curved cupola roof detail
I.	Side grab rail touches rivet 2	Space between side grab rail and rivet 2	Space between side grab rail and rivet 2	Side grab rail touches rivet 3
J.	No extra rivet on ends above door	No extra rivet on ends above door	Extra rivets on ends above door	Extra rivets on ends above door
K.	No die crack on roof	No die crack on roof	Die crack on roof	No die crack on roof
L.	No supports for catwalk overhang	No supports for catwalk overhang	No supports for catwalk overhang	Brackets support catwalk overhang

Die 1A
Same as above except
(E.) 4 rivets below windows 3 and 4

Die 2A
Same as above except
(E.) 4 rivets below windows 3 and 4

Die 3A
Same as above except
(H.) low, long cupola roof railing

Die 3B
Same as 3 except
(G.) wedges are present
(H.) low, long cupola roof railing

Die 3C
Same as 3 except
(C.) reinforced roof (plug for the 6557 Smoking Caboose and the 6017-100 B&M (1959) and possibly others);
(E.) 4 rivets below windows 3 and 4;
(G.) wedges present;
(H.) low, long cupola roof railing

Gd. V.G. Exc. Mt.

1007 LIONEL LINES SP Die 3, 1948-52, Scout caboose with Scout trucks, "1007" behind "LIONEL LINES" on left side, "1007" in front of "LIONEL LINES" on right side. These locations imply that the same stamp was used on both sides.
(A) Red with white lettering   1   1.50   2   3
(B) Lighter red with white lettering   1   1.50   2   3
(C) Orange-red with white lettering   1   1.50   2   3

2257 LIONEL SP Die 1, 1948, metal trucks with two operating coil couplers, two brakewheels, "2257" centered on side under cupola
(A) Not illuminated, no stack, red with white lettering, no tool boxes
                                             2   3   4   6
(B) Illuminated, stack, tuscan with white lettering, and tool boxes
                                             5   7   10   12
(C) Same as (A) but tuscan, Kotil Collection   2   3   4   6
(D) Same as (B) but red, Kotil Collection   5   7   10   12

2357 LIONEL SP Die 1 or 2, 1948, metal trucks with two operating coil couplers, two brakewheels, two ladders, brown stack, tool boxes, illuminated, window inserts, "2357" centered under cupola
(A) Red with white lettering   5   7   10   15
(B) Tuscan with white lettering   5   7   10   15
(C) Same as (B), but brakewheels mounted towards platform, not towards outside, Fleming Collection
                                             5   7   10   15

94

1007	6017[L]
2257	6017-50
2357	6027
4357	6037
6017	6047
6017-200	6057

N5C CABOOSE

2419 D. L. & W. Work Caboose 1946-47, gray with black lettering, die-cast frame; handrails, ladders, two tool boxes, brakewheels, die-cast smoke stack
(A) Metal trucks with open type early coil couplers, 1946 15 22 30 50
(B) Metal trucks with regular coil couplers, 1947 15 22 30 50

2420 D. L. & W. Work Caboose 1946-49, gray with black lettering, die-cast frame; handrails, ladders, two tool boxes, brakewheels, die-cast smokestack and search light
(A) Metal trucks with open type early coil couplers, 1946 20 30 40 75
(B) Metal trucks with regular coil couplers, 1947 20 30 40 75
(C) Darker gray cab and tool boxes on light gray frame, Ocilka Collection 20 30 40 75

2457 PENNSYLVANIA N5, 1946-47, metal body with white lettering, black frame, smokestack, illuminated, window inserts, metal couplers, "477618" appears on car sides, pierced cupola end windows. Some lettered. "Eastern Division" Ely reports. (We need to know which are and which are not.)
(A) Glossy red body, black window frames, whirly wheels, steps, front and rear cupola windows, rivet detail on roofwalk, two operating coil couplers, Foss observation 7 10 15 20
(B) Same as (A) but plain wheels, one operating coil coupler 7 10 15 20
(C) Semi-gloss red paint, black window frames, plain wheels, steps, no cupola end windows, no rivet detail on roofwalk, two operating coil couplers, Foss observation 7 10 15 20
(D) Brown body, red window frames, whirly wheels, no steps, front and rear cupola windows, no roofwalk rivet detail underscored "2457" on bottom, Foss observation 7 12 15 18
(E) Glossy red body, black window frames, no "EASTERN DIV.," front and rear cupola windows, plain wheels, no steps, staple-end metal trucks, one late coil coupler, no rivet detail on catwalk, "2457" on bottom in silver, "BLT. 4.41 N5 P.R.R." on lower right of car side, white heat-stamped lettering, battery box on frame, plastic air compressor mounted on metal channel, LaVoie Collection 7 10 15 18

2472 PENNSYLVANIA N5, 1945-47, red metal body with white lettering, black frame, no window inserts, no stack, metal trucks, one operating coil coupler, "477618" on car sides.
(A) Pierced cupola end windows, lettered "EASTERN DIV.," Lemieux Collection 4 6 8 12
(B) Unpierced cupola end windows, lettered "EASTERN DIV.," late coil couplers, bottom rubber stamped "2472;" Kotil and Lemieux Collections 4 6 8 12

2857 N Y C 1946, scale detailed caboose, catalogued, but not manufactured
Not Manufactured

2957 N Y C Circa 1946, originally manufactured 1940-42, refitted with postwar staple-end trucks with coil couplers by either Lionel service stations or owner 100 200 300 400

4357 PENNSYLVANIA N5, 1948-50, red metal body with white lettering, black frame, green and white "ELECTRONIC CONTROL" decal, electronic control receiver 25 37 50 75

4457 PENNSYLVANIA 1946-47, N5, red metal body with white lettering, black frame, green and white "ELECTRONIC CONTROL" decal, electronic control receiver 25 37 50 75

6007 LIONEL LINES 1950, SP Die 3, Scout caboose with Scout trucks, only trim is front and rear railings, screws fasten body and frame.
  1 1.50 2 3

6017 LIONEL LINES SP Dies, 1951-61, only trim is front and rear railings
(A) Die 2, gray painted black plastic with black lettering, black frame, plastic Timken trucks, tab fasteners, "6017" on rear left side and front right side, one operating disc coupler 7 11 15 20
(B) Red with white lettering, black frame, metal trucks 1 1.50 2 3
(C) Light tuscan, painted black plastic, white lettering, black frame, Timken trucks with one magnetic tab coupler 1 1.50 2 3
(D) Light tuscan painted mustard plastic; lighter tuscan than (C), Timken trucks, one magnetic tab coupler 1 1.50 2 3
(E) Same as (C) but very light tuscan painted orange plastic
  1 1.50 2 3
(F) Same as (C) but dark tuscan painted orange plastic 1 1.50 2 3
(G) Die 4, dark tuscan painted black plastic, black frame with tab fasteners
  1 1.50 2 3

6167

6257-100

6257

6357

6357[F]

2957

2420 D.L. & W.

6119-25 D.L. & W.

6420 D.L. & W

6429 D.L. & W.

6814 Lionel Rescue

6824 U.S.M.C. Rescue

Top Row: Bay Window Cabooses, lower rows: Work Cabooses

(H) Dark tuscan painted tuscan plastic, black frame with tab fasteners, Timken trucks, two couplers, one operating coupler   1.50   2   2.50   3

(I) Die 4, dark tuscan painted red plastic, Timken trucks, one operating disc coupler, black frame with tab fasteners   —   1.50   2   3

(J) Flat maroon-tuscan paint, bar-end metal trucks, magnetic coupler, black frame with screw fasteners for body   1   1.50   2   3

(K) Same as (J) but shiny maroon-tuscan paint   1   1.50   2   3

(L) "LIONEL" rather than "LIONEL LINES," "6017" underscored, bar-end metal trucks, one operating coupler, black frame with screw body fastener, shiny maroon-tuscan paint   2   3   4   6

(M) Brown plastic body, metal trucks, Pauli Collection   1   1.50   2   3

(N) Die 3B, unpainted shiny maroon plastic; white "LIONEL LINES" between third and fourth windows and "6017" between first and second windows on lower half of one side; on other side "LIONEL LINES" between windows one through three and "6017" below second cupola window, on lower half; truck detail not known, Edmunds Collection   1   1.50   2   3

(O) Die 1A, flat brown-maroon painted black plastic, same lettering as "N", truck detail not known, Edmunds Collection   1   1.50   2   3

(P) Die 1A, brown painted black plastic, same lettering as "N" Timken trucks, one disc-operating coupler, Stem Collection   1   1.50   2   3

6017-50 UNITED STATES MARINE CORPS 1958, SP Die 1A, dark blue with white lettering, black frame with tab body fasteners, "601750" on front left side and rear right side, Timken trucks, one operating coupler   12   17   25   50

6017-100 BOSTON AND MAINE 1959, 1964-65, SP Dies 3C and 4, blue with white lettering, "6017" under cupola on both sides, black frame with tab body fasteners, Timken trucks, one operating coupler; catalogued as 6017-100 but only "6017" appears on car, Powell Collection. Information needed about following variation types:

(A) Medium blue   7   11   15   30
(B) Lighter blue, Pauli Collection   7   11   15   25
(C) Purplish blue, Pauli Collection   40   65   120   175

6017-185 A.T. & S.F. 1959, SP Die 4, gray with red lettering, galvanized frame, tab body fasteners, no end rails, "6017" on rear left and front right sides, catalogued as "6017-185" but "6017" appears on car

(A) Timken trucks, one fixed coupler   5   7   15   25
(B) Front Timken truck with operating coupler, rear arch bar truck with fixed coupler   5   7   15   25
(C) Timken trucks, one operating coupler, one fixed coupler, SP Die other than 4   5   7   15   25
(D) Same as (C), but black frame, square end railings, stack plug flush with roof and reinforced from below, George Cole Collection   5   7   15   25

See also 6017-225 and 6017-235

6017-200 UNITED STATES NAVY 1960, SP Die 4, light blue with white lettering, black frame with tab body fasteners, Timken trucks, one operating coupler; catalogued as "6017-200," but "6017" appears on car (A) As described above   15   22   30   50

(B) Light blue body with aqua tint, blue platform and steps, tall stack, metal ladders and platform ends, battery boxes, clear plastic window inserts, bar-end metal trucks, two magnetic couplers, Hopper Collection   NRS

6017-225 A.T. & S.F. SP Die 4. Red tint with white lettering, galvanized frame with tab body fasteners and no end rails, Timken trucks with operating front coupler and fixed rear coupler, "6017" on left rear and right front sides. See 6017-235 and 6017-185 for other versions of A.T. & S.F.

(A) Red painted black plastic, Foss Collection   7   11   18   35
(B) Bright red with orange tint   7   11   18   35

6017-235 A.T. & S.F. SP Die 4, bright red painted black plastic, white lettering, one "6017" (not 6017-235), boxes stamped "6017-235," black frame, with end rails, tab body fasteners, Timken trucks, one disc-operating coupler, Kotil Collection   NRS

6027 ALASKA 1959, SP Die 2A, blue with yellow lettering, black frame with tab body fasteners. Timken trucks with one operating disc coupler, "6027" on rear left and right sides   15   22   30   50

6037 LIONEL LINES 1952-54, SP Die 3A, Scout trucks, black frame with screw body fasteners, (these are unusual since Scout trucks usually have Scout couplers, but the 6037 has knuckle couplers. See the 6002 NYC Gondola for another example of this arrangement).

(A) Brown with white lettering, one magnetic coupler, Die 3A   1   1.50   2   3
(B) Reddish-brown with white lettering, one magnetic coupler, Die 3A   1   1.50   2   3
(C) Same as (B) but lighter brown, Die 3A   1   1.50   2   3
(D) Same as (A) but two operating couplers   1   1.50   2   3
(E) Same as (A) but orange-red with white lettering, Cole Collection   1   1.50   2   3

6417-25

2472

6437-25

2457

6447

6517-1966 T.C.A.

6427-500

99

6047 LIONEL LINES 1962, black frame with tab body fasteners, Die 2A or 4
(A) SP Die 2A, medium red, white lettering, arch bar trucks, one fixed coupler   1   1.50   2   3
(B) SP Die 2A, medium red, white lettering, one arch bar truck with fixed coupler, one Timken truck without coupler   1   1.50   2   3
(C) SP Die 4, light red, white lettering arch bar trucks, one fixed coupler   1   1.50   2   3

6057 LIONEL LINES 1959-62, black frame with tab body fasteners
(A) SP Die 1A, medium red, Timken trucks, one operating coupler   1   1.50   2   3
(B) Same as (A) but slight pink tint to red   1   1.50   2   3
(C) SP Die 4, slight orange tint to red, Timken trucks, one operating coupler   1   1.50   2   3
(D) Brown with white lettering   1   1.50   2   3

6057-50 LIONEL LINES 1962, SP Die 4, orange with black lettering, black frame with tab body fasteners, Timken trucks, one operating coupler
                                                                4   7   15   25

6058 C & O 1961, SP Die 4, yellow with black lettering, black frame with tab body fasteners, Timken trucks, one operating coupler   10   15   20   35

6059-50 M St L 1961-63, SP Die 4, Timken trucks, one operating disc coupler, one fixed coupler; black frame with tab body fasteners
(A) Dark maroon with white lettering   3   4   8   15
(B) Lighter maroon than (A) with white lettering   3   4   8   15

6059-60 MStL 1963-69, SP Die 4, black frame with tab body fasteners, Timken trucks
(A) Unpainted shiny red plastic, one disc-operating coupler, one fixed coupler   3   4   8   15
(B) Unpainted flat red plastic, one disc-operating coupler 3   4   8   15
(C) Red painted gray plastic, one disc-operating coupler   3   4   8   15

6067 NO LETTERING 1962, SP Type, not illustrated, more information requested   1   1.50   2   3

6119 D.L.&W. 1955-56, Work Caboose, low stack
(A) Stamped, flat black frame, white "LIONEL" with serifs, red cab and tool boxes; metal trucks, one tab-operating coupler   6   9   12   15
(B) Same as (A) but shiny black frame   6   9   12   15
(C) Stamped gray frame, black "LIONEL" without serifs, gray cab and tool boxes, metal trucks, one tab-operating coupler   6   9   12   15
(D) Same as (C) but darker gray frame, cab and boxes   6   9   12   15
(E) Stamped brown frame, white "LIONEL" with serifs, brown cab, tool boxes, metal trucks, tab-operating couplers   7   11   18   25
(F) Stamped black frame, white "LIONEL" without serifs, red cab, gray tool boxes, metal trucks, tab-operating couplers   6   9   12   15
(G) Same as (F) but no lettering on frame, smooth area on cab lettered "BUILT BY LIONEL," plastic trucks   6   9   12   15
(H) Same as (F) but lettered "LIONEL" with serifs, plastic trucks
                                                                6   9   12   15

6119-25 D.L. & W. 1957-59, Work Caboose, orange with black lettering, stamped frame, bar-end metal trucks   10   15   20   30

6119-25 D.L. & W. Circa 1960, Work Caboose, stamped gray frame, black "LIONEL" without serifs, gray cab, one large bin instead of tool boxes, metal trucks, one tab-operating coupler, box marked "6119-25," car not numbered, Mitarotonda Collection   NRS

6119-100 D.L. & W. 1963-66, Work Caboose, red cab, black stamped frame, gray tool boxes, plastic trucks   4   6   8   12

6119-25 NO LETTERING Circa 1960, Work Caboose, olive drab, Timken trucks, one disc-operating coupler, one fixed coupler   6   9   12   15

6120 NO LETTERING, circa 1962, work caboose, unpainted yellow plastic cab and low-walled open bin. The car is the same as the 6119 and 6129 illustrated in color on page, but it is all yellow with no lettering. No part numbers are embossed on the yellow plastic pieces. Car bus arch-bar trucks with one dummy coupler; black metal rear railing is integral to frame. The cab roof shows where the die has been changed to plug the smokestack hole. Black painted integral plastic ladder on one side, but there is some question as to whether this ladder was painted at the factory. Readers are asked to comment about whether their pieces are similarly painted. Lord observations.

(A) Flat black stamped frame   4   6   8   12
(B) Shiny black stamped frame   4   6   8   12

6130 SANTA FE 1965-68, Work Caboose, stamped black frame, unlettered frame sides, unlettered builder's plate on cab, plastic trucks
(A) Red cab and tool boxes with pinkish cast, shiny frame, lettering on tool boxes   6   9   12   15
(B) Red cab and tool boxes, shiny frame, lettering on tool boxes
                                                                6   9   12   15
(C) Red cab and tool boxes with slight orange tint, lettering on tool boxes
                                                                6   9   12   15
(D) Orange-red cab and tool boxes, lettering on tool boxes
                                                                6   9   12   15
(E) Red cab, gray tool boxes, no lettering on tool boxes   6   9   12   15
(F) Orange-red cab and tool boxes, lettering on tool boxes, "LIONEL" on frame, Pauli Collection   6   9   12   15

6157 Reported but not verified, more information needed.

UNLETTERED & UNNUMBERED CABOOSES

Lionel made a number of unlettered and unnumbered cabooses. These often came with inexpensive sets and the omission of letters and numbers probably can be explained by cost reduction. We have had difficulty in matching the catalogue numbers as they appear in the Service Manual with these un-numbered cabooses. Numbers do appear on their boxes. We would appreciate very much your assistance in matching cabooses with numbers. We have made some matches below. Known numbers are:

6167-25 (red) body, body mold number 6059-2; 6167-50 (yellow) body, body mold number 6167-52; 6167-100 (body color unknown), body mold number 6167-102; 6167-125 (red) body, body mold number 6059-2, and 6167-150 (body color unknown), body mold number 6167-102.

6167 LIONEL LINES 1963, SP Die 4, galvanized frame with tab-fastened body, Timken trucks
(A) Red plastic body, white lettering, one disc-operating coupler, one fixed coupler   1   1.50   2   3
(B) Flat red plastic body, white lettering, one disc-operating coupler, one fixed coupler   1   1.50   2   3
(C) Same as (A) but only one disc coupler, Kotil Collection
                                                                1   1.50   2   3

6167-25 NO LETTERING, SP Type 4 red unpainted plastic body, galvanized underframe, Timken trucks with one dummy coupler, frame with tab-fastened body, no end rails, came with set no. 11420 (1964) with 1061 loco and 6112 gondola in box probably numbered 6042-50, confirmation requested, Light Collection   1   2   3   5

6167-50 NO LETTERING 1964, SP Die 4, yellow unpainted plastic body, galvanized underframe, Timken trucks, fixed couplers, frame with tab-fastened body, no end rails   1   1.50   4   8

6167-85 UNION PACIFIC 1964-69, SP Die 4, unpainted yellow plastic body, black lettering, Timken trucks, one disc-operating coupler, one fixed coupler; frame with tab-fastened body, only "6167" appears on car
(A) One disc-operating coupler, one fixed coupler   6   9   15   25
(B) Only one disc-operating coupler, Kotil Collection   6   9   15   25

6167-100 NO LETTERING 1964, SP Die 4, light red unpainted body, Timken trucks, one fixed coupler, galvanized frame with tab body fasteners and no end rail   1   1.50   2   3

6167-125 NO LETTERING 1964, SP Die 4, arch bar trucks, one fixed coupler, frame with tab body fasteners, with end rail
(A) Dark brown unpainted plastic   1   1.50   2   3
(B) Medium red unpainted plastic   1   1.50   2   3
(C) LIONEL LINES, 6167 only on caboose, SP-4 die, Timken plastic trucks, one disc and one dummy coupler, part of set no. 11430, Winton Collection
                                                                1   1.50   2   3

6167-150 NO LETTERING. More information requested

6219 C&O 1960, Work Caboose, stamped flat black frame, blue cab with yellow lettering, blue tool boxes, Timken trucks, one disc-operating coupler   10   15   25   50

6257 LIONEL 1948-56, SP Dies, metal trucks, one operating coupler, frame fastened to body with screws
(A) "6257" is underscored, partially filled double circle around "L," red, painted black plastic brakewheel, Die 2   1   1.50   2   3

100

(B) Same as (A) but unpainted red plastic body, one brakewheel, original box stamped "25 LIONEL 25," Kotil Collection   1   1.50   2   3
(C) Same as (A) but unpainted red plastic body and partially filled double circle   1   1.50   2   3
(D) Same as (A) but circle not filled in   1   1.50   2   3
(E) Same as (A) but black plastic painted duller red   1   1.50   2   3
(F) Same as (A) but black plastic painted brownish-red   1   1.50   2   3
(G) "6267" is underscored, no "L"   1   1.50   2   3
(H) "SP" above underscored "6257," black plastic painted red   1   1.50   2   3
(I) "SP" above underscored "6257," clear plastic painted flat red (compared to (H)), lighted, light may have been added after piece left factory   1   1.50   2   3
(J) "SP" above underscored "6257," clear plastic painted brownish-red as compared to (K), (L) and (M)   1   1.50   2   3
(K) "SP" above underscored "6257," black plastic painted brownish-red, "S" is thicker than on other 6257s   1   1.50   2   3
(L) Same as (K) but regular "S"   1   1.50   2   3
(M) "SP" above underscored "6257," black plastic painted shiny brownish-red when compared to (J), (K) and (L)   1   1.50   2   3
(N) Same as (B) but no brakewheel, box stamped "50 LIONEL 50," Kotil Collection   1   1.50   2   3
(O) Red painted black plastic, white "SP" above underscored "6257" between third and fourth windows, "LIONEL" beneath first and second windows, "C 40-1 BUILT 9-47" beneath "LIONEL," Edmunds Collection   1   1.50   2   3

6257-25 LIONEL Die 3A, "L" in double circle, underscored "6257," unpainted bright red plastic body, metal trucks, one brakewheel, "6257-25" on box end, car marked only "6257," Kotil Collection   1   1.50   2   3

6257-50 LIONEL Die 1 or 3A, box end marked "6257-50," car marked only "6257"
(A) "L" in double circle, "6257" underscored, unpainted bright red plastic body, no brakewheel, metal trucks, Die 1, Kotil Collection   1   1.50   2   3
(B) No "L" in circle, "6257" underscored, unpainted bright red plastic body, no brake wheel, metal trucks, Die 3A, Kotil Collection   1   1.50   2   3

6257-100 LIONEL LINES 1956-63, SP Die 4, red unpainted plastic, stack, Timken trucks, one disc-operating coupler, tabs fasten black frame and body, "6257-100" catalogue number, only "6257" on car   1   1.50   2   3

6257X LIONEL LINES 1948 catalogue, page 5; came with two couplers instead of the usual one with the 6257 because it was part of the 1656 switcher outfit; Foss and Hutchinson observations   **NRS**

6357 LIONEL 1948-57, SP Dies, smoke stack, bar-end metal trucks, "6357" underscored, "SP" above "6357" underscored, lighted, screws fasten black base to body, one operating coupler, "C-40-1" and "BUILT 9-47," brakewheel, except as noted
(A) Brownish-red painted black plastic, two operating couplers, no stack   4   6   8   12
(B) Shiny maroon painted black plastic, one operating magnetic coupler   4   6   8   12
(C) Duller maroon painted black plastic   4   6   8   12
(D) Black plastic painted maroon, Timken trucks   4   6   8   12
(E) A.T. & S.F., SP Die 4, (not LIONEL), "6357" not underscored, black plastic painted red, Timken trucks, one disc-operating coupler. Usually screw fasteners came only with tab frame body fasteners. Without "C-40-1," "BUILT 9-47," and "SP." This caboose is probably as scarce as the tuscan Lehigh Valley, but it has not received the publicity. Came in "over and under" set only, 1960; Stein and Degano observations   150   250   350   500
(F) SP Die 4, gray plastic painted maroon, Timken trucks, one disc-operating coupler, ladder, without "SP"   5   7   10   14
(G) Black plastic painted maroon, without "SP"   4   6   8   12
(H) Black plastic painted bright red, Pauli Collection, Die 1, staple-end trucks   4   6   8   12
(I) Same as (A) but staple-end trucks, one wire wound coupler, 1948, Hutchinson Collection   4   6   8   12

6357-25 SP Die 2, "L" in double circle over underscored "6357," ("6357-25" does not appear on car sides), lighted, stack, brakewheel, black base, screws fasten body to frame, bar-end metal trucks, one operating magnetic coupler

(A) Reddish-maroon painted; black plastic   4   6   8   12
(B) Maroon painted black plastic   4   6   8   12
(C) Brownish-maroon painted black plastic   4   6   8   12
(D) Gray with red lettering   —   —   1000   —

N 5 C CABOOSE CATALOGUE NUMBERS

We are following the recommendation of Joseph Kotil and are recataloguing the 6417-N5C cabooses. The following numbers come from **GREENBERG'S REPAIR AND OPERATING MANUAL FOR LIONEL TRAINS,** Third Edition, page 309, and represent a change from the previous Price Guides.

6417 PENNSYLVANIA 1953-57, N5C, "536417" on side, tuscan with white lettering, lights, bar-end metal trucks (PT-1 and 479-1), two operating couplers, lettered "BLT 2-53." (The part number for the caboose body is 6417-3.)
(A) With "NEW YORK ZONE"   7   11   15   25
(B) Without "NEW YORK ZONE"   10   15   20   30
(C) Gray painted black plastic shell, dark maroon "NEW YORK ZONE" in sans-serif, "BLT 2-53," "L" in circle, plug in light unit, bar-end metal trucks, operating tab couplers, Degano Collection   **NRS**
(D) Lime green painted black plastic shell, dark maroon "NEW YORK ZONE" in sans-serif, "BLT 2-53," one operating coupler, no tabs, Degano Collection   **NRS**

64173 See 6417-25

6417-25 LIONEL LINES 1954, N5C, "64173" on side, tuscan with white lettering, lettered "BLT 11-53." In previous editions, this car was numbered 6417-53. (The part number for the caboose body is 6417-26.)
(A) Magnetic couplers with tabs   7   11   15   25
(B) Magnetic couplers, no tabs, Kotil Collection   7   11   15   25

6417-50 LEHIGH VALLEY 1954, N5C, numbered on side "641751," lettered "BLT 6-54," Lionel "L" in circle on lower right car side, bar-end metal trucks (PT-1), magnetic couplers, apparently not lighted. (Listed as 6417-51 in last edition but changed to correspond to Service Manual entry which lists the body part number as 6417-50.)
(A) Tuscan with white lettering, tab couplers   —   —   1000   —
(B) Gray with red lettering   20   30   40   60
(C) Tuscan with gold lettering, Degano Collection   —   —   1200   —
(D) Gray, painted clear plastic shell, blue heat stamped lettering "BLT 6-54," "L" in circle on lower right, plastic window inserts, press in light unit, bar-end trucks, magnetic operating couplers without tabs, Degano Collection   —   —   1000   —

6417-51 See 6417-50

6419 DL&W 1950, 1956-57, Work Caboose, bar-end metal trucks, two magnetic couplers, die-cast frame (#2419), "D L & W 6419" on cab side and black "LIONEL LINES" lettering on frame side, smokestack on roof, brakewheel at each end, steps at each corner. In 1950, Lionel also offered a deluxe version of the 6419, the 6420 with searchlight (see below). In 1956, after a five year absence, the 6419 was offered as part of the Virginian set whose number is believed to be 2267W. The 6419 was also offered for separate sale. In 1957, the caboose was again offered as part of Set 2281W headed by a single motor 2243 Santa Fe F-3 AB catalogued as O gauge. (See 2243 for this interesting tale.) The caboose was also offered for separate sale again in 1957. Lord comments.
(A) Black marble plastic painted dark gray   10   15   20   30
(B) Pink plastic painted light gray   10   15   20   30
(C) Orange plastic, catalogued but not manufactured   **Not Manufactured**

6419-57 N & W 1957, Work Caboose, bar-end metal trucks, one magnetic tab coupler, low stack, medium gray die-cast frame, "LIONEL LINES" in black letters, light gray boxes, light gray cab with "576419" in black   25   35   45   80

6420 D.L. & W. 1949-50, Work Caboose, staple-end metal trucks, coil couplers, dark gray die-cast frame with black "LIONEL LINES," dark gray cab, searchlight, tall stack, two brakewheels, dark gray tool boxes   37   50   75   125

6427 LIONEL LINES 1955-60, N5C, numbered "64273" on side, lights, tuscan with white lettering, "BLT 11-53," bar-end metal trucks, single tab magnetic coupler. "6427," the "official" Lionel number, is used in the Service Manual and 6427-3 is the part number for the body. Numbering in this edition now corresponds to Lionel's.   6   9   15   25

101

64273 See 6427

6427-60 VIRGINIAN 1958, N5C, dark blue with yellow lettering, "6427" on side, "BLT 8-58," lighted, bar-end metal trucks, one tab magnetic coupler. (Body is part number 6427-63.)   50   75   110   175

6427-500 PENNSYLVANIA 1957-58, N5C, from "Girl's Set," numbered "576427" on side, lighted, bar-end metal trucks, one coupler. Reproductions have been made and are reportedly marked.
(A) Sky blue with white lettering, production model   50   75   100   200
(B) Flat yellow finish on black plastic body, extremely heavy white heat-stamped letters and numbers, one brakewheel, preproduction Lionel color sample not produced, Degano Collection   —   —   1000   —
(C) Semi-gloss yellow paint on black plastic body and black heat-stamped lettering which is heavier nearer the A and lighter nearer the P; tab-operating coupler, roller shows considerable wear; preproduction Lionel color sample not produced, Degano Collection   —   —   1000   —
(D) Pink painted black plastic body, very heavily heat-stamped in white, bar-end metal trucks, one magnetic operating coupler, plastic window inserts, preproduction color sample for Girl's Set not produced, Degano Collection   —   —   1000   —

6427 A.T. & S.F. 1960, N5C, catalogued but not manufactured
                                                    Not Manufactured

6429 D.L. & W. 1963, Work Caboose, light gray cab, medium gray tool boxes, light gray die-cast frame, bar-end metal trucks, one tab, magnetic coupler, two brakewheels, short stack   10   20   30   50

6437-25 PENNSYLVANIA 1961-68, N5C, tuscan with white lettering, "BLT 2-53," lighted, Timken trucks, one operating coupler; "6437" on side
(A) Timken trucks   6   9   15   25
(B) Metal trucks   6   9   15   25

6447 PENNSYLVANIA 1963, N5C, tuscan with white lettering, "BLT 2-53," non-illuminated, used in one Super 0 set, Timken trucks, one coupler   20   30   50   100

6457 LIONEL 1949-52, SP type, "L" in double circle over underscored "6457," "LIONEL" under first two windows, "C-40-1" and "BUILT 9-47" centered in two lines under "LIONEL," lighted, smokestack, ladders, battery box, two brakewheels, two operating couplers, black box fastens with screws to body, "blt. 9-47." Schmaus Observation
(A) Brown painted black plastic; staple-end metal trucks, black stack, Die 1.   6   9   12   17
(B) Brownish-maroon painted black plastic, bar-end metal trucks, black stack   6   9   12   18
(C) Brown painted black plastic, staple-end metal trucks, brown stack, Die 1   6   12   25   45
(D) Same as (C) but Die 2, Kotil Collection   6   9   12   18

6517 LIONEL LINES 1955-59, Bay Window, red with white lettering, lighted, stack, 0-27 passenger trucks, two operating couplers
(A) "BLT 12-55" and "LIONEL" underscored   20   30   50   75
(B) "BLT 12-55" and "LIONEL" not underscored   25   32   60   90
(C) Same as (B) but missing all bay markings and radio wave on side **NRS**

6517-75 ERIE 1966, Bay Window, with white lettering, stack, lighted, 0-27 passenger trucks, two operating couplers
(A) Tuscan   135   190   275   350
(B) Orange painted black plastic, one of three Lionel preproduction color samples; car base rubber stamped "6517-75" and "LIONEL" in silver, Degano Collection   —   —   1500   —

6517-1966 T.C.A. Convention bay window caboose, 1966, dull orange painted body with white "TCA" on caboose bay, white TCA logo at left of bay, octagonal convention data lettering to right of bay in white, Timken 4-wheel passenger die-cast trucks, two magnetic couplers. 700 produced for convention in Santa Monica. It has been reported that Lionel mistakenly produced the first 500 cars in red and had to repaint them orange.   —   —   250

6557 LIONEL 1958-59, SP Die 3C, with smoke unit, black plastic painted brown, white lettering, "BUILT 9-47," bar-end metal trucks, tab magnetic coupler
(A) Regular cat walk   50   75   100   175
(B) Slightly raised hump on catwalk   50   75   100   175

6657 Rio Grande 1957-58, SP Die 1 or 2, yellow body with silver lower band, black lettering, bar-end metal trucks, tab magnetic coupler, smokestack, lighted
(A) Without smoke unit   50   75   100   125
(B) With brown smoke unit,   **NRS**
(C) With white smoke unit, Powell Collection   **NRS**

6814-1 LIONEL 1959-61, Work Caboose, "RESCUE UNIT," short stack, white cab and tool boxes, red lettering, light gray base, man, two stretchers, oxygen tank unit, Timken trucks, two couplers, "6814" appears on car
(A) As described above   20   30   40   60
(B) Same as (A) but with Red Cross emblem on plastic yard type stand   50   75   100   130
(C) Black frame, no stretchers, man or oxygen tanks, "LIONEL" in white sans serif lettering on frame side, no brakewheels, Timken trucks, one disc-operating coupler, one fixed coupler, made by Lionel for Sears set no. 9820, circa 1964. For background, see 3666 boxcar and 240 loco and tender, made by Lionel for Sears with No. 240 steamer, circa 1968, Lebo and Powell Collections   30   40   50   100

6824 U.S.M.C. 1960, Work Caboose, "RESCUE UNIT," short stack, olive drab cab, tool boxes, white lettering, man, two stretchers, oxygen tank unit, Timken trucks, two couplers   25   37   50   75

6824 RESCUE UNIT Circa 1960, Work Caboose, no number on car, short stack, olive drab cab and tool boxes, white cross, black frame with white serif "LIONEL," Timken trucks, tab front coupler, no rear coupler, Catalano observation   15   25   40   75

NO NUMBERS

(A) SP Die 4, olive drab unpainted plastic, galvanized base, tabs fasten base to body, one fixed coupler, open on top, Timken trucks, no lettering, no back railing, resembles olive drab hopper, gondola and turbo missile cars, Wilson Collection. We need to learn this car's catalogue number and set number.
                                                         NRS

SP Types: See 6067, 6167-50, 6167-100 and 6167-125

Work Caboose: See 6119-25, 6120, 6824

Chapter VI
CRANES AND SEARCHLIGHTS

Note differences in the width and spacing of the word Lionel on the frames of the 2460 and 6560-25 on the bottom row.

Gd. V.G. Exc. Mt.

2460 BUCYRUS ERIE Crane, 1946-50, black with white lettering with serifs, "LIONEL LINES" in single arch on cab, Irvington-type six-wheel trucks with coil couplers, die-cast frame
(A) "LIONEL LINES" in single arch on black cab   20   30   40   75
(B) "LIONEL LINES" in single arch on gray cab   30   45   60   100
(C) "LIONEL LINES" in two arched lines, factory production, Latina Observation   20   30   40   75
(D) "LIONEL LINES" with top line arched and bottom line straight; red cab on black base, no cab smokestack and no cutout for stack, Catalano Observation   20   30   40   75
(E) Same as (D), but black cab on black base, Lahti Collection   20   30   40   75

2560 LIONEL LINES Crane 1946-47, continuation of prewar 2660 design with modifications, light yellow metal cab with red roof, "2560" rubber stamped on cab, staple-end metal trucks, coil-operated couplers
(A) Brown boom   10   15   20   40
(B) Green boom   10   15   20   40
(C) Black boom   10   18   30   50
(D) Brown cab, catalogued but not manufactured   **Not Manufactured**

3360 BURRO CRANE See Chapter I.

4460 BUCYRUS ERIE Crane car, shown in 1950 Advance Catalogue for Electronic Set, but never made   **Not Manufactured**

6460 BUCYRUS ERIE Crane, 1952-54, bar-end metal four-wheel trucks, die-cast frame
(A) Black with white cab lettering, "LIONEL LINES" without serifs in two lines; "LIONEL LINES" on frame in white bold serif letters, Griesbeck Collection   12   17   25   40
(B) Same as (A) but light, condensed letters on frame, Griesbeck Collection   12   17   25   40
(C) Gray plastic painted red with white lettering, "LIONEL LINES" without serifs in two lines   20   30   40   60
(D) Black with white lettering, "LIONEL LINES" with serifs in one arched line, not factory production   10   15   20   28

6460-25 BUCYRUS ERIE Crane, listed in 1954 catalogue with red cab, but never made   **Not Manufactured**

6560 BUCYRUS ERIE Crane, 1955-58, black plastic frame, large smokestack, "LIONEL LINES" in two lines, top line arched, bottom line straight, crank wheel with short handle, cab fastened to base with clips, four-wheel trucks
(A) Gray cab, black lettering, bar-end metal trucks, magnetic tab couplers   15   22   30   50
(B) Red cab, white lettering, bar-end metal trucks with magnetic tab couplers (Type VI). Box end flags marked: "No. 6560 OPERATING WORK CRANE LIONEL 25." This is clearly a different unit than 6560-25 shown below variety (E) as the next entry. That car is marked "656025" on its frame, while this car is marked "6560" only. We would appreciate reader comments about the dating of both units and the explanation for this odd numbering situation. Yeckel Collection   10   15   20   40
(C) Same as (B) but Timken trucks, disc-operating couplers, solid wheel on cab side, very dark blue base, part of Hagerstown 1969 set, Catalano observation   12   17   25   40
(D) Red-orange cab, strikingly different from usual red, bar-end metal trucks, magnetic couplers, no number on frame side, Griesbeck Collection   10   15   20   40
(E) Same as (B) but solid wheel on cab side, LaVoie Collection   10   15   20   40

6560-25 BUCYRUS ERIE Crane, 1956, red cab with white lettering, plastic frame numbered "6560-25," four-wheel trucks, "LIONEL LINES" in two lines, stack   22   30   50   100

SEARCHLIGHTS

3520 SEARCHLIGHT 1952-53, "LIONEL LINES" on gray die-cast frame, orange diesel generator unit, steps, bar-end metal trucks, one brakewheel, die-cast searchlight revolves by vibrator mechanism, remote control on-off switch for searchlight
(A) "LIONEL LINES," sans serif lettering   15   22   30   50
(B) "LIONEL LINES," with serif lettering, Griesbeck Collection   NRS

3530 GENERATOR See Box Cars.

3620 SEARCHLIGHT 1954-56, "LIONEL LINES" in sans serif lettering on gray die-cast frame (lettering is found in both light and heavy faces), orange diesel generator, steps, bar-end metal trucks, one brakewheel, searchlight revolves by vibrator mechanism, no remote control on-off switch, Parvin Observation
(A) As described above   **12 17 25 40**
(B) Gray die-cast flatcar base, "3620 LIONEL LINES 3620" rubber-stamped in black sans serif letters, bright red-orange generator and bright red-orange searchlight housing. NOTE: A detachable variation such as the searchlight housing raises the inevitable question of substitution. In this case, however, the color of the housing and the generator are perfectly matched. This car is probably genuine and may be unique. Art Tom Collection   **NRS**

3650 EXTENSION SEARCHLIGHT 1956-59, gray die-cast base, black lettering, "LIONEL LINES" without serif, gray plastic searchlight unit on red base held by magnet to steel plate in die-cast frame, gray generator, red reel with green cord and crank supported on black frame, bar-end metal trucks, magnetic tab couplers
(A) Light gray die-cast frame, two brakewheels   **10 15 25 60**
(B) Dark gray die-cast frame, one brakewheel   **10 15 25 60**
(C) Same as (A), but olive tint to paint on gray frame, Blotner Collection   **NRS**

6520 SEARCHLIGHT 1949-51, gray die-cast base, die-cast searchlight, staple-end metal trucks, magnetic couplers, on-off switch, manual rotation of light, one brakewheel, steps

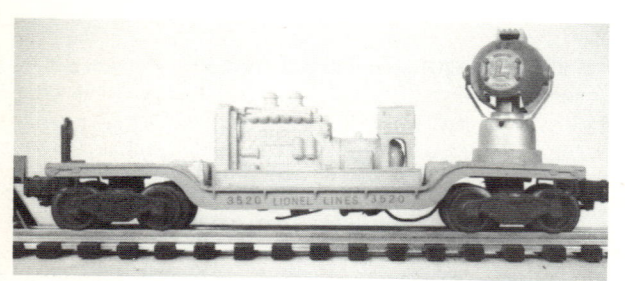

6520

3520

3650

3620

6822

(A) Green diesel generator, shiny smooth gray light housing
                                                          37 50 75 125
(B) Green diesel generator, crinkle gray light housing **37 50 75 125**
(C) Orange diesel generator, gray crinkle light housing **15 22 30 50**
(D) Maroon diesel generator, gray crinkle light housing **15 22 30 50**
(E) Maroon diesel generator, smooth gray light housing **15 22 30 50**
(F) Tan diesel generator, gray metallic enameled light **75 115 150 225**

6822 SEARCHLIGHT 1961-69, red frame with white lettering, blue man, Timken trucks, disc-operating couplers
(A) Black lighting unit base, gray searchlight housing **7 10 15 30**
(B) Gray lighting unit base, black searchlight housing **7 10 15 30**

FLAT CARS

3330

3349[A]

3361-55

3362

3362

3410

3413

3451

3460

3461

3470

3509

3510[B]

3519

Chapter VII
FLAT CARS

	Gd.	V.G.	Exc.	Mt.

1877 FLAT WITH FENCE AND HORSES 1959-62, brown unpainted plastic body, white lettering, six horses   20   30   40   60

[1877] NO NUMBER circa 1960-65, 1877 Type. Car catalogue number does not appear on car, hence appears in parentheses.
(A) Flat car with logs, unpainted gray plastic, three logs, no stakes, Timken trucks, one disc-operating coupler, one fixed coupler   1   2   3   5
(B) Flat without stakes or load, unpainted brown plastic, arch bar trucks, fixed couplers   1   1.50   2   4
(C) Flat without stakes or load, unpainted gray plastic, arch bar trucks, fixed couplers, Edmunds Collection. Used for Sears military tank car flat, Bohn comment   1   1.50   2   4
(D) Flat with yellow auto, part of set 19142-100, Dupstet Collection   NRS

1887 FLAT WITH FENCE AND HORSES 1959, tuscan with yellow lettering and fence, six horses, part of uncatalogued Sears 0-27 set
   60   85   125   170

2411 FLAT WITH BIG INCH PIPES 1946-48, same die-cast frame as 2419 Work Caboose, three black metal pipes with grooves at end, or three wood logs; staple-end metal trucks, coil coupler, gray die-cast frame (same as 2419 Work Caboose) with black serif lettered "LIONEL LINES," six black stakes, four steps, two sets of end rails
(A) 1946, metal pipes, Foss comment   3   6   10   15
(B) 1947-48, wood logs, Foss comment   3   6   10   15

2461 TRANSFORMER CAR 1947-48, gray die-cast depressed center belly frame with black serif lettered "LIONEL LINES," staple-end metal trucks, coil couplers with sliding shoes, two brakewheels
(A) Black transformer, small white decal on one side with "Transformer" and "L" in circle   11   17   25   35
(B) Red transformer, same decal as (A)   11   17   25   35
(C) Red transformer, same decal as (A), no lettering on frame
   11   17   25   35

[3309] TURBO MISSILE LAUNCHING CAR circa 1960. Also see 3349.
(A) Light red plastic car, no number or lettering, blue launch mechanism, red missile, blue missile holder, arch bar trucks, fixed couplers, Royer comment. Note that 3309 does not have an extra missile rack while 3349 does
   12   25   35   50

(B) Same as (A) but cherry red, Royer comment   12   25   35   50
(C) Same as (A) but light blue launcher, Timken trucks, Royer comment
   12   25   35   50
(D) Same as (A), except gray "General" type flat car, Blotner Collection
   NRS

3330 FLAT WITH OPERATING SUBMARINE KIT 1960-62, flat (6511-2 on underside) with disassembled submarine requiring assembly, blue car, white lettered "LIONEL" with serifs, Timken trucks, disc-operating couplers, gray submarine lettered "U.S. Navy, No.3830"   20   35   50   75

3349 TURBO MISSILE LAUNCHING CAR Circa 1960, also see 3309. Note that 3349 has an extra missile rack that 3309 does not have. 3349 came with set 19142-100. It also came with other sets. No number or lettering, light red or olive drab plastic car with blue launch mechanism, red and white missiles, blue missile holder, Timken trucks. Operating couplers, Royer comment.
(A) Light red body   10   15   25   50
(B) Olive drab body, Marine Corp markings   10   15   25   50

3361-55 LOG DUMP 1955-58, unpainted gray plastic with black lettering, bar-end metal trucks, magnetic tab couplers, metal channel runs car length and holds operating mechanism
(A) "LIONEL LINES" with serif   8   15   20   30
(B) "LIONEL LINES" without serif   8   15   20   30

3362 FLAT WITH HELIUM TANKS or LOGS 1961-63, dumps three silver painted wooden tanks or three large dark-stained logs, unpainted dark green plastic body, mold no. 2, with LIONEL LINES serif lettering, "LD LMT 128800, LT WT 40200, CAPY 100000" in white sans-serif lettering, metal channel runs length of car, magnetic operation, Timken plastic trucks, one disc and one dummy coupler
(A) With helium tanks   8   15   25   40
(B) With logs, Popp Collection   8   15   25   40

3364 LOG DUMP 1965-69, dumps three large dark-stained logs, mechanism similar to 3362; not illustrated   7   10   15   20

3409 HELICOPTER LAUNCHING CAR 1961-62, helicopter with black plastic spring wound launch mechanism, manually cocked and released; light blue unpainted flat car, white lettering; gray "Navy" plastic helicopter with simulated door, black lettering, clear plastic front bubble, black plastic skid, single propeller, yellowish tail end piece and rotor, arch bar trucks, fixed couplers, Pauli Collection **14 25 35 60**

3409 SATELLITE CAR Circa 1961, uncatalogued, light blue flat, white lettering, manual release, black and silver satellite, yellow microwave disc on gray superstructure, Timken trucks, operating disc couplers, Wilson Collection **NRS**

3410 HELICOPTER LAUNCHING CAR 1961-62, same as 3409 but with Timken trucks, disc-operating couplers **13 20 30 40**

3413 MERCURY CAPSULE CAR 1962-64, car launches rocket into air, Mercury capsule separates and returns via parachute. Red plastic frame, white lettered "LIONEL," no numbers, gray superstructure with red rocket launcher; gray Mercury capsule nose with parachute inside of rocket, red rocket base; Timken trucks, one disc-operating coupler, one fixed coupler **20 35 45 75**

3419 REMOTE CONTROLLED HELICOPTER LAUNCHING CAR 1959-65, similar to 3409 in function but with two slots on top and large two inch black winder designed to be released (after manually cocked) by UCS magnet track; with alternate manual lever and lock lever on car top near black plastic piece which holds copter tail assembly rigid prior to flight, flat car mold number 3419-30
(A) Light blue body, same helicopter as 3409 **13 25 35 50**
(B) Medium blue body, 1 1/4 inch diameter winder, same helicopter as 3409 **13 25 35 50**
(C) Royal blue body, gray helicopter with two top rotors and four tips, 2 inch winder **13 25 35 50**
(D) Dark blue, almost purple, two control levers on car's top surface, all yellow helicopter (see 3429 for copter description) **13 25 35 50**
(E) Aqua blue body, helicopter with two top rotors and four tips **13 25 35 50**
(F) Same as (C) but helicopter as in (E) Mitarotonda comment **13 25 35 50**

3429 U.S.M.C. 1960, U.S. MARINE CORPS operating helicopter car, olive drab paint over blue plastic car, white lettering, same mechanism as 3419, all yellow helicopter with three windows behind bubble, one porthole in rear section, one blade, same as 3419(D). One control lever on car's top surface, other on car's side; winder could be remotely released **14 25 35 50**

3451 LOG DUMP 1946-47, black die-cast base, white lettering, staple-end metal trucks, coil couplers
(A) 1946, shaft retainers for the swivel movement are riveted with round head rivets from the top and swaged from the bottom; nickel-sized hole between second and third set of stakes; heat-stamped lettering **10 15 20 35**
(B) 1947, shaft retainer rivets are integral to casting and swaged from top, hole about size of half dollar on frame, heat-stamped lettering **10 15 20 35**
(C) Same as (B) but rubber stamped lettering, Latina Collection **10 15 20 35**

3460 FLAT WITH TRAILERS 1955, red unpainted plastic flat car, mold number 6511, white lettering, metal strip holds trailers, bar-end metal trucks, magnetic tab couplers, trucks fastened to frame by metal plate; metal plate slides into two slots at each end of car; trailers are dark green with aluminum sign reading "LIONEL TRAINS," end decal reads "FRUEHAUF DURAVAN," lower right hand decal reads "FRUEHAUF," van with single axle, four wheels **10 20 25 40**

3461 LOG DUMP 1949-55, five logs stained dark brown, white lettering, "LIONEL LINES," one brakewheel
(A) 1949-53, black die-cast frame and dump unit; staple-end metal trucks, magnetic couplers **10 20 25 40**
(B) 1954-55, green die-cast frame, black dump unit, bar-end metal trucks, magnetic couplers **14 20 35 50**
(C) 1952-55, black die-cast frame and dump unit, bar-end metal trucks, magnetic couplers, Kaiser Collection **10 20 25 40**

3470 TARGET LAUNCHER 1962-64, dark blue unpainted flat car, mold #6511-2, no lettering; white superstructure with red letters, red lever on top activates motor; blue balloon carriage on top; car came with Lionel balloons, which when inflated and motor was turned on would raise the balloon approximately one inch above the balloon carrier, the balloon would then follow the moving car; with two dry cell batteries for operation; Timken trucks, disc couplers
(A) As described above **12 25 40 60**
(B) Same as (A), but light blue unpainted flat car, Blotner Collection **12 25 40 60**

3509 MANUALLY OPERATED SATELLITE CAR 1961, not catalogued, green car, white lettering, black and silver satellite, yellow microwave disc, gray superstructure holds yellow microwave disc; manually-operated by side lever, Timken trucks, disc couplers **9 15 22 30**

3510 RED SATELLITE CAR 1961-62, black and silver satellite, arch bar trucks, fixed couplers

107

3535

3540

3545

6121[A]

6151[A]

6175 [note wrong load]

6262

6264

6362-55

6404

6405

6413

6414

6414

(A) Darker red car, gray superstructure, yellow microwave disc
13	25	35	50

(B) Red car, no superstructure   9   20   27   40

3512 LADDER CO. 1959-61, red unpainted plastic body, white lettering, truck mechanism causes light shield to rotate causing light rotation, man rotates at other car end; mechanism uses rubber belt which almost always deteriorates; Timken trucks, disc couplers, three small metal nozzles, two ladders

(A) Common black ladder   22   35   50   70
(B) Silver ladder   32   45   65   120

3519 REMOTE CONTROL SATELLITE CAR 1961-64, green base, white letters, gray superstructure with yellow microwave disc, black and silver satellite, Timken trucks, disc couplers; car activated manually by lever on side or by remote control track, mold #3479-30   8   15   25   35

3535 AEC SECURITY 1960-61, black base, mold #6511-2, red building, white letters, gray gun on roof, gray rotating type searchlight with vibrator motor, Timken trucks, disc couplers, one pickup roller. Same body used for 520 Box Cab Electric (p. 9)   19   35   50   90

3540 OPERATING RADAR CAR 1959-60, red car base, mold #6511-2, white letters, gray superstructure with yellow microwave disc; black and silver radar antenna; blue seated man with flesh colored hands and face; radar unit panel similar to 44 Rocket Launcher with dials and gauges; lighted green radar screen with black lines and white dots; rotating radar tower powered by rubber band drive attached to disc and axle; rubber band usually deteriorates; one roller pickup for radar screen light   22   55   75   125

3545 LIONEL TV CAR 1961-62, black base, white letters, blue superstructure with blue TV camera and base; blue man with flesh colored face and hands in seated position looking into TV projection screen; screen shows a Santa Fe diesel coming and an open railroad track in the direction the car is moving; to the rear of seated figure is a movable light structure that "illuminates" the cameraman's subject; TV cameraman rotates by rubber band drive attached to disc and axle; rubber band usually deteriorates
   20   45   65   115

3820 FLAT WITH OPERATING SUBMARINE 1960-62, olive drab car, mold #6511-2, white lettered "USMC," gray submarine marked "U.S. NAVY 3830," Timken trucks, disc couplers   17   25   35   65

3830 FLAT WITH OPERATING SUBMARINE 1960-63; blue car, mold #6511-2, white lettered "LIONEL," gray submarine with black lettered U.S. NAVY 3830," Timken trucks, disc couplers   12   25   35   60

NOTE: There are three different 6111 flat cars

6111 FLAT WITH LOGS 1955, yellow painted stamped steel car, black serif lettered "LIONEL," three logs, bar-end metal trucks   1   1.50   2   4

6111 FLAT WITH UNKNOWN LOAD Circa 1955-56, painted stamped steel frame; frame similar to preceeding 6111, probably held pipes or logs, pipe or log holders.
(A) Gray painted frame "LIONEL" in sans-serif lettering, Timken trucks, disc couplers, Schreiner and Light Collections   **NRS**
(B) Light gray painted frame, "LIONEL" in serif lettering, metal trucks, Kotil Collection   **NRS**
(C) Dark gray painted frame, "LIONEL" in serif lettering, Timken trucks, Kotil Collection   **NRS**
(D) Same as (C) but "LIONEL" in sans-serif lettering, Kotil Collection   **NRS**
(E) Dark blue gray painted frame, "LIONEL" in serif lettering, Timken trucks, Kotil Collection   **NRS**

6111 FLAT WITH PIPES 1957, red painted stamped steel car, white serif lettered "LIONEL," pipes
(A) Lettering with serifs   1   1.50   2   4
(B) Lettering without serifs   1   1.50   2   4

6121 FLAT WITH PIPES 1955, yellow painted stamped steel, black lettered "LIONEL," three pipes
(A) Lettering with serifs   1   1.50   2   4
(B) Lettering without serifs   1   1.50   2   4

6151 FLAT CAR WITH PATROL TRUCK 1958, yellow stamped steel car, black serif lettering, steps, bar-end metal trucks, magnetic couplers
(A) White plastic patrol truck cab lettered "LIONEL RANCH," in black, with longhorns insignia; black plastic body lettered "RANGE PATROL," truck made by PYRO   12   25   40   60
(B) Orange steel car, Degano Collection   17   25   40   50

6175 FLAT CAR WITH ROCKET Red and white rocket with blue letters, gray rocket rack, Timken trucks, disc couplers
(A) Black plastic car, Type A #6424-11 mold, white lettering, Ocilka Collection   19   35   55   75
(B) Same as (A), but Type (B) 6424-11 mold, Ocilka Collection
   12   25   40   50
(C) Red plastic car, mold #6511-2, white lettering   10   15   20   40

6262 FLAT WITH WHEELS 1956-57, white lettering, gray superstructure with eight sets of Lionel wheels and axles; bar-end metal trucks, magnetic tab couplers
(A) Black flat car, mold #6424-11   9   18   25   40
(B) Red flat car   20   40   65   100

6264 FLAT WITH LOG LOAD 1957, lumber for fork lift car, red plastic car, mold #6511-2, white lettering, brown lumber rack, black stakes, one brakewheel, bar-end metal trucks, magnetic couplers; truck mounting plates that fit into car grooves   12   25   35   60

6311 FLAT 1955, reddish-brown metal body with pipes, mold #6511-2; bar-end metal trucks, magnetic tab couplers, truck mounting plates that fasten with screws, Pauli Collection   1   1.50   2   4

6343 BARREL RAMP CAR 1961-62, red with white lettering, Timken trucks, disc couplers with 6 stained brown barrels, part of set No. 11222
   8   15   20   40

6361 FLAT WITH TIMBER 1960-61, 64-69; green plastic, three wooden sticks with bark held by chains with spring on underside; metal channel provides support for car; Timken trucks, disc couplers
(A) White lettering   9   17   25   40
(B) No lettering, gold chains, Degano Collection   11   20   35   75

6362-55 TRUCK CAR 1956, carries three Lionel trucks without couplers, bar-end trucks, Mitarotonda comment
(A) Clear plastic painted orange, magnetic tab couplers, serif lettering
   7   14   30   45
(B) Orange plastic, magnetic couplers, sans-serif lettering
   7   14   30   45
(C) Orange unpainted plastic, serif lettering, magnetic couplers, Kotil Collection   8   15   20   40
(D) Same as (B) but sans-serif lettering, Mitarotonda and Kotil Collections
   8   15   20   40

6401-50 FLAT CAR Circa 1960?, olive drab plastic car, probably mold #1877-3 although Service Manual cites part number 6401-51 as frame. Probably has no number or lettering, Timken trucks, one operating coupler, one fixed coupler. Confirmation requested: car number probably appears on box end.

6401 FLAT WITH VAN Light gray car with gray two wheel van, Timken trucks, one disc coupler, one fixed coupler, Pauli Collection
   3   7   12   20

6402 FLAT WITH REELS OR BOAT, medium gray plastic car, mold #1877-3
(A) 1964, orange reels marked "LIONEL," elastic bands hold reels in place; base from General flat car   3   6   9   15
(B) 1969, blue boat   4   8   12   20

6402-50 FLAT CAR WITH CABLE REELS, 1964, medium gray plastic car, mold #1877-3 from General flat car, although Service Manual calls for part number 6402-51. "6402" on car side. Orange reels marked "LIONEL," elastic bands hold reels in place, Timken trucks, one operating coupler, one fixed coupler.   2   3   5   11

6404 FLAT CAR not catalogued in 1960 Consumer catalogue, but shown in 1960 Advance Catalogue. Black body with struts, base from General flat car, arch bar trucks, dummy couplers. Came with red auto; description of auto requested. Part of special low-price set No. 1109, "The Huntsman Steamer... designed for the toy market and ... not ... included in the Lionel consumer catalogue." For more information about this set, see the entry for 1060 in the steam locomotive section. Car was possibly also offered as a Merchant's Green Stamp premium car, and possibly by other mass merchandisers as a low-price "leader." We would like information from the 1960 Merchants'

MILITARY & SPACE ITEMS

6424

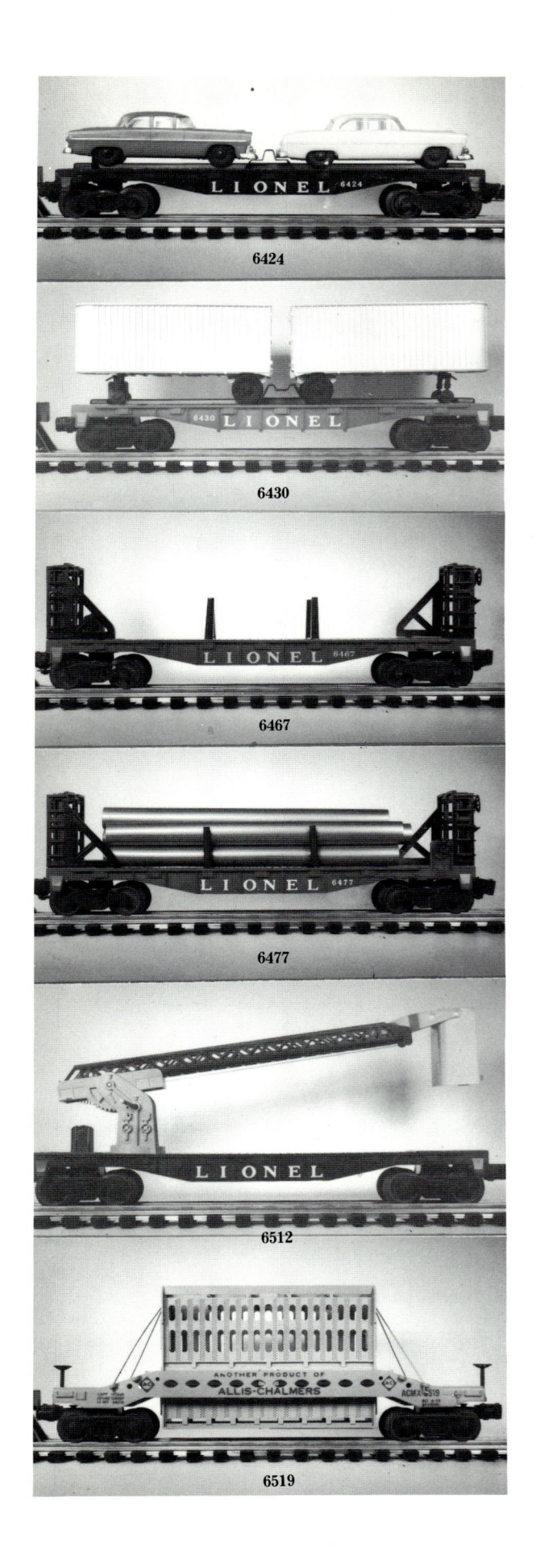

6430

6467

6477

6512

6519

6544

6630

6640

6651

6660

6670

111

Green Stamp catalogue. Fleming Collection and observations
14 22 35 60

6405 FLAT WITH TRAILER 1961, brown plastic flat, mold #1877-3 with struts; Timken trucks, disc couplers; yellow trailer marked "Made in the U.S. of America, The Lionel Corporation, New York, New York," trailer has single axle with two wheels while Piggyback outfit trailer has single axle with four wheels
7 10 15 30

6406 FLAT WITH AUTO Circa 1960?, probably mold 1877-3 although Service Manual cites part number 6406-3 as frame. Frame color unknown; probably has no number or lettering. (If it did have lettering or numbering it would likely have been brought to our attention as an omission.) Load was listed as a yellow auto, part number 6406-30. Probably Timken trucks, one operating coupler, one fixed coupler. Confirmation requested: car number probably appears on box end. This request for confirmation was also printed in the 1981 edition of this book. The car probably does not exist.

6407 FLAT WITH ROCKET 1963, red flat car, no numbers, white letters, gray superstructure holds large white and red rocket with blue nose
(A) Nose is a pencil sharpener that can be removed and used; rocket does not launch
45 90 160 275
(B) Nose is not a pencil sharpener. Catalano comment
42 80 140 250

6409-25 FLAT With unknown load, if any. Red body, body mold number "6511-2," no number, no brakewheel, white lettered "LIONEL," arch bar truck, fixed couplers believed to be from Set 11311, 1963 Catalogue, page 3; confirmation of item and set number requested, Schreiner Collection **NRS**

6411 FLAT WITH LOGS 1948-50, gray die-cast frame rubber stamped "6411" on underside, black "LIONEL LINES" serif lettering, two brakewheels, end railings, logs. Not illustrated.
(A) Staple-end metal trucks, coil couplers, 1948, I. D. Smith Collection
3 5 6 10
(B) Same as (A), but magnetic couplers, 1949-50, I. D. Smith and Schmaus Collections
3 5 6 10

6413 MERCURY PROJECT CAPE CANAVERAL 1962-63, blue plastic car, white letters, two gray Mercury capsules held by bands with cloth coating; metal plates hold capsules, Timken trucks, disc couplers
(A) Powder blue car, Wilson Collection
10 20 25 50
(B) Aquamarine car, Wilson Collection
10 20 25 50

6414 AUTO LOADER 1955-57, red base, white letters, black metal superstructure, white letters
(A) Premium cars with windshields, bumpers, rubber tires; car colors vary yellow, red, blue and white. "6414" on right side of car, bar-end metal trucks, magnetic tab couplers
8 15 20 40
(B) Premium cars with windshields, bumpers, rubber tires; colors of cars vary, "6414" on left side
8 15 20 40
(C) Four red premium cars with gray non-chrome bumpers, bar-end metal trucks, magnetic tab couplers, "6414" on right
8 15 20 40
(D) Four cheap cars without bumpers, wheels or windshields, two red cars and two yellow cars; simulated wheels on the exterior with an interior space where the axle would have been attached; red cars have attachment for axle, yellow cars do not, "6414" on left side; Timken trucks, disc couplers
8 15 20 40
(E) Decaled version made for Glen Uhl by Lionel; 200 reportedly made with black decals, yellow letters, red autos; have gray plastic bumpers, black wheels, Timken trucks, one disc coupler, one fixed coupler; "6414" on decal, not on flat car
15 30 40 65
(F) 1966, Four red premium cars with gray non-chrome bumpers, Timken trucks with disc operating couplers, "6414" on left, Hutchinson Collection
8 15 20 40
(G) Four dark brown premium cars with chrome bumpers, 6414 to right, bar-end metal trucks, magnetic couplers, Art Tom Collection **NRS**
(H) Four medium green premium cars with chrome bumpers, 6414 to left, Timken plastic trucks, one disc-operated and one fixed coupler, Art Tom Collection **NRS**

6416 BOAT LOADER CAR 1961-63, red base, white letters, black metal superstructure with white letters, four boats, Timken trucks, disc couplers
(A) Boats with white hull, blue top, brown interior
25 40 60 125
(B) All red boats, Wilson Collection
23 37 50 100
(C) Boats with white hull, blue top and red inner shells, Blotner Collection
25 40 60 125

6418 FLAT WITH U.S. STEEL GIRDERS 1955, depressed center, die-cast gray body, four trucks with bar-ends, magnetic tab couplers. For 0 Gauge only, will not pass through 0-27 switches, Knight comment
(A) All orange "LIONEL" girder. Catalano comment
17 30 40 75
(B) Pinkish-orange girders with black "U.S. STEEL" lettering. Catalano comment
17 30 40 75
(C) Black girders with white "U.S. STEEL" lettering, and numbered "6418" on lower right. Degano comment
25 37 50 85
(D) Red girders with white "U. S. STEEL" lettering, Blotner Collection
25 37 50 85

6424 FLAT WITH TWO AUTOS 1956-59, black plastic flat car with white lettering, black metal superstructure to keep autos from falling off; bar-end metal trucks, magnetic tab couplers
(A) Mold #6424-11, bar-end metal trucks, magnetic tab couplers, number on right, Kotil Collection
8 15 20 40
(B) Mold #6424-11, Timken trucks, disc couplers, number on right, Kotil Collection
8 15 20 40
(C) Mold #6511-2, Timken trucks, disc couplers, number on left, Kotil Collection
8 15 20 40
(D) Same as (A) but flat red car
12 25 50 90

6430 FLAT CAR WITH COOPER-JARRETT VANS 1955-58, red plastic base, mold #6511-2, white lettering; trucks are fastened to plate, plate slides into car
(A) "6430" appears on right side of car, regardless of how car is held; trailer mounting unit is screwed onto car; COOPER-JARRETT VAN is gray plastic with an aluminum sign with an orange arrow and black lettering
7 15 20 35
(B) "6430" appears on the left side of car, regardless of how car is held see next entry, 6431
7 15 20 35
(C) COOPER-JARRETT VAN in white plastic
7 15 20 35
(D) Two dark green plastic trailers, metal signs on sides lettered "Lionel Trains," small decal on right front of each trailer lettered "fruehauf," also decal center top front of each trailer lettered "FRUEHAUF Dura-Van," trailers with four rubber tires, bar-end metal trucks, magnetic tab couplers, one brakewheel, 1955-58, Powell Collection
7 15 20 35
(E) Same as (A), except Cooper-Jarrett signs are copper-colored, not aluminum, Blotner Collection
7 15 20 35

6431 FLAT WITH VANS 1965, red plastic flat, mold #6424-11, with white lettering and numbers; "6430" appears on left side regardless of how car is held; 6431 is a special with a Midge Toy tractor and two white unlettered trailers; the red die-cast tractor is marked: "Midge Toy, Rockford, Illinois, U.S.A., Patent 2775847," tractor has fifth wheel, a plug that fits into an enlarged hole in the trailer; the trailer mounting bracket and the flat car trucks are riveted to the car; Timken trucks, disc couplers, one brakewheel
20 40 50 75

6440 FLAT WITH VANS red unpainted plastic flat car, mold 6511-2, white LIONEL lettering and "6440" to left, Timken plastic trucks
(A) 1960, no van mounting units, two gray unpainted plastic vans with side slots for nameplates, but nameplates are absent, bottom of vans embossed "MADE IN U.S. OF AMERICA/THE LIONEL CORPORATION/NEW YORK, N.Y." in three lines, trailers have one 2-wheel axle each, two disc-operating couplers, box marked "No. 6440 FLAT CAR WITH PIGGY BACK VANS," Blotner, Landry, Marshall, Shewmake, Surratt and Toone Collections
15 25 40 60
(B) 1961, same as (A), except vans have "COOPER-JARRETT" nameplates and car has one disc-operating and one dummy coupler, Ocilka Collection
15 25 40 60
(C) Same as (B), except two disc-operating couplers, Sykes Collection
15 25 40 60

6461 TRANSFORMER CAR 1949-50, gray die-cast depressed center base, black lettering, black plastic transformer with white decal, two brakewheels, steps, staple-end metal trucks, magnetic couplers, see color illustration, Lord observation
12 22 30 45

6467 BULKHEAD CAR 1956, red flat with black bulkheads with stakes and white lettering, mold #6511-2, called "Miscellaneous Car," bar-end metal trucks, magnetic tab couplers
13 25 35 50

6469 LIONEL LIQUIFIED GASES 1963, red car, mold #6424-11, Die 2, white letters, no numbers, large liquified gas cylinder lettered "Lionel,"

"ERIE," and "6469." 6467 is often found with this liquified gas cylinder but it did not come with it; Timken trucks, disc couplers, see color illustration, Ocilka Collection   16   30   45   75

6475 Vat Cars. See Chapter XII, Vat Cars

6477 BULKHEAD CAR WITH PLASTIC PIPES 1957-58, red base, black bulkheads, white letters, stakes, called "Miscellaneous Car," bar-end metal trucks
(A) Bar-end metal trucks, magnetic couplers   13   25   35   60
(B) Timken trucks, disc couplers, Pauli Collection   13   25   35   60

6500 FLAT WITH BONANZA PLANE 1962, 65, black flat car, white lettering, no number on car, Timken trucks, disc couplers, red and white plane, one wing lettered "N2742B," see color illustration
(A) Plane has red top and white bottom. Catalano comment
                                                32   65   85 145
(B) Plane has white top, red bottom. Catalano comment 37   75 100 175
(C) Same as (B), but gray "General" flat car, Blotner Collection
                                                37   75 100 175

6501 FLAT WITH JET BOAT 1963, red base, white lettered "LIONEL," mold #6511-2, Timken trucks, disc couplers, boat with white hull, brown decal, no lettering, boat uses baking soda mixed with water to create a gas given off at nozzle   17   30   40   70

6502-50 FLAT WITH BRIDGE GIRDER 1962, No number, blue unpainted plastic car, mold #6511-2, orange unpainted Lionel bridge side, Timken trucks, fixed couplers
(A) Blue unpainted plastic   1   1.50   2   4
(B) Deeper blue unpainted plastic   1   1.50   2   4
(C) Same as (A) but one disc coupler, one fixed coupler 1   1.50   2   4

6502-75 FLAT WITH BRIDGE GIRDER 1962, probably no number, blue car with white lettering and orange girder, mold 6511-2, Morse observation **NRS**

6511 FLAT WITH PIPES 1954-56, white lettering, black stakes, three aluminum colored plastic pipes, bar-end metal trucks, steel truck mounting plate
(A) Brown flatcar, white lettering, magnetic tab couplers 3   7   9   12
(B) Dark red flat car, white lettering, magnetic couplers   3   7   9   12
(C) Same as (B) but die-cast truck mounting bracket   3   7   9   12

6512 CHERRY PICKER CAR 1962-63, black or blue base, mold #6511-2, white letters, no number on car, orange structure at end of ladder with gray man inside, structure swivels to outside, black metal ladder extends twice the length of unextended ladder, gray superstructure holds ladder, Timken trucks, disc couplers
(A) Black base   19   35   50   85
(B) Blue base   **NRS**

6518 TRANSFORMER CAR 1956-58, gray die-cast depressed center car, black transformer, four trucks, for O Gauge only, will not pass through 0-27 switches, Knight comment   18   35   55   85

6519 ALLIS CHALMERS 1958-61, condenser car, orange base, blue letters, gray condenser held by metal bars, two brakewheels, often broken, Timken trucks, disc couplers
(A) Orange base   11   18   25   40
(B) Darker orange base   11   20   30   50

6544 MISSILE FIRING CAR 1960-64, blue frame, gray launcher, red firing knob, four white small rockets, Timken trucks, disc couplers, two brakewheels
(A) White lettered console, Degano comment   14   23   33   55
(B) Black lettered console, Degano comment   20   35   70 110

6561 REEL CAR WITH DEPRESSED CENTER 1953-56, die-cast gray frame, black lettering, two plastic reels marked "LIONEL," wound with aluminum coil, same base as searchlight car with modification to hold reels, steps, two brakewheels, bar-end metal trucks, see color illustration
(A) Gray plastic reels   6   12   15   25
(B) Orange plastic reels, Pauli collection   6   12   15   25

6630 IRBM LAUNCHER 1960-64, black car, white letters, blue superstructure with black missile firing ramp, pushing levers cock launching unit, ramp rises to a 30 to 45 degree angle prior to takeoff due to air pressure generated by bellows at front end, red and white missile with blue tip, arch bar trucks with fixed couplers   17   35   45   65

6640 U S M C LAUNCHER 1960, olive drab car and superstructure, black firing ramp, same mechanism as 6630, white rocket with blue tip
                                                20   35   50   85

6650 I R B M LAUNCHER 1959-63, red car base, mold 6424-11, Die 2, blue superstructure, white letters, black firing ramp, white and red missile with blue nose, same mechanism for 6630, Timken trucks, disc couplers
                                                13   25   35   60

6651 U S M C CANNON Circa 1960-61, not catalogued, olive drab car, gun and superstructure, mold #6511-2, white lettering, fires four projectiles, Timken trucks, disc-operating couplers   17   35   50   75

6660 FLAT CAR WITH CRANE 1958, dark red flat, mold #6424-11, white lettering, two black metal bases, outriggers, ochre-boom, Timken trucks, disc couplers
(A) Silver crank handles, hook on cable end, Catalano comment
                                                17   35   55   70
(B) Black crank handles, round bar magnet inside of red plastic housing on cable end, Catalano comment   17   35   55   70

6670 FLAT CAR WITH BOOM 1959-60, red unpainted body, yellow boom, no outriggers, Timken trucks, disc-operating couplers. Note that two varieties follow. We would like to learn which of these types came with which sets.
(A) Darker red body, mold 6511-2, "6670" to right of "LIONEL", Fleming Collection   13   25   35   50
(B) Brighter red body, mold 6424-11, "6670" to left of "LIONEL", Fleming Collection   13   25   35   50

6800 FLAT WITH AIRPLANE 1957-60, red car, mold #6424-11, black and yellow Beechcraft Bonanza airplane
(A) Plane with black upper and yellow lower fuselage, Timken trucks, disc couplers, "6800" to left of "LIONEL" 16   25   38   55
(B) Plane with yellow upper and black lower fuselage, metal trucks attach via metal plates and slots and screws, "6800" to right of "LIONEL"
                                                16   25   38   55
(C) Same as (A), but lighter red body which has four off-center holes as in 6805, mold 6424-11, Ocilka Collection   16   25   38   55

6801 FLAT WITH BOAT 1957-60, red plastic body, white lettering, boat usually with cream deck and clear windshield, boat numbered 6801-60, Timken trucks, disc couplers, "6801" usually left of "LIONEL"
(A) Turquoise boat hull, flat car mold #6511-2 12   22   35   55
(B) Same as (A) but mold #6424-11, Warswick Collection 12   22   35   55
(C) Medium blue hull, flat car mold #6511-2   12   22   35   55
(D) Brownish-yellow hull   12   22   35   55
(E) White hull, brown deck, bar-end metal trucks, metal plates fasten trucks to base, "6801" to right of "LIONEL," flat car mold #6511-2
                                                12   22   35   55

6802 FLAT WITH BRIDGE 1958-59, red flat, white lettering, black plastic bridge sides lettered in white "U.S. STEEL," one brakewheel, "6802" to left of "LIONEL," Timken trucks, disc couplers
(A) Flat car mold #6424-11   4   7   11   17
(B) Flat car mold #6511-2, Pauli Collection   4   7   11   17

6803 FLAT CAR WITH TANK AND TRUCK 1958-59, two gray U.S.M.C. vehicles, tank and truck with microwave disc, flat car mold #6424-11, Timken trucks, disc couplers   20   35   45   70

6804 FLAT WITH U.S.M.C. TRUCKS 1958-59, red plastic flat, mold #6424-11, white lettering, #6804 to left of "LIONEL," gray U.S.M.C. trucks, one with microwave disc, one with two guns   22   35   45   70

6805 ATOMIC DISPOSAL FLAT CAR 1958-59, red plastic car, mold #6424-11, white letters, "6805" on left side, two Super 0 rails run car length, two removable grayish-tan or gray disposal containers with red and black lettered "RADIOACTIVE WASTE" in black and "DANGER" in red, each letter of "DANGER" is underlined, containers have red flashing lights, bar-end metal trucks, magnetic tab couplers. The gray canisters are much rarer than the grayish-tan. However, the Fundimensions' re-run comes with gray canisters. Is there a way to discriminate the Fundimensions' production from the earlier gray canisters? Lebo comment.
(A) Gray canisters   **NRS**
(B) Grayish-tan canisters   13   25   35   60

6806 FLAT WITH U.S.M.C. TRUCKS 1958-59, red plastic flat, mold #6424-11, white lettering, "6806" on left side, Timken trucks, disc couplers

113

6801

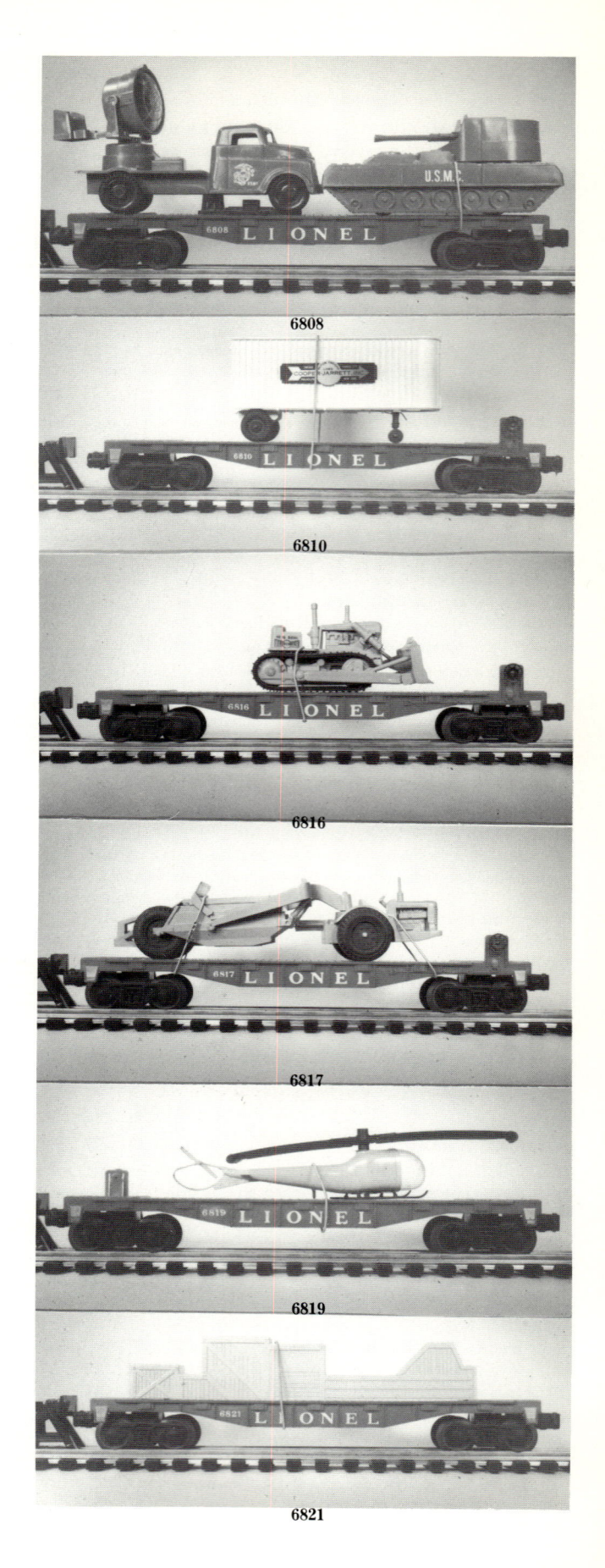

6803

6804

6805

6806

6807

6808

6810

6816

6817

6819

6821

114

(A) Two gray plastic U.S.M.C. trucks: one with radar disc truck, other a hospital truck with U.S. Navy insignia on van rear   21   35   45   75
(B) Gray U.S.M.C. radar disc truck, and gray plastic open-windowed snack bar truck with lettering "MOBILE USO CANTEEN" with small chimney, door with white anchor, Lionel Train & Seashell Museum comment.   **NRS**

6807 LIONEL FLAT WITH BOAT 1958-59, red plastic flat, mold #6511-2, white lettering, "6807" on left, large gray amphibious type boat, known as DKW, Timken trucks, disc couplers   21   35   50   80

6808 LIONEL FLAT WITH U.S.M.C. TRUCKS 1958-59, red plastic flat, mold #6424, "6808" on left, Timken trucks, disc couplers, one U.S.M.C. gray mobile searchlight truck, one gray two gun tank   21   35   50   80

6809 LIONEL FLAT WITH U.S.M.C. TRUCKS 1958-59, red plastic flat, mold #6424-11, white lettering, "6809" on left, Timken trucks, disc couplers, gray U.S.M.C. trucks: one with cannon, other hospital van with U.S. Navy insignia
(A) Hospital van with Navy insignia on one side   21   35   45   75
(B) Hospital van with Navy insignia on both sides   21   35   45   75

6810 LIONEL FLAT WITH TRAILER 1958, red plastic flat, mold #6424-1, white lettering, "6810" on left, Timken trucks, disc couplers, white trailer, black painted plate with copper colored arrow, black and white lettered "COOPER JARRETT INC"   9   15   20   30

6812 TRACK MAINTENANCE CAR 1959, red plastic flat, white lettering "6812" on left, Timken trucks, disc couplers, superstructure with blue men, platform cranks up and if cranked up far enough will come out
(A) All dark yellow superstructure   9   17   25   40
(B) Superstructure with black base and gray top, flat car mold #6511-2
                                         9   17   25   40
(C) Gray base, black top   9   17   25   40
(D) All cream base and top   25   40   60   100
(E) Dark yellow base, gray top, Askenas comment   **NRS**
(F) Black base, black top, Askenas comment   **NRS**
(G) Black base, dark yellow top, Askenas comment **NRS**
(H) Light yellow base and top, Askenas comment   **NRS**

6816 FLAT WITH ALLIS-CHALMERS BULLDOZER 1959-60, red or black plastic flat, mold #6424-11, white letters, "6816" on left, Timken trucks, disc couplers, orange plastic Allis-Chalmers bulldozer, black rubber treads, lettered "HD 16 Diesel" torque converter
(A) Red plastic car   15   30   45   70
(B) Black plastic car, Wirtz Collection   **NRS**

6817 FLAT WITH ALLIS-CHALMERS SCRAPER 1959-60, red plastic flat, mold #6424-11, white lettering, "6817" on left, Timken trucks, disc couplers, orange plastic scraper with black rubber tires   16   30   45   70

6818 TRANSFORMER CAR 1958, red plastic base, white lettering, one brakewheel, black plastic transformer with heat-stamped lettering on one side, Timken trucks, disc couplers
(A) Base mold #6424-11   5   10   12   25
(B) Base mold #6511-2   5   10   12   25

6819 FLAT WITH HELICOPTER 1959-60, red plastic car, mold #6424-11, white lettering, "6819" on left, Timken trucks, disc couplers, gray helicopter with separate yellow plastic tail section, single black rotor, clear plastic nose, operating-type helicopter without launching mechanism, Ocilka Collection   9   17   24   40

6820 FLAT WITH HELICOPTER 1960-61, blue painted black plastic flat car, white letters, "6820" on left, mold #6424-11, Timken trucks, disc couplers, gray Navy helicopter, separate yellow plastic tail section, single black rotor, clear plastic nose, with "Little John" missiles, operating type helicopter without launching mechanism
(A) As described above   16   35   45   60
(B) Same as (A), except darker blue flat car, Blotner Collection
                                        16   35   45   60

6821 FLAT WITH CRATES 1959-60, red unpainted plastic flat car, mold 6424-11, Die 2, white lettering "6821" on left side, Ocilka Collection. The same crate structure had been used on the 3444 Animated Gondola, La Voie observation   7   15   19   25

6822 SEARCHLIGHT CAR See "Cranes and Searchlights"

6823 FLAT WITH IRBM MISSILES 1959-60, red plastic car, mold #6424-11, white lettering, "6823" on left, Timken trucks, disc couplers, two red and white missiles with blue tips, front of one missile fits into rear of other missile, same missiles as on 6630 and 6640 missile launching cars
                                        12   22   31   45

6825 FLAT WITH TRESTLE BRIDGE 1959-60, red plastic car, mold #6511-2, white lettering, "6825" on left side, Timken trucks, disc couplers, with bridge apparently designed for HO rolling stock
(A) Black bridge   8   15   20   30
(B) Gray bridge   8   15   20   30

6826 FLAT WITH CHRISTMAS TREES 1959-60, red plastic base, mold #6511-2, "6826" on left, Timken trucks, disc couplers, several scrawny trees
                                        14   25   32   50

6827 FLAT WITH P & H STEAM SHOVEL 1960-63, black plastic car, mold #6424-11, Die 2, white lettering, "6827" on left side, Timken trucks, disc couplers, came as kit, shown assembled, one long stake on car, Ocilka observation   14   30   45   70

6828 FLAT WITH P & H CRANE 1960-63, 68, black or red plastic flat car, mold #6424-11, "6828" on left, Timken trucks, disc couplers, crane with black chassis, yellow or yellow/orange cab, lettered "HARNISCHFEGER MILWAUKEE WISCONSIN" and "P & H" embossed on cab and on boom near top
(A) Yellow cab, black flat car   16   25   38   60
(B) Yellow-orange cab, red flat car   16   25   38   60

6830 FLAT WITH OPERATING SUBMARINE 1960-61, blue plastic car, mold #6511-2, white letters, "6830" on left, Timken trucks, disc couplers, "U.S. NAVY SUBMARINE 6830," gray with black letters
                                        16   25   38   60

6844 FLAT WITH MISSILES Circa 1960, black plastic flat car, mold #6424-11, white lettering, "6844" to left, Timken trucks, disc couplers, gray superstructure holds six white Lionel missiles
(A) As described above   16   25   35   60
(B) Same as (A), but red unpainted plastic flat car, light gray missile superstructure, Art Tom Collection   **NRS**

NO NUMBER See 1877, 3309, 3349

One of the areas for future research is determining the catalogue numbers and loads of the no number flat cars, gondolas, cabooses and hoppers produced by Lionel. The following is a listing of reported cars. One method of identification is from original boxes and/or original set components. If you have "no number" cars in original boxes or with original sets, we would appreciate very much your assistance.

(A) Red plastic flat car, mold #6511-2, white lettered "LIONEL" (serif or sans-serif?), Timken trucks, one disc coupler, one fixed coupler, Pauli Collection   1   1.50   2   3
(B) Same as (A) but two fixed couplers   1   1.50   2   3
(C) Olive drab flat car. See 6401-50   1   1.50   2   3
(D) Flat with yellow autos. See 6406   1   1.50   2   3
(E) Red plastic flat car, mold #6511-2, white lettered "LIONEL" (serif or sans-serif?), arch bar trucks, two fixed couplers, no brakewheel, Kotil Collection   1   1.50   2   3
(F) Same as (E) but no lettering, Timken trucks   1   1.50   2   3
(G) Black plastic flat car, mold #6511-2, white lettered "LIONEL" (serif or sans-serif?) arch bar trucks, two fixed couplers, no brakewheel, Kotil Collection   1   1.50   2   3
(H) Blue plastic flat car, mold #6511-2, no lettering, arch bar trucks, two fixed couplers, no brakewheel, Kotil Collection   1   1.50   2   3
(I) Same as (H) but Timken trucks, Kotil Collection   1   1.50   2   3
(J) Gray flat car with green tank. The flat car is embossed with mold 1877-3 and also embossed "MADE IN U.S. OF AMERICA/THE LIONEL CORPORATION/NEW YORK, N.Y." on its underside. No other lettering or numbering is present. Car has Timken plastic trucks with one disc-operating and one dummy coupler. The moss-green tank has a swivel turret and two molded green plastic wheel/axle sets. The tank is lettered "Q" inside the turret. This car came in a military set made for Sears with a 240 locomotive. For details of this set, see the entries for the 240 steam loco and the 3666 cannon-firing box car. Vergonet, Bohn and Jarman Collections. Illustrated on page 110.   50   100   150   200

(K) 6511-type flat, all red, white "LIONEL," no number, arch bar trucks, fixed couplers, no brakewheel, no load, 6511-2 mold, may be 6409-25 from set 11311 in 1963 catalogue, page 3, reader comments invited, Schreiner Collection   **NRS**

6828

6844

6823

6825

6826

6827

6830

116

Chapter VIII
GONDOLAS

	Gd.	V.G.	Exc.	Mt.

1002 LIONEL 1949, white lettering, from the Scout set, with Scout couplers, 8 inches long

(A) Blue unpainted plastic	1	1.50	2	3
(B) Black unpainted plastic	1	1.50	2	3
(C) Silver with black lettering	40	60	100	150
(D) Yellow with black lettering	30	60	100	150
(E) Red with white lettering				NRS
(F) Light blue with black lettering				NRS

2452 PENNSYLVANIA 1945-47, black body, white lettering, black metal underframe held to body by four filister head screws in corners of body floor, steps at corners, builtdate "NEW 12-45", usually brakewheels; always found with staple-end trucks.

Body Mold Type Ia, rectangular opening approximately 2 x 2 in center of floor in body does not go through metal frame. The opening was designed to fit a frame supporting the electronic control unit found in No. 4452.

(A) 1945, whirly wheels, thick axles, early coil couplers with fiber bar showing on bottom, one pick up shoe on each end, 2452 stamped in silver on bottom, Vagner Collection   2 3 5 8
(B) 1945, same as (A) except dished wheels, without raised area around axles on back of wheels, Kotil and Vagner Collections   2 3 5 8
(C) 1946, same as (A) except thin axles and regular wheels, Vagner Collection   2 3 4 7
(D) 1947, regular wheels, late coil couplers with pickup shoe on metal plate which is fastened to axles. otherwise same as (A), Kotil and Rohlfing Collections   2 3 4 7
(E) 1947, same as (D) except stamped 2452X on bottom indicating no brakewheels were installed, Kotil Collection,   2 3 4 7
Body mold Type Ib, round opening approximately 1" in diameter in center of floor in body does not go through metal frame.
(F) 1947, regular wheels, late coil couplers, brakewheels and steps, not stamped on bottom otherwise same as (D), Vagner Collection   2 3 5 7

(G) 1947, same as (F) except stamped 2452X on bottom indicating no brakewheels were installed. Vagner Collection   2 3 5 7

3444 ERIE 1957-59, cop chases hobo, vibrator motor, unpainted red plastic body with white lettering, on/off switch, "BLT 2-57"
(A) Tan colored crates   17 30 40 55
(B) Clear unpainted plastic crates, Piker Collection   NRS

3562-1 A.T.&.S.F. 1954, operating barrel, car man "unloads" barrels, black with white lettering, "Built 5-54," six wooden barrels, plastic unloading bin
(A) Black body with black central barrel trough, Catalano observation   25 50 75 100
(B) Black body with yellow trough   25 50 75 100

3562-25 A.T.&.S.F. 1954, operating barrel car, man "unloads" barrels, "NEW 5-54," six wooden barrels, plastic unloading bin
(A) Gray-painted plastic body with blue lettering, bar-end metal trucks, magnetic couplers, body has molded plastic tab to hold base upon which a man is attached so that barrels are not dumped in transit. A metal tab fits into the gap between the plastic tab and the side edge to lock the man into place, Lemieux Collection   10 15 20 40
(B) Same as (A), but does not have molded plastic tab, Lemieux Collection
    10 15 20 40
(C) Gray with red lettering   40 60 80 150

3562-50 A.T.&.S.F. 1955-57, operating barrel car, man "unloads" barrels, "NEW 5-54," six stained wooden barrels, plastic unloading bin, plastic tab to lock base holding man into place, bar-end metal trucks, magnetic couplers with tabs
(A) Bright yellow unpainted plastic, black lettering   10 15 25 50
(B) Darker yellow painted clear plastic body, black lettering, LaVoie Collection   20 35 50 70

3562-75 A.T.&.S.F. 1958, operating barrel car, man "unloads" barrels, "NEW 5-54," six wooden barrels, plastic unloading bin, orange with black lettering   16 30 40 70
(C) Cream painted clear plastic body, black lettering, black painted trough,

6462 "N" in second panel from left, "N.Y.C" in serif letters, line under "6462," two lines of weights, no brakewheel, no steps, no "new" date, magnetic tab couplers, bar-end trucks.

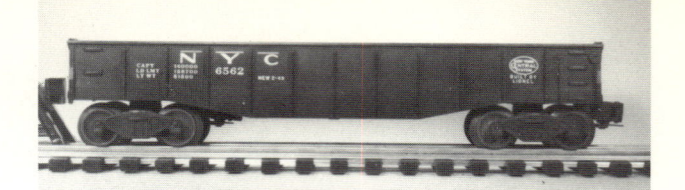

6562 "N" in third panel, "N.Y.C." is overscored, "N.Y.C." in sans serif lettering, no line under or over "6562," three lines of weights, no brakewheels, no steps, "NEW 2-49," magnetic tab couplers, bar-end trucks.

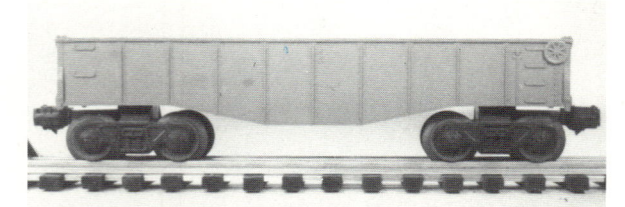

Catalogue number not known. Note molded brakewheel.

Art Tom Collection **NRS**

4452 PENNSYLVANIA 1946-48, special black gondola with white lettering for electronic control set with electronic control unit 30 45 60 80

6002 N.Y.C. 1949, black unpainted plastic body with white lettering, "BLT 2-49," 9 9/16 inches long, Scout trucks with magnetic couplers
 2 6 8 15

6012 LIONEL 1955-56, black unpainted plastic with white lettering, 8 inches long, no brakewheel, bar-end metal trucks, magnetic tab couplers, Cole and Kruelle Collections 1 1.50 2 3

6032 LIONEL 1952-53, black unpainted plastic, Scout trucks, operating magnetic couplers, 8 inches long, no brakewheel, white lettering
 1 1.50 2 3

6042 LIONEL Uncatalogued, 8 1/8 inches long, detailed undercarriage and box interior, unpainted plastic, white lettering, fixed couplers open at top, brakewheel embossed in plastic car sides, red or white canisters
(A) Black unpainted plastic, arch bar trucks, Kotil Collection
 1 1.50 2 3
(B) Blue unpainted plastic, arch bar trucks, Kotil Collection
 1 1.50 2 3
(C) Blue unpainted plastic, Timken trucks, Kotil Collection
 1 1.50 2 3

6042-125 LIONEL same as 6042 but blue unpainted plastic, numbered "6042"
(A) Blue unpainted plastic 1 1.50 2 3
(B) Shinier blue unpainted plastic 1 1.50 2 3

6062 N.Y.C. 1959-64, glossy black plastic body, white lettering, "N.Y.C" overscored, "6062" underscored, "NEW 2-49," Timken trucks, disc-operating couplers
(A) Detailed plastic undercarriage similar to 6042, "6462-2" mold, Schreiner Collection 3 7 10 15
(B) Stamped metal undercarriage similar to 6462, Schreiner Collection
 3 7 10 15

6062-50 N.Y.C. circa 1968-69, glossy black unpainted plastic, "N.Y.C." overscored, "6062" underscored (not 6062-50), no "NEW 2-49," (compare with 6062 previously), 9 9/16 inches long, detailed plastic undercarriage, no brakewheels molded on side, body mold "6462-2" on base underside, 6062-50 appears only on the box end. Car has Timken plastic trucks, one disc-operating coupler and one fixed coupler, two red unpainted plastic canisters with "LIONEL" molded on top. This car came in an orange and white box lettered "LIONEL" in large white letters and then "LIONEL TOY CORPORATION/HAGERSTOWN, MARYLAND." Talley and Falter Collections 2 4 8 14

6112 LIONEL Circa 1956-58, 8 inches long, plain undercarriage and box interior, disc-operating couplers. Truck undersides come with many different numbers, for example, 5 and 3, 7 and 2, 2 and 0, 4 and 8 etc., appear on blue cars, according to Griesbeck
(A) White unpainted plastic body, black lettering, four red canisters, Timken trucks 4 7 11 15
(B) Blue unpainted plastic body, white lettering. Timken trucks, 3 black-lettered white canisters, hard to find, Bohn comment 1 1.50 6 3
(C) Black with white lettering, Timken trucks, three red canisters, Schreiner Collection 1 1.50 2 3
(D) Same as (C) but bar-end metal trucks, sheet metal clip holds truck to frame, Kotil Collection 1 1.50 2 3

(6112) LIONEL Circa 1960, olive drab or blue, 8 inches long, plain undercarriage and box interior, brakewheels molded on side, body mold number "6112-86" molded into base underside, Timken trucks, catalogue number uncertain, parentheses indicate number does not appear on car, original box will probably provide catalogue number
(A) Unpainted blue plastic, one tab and one fixed coupler, Schreiner Collection 1 2 3 4
(B) Unpainted olive drab plastic, disc-operating couplers, came with olive drab flat (3349) and olive drab work caboose (6824), set number unknown. Source: Catalano and Wilson 7 11 18 29
(C) Same as (A), but two non-operating couplers. This car was apparently sold in set no. 11420 (1964) with a 1061 loco and 6167-25 caboose. The gondola box was probably numbered 6042-250, but confirmation of this is requested. Light Collection 1 2 3 4

6112-135 LIONEL Black plastic body, 8 inches long, operating tab couplers, three white "LIONEL AIR ACTIVATED CONTAINER," numbered "6112" on car although box numbered "6112-135," Catalano observation
 1 2 3 4

6142 LIONEL 1961-66, 70, 8 1/8 inches long, detailed undercarriage, box interior and sides, unpainted plastic, white lettering, Timken trucks, one disc-operating coupler, one fixed coupler
(A) Black unpainted plastic 1 1.50 2 3
(B) Black unpainted plastic, 1970, with Bettendorf trucks (introduced by MPC about 1970), one manual-operating coupler with plastic tab, one fixed coupler with open top, with "old" Lionel number, probably from leftover bodies. (Similar combinations are also seen with hoppers.) 1 1.50 2 3

6142-50 LIONEL 1961-63, Unpainted shiny green plastic, white lettering "LIONEL" and "6142," Timken plastic trucks with one disc-operating and one dummy coupler, one molded brakewheel each side, body mold 6112-86, no built date, two red canisters. Possibly included in 1065 diesel set in 1961. I. D. Smith observation 1 1.50 2 3

Need information as to whether 6142-50 has a body mold number.

6142-75 LIONEL Same as 6142 but unpainted blue plastic, 1961-63, numbered "6142," with white canisters, 6112-88. Need information as to whether 6142-75 has a body mold number 1 1.50 2 3

6142-100 LIONEL Light green unpainted plastic body, no lettering, mold no. 6112-85. Molded brakewheels, Timken plastic trucks, one disc-operating and one dummy coupler, two white 6112-88 canisters, part of set no. 11430. Further confirmation rquested, Winton Collection 1 1.50 2 3

118

2452

2452[B or C]

2452[F]

3444

4452

6002

6012

6032

6042

6062

6112

6142

6162

6162-60

6342

6462

[Photo: gondola cars with barrels, labeled 3562-1, 3562-25, 3562-25, 3562-50, 3562-75]

6142-150 LIONEL Same as 6142 above but unpainted blue plastic, circa 1961-63?, with "6142" numbered cable reels. Need information as to whether 6142-150 has a body mold number   1   1.50   2   3

6142-175 LIONEL Probably similar to 6142 above although body's part number differs from previous entries, circa 1961-63? numbered "6142." Need information as to whether 6142-175 has a body mold number   1   1.50   2   3

6162 N.Y.C. 1961-69, unpainted plastic body, white lettering, 9 9/16 inches long, "N.Y.C." overscored, "6162" underscored
(A) Red, no "new" date, Timken trucks, one disc-operating coupler, one fixed coupler, heavy heat-stamped letters   2   5   7   10
(B) Blue, "NEW 2-49," Timken trucks, two disc-operating couplers   2   5   7   10
(C) Aqua blue, "NEW 2-49," Timken trucks, two disc-operating couplers, two brake wheels. Pauli Collection   2   5   7   10
(D) Blue, no "new" date, Timken trucks, disc-operating couplers, Griesbeck Collection   3   5   7   10

6162-60 ALASKA 1959, yellow unpainted plastic body, dark blue lettering, bar-end metal trucks, magnetic tab couplers, four white canisters with set #1611, 9 9/16 inches long. This has also been reported with plastic trucks with disc couplers. We need reader confirmation of both types
   25   37   50   75

6342 N.Y.C. 1956-58, and 1966-69, special gondola for culvert loader with black metal channel, culverts fall down channel, 9 9/16 inches long, red unpainted plastic, white lettering, "N.Y.C." overscored, three lines of weights, "6342" not overscored, came with 348 culvert unloader
(A) No "new" date, Timken trucks, 1965-69, Hutchinson observation
   7   10   15   25
(B) "NEW 2-49," bar-end metal trucks, magnetic tab couplers
   7   10   15   25
(C) "NEW 2-49," orange-red plastic body   7   10   15   25

6452 PENNSYLVANIA 1949, see next entry

6462 PENNSYLVANIA 1947-48, short, 8 inches long, dark maroon plastic body painted black, white lettering, quarter sized hole in center of plastic body, metal underframe, stamped "6452" "6462" on car sides, brakewheel disc with center holes, without brakewheel, staple-end metal trucks, coil couplers, sliding shoes.   1   1.50   2   5

6462 N.Y.C. 1949, 9 9/16 inches long. Note that variation letters differ from those in the last edition. The cars are now arranged by color, although some varieties are found under 6462-25, 6462-75 and 6462-125. Note: Black cars come with 6 straight-sided solid wooden drums. Other colors came with 6 brown stained turned wood barrels with ribs, Bohn comment

BLACK CARS

(A) Unpainted black plastic body, "N" in second from left panel, "6462" underscored, staple-end metal trucks, "NEW 2-49," three lines of weights, high gloss metal underframe, brakewheels and steps   2   3   5   8
(B) Same as (A) but black painted opaque blue plastic, Kotil Collection
   2   3   5   8
(C) Same as (A) but black painted gray plastic, Kotil Collection
   2   3   5   8
(D) Same as (A) but black painted green plastic, Kotil Collection
   2   3   5   8
(E) Same as (A) but flat black painted brown plastic, Dorn Collection
   2   3   5   8
(F) Same as (A) but only two lines of weights, no brakewheels
   2   3   5   8
(G) Flat black painted shiny black plastic body, "N" in second from left panel, "6462" underscored, "NEW 2-49," two lines of weights, no brakewheels, bar-end metal trucks, magnetic couplers   2   3   5   8
(H) Same as (G) but unpainted black plastic, Kotil Collection
   2   3   5   8
(I) Flat black painted shiny black plastic, "N" in second from left panel, "6462" underscored, no "new" date, two lines of weights, no brakewheels, Type VI bar-end metal trucks, magnetic couplers, Crile and Clark Collections   2   3   5   8
(J) Same as (I), but unpainted black plastic body, Kaiser Collection
   2   3   4   6

RED CARS   1950-52, 1954-56

(L) Dark painted light colored plastic body, metal underframe, no lines over "N.Y.C.," "N" in second panel from left, line under "6462," no "new" date, two lines of weights, no brakewheel, no steps, bar-end metal trucks
   2   5   8   10
(M) Same as (L) but shiny red painted clear plastic, Kotil Collection
   2   5   8   10
(N) Same as (L) but shiny red painted light blue plastic, Kotil Collection
   2   5   8   10
(O) Bright red paint over black plastic, white lettering, metal underframe, no lines over "N.Y.C.," "N" in second panel from left, line under "6462," no "new" date, two lines of weights, no brakewheel, no steps, bar-end metal trucks   2   5   8   10
(P) "General" red paint over dark gray plastic body, white lettering, "N" in second panel from left, line under "6462," "NEW 2-49," staple-end metal trucks, two lines of weights, two brakewheels, Pauli Collection
   2   5   8   10

120

(Q) Same as (L), but same maroon color as 6456 Lehigh Valley hopper, Sipple Collection   2   4   8   10

(R) Dark red paint over clear plastic, white lettering, metal underframe, no line under "6462," "NEW 2-49," staple-end metal trucks, three lines of weights, steps and two brakewheels, Falter Collection   2   4   8   10

(S) Same as (R), except medium red paint and two lines of weights, Lahti Collection   2   4   8   10

GREEN CARS 1954-56

(T) Green paint over black plastic body, white lettering, metal underframe, lines over "N.Y.C.," "N" in third panel from left, line under "6462," "NEW 2-49," bar-end metal trucks, three lines of weights, no brakewheel, no steps   3   5   9   14

(U) Darker green body than (S), white lettering, dull black metal underframe, no lines over "N.Y.C.," "N" in second panel from left, line under "6462." no "new" date, bar-end metal trucks, tab magnetic couplers, two lines of weights, no brakewheels, no steps, 3/16 inch diameter hole in underframe center   3   5   9   14

(V) Flat medium green paint over black plastic body, white lettering, metal underframe, no lines over "N.Y.C.," line under "6462," no "new" date, metal trucks, magnetic couplers, two lines of weights, Warswick Collection   3   5   9   12

(W) Same as (T) but no tabs on couplers, no hole in underframe, dark cream lettering, two brakewheels, Pauli Collection. This version may not have originally come with brakeweels. We would appreciate it if our readers would provide additional confirmation.   3   5   9   12

6462-25 Green painted black plastic body, very white lettering, metal underframe, no lines over "N.Y.C," "N" in second panel from left, line under "6462," no "new," two lines of weights, no hole in underframe, no steps, no brakewheels, bar-end metal trucks, magnetic couplers without tabs, numbered "6462" only, "6462-25" is catalogue number that appears on box

(A) Green painted black plastic body, Kotil Collection   3   5   9   12

(B) Darker green, than (A), Pauli Collection   3   5   9   12

6462-75 Red painted black plastic body, white lettering, lines over "N.Y.C.," "N" in third panel from left, "NEW 2-49," three lines of weights, bar-end metal trucks, magnetic couplers, numbered "6462," "6462-75" is catalogue number that appears on box.

(A) Bright red paint, Pauli Collection   3   5   9   14

(B) Shiny darker red, Kotil Collection   3   5   9   14

(C) Dull red, Kotil Collection   3   5   9   14

6462-125 Red unpainted plastic body, 1949 only, white lettering, metal underframe, lines over "N.Y.C.," "N" in third panel, line under "6462," "NEW 2-49," three lines of weights, no brakewheel, no steps, bar-end metal trucks, magnetic tab couplers, only "6462" appears on car, "6462-125" is catalogue number that appears on box. Also see 6562. Kotil Collection

(A) Dull red, Kotil Collection   3   5   9   14

(B) Shiny red, no line under 6462, Griesbeck Collection   3   5   9   14

6462-500 N.Y.C. Pink painted body, black lettering, from Girl's Set, lines over "N.Y.C.," "N" in third panel from left, line under "6462," "NEW 2-49," bar-end metal trucks, magnetic tab couplers, three lines of weights, no brakewheel, no steps, note that 6462, not 6462-500, appears on car   40   75   100   150

6562 N.Y.C. 1956-58, metal underframe, lines over "N.Y.C.," "N" in third panel from left, no line under "6562," "NEW 2-49," bar-end metal trucks, magnetic tab couplers, three lines of weights, no brakewheels, no steps, 9 9/16 inches long, 3/16 inch hole in center of metal base, Degano observation

(A) Unpainted gray plastic, maroon lettering, gray plastic is lighter and less shiny than (D), magnetic couplers with tabs, no mold number, metal base, Fleming Collection   7   13   25   40

(B) Red unpainted plastic body, white lettering   7   13   25   40

(C) Black unpainted plastic body, white lettering   7   13   25   40

(D) Unpainted gray plastic, red lettering, gray plastic is darker and more shiny than (A), magnetic couplers without tabs, no mold number, metal base, Fleming Collection.   7   12   25   40

6562-1 Red unpainted plastic body, white lettering, metal underframe, lines over "N.Y.C.," "N" in third panel, line under "6462," "NEW 2-49," bar-end metal trucks, magnetic tab couplers, three lines of weights, no brakewheel, no steps, came with four red canisters, box marked "6562-1" and "25" rubber stamped after "LIONEL" on box end, although only "6462" appeared on car.

This car with an unknown load also came in a box marked "6462-125." Kotil Collection   3   5   9   14

NO NUMBER 8 1/8 inches long, detailed undercarriage and box interior, blue unpainted plastic, no lettering, Timken trucks, fixed couplers, "61 12-86" mold number embossed in bottom, catalogue number not known, Schreiner Collection   1   1.50   2   3

NO NUMBER Green unpainted plastic, short gondola, length unknown, interior detail unknown, Timken trucks, one fixed coupler, one disc-operating coupler, mold number and catalogue number not known, Schreiner Collection   1   1.50   2   3

NOTE: On those 9 9/16" cars with a metal underframe, the mold number (part number) is under the metal under frame.

For a detailed analysis of 9 9/16" gondolas see Appendix by Richard Vagner

Chapter IX
HOPPERS AND DUMP CARS

Hopper Body Types

All trucks attached with metal plates have steps on side

Type I

Raised posts with screws for trucks

Trucks attached with metal plate, 2 screws

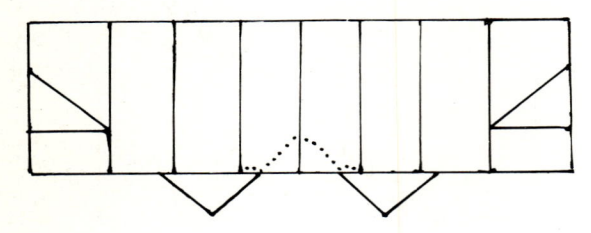

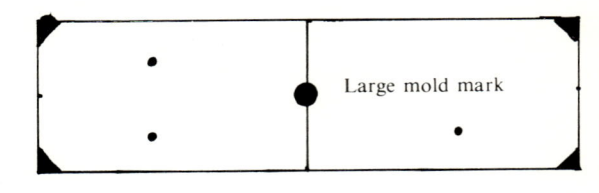

Large mold mark

Type II Same as I, but cutout for operating dump

Same as I, but cutout for operating dump

Type III

Raised posts with screws for trucks; metal plate, 2 screws

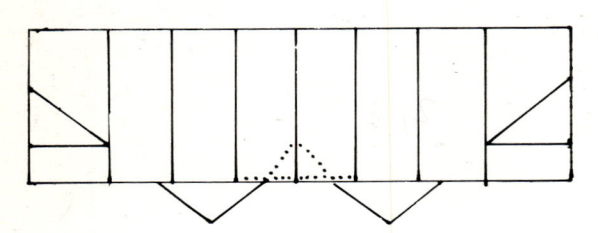

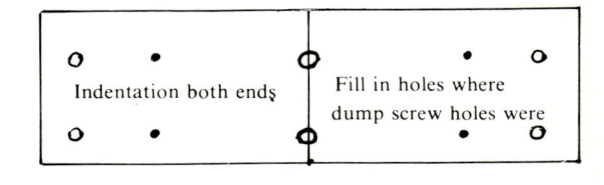

Indentation both ends   Fill in holes where dump screw holes were

Type IV Same as III, but cutout for operating dump

Same as II, but cutout for operating dump

Type V Same as III

Raised posts, no screws; metal plate with tub

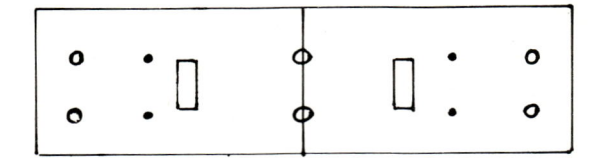

Type VI.

Rivet to post

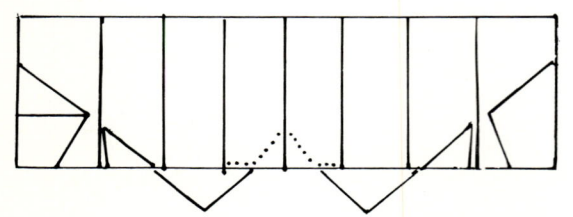

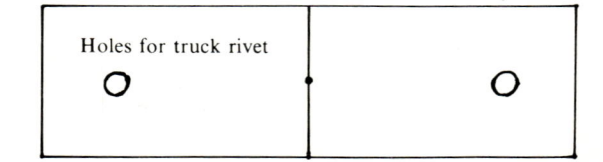

Holes for truck rivet

122

2456

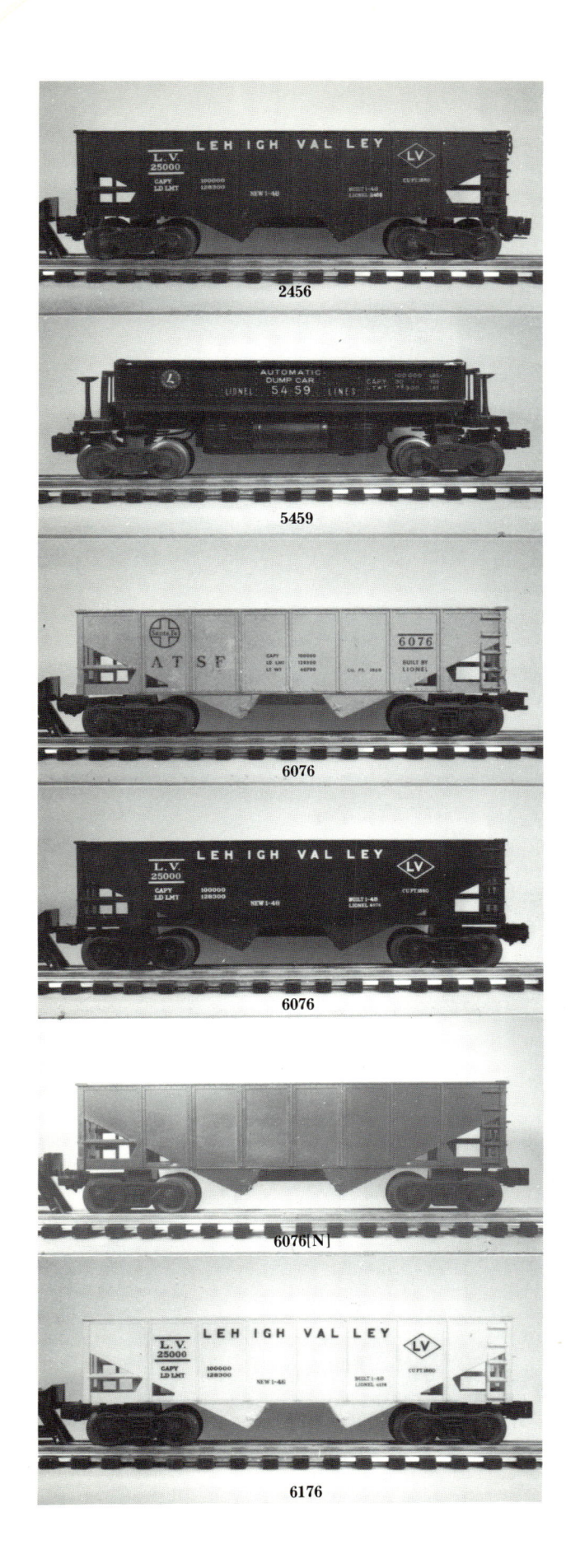

5459

6076

6076

6076[N]

6176

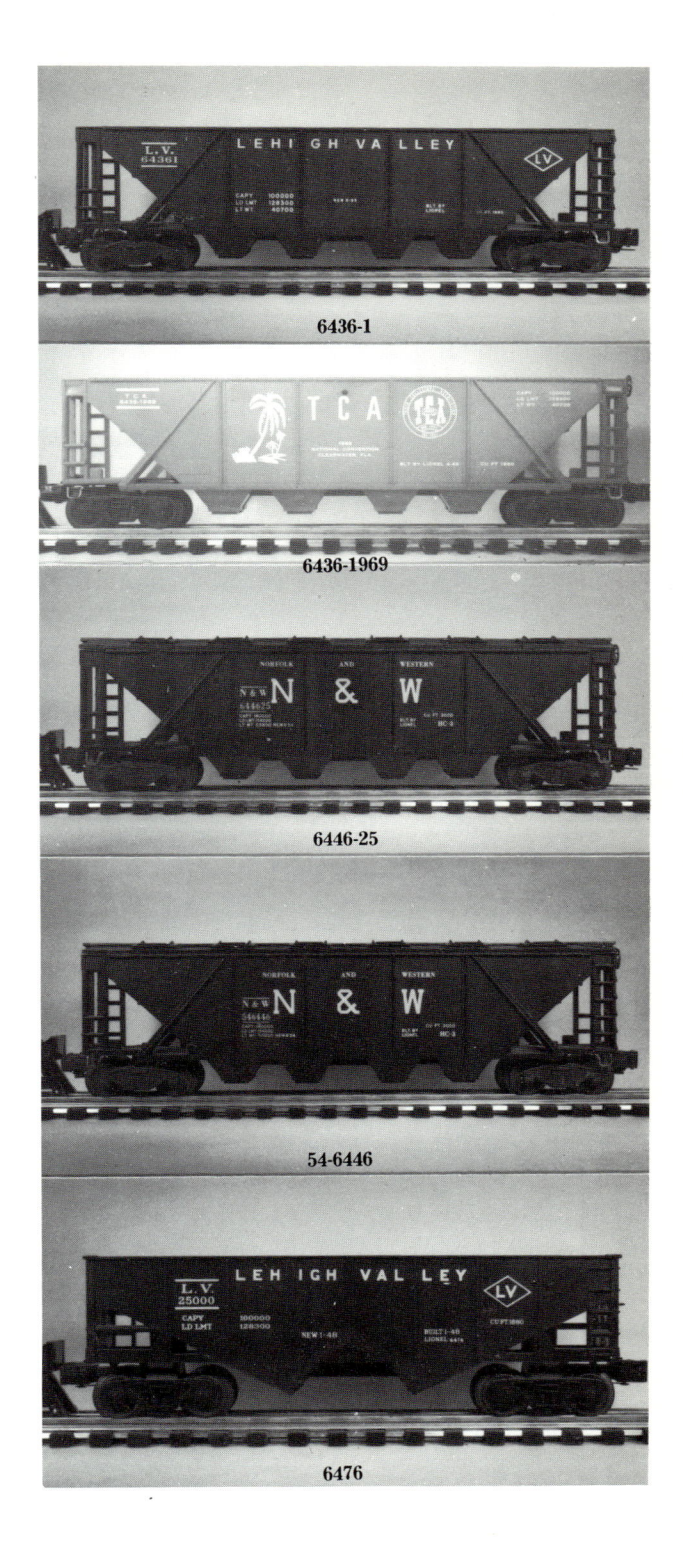

6436-1

6436-1969

6446-25

54-6446

6476

			Gd.	V.G.	Exc.	Mt.

2456 LEHIGH VALLEY Type I body, white lettering, "NEW 1-48," and "BLT-I-48," two brakewheels, staple-end metal trucks, coil couplers, steps, 8 9/16 inches long

(A) Flat black — 5 7 12 15
(B) Shiny black paint over marbled plastic — 5 7 12 15

2856 B & O 1946, scale detailed hopper car; catalogued but not manufactured — **Not Manufactured**

2956 B & O Circa 1946, scale detailed hopper car from 1940-42; black die-cast body, white lettering, "BLT 3-27," "532000," "2956," working die-cast bottom hatches, staple-end metal trucks, coil couplers, apparently not manufactured after 1942; car most likely converted from tinplate trucks to staple-end trucks by service station or owner — 90 160 200 320

3359-55 LIONEL LINES 1955, twin gray bins which tilt, red simulated power unit mounted on black bar-end metal trucks, magnetic tab couplers, came with two OTC contractor, long receiving bin and 96C controller — 9 15 20 30

3456 N & W 1951-55, black with white lettering, "BLT 8-50," "NEW 8-50," operating bottom hatches, steps, brakewheels, 8 9/16 inches long
(A) Black paint on colored plastic, Type II body, staple-end metal trucks — 12 20 25 40
(B) Black paint on brown plastic, Type IV body — 12 20 25 40
(C) Black paint on blue plastic, Type IV body — 12 20 25 40
(D) Light blue with red lettering — NRS
(E) Black paint on white plastic, type IV body, Kotil Collection — NRS

3459 LIONEL LINES 1946-48, "AUTOMATIC DUMP CAR," bin dumps, black frame and simulated dump mechanism, two brakewheels, staple-end metal trucks
(A) 1946, unpainted aluminum bin with blue lettering, staple-end metal trucks — 40 60 80 100
(B) 1946-47, black painted bin, white lettering, staple-end metal trucks — 9 15 20 30
(C) 1948, green painted bin, white lettering — 20 25 35 50

3469 LIONEL LINES 1949-55, "AUTOMATIC DUMP CAR," bin dumps, black frame and simulated dump mechanism, two brakewheels, bar-end metal trucks — 9 12 20 30

3559 COAL DUMP CAR 1946, rerun of 3659 prewar car with new staple-end metal trucks, black frame and end unit, red bin, silver/white "3559" rubber stamped on underside
(A) Early coil couplers, open truck underside — 7 10 15 25
(B) Regular coil couplers — 7 10 15 25

5459 LIONEL LINES 1946, "AUTOMATIC DUMP CAR" with green and white "ELECTRONIC CONTROL" decal, black car with white lettering, electronic control receiver hidden inside frame of car; staple-end metal trucks, coil-operated couplers — 22 35 50 80

546446 See 6446-1 or 6446-25.

6076 [A-C] A T S F 1963, Type VI body, gray plastic, black lettering, "BUILT BY LIONEL," no date, no brakewheels, special promotional set for Libby (#19263) 8 9/16 inches long
(A) Timken trucks, one disc-coupler, one fixed coupler — 9 15 20 30
(B) Arch bar trucks, fixed couplers — 9 15 20 30
(C) One Timken truck with disc coupler; one arch bar truck with fixed coupler — 9 15 20 30

6076 [D-J] LEHIGH VALLEY Type VI body, 8 9/16 inches long, no brakewheels
(D) Gray body, black lettering, "BUILT 1-48," no "new" date, Timken trucks, one disc coupler, one fixed coupler — 4 6 8 12
(E) Black body, white lettering, "BUILT 1-48," "NEW 1-48," Timken trucks, one disc coupler, one fixed coupler — 4 6 8 12
(F) Same as (E) but arch bar trucks, fixed couplers — 4 6 8 10
(G) Same as (E) but without "new" dates — 4 6 8 10
(H) Same as (E) but without "built" and "new" dates, Pauli Collection — 4 6 8 10
(I) Red with white lettering, "Built 1-48" "NEW 1-48," arch bar trucks fixed couplers — 4 6 8 10
(J) Same as (E) but fixed couplers, Kotil Collection — 4 6 8 10
(K) Dull yellow painted Type VI gray body, black lettering, "NEW 1-48", "BUILT 1-48", "CAPY 100000; LO LMT 128300; CU. FT. 1860". Timken plastic trucks, one disc-operating and one dummy coupler, no brakewheel, Sekely Collection — 2 3 5 6
(M) NO LETTERING, Type VI body, unpainted olive drab, Timken trucks, one disc-coupler, one fixed coupler, with open top, Wilson Collection — 1.50 2 3 5
(N) NO LETTERING, Type VI unpainted gray plastic body, Timken trucks, fixed couplers, Griesbeck and Kotil Collections — 1.50 2 3 5
(R) NO NUMBER LEHIGH VALLEY, black Type VI body, white lettered "CAPY 100000 LD LMT 128300 CU FT 1860," no "BLT" date, no "NEW" number, Timken trucks, Schreiner Collection. (We need assistance in identifying Lionel's number for this car. The original box probably bears the Lionel catalogue number.) — NRS

NOTE: The Lionel Service Manual lists three 6176 varieties: 6176-25 with 6176-2 body, 6176-50 with 6076-88 body and 6176-75 with 6176-76 body. All have Timken trucks, one disc and one fixed coupler. We believe that these Lionel numbers correspond to one or another of our body types and descriptions. Of particular help would be information corroborating box numbers and body mold numbers with our descriptions and body types.

6176[A-I] LEHIGH VALLEY Type VI body, no brakewheel
(A) Dark yellow, blue lettering, "NEW 1-48," "BUILT 1-48," "LIONEL 6176," Timken trucks, one disc coupler, one fixed coupler — 3 5 7 10

124

(B) Same as (A), but without "new" date 3 5 7 10
(C) Same as (A), but medium yellow 3 5 7 10
(D) Light yellow, black lettering, "new" not present, "BUILT 1-48" and "LIONEL 6176" both present, Timken trucks, disc couplers
3 5 7 10
(E) Same as (D), but one disc coupler, one fixed coupler 3 5 7 10
(F) Light yellow, black lettering, "NEW 1-48," "BUILT 1-48" and "LIONEL 6176"all missing, Pauli Collection 3 5 7 10
(G) Gray with black lettering, "NEW 1-48" not present, "BUILT 1-48" present, Timken trucks, one disc coupler, one fixed coupler 3 5 7 10
(H) Same as (A), but black lettering. Part of set no. 11430, Kotil and Winton Collections 3 5 7 10
(I) Same as (G), but with "NEW 1-48," Kotil Collection 3 5 7 10

6176[P] NO LETTERING, deep bright yellow, Type VI body, Timken trucks, one disc coupler, one fixed coupler, from set #11430, Edwards Collection
2 4 7 10

6346-56 ALCOA 1956, 50 ton quad hopper, aluminum with blue lettering, "NEW 6-56," hatch covers, Alcoa labels, no center brace hole, brakewheel, bar-end metal trucks, magnetic couplers 12 25 30 45

6436-1 LEHIGH VALLEY 1955, uncatalogued, 50 ton quad hopper, gray plastic painted black, white lettering, "NEW 3-55," no covers, bar-end trucks, magnetic tab couplers, brakewheels
(A) Center spreader bar holes 8 15 20 30
(B) Without center spreader bar holes 15 30 40 55

6436-25 LEHIGH VALLEY 1955, 50 ton quad hopper, no covers, maroon with white lettering, "NEW 3-55", brakewheels, bar-end metal trucks, magnetic couplers 8 15 20 30

6436 See 6436-110

6436-100 - see 6436-110

6436-110 LEHIGH VALLEY 1963-68, 50-ton quad hopper, red painted gray plastic with white lettering, spreader, no covers, Timken trucks, magnetic couplers, brakewheel. Car may be numbered 6436 or 6436-100. See variations below. Car may or may not have lettering "NEW 3-55". All cars have "BLT BY LIONEL", but we do not know if all varieties have built dates.
(A) Numbered only "6436", no new or built dates, came in box numbered 6436-110, Fleming Collection 10 22 30 55
(B) Numbered "6436-100",has "NEW 3-55", no built date, came in box numbered 6436-110, Kotil Collection 40 60 90 125
(C) Numbered "6436-100" without new or built date, came in box numbered 6436-110, Kotil Collection 10 22 30 55

6436-1969 TCA 1969, uncatalogued, 50 ton quad hopper, special 1,000 run for 1969 TCA Convention, "BLT BY LIONEL 4-69" spreader bar, no cover, red painted body with white convention data and lettering, white palm tree and white TCA logos. Timken plastic trucks, disc-operating couplers
— — 100 135

6436-500 LEHIGH VALLEY 1957-58, 50 ton quad hopper from Girl's Set, numbered "643657" and "NEW 3-55"
(A) Lilac car with maroon lettering 45 90 125 170
(B) Burgundy painted black plastic shell, white heat-stamped lettering, "NEW 3-55," one metal spreader bar; Lionel preproduction paint sample, Degano Collection — — 1000 —

6446-1 N & W 1954-55, 50 ton quad hopper, "NEW 6-54," "546446" on side, bar-end metal trucks, roof with twelve covers, brakewheel. (In earlier editions this item was catalogued as a 54-6446 and variations had different letter designations.)
(A) Gray plastic body painted gray, black lettering, covers, "BLT BY LIONEL," 13 25 35 60
(B) Light gray, black lettering 13 25 35 60
(C) Gray plastic body painted gray, black lettering, without center brace hole, magnetic couplers 13 25 35 60
(D) Gray body, brace holes and brace, no roof, plastic trucks, 1963 couplers 13 25 35 60

6446-25 N & W 1955-57, 50 ton quad hopper, numbered "546446," and "NEW 6-54," roof with twelve covers. (Note: We have changed hopper classifications from previous editions so that our numbers correspond to Lionel's cataloging system.)
(A) Black painted gray plastic, white lettering, no center brace hole, bar-end metal trucks, magnetic couplers, brakewheel "BLT BY LIONEL NEW 6-54;" box end lettered "6446 CEMENT CAR 25 LIONEL 25," Kotil Collection 9 15 25 45
(B) Same as (A) but center brace hole with brace, tab magnetic couplers 9 15 25 45
(C) Gray unpainted plastic, black lettering. Center brace hole, no brace, Timken trucks, disc-operating couplers, part of set #13098, 1963, Powell Collection 10 20 35 50
(D) Light gray unpainted plastic, black lettering, no information about brace holes, trucks, lettering content; box end marked "6446 CEMENT CAR," Kotil Collection 10 15 25 40
(E) Royal blue, white lettering, produced by MPC, 1970-71; listed here for your convenience 20 45 80 125

(M-Q) Specials made for N & W that are rare and very desirable, but are not catalogued.
(M) Gold with white lettering — — 1000 —
(N) Pink with black lettering — — 1000 —
(O) Light blue plastic painted light blue, white lettering — — 1000 —
(P) Same as (G) but with covers and center brace holes — — 1000 —
(Q) Silver with white lettering — — 1000 —

125

54-6446 N&W 1954, 50 ton quad hopper, "NEW 6-54," bar-end metal trucks, brakewheel
(A) Gray plastic body painted black, white lettering, center brace hole with brace, tab magnetic couplers　　20　35　45　65
(B) Gray plastic body painted black, white lettering, without center brace hole, with covers, magnetic couplers　　16　25　35　50
(C) Gray plastic body painted gray, black lettering, without center brace hole, with covers, magnetic couplers, Kotil Collection　　16　25　35　50

6456 LEHIGH VALLEY 25000 "NEW 1-48," "BUILT 1-48," steps, brakewheels, except as noted

Type I Bodies
(A) Maroon with white lettering, staple-end trucks　　5　7　9　12
(B) Black with white lettering, bar-end metal trucks　　5　7　9　12
(C) Faded brown with white lettering, staple-end metal trucks　　5　7　9　12
(D) Same as (B), staple-end trucks, Kotil and Rohlfing Collections　　5　7　9　12
(E) Maroon with cream lettering, staple-end trucks, Griesbeck Collection　　5　7　9　12

Type III Bodies
(H) Gray with maroon lettering, bar-end metal trucks　　5　7　9　12
(I) Shiny red paint over opaque body, yellow lettering, bar-end metal trucks　　15　22　40　70
(J) Maroon with white lettering, bar-end metal trucks　　5　7　9　12
(K) Dark maroon with white lettering, staple-end metal trucks　　5　7　9　12
(L) Black with white lettering, bar-end metal trucks　　5　7　9　12
(M) Reddish-maroon with white lettering, bar-end metal trucks　　5　7　9　12
(N) Same as (I) but white lettering, Degano Collection　　**NRS**

Type V Bodies
(S) Shiny black unpainted plastic, white lettering, bar-end metal trucks, no brakewheel
(T) Shiny black unpainted plastic, white lettering, Timken trucks, disc-operating couplers　　5　7　9　12
(U) Flat black unpainted plastic, white lettering, Timken trucks, disc-operating couplers　　5　7　9　12

Type VI Bodies
(X) Shiny black unpainted plastic, white lettering, Timken trucks, disc-operating couplers, no brakewheels　　5　7　9　12

6476 LEHIGH VALLEY 25000 "NEW 1-48," "BUILT 1-48,"
(A) Type V red plastic body, white lettering, bar-end metal trucks, magnetic tab couplers, brakewheels, steps　　5　7　9　12

(B) Type V gray plastic body, black lettering, Timken trucks, disc-operating couplers, steps　　5　7　9　12
(C) Type V red plastic body, white lettering, Timken trucks, disc-operating couplers, steps, no brakewheels　　5　7　9　12
(D) Type V darker red plastic body, white lettering, Timken trucks, disc-operating couplers　　5　7　9　12
(E) Type VI red plastic body, white lettering, Timken trucks, disc-operating couplers　　5　7　9　12
(F) Type VI pale red plastic body, white lettering, Timken trucks, disc-operating couplers　　5　7　9　12
(G) Type VI black unpainted plastic body, white lettering, Timken trucks, disc-operating couplers, Maher Collection　　5　7　9　12
(H) Type V black unpainted plastic body, white lettering, steps, Timken trucks, disc-operating couplers, Kotil Collection　　5　7　9　12

6476-125 LEHIGH VALLEY Listed in Service Manual, probably with "6476" on side and "6476-125" on original box; more information requested　　**NRS**

6476-135 LEHIGH VALLEY Listed in Service Manual, probably has "6476" on side and "6476-135" on original box; more information requested　　**NRS**

6536 M St L 1955, 1963, 50 ton quad hopper, red painted black plastic, white lettering, center brace, no covers, "BLT 6-58," no brakewheel, Timken trucks, one disc-operating coupler, one fixed coupler　　12　17　25　40

6636 ALASKA 1959, 50 ton quad hopper, black plastic body with orange/yellow lettering, does not have Eskimo shown in catalogue, no covers, center brace, Timken trucks, disc-operating couplers
(A) No brakewheel　　17　25　35　60
(B) Brakewheel, Patton Collection　　17　25　35　60

6736 DETROIT & MACKINAC 1960, 50 ton quad hopper, red plastic, white lettering, no covers, center brace, Timken trucks, disc-operating couplers　　17　25　35　60

546446 See 6446-I or 6446-25

NO LETTERING: See 6076 (J-K)

126

Chapter X
PASSENGER CARS

Gd. V.G. Exc. Mt.

1865 WESTERN & ATLANTIC 1959-62, 1860-Type coach, yellow with brown roof and lettering, unlighted, fixed couplers
(A) As described above   13   17   25   35
(B) Same as (A), except has interior illumination, Klaassen Collection   **NRS**

1866 WESTERN & ATLANTIC 1959-62, 1860-Type mail-baggage
(A) Yellow with brown roof and lettering   17   20   25   35
(B) Unpainted lemon yellow, no lettering   **NRS**
(C) Same as (A), except has interior illumination, Klaassen Collection   **NRS**

1875 WESTERN & ATLANTIC 1959-62, coach, yellow with tuscan roof and lettering, offered separately, similar to 1865   40   60   90   120

1875W WESTERN & ATLANTIC 1959-62, coach with whistle; yellow with tuscan roof and lettering, lights, came with Five Star General Set, lighted, operating couplers   40   60   80   100

1876 WESTERN & ATLANTIC 1959-62, mail-baggage, lights, came with Five Star General Set; similar to 1866   25   40   60   90

1885 WESTERN & ATLANTIC, 1959, blue with white lettering, brown top, lighted, uncatalogued by Lionel. Offered by Sears as part of set 79 N 0966 with 1886 mail-baggage car, 1887 flat car with horses and 1882 engine, Weiss Collection   75   150   250   350

2400 MAPLEWOOD 1948-49, Pullman, "LIONEL LINES," green sides, yellow window outlines, white lettering, gray roof, lights   15   20   35   50

2401 HILLSIDE 1948-49, observation, matches 2400   15   20   35   50

2402 CHATHAM 1948-49, Pullman, matches 2400   15   20   35   50

2404 SANTA FE 1964-65, Vista Dome, aluminum paint on plastic with blue lettering, not illuminated   12   18   22   30

2405 SANTA FE 1964-65, Pullman, matches 2404   12   18   22   30

2406 SANTA FE 1964-65, observation, matches 2404   12   18   22   30

2408 SANTA FE 1964-65, Vista Dome, aluminum paint on plastic, blue lettering, window inserts, matches 2404   12   18   22   30

2409 SANTA FE 1964-65, matches 2408   12   18   22   30

2410 SANTA FE 1964-65, observation, matches 2408   12   18   22   30

2412 SANTA FE 1959-63, Vista Dome, silver with blue stripe through windows, lights   12   20   30   40

2414 SANTA FE 1959-63, Pullman, matches 2412   12   20   30   40

2416 SANTA FE 1959-63, observation, matches 2412   12   20   30   40

2421 MAPLEWOOD 1950, 1952-53, Pullman, "LIONEL LINES"
(A) Aluminum painted sides, gray roof, black stripe, 1951
   15   20   30   37
(B) Aluminum painted sides, silver roof and no stripes   20   22   34   40

2422 CHATHAM 1950, 1952-53, Pullman, "LIONEL LINES"
(A) Matches 2421 (A)   12   25   31   37
(B) Matches 2421 (B)   12   25   34   40

2423 HILLSIDE 1950, 1952-53, observation
(A) Matches 2421 (A)   12   25   31   37
(B) Matches 2421 (B)   12   25   34   40

2429 LIVINGSTON 1950, 1952-53, Pullman
(A) Matches 2421 (A), (No prices, existence questionable)
(B) Matches 2421 (B)   13   25   35   50

2430 PULLMAN 1946-47, blue and silver sheet metal
(A) Silver letters, staple-end trucks, early coil couplers
   12   15   25   40
(B) White letters, staple-end trucks, later coil couplers
   12   15   25   40

2431 OBSERVATION 1946-47, blue and silver sheet metal, matches 2430
(A) Silver letters, staple-end trucks, early coil couplers
   12   15   25   40
(B) White letters, staple-end trucks, later coil couplers
   12   15   25   40

2432 CLIFTON 1954-58, Vista Dome, "LIONEL LINES," aluminum paint with red lettering, lights   12   20   30   40

2434 NEWARK 1954-58, Pullman, matches 2432   12   22   30   40

2435 ELIZABETH 1954-58, Pullman, matches 2432   12   22   30   40

NOTE: There are two different passenger cars numbered 2436.

2436 SUMMIT 1954-58, observation, "LIONEL LINES," silver with red lettering, lights, matches 2432   12   20   30   48

2436 MOOSEHEART 1957-58, observation, "LIONEL LINES," aluminum painted plastic, red lettered "Mooseheart," came as part of a conventional passenger set, 1608W in 1958, as well as part of an unusual set with a Railway Express refrigeration car REX6572 in green with gold lettering and a 215 Burlington Alco A unit in red trim. Price for Mooseheart only
   25   40   60   80

2440 PULLMAN 1946-47, sheet metal body, staple-end metal trucks, coil couplers, Ervin observations
(A) Blue with silver roof and lettering, early coil trucks, 1946
   15   22   30   45
(B) Green with dark green roof, yellow window inserts, white lettering, 1947
   15   22   30   45

2441 OBSERVATION 1946-47, matches 2440
(A) Matches 2440 (A)   15   22   30   45
(B) Matches 2440(B)   15   22   30   45

NOTE: Lionel used "2442" for two different passenger cars.

2442 PULLMAN 1946-47, brown sheet metal, gray windows, lights, staple-end metal trucks, coil couplers, Ervin observation
(A) Silver letters, 1946   15   22   30   45
(B) White letters, 1947   15   22   30   45

2442 CLIFTON 1955-56, Vista Dome, "LIONEL LINES," aluminum paint, red window stripe, lights   15   25   35   50

2443 OBSERVATION 1946-47, matches 2442 PULLMAN
(A) Silver letters, 1946   15   22   30   45
(B) White letters, 1947   15   22   30   45

2444 NEWARK 1955-56, matches 2442 CLIFTON   15   25   35   50

2445 ELIZABETH 1955-56, matches 2442 CLIFTON   18   30   40   65

2446 SUMMIT 1955-56, matches 2442 CLIFTON   15   25   35   50

2481 PLAINFIELD 1950, Pullman, "LIONEL LINES," yellow with red stripes, part of 1950 Anniversary Set with 2482, 2483 and 2023(A) diesel. Price for 2481 only   40   60   90   125

2482 WESTFIELD 1950, Pullman, matches 2481   40   60   90   125

2483 LIVINGSTON 1950, observation, matches 2481   40   60   90   125

2521 PRESIDENT McKINLEY 1962-66, "OBSERVATION," extruded aluminum with black lettering and gold stripe, lights   40   60   75   100

2522 PRESIDENT HARRISON 1962-66, "VISTA DOME," matches 2521
   40   60   75   100

2523 PRESIDENT GARFIELD 1962-66, "PULLMAN," matches 2521
   40   60   75   100

2530 RAILWAY EXPRESS AGENCY 1953-1960, large-door versions 1953 only; small-door versions 1954-60, Weiss comment.
(A) Small doors, name plate between doors, "LIONEL LINES" not present
   50   70   85   110

SMALL PASSENGER SETS

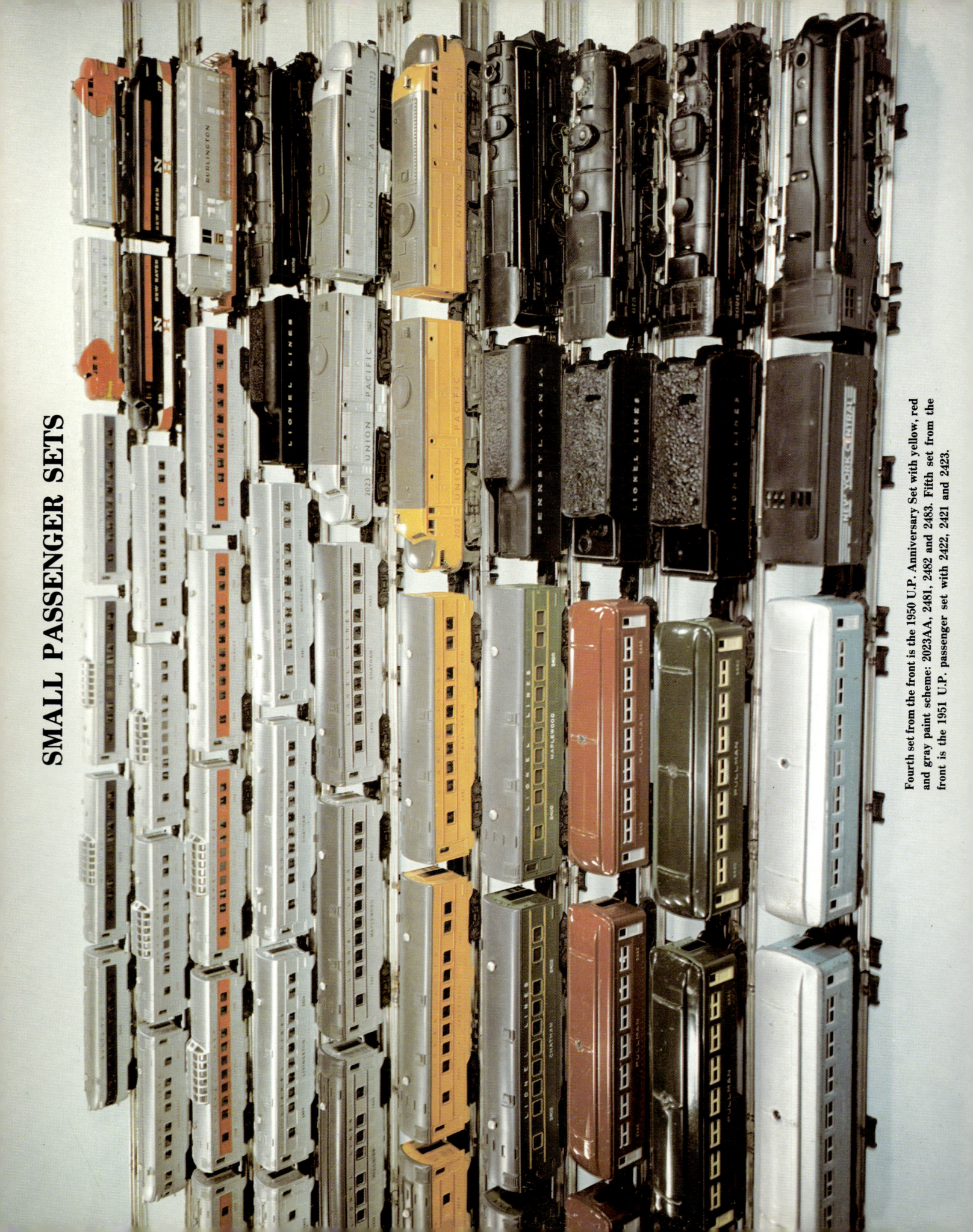

Fourth set from the front is the 1950 U.P. Anniversary Set with yellow, red and gray paint scheme: 2023AA, 2481, 2482 and 2483. Fifth set from the front is the 1951 U.P. passenger set with 2422, 2421 and 2423.

(B) Small doors, name plate partially below doors, no dots before or after "LIONEL LINES"   50   70   85   110
(C) Small doors, name plate partially below doors, with dots before and after "LIONEL LINES"   50   70   85   110
(D) Large doors, 1953 only, name plate partially below doors, no dots before or after "LIONEL LINES", Weiss comment.   120   150   190   260

2531 SILVER DAWN 1952-60, observation, extruded aluminum, lights
(A) Glued plates, dots before and after "LIONEL LINES" and "SILVER DAWN"   25   37   50   75
(B) Plates with round-head rivets   25   37   50   75
(C) Plates with hex-head rivets   25   37   50   75
(D) Glued plates, wide flat channels, 1955-60   40   60   80   100

2532 SILVER RANGE 1952-60, Vista Dome, extruded aluminum, "LIONEL LINES," lights
(A) Glued plates   25   37   50   75
(B) Plates with round-head rivets   25   37   50   75
(C) Plates with hex-head rivets   25   37   50   75
(D) Glued plates, wide flat channels, 1955-60   40   60   80   100

2533 SILVER CLOUD 1952-60, Pullman, extruded aluminum, "LIONEL LINES," lights
(A) Glued plates, dots before and after "LIONEL LINES"   25   37   50   75
(B) Plates with round-head rivets   25   37   50   75
(C) Plates with hex-head rivets   25   37   50   75
(D) Glued plates, wide flat channels, 1955-60, dots before and after "LIONEL LINES"   40   60   80   100

2534 SILVER BLUFF 1952-60, Pullman, extruded aluminum, "LIONEL LINES," lights
(A) Glued plates   25   37   50   75
(B) Plates with round-head rivets, 1952-53   25   37   50   75
(C) Plates with hex-head rivets   25   37   50   75
(D) Glued plates, wide flat channels, 1955-60, dots before and after "LIONEL LINES" and "SILVER BLUFF"   40   60   80   100

THE CONGRESSIONAL SET: 2340 or 2360 GG-1, 2541, 2542, 2543 and 2544

2541 ALEXANDER HAMILTON* 1955-56, extruded aluminum observation, "PENNSYLVANIA," lights   50   75   95   130

2542 BETSY ROSS* 1955-56, Vista Dome, Pullman, matches 2541   50   75   95   130

2543 WILLIAM PENN* 1955-56, Pullman, matches 2541   50   75   95   130

2544 MOLLY PITCHER* 1955-56, Pullman, matches 2541   50   75   95   130

THE CANADIAN PACIFIC SET As catalogued this set consisted of a 2373AA F-3 diesel, three 2552 Vista Domes and one 2551 observation. Lionel dealers encountered sales resistance to this combination and so the 2553 and 2554 were often substituted for two 2552 Vista Domes.

2551 BANFF PARK. 1957, extruded aluminum observation, "CANADIAN PACIFIC," lights   75   110   150   185

2552 SKYLINE 500* 1957, Vista Dome matches 2551   75   110   140   185

2553 BLAIR MANOR* 1957, Pullman, matches 2551   100   135   160   200

2554 CRAIG MANOR* 1957, Pullman, matches 2551   100   135   160   200

2561 VISTA VALLEY 1959-61, extruded aluminum observation, "SANTA FE," lights
(A) "SANTA FE" in small letters   35   50   75   100
(B) "SANTA FE" in large letters   35   50   75   100

2562 REGAL PASS* 1959-61, Vista Dome, matches 2561
(A) "SANTA FE" in small letters   35   50   75   100
(B) "SANTA FE" in large letters   35   50   75   100

2563 INDIAN FALLS* 1959-61, Pullman, matches 2561
(A) "SANTA FE" in small letters   35   50   75   90
(B) "SANTA FE" in large letters   35   50   75   90

NOTE: Lionel used 2625 for three passenger cars with different names.

* Excellent reproductions have been made by Williams Electric Trains. In 1979 Fundimensions reissued the Congressional Set with different numbers.

2625 IRVINGTON* 1946-50, Pullman, "LIONEL LINES," bakelite body painted tuscan, white lettering, six-wheel metal trucks with plastic side frames, lights
(A) Plain window inserts   50   75   100   140
(B) Window inserts with silhouetted people, 1950   50   75   100   140

2625 MANHATTAN 1946-47, Pullman, matches 2625(A) IRVINGTON   60   90   120   180

2625 MADISON 1946-47, Pullman, matches 2625(A) IRVINGTON   60   90   120   180

2626 OBSERVATION 1946, shown in advance catalogue but not made.   **Not Manufactured**

2628 MANHATTAN 1948-50, Pullman, matches 2625 IRVINGTON
(A) Plain window inserts   50   75   100   140
(B) Window inserts with silhouetted people, 1950   50   80   110   140

2627 MADISON 1948-50, Pullman, matches 2625 IRVINGTON
(A) Plain window inserts   50   75   100   140
(B) Window inserts with silhouetted people, 1950   50   80   110   140

2630 PULLMAN 1946, light blue sheet metal body, gray roof, gray window inserts, staple-end metal trucks, coil couplers, same number as prewar unit but with different couplers and a darker gray   15   22   30   50

2631 OBSERVATION 1946, matches 2630   15   22   30   50

6440 PULLMAN 1948-49, green sheet metal body, dark green roof, white lettering, yellow windows, lights, metal trucks and magnetic couplers, Ervin observation   15   22   30   50

6441 OBSERVATION 1948-49, matches 6440   15   22   30   50

6442 PULLMAN 1949, brown sheet metal body and roof, gray windows, lights, metal trucks and magnetic couplers   18   30   40   60

6443 OBSERVATION 1949, matches 6442   18   30   40   60

* Williams Electric Trains and Edward Kramer have made excellent reproductions of the 2625-2628 series passenger coaches.

2531[C] Hex head rivets

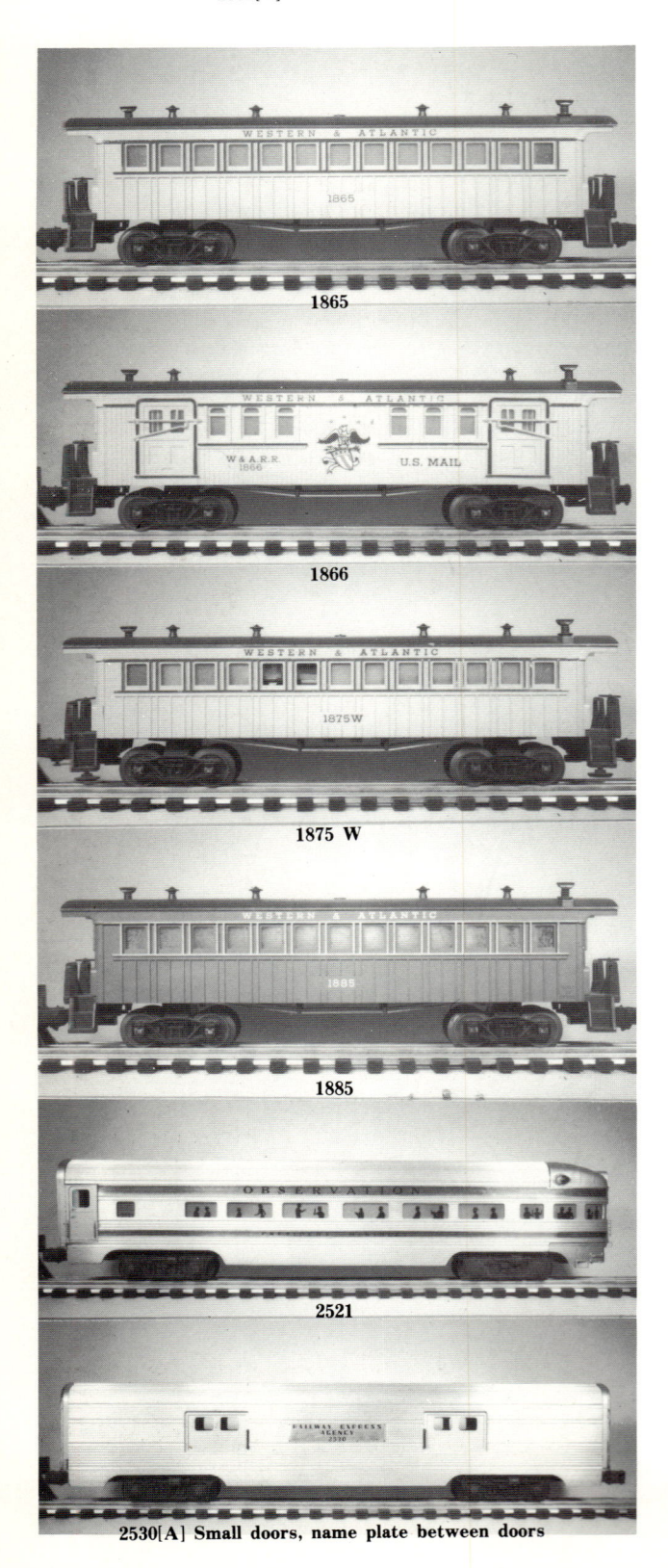

2531[B] Round head rivets

1865

1866

1875 W

1885

2521

2530[A] Small doors, name plate between doors

2530 [B] or [C] small doors, name plate partially below doors

2530[D] large doors

2531 SILVER DAWN

2532 SILVER RANGE

2534 SILVER BLUFF

2541 ALEXANDER HAMILTON

2551 BANFF PARK

130

2561[A] VISTA VALLEY

2561[B] VISTA VALLEY

2400 MAPLEWOOD

2404 SANTA FE

2408 SANTA FE

2412 SANTA FE

2421[A] MAPLEWOOD

2421 [B] MAPLEWOOD

2430 PULLMAN

2432 CLIFTON

2436 MOOSEHEART

2440[B] PULLMAN

2442 PULLMAN

2442 CLIFTON

2481 PLAINFIELD

2625 MADISON

2627 MADISON

6440 PULLMAN

6442 PULLMAN

TANK CARS

2555

2755

2955

6015

6025

6035

6045

6315

6463

6465

6465

Chapter XI
TANK CARS

[Photo showing tank cars labeled: 2855, 6415, 2855, 6425, 6555, 6315]

Gd. V.G. Exc. Mt.

1005 SUNOCO 1948-50, single dome, gray tank, tank fastened to frame by tabs, from Scout set with Scout couplers
(A) Chemically blackened frame, Pauli Collection 1 2 3 6
(B) Shiny black frame, Pauli Collection 1 2 3 6
(C) Dull black frame 1 2 3 6

2465 SUNOCO 1946-48, two domes, silver tank with black or blue decal lettering, yellow diamond, staple-end metal trucks, coil couplers, steps
(A) "SUNOCO" extends beyond diamond, blue decal lettering, Kotil Collection 2 3 5 8
(B) "SUNOCO" completely within diamond; contains line "TESTED 5-10-23 PRESSURE 60 LBS AT MILTON PA. BY A.C. & F. CO.," black decal lettering, Kotil Collection 2 3 5 8
(C) "SUNOCO" extends beyond diamond, blue stamped lettering, Kotil Collection 4 6 10 16
(D) "SUNOCO" completely within diamond, "CAPACITY 8000 GALS" on diamond decal, other decal reads "...TESTED 3-31-25 PRESSURE 25 LBS. AT MARCUS HOOK PA. BY SUN OIL CO." and in smaller letters on same decal "TESTED 5-10-23 PRESSURE 60 LBS. AT MILTON PA. BY A. C & F.CO.," magnetic couplers, "2465" does not appear on tank where number often appears on decal, the word "TANK" appears, white rubber stamped "2465" on base underside, Edmunds Collection 4 6 10 16
(E) "GAS SUNOCO OILS" all within diamond in black lettering, diamond located on center of car; only other lettering is "2465" rubber stamped on frame bottom, Type II trucks. This car is illustrated on page 2 of the 20-page version of the Lionel 1946 catalogue, Dunn Collection **NRS**

2555 SUNOCO 1946-48, single dome, silver tank, yellow diamond, staple-end metal trucks, coil couplers, one brakewheel, screws fasten frame and tank
(A) Black decal lettering, "GAS SUNOCO OILS," all within diamond, "S.U.N.X. 2555" in large decal letters, early coil couplers, Kotil Collection 10 15 26 35
(B) Same as (A) but later coil couplers, Kotil Collection 10 15 26 35

(C) Blue decal lettering, "SUNOCO" extends beyond diamond, black decal lettering "S.U.N.X. 2555," late coil couplers, Kotil Collection 10 15 26 35
(D) Blue decal lettering, "SUNOCO" extends beyond diamond, "2555" not on side, late coil couplers, Kotil Collection 10 15 26 35
(E) Same as (C), but magnetic couplers. Original box is marked "6555" and original "2555" box marking is obliterated by rectangular overstamp. Came as part of 1949 set no. 2151, Donangelo Collection **NRS**

2755 S.U.N.X. 1945, single dome, silver tank, black decal lettering, "GAS SUNOCO OILS" all within diamond, staple-end metal trucks, early coil couplers without bottom plate, black brakewheel, screws fasten frame and tank, four steps on frame
Note: 2755 was made before World War II and is found with a gray tank and box couplers.
(A) Whirly wheels 20 30 60 85
(B) Dish wheels, thick axles, Kotil Collection 20 30 60 85

2855 S.U.N.X. 1946, single dome, black tank, white decal lettering, staple-end metal trucks, coil couplers, black brakewheel, four steps, screws fasten tank and frame
(A) "GAS SUNOCO OILS" within diamond, see color illustration 40 60 80 150
(B) "GAS OILS" omitted from diamond, "SUNOCO" goes beyond diamond 40 60 80 150
(C) Same as (B) but gray tank, see color illustration 45 70 90 165

2955 S.U.N.X. 1940-42, 1946, single dome, black die-cast tank and frame
(A) Stamped steel tinplate trucks, box coupler, 1940-42 110 175 300 460
(B) Staple-end metal trucks, coil couplers, circa 1946 110 175 275 375
(C) Same as (B) but "SHELL" 75 125 175 275

134

6015 SUNOCO 1954-55, single dome, 8 inches long, "LIONEL LINES," bar-end metal trucks, body fastened to frame by tabs, frame has two indentations on each side
(A) Yellow unpainted plastic tank, black lettering, magnetic tab couplers, Kotil Collection   2   4   6   8
(B) Dark yellow tank, black lettering, magnetic couplers   2   4   6   8
(C) Yellow painted gray plastic, Kotil Collection   2   4   6   8

6025 GULF 1956-57, single dome, 8 inches long, "LIONEL LINES," body fastened to black frame with tabs
(A) Orange tank, blue lettering, Timken trucks, disc couplers
    2   4   6   8
(B) Gray tank, blue lettering, bar-end metal trucks, magnetic tab couplers
    2   4   7   10
(C) Black tank, white lettering, bar-end metal trucks, magnetic tab couplers
    2   5   7   10

6035 SUNOCO 1952-53, single dome gray tank, black lettering, body fastened to frame with tabs, Scout trucks, magnetic couplers   1   2   3   4

NOTE: There are two different 6045 tanks.

6045 CITIES SERVICE 1960, not catalogued, two domes, green tank, white lettering "CSOX 6045," body fastened to gunmetal frame with tabs, arch bar trucks, fixed couplers   6   9   12   20

6045 LIONEL LINES 1958, 1963, two domes, "L" in circle, body fastened to frame with tabs
(A) 1958, light gray tank, blue lettering, Timken trucks, disc couplers, "BLT 1-58"   2   4   6   8
(B) 1963, orange tank, black lettering, Timken trucks, disc couplers, no built date   2   5   7   10
(C) Same as (A) but arch bar trucks, fixed couplers, Strong Collection
    2   4   6   8

NOTE: There are three different 6315 tanks

6315 GULF 1956-59, chemical single dome, metal catwalk around dome; screws fasten tank and frame, "BLT 1-56"; see color illustration
(A) Burnt-orange and black tank, bar-end metal trucks, magnetic tab couplers   15   22   30   40
(B) Same as (A) but redder-orange   15   22   30   40
(C) All orange tank, Timken trucks, disc couplers   8   12   15   25
(D) Same as (C), no built date   8   12   15   25

6315 LIONEL LINES 1963-66, chemical single dome, metal catwalk around dome, ladder, screws fasten tank and frame, orange tank, black lettering, Timken trucks, disc couplers   7   12   15   25

6315-1972 TCA 18th NATIONAL CONVENTION 1972, chemical single dome, special for TCA, limited run of 2,000, bar-end metal trucks, magnetic tab couplers; manufactured by MPC but listed here because of number
    —   —   50   80

6415 SUNOCO 1953-55, three domes, silver tank, body fastened to black frame with screws; see color illustration
(A) Black lettering "6600 GALS," "6415" to right of dome, bar-end metal trucks, magnetic tab couplers, silver brakewheels   5   7   10   15
(B) Same as (A) but "6415" not on tank   5   7   10   15
(C) Same as (A) but blue lettering, Timken trucks, disc couplers, black brakewheels   6   8   12   20
(D) Black lettering, "8000 GALS," "6415" to right of dome, bar-end metal trucks, magnetic tab couplers, silver brakewheels, Kotil Collection
    5   7   10   15
(E) Same as (D) but "TANK," instead of "6415," Schreiner Collection
    5   7   10   15

6425 GULF 1956-58, three domes, silver tank, orange GULF circle, blue lettering, "BLT 2-56," black frame, bar-end metal trucks, magnetic tab couplers; see color illustration   7   11   18   30

6463 ROCKET FUEL 1962-63, two domes, body fastened to black frame with tabs, Timken trucks, disc couplers
(A) Blue tank, white lettering   NRS
(B) White tank, red lettering   6   8   15   25

NOTE: There are four different road names found on 6465s: SUNOCO, LIONEL LINES, CITIES SERVICE AND GULF.

6465 SUNOCO 1948-50, two domes, silver tank, blue lettering, yellow decal background, two wire handrails
(A) Indentation on center of both frame sides, "6465" stamped on bottom, last line of test block reads "TANK," frame steps, staple-end metal trucks, magnetic couplers   2   3   4   9
(B) Same as (A) but 3/8 inch hole near frame center, Kotil Collection
    2   3   4   9
(C) Same as (A) but 3/8 inch hole near frame center, no steps, Kotil Collection   2   3   4   9
(D) Same as (A) but 3/8 inch hole near frame center, no steps, no frame indent; frame has notch like 3472 milk, Kotil Collection   2   3   4   9
(E) Same as (A) but no frame indentations, bar-end metal trucks
    2   3   4   9
(F) Same as (A) but no frame indentations, bar-end metal trucks, light yellow decal background   2   4   6   10
(G) Same as (A) but last line of test block reads "6465"   2   4   6   10
(H) No indentation on frame, "6465" is last line of test block, no number on frame, no steps, bar-end metal trucks, magnetic couplers
    2   4   6   10
(I) Same as (H) but magnetic tab couplers   2   4   6   10
(J) No frame indentation, 3/8 inch hole, three small holes, staple-end trucks, Kotil Collection   2   4   6   10
(K) Same as (J) but bar-end trucks, Kotil Collection   2   4   6   10
(L) Same as (J) but bar-end trucks, no small holes, Kotil Collection
    2   4   6   10
(M) No frame indentation, four holes which appear accidentally punched, Kotil Collection   2   4   6   10
(N) No frame indentation, 3/8 inch hole, "6465" on right under "AT MARCUS HOOK PA. BY SUN OIL.", Kotil Collection   2   4   6   10
(O) Dark silver tank, no frame indentations, last line of test block reads, "TANK," staple-end trucks, magnetic couplers, no steps
    7   11   15   25

6465 GULF 1958, two domes, black painted black plastic tank, black metal frame, plastic simulated handrails around tank, no frame indentations, white lettering, "LIONEL LINES," last line of test block reads "6465," orange GULF disc, no steps, no rubber stamping on bottom, Timken trucks, disc couplers
(A) As described above, Foss Collection   23   35   50   100
(B) Same as (A), except unpainted black plastic tank, Mueller Collection
    23   35   50   100

6465-60 GULF 1958, two domes, gray painted black plastic tank, dark gunmetal frame, plastic simulated handrails around tank, no frame indentation, blue lettering, "LIONEL LINES," last line of test block reads "6465," orange GULF disc, no steps, no rubber stamping on bottom, Timken trucks, disc couplers, "6465-60" appears on box end, but only "6465" on car, Rohlfing Collection   6   9   12   20

6465 LIONEL LINES 1958-59, two domes, "L" in circle, plastic simulated handrails around tank, no frame steps, no number rubber stamped on bottom; no frame indentations
(A) Black unpainted plastic tank, white lettering; "BLT 1-58," Timken trucks, disc couplers   5   7   9   18
(B) Orange unpainted plastic tank, black lettering, no built date, Timken trucks, one disc coupler, one fixed coupler   4   6   8   16
(C) Same as (B), but black ends and lettered "BLT BY LIONEL" on tank side at center. Location of lettering similar to that shown as (B) orange in lower right corner of page 133, I. D. Smith observation   4   6   8   16

6465 CITIES SERVICE 1960-62, two domes, green painted black plastic, plastic simulated handrails around tank, white lettering "C S O X," no frame steps, no number rubber stamped on bottom, no frame indentations, Timken trucks, disc couplers   6   10   15   25

6555 SUNOCO 1949-50, single dome, silver tank, staple-end metal trucks, magnetic couplers, brakewheel, ladders, handrails
(A) "SUNOCO" goes beyond diamond   9   15   20   30
(B) "GAS SUNOCO OILS" all within diamond, bold black lettering, decal shaped, Kotil Collection   8   15   20   30
(C) "SUNOCO" beyond diamond, less bold blue-black lettering, round corner decal, Kotil Collection   8   15   20   30

Chapter XII
VAT CARS

NOTE: There are three different vat cars numbered 6475.

	Gd.	V.G.	Exc.	Mt.

6475 LIBBY'S CRUSHED PINEAPPLE Light or aqua car with white and silver labels and red and blue letters
(A) Timken trucks, disc couplers   20   30   40   65
(B) Arch bar trucks, fixed couplers   20   30   40   65
(C) Aqua, Timken trucks, fixed couplers, Kotil Collection
                                     20   30   40   65
(D) Light blue, Timken trucks, fixed couplers, Kotil Collection
                                     20   30   40   65

Reproductions of the (B) vat labels have been made. These reproductions do not have the word "PICKLES" on the side.

6475 HEINZ 57 Tan car with brown roof, green lettering, green vat labels with red lettering. A reliable informant has suggested that the HEINZ 57 cars were "the product of a lark and not genuine Lionel." More information is needed about this car.   40   60   80   100

6475 PICKLES Tan car body, brown roof, black "TLCX" at left of body base, car number in black at right
(A) Yellow vats with black slats, red lettered "PICKLES"
                                     10   15   25   40
(B) Same as (A), but no slats, factory error. Reproductions of these vats without slats have been made, but they do not have the word "PICKLES" on the side, as do the originals, Blotner Collection   10   15   25   40
(C) Same as (A), but light brown vats, Blotner Collection   NRS
(D) Same as (A), but red vat lettering is missing, Blotner Collection   NRS

6475 Libby's

6475 Heinz 57

6475 Pickles

6475[B] No Slats

Chapter XIII
FUNDIMENSIONS DIESELS & ELECTRICS

INTRODUCTION
The introduction analyzes the following diesel bodies: GM Yard Switcher, F-3 Unit, Alco, GP-7 and GP-9, U36B and GP-20. It also discusses GP and U36B motors and diesel railing types.

ALCO BODY TYPES

Type I
1. Open slot on front pilot for coupler
2. Closed slot number board
3. "LIONEL MPC" builder's plate at lower rear

Type II
1. Open slot on front pilot for coupler
2. Open slot number board
3. "LIONEL MPC" builder's plate behind cab door

Type III
1. Open slot on front pilot for coupler
2. Closed slot number board
3. No builder's plate

Type IV
1. Closed slot on front pilot, no coupler
2. Open slot number board
3. "LIONEL MPC" builder's plate behind cab door

Type V
1. Open slot on front pilot, no strut
2. Open slot number board
3. "LIONEL" only on builder's plate behind cab door

Type VI
1. Closed slot on front pilot
2. Open slot number board
3. "LIONEL" only on builder's plate behind door

GP-7 and GP-9 Body Types
The difference between a Lionel GP-7 and a GP-9 is the addition of a snap-on plastic dynamic brake casting. The GP-7 and 9 bodies show a progression not unlike those of the F-3s, Alcos and Yard Switchers. Fundimensions made changes in body design to solve decorating problems or to coordinate body design with other production changes. We have identified five basic bodies:

Body Type I 8030, 8031
(A) One piece inserted in the body to form two headlight lenses, two marker light lenses and two number boards with actual numbers.
(B) Hinges on side door panels beneath the road name.
(C) Builder's plate carries the LIONEL and MPC logo.
(D) No indentations for stamped steel handrails since wire handrails used.
(E) Louvers on hatch panels beneath the numerals 8030.
(F) Two steps from the cab to the frame.

Body Type II 8250 Santa Fe, same as Type I, but:
(A) No numbers on number boards.
(B) No hinges on side door panels near the road name.

Body Type III Early 1976, 8576 Penn Central, same as II, but:
(C) Builder's plate carries only the LIONEL name.
(D) Indentations in the cab side (addition of Type IV railings), since stamped steel handrails are added.

Body Type IV Early 1978, 8866 Minneapolis and St. Louis, same as III, but:
(E) No louvers (but numbers) on the hatch panel on the cab below the window.
(F) One step only from the cab to the frame.

Body Type V Later 1978, 8854 C.P. Rail, same as IV, but:
(G) No indentations in the cab because Type IV railing used.

U36B Body Types
Type I: No indentations for handrails
Type II: Indentations for handrails

GP-20 Body Types
Type I: No indentations for handrails
Type II: Indentations for handrails

GP and U36B Motor Types
Type I: 8010-127 has two circular pickups as found on the old-style Scout. The pickups did not bridge the switches so Fundimensions added a pickup to the dummy truck on its later production. This pickup was similar to the old Lionel GP-style pickup.

Type II: 8250-125 has two roller pickups which are similar to those found on MPC tenders and passenger cars. The rollers are attached to a shoe that slides under a brass spring plate on the truck. Fundimensions also added a pickup to the dummy trucks on its initial motor run. All GPs and U36Bs have two operating couplers, stamped metal frames and plastic steps attached to both trucks, and powered units have three position E-units. All GP-20s have LIONEL builder's plates, U36Bs do not have any. Early MPC, GP-7 and GP-9 production included a Lionel MPC builder's plate. On later production the MPC part of the logo was dropped.

Diesel Railing Types
Type I Stamped Metal Post Made apparently from Lionel flat car stakes with a handrail passing through the stakes, railing end holes in north and south cab sides, oversized but sturdy.

Type II Plastic Posts - Handrail Combination Better scaled but fragile, railing end holes in north and south cab sides.

Type III Stamped Metal Railing Riveted to frame, with large rivets for end railings, railing is turned into cab with indentations on east and west cab sides.

Type IV Metal Railing Railing spot-welded to frame, but not connected to cab, indentations in cab filled in and railing simply lies along cab side. The change from Type III to IV apparently occurred in mid-1978 because the 8866 is a Type IV. End railings are an integral part of its frame and were formed with the frame and not separately as in Type III. (Note: Some copies of the 8866 were apparently made with Type III railings).

634 SANTA FE Circa 1970, NW-2 Yard Switcher, rerun of 1965-66 unit, chrome-plated plastic bell and radio antenna.   15   22   30   50

1776 NORFOLK & WESTERN 1976, powered GP-9, Type II plastic railings, painted red, white and blue body with flat gold lettering, silver circle of thirteen stars, black underframe, lights, nose decal, Type II motor, no pickup on dummy truck, no MPC logo. This is actually catalogued as 8559 but is listed here for your convenience.

(A) Gloss red paint	—	—	50	95
(B) Flat red paint	—	—	50	95
(C) Same as (A) but no circle of stars	—	—	90	175

1776 SEABOARD COAST LINE 1976, powered G.E. U36B, stamped metal railings, red, white and blue body with blue lettering, no lettering on frame, black underframe, lights, nose decal, Type II motor, no pickup on dummy truck, no MPC logo

(A) No lettering on frame   —   —   50   80
(B) White "SEABOARD COAST LINE" on frame   —   —   60   90
(C) Same as 1776 (B) but with medium white "SEABOARD COAST LINE" on frame   —   —   50   90
(D) Special for TCA with TCA logo and three TCA passenger cars   —   —   —   205

137

1776[C]

1776[A]

1776

1776[E]

1776[B]

ALCO DIESELS

8020	8020
8020	8022[A]
8025	8025
8252	8253
8351	8563
8361	8362

1776 BANGOR AND AROOSTOOK 1976, powered GP-9, "Jeremiah O'Brien," catalogued as 8665, Type III railing, red, white and blue with red, white and blue lettering, catalogued and sold with a 9176 caboose, "8665" not on engine, silver truck side frames, lights, nose decal, no MPC logo, "LIONEL" builder's plate, Type III body — — 60 85

1976 See 1776(E)

4935 PENNSYLVANIA See 8150

7500 LIONEL 75th ANNIVERSARY 1975-76, powered G.E. U36B diesel, part of set 1505, red, silver and black body, black frame, lights, "7500" on box — — 60 85

8010 A T & S F 1970, NW-2 Yard Switcher, blue with yellow lettering — — 20 32

8020 SANTA FE 1970-76, powered Alco FA-2 A unit, red and silver body, lights, comes with 8021 or 8020 dummy
(A) Powered 8020, Type I body — — 19 27
(B) SANTA FE, 1970-71, dummy Alco FA-2 A unit, red and silver body — — 13 19
(C) Blue and silver body — — 13 19

8021 SANTA FE 1971-72, 1974-76, dummy Alco FA-2 B unit, red and silver body, "SANTA FE" under vents — — 10 15

8022 SANTA FE 1971, powered, Alco FA-2, A unit, blue and yellow freight colors, uncatalogued, made for J.C. Penney, lights
(A) With nose decal — — 20 30
(B) Without nose decal — — 20 30
(C) Powered and dummy A unit set, numbered "8022," only fifty sets, made for J.C. Penney's, Ann Arbor, Michigan, store, Catalano observation **NRS**

8025 CANADIAN NATIONAL 1971, Alco FA-2 AA units, one powered, other dummy, both with same number, not catalogued, Parker Brothers distribution in Canada, imported by U.S. dealers. Price for both units — — 40 55

8030 ILLINOIS CENTRAL 1970-71, powered GP-9, white and orange body with black lettering, one pickup on power truck, pickup on dummy truck, black frame, lights, Type I motor, LIONEL/MPC builder's plate, Type I body, loop pickup may or may not supplement pickup on dummy truck
(A) Lighter orange, Type I motor, Type I railing, nose decal, loop — — 35 45
(B) Darker orange, Type II railing, no nose decal, Type II motor — — 35 45
(C) ITT Special Limited Edition Railway Set for Marine Expo 9 at Washington, D.C., fall, 1975, registered as "ISBN 0-912276-13-4" and "LC 74-29700" with Library of Congress, "ITT Cable-Hydrospace" glossy black sticker with gold letters placed over "ILLINOIS CENTRAL" on loco side, no end decal. Twenty-five sets, each with an 8030 engine, 8254 dummy with the same sticker, three bright blue over-painted 9113 N & W hoppers with clear central decals with white lettered "cable ITT car," one hopper with an orange cover, 9160 caboose with black sticker with gold letters, Catalano observation, two engine-four car set — — 400
(D) Same as (B) but with nose decal and extra set of pickups, Rohlfing Collection — — 35 45

8031 CANADIAN NATIONAL 1970-71, powered GP-7, black and orange body, white lettering, lights, no nose decal, Type I motor, pickup on dummy, Lionel/MPC builder's plate, Type II body
(A) Type I railing, Canadian edition — — 35 50
(B) Type II railing — — 30 40

8050 DELAWARE & HUDSON 1980, powered U36C, silver body, blue top, six-wheel trucks, matching 8051 dummy available separately, 8050 only — — 95

8051 DELAWARE & HUDSON 1980, dummy U36C, matches 8050 set — — 45

8054 C & S BURLINGTON 1980, dual-motored F-3 A unit, metallic silver body with black and red markings, known as Texas Zephyr (C & S stands for Colorado and Southern, a group of railroads acquired by Burlington in 1908 and run as a division), matching dummy A unit (8055) and B unit (8062) available, 8054 A unit only — — 115

8055 C & S BURLINGTON 1980, dummy F-3 A unit, illuminated, matches 8054, 8055 only — — 80

8054 and 8055 Set — — 195

8056 CHICAGO & NORTH WESTERN 1980, dual-motored FM Trainmaster, magnetraction, six-wheel trucks — — 200

8057 BURLINGTON 1980, NW-2 Yard Switcher, red and gray, lettered "Way of the Zephyrs," two-position reverse unit, disc-operating couplers — — 65

8059 PENNSYLVANIA 1980, F-3 B unit, dummy, Brunswick green, matches 8952 and 8953 F-3 A units, clear plastic portholes — — 150

8060 PENNSYLVANIA 1980, F-3 B unit, dummy, tuscan matches 8970 and 8971 F-3 A units, clear plastic portholes — — 90

8061 WM 1980 WESTERN MARYLAND Powered U36C, yellow and orange body with blue roof, three-position reverse unit, six-wheel trucks, from No. 1070 Royal Limited Set — — 95

8062 BURLINGTON 1980, F-3 B unit, dummy, matches 8054 and 8055 F-3 A units, clear plastic portholes — — 100

8063 SEABOARD 1980, powered SD-9, black with yellow band with red trim and yellow frames, six-wheel trucks with blind center wheels and rubber tires on the three wheels on geared side, three-position reverse, disc-operating couplers with small tabs, heavy stamped steel railing — — 85

8064 FLORIDA EAST COAST 1980, powered GP-9, red and yellow, catalogued with black trucks but made with silver trucks, three-position reverse unit — — 65

8065 FLORIDA EAST COAST 1980, dummy GP-9, matches 8064 — — 35

8064 and 8065 pair — — 110

8066 T P W 1980 [TOLEDO, PEORIA & WESTERN,] Powered GP-20, red and white, three-position reverse unit, catalogued with dynamic brake unit on roof, but made without brake unit, came with No. 1072 Cross Country Express Set. Catalogue shows orange color, but not produced that way. — — 65

8067 TEXAS AND PACIFIC 1980, powered Alco FA-2 unit, two-position reverse unit, blue and white, illustrated as part of No. 1051 Texas & Pacific Diesel Set **Not Manufactured**

8068 THE ROCK "1980" on loco cab, powered GP-20, 1980 annual LCCA convention issue, 2,700 made. — — 125

8071 VIRGINIAN 1980, powered SD-18, blue and yellow, also see 8072, six-wheel trucks, silver truck sides. — — 100

8072 VIRGINIAN 1980, dummy SD-18, matches 8071 engine — — 55

8071 and 8072 Set — — 150

8111 DT & I 1971-74, NW-2 Yard Switcher, illuminated headlight, hand reverse
(A) Two green marker lights — — 20 30
(B) Two red marker lights — — 20 30

8150 PENNSYLVANIA 1981, dual-powered GG-1 electric, green painted die-cast body with five gold stripes, magnetraction, three-position reverse unit, green painted die-cast body — — 225 320

8151 BURLINGTON 1981 powered SD-28, red with gray top, white nose stripes, white frame, numbers and letters, six-wheel trucks, from No. 1160 Great Lakes Limited set — — 80

8152 CANADIAN PACIFIC 1981, powered SD-24 flat top diesel, maroon and gray, with two yellow side stripes, three horizontal nose stripes, white frame, yellow numbers, maroon "Canadian Pacific" in script on gray background, horn, six-wheel trucks, from No. 1158 Maple Leaf set — — 80 120

8153 READING 1981, powered NW-2 Yard Switcher, dark green front and top, black frame, yellow sides, dark green numbers and logo, from No. 1154 Reading Yard King set — — 32 45

8154 ALASKA 1981-82, powered, NW-2 Yard Switcher, dynamic air brake, same paint scheme as Lionel 614 — — 60 89

8155 MONON 1981-82, powered U36B, gold sides and ends with dark blue roof and dark blue band running along cab bottom, also see 8156 — — 75

140

FUNDIMENSIONS GM YARD SWITCHER BODY TYPES

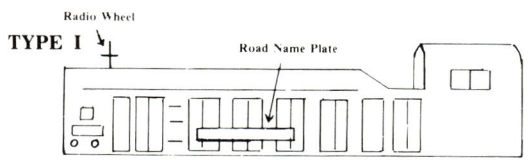

TYPE I
Maintenance ladders with three steps, little doors and road name plate

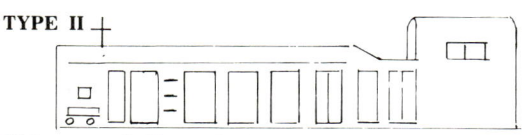

TYPE II
Maintenance ladder with three steps, no little doors, no road name plate

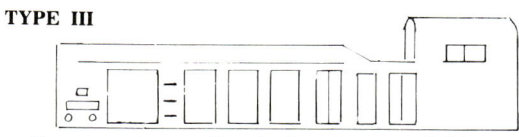

TYPE III
Large panel, no radio wheel, maintenance ladder with three steps

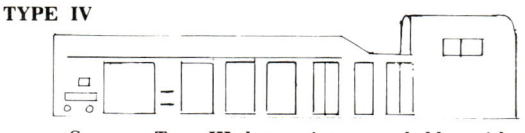

TYPE IV
Same as Type III, but maintenance ladder with two steps

TYPE V
Same as Type III, but maintenance ladder with one step

FUNDIMENSIONS F-3 A UNIT BODY TYPES

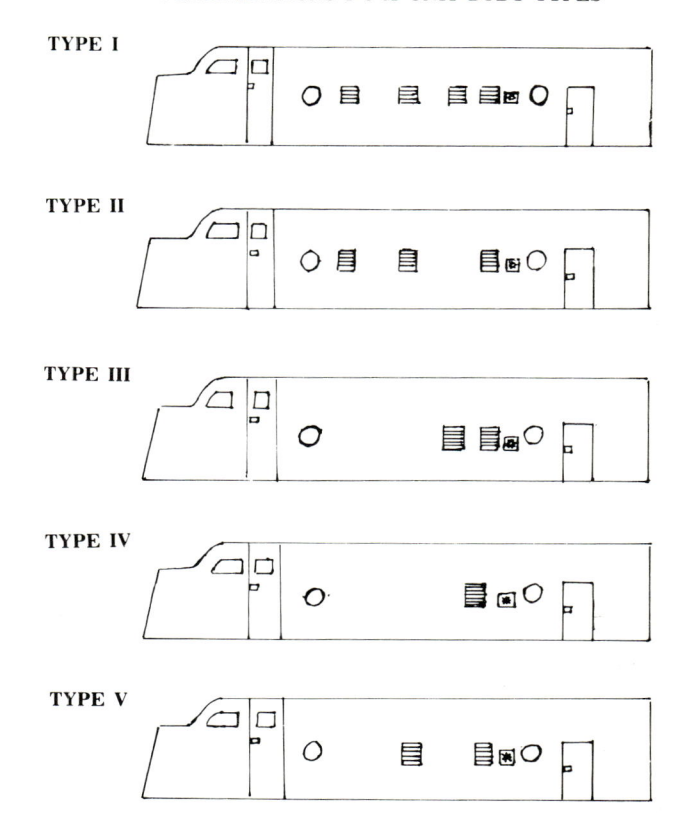

TYPE I

TYPE II

TYPE III

TYPE IV

TYPE V

8156 MONON 1981-82, dummy U36B, matches 8155 — — — 50

8155 and 8156 Pair — — — 125

8157 SANTA FE 1981, dual-powered FM Trainmaster, blue with yellow trim, numbers and letters, electronic horn — — 195 260

8158 DULUTH MISSABE 1981-82, powered GP-35, maroon with yellow middle side band, white numbers and letters, also see 8159 — — — 70

8159 DULUTH MISSABE 1981-82, dummy GP-35, matches 8158 — — — 45

8160 BURGER KING 1981-82, powered GP-20, yellow body with red top, frame, numbers and letters, from Favorite Food Freight, available only as separate sale item — — 47 70

8161 L.A.S.E.R. 1981-82, Gas Turbine, bright chrome, blue lettering, part of No. 1150 L.A.S.E.R. Train set, a return to a late 1950's-type Lionel space set, D.C. powered — — 20 25

8162 ONTARIO NORTHLAND 1981, powered SD-18, also see 8163, part of the "Fall Release Items," blue with yellow trim and lettering — — 75 100

8163 ONTARIO NORTHLAND 1981, dummy SD-18, also see 8162 — — 40 60

8164 PENNSYLVANIA 1981, F-3 B unit, green body, with horn. Distributors were required to purchase nearly $800 of goods to acquire one. Matches 8952-53 AA pair. — — — 175

8250 SANTA FE 1972-75, powered GP-9, Type II railing, black & yellow body with yellow lettering, black underframe, nose decal, Type II motor, pick-up on dummy truck, Lionel/MPC builder's plate, Type II body — — 40 50

8252 DELAWARE & HUDSON 1972, powered Alco FA-2 unit
(A) Dark blue and silver body, two-position E-unit, Type IV body, D & H decal on side and nose, blank number boards, no front coupler — — 25 35
(B) Similar to (A) but factory prototype as shown in 1972 catalogue with lighter blue, almost powder blue paint, number boards read "8022," D & H decal on side but road name and number not printed out. Road name and number shown in 1972 catalogue are printer overlay. Front coupler, side ladder steps do not line up with door, believed to be one of a kind, Philip Mace Catalano Collection, value with 8253(C) — — — 550

8253 DELAWARE & HUDSON 1972, dummy Alco FA-2 A unit, matches 8252
(A) Dark blue, with side decal — — 20 30
(B) Dark blue without side decal — — 20 30
(C) Light blue, almost powder blue, matches 8252(B), yellow sticky strip along bottom unlike painted yellow strip on 8252(B), ladders do not line up with door. With D & H decal but without number or name on side. 1972 catalogue shows prototype with name and number but these are printer overlay, Philip Mace Catalano Collection, see 8252 (B) for value.

8254 ILLINOIS CENTRAL 1972, dummy GP-9, Type II railings, black lettering, orange plastic body with white stripe, no lights, nose decal, Lionel/MPC builder's plate, black frame — — 20 25

8255 SANTA FE 1972, dummy GP-9, matches 8250, but not lighted — — 20 35

8258 CANADIAN NATIONAL 1972, dummy GP-7, Type II railings, black and orange body with white lettering, no lights, no nose decal, Lionel/MPC builder's plate — — 21 25

8260 SOUTHERN PACIFIC 1982, dual-motored F-3 A unit in distinctive red, orange, white and black "Daylight" paint scheme, three-position reverse unit, one-axle magnetraction, one operating coupler on front, fixed coupler on rear, illuminated number boards, portholes, part of Spring Collector Series and reportedly a limited edition, comes with matching dummy 8262. Price for both units: — — 210 280

Five matching passenger cars available as separate sales only.

8261 SOUTHERN PACIFIC 1982, dummy F-3 B unit, matches 8260 — — — 175

8262 See 8260

8263 SANTA FE 1982, powered GP-7, blue and yellow, operating couplers, electronic reverse unit, split-field motor, electronic 3-position reversing unit — — 35 50

141

GP-7, GP-9 and GP-20 DIESELS

8030 GP-9

8031 GP-7

8359 [A] GP-7

8250 GP-9

8352 GP-20

GP-7, GP-9 and GP-20 DIESELS

8353 GP-7

8357 GP-9

8360[B] GP-20

8454 GP-7

8463 GP-20

8264 CANADIAN PACIFIC 1982, gray and maroon snowplow, reportedly similar to No. 53 Rio Grande from 1957-60 — — 60 90

8265 SANTA FE 1982, powered SD-40, new cab design, Type C six-wheel trucks, twin motors, magnetraction, horn — — 250 300

8266 NORFOLK AND WESTERN 1982, SD-24, maroon body with yellow trim, three-position reverse unit, die-cast six-wheel trucks, operating couplers, illuminated number boards, electronic diesel horn, part of No. 1260 Continental Limited set issued in Spring Collector Series **NRS**

8268 T & P Express set, 1982, No. 1253 in 1983. To solve traction problems, Lionel made available two iron weights with a piece of foam with double sided adhesive for Service Station installation. It is reported that 1983 production will include the weights. The set sold exceptionally well in 1982. 1983 set price is $130. A unit only. — — 50 60

8269 T & P 1982-83, matches 8268, dummy unit — — 25 30

8350 U.S. STEEL 1974-75, Gas Turbine, 0-4-0, maroon plastic body with silver lettering, DC motor, forward and reverse by polarity, reverse on power packs, motor will burn out if run on AC — — 7 10

8351 SANTA FE 1973-74, powered Alco, FA-2 A unit, blue and silver body, Sears set — — 20 25

8352 SANTA FE 1973-75, powered GP-20, plastic railings, dark blue and yellow body with yellow lettering, black underframe, no decal, Type II — — 30 40

8353 GRAND TRUNK 1974-75, powered GP-7, Type II railings, gray plastic body painted blue and orange, white lettering, lights, Type II motor, Lionel/MPC builder's plate, Type II body — — 36 43

8354 ERIE 1973-75, NW-2 Yard Switcher, black plastic body, heat-stamped gold lettering, lights
(A) Type III body — — 30 40
(B) Type IV body — — 30 40

8355 SANTA FE 1973-75, dummy GP-20, matches 8352, electronic diesel horn, pickup on one truck — — 50 60

8356 GRAND TRUNK 1974-75, dummy GP-7, matches 8353, no lights — — 20 25

8357 PENNSYLVANIA 1973-75, powered GP-9, Type II railings, gray plastic body painted dark green, gold lettering, lights, no nose decal, Type II motor, black frame, Lionel/MPC builder's plate, Type II body, 9,000 made — — 45 65

8358 PENNSYLVANIA 1973-75, dummy GP-9, matches 8357, no lights, a few units are known to have been made with horns
(A) No horn — — 20 30
(B) With factory installed horn — — 50 60

8359 CHESSIE 1973, powered GP-7, Type II railings, special gold paint for GM's 50th anniversary with blue lettering, reported that 9,000 made. "8359" not on loco, lights, nose lettering, Type II motor, black frame, Lionel/MPC builder's plate, Type II body
(A) All blue "B & O" and "GM 50" lettering, painted nose, Mitchell Collection — — 70 80
(B) Without "B & O" and "GM 50" but with nose decal **NRS**

8360 LONG ISLAND 1973-74, powered GP-20, Type II railings, charcoal gray painted body with silver lettering, no nose decal, lights, Lionel/MPC builder's plate, Type II body
(A) Black frame — — 35 45
(B) Black frame with painted red stripe — — 45 60

8361 WESTERN PACIFIC 1973-74, powered Alco, FA-2, A unit, silver and orange body, see 8362 for matching B unit, lights — — 21 33

8362 WESTERN PACIFIC 1973-74, dummy Alco, FA-2B unit, matches 8361 — — 15 20

8363 BALTIMORE & OHIO 1973-75, powered F-3 A unit, dark blue plastic body painted light blue with white and gray top, yellow lettering on black stripe, Type I body, lights. See next entry for matching dummy A unit. — — 75 90

8364 BALTIMORE & OHIO 1973-75, dummy F-3 A unit matches 9863 — — 40 55

8365 CANADIAN PACIFIC 1973, powered F-3 A unit, Type I body, reportedly that only 2,500 manufactured, not catalogued,1973 Service Station Special, for matching dummy A unit see 8366
(A) Gray plastic body painted brown and gray — — 120 140
(B) Blue plastic body painted brown and gray — — 120 140

8366 CANADIAN PACIFIC 1973, dummy A unit
(A) Matches 8365 (A) — — 75 85
(B) Matches 8365 (B) — — 75 85

8367 LONG ISLAND 1973, dummy GP-20, matches 8360, electronic diesel horn
(A) Plain frame — — 50 60
(B) Red stripe on frame — — 55 65

8368 ALASKA RAILROAD 1983, 2-4-2, motorized unit, yellow and blue with blue lettering "ALASKA RAILROAD 8368" and eskimo logo. Silver finished bell, operating headlight, operating couplers, die-cast frame, three-position E unit — — 80 90

8369 ERIE LACKAWANNA 1983, powered GP-20, dual DC motors, operates on AC or DC, operating headlight, electronic 3-position reverse, one operating coupler, only offered for separate sale in Traditional Series catalogue, shown in catalogue as blue and tuscan engine, but made in gray and tuscan Erie Lackawanna colors. Lionel also made a matching 6425 caboose. — — 60 75

8370 NEW YORK CENTRAL 1983, powered F-3A unit, dual motors with eight wheel magnetraction, 3-position reverse unit, headlight, illuminated number boards, portholes, operating coupler at front end. Note matching

8350 U.S. STEEL

8371 and 8372 and passenger cars. In 1948-49 Lionel offered a N.Y.C. F-3 as 2333, 8370 and 8372 as a pair: 300 — — 225 250

8371 NEW YORK CENTRAL 1983, dummy F-3B unit matches 8370 and 8372. Electronic diesel horn, portholes, not illuminated, dummy couplers. — — 60 75

8372 NEW YORK CENTRAL 1983, dummy F-3A unit, headlight, illuminated number boards, portholes, operating coupler at cab end. Matches 8370 and 8372. — — 60 75

8374 BURLINGTON NORTHERN 1983, DC powered NW-2 Yard Switcher, rectifier for AC or DC operation, green and black plastic body, white lettering and logo, black enameled frame, two red indicator lights and operating headlight, two disc operating couplers, three-position electronic reversing unit, only offered for separate sale in Traditional Series Catalogue. Lionel also made a matching 6427 caboose. — — 45 55

8375 CHICAGO & NORTHWESTERN 1983, DC powered GP-7, dual motors with rectifier for AC or DC operation, headlight, operating couplers, electronic reverse unit, yellow and green body, part of set No. 1354 Northern Freight Flyer, set price: 160 — — 50 65

8376 UNION PACIFIC 1983, powered SD-40, magnetraction, six-wheel die-cast metal trucks, headlight, electronic diesel loco, 3-position reverse unit, operating couplers at both ends, catalogued as part of the yellow and gray body with red stripe, green hood top. Part of a special limited edition set, No. 1361 Gold Coast Limited with 9290 barrel car, 9888 reefer, 9468 box car, 6114 hopper, 6357 tank and 6904 caboose. Set currently brings $375, LaVoie comment — — 200 225

8377 US 1983, switcher, 0-4-0, olive drab, engine does not have applied lettering as shown in the Traditional Series Catalogue. Lionel supplied a decal sheet for the operator. This loco is part of the low price introductory set No. 1355 Commando Assault Train with 6561 flat with cruise missile, 6562 flat

GP-7, GP-9 and GP-20 DIESELS

8550 GP-9

8562 GP-20

8576 GP-7

8654 GP-9

8666 GP-9

with crates, 6564 flat with tanks, 6435 caboose, playmat, figures and supply depot kit. Set price $50. — — 20 25

8379 PENNSYLVANIA 1983, motorized fire-fighting car, tuscan body with black bumpers and wheels, white fire nozzle, seat, outriggers and hose reel. Black clad fireman with flesh colored hands and face. Highly detailed body, gold plastic bell, illuminated red dome light atop cab. Bump reverse. Gold "PENNSYLVANIA" PRR Keystone and "6521" on side of body; number is divided in center by Keystone. Catalogue number may change. Fall Collector Center, LaVoie report **NRS**

8380 LIONEL LINES 1983, powered SD-28, dark blue upper body, upper cab and nose top, orange lower body, and nose. Black frame, red, white and blue Lionel logo on cab side and nose, six-wheel trucks Type IV handrails. Blue number is below the logo on the cab, blue "LIONEL LINES" in modern sans-serif lettering below color division, lighted cab, chromed plastic five-horn unit atop cab, squared off cab roof, Fall Collector Center, LaVoie report — — —

8452 ERIE 1974, powered Alco FA-2 A unit, black plastic body painted green with yellow lettering, lights, see next entry for B unit — — 18 22

8453 ERIE 1974, dummy Alco FA-2 B unit matches 8452 A unit (in previous entry) — — 14 18

8454 RIO GRANDE 1974-75, powered GP-7, Type II railings, black body with orange lettering, yellow hash marks, black frame, lights, Type II motor, Lionel/MPC builder's plate, Type II body — — 35 45

8455 RIO GRANDE 1974-75, dummy GP-7, matches 8454, no lights — — 15 20

8460 MKT 1973-75, NW-2 Yard Switcher, gray plastic body painted red, white lettering, manual forward and reverse, Type IV body, dummy coupled — — 22 28

8463 CHESSIE 1974, powered GP-20, Type II railings, blue, orange and yellow body with blue lettering, limited edition of 10,000, lights, black frame, nose decal, Type II motor, "LIONEL" logo — — 60 85

8464 RIO GRANDE 1974, powered F-3 A unit, yellow body with black lettering, silver roof, solid portholes, lights, only 3,000 manufactured, uncatalogued 1974 Service Station Special, Type I body — — 54 61

8465 RIO GRANDE 1974, dummy F-3 A unit, matches 8464, 3,000 manufactured, lights, Type I body — — 34 40

8466 AMTRAK 1974-75, powered F-3 A unit, silver body and sides, black roof and nose hood, red and blue logo, sealed portholes, lights, Type III body — — 70 90

8467 AMTRAK 1974-75, dummy F-3A unit, matches 8466 — — 40 55

8468 BALTIMORE & OHIO 1974, dummy F-3 B unit, blue body with white lettering, sealed portholes, matches 8363 and 8364 A units
(A) Top edge of sides not painted — — 50 70
(B) Top edge of sides painted — — 50 70

8469 CANADIAN PACIFIC 1974, dummy F-3 B unit, sealed portholes, matches 8365, 8366, top edge of side not painted maroon — — 55 75

8470 CHESSIE 1974, powered G.E. U36B, stamped metal railings, blue, orange and yellow body with blue lettering, from Grand National set, black frame, lights, nose decal, Type II motor, no MPC logo. Shown in 1974 catalogue with large emblem and lettering, but not produced that way. — — 60 75

8471 PENNSYLVANIA 1973-74, NW-2 Yard Switcher, dark green body with yellow lettering, red Keystone on cab sides — — 45 60

8473 COCA COLA 1975, NW-2 Yard Switcher, red body with white lettering, two-position reverse
(A) "Three step" variety, Type III body — — 24 31
(B) "Two steps," Type IV body — — 20 27
(C) "One step," Type V body — — 21 28

8474 RIO GRANDE 1975, dummy F-3 B unit, yellow and green body, silver roof, sealed portholes, matches 8464, 8465 — — 45 60

8475 AMTRAK 1975, dummy F-3 B unit, silver body and sides, black roof, red and blue logo, sealed portholes, matches 8466, 8467 — — 45 60

8477 NEW YORK CENTRAL 1984, powered GP-9, AC motor, operates on either AC or DC, magnetraction, diesel horn, three-position E type reverse unit, operating headlights, operating couplers, die-cast truck side frames, steel frame, and handrails — — — —

8550 JERSEY CENTRAL 1975, powered GP-9, Type II railings, red and white painted body with white lettering, black frame, lights, nose decal, Type II motor, no pickup on dummy truck, "LIONEL" builder's plate — — 35 50

8551 PENNSYLVANIA 1975, powered, "Little Joe" G.E. EP-5 electric, tuscan body with gold stripes on body and lettering, lights, two pantographs, can be wired for overhead operation on catenary, separate motor and power truck — — 65 80

8552 SOUTHERN PACIFIC 1975, powered Alco FA-2 A unit, orange body with white stripes, lights, set of three with 8553, 8554, price for set — — 70 90

8553 SOUTHERN PACIFIC 1975, dummy Alco FA-2 B unit matches 8552. (Only B unit dummy with operating couplers at both ends, wheel base altered to accommodate trucks.) Set price with 8552, 8554 — — 70 90

8554 SOUTHERN PACIFIC 1975, dummy Alco FA-2 A unit, matches 8552, price for set — — 70 90

8555 MILWAUKEE ROAD 1975, powered F-3 A unit, gray and orange body, sealed portholes, lights, Type II mold, uncatalogued 1975 Service Station Special — — 70 90

8556 CHESSIE 1975-76, NW-2 Yard Switcher, yellow and blue, lights, Type V body — — 40 55

8557 MILWAUKEE ROAD 1975, dummy F-3 A unit, gray and orange body, matches, 8555 Type II body — — 45 60

8558 MILWAUKEE ROAD 1976, powered GEEP-5 electric, brown, orange and black body, lights, two silver pantographs, can be wired for catenary operation, separate motor and power truck — — 60 70

8559 N & W 1776 1975, see 1776 (A),(B) and (C)

8560 CHESSIE 1975, dummy G.E. U36B, matches 8470, lights, pickup on one truck. Some reports stress this is not quite an exact match for the 8470. Further information needed — — 33 40

8561 JERSEY CENTRAL 1975-76, dummy GP-9 matches 8550, not lighted — — 15 22

8562 MISSOURI PACIFIC 1975-76, powered GP-20, Type II railings, blue with white lettering, hash marks, black underframe, Type II motor — — 35 43

8563 ROCK ISLAND 1975, powered Alco FA-2 A unit, red body with white letters, yellow stripe, closed pilot, uncatalogued, available only in Sears set — — 31 38

8564 UNION PACIFIC 1975, powered G.E. U36B, Type III railing, gray and yellow body with red stripe, from North American set, black frame, lights, nose decal, Type II motor — — 55 68

8565 MISSOURI PACIFIC 1975-76, dummy GP-20, matches 8562, a few with horns are known to exist
(A) No horn — — 19 24
(B) With horn — — 55 65

8566 SOUTHERN 1975-77, powered F-3 A unit, green body with gray stripes, sealed portholes, lights, Type IV body, gold lettering — — 80 120

8567 SOUTHERN 1975-77, dummy F-3 A unit, matches 8567 — — 72 110

8568 PREAMBLE EXPRESS 1975, powered F-3 A unit, red, white and blue body, sealed portholes, Spirit of 76, East Coast Clearance Engine, lights, Type IV body. No dummy unit made — — 50 63

8569 SOO 1975-77, NW-2, Yard Switcher, red body with white lettering, lights, dummy couplers, two-position reverse — — 23 33

8570 LIBERTY SPECIAL 1975, powered Alco FA-2, blue top, white body, with red nose and stripe, lights — — 30 40

8571 FRISCO 1975-76, powered G.E. U36B, Type III railing, white and red with red lettering, black frame, lights, no nose decal, Type II motor — — 45 59

GP-7, GP-9, and GP-20 DIESELS

8750 GP-7

8757 [A] GP-9

8759 GP-9

8763 GP-9

8772 GP-20

8572 FRISCO 1975-76, dummy G. E. U36B matches 8571, lights, pickup on one truck — — 25 29

8573 UNION PACIFIC 1975, dummy G. E. U36B, stamped metal railing, matches 8564, except no lights, pickup on one truck, with horn, reported that only 1,200 made — — 90 110

8575 MILWAUKEE ROAD Dummy F-3B unit, matches 8555 — — 32 37

8576 PENN CENTRAL 1975-76, powered GP-7, Type III railings, black body with white lettering
(A) Door outline shows through PENN CENTRAL lettering, black frame, lights, nose decal, Type II motor, Lionel/MPC builder's plate — — 40 50
(B) Same as (A) but door outline painted solid, "LIONEL" builder's plate, Type III body — — 40 50

8650 BURLINGTON NORTHERN 1976-77, powered G.E. U36B, Type III railing, black and green body with white lettering, hash marks, black frame, lights, Type II motor — — 40 50

8651 BURLINGTON NORTHERN 1976-77, dummy G.E. U36B matches 8650, lights, pickup on one truck — — 25 35

8652 SANTA FE 1976-77, powered F-3 A unit, red and silver, lights, sealed portholes, Type V mold — — 70 95

8653 SANTA FE 1976-77, dummy F-3 A unit, matches 8562, Type V mold — — 60 85

8654 BOSTON & MAINE 1976, powered GP-9, Type III railings, blue, white and black body, white and black lettering, white frame, lights, no nose decal, "LIONEL" builder's plate, Type III body — — 40 46

8655 BOSTON & MAINE 1976, dummy GP-9 matches 8654, not lighted — — 20 25

8656 CANADIAN NATIONAL 1976, powered Alco FA-2 A unit, orange, black and white, lights, three-position reverse — — 30 35

8657 CANADIAN NATIONAL 1976, dummy Alco FA-2 B unit, matches 8656 — — 20 25

8658 CANADIAN NATIONAL 1976 dummy Alco FA-2 A unit, matches 8656 — — 25 35

8659 VIRGINIAN 1976-77, G.E. EL-C rectifier electric, blue body with yellow stripe and lettering, yellow frame, can be wired for catenary, separate motor and power truck
(A) Thin, light colored nose decal — — 75 95
(B) Same as (A) but with thick, light colored nose decal — — 75 95
(C) Same as (A) but with regular dark yellow nose decal — — 75 95

8660 C P RAIL 1976,77, NW-2 Yard Switcher, red body with white lettering, lights — — 25 40

8661 SOUTHERN Dummy F-3B unit, not lighted — — 35 40

8664 AMTRAK 1976-77, powered Alco FA-2 A unit, light, fixed rear coupler, body has black roof and nose top, silver sides and nose skirt, red nose and blue lettering — — 20 30

8665 BANGOR AND AROOSTOOK See 1776

8666 NORTHERN PACIFIC 1976, powered GP-9, stamped metal railings, black and gold body with red stripe, gold and red lettering, 1976 Service Station Special, not catalogued, gold frame, lights, no nose decal, Type II motor, no MPC logo — — 90 100

8667 AMTRAK 1976-77, dummy Alco B unit, black roof and nose top, silver sides and nose skirt, red nose, blue lettering, matches 8664, difficult to find — — 15 20

8668 NORTHERN PACIFIC 1976, dummy GP-9, matches 8666 — — 35 40

8669 ILLINOIS CENTRAL 1976, powered G.E. U36B, stamped metal railings, white and orange with black lettering, from Illinois Central set, black frame, Type II motor, nose decals — — 45 60

8670 CHESSIE 1976, Gas Turbine, 0-4-0, yellow body with blue trim, fixed couplers, DC motor, polarity reversed, runs only on DC, sliding shoe pickup, not lighted — — 8 10

8750 THE ROCK 1977, powered GP-7, Type III railings, blue and white body with white and blue lettering, white frame, lights, nose decal, Type II motor, "LlONEL" builder's plate, Type III body — — 35 45

8751 THE ROCK 1977, dummy GP-7, matches 8750, no lights — — 20 25

8753 PENNSYLVANIA 1977, powered GG-1 electric, wine red with gold stripes, two motors, magnetraction, 6000 produced, not catalogued — — 250 290

8754 NEW HAVEN 1977-78, powered G.E. EL-C rectifier electric, lights, black roof, orange sides, white stripes, black lettering, black frame, can be wired for catenary, separate motor and power truck — — 65 75

8755 SANTA FE 1977-78, powered G.E. U36B, stamped metal railing, blue and yellow body with blue and yellow lettering, silver metal truck side frame, yellow frame, lights, nose decal, Type II motor — — 35 50

8756 SANTA FE 1977-78, dummy G.E. U36B matches 8755, not lighted — — 20 29

8757 CONRAIL 1977-78, powered GP-9, Type III railing, gray plastic body painted blue, white lettering, lights, nose decal, Type II motor, no pickup on dummy truck, no MPC logo
(A) Black underframe and railings — — 35 40
(B) White underframe and railings — — 35 40

8758 SOUTHERN 1978, GP-7 dummy matches 8774, green and white. This unit is unique in that it has a lower number than does its powered unit — — 30 40

8759 ERIE LACKAWANNA 1977-79, powered GP-9, Type III railing, gray plastic body painted gray, tuscan and yellow, yellow lettering, yellow frame, lights, nose decal, Type II motor, no MPC logo — — 32 41

8760 ERIE LACKAWANNA 1977-79, dummy GP-9, matches 8759 — — 22 27

8761 GRAND TRUNK 1977-78, NW-2 Yard Switcher, blue, white and orange paint, three-position E-unit, two disc-operating couplers, light — — 30 40

8762 GREAT NORTHERN 1977-78, powered G.E. EP-5 electric, gray plastic painted dark green and orange, yellow lettering and stripes, four red and white logos, two large decals on nose, two pantographs, can be wired for catenary, separate motor and power truck — — 70 80

8763 NORFOLK & WESTERN 1977-78 powered GP-9, Type III railing, gray plastic painted black, white lettering, black frame, lights, nose decal, Type II motor, no MPC logo — — 35 45

8764 B & O 1977, powered Budd RDC passenger car, gray plastic body painted silver with blue lettering, metal frame, plastic battery box hangs from frame, three-position E-unit with lever on bottom, two disc-operating coup-

8670 Chessie

lers, rubber tread on two wheels with gears, F-3-type power trucks with plastic two step assembly. (The plastic assembly formerly appeared on the Lionel 44 ton dummy truck.) This is a remanufacture of the Lionel 1950's version and differs from it in the following ways: the reissues have different numbers, a plastic trim horn replaces a metal trim horn, rubber tire traction replaces magnetraction and highly shiny silver paint replaces flat silver/gray paint — — 60 80

8765 B & O 1977, dummy Budd RDC baggage/mail, "US Mail Railway Post Office," "Budd RDC" in blue letters pierced by red line on small decal, lights, two disc-operating couplers, gray plastic painted silver with blue lettering — — 30 40

GP-7, GP-9 and GP-20 DIESELS

8774 GP-7

8775 GP-9

8776 GP-20

8854 GP-9

8866 GP-9

8766 B & O 1977, powered Budd RDC baggage/mail, gray plastic painted shiny silver with blue lettering, lights, part of uncatalogued 1977 Service Station Special set No. 1766 and 8767 and 8768, price for set
— — **150 170**

8767 B & O 1977, dummy Budd RDC passenger car matches 8766, part of set with 8766 and 8768, price for set — — **150 170**

8768 B & O 1977, dummy Budd RDC passenger car, matches 8766, part of set with 8766 and 8767, price for set — — **150 170**

8769 REPUBLIC STEEL 1977, DC-powered, Gas Turbine, blue with yellow trim, fixed couplers, sliding contact pickups, for use with DC current only
— — **7 10**

8770 E. M. D. 1977, NW-2 Yard Switcher, General Motors E. M. D. factory demonstrator paint scheme, blue and white body with white lettering, lights.
(A) Two disc-operating couplers, three-position E-unit — — **40 50**
(B) Fixed couplers, two-position reverse unit — — **30 40**

8771 GREAT NORTHERN 1977, powered G.E. U36B, Type III railing, gray plastic painted black, white and blue with white lettering, from Rocky Mountain Special set, black frame, lights, Type II motor — — **50 60**

8772 G M & O 1977, powered GP-20, Type III railing, gray plastic body painted red and white, from Heartland set, white frame, lights, nose decal, Type II motor, "LIONEL" logo — — **45 61**

8773 MICKEY MOUSE 1977-78, powered G.E. U36B gray plastic body painted red and white with Mickey, Pluto and Donald. This item has shown greater appreciation than any other Fundimension engine
— — **150 165**

8774 SOUTHERN 1977-78, powered, GP-7, small pickup rollers mounted on power truck, gray plastic body painted green and white, gold stripe and gold lettering, Southern decal at front end, black frame, Type IV railing, Type III body, Type II motor — — **35 45**

8775 LEHIGH VALLEY 1977-78, powered GP-9, gray plastic body painted bright red, yellow heat-stamped lettering and stripe, Type III railing, Type III cab, three-position E-unit — — **35 45**

8776 C & N W 1977-78, powered GP-20, gray plastic body painted yellow and very dark green, green lettering, red, white, and black decal beneath cab window, number boards do not have numbers, black frame, Type III railing
— — **35 45**

8777 SANTA FE 1977-78, dummy F-3 B unit matches 8652, fixed couplers at both ends, Santa Fe decal on side, no portholes, no separate grate units
— — **35 45**

8778 LEHIGH VALLEY 1977-78, dummy GP-9, matches 8775, not lighted
— — **26 30**

8779 C & N W 1977-78, dummy GP-20, matches 8776, not lighted, two disc-operating couplers — — **26 29**

8850 PENN CENTRAL 1978-79, powered GG-1 electric, black painted diecast body with white "PENN CENTRAL" and Penn Central logo on side, two magnetraction motors, magnetic couplers, headlamps at both ends, operating pantographs with black insulators, shiny metal shoes on pantographs, E-unit lever goes through roof. This engine has not sold as well as the first GG-1 rerun and substantial supplies exist. However, according to reliable sources, fewer black GG-1s were made than 8753s.
— — **190 220**

8851 NEW HAVEN 1978-79, powered A unit, Type VI body, three ridges run from the cab door to the rear of the side, gray plastic body painted silver-white, orange and black. "NH" in white letters on nose, the "N" has no serifs on the bottom right side - this matches the original Lionel F-3 New Haven but differs from the way NH is shown on the box cars. Silver painted frame, black truck side frames, disc-operating front coupler, two motors, rubber tires, came with 8852 as set, price for set — — **150 175**

8852 NEW HAVEN 1978-79, dummy F-3 A unit, Type VI body, matches 8851, lights, came with 8851 as set, price for set — — **150 175**

8854 CP RAIL 1978-79, GP-9, gray plastic body painted red, white and black, white lettering, white and black CP design. Black truck sides, two disc-operating couplers, two geared wheels with rubber tires, Type IV railing, came with Great Plains Express set, LIONEL builder's plates, Type V body — — **50 60**

8855 MILWAUKEE ROAD 1978, powered SD-18, the first in the SD-18 locomotive series, it is a combination of a U36B chassis with six-wheel trucks and a GP-20 cab/hood unit with added dynamic brake and five unit horn cluster. Because of the increased truck size, the "battery box" was redesigned and now reads "LIONEL MT. CLEMENS MICHIGAN 28045." Two disc-operating couplers, three-position reverse unit, rubber tires on end geared wheels (center wheels are blind). (For better operation note that center blind drivers are often too high and cause the rubber tire drivers to lose traction, particularly under a heavy load. Solution: hold the running engine upright and gently place a fine file against the blind driver and reduce its diameter.) Gray plastic body painted dull orange and black, black and white lettering, red and white logo underneath cab window, light, two disc-operating couplers, three-position E-unit. Sold only as part of the specially boxed Milwaukee Road set and not available for separate sale. Most sets are believed to have been sold to collectors and not run, matching dummy not available, five horn cluster and bell, Type IV frame, Type II motor
— — **80 90**

8857 NORTHERN PACIFIC 1978-80, powered G.E. U36B, gray plastic painted black with orange band along base, yellow cab end, yellow frame and rails, burnished truck side frames, Ying/Yang logo on cab decal, disc-operating couplers, five unit plastic horn on hood roof, three-position E-unit, Type IV railing, Type II motor — — **42 51**

8858 NORTHERN PACIFIC 1978-80, dummy G.E. U36B, matches 8857, not lighted
(A) No horn — — **25 30**
(B) With horn — — **50 60**

8859 CONRAIL 1978-80, 82, powered G.E. EL-C rectifier electric, gray plastic body painted blue, white lettering and Conrail design, two disc-operating couplers, black truck side frames, one operating pantograph, shiny metal pantograph shoe, can be wired for catenary operation, separate motor and power truck — — **70 85**

8860 ROCK 1978-79, powered NW-2 Yard Switcher, gray plastic body painted blue, black and white lettering and logo, white enameled frame, white nose with two pronounced red indicator lights, blue paint around headlight, two disc-operating couplers, three-position E-unit, rubber tires on two geared wheels, plastic unit suspended from frame behind E-unit, Type II motor — — **35 40**

8861 SANTA FE 1978-79, powered Alco FA-2 A unit, red and silver paint, light, two-position reverse, Type II motor — — **25 30**

8862 SANTA FE 1978-79, dummy Alco FA-2, matches 8861
— — **20 25**

8864 NEW HAVEN 1978, dummy F-3 B unit, matches 8851 and 8852, not lighted — — **33 39**

8866 MINNEAPOLIS & ST. LOUIS 1978, GP-9 powered Service Station Special sold by Lionel to Service Stations for their exclusive sale as part of a special set. This is the only item not available for separate sale in the 1978 Service Station Special set. Gray plastic body painted red and white, blue cab roof, white and red lettering, red and white logo beneath cab windows and on hood front, two disc-operating couplers, three-position E-unit, rubber tires on two geared wheels, Type IV body, Type III railing with cab indentations. (Note that the matching 8867 dummy unit has a Type IV railing. This fact supports the belief that the railing design change occurred in 1978.)
A. Type III body & railing (see illustration) — — **70 80**
B. Type IV body & railing — — **70 80**

8769 Republic Steel

R D C

8764

8765

8868

8869

8870

8871

8867 MINNEAPOLIS & ST. LOUIS 1978, dummy GP-9, matches 8866, lighted (apparently the only GP-9 dummy with lights) Type IV railing, two disc-operating couplers — — 35 40

8868 AMTRAK 1978, 80, powered Budd RDC baggage/mail unit, gray plastic body painted silver, blue lettering, white band through windows with red and blue stripes, lights, three-position reverse unit, two disc-operating couplers, Pauli Collection — — 60 80

8869 AMTRAK 1978, 80, dummy Budd RDC passenger car, lighted, two disc-operating couplers, matches 8868 — — 30 40

8870 AMTRAK 1978, 80, dummy Budd RDC passenger car, lighted, matches 8868 — — 30 40

8871 AMTRAK 1978, 80, dummy Budd RDC baggage/mail, matches 8868, lighted, two disc-operating couplers — — 30 40

8872 SANTA FE 1978-79, gray plastic body painted yellow and blue, blue and yellow lettering, Santa Fe decal on nose, yellow frame (see 8855 for SD-18 background), six-wheel trucks, two disc-operating couplers, Type IV handrails, one light, three-position reverse unit — — 60 75

8873 SANTA FE 1978-79, dummy, lights, matches 8872. The second digit of the number of every Lionel-MPC steam, diesel or electric locomotive indicates the year of manufacture. — — 35 43

8950 VIRGINIAN 1978, dual-motored, magnetraction, Fairbanks Morse Trainmaster, rerun of 1950's loco with new number and other modifications, not illustrated — — 200 220

8951 SOUTHERN PACIFIC 1979, dual-motored, magnetraction, Fairbanks Morse, rerun of prototype Trainmaster shown at 1954 Toy Fair with new number, and other modifications, not illustrated — — 230 267

8952 PENNSYLVANIA 1979, F-3 A unit, Type VII body, powered, comes with matching dummy A unit 8953, gray plastic body painted Brunswick green, five gold stripes, portholes with clear plastic lenses, nose grab irons, frost-white cab windows, two motors, each motor has two geared wheels with rubber tires and a single pickup roller, disc-operating coupler on front, fixed coupler on rear, steps on rear, red, black and gold Keystone nose decal, five stripes merge on nose, decal, gold stripes and lettering are electrocals. (Note that the area in which the electrocal is applied has a flat finish readily visible when the train is held upon its side.) Has clear number boards without numbers, price includes 8953 — — 210 255

8953 PENNSYLVANIA 1979, F-3 A unit, dummy, matches 8952, see 8952 for information

8955 SOUTHERN 1979, U36B gray plastic body painted green and white with gold lettering, five horn cluster on roof, brakewheel on hood near cab, gold stripe runs completely around cab, "SOUTHERN RAILROAD" decal on hood near cab, Type IV frame, two disc-operating couplers, geared motor wheels with rubber tires, not illustrated — — 50 60

8956 SOUTHERN 1979, U36B dummy, matches 8955 — — 29 33

8957 BURLINGTON NORTHERN 1979, powered GP-20, two-tone green body, white lettering, no stripe — — 46 53

8958 BURLINGTON NORTHERN 1979, GP-20 dummy, matches 8957 — — 26 31

8960 SOUTHERN PACIFIC 1979, G.E. U36C, powered, basically a U36B frame and cab with six-wheel trucks with added brakewheel on cab, two small marker lights near forward facing hood, Type IV frame, shortened battery box, two disc-operating couplers with tabs, bright red-orange and yellow "Daylight" colors, white lettering — — 85 95

8961 SOUTHERN PACIFIC 1979, G.E. U36C dummy, matches 8960 — — 35 45

8962 READING 1979, U36B, powered, green and yellow body, "BEE LINE SERVICE," die-cast trucks, metal wheels and handrails, disc-operating couplers, one working headlight, illuminated number plates without numbers and three-position reverse unit, Miller observation, Part of Quaker City Limited set — — — 70

8970 PENNSYLVANIA 1979-80, dual-motored F-3 A unit, tuscan painted body, five gold stripes, grab bars, clear portholes, price includes matching 8971 dummy — — 150 170

8971 PENNSYLVANIA 1979-80, F-3 dummy, matches 8970, for price see 8970

152

NW SWITCHERS

8010

8111

8354

8460

8471

8473

8473

8556

8569

8660

153

F-3 DIESELS

F-3 DIESELS

GG-1 AND EP-5 ELECTRICS

8753 GG-1

8850 GG-1

8851 EP-5

8558 EP-5

8762 EP-5

G.E. EL-C ELECTRICS & DIESELS

8659 G.E. EL-C

8754 G.E. EL-C

8859 G.E. EL-C

8855 SD-18

8872 SD-18

U36B DIESELS

7500 U36 B

8470 U36B

8564 U36B

8571 U36B

8650 U36B

U36B and U36C diesels

8669 U36B

8755 U36B

8771 U36B

8857 U36B

8960 U36C

8701 General

8140 Southern

8303 Jersey Central

8702 Southern Crescent

8801 Blue Comet

8900 Santa Fe

Chapter XIV

FUNDIMENSIONS STEAM LOCOMOTIVES

            Gd. V.G. Exc. Mt.

3 UNION PACIFIC 1981, see 8104.

3 W. & A. R.R. 1977, see 9701

611 See 8100

659 See 8101

783 See 8407

3100 GREAT NORTHERN 1981, 4-8-4, Famous American Railroad Series #3; whistle, electronic Sound of Steam, magnetraction, three-position E-unit, green and silver boiler (front of boiler - to stack - in silver), "elephant ears," terra-cotta cab roof, black sand and steam domes, white-edged running board; black streamlined tender with GREAT NORTHERN logo on side, superb "runner"   —   —   230   260

4449 See 8307

4501 See 8309

8001 NICKEL PLATE 1980, 2-6-4, plastic K-4 loco, remake of 2025/675 die-cast steamer from late 40s. This (with 8007) is the first Lionel six-wheel driver plastic locomotive, DC-powered engine   —   —   30   41

8002 UNION PACIFIC 1980, 2-8-4, Berkshire, second in Fundimension's Famous American Railroad Series (FARR); two-tone gray boiler, yellow-edged running board, electronic whistle, electronic sound of steam, magnetraction, smoke, three-position reverse unit; gray tender with dark gray center band, yellow lettered "UNION PACIFIC," with (FARR) DIAMOND LOGO. The UP prototype is actually a 4-8-4 Northern since the U P did not use a 2-8-4 Berkshire, first loco with smoke deflectors astride the boiler, Bohn comment   —   —   275   350

8003 CHESSIE 1980, 2-8-4; die-cast Berkshire. This locomotive marked an important development in Fundimensions' history, the rerun of the 2-8-4 Berkshire, Lionel's top-of-the-line postwar steam engine. Fundimensions also offered handsome matching passenger cars as separate sale items. The Chessie Steam Special engine and cars were based on a prototype Chessie train tour which actually toured the United States to celebrate the 150th Anniversary of American railroading. The model engine featured an electronic whistle, electronic Sound of Steam, smoke, magnetraction and a three-position reverse unit. The engine boiler is light gray (forward of the bell) and dark gray (behind the bell); it has a yellow-edged running board, yellow and red stripes beneath the cab window and "8003" under cab window. Dark gray tender with six-wheel trucks and large yellow area topped by orange band, "Chessie System" lettering on side. The engine as delivered did not run well. After adjustments it ran better, and its sound, properly synchronized, is delightful, Miller observation   —   —   325   350

8004 ROCK ISLAND & PEORIA 1980, 1982, 4-4-0, General chassis but modeled after a loco built by the Rock Island and Peoria Railroad in the late 1800s for the World's Fair, engine has chrome boiler, tuscan cab and steam chest, black stack and boiler bands, smoke and two-position reverse unit; tender has tuscan sides with mountain mural   —   —   100   130

8005 A T S F 1980, 82, 4-4-0, General chassis, D C powered, very lightweight locomotive, red and maroon engine with gold trim; 8005T tender with gold rectangle trim with ATSF. Came as part of No. 1053 THE JAMES GANG set with three cars, figures and building. Price for engine and tender only   —   —   25   30

8006 ATLANTIC COAST LINE 1980, 4-6-4, gunmetal-painted die-cast boiler, one piece boiler front with "LIONEL" cast beneath the headlight and numbered "2065-15" on inside, steam chest side is decorated in white with a rectangle; inside of the rectangle is another rectangle with rounded corners. The engine, known as "The Silver Shadow," has white tires and a high gloss black paint beneath the white painted running board edge. The New York Central-style tender has a water scoop; two-thirds of the prototype tender was a coal bunker. The line of rivets that descends from the rear of the coal bunker indicates the demarcation between water and coal in the prototype. This model was made for J.C. Penney as a special item and was not catalogued by Lionel. It came with a display track mounted on a wooden base in a clear plastic case. Only 2,200 reportedly were manufactured and these were sold out immediately. Many collectors believe that this item has unusual appreciation potential, Degano and White observations   —   —   275   325

8007 NEW YORK, NEW HAVEN & HARTFORD 1980, 2-6-4, plastic K-4 loco with silver boiler front, a remake of 2025/675 die-cast steamer from later 40s. This is the first time Lionel has ever made a six-driver plastic locomotive. Loco, with smoke, gold-striped running board edge; square-backed 8007T tender with gold "NEW YORK, NEW HAVEN & HARTFORD" stripe and mechanical Sound of Steam. The K-4 prototype appeared only on the Pennsylvania Railroad, but Fundimensions' management reportedly liked the New Haven logo. Came as part of No. 1050 NEW ENGLANDER set. DC-powered engine   —   —   30   40

8008 CHESSIE 1980, 4-4-2, dark blue painted die-cast loco with yellow-painted running board edge, smoke, red fire box light; dark blue 8008T tender with large yellow area topped with orange stripe and Chessie System logo and mechanical Sound of Steam. Came as part of No. 1052 CHESAPEAKE FLYER set. DC-powered engine   —   —   40   50

8040 NICKEL PLATE 1970, 2-4-2, black plastic body
(A) White flat lettering, slope-back tender   —   —   15   20
(B) Same as (A) but raised letters and short box tender, 1972   —   —   15   20

8041 NEW YORK CENTRAL 1970, 2-4-2, silver gray body, white lettering, red stripes   —   —   16   22

8042 GRAND TRUNK WESTERN 1970, 2-4-2, black, die-cast metal body, white lettering
(A) Thin cab floor   —   —   10   15
(B) Thick cab floor   —   —   10   15

8043 NICKEL PLATE 1970, 2-4-2, black plastic body with white lettering, slope-back tender, manufactured for Sears   —   —   15   20

8062 GREAT NORTHERN 1970, catalogued but not manufactured
                     Not Manufactured

8100 NORFOLK & WESTERN 1981, 4-8-4, J Class, streamlined engine, whistle, electronic Sound of Steam, three-position reverse unit, engine and tender paint match extruded aluminum Powhatan Arrow passenger cars. These cars were available only as separate sale items. This N & W was the first Lionel engine to simulate steam smoke actually issuing from its steam cylinders. (Marx introduced this feature many years before.) "611" appears on the side of the engine; tender with long stripe and six-wheel trucks, "8100" appears on box only.   —   —   375   395

8101 CHICAGO & ALTON 1981, 4-6-4, maroon-painted die-cast engine, based on "The Red Train," whistle, electronic Sound of Steam, three-position reverse unit, smoke; maroon die-cast tender with red frame, gold numbered "659" on side, "8101" appears only on box. Matching passenger cars available for separate sale. Tender is a remake of Lionel 224 tender, out of production for 40 years   —   —   225   250

8102 UNION PACIFIC 1981-82, 4-4-2, dark gray painted die-cast boiler with yellow-edged running board, yellow numbers and letters; electronic Sound of Steam, smoke, headlight, two-position reverse unit, traction tires and 8102T square-back tender. Part of No. 1151 Union Pacific Thunder Freight and No. 1153 Union Pacific Thunder Freight Deluxe, made for J.C. Penney sets   —   —   35   55

8104 UNION PACIFIC 1981, 4-4-0, General-type loco, green cab, pilot, lamp, wheel spokes and bell, black stack, chrome-finished boiler, "3" appears on side of headlamp and under cab window; it was sold by J.C. Penney as an uncatalogued special called "The Golden Arrow"; loco with wooden base and plastic cover

161

8200 Kickapoo

(A) As described above — — 175 200
(B) Same as (A), except came with one arch bar truck on front of tender and one Bettendorf truck on rear, probable factory error, Moyer Collection
NRS

8140 SOUTHERN 1971, 2-4-0 or 0-4-0, mechanical Sound of Steam, green and black body with gold lettering on tender cab
(A) 2-4-2 — — 15 20
(B) 0-4-0 — — 15 20

8141 PENNSYLVANIA 1971, 2-4-2, gray plastic and red stripe body, mechanical Sound of Steam, smoke, headlights
(A) White lettering, from set 1183 — — 15 20
(B) Same as (A), except heat-stamped red lettering. This was the version separately sold, Riley Collection — — 15 20

8142 CHESAPEAKE & OHIO 1971, 4-4-2, black die-cast metal body, white lettering, smoke
(A) Electronic Sound of Steam — — 26 40
(B) Electronic whistle — — 40 65

8200. KICKAPOO DOCKSIDE 1972, 0-4-0 Switcher, black plastic body, gold lettering and trim — — 17 25

8203 PENNSYLVANIA 1972, 2-4-2, Columbia-type, electronic Sound of Steam, charcoal black plastic body, red stripe and lettering
— — 25 35

8204 CHESAPEAKE & OHIO 1972, 4-4-2, black die-cast metal body, Sound of Steam, whistle, smoke, headlight — — 42 66

8206 NEW YORK CENTRAL 1972-74, 4-6-4, metal die-cast body, Sound of Steam, smoke, whistle, headlight, white lettering
(A) Flat charcoal black body — — 120 150
(B) Shiny black body — — 120 150

8209 PIONEER DOCKSIDE SWITCHER 1972, 0-4-0
(A) With four-wheel tender, from Kickapoo Valley set — — 25 33
(B) No tender — — 15 20

8210 COWEN 1982, 4-6-4, Hudson, gold and burgundy painted die-cast engine, headlight, smoke, magnetraction, die-cast tender with six-wheel trucks, electronic whistle, electronic Sound of Steam, simulated gold "Joshua Lionel Cowen" nameplate. Note: When boxes are opened many units are reported to have broken rear trucks, Deitrich observation
— — 240 275

8212 BLACK CAVE 1982, 0-4-0, black plastic body, slope-back tender, with glow-in-the-dark decal, D C motor, part of No. 1254 Black Cave Flyer set
— — 15 20

8213 RIO GRANDE 1982-83, 2-4-2, die-cast metal body; smoke, headlight, electronic reversing unit, split-field motor, tender with mechanical Sound of Steam, part of No. 1252 Heavy Iron — — 60 70

8214 PENNSYLVANIA 1982-83, 2-4-2, die-cast metal body, headlight, smoke, electronic reverse unit, split-field motor; tender with mechanical Sound of Steam — — 60 75

8300 SANTA FE 1976, 2-4-0 — — 15 22

8302 SOUTHERN 1973-76, 2-4-0, mechanical Sound of Steam, black plastic body painted green, plastic silver bell on top, headlight, MPC logo on both sides; from Set 6-1384, oil-type tender — — 25 33

8209 Pioneer

8303 JERSEY CENTRAL 1973-74, 2-4-2, electronic Sound of Steam, smoke, blue plastic body, light blue and gold lettering, dark blue trim
— — 20 25

NOTE. There are four different 8304 locomotives

8304 ROCK ISLAND 1973-74, 4-4-2, black die-cast body, electronic Sound of Steam, white lettering — — 30 42

8304 BALTIMORE & OHIO 1975, 4-4-2, black die-cast body, white lettering, electronic Sound of Steam — — 40 60

8304 CHESAPEAKE & OHIO 1974-77, 4-4-2, black die-cast body, gold lettering, electronic Sound of Steam, smoke — — 31 42

8304 PENNSYLVANIA 1974, 4-4-2, black die-cast body, gold lettering, electronic Sound of Steam, smoke, headlight — — 30 40

8305 MILWAUKEE ROAD 1973, 4-4-2, black die-cast body, gold lettering, red stripe on tender, electronic Sound of Steam, smoke, headlight
— — 40 53

8306 PENNSYLVANIA 1974, 4-4-2, black plastic body, smoke, Sound of Steam — — 25 30

8307 SOUTHERN PACIFIC 1983, 4-8-4, "Southern Pacific Daylight," "4449" below cab window and on boiler front, vertical dual headlights, magnetraction, smoke from stack and "simulated" steam (actually smoke from generator) from cylinders, three-position E unit, electronic Sound of Steam and whistle. Orange, white, and black paint scheme, silver boiler front. Matching passenger cars were available for separate sale.

Catalogue portrays a 2046-W coal tender, but production version has prototypical oil-burning tender and "99" unlighted number boards halfway down the top of the boiler sides. Early reports indicate that this locomotive is an outstanding runner. — — 400 425

8308 JERSEY CENTRAL 1974, 1973, 2-4-2, made for Sears
— — 25 34

8309 SOUTHERN 1983, 2-8-2, gold, "4501" beneath loco cab window and "SOUTHERN" and "FAMOUS AMERICAN RAILROAD SERIES" on tender side. Die-cast loco is green with silver boiler front and red cab roof. Frieght cars with special FARR 4 markings: 6104 hopper, 6306 tank, 9451 box car, 9887 reefer, and 6431 caboose were available for separate sale.
— — 260 290

8309 JERSEY CENTRAL 1974, uncatalogued, 2-4-2 — — 25 35

NOTE: The following five locos are similiar except for their road names and paint schemes

8310 NICKEL PLATE 2-4-0, black die-cast body, gold lettering, slope-back tender — — 30 40

8310 JERSEY CENTRAL 2-4-0, uncatalogued, black die-cast body, gold lettering, mechanical Sound of Steam, made for Sears — — 30 40

8310 NICKEL PLATE ROAD 1974-75, 2-4-0, black die-cast body, gold lettering, slope-back tender lettered "NICKEL PLATE ROAD"
— — 30 40

8310 JERSEY CENTRAL 1974-75, uncatalogued, 2-4-0, black die-cast body, gold lettering, mechanical Sound of Steam — — 30 40

162

8303

8304

8506

8305

8600

8310 Nickel Plate

8601

8310 Jersey Central

8602

8603

8502

8703

163

8310 A T S F 1974-75, 2-4-0, black die-cast body, gold lettering, slope-back tender lettered "A T S F," made for Sears, Haffen Collection
— — 30 40

8311 SOUTHERN 1973, uncatalogued, black body, made for J.C. Penney
— — 12 17

8313 SANTA FE 1983, 0-4-0, black plastic loco body with gold boiler front, stack and bell, gold numbering 8313 under cab window and gold Santa Fe logo and A.T. & S.F. on slope-back tender. DC powered, no headlight, fixed coupler on tender. This is the same loco model that appeared in the Black Cave set and is noteworthy for how few pieces of metal are used in its construction. Part of set No. 1352, Rocky Mountain Freight shown in Traditional Series catalogue. Set value: $50. Loco and tender price:
— — — 15

8314 SOUTHERN STREAK 1983, 2-4-0, dark green plastic loco body with headlight, DC powered, white number "8314" under cab window and white lettering "SOUTHERN STREAK" on tender sides, square back oil type tender with hatch and mechanical Sound of Steam, fixed coupler on tender. Part of Set 1353, Southern Streak shown in Traditional Series Catalogue. Set price: $60. Loco and tender price:
— — 17 20

8314 B & O 1983, 4-4-0, General style plastic loco with blue boiler and stack, black pilot, steam cylinders and cab and black tender. White letter: "8315" beneath cab windows and "B & O" on tender sides. DC motor with rectifier for AC operation as well as DC operation, illustrated with non-illuminating headlight but made with fixed coupler on tender, electronic 3-position reverse unit, part of Set No. 1351, Baltimore and Ohio shown in Traditional Series Catalogue. Set price: $110. Loco and tender price:
— — 45 50

8406 NEW YORK CENTRAL 1984, 4—4, 1/4" scaler die-cast Hudson, 23" long, smoke unit with emissions from stack and steam chest, magnetraction, three-position E type reverse unit, operating headlight, electronic Sound of Steam; 2426 die-cast tender with six-wheel trucks, operating coupler, and whistle. This is a rerun of the 773 introduced in 1950.
— — — 575

8500 PENNSYLVANIA 1976, 2-4-0, black plastic body, gold lettering, mechanical Sound of Steam
— — 15 21

8502 SANTA FE 1975, 2-4-0, black plastic body, gold lettering, slope-back tender
— — 14 20

8506 PENNSYLVANIA 1976-77, 0-4-0, black die-cast body, gold lettering, slope-back tender with red light which lights only when loco is in reverse
— — 60 80

8510 PENNSYLVANIA 1975, not catalogued, 0-4-0, slope-back tender, made for Sears
— — 12 16

8600 NEW YORK CENTRAL 1976, 4-6-4, black die-cast body, white lettering, electronic Sound of Steam, smoke, magnetraction, silver boiler front, shown as 646 in 1976 catalogue, part of Empire State Express set
— — 140 170

8601 ROCK ISLAND 1976-77, 0-4-0, black plastic body, large white numbers on cab, slope-back tender with red ROCK ISLAND logo — — 12 17

8602 RIO GRANDE 1976-78, 2-4-0, plastic body, white lettering; 89021 tender with mechanical Sound of Steam
— — 15 23

8603 CHESAPEAKE & OHIO 1976-77, 4-6-4, black die-cast body, white lettering, silver boiler front, electronic Sound of Steam, headlight, smoke, rubber tires, tender lettered "CHESAPEAKE & OHIO," over 19 1/2 inches long. The earlier Baldwin disc drivers had polished steel rims, but when reports of corrosion arose, Fundimensions changed production to white-painted driver rims. The painted rims are probably more scarce. LaVoie comments
(A) Polished steel driver rims, LaVoie Collection — 100 135 175
(B) White-painted driver rims, Boehmer Collection — 110 150 190

8701 GENERAL 1977-78, 4-4-0, cab numbered No. 3, rerun of Lionel 1882 General, 1959-62, black plastic boiler, and frame, red cab, gold boiler bands, dome and bell, yellow lettering, headlight, smoke, two-position reverse, black plastic tender with yellow lettered "Western & Atlantic"
— — 85 100

8702 CRESCENT LIMITED 1977, 4-6-4, also known as Southern Crescent, green painted die-cast boiler with silver painted boiler front, gold crescent and border on steam chest, crescent emblem and "8702" in gold on cab, magnetraction, white-outlined drivers, liquid smoke. This locomotive appears to have exactly the same castings as the 646. Originally the 8702 came in flat green, the second run was in shiny green; it appears that equal quantities were produced. The tender is painted green with a black coal pile, lettered "CRESCENT LIMITED" in gold with gold border, Bettendorf trucks, Sound of Steam
— — 225 275

8703 WABASH 1977, 2-4-2, black plastic body, white stripe on loco and tender, electronic Sound of Steam, smoke, headlight — — 23 32

8800 LIONEL LINES 1978-81, 4-4-2, die-cast boiler, red marker lights, battery box on pilot, similar to Lionel 2037 with the following modifications: the marker lights, which protrude above the boiler on a 2037, were moved to a more protected location inside the boiler front; the "Made by Lionel" builder's plate was replaced with a Lionel/MPC logo, and the valve gear was given a moving control rod reminiscent of the 1666. The main rod is heavily sculptured with ridges; there is a side rod; liquid smoke unit, two-position reversing unit; a wire connects the tender and loco, with electronic Sound of Steam in the 8800T tender and a fixed rear tender coupler. Tender base is marked "8141T-10" and has a large black "L" in white and black box and "LIONEL LINES" in sans-serif rounded letters across its side. (Same engine as Chesapeake Flier with one rubber tire on loco.)
— — 50 62

8801 BLUE COMET 1979-80, 4-6-4, dark blue upper boiler section, lighter blue lower boiler section, gold outlined steam chest, "8801" in gold on cab, decal on loco feedwater tank reads "THE BLUE COMET;" "LIONEL" on small plate beneath headlight; six-drivers outlined in white, blind center drivers, plastic trailing trucks, side frames and a modified 646 boiler. A major modification is its feedwater tank which has a 665 boiler front with marker lights on the boiler front door and a small name plate beneath the headlight. The tender's paint design is similar to the loco's with a dark blue upper section, black coal pile, light blue lower section with gold circle and gold lettered "NEW JERSEY CENTRAL." The Blue Comet brings back memories of the top-of-the-line or classic Standard and 0 Gauge locomotives of the 1930s. The Blue Comet has met with great popularity. — — 200 230

8803 SANTA FE 1979, 0-4-0, black plastic engine with silver boiler front and red plastic drivers, two-position reverse, 8803T square-back tender with Santa Fe logo. Part of No. 1860 Timberline set, No. 1862 Logging Empire set, No. 1892 Penney Logging Empire, No. 1893 Toys-R-Us-Logging Empire
— — 10 15

8900 A.T.S.F. 1979, 4-6-4, black painted die-cast boiler with silver painted boiler front, green marker lights, tuscan painted cab roof, magnetraction, same boiler as 2065 without the feedwater tank; rear trailing truck has same side frames as 2065, side configuration same as 2065 but brighter, shinier plating; nylon gears substitute for metal gears. Tender has "8900" in very large white numerals and a small diamond-shaped block outlined in gold with gold lettered "Famous American Railroad Series" with a spike (indicates it is first in a series); water scoop pickup, Sound of Steam inside tender (power pickup for Sound of Steam comes in part from tender trucks and in part from wire from loco); fixed coupler on rear of tender with rear number plate "2671W-6," gray wheels on tender. Our search indicates that most if not all pre-Fundimensions 2671-W tenders did not carry a plate with such a number. The number has been carried on the tender plate since MPC began using this tender
— — 190 225

8902 ATLANTIC COAST LINE 1979-82, 2-4-0, black plastic engine, DC-powered, 8902T slope-back tender with ATLANTIC COAST LINE logo; available as part of No. 1960 and No. 1993 Midnight Flyer sets, No. 1990 Mystery Glow Midnight Flyer and No. 1155 Cannonball Freight set
— — 15 20

8903 RIO GRANDE 1979, 2-4-2, black plastic engine, DC-powered, 8602T tender with mechanical Sound of Steam; white script "Rio Grande." Available as part of No. 1963 Black River Freight set — — 15 20

8904 WABASH 1979, 81, 2-4-2 die-cast engine with white stripe along running board, smoke working headlight, two-position reverse unit, AC-powered; 8904T oil-type tender with or without mechanical Sound of Steam; dark-lettered "WABASH" on white stripe across tender side, from No. 1962 Wabash Cannonball set or No. 1991 Wabash Deluxe Express
(A) With mechanical Sound of Steam, 8906T — 22 27 32
(B) Without mechanical Sound of Steam, 8904T — 20 25 30

8905 SWITCHER 0-4-0, 1979, plastic engine, no headlight, diamond-shaped stack, D C-powered, fixed coupler, no tender; part of No. 1965 Smokey Mountain Line
— — 10 15

8040[A]

8040[B]

8142

8041

8203

8042

8206

8140

8304

8140

8304

8141

8304

Chapter XV
FUNDIMENSIONS ACCESSORIES

                                                     Gd. V.G. Exc. Mt.

2110 GRADUATED TRESTLE SET 1971-83, twenty-two pieces graduated from 3/16 to 4 3/4 inches high   2   5   7   10

2111 ELEVATED TRESTLE SET 1971-83, ten 4 3/4 inch piers
(A) Gray plastic   2   4   6   9
(B) Brown plastic   2   3   6   9

2122 EXTENSION BRIDGE 1977-83, two gray plastic piers, plastic bridge, requires assembly, 24 inches long by 5 inches wide, piers 7 inches high, overall height with piers is 11 3/4 inches
(A) Brown sides and top   —   7   9   15
(B) Brown sides and maroon top, Piker Collection   —   7   9   15

2125 WHISTLING FREIGHT STATION 1971   8   10   12   18

2126 WHISTLING FREIGHT SHED 1976-83, brown plastic base, off-white yellow shed, green door and windows, opaque window in non-opening door, green tool shed lid, brown plastic roof, whistle   7   9   12   20

2127 DIESEL HORN SHED 1976-83, height 4 7/8 inches, base 6 inches by 6 inches, battery-operated nine volt transistor battery not included. Diesel horn remote controlled, light tan plastic base, red building, white tool shed lid, white door, frosted window, gray roof   7   10   12   20

2128 AUTOMATIC SWITCHMAN 1983, animated blue switchman waves flag at train approach. Appears to be a reissue of 1047 from 1959-61. Reader comments requested on differences, if any   —   —   —   27

2129 FREIGHT STATION 1983, maroon platform, tan building with brown windows and door, green roof, black picket fence with billboards reading "Cheerios," "Wheaties," and "Gold Seal." Also several wall posters, illuminated, number of bulbs not known. The catalogue shows the station with white walls. 15" long, 5" wide and 5 1/2" high. This is a reissue of 256 from 1950-53. Reader comments appreciated on the differences between 2129 and 256.   —   —   16   20

2133 FREIGHT STATION 1972-83, maroon plastic base, white plastic side with green windows and doors, green roof, box at one time made by Stone Container Corporation, Detroit, Michigan, white corrugated box with colored picture of station on lid, illuminated in 1983, reissue of 133 from 1957-66   7   10   12   19

2140 AUTOMATIC BANJO SIGNAL 1970-83, as train approaches, red light turns on, "stop" arm swings, die-cast construction, 7 1/2 inches high   6   8   12   20

2145 AUTOMATIC GATEMAN 1970-83, gateman rushes from lighted shed as train approaches, then flags train with his lantern and returns to shed after train passes, green metal base with green cardboard bottom, white shed with brown door and window, frosted plastic windows, brown roof, brown tool shed lid, pressure contactor, lock-on, reissue of 1945   8   12   15   26

2151 SEMAPHORE 1978-83, raises as train approaches   6   8   12   20

2152 AUTOMATIC CROSSING GATE 1977-83, black plastic base, white plastic gate with gray weights, on bottom "#252 Crossing Gate," with pressure contactor   5   7   11   17

2154 AUTOMATIC HIGHWAY FLASHER 1970-83, red light blinks alternately as train passes, 8 3/4 inches high with special track clip   6   10   14   19

2156 STATION PLATFORM 1970-71, rerun of 156 with changes, green plastic base, illuminated, underside of base reads, "CAT. NO. 2156 STATION PLATFORM," and "LIONEL MT. CLEMENS MICH. MADE IN USA," Grossano Collection   **NRS**

2162 AUTOMATIC CROSSING GATE AND SIGNAL 1970-83, black plastic base, white gate with red stripes, red bulbs with pins, pressure contactor, lock on   7   11   15   20

2163 AUTO BLOCK TARGET SIGNAL 1970-78, green light switches to red as train approaches, 7 1/2 inches high, contactor, L-19R red bulb, L-19G green bulb, both with pins   —   7   9   14

2170 STREETLAMPS 1970-83, three per package   3   5   6   8

2171 GOOSE NECK LAMPS 1980-83, two lamps, reissue of 1961-63   5   6   7   11

2175 SANDY ANDY 1976-79, mechanically-operated gravel loader, plastic kit   6   8   10   12

2180 ROAD SIGN SET 1977-83, plastic signs, attached as shown   —   —   2   3

2181 TELEPHONE POLES 1977-83, 10 poles, each 7 inches high   —   —   2   4

2195 FLOODLIGHT TOWER 1970-72, eight lights, unpainted aluminum tower, light bracket and reflectors, tan base, "LIONEL" on two tabs near top of tower, Brad Thomas Collection   7   10   15   20

2199 MICROWAVE TOWER 1972-75, black plastic base, gray plastic tower, black plastic top with three operating blinking light tips   6   12   19   25

2214 GIRDER BRIDGE 1970-83, metal base, black or brown painted or brown anodized, gray plastic side embossed "LIONEL," comes knocked down or assembled. If knocked down plastic sides must be screwed on with eight Phillips head screws, 10 inches long, 4 1/2 inches wide, Rohlfing Collection   —   1   2   5

2256 STATION PLATFORM 1973-81, green base, plastic, metal post, black plastic center, fence, red unpainted plastic roof, not lighted   3   5   6   10

2256 STATION PLATFORM Overprinted heat-stamped in white "21 TCA National Convention, Orlando, Florida, June 19-26, 1975"   —   12   15   20

2280 BUMPERS
(A) Three to a package, early version with open area, 1973-75   —   —   1   2
(B) Later version with closed area, 1974-80, 83   —   —   2   3

2282 BUMPER 1983, black die-cast body which attaches to the track with screws; black plastic shock absorber, red illuminated jewel atop body. Reissue of 260 bumper from the 1950's with a color change. Illustrated in the 1983 Fall Collector's Brochure, LaVoie comment   —   —   —

2290 LIGHTED BUMPERS 1974-83, pair   2   3   4   6

2300 OIL DRUM LOADER 1983, reissue of No. 779 American Flyer accessory from 1955-56. Reader comments and differences between 779 and 2300 appreciated. Listed here as well as in our American Flyer book because it appeared in a Fundimensions' catalogue and will be found with Lionel trains.   —   —   —   75

2301 OPERATING SAWMILL 1981-83, maroon plastic base, white mill building, red door, gray shed, red lettering on window facing track, white crane, simulates the transformation of logs into dressed lumber, vibrator mechanism moves lumber. Length 10 1/2 inches, width 6 inches, height 6 inches. Reissue of 464 from 1956-60. Reader comments on the differences between 464 and 2301 appreciated.   —   —   40   60

2302 U.P. GANTRY CRANE 1981-82, maroon crane housing and boom, black platform spans track and runs on its own wheels, manually-operated, reproduction of 282 from 1954 but without motor and remote control   —   —   —   34

2305 OIL DERRICK 1981-83, walking beam rocks up and down, bubbling pipe simulates oil flow, hand-operated winch, ladder, barrels, red-painted sheet metal base, reissue of 455 from 1950-54   —   —   53   69

2306 OPERATING ICE STATION 1982-83, with reefer, reissue of 352 from 1955-57   —   —   60   81

2308 ANIMATED NEWSSTAND 1982-83, reissue of 128 from 1957-60   —   —   40   57

2309 MECHANICAL CROSSING GATE 1982-83, operated by weight of train   —   —   2   4

2122

2125

2127

2133

2140

2145

2152

2154

2162

2163

2175

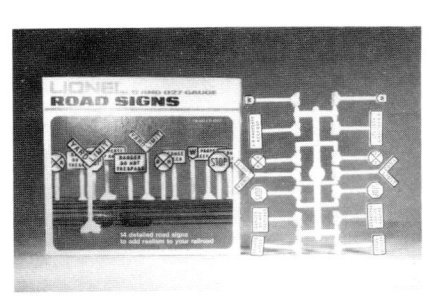

2180

167

2310 MECHANICAL CROSSING GATE AND SIGNAL 1973-75, activated by weight of train, black and white plastic, requires assembly
— 2 3 5

2311 MECHANICAL SEMAPHORE 1982-83, operated by weight of train
— — 2 4

2312 MECHANICAL SEMAPHORE 1973-75, activated by weight of train, flag raises and green signal illuminates as train approaches, flag lowers and red signal illuminates after train passes, contact track — 3 5 6

2313 OPERATING FLOODLIGHT TOWER 1975-83, black plastic base, red plastic tower, black plastic top, eight miniature lights, two binding posts on bottom 7 10 12 19

2314 OPERATING SEARCHLIGHT TOWER 1975-83
(A) Black plastic, two searchlights 4 6 10 13
(B) Same as 2314 (A) but black base, gray tower, gray top, not illustrated, Eddins Collection 4 7 10 13
(C) Same as 2314 (A) but red tower, not illustrated, Eddins Collection
4 7 10 13

2315 See 2324

2316 REMOTE GANTRY CRANE 1983, reissue of 282. Reader comments on the similarities and differences of the 282 and 2316 would be appreciated.
— — — 65

2317 DRAWBRIDGE 1975-81, brown plastic piers, gray span, five pressure binding posts visible on right side of illustration, olive green tender house with terra-cotta roof, brown door and steps, with one full length of 0-27 track and two half sections — 9 15 19

2318 CONTROL TOWER 1983, reissue of 192. Reader comments on the similarities and differences between 192 and 2318 would be appreciated.
— — 45 52

2319 WATCHTOWER Lighted, 1975-80 — 6 10 12

2320 FLAG POLE KIT 1983, reissue of 89 from 1956-58. Reader comments on the similarities and differences between 89 and 2320 would be appreciated. — — 3 5

2324 COALING STATION 1983, reissue of 497 from 1953-58. The catalogue text describes this as 2315 but Lionel's inventory number is believed to be 2324. Reader comments on the similarities and differences between 497 and 2324 would be appreciated. — — — 80

2494 ROTARY BEACON 1972-74, red sheet metal tower with revolving beacon powered by vibrator motor, beacon projects red and green illumination, over 11 1/2 inches high, red stamped metal base 5 inches by 5 inches, black ladder, black and aluminum nameplate on base, two clips on underside of base for wires, Cole and Kruelle Collections 7 12 14 18

2709 RICO STATION 1981-83, large plastic kit, 22 inches long by 9 inches wide, different versions were reportedly made. We believe that the 2797 from 1976 was in a different color. Reader comments appreciated.
5 9 15 20

2710 BILLBOARDS 1970-83, five per package, signs vary
.50 1 2 4

2714 TUNNEL 1975-77, 15 1/2 x 13 1/2 x 10 inches, two-piece construction
2 3 5 7

2717 SHORT EXTENSION BRIDGE 1977-83, 10 x 6 1/2 x 4 1/2 inches, plastic kit — 1 2 4

2718 BARREL PLATFORM 1977-83, plastic kit includes figure, barrels, tools, lamp, ladder and building, 4 x 4 x 3 1/2 inches — 1 2 4

2719 SIGNAL TOWER 1977-83, described as "Watchman Shanty" in catalogue, 7 inches high, 4 x 4 1/2 inches, plastic kit — 1 2 4

2720 LUMBER SHED 1977-83, plastic kit includes workman, shed, table, lumber, tools, ladder, 4 inches high, 6 inches long, 3 1/2 inches wide
— 1 2 4

2721 LOG LOADING MILL 1979, red plastic kit, manual operation, pressing a lever causes plastic log to be released and roll down ramp, part of inexpensive "Workin' On The Railroad" sets NRS

2722 BARREL LOADER 1979, green plastic kit, manual operation, workman pushes barrel down a chute, part of inexpensive "Workin' On The Railroad" sets NRS

2784 FREIGHT PLATFORM 1981-83, snap together realistic O scale plastic kit with opening door 2 3 6 9

2785 ENGINE HOUSE 1974-77, plastic kit — 15 20 30

2786 FREIGHT PLATFORM 1974-77, freight shed with platform, plastic kit
— 3 4 7

2787 FREIGHT STATION 1974-77, 83, highly detailed O scale plastic kit
3 5 7 10

2788 COALING STATION 1975-77, plastic kit, coal may be mechanically dumped 5 9 11 15

2789 WATER TOWER 1975-80, water tower on brick structure, plastic kit
— 3 7 9

2790 BUILDING KIT ASSORTMENT 1983, details needed NRS

2791 CROSS COUNTRY SET 1970-71 — 3 4 6

2792 LAYOUT STARTER PAK 1980-83, snap-together extension bridge kit, barrel platform kit, lumber shed kit, 10 telephone poles, 14 road signs, 5 billboards and a Track Layout Book — — 15 20

2792 WHISTLE STOP SET 1970-71 — 3 4 6

2793 ALAMO JUNCTION SET 1970-71 — 3 4 6

2796 GRAIN ELEVATOR 1977, 16 inches high, 16 inches long, 13 inches wide, plastic kit — 11 13 20

2797 RICO STATION 1976, large plastic kit 22 x 9 x 9 inches high, modeled after Rico, Colorado, station — 9 15 17

2900 LOCKON 1970-83 .20 .40 .50 1

2901 TRACK CLIPS 1970-83, 12 pack — 1 2 5

2905 LOCKON & WIRE 1972-83, blister pack — .70 .85 1.50

2909 SMOKE FLUID 1977-82, for locos made after 1970 — 1 1.50 3

2927 MAINTENANCE KIT 1977-83, consists of lubricant, oiler, track cleaning fluid, track cleaner, rubber eraser, all mounted on a piece of cardboard and shrink-wrapped 1 2 3 5

2951 TRACK LAYOUT BOOK 1976-80, 83, — .50 .75 2

2952 TRACK ACCESSORY MANUAL — — .75 1

2953 TRAIN & ACCESSORY MANUAL 1977-83 — — 1.25 2

2960 LIONEL 75th ANNIVERSARY BOOK 1976 — 6 8 10

9195 ROLLING STOCK ASSORTMENT 1979. Lionel offered a 12 car assortment of its inexpensive cars for mass market sales (contrasted with collector market sales). Lionel provided two each from the following categories: short box car, short hopper, long gondola, short tank, work caboose and flat car with fences. Each car has Bettendorf plastic trucks with one operating disc coupler and one fixed coupler. However, the specific road names and colors included probably changed during the production period to fit Fundimensions' convenience. We would appreciate reader listings of the contents of their assortments. Some cars needed assembly by purchaser. Bohn comments

TRANSFORMERS

4060 POWER MASTER 1980-83, fixed AC and variable DC output, direction reverse switch, automatic circuit breaker 6 9 12 30

4090 POWER MASTER 1978-81, 83, AC output, right lever controls speed, left lever controls direction, fixed voltage taps, automatic circuit breaker
10 15 20 55

4150 TRAIN MASTER TRANSFORMER — 3 6 12

4250 TRAIN MASTER TRANSFORMER — 3 6 12

4651 TRAIN MASTER 1978-79, lever controls speed, two posts with button on one post for forward and reverse, automatic circuit breaker
— — 2 3

5900 AC/DC CONVERTER 1979-81, 83 — — 4 6

8190 DIESEL HORN 1981, electronic package that can be adapted to engines or rolling stock, operated by whistle button on older transformer, includes circuit board, speaker, track and pickups — — — 25

027 TRACK

5012 CURVED TRACK 1980, 83, 4 on card — — 2.20 3.50

2181

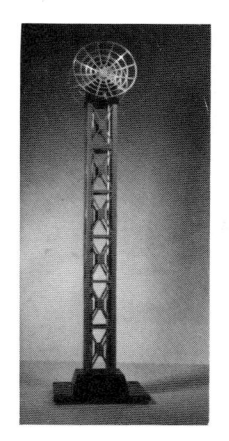

2199

2214

2310

2312

2313

2314[A]

2317

2494

2256

2256[B]

2280[A]
2280[B]
2290

169

2285

2787

2788

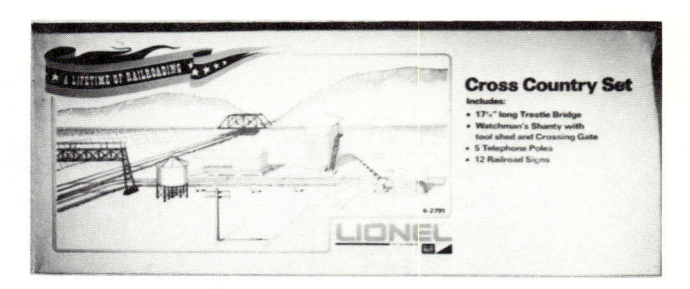

2791

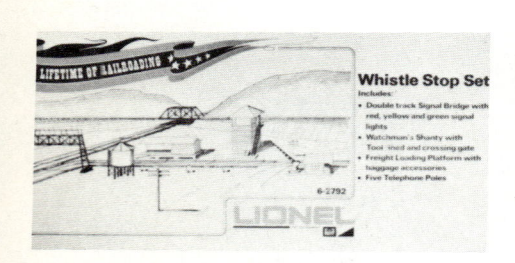

2792

2793

2789

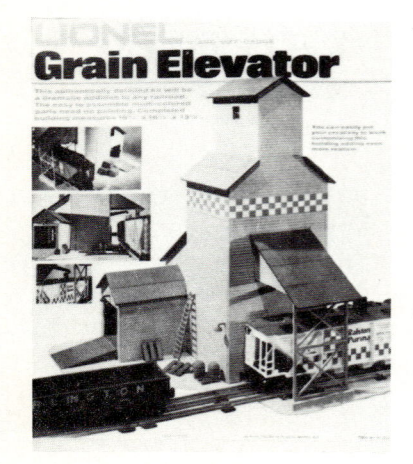

2796

29005

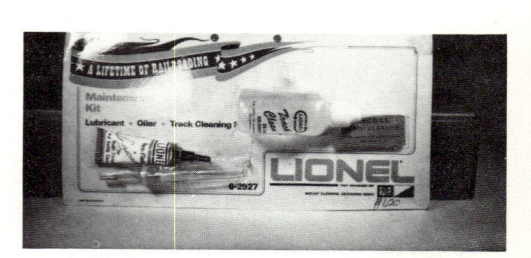

2927

170

5013 CURVED TRACK	.10	.30	.50	.55
5014 HALF-CURVED TRACK 1980-83	.20	.40	.50	.75
5017 STRAIGHT TRACK 1980-83, 4 on card	—	—	3.50	3.50
5018 STRAIGHT TRACK	.20	.40	.50	.75
5019 HALF-STRAIGHT TRACK	.20	.40	.50	.75
5020 90 DEGREE CROSSOVER	1.50	3	3.50	4.75
5023 45 DEGREE CROSSOVER	1.50	3	4	6.50
5030 LAYOUT BUILDERS SET 1978-80, 83, pair of manual switches, 2 curved, 6 straight track	10	14	17	25
5033 CURVED TRACK Bulk packed, but sold individually	.10	.20	.30	.75
5038 STRAIGHT TRACK Bulk packed, but sold individually	.10	.20	.30	.75
5041 0-27 INSULATOR PINS 12 per pack	—	—	.50	1
5042 0-27 STEEL PINS 12 per pack	—	—	.40	.75
5113 0-27 WIDE RADIUS TRACK 16 sections make a 54 inch diameter circle per piece	—	—	1.10	1.50
5149 REMOTE UNCOUPLING TRACK	—	2.50	3.50	7.25

0-27 SWITCHES

5021 MANUAL SWITCH, LEFT	4	7	8	13
5022 MANUAL SWITCH, RIGHT	4	7	8	13
5027 PAIR MANUAL SWITCHES	8	13	15	26
5090 3 PAIR MANUAL SWITCHES 1983	—	—	60	80
5121 REMOTE SWITCH, LEFT	7	11	14	20
5122 REMOTE SWITCH, RIGHT	7	11	14	20
5125 PAIR REMOTE SWITCHES	14	20	28	40

0 GAUGE TRACK, SWITCHES & UNCOUPLERS

5132 REMOTE SWITCH, RIGHT With controller	15	20	33	40
5133 REMOTE SWITCH, LEFT With controller	15	20	33	40
5193 3 PAIR REMOTE SWITCHES 1983	—	—	90	110
5500 STRAIGHT TRACK	—	.30	.75	1.25
5510 CURVED TRACK	—	.30	.75	1.25
5530 REMOTE UNCOUPLING SECTION With controller	6	9	11	13
5540 90 DEGREE CROSSOVER	3	5	7	8
5543 INSULATOR PINS 12 per pack	.25	.50	.75	1
5545 45 DEGREE CROSSOVER 1982	—	—	—	13
5551 STEEL PINS 12 per pack	.25	.50	.75	1
5572 WIDE RADIUS CURVED TRACK 16 pieces make a circle with a 72" diameter. Per piece	.50	.75	1.25	2.50

PERIPHERAL ITEMS

JC-1 LIONEL JOHNNY CASH RECORD ALBUM 33 1/3 speed
— 2 3 6

7-1110 HAPPY HUFF'N PUFF train set, 1975, Fundimensions pre-school toy push train similar to those made by Fisher-Price and Playskool, whimsical old-fashioned 4-wheel steamer and two gondolas embossed with two large squares on their sides. Train is made of plastic simulated to look like wood. Wheels fastened with metal axles. Loco has smile-mouth and eye decorations. Came with a circle of two-rail plastic track and a story booklet showing "how Happy Huff'n Puff got his name." Bohn and LaVoie comments
— 4 7 9

7-1200 GRAVEL GUS 1975, a three-piece road construction set consisting of a grader with a large squared head seated on the chassis (presumably Gus) and two side dump cars. The grader has four large wheels and swivels in the center with a removable pusher blade. The two cars each have one axle with two large wheels, with the first car resting on the grader and the second car resting on the rear of the first car. The set is made from plastic simulated to resemble wood. It came with a full-color story booklet. Weisblum comments **NRS**

7-1300 GRAVEL GUS JUNIOR 1975, appears to be identical to 7-1200 Gravel Gus, except has only one side dump car, Bohn comment **NRS**

7-1400 HAPPY HUFF'N PUFF JUNIOR 1975, essentially similar to 7-1100 Happy Huff'n Puff, except does not include circle of track, loco has much thicker smokestack and gondolas are not embossed with large squares. These four pre-school toys were apparently offered only in 1975 through large toy outlets. Their success would have been an asset to Fundimensions, but they were launched into the teeth of a highly competitive pre-school market long dominated by giants such as Fisher-Price and Playskool. Bohn and LaVoie comments **NRS**

NO NUMBER LIONEL CLOCK 1976-77, made by American Sign and Advertising Services, Inc., 7430 Industrial Road, Industrial Park, Lawrence, Kentucky, 41042, white dial with black hand, red second hand, red field on bottom with white "LIONEL," available to Service Stations for $20-$25
— — 25 30

NO NUMBER LIONEL PENNANT Plastic, white background, black trim on edge, black "LIONEL," left arrow red, right side arrow blue, "A LIFETIME INVESTMENT IN HAPPINESS" in black, 45 inches wide, 29 1/2 inches high
— — 2 4

NO NUMBER BLACK CAVE VINYL PLAYMAT 1982, from No. 1254 Black Cave Flyer set, 30 inches x 40 inches, from set No. 1355
— — — 10

NO NUMBER COMMANDO ASSAULT TRAIN PLAYMAT 1983, 30 inches x 40 inches, from set No. 1355
— — — 10

NO NUMBER ROCKY MOUNTAIN FREIGHT PLAYMAT 1983, 36 inches x 54 inches, from set No. 1352
— — — 3

NO NUMBER STATION PLATFORM 1983, 23 inches x 3 1/2 inches x 5 inches, similar to 2256 Station Platform, details requested, part of set No. 1351
— — — 10

NO NUMBER CANNONBALL FREIGHT VINYL PLAYMAT 1982, 36 inches x 54 inches, 2-piece mat, from set No. 1155
— — — 5

NO NUMBER L.A.S.E.R. VINYL PLAYMAT 1982, 36 inches x 54 inches, mat from set No. 1150
— — — 5

Chapter XVI
FUNDIMENSIONS HOPPERS

                                              Gd.   V.G.   Exc.   Mt.

6100 ONTARIO NORTHLAND 1981-82, blue sides and cover, yellow trim — — 17 25

6101 BURLINGTON 1981, green sides and cover, white lettering — — 13 16

6102 GREAT NORTHERN 1981, tuscan body and cover, white lettering, FARR Series 3 logo, disc-operating couplers, from Famous American Railroad Series 3, available only as separate sale — — 11 13

6103 CANADIAN NATIONAL 1981, gray with red lettering, tuscan cover, die-cast sprung trucks, part of No. 1158 MAPLE LEAF LIMITED set — — 30 35

6104 SOUTHERN 1983, black body with coal load, gold lettering and FARR 4 logo. Available for separate sale. Caponi comment NRS

6105 READING 1982, tuscan, operating hopper — — 17 20

6106 N W 1982, gray with black lettering, black cover, die-cast sprung 0 trucks, disc-operating couplers, part of No. 1260 Continental Limited set NRS

6107 SHELL 1982 — — 12 14

6109 C & O 1983, operating car with opening bins, black body, white lettering. NRS

6110 MISSOURI PACIFIC 1983, black with white lettering available for separate sale. — — — 14

6111 L & N 1983, gray with red lettering, available for separate sale — — — 14

6113 ILLINOIS CENTRAL 1983, black with white lettering, sold as part of 1354 Northern Freight Flyer set. — — — 10

6114 C N W 1983, black body and cover, yellow lettering and logo, available only as part of No. 1361 Gold Coast Limited set. NRS

6115 SOUTHERN 1983, gray with red lettering, sold as part of 1353 Southern Streak set. — — — 10

7504 LIONEL 75th ANNIVERSARY 1975   5   8   12   14

9010 GREAT NORTHERN 1971, blue body, white lettering, plastic brakewheels, metal wheels, one manumatic coupler, one fixed coupler, MPC logo
(A) Medium blue body, Timken trucks, "1-70"   1   2   3   5
(B) Light blue body, Timken trucks, "1-70"   1   2   3   5
(C) Medium light blue body, Timken trucks, "7-70"   1   2   3   5
(D) Light blue body, Bettendorf trucks, "1-70"   1   2   3   5

9011 GREAT NORTHERN 1971, 79, medium blue body, white lettering, "7-70," Bettendorf trucks, plastic wheels, one manumatic coupler, one fixed coupler
(A) Externally-mounted brakewheel, MPC logo   3   4   5   6
(B) Built-in brakewheel, MPC logo   3   4   5   6
(C) Built-in brakewheel, no MPC logo   3   4   5   6
(D) Deep royal blue mold — — 120 165

9012 T A & G 1971-72, 79, blue body, white lettering, built-in brakewheel, "1-70," Bettendorf trucks, plastic wheels, one manumatic coupler, one fixed coupler, MPC logo
(A) Dark blue body (navy)   2   3   5   7
(B) Bright blue body (royal blue) — — 22 40

9013 CANADIAN NATIONAL 1972-74, 79, red body, white lettering, built-in brakewheel, "1-72," Bettendorf trucks, plastic wheels, one manumatic coupler, one fixed coupler, MPC logo
(A) Dark red body   2   3   4   5
(B) Medium red body   2   3   4   5
(C) Light red body   2   3   4   5

9015 READING 1973-74, 79, brown body, yellow lettering, built-in brakewheel, "1-73," Bettendorf trucks, metal wheels, one disc coupler, one fixed coupler, no MPC logo   3   5   7   10

9016 CHESSIE 1975-79, yellow body, blue lettering, built-in brakewheel, "1-75," Bettendorf trucks, metal wheels, one operating coupler, one fixed coupler, no MPC logo
(A) Yellow body   1   2   3   4
(B) Light yellow body   1   2   3   4

9018 D T & I 1978, 1981, yellow body, black heat-stamped lettering, plastic brakewheel, "BLT 1-78," Bettendorf trucks, one manumatic coupler, one fixed coupler   2   3   5   8

9028 B & O 1978, dark blue body, yellow lettering, Chessie emblem, plastic brakewheel, "BLT 1-78," Bettendorf trucks, plastic wheels, one manumatic coupler, one fixed coupler   3   4   6   8

9034 LIONEL LEISURE Kiddie City — — 12 14

9038 CHESSIE 1978, 80-81, plastic trucks and wheels, one operating coupler, one fixed coupler   1   2   3   4

9079 GRAND TRUNK 1977, deep blue body, white lettering, built-in brakewheel, "1-77," Bettendorf trucks, metal wheels, one disc coupler, one fixed coupler, no MPC logo   5   7   9   12

9110 B & O 1971, black body, "2-71," builder's plate, not covered, metal truck plate holders
(A) Gray lettering, reportedly only 1,000 made   12   20   30   40
(B) White lettering   6   8   10   15

9111 N & W 1972, not covered, builder's plate, metal plate holding truck
(A) Brown body, white lettering   5   7   10   15
(B) Dark red body, white lettering, less than 40 reportedly produced — — — 85
(C) Brown body, white decal lettering, prototype, rare NRS

9112 D & R G Orange body, black lettering, orange cover, builder's plate, metal plate holding truck
(A) Light orange body, raised lettering   3   5   7   9
(B) Light orange body, flat lettering   3   5   7   9
(C) Darker orange body, flat lettering   3   5   7   9

9113 N & W 1973, gray body, black lettering, uncatalogued, from 1973 Service Station set, not covered, builder's plate, metal plate holding trucks   7   9   12   15

9114 MORTON'S SALT 1975-76, navy blue body, white and yellow lettering, yellow cover, builder's plate, metal plate holding trucks   3   4   6   8

9115 PLANTER'S PEANUTS 1974-76, light blue body, yellow lettering, yellow cover, builder's plate, metal plate holding trucks   3   4   6   8

9116 DOMINO SUGAR 1974-76, gray body, blue lettering, navy blue cover, builder's plate, metal plate holding trucks   3   4   6   8

9117 ALASKA 1974-76, black body, black cover, from 1974 Service Station set
(A) Orange-yellow lettering, builder's plate   6   8   10   14
(B) Light yellow lettering, builder's plate   6   8   10   14
(C) Light yellow lettering, no builder's plate   6   8   10   14

9118 CORNING 1974, white and mist green body, covered, LCCA 1974 Convention car, 2,000 made — — 55 64

9119 DETROIT & MACKINAC 1975, red body, white lettering, shiny red cover, "1-76," 1975 Service Station set, no builder's plate, metal plate holding trucks   4   5   6   8

9130 B & O 1970-71, light blue paint on gray plastic, white lettering, "1-70," not covered
(A) Plastic plate holding trucks   6   8   10   12
(B) Metal plate holding trucks   10   12   15   25

9134 VIRGINIAN 1976-77, white body, blue lettering, blue cover, plastic plate holding trucks
(A) No builder's plate   7   9   11   14
(B) Builder's plate   7   9   11   14
(C) Silver cover, LaVoie Collection NRS

7504

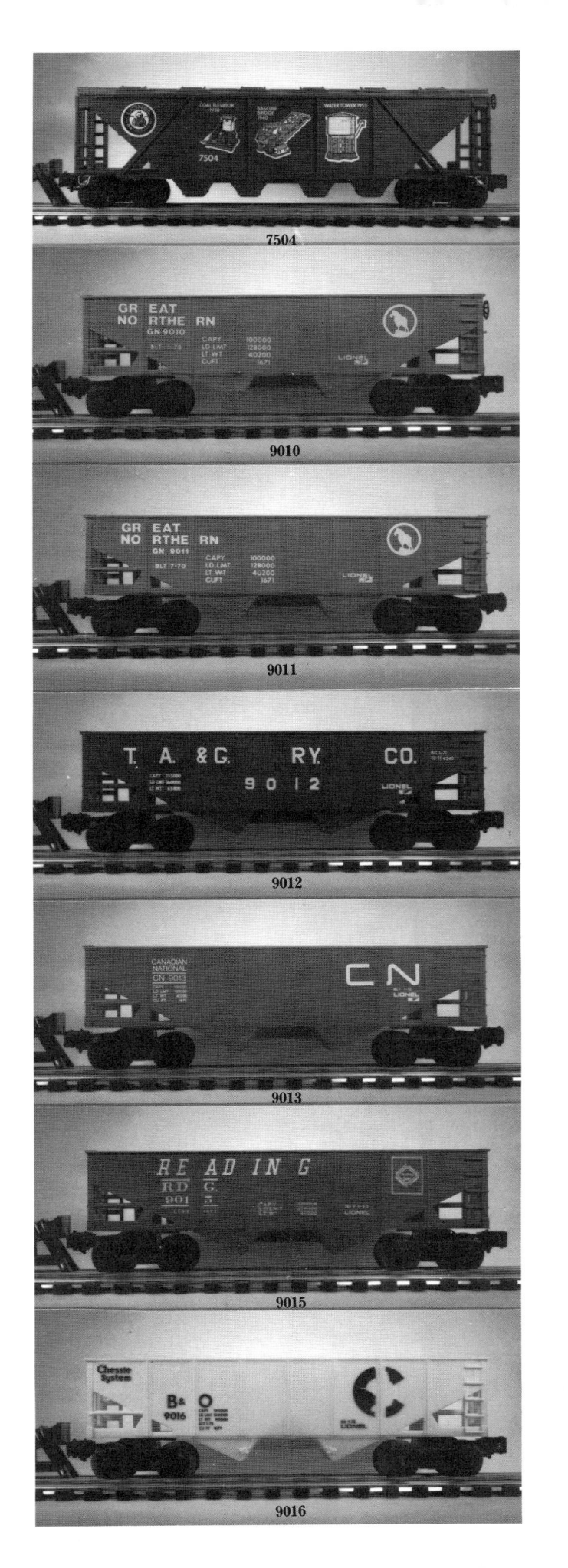

9010

9011

9012

9013

9015

9016

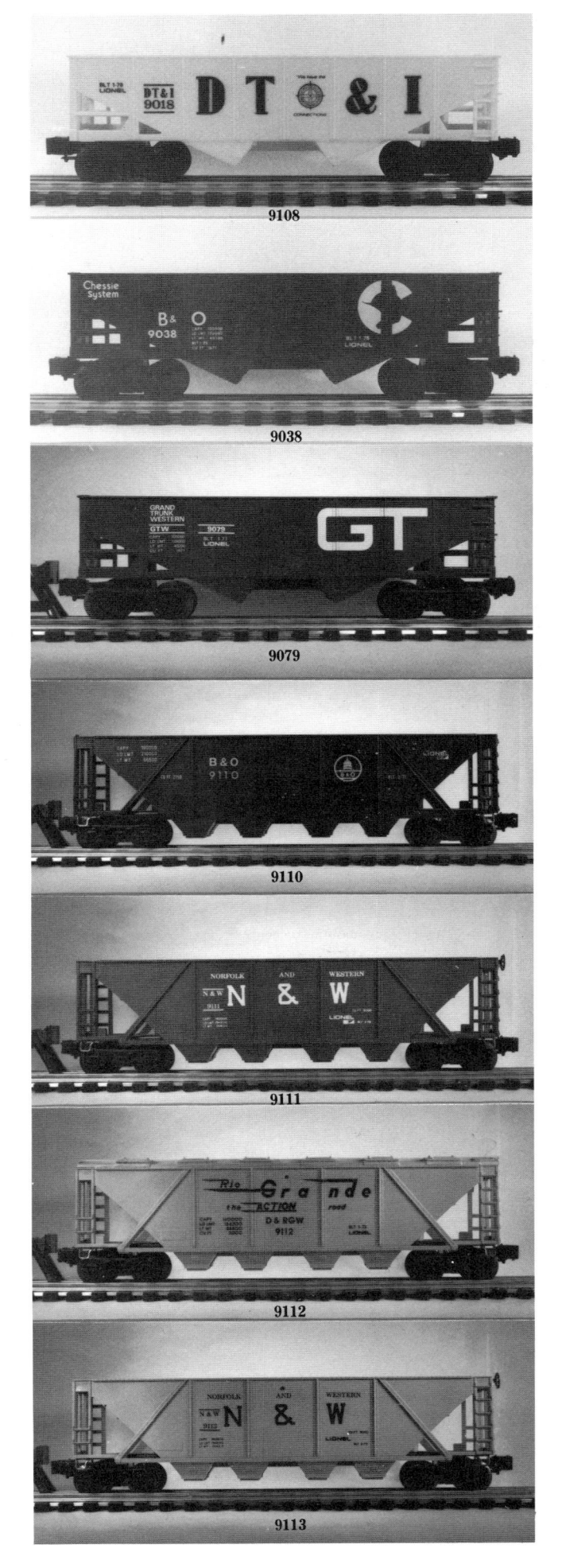

9108

9038

9079

9110

9111

9112

9113

9135 N & W 1971, blue or purple body, white lettering, royal blue cover, "9-70," usually Bettendorf trucks, metal plate holding trucks, from N & W set
(A) Royal blue body, no builder's plate   6   8   10   12
(B) Royal blue body, builder's plate   6   8   10   12
(C) Purple body, builder's plate, 3,000 manufactured   6   8   10   12
(D) Light blue body, builder's plate, Timken trucks   6   8   10   12
(E) Same as (D) but covers glued on by factory   6   8   10   12
(F) Flat Navy blue painted blue plastic body, glossy unpainted darker blue cover, light gray lettering instead of white, builder's plate, MPC logo, "9-70," Bettendorf trucks. It is possible that this particular version was issued in 1974 as part of the "Spirit of America" diesel set. Reader comments invited. LaVoie Collection   **NRS**

9213 M & St L 1978, red, white lettering, cover, sprung die-cast trucks, part of Service Station Set from 1978   —   —   13   15

9260 REYNOLDS ALUMINUM 1975-78, "NAHX 9260," blue body, silver lettering, "1-75," metal plate holding trucks, silver cover with blue hatches
(A) No builder's plate   4   5   7   9
(B) Builder's plate   4   5   7   9

9261 SUNMAID 1975-76, "GACX 9261," red body, yellow and white lettering, yellow cover, "Raisin Lady," "1-75," no builder's plate, metal plate holding trucks   4   5   7   9

9262 RALSTON-PURINA RPFX9262 1975-76, white body, red and white checks, red and black lettering, "1-75," red and black covers, no builder's plates, metal plate holding trucks   10   15   20   28

9263 PENNSYLVANIA 1975-77, tuscan body, white lettering, black cover, "1-76," no builder's plate
(A) Metal plate holding trucks   6   8   10   14
(B) Plastic plate holding trucks   6   8   10   14
Note: a few boxes were mislabeled Penn Central but the cars inside were labeled properly.

9264 I C 1975-77, orange body, black lettering, black cover, Bettendorf trucks
(A) Metal plate holding trucks, no builder's plate   6   8   10   14
(B) Same as (A) but plastic plate holding trucks   6   8   10   14
(C) Same as (A) but builder's plate   6   8   10   14
(D) Plastic plate holding trucks, builder's plate   6   8   10   14
(E) Same as (A) but stamped "TCA MUSEUM EXPRESS," 108 model Rohlfing Collection   **NRS**

9265 W M 1975-77, "Chessie System," yellow body, blue lettering, blue cover, "1-75," no builder's plate
(A) Metal plate holding trucks   6   8   10   14
(B) Plastic plate holding trucks   6   8   10   14

9266 SOUTHERN 1976, gray plastic painted silver, black lettering, red cover, plastic plate holding trucks
(A) Builder's plate   12   18   25   30
(B) No builder's plate   8   12   16   20

9267 ALCOA Gray body, blue lettering, silver cover, no builder's plate, standard 0 series with standard 0 trucks.   10   13   15   20

9276 PEABODY 1978, yellow body, dark green lettering, "BLT 1-78," sprung die-cast trucks, disc couplers, hole for center bar, no bar, part of Milwaukee Limited set   —   —   15   20

9286 B & L E Orange body, black lettering, black cover, builder's plate, plastic plate holding trucks   6   8   10   14

9304 C & O 1973-76, blue body, yellow lettering, coal carrier tilts   4   5   7   9

9306 C & O 1974-76, blue body, yellow lettering, coal carrier tilts, operating coupler   4   6   8   10

9311 U P 1978, coal dump with black coal, Bettendorf trucks, one disc coupler, one fixed coupler, load dumps when operating disc pulled down   3   5   7   9

9322 A.T.S.F. 1979, red plastic body painted red, white lettering, black and white Santa Fe logo, diamond shaped herald "Famous American Railroad Series 1" in gold, plastic brakewheel, hole for center brace, no center brace, covers   —   —   12   15

9330 KICKAPOO VALLEY 1972, four wheels
(A) Green   1   2   3   4
(B) Red   1   2   3   4
(C) Yellow   1   2   3   4

9333 PENNSYLVANIA POWER & LIGHT 1979, tuscan body, yellow lettering, die-cast sprung trucks, disc-operating couplers with small tabs, no

9330 Kickapoo Valley

spreader bar, from No. 1971 Quaker City Limited set, an excellent copy of the Bethlehem Steel Corporation prototype   —   —   25   30

9358 SAND'S OF IOWA 1980, LCCA 1980 National Convention car, 4,500 made   —   —   20   25

9366 U.P. 1980, disc-operating couplers, red, white and blue UNION PACIFIC logo, FARR Series 2 logo, from Famous American Railroad Series 2, only available as separate sale   —   —   11   14

9371 ATLANTIC SUGAR 1980, yellow sides and cover, die-cast sprung trucks, disc-operating couplers, from No. 1071 Mid Atlantic Limited set   —   —   11   14

9374 READING 1980-81, black sides, white lettering, disc-operating couplers, from No. 1072 Cross Country Express   —   —   25   30

9384 GREAT NORTHERN 1981, black with white lettering, bins open by remote control, die-cast sprung trucks, disc-operating couplers, from No. 1160 Great Lakes Limited set   —   —   50   60

9114

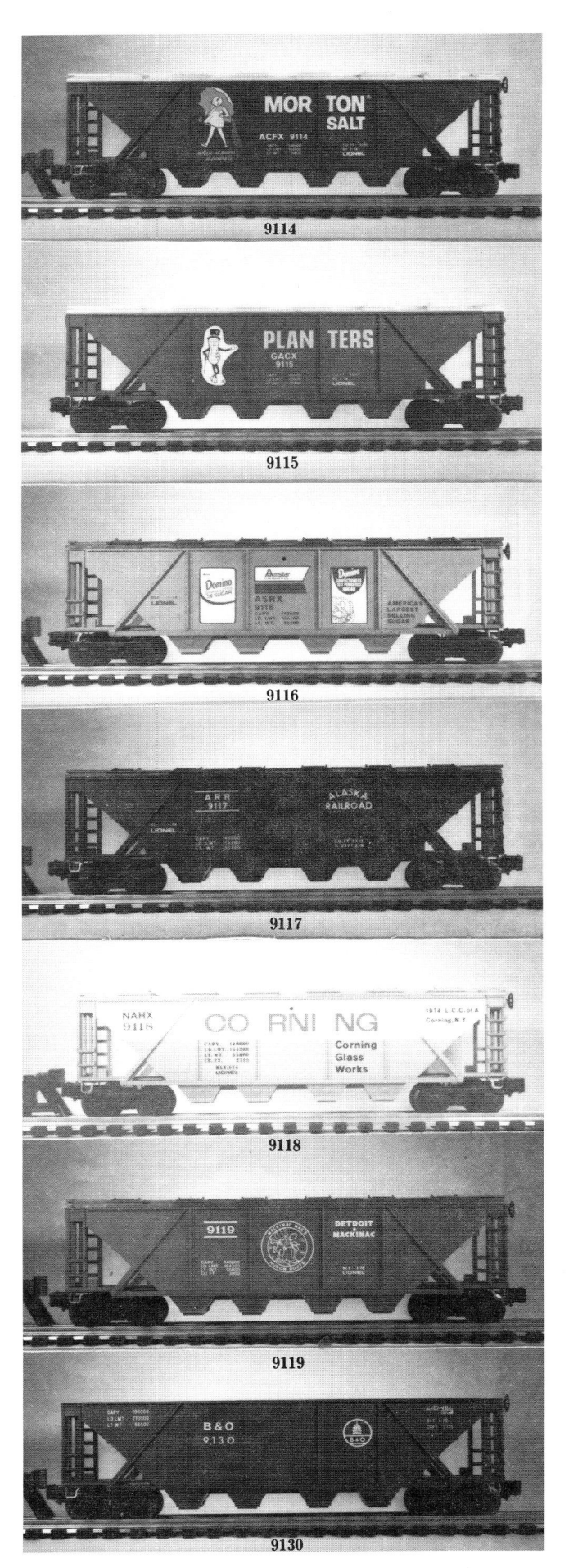

9115

9116

9117

9118

9119

9130

9134

9135

9260

9261

9262

9263

9264

175

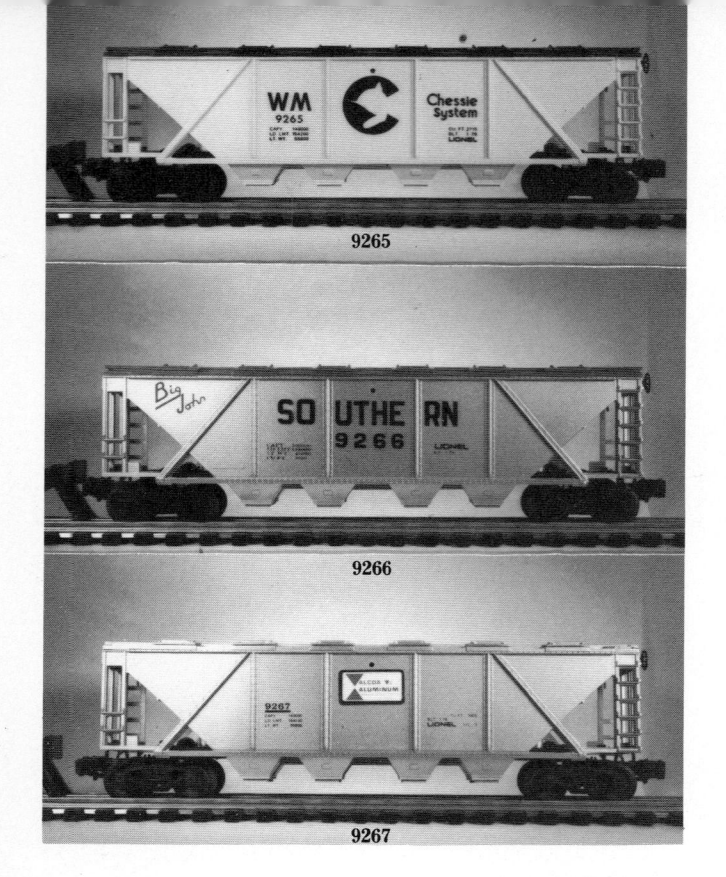

9200 and 9700 Box Car Body Characteristics*
Body Mold Types Type I - IV Lionel Postwar (pre-1970) Type V - IX Fundimensions (from 1970 on)

Door Guides
M: two metal door guides
P: two plastic door guides
S: one single plastic and one set of hooks on bottom of door

Trucks
T: Timken trucks
B: Bettendorf trucks
S: Standard "O" sprung trucks

Frames
I: With bubble and two holes
II: Without bubble, with two holes
III: Without bubble, with two holes and lettering

Miscellaneous
Starting with car #9709, the MPC logo appears on the car's side beneath the word LIONEL, it is missing on all other 9700 cars.

9200 and 9700 BOX CAR VARIATIONS

TYPE V BODY
(A) One partially complete rivet row
(B) Blank end plates
(C) Metal or plastic door guides at top and bottom

TYPE VI BODY [also known as '70 Body]
(A) Absence of even partially complete rivet row
(B) Blank end plates
(C) Metal or plastic door guides at top and bottom

TYPE VII BODY [also known as '71 Body]
(A) Absence of even partially complete rivet row
(B) "9200" on one end plate, "LIONEL MPC" logo on other
(C) Metal or plastic door guide at top and bottom

TYPE VIII BODY
(A) Absence of even partially complete rivet row
(B) "9200" on one end plate, "LIONEL MPC" logo on other
(C) One plastic door guide at top, hooks on bottom

TYPE IX BODY [also known as '72 Body]
(A) Absence of even partially complete rivet row
(B) "9700" on one end plate, "LIONEL MPC" logo on other
(C) One plastic door guide at top, hooks on bottom

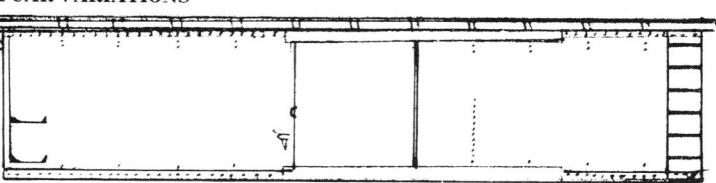

One partially complete rivet row

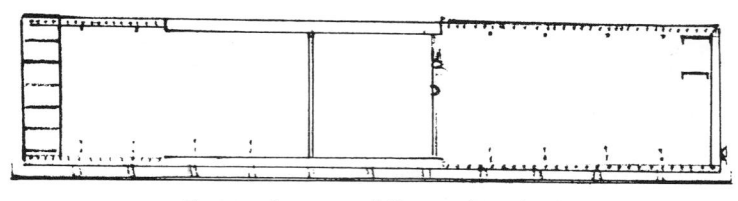

Absence of even partially complete rivet row

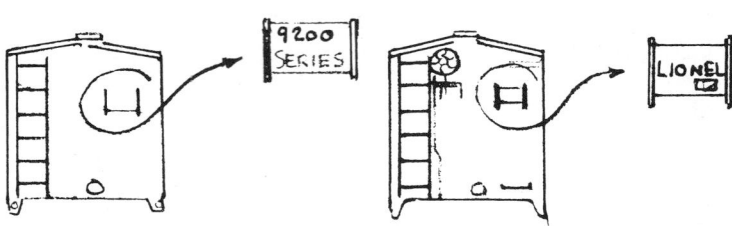

In our description we have omitted the body mold types '70, '71 and '72 as found in the last edition since these are now redundant to our new classification.
In this edition we have completely rewritten the 9200 and 9700 series box car descriptions to conform to the general pattern of this book. Common elements are described first and varying characteristics follow under subheadings (A), (B), etc. This method focuses the reader's attention on the varying elements and makes identification easier. Drawing by Bob Fox

176

Chapter XVII
FUNDIMENSIONS BOX CARS, REEFERS & STOCK CARS

                                                                               Gd. V.G. Exc. Mt.

0512 TOY FAIR 1981, reefer   —   —   75   110

0780 LIONEL RAILROADER CLUB BOX CAR 1982, white painted white body, red painted white doors, red roof and ends, Type IX body, Bettendorf trucks. Black electrocal of steam loco front end at right of door. Red "1982" and black "SPECIAL EDITION THE INSIDE TRACK" to left of door. "LIONEL" and "0780" in red and "RAILROADER CLUB" in black to right of door. This car was only available to members of the Lionel Railroader Club, a Fundimensions sponsored organization. Francis Stem Collection   **NRS**

1018-1979 TCA MORTGAGE BURNING CEREMONY CAR 1979, Light tan painted gray plastic body, light yellow painted white door, Hi-Cube box car, orange, black and red rectangular mortgage burning logo at left, orange Toy Train Museum logo and black lettering at right. There is an intriguing story behind the making of this car. In 1978, the TCA held its convention in Boston. The 9611 "Flying Yankee" hi-cube box car was produced for this convention in official Boston and Maine sky blue and black (see 9611-1978 entry). Large anticipated sales of the Flying Yankee car never materialized, and at convention's end the TCA found itself in possession of a considerable backlog of unsold cars. In the next year, the organization was to finish paying the mortgage on its museum in Strasburg, Pa. Rather than order a special car, the TCA shipped its entire backlog of 9611 Flying Yankee cars to the Pleasant Valley Process Company of Cogen Station, Pennsylvania. There, the Flying Yankee cars were repainted into the Mortgage Burning Ceremony car. Faint traces of the original black paint show through the light tan paint on the ends and roof. Bratspis observation   —   —   —   125

5700 OPPENHEIMER 1981, SAUSAGE CASINGS, dark green "weathered" paint, standard 0 sprung trucks, disc-operating couplers, the first in the "Turn of the Century" series   —   —   14   18

5701 DAIRYMEN'S LEAGUE 1981, milk reefer, off-white "weathered" paint, standard 0 sprung trucks, disc-operating couplers —   —   11   14

5702 NATIONAL DAIRY DESPATCH 1981, Universal Carloading & Distributing Co., red and silver "weathered" paint, standard 0 sprung trucks, disc-operating couplers   —   —   11   14

5703 NORTH AMERICAN DESPATCH 1981, "FRIGICAR," light and dark brown "weathered" paint, standard 0 sprung trucks, disc-operating couplers   —   —   11   14

5704 BUDWEISER 1981, "weathered" paint, standard 0 sprung trucks, disc-operating couplers   —   —   14   18

5705 BALL GLASS JARS 1981, "weathered" paint, standard 0 sprung trucks, disc-operating couplers   —   —   11   14

5706 LINDSAY BROS 1981, BINDER & TWINE, "weathered" paint standard 0 sprung trucks, disc-operating couplers   —   —   14   18

5707 AMERICAN REFRIGERATION 1981, "weathered" paint, standard 0 sprung trucks, disc-operating couplers   —   —   11   14

5708 ARMOUR 1982-83, wood-sheathed reefer, white sides, tuscan end and roof   —   —   12   15

5709 REA 1982-83, wood-sheathed reefer, green painted body   —   —   12   15

5710 CANADIAN PACIFIC 1982-83, wood-sheathed reefer, tuscan body   —   —   12   15

5711 COMMERCIAL EXPRESS 1982-83, wood-sheathed reefer   —   —   12   15

5713 COTTON BELT 1983, wood-sheathed reefer, yellow sides, brown roof and ends, disc-operating couplers   —   —   —   15

5714 MICHIGAN CENTRAL 1983, wood-sheathed reefer, white sides, blue roof and ends, disc-operating couplers   —   —   —   15

5715 SANTA FE 1983, wood-sheathed reefer, orange sides, disc-operating couplers   —   —   —   15

5716 VERMONT CENTRAL 1983, wood-sheathed reefer, white sides, blue roof and ends, disc-operating couplers   —   —   —   15

5717 A.T.S.F. 1983, bunk car   —   —   —   20

5718 See 9849

6464-500 See Chapter IV for listing

6464-1970 See Chapter IV for listing

7301 N & W 1982, cattle car, brown and white lettering, standard O trucks, disc-operating couplers, from Continental Limited set   —   —   —   35

7302 T & P 1983, cattle car, brown with white lettering   —   —   —   10

7304 SOUTHERN 1983, tuscan sides, two lighter brown doors on each side, "SOUTHERN" and "9459" in white to the left of doors, circular Southern logo to the right of the doors, metal door guides, gold "Famous American Railroads 4" logo, disc-operating couplers, Standard O die-cast trucks, La-Voie comment   —   —   —   —

7501 LIONEL 75th ANNIVERSARY 1975, Cowen picture, blue body, silver roof, 9700 type car   —   7   10   14

7502 LIONEL 75th ANNIVERSARY 1975, reefer, innovations, yellow body, blue roof   —   7   10   14

7503 LIONEL 75th ANNIVERSARY 1975, reefer famous engines, beige body, brown roof   —   7   10   14

7505 LIONEL 75th ANNIVERSARY 1975, 9700 series box, accessories, silver body, red roof   —   7   10   14

7506 LIONEL 75th ANNIVERSARY 1975, 9700 series box, famous catalogues, green body, gold roof   —   7   10   14

7507 LIONEL 75th ANNIVERSARY 1975, reefer logos, white body, blue roof   —   7   10   14

7509 KENTUCKY FRIED CHICKEN 1981-82, reefer with white sides, tuscan roof and ends, red lettering, Colonel Sanders electrocal, disc-operating couplers, from Favorite Food Freight, available only as separate sale   —   —   10   14

7510 RED LOBSTER 1981-82, reefer with white sides, black roof and ends, red lettering, lobster electrocal, disc-operating couplers, from Favorite Food Freight, available only as separate sale   —   —   20   25

7511 PIZZA HUT 1981-82, reefer with white sides, red roof and ends, red lettering, hut electrocal, disc-operating couplers, from Favorite Food Freight, available only as separate sale   —   —   10   14

7515 DENVER MINT 1981, light gold paint on clear plastic, stack of silver ingots inside car, standard O trucks   —   —   35   45

7517 PHILADELPHIA MINT 1982, clear plastic body painted burnished bronze, coin slot circular grates at each end, silver bullion inside, standard 0 trucks, disc-operating couplers, from Spring '82 Collector Center. Similar type box cars are 7515, 9319, 9320 and 9349   —   —   25   30

7518 CARSON CITY MINT 1983, clear plastic body painted black. Die-cast sprung trucks, disc-operating couplers, available as separate item. Similar items are 7515, 7517, 9319, 9320 and 9349.   —   —   —   20

SPIRIT OF 76 SERIES CARS
TYPE I AND TYPE II BODIES

TYPE I: Black metal strip runs car length and is used to attach trucks. Underneath the strip at each end are square holes. Black metal strip is attached to the bottom of the car by one screw, the trucks then attach to the black strip.

TYPE II: No strip version with a round hole at each end on the bottom. Round hole is for the screw that holds the one-piece roof and ends to the car sides.

7601 DELAWARE 1975-76

(A) Type I light yellow body painted light yellow, light yellow door painted light yellow, blue roof painted blue, gold diamond in flag, Mitarotonda Collection   —   5   9   12

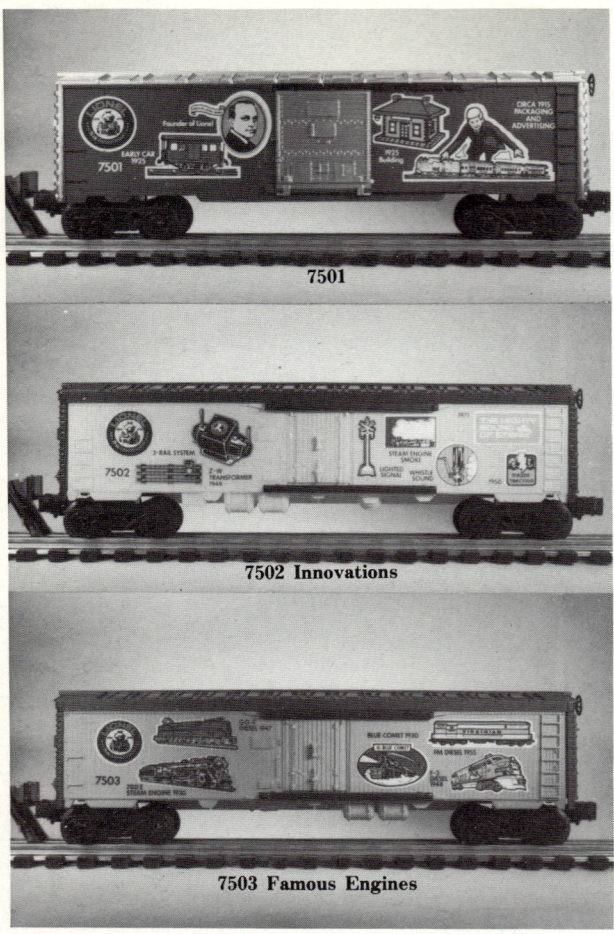

7501

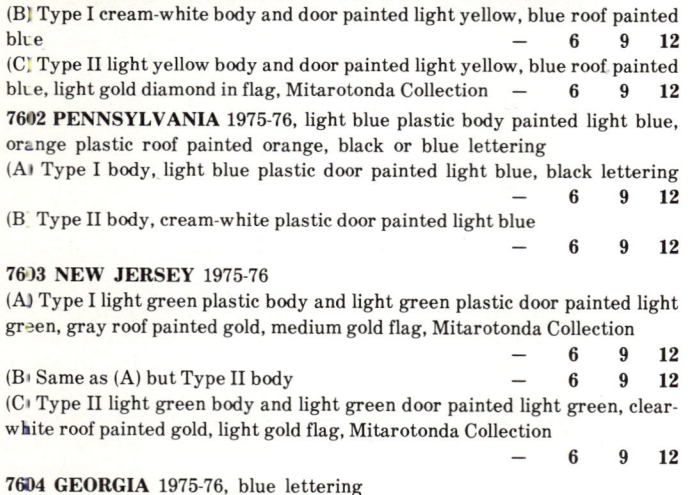

7502 Innovations

7503 Famous Engines

7505 Accessories

7506 Famous Catalogues

7507 Logos

(B) Type I cream-white body and door painted light yellow, blue roof painted blue — 6 9 12
(C) Type II light yellow body and door painted light yellow, blue roof painted blue, light gold diamond in flag, Mitarotonda Collection — 6 9 12

7602 PENNSYLVANIA 1975-76, light blue plastic body painted light blue, orange plastic roof painted orange, black or blue lettering
(A) Type I body, light blue plastic door painted light blue, black lettering — 6 9 12
(B) Type II body, cream-white plastic door painted light blue — 6 9 12

7603 NEW JERSEY 1975-76
(A) Type I light green plastic body and light green plastic door painted light green, gray roof painted gold, medium gold flag, Mitarotonda Collection — 6 9 12
(B) Same as (A) but Type II body — 6 9 12
(C) Type II light green body and light green door painted light green, clear-white roof painted gold, light gold flag, Mitarotonda Collection — 6 9 12

7604 GEORGIA 1975-76, blue lettering
(A) Type I light blue body painted light blue, clear-white door painted light blue, clear-white roof painted red, red flag, yellow-gold bars and stripes border, Mitarotonda Collection — 6 9 12
(B) Type I cream-white plastic body and door painted light blue, red roof painted flat red, Eddins Collection — 6 9 12
(C) Type II light blue body and door painted light blue, red roof painted dark red, dark red flag, lighter gold bars and stripes border, Mitarotonda Collection — 6 9 12
(D) Type II light blue plastic body and door painted light blue, glossy red roof painted glossy deep red, Eddins Collection — 6 9 12

7605 CONNECTICUT 1975-76, black lettering
(A) Type I body, cream-white plastic body and door painted medium pale blue, blue roof painted medium pale blue — 6 9 12

(B) Type II body, medium pale blue plastic body and door painted medium pale blue, dark blue roof painted dark blue — 6 9 12
(C) Same as (A) but white roof painted dark blue, Mitarotonda Collection — 6 9 12

7606 MASSACHUSETTS 1975-76, black lettering
(A) Type 1 body, cream-white plastic body and door painted light yellow, cream-white roof painted white — 6 9 12
(B) Type I body, cream-white plastic body and door painted medium yellow, cream-white roof painted white — 6 9 12
(C) Type I body, shiny white plastic body and door painted dark yellow, cream-white roof painted white, flag is bordered in dark gold, purple crest, light purple shadowing, Mitarotonda Collection — 6 9 12
(D) Type II body, shiny white plastic body and door painted very dark yellow, cream white roof painted white, flag is bordered in yellow gold, dark blue crest, light blue shadowing, Mitarotonda Collection — 6 9 12

7607 MARYLAND 1975-76, black lettering
(A) Type I body, white plastic body and door painted light yellow, white roof painted black, checkered quadrants of the flag are alternating gold and black squares, gold flagstaff is topped by a dark gold eagle, Mitarotonda Collection — 6 9 12
(B) Type II body, light yellow body and door painted light yellow, yellow and black checkered flag quadrants, light gold cross tops flagstaff, black roof painted black, Mitarotonda Collection — 6 9 12
(C) Type II body, cream-white plastic body and door painted mustard, cream-white roof painted black — 6 9 12
(D) Type I body, cream-white plastic body and door painted dark yellow, cream-white roof painted black — 6 9 12
(E) Type II light yellow body and door painted light yellow, black roof painted black, black and yellow alternating flag quadrant squares, white quadrants slightly shadowed, yellow-gold cross tops yellow-gold flagstaff, Mitarotonda Collection — 6 9 12

7608 SOUTH CAROLINA 1975-76, black lettering
(A) Type I body, dark yellow body and door painted mustard, brown roof

SPIRIT OF 76 BOX CARS

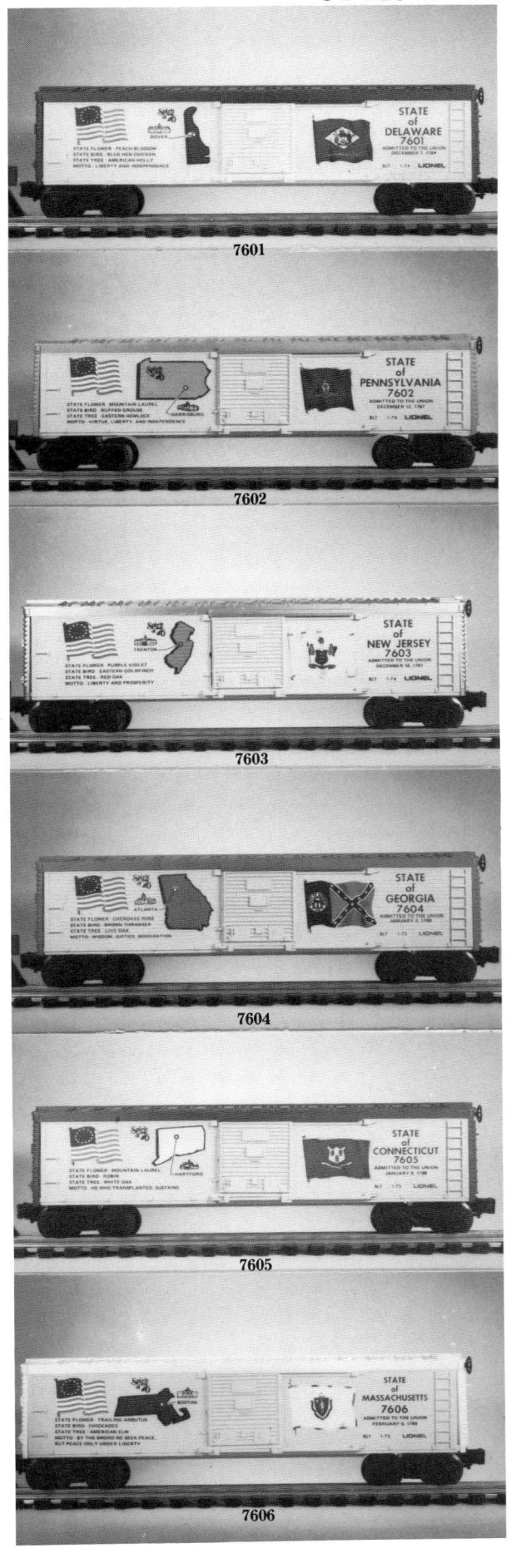

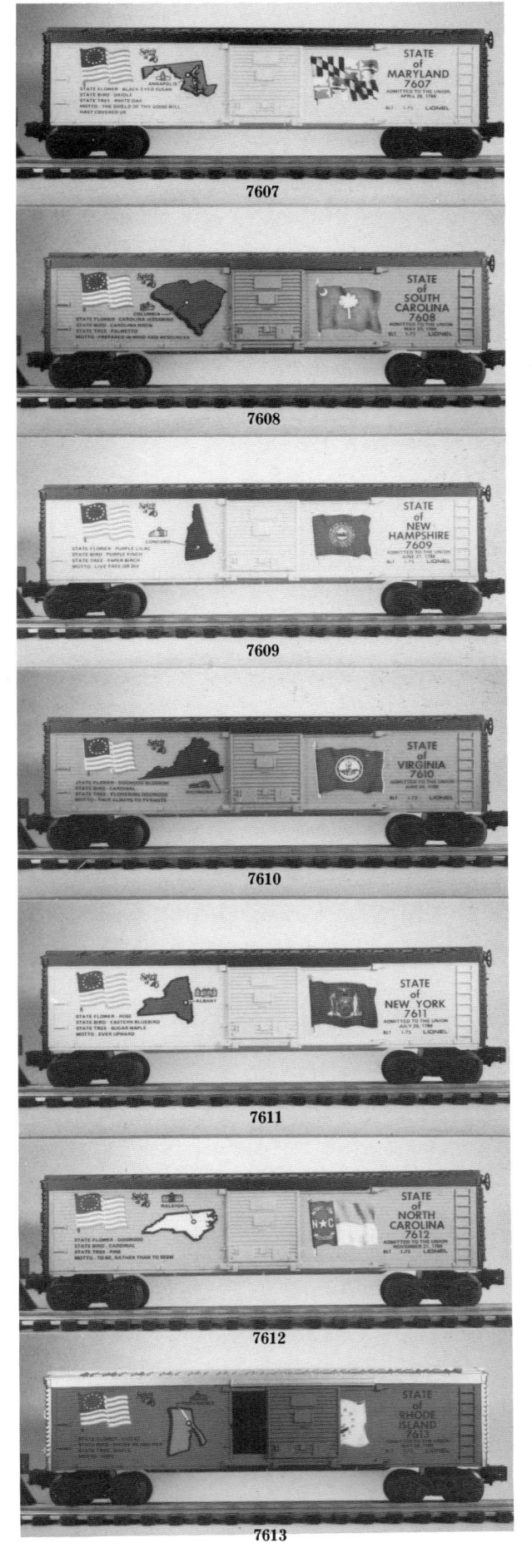

7601

7602

7603

7604

7605

7606

7607

7608

7609

7610

7611

7612

7613

painted chocolate brown, Mitchell and Mitarotonda Collections
— 6 9 12
(B) Same as (A) but white door painted darker mustard, Mitarotonda Collection — 6 9 12
(C) Type II body, dark mustard plastic body and medium mustard door painted dark mustard, mustard roof painted chocolate brown, medium blue flag
— 6 9 12

7609 NEW HAMPSHIRE 1975-76, black lettering
(A) Type I body, dark yellow plastic body and door painted dark yellow, light green roof painted dark green — 6 9 12
(B) Type II body, dark yellow plastic body painted dark yellow, dark yellow door painted dark yellow, green roof painted dark green, dark blue flag bordered in light gold with light gold leaves and printing on the flag, Mitarotonda Collection — 6 9 12
(C) Same as (A) but Type II body and white border around right side of map, half moon on map by star — 6 9 12
(D) Type I body, dark yellow plastic body painted dark yellow, white door painted dark yellow, white roof painted dark green, purple flag bordered in gold, gold leaves and printing on flag, Mitarotonda Collection **NRS**

7610 VIRGINIA 1975-76, black lettering
(A) Type I body, cream-white plastic body and door painted orange, cream-white roof painted dark blue 25 50 100 125
(B) Type I body, orange plastic body and door painted orange, blue roof painted blue, quarter moon on map 25 50 100 125
(C) Same as (B) but Type II body 25 50 100 125
(D) Type I body, cream-white body painted orange, orange door painted orange, dark blue roof painted dark blue, Mitarotonda Collection
25 50 100 125

7611 NEW YORK 1975-76, black lettering
(A) Type I cream-white plastic body and medium yellow door painted light yellow, dark blue roof painted dark blue — 15 30 40
(B) Type II cream plastic body and medium yellow door painted dark yellow, near perfect flag, dark blue roof painted dark blue — 15 30 40
(C) Type II cream plastic body and medium yellow door painted dark yellow, flag with red border, dark blue roof painted dark blue — 15 30 40
(D) Type II dark cream plastic body and medium yellow door painted dark yellow, flag with red and white border, dark blue roof painted dark blue
— 15 30 40
(E) Type II cream plastic body and white door painted medium yellow, flag with white border, dark blue roof painted dark blue — 15 30 40
(F) Type I pale yellow body and medium yellow door painted dark yellow (door darker than body) clear-white roof painted dark blue, Mitarotonda Collection — 15 30 40
(G) Type I medium yellow body and medium yellow doors painted dark yellow (doors darker than body) clear-white roof painted dark blue, Mitarotonda Collection — 15 30 40

7612 NORTH CAROLINA 1975-76, black lettering
(A) Type I cream plastic body painted dark mustard, yellow door painted medium mustard, slight contrast between door and darker body, cream-white roof painted black, flag heavily shadowed in blue tint, yellow letters and banners subsequently show green tint, Mitarotonda Collection
— 9 12 14
(B) Type I white plastic body and cream door painted light mustard, cream-white roof painted black — 9 12 14
(C) Type II mustard body and mustard door painted dark mustard, no contrast between door and body, black roof painted black, flag in light shadow, blue portion is dark blue, Mitarotonda Collection — 9 12 14
(D) Type II dark yellow body painted light mustard, yellow door painted dark mustard, large contrast between darker door and body, black roof painted black, flag in medium shadow, red portion is light red, Mitarotonda Collection — 9 12 14

7613 RHODE ISLAND 1975-76, black lettering
(A) Type I body, aqua-blue plastic body and door painted green, gray roof painted gold — 9 12 14
(B) Type II body, green plastic body and door painted green, white roof painted gold — 9 12 14
(C) Type I body, aqua-blue body painted dark green, dark green door painted dark green, green roof painted gold, Mitarotonda Collection **NRS**

7700 UNCLE SAM 1976, white painted body and door, red painted roof, plastic top door guides with molded hook on bottom, white and black lettering
(A) Opaque-white plastic body and door 25 35 50 60
(B) Translucent-white plastic body 25 35 50 60

7701 CAMEL 1976-77, brown, black and silver lettering, plastic top door guides with molded hook on bottom, dark brown roof
(A) Opaque-white plastic body and doors painted medium yellow
— 4 6 9
(B) Same as (A) but medium dark yellow body and light yellow doors
— 4 6 9
(C) Same as (A) but dark yellow body and doors — 4 6 9
(D) Translucent-white plastic body painted light yellow, dark yellow doors
— 4 6 9

7702 PRINCE ALBERT 1976-77, red plastic body painted red and yellow, door painted yellow, black roof, yellow, black and white lettering, plastic top door guides with molded hook on bottom — 4 6 9

7703 BEECH-NUT 1976-77, opaque-white plastic body painted white, red roof and blue doors painted blue, blue and red lettering, plastic top door guides with molded hook on bottom — 4 6 9

7704 WELCOME TOY FAIR 1976 (U S Toy Fair) opaque-white plastic body painted white, red roof, translucent-white doors painted blue, blue and red lettering, plastic top door guides with molded hook on bottom
— 60 110 125

7705 TOY FAIR 1976 (Canadian Toy Fair) opaque-white plastic body painted white, red roof, translucent-white door painted red, red lettering, plastic top on door guides with molded hook on bottom — — 250 350

7706 SIR WALTER RALEIGH 1977-78, opaque-white plastic body painted orange, blue roof, translucent-white door painted gold, white lettering, plastic top on door guides with molded hook on bottom — 4 6 9

7707 WHITE OWL 1977-78, opaque-white plastic body painted white, brown roof, translucent-white door painted gold, brown lettering, plastic top door guides with molded bottom hook — 4 6 9

7708 WINSTON 1977-78, red plastic body painted red, gold roof, translucent-white door painted gold, white and red lettering, plastic top door guides with molded bottom hook — 4 6 9

7709 SALEM 1978, green painted sides, gold door and roof
— 4 6 9

7710 MAIL POUCH 1978, white painted sides, tuscan roof and door
— 4 6 9

7711 EL PRODUCTO 1978, white sides, gold door, dark red roof and ends
— 6 8 12

7712 A T S F 1979, yellow sides, silver roof, part of Famous American Railroad Series — 8 10 14

7800 PEPSI 1977, white plastic body painted white, red roof and ends, blue doors painted blue, red and blue lettering, 1972 Type body, single door guides, Bettendorf trucks, Type III frame, "LIONEL" on right side
— 6 10 14

7801 A & W 1977, white plastic body painted yellow, orange roof and ends, brown lettering, white doors painted brown, 1972 Type body, single door guides, Bettendorf trucks, Type III frame, "LIONEL" on right side
— 4 7 9

7802 CANADA DRY 1977, green plastic body painted green, gold roof and ends, cream door painted gold, white and gold lettering, 1972 Type body, single door guides, Bettendorf trucks, Type III frame, "LIONEL" on left side — 4 7 9

7803 TRAINS N TRUCKING white body, gold roof, green lettering
10 15 20 30

7806 SEASONS GREETINGS 1976, silver painted body, green door, white lettering, 1972 Type body — 60 90 110

7807 TOY FAIR 1977, green and gold painted body, gold painted door, red and green lettering, 1972 Type body mold — 60 95 135

7808 NORTHERN PACIFIC Brown with silver roof, black door, silver lettering, known as "The Pig Palace" 10 15 30 40

7809 VERNORS 1978, yellow painted sides, black roof and door
— 4 7 9

7810 CRUSH 1978, orange painted sides, green roof, ends and door
— 4 7 9

PLUG DOOR BOX CARS

7811 DR. PEPPER 1978, dark orange painted roof, dark brown body, white lettering — 4 7 9

7812-1977 TCA Convention Stock Car, 1977, Brown cattle car body, brown-yellow plastic plaque inserted in place of double doors, center metal door guide removed. Yellow lettering on car body, "23rd NATIONAL CONVENTION/HOUSTON/ TEXAS/JUNE 1977." Brown lettering and logos on plaque. Bettendorf trucks — — 30 35

7813 SEASONS GREETINGS 1977 — — 90 100

7814 SEASONS GREETINGS 1978 — — 100 125

7815 TOY FAIR 1978 — — 100 120

7900 OUTLAW CAR 1982-83, orange stock car with outlaw and sheriff who move in and out of car windows as car moves, mechanism like Horse Transport Car — — 11 14

7901 LIONEL LINES 1982-83, cop and hobo car, "HYDRAULIC PLATFORM MAINTENANCE CAR," one figure moves from car platform to overhead trestle while other figure moves from trestle to car platform — — 18 20

SMALL PLUG DOOR BOX CARS

7902 A.T.S.F. 1982-83, red plastic plug door, white lettering, from No. 1353 Southern Streak set (1983) — — 6 8

7903 ROCK 1983, blue plastic plug door box car, white lettering, one fixed coupler, one disc-operating coupler, metal wheels, Caponi comment — — — 8

7904 SAN DIEGO ZOO 1983, red plastic car with giraffe, with white lettering "SAN DIEGO ZOO/BLT 1983/LIONEL," disc-operating couplers, rerun of 3376 and 3386 from 1960s. With tell-tale and trip clip. Catalogue shows car numbered "7903" in error. — — — 22

7909 L & N 1983, blue plastic, plug door box car, yellow lettering, fixed couplers, plastic trucks, part of No. 1352 Rocky Mountain Freight — — — 10

9035 CONRAIL 1978-82, blue body, white lettering — — 2 4

9037 CONRAIL 1978-81, brown or blue body, white lettering, plastic trucks and wheels
(A) Brown — — 3 5
(B) Blue — — 3 5

9040 WHEATIES 1970, orange body, white and blue lettering, MPC logo
(A) Type V body, Timken trucks, one operating coupler, one fixed coupler, plastic wheels 1 1.50 2 4
(B) Type IV body, Bettendorf trucks, one operating coupler, one fixed coupler, plastic wheels 1 1.50 2 4
(C) Type V body, Bettendorf trucks, one operating coupler, one fixed coupler, plastic wheels 1 1.50 2 4
(D) Type V body, Bettendorf trucks, one operating coupler, one manumatic coupler, metal wheels 1 1.50 2 4

9041 HERSHEY'S 1971, silver lettering, metal wheels, one operating coupler, one fixed coupler, MPC logo
(A) Type IV chocolate body, Timken trucks, plastic wheels, silk screened lettering, Askenas Collection 1 1.50 2 4
(B) Type V dark chocolate body, Bettendorf trucks, plastic wheels 1 1.50 2 4
(C) Type V maroon body, Bettendorf trucks, two fixed couplers 1 1.50 2 4
(D) Same as (C) but one disc coupler, one fixed coupler, Askenas Collection 1 1.50 2 4
(E) Type IV chocolate body, Bettendorf trucks, Rohlfing Collection 1 1.50 2 4

9042 AUTOLITE 1972, Type V white body, black and orange lettering, Bettendorf trucks, one operating coupler, one fixed coupler, metal wheels, MPC logo 1 1.50 2 4

9043 ERIE LACKAWANNA 1973-74, gray body, wine lettering, Type V body, Bettendorf trucks, one operating coupler, one manumatic fixed coupler, plastic wheels, no MPC logo 1 1.50 2 4

9044 D & R G W 1975,79, orange body, black lettering, Type V body, Bettendorf trucks, one operating coupler, one manumatic fixed coupler, no MPC logo 3 4 6 8

9045 TOYS "R" US White body, orange and black lettering, Type V body, Bettendorf trucks, one operating coupler, one manumatic fixed coupler, plastic wheels, no MPC logo 15 22 30 40

9046 TRUE VALUE White body, red and black lettering, Type V body, Bettendorf trucks, one operating coupler, one fixed coupler, metal wheels, no MPC logo 15 22 30 40

9047 TOYS "R" US White body, orange and black lettering, Type V body, Bettendorf trucks, one operating coupler, one manumatic dummy coupler, plastic wheels, no MPC logo — 10 19 25

9048 TOYS "R" US White body, orange and black lettering, Bettendorf trucks, one operating coupler, one manumatic coupler, plastic wheels 7 10 19 25

9052 TOYS "R" US White body, orange and black lettering, Bettendorf trucks, one operating coupler, one manumatic coupler, plastic wheels 7 10 19 25

9053 TRUE VALUE Green plug door box car with True Value electrocal NRS

9054 JC PENNEY Orange body, black lettering, "75th Anniversary" NRS

No Number TOYS "R" US Plug door box car, orange and black lettering, "GEOFFREY POWER" NRS

MINI MAX BOX CAR

9090 MINI MAX 1971, light blue body, white door, blue lettering, four wheels
(A) Three roof brackets, "G" is in fourth panel from right 6 9 12 15
(B) Same as (A) but without three roof brackets 6 9 12 15
(C) Same as (A) but without three roof brackets and USLX 9090 lettering on lower left side — — 17 25
(D) Three roof brackets, "G" is in fourth panel from left 6 9 12 15

9200 SERIES BOX CARS

9200 ILLINOIS CENTRAL Several body types, black and white lettering
(A) Type VI body, metal door guides, flat orange painted orange body and doors, Timken trucks, Type I frame, IC spread 4 6 8 11
(B) Type VII body, metal door guides, glossy orange painted orange body and doors, Timken trucks, Type I frame, IC close 4 6 8 11
(C) Same as (B) but plastic door guides 4 6 8 11
(D) Same as (B) but plastic door guides, Bettendorf trucks, IC spread 4 6 8 11
(E) Same as (B) but dull dark orange painted orange body, IC spread 4 7 9 12
(F) Type VIII body, flat orange painted gray body and doors, Bettendorf trucks, Type II frame, IC spread 4 7 9 12
(G) Same as (F) but Type IX body 4 7 9 12
(H) Type IX body, glossy orange painted orange body, flat orange painted gray doors, Bettendorf trucks, Type II frame, IC spread 4 7 9 12

9201 PENN CENTRAL Type VI body, metal door guides, white lettering, Timken trucks, Type I frame
(A) Jade green painted jade green plastic body and door 7 10 12 17
(B) Dark green painted dark green plastic body and door 7 10 12 17

9202 SANTA FE Type VI body, metal door guides, Timken trucks, Type I frame, all have red painted red bodies except (A), all have white lettering except (A)
(A) Orange painted orange body, black painted black door, black lettering, prototype, 1 of 69 — — 675 800
(B) Silver painted gray door 12 17 25 35
(C) Same as (B) but only two dots on left side of door 12 17 25 35
(D) Gray painted gray door 12 17 25 35

9203 UNION PACIFIC Type V body, metal door guides, yellow painted yellow doors, blue lettering, Timken trucks, Type I frame
(A) Yellow painted yellow body 9 15 20 30
(B) Light yellow painted light yellow body 9 15 20 30

9204 NORTHERN PACIFIC White and black outline letters, Type I frame, Timken trucks except as noted
(A) Type VI body, dark green painted dark green body and shiny green door, metal door guides, dark red logo insert, built date 10 22 30 35
(B) Same as (A) but light red logo insert 10 22 30 55

0-27 Plug Door Box Car Types

I.
II.
III.
IV.

V. Same as IV but with LIONEL MPC on end board - 9040 series

(C) Type VII body, apple green painted apple green body and door, no built date, metal door guides   10   17   28   35
(D) Same as (C) but plastic door guides and Bettendorf trucks   10   17   28   35

9205 NORFOLK & WESTERN Type VI body, metal door guides, white lettering, Timken trucks except as noted, Type I frame
(A) Dark blue painted dark blue body and navy blue door   5   7   10   12
(B) Same as (A) but Bettendorf trucks   5   7   10   12
(C) Medium blue painted medium blue body and navy blue door   5   7   10   12
(D) Royal blue (reddish-blue) painted royal blue body and door   5   7   10   12

9206 GREAT NORTHERN White lettering, metal door guides, Timken trucks except as noted, Type I frame
(A) Type VI body, light blue painted body and door   5   7   10   12
(B) Type VII body, paler blue painted paler blue body and light blue door   5   7   10   12
(C) Type VII body, palest blue painted palest blue body and light blue door, Bettendorf trucks   5   7   10   12

9207 SOO Type VII body, Type I frame
(A) White painted sides and black painted roof on white plastic body with red painted red door, black lettering, metal door guides, Bettendorf trucks, preproduction sample, one of twenty-four   —   —   —   225
(B) Same as (A) but all white painted car   —   —   —   225
(C) Red painted red body and red door, white lettering, Timken trucks, metal door guides   4   6   9   12
(D) Flat red painted red body and door, white lettering, Bettendorf trucks, metal door guides   4   6   9   12
(E) Shiny red painted red body and door, white lettering, Bettendorf trucks, plastic door guides   4   6   9   12

9208 C P RAIL Type VII body, black lettering, Type I frame
(A) Medium yellow painted medium yellow body and door; metal door guides, Bettendorf trucks   4   6   9   12
(B) Light yellow painted light yellow body and door, metal door guides, Bettendorf trucks   4   6   9   12
(C) Light yellow painted light yellow body, light yellow painted medium yellow door, plastic door guides, Timken trucks   4   6   9   12
(D) Dark yellow painted dark yellow body, dark yellow painted medium yellow door, Timken trucks, plastic door guide   4   6   9   12
(E) Same as (D) but Bettendorf trucks   4   6   9   12

9209 BURLINGTON NORTHERN Type I frame, white lettering
(A) Type VII body, apple green painted apple green body and dark green painted dark green door, Timken trucks, metal door guides   4   6   9   12
(B) Type VII body, dark green painted dark green body and doors, metal door guides, Bettendorf trucks   4   6   9   12
(C) Same as (B) but Type VIII body   4   6   9   12
(D) Same as (B) but Type IX body   4   6   9   12
(E) Same as (B) but plastic door guides   4   6   9   12

9090 General Mills
MINI MAX BOX CARS

(F) Same as (A), but Type VII body and plastic door guides, Knopf Collection   4   6   9   12

9210 B & O Auto car, Type VII body, metal door guides, Type I frame, white lettering, Lionel doors with different colors added outside the factory, all Bettendorf trucks except (A)
(A) Black painted black body and doors, Timken trucks   4   6   9   12
(B) Same as (A) but dark blue painted dark blue doors   4   6   9   12
(C) Same as (A) but light green painted light green doors   4   6   9   12
(D) Same as (A) but orange painted orange doors   4   6   9   12
(E) Same as (A) but burnt-orange painted burnt-orange doors   4   6   9   12
(F) Same as (A) but turquoise painted turquoise doors   4   6   9   12

9211 PENN CENTRAL Type VII body, except for (A), silver painted gray doors, white lettering, Type I frame
(A) Jade green painted Type VI jade green body, Timken trucks, 1000 made, no end imprints, metal door guides   6   10   15   20
(B) Jade green painted jade green body, Bettendorf trucks, metal door guides   6   10   15   20
(C) Pale green painted pale green body, Timken trucks, metal door guides   6   10   15   20
(D) Medium green painted medium green body, Timken trucks, metal door guides   6   10   15   20
(E) Same as (D) but plastic door guides   6   10   15   20
(F) Same as (D) but Bettendorf trucks   6   10   15   20
(G) Dark green painted dark green body, Bettendorf trucks, plastic door guides   6   10   15   20

9212 Assigned to Lionel Collector's Club of America, 1976 Flat Car
9213 Not assigned

9214 NORTHERN PACIFIC Type VII maroon plastic body except for (D), white and black outlined lettering, Type I frame, metal door guides, red oxide painted maroon doors
(A) Flat red oxide painted body, Bettendorf trucks   5   7   10   12
(B) Red oxide painted body, Timken trucks   5   7   10   12
(C) Red oxide painted Type IX tuscan body, tuscan painted tuscan door, Bettendorf trucks, Type II frame   6   11   15   18

9215 NORFOLK & WESTERN Type VII body, silver painted gray doors, white lettering, Type I frame
(A) Royal blue painted royal blue Type VI plastic body, plastic door guides, Timken trucks, 1000 manufactured   10   15   20   30
(B) Dark blue painted dark blue body, metal door guides, Bettendorf trucks   4   6   8   10
(C) Same as (B) except plastic door guides   4   6   8   10
(D) Same as (B) except plastic door guides and Timken trucks   4   6   8   10

9217 SOO 1982, operating box, plunger opens door, worker moves towards door, tuscan painted car, white lettering, die-cast trucks, disc-operating couplers   —   —   10   15

9218 MONON 1981-82, operating box, plunger opens door, worker moves towards door, die-cast trucks, disc-operating couplers   —   —   10   15

183

7800 BOX CARS

9200 SERIES BOX CARS

9219 MISSOURI PACIFIC 1983, operating car with plunger mechanism, door opens, worker moves toward door, blue sides with gray stripe and gray ends and roof. Reissue of 3494-150 M.P. from 1956. Reader comments on the differences and similarities of these cars would be appreciated.
— — — 26

9220 BORDEN 1983, operating milk car — — — 8

9221 POULTRY DISPATCH, 1983, reissue of 3434 from 1959-60
— — — 30

9230 MONON Type VII body (A-C) and Type IX body (D-E), white lettering, Bettendorf trucks
(A) Tuscan painted maroon body, red oxide painted maroon doors, Type I frame, metal door guides 4 6 8 10
(B) Same as (A) but red oxide painted red oxide body 4 6 8 10
(C) Flat red oxide painted flat red oxide body, red oxide painted maroon doors, Type I frame, plastic door guides 4 6 8 10
(D) Tuscan painted tuscan body, tuscan painted tuscan doors, Type I frame
4 6 8 10
(E) Same as (D) but Type II frame 4 6 8 10

9280 A T S F 1978-80, horse transport car, white horses bob in and out, red with white lettering 4 6 8 11

9301 U.S. MAIL 1975-83, red, white and blue painted red plastic body and door, white and black lettering, 1972-Type body mold, Bettendorf trucks, Type I frame, single door guides, "LIONEL" on left, man tosses mail sack when door is opened by plunger.
(A) Dark blue paint, MPC plate 6 10 13 20
(B) Light blue paint, MPC plate 6 10 13 20
(C) Medium blue paint, no MPC plate 6 10 13 20
(D) Light blue paint, no MPC plate 6 10 13 20

9305 SANTA FE 1980, 82, stock car with bobbing figures, from James Gang set — — 10 14

9308 AQUARIUM CAR 1981-83, reissue of 3435 from 1959-62
— — 50 60

9319 TCA SILVER JUBILEE 1979, gloss dark blue body, silver bullion car for TCA's 25th anniversary, silver bullion, white lettering on clear sides, special coin available only at TCA's National Convention, coin sits in car slot but does not fall into car, coin lettered "TCA 25 Years," coin about size of half dollar, 6,000 made
(A) Car only — — 60 85
(B) Car with coin — — 70 90

9320 FORT KNOX GOLD RESERVE 1979, clear plastic body, painted silver, coin slot, circular grates at each end, "gold reserve" inside, sprung die-cast trucks, disc couplers, from Southern Pacific Limited set
— — 65 75

9339 GREAT NORTHERN 1979-81, 83, green plastic plug door box car, white lettering, part of 1980-81 No. 1960 Midnight Flyer set (1980-81) and part of No. 1252 Heavy Iron set (1983), operating couplers (1983)
— — 2 4

9349 SAN FRANCISCO MINT 1980, dark maroon body, gold letering, gold ingots stacked inside car, Standard "O" trucks — — 40 50

9359 NATIONAL BASKETBALL ASSN 1980, plug door box car, came in year-end special only, many labels provided with car so that the purchaser could decide which to place on car — — 12 18

9360 NATIONAL HOCKEY LEAGUE 1980, plug door box car, Stanley Cup, came in year-end special, many labels provided so that car purchaser could decide which to place on car — — — 18

9361 Not Used 1980, this number was for the National Football League Car. At the last minute the League withdrew permission (perhaps they wanted a fee, which Lionel did not want to pay) and production was cancelled
Not Manufactured

9362 MAJOR LEAGUE BASEBALL 1980, came in year-end special, many labels provided with car, each for a different team, purchaser to decide which to place on car — — 12 18

9365 TOYS "R" US 1979, part of No. 1993 TOYS "R" US Midnight Flyer set
— — 10 15

9376 SOO 1981, part of uncatalogued No. 1157 Wabash Cannonball set
— — 10 15

9388 TOYS "R" US 1981, part of No. 1159 TOYS "R" US Midnight Flyer set
— — 10 15

9400 CONRAIL 1978
(A) Tuscan painted tuscan plastic body and door, white lettering, 1972-Type body mold, single door guides, Bettendorf trucks, Type III frame, "LIONEL" on left 3 5 7 9
(B) Same as (A) but brown painted brown body and door
3 5 7 9

9401 GREAT NORTHERN 1978, pale green painted pale green plastic body and door, white lettering, Bettendorf trucks, 1972-Type body mold, single door guides, Bettendorf trucks, Type III frame, "LIONEL" on left
3 5 7 9

9402 SUSQUEHANNA 1978, green painted green plastic body and door, gold lettering, 1972-Type body mold, single door guides, Bettendorf trucks, Type III frame, "LIONEL" on left 7 9 12 15

9403 S C L 1978, (Seaboard Coast Line); black painted black plastic body and door, yellow lettering, 1972-Type body mold, single door guides, Bettendorf trucks, Type III frame, "LIONEL" on right 3 5 7 9
(A) Yellow lettering 4 6 8 10
(B) Extremely bold yellow lettering 4 7 9 15
(C) Shiny white lettering — — — 145

9404 NICKEL PLATE 1978, wine and silver painted wine body and door, black and white lettering, 1972-Type body mold, single door guides, Bettendorf trucks, Type III frame, "LIONEL" on left 3 5 7 9

9405 CIRR 1978, (Chattahoochie Industrial Railroad), silver painted gray plastic body and door, orange and black lettering, 1972-Type body mold, single door guides, Bettendorf trucks, Type III frame, "LIONEL" on left
3 5 7 9

9406 D & R G W 1978, "Rio Grande," white and brown painted white plastic body, brown painted brown plastic door, black and red lettering, 1972-Type body mold, single door guides, Bettendorf trucks, Type III frame, "LIONEL" on right, "Cookie Box" 3 5 7 9

9407 UNION PACIFIC 1978, "LIVESTOCK DISPATCH," gray and yellow painted yellow plastic body, black painted black doors, red lettering, Type I mold, three metal door guides, Bettendorf trucks, Type I frame, "LIONEL" on right 7 9 12 15

9408 LIONEL LINES 1978, "CIRCUS CAR," white and red painted white plastic body, white painted white plastic door, red lettering, Type I mold, three metal door guides, sprung die-cast trucks Type I, frame, "LIONEL" on left, red painted catwalk, part of Minneapolis & St. Louis Service Station Set
7 9 12 15

9411 LACKAWANNA 1978, tuscan painted tuscan plastic body and door, white lettering, 1972-Type body mold, single door guides, standard 0 trucks, Type III frame, "LIONEL" on right, part of Milwaukee Special Set
7 9 12 17

9412 R F & P 1979, "RICHMOND FREDERICKSBURG POTOMAC," blue painted body, white lettering 7 9 12 15

9413 NAPIERVILLE JUNCTION 1979, yellow painted sides, red painted roof and ends, black lettering 4 6 8 10

9414 COTTON BELT 1980, tuscan body, white lettering, blue lightning streak, disc-operating couplers 4 6 8 10

9415 PW 1979, "PROVIDENCE & WORCESTER RAILROAD," red painted body, white and black lettering 4 6 8 10

9416 M D & W 1979 (Minnesota, Dakota & Western), white and green painted body, green door 4 6 8 11

9417 C P RAIL 1979, black, white and red sides, gold letters, from Great Plains Express set. Some sets included this car, others a 9729 car identical except for number — — 25 35

9418 FARR 1979, Famous American Railroad Series railroad emblem car with markings of Southern, Santa Fe, Great Northern, Union Pacific and Pennsylvania Railroads, emblem of FARR series reads #1 — — 40 58

9419 UNION PACIFIC 1980, tuscan sides, black roof, FARR Series 2 (Famous American Railroads), sold separately — — 14 16

9420 B.& O. 1980, Sentinel, dark blue and silver, same color scheme as 9801 Standard O series car — — 12 15

9421 MEC 1980, yellow sides, "MAINE CENTRAL" logo — — 7 9

9422 E J & E 1980, turquoise and orange (Elgin, Joliet & Eastern)
— — 7 9

9319 TCA SILVER JUBILEE

9320 Fort Knox

9423 NEW YORK, NEW HAVEN & HARTFORD 1980, tuscan with white script — — 7 9

9424 T P W 1980, red sides, silver roof and ends, white lettering "TOLEDO PEORIA & WESTERN," disc-operating couplers — — 7 9

9425 BRITISH COLUMBIA 1980, dark green sides and roof, lighter green door, white lettering, yellow and white logo, disc-operating couplers, automobile car with two dark green doors and two light green doors, one of each per side — — 12 15

9426 CHESAPEAKE & OHIO 1980, blue and yellow sides, silver roof and ends, yellow and blue lettering, disc-operating couplers — — 7 9

9427 BAY LINE 1980
(A) Green body with yellow logo, green lettering, "THE BAY LINE" inside of broad yellow stripe; white number and technical data — — 7 10
(B) Similar to (A) but logo and stripe are white — — — 135

9428 T P & W 1980, distinctive green and yellow livery, very different from 9424, disc-operating couplers, available only with No. 1072 CROSS COUNTRY EXPRESS set — — 22 30

9429 THE EARLY YEARS 1980, "COMMEMORATING THE 100th BIRTHDAY OF JOSHUA LIONEL COWEN" (car came in a special limited edition box as did the 9429, 9430, 9431, 9432 and 9433) — — — 30

9430 THE STANDARD GAUGE YEARS 1980 "....100th BIRTHDAY....," matches 9429 — — 20 25

9431 THE PREWAR YEARS 1980, matches 9429 — — 20 25

9432 THE POSTWAR YEARS 1980, matches 9429, available only with No. 1070 Royal Limited set — — 55 62

9433 THE GOLDEN YEARS 1980, matches 9429, available only with No. 1071 Mid-Atlantic set — — 45 60

9434 JOSHUA LIONEL COWEN-THE MAN 1980, the last car in the series; series began with 9429 — — 80 110

9436 BURLINGTON 1981, red with white lettering, disc-operating couplers, die-cast sprung trucks, came with No. 1160 Great Lakes Limited set — — 30 40

9437 NORTHERN PACIFIC 1981, stock car, white lettering, die-cast sprung trucks, disc-operating couplers, from No. 1160 Great Lakes Limited set — — 30 40

9438 ONTARIO NORTHLAND 1981, tuscan with yellow ends, three tilted Zs in yellow on side, disc-operating couplers — — 12 15

9439 ASHLEY, DREW & NORTHERN 1981, green with white door and lettering, yellow, green and white logo, disc-operating couplers — — 7 9

9440 READING 1981, yellow with green lettering, die-cast sprung trucks, disc-operating couplers, from No. 1158 Maple Leaf Limited set — — 27 35

9441 PENNSYLVANIA 1981, tuscan with white stripe, white and red lettering; "MERCHANDISE SERVICE," die-cast sprung trucks, disc-operating couplers, from No. 1158 Maple Leaf Limited set — — 27 35

9442 CANADIAN PACIFIC 1981, white sides, maroon lettering, disc-operating couplers — — 9 12

9443 F E C 1981, tuscan sides, white lettering, "FLORIDA EAST COAST RAILWAY" — — 7 9

9444 LOUISIANA MIDLAND 1981, white sides, tuscan ends, red and blue lettering, disc-operating couplers — — 7 9

9445 VERMONT NORTHERN 1981, yellow sides and end, disc-operating couplers — — 7 9

9447 PULLMAN STANDARD 1981, "This is the 1,000,000th," disc-operating couplers, silver with black lettering — — 14 17

9448 A T S F 1981, double-door cattle car, brown with white lettering, black doors, from No. 1154 READING YARD KING set — — 12 15

9449 GREAT NORTHERN 1981, dark green and red; disc-operating couplers; GREAT NORTHERN goat logo, FARR Series 3 logo, Famous American Railroads, Series 3, car sold separately — — 10 13

9450 GREAT NORTHERN 1981, cattle car, FARR Series 3, car sold separately — — 12 15

9451 SOUTHERN 1983, tuscan box car, yellow lettering, FARR Series 4, die-cast Standard O sprung trucks, car sold separately — — — 18

9452 WESTERN PACIFIC 1982-83, tuscan painted body, white lettering, disc-operating couplers — — 9 12

9453 M P A 1982-83, blue painted body, white lettering, disc-operating couplers — — 9 12

9454 NEW HOPE & IVYLAND 1982-83, green painted body, white lettering, disc-operating couplers — — 9 12

9455 MILWAUKEE ROAD 1982-83, yellow painted body, black lettering, disc-operating couplers — — 9 12

9461 NORFOLK SOUTHERN 1982, tuscan body, yellow doors, standard 0 trucks, disc-operating couplers, from Continental Limited set — — 28 38

9462 SOUTHERN PACIFIC 1983, white sides, blue roof and ends, sliding doors, disc-operating couplers — — — 13

9463 TEXAS & PACIFIC 1983, yellow sides and roof, sliding doors, disc-operating couplers — — — 13

9464 N C & St L 1983, red car with orange stripe on side, white lettering, sliding doors, disc-operating couplers — — — 13

9465 A T S F 1983, blue with yellow lettering and logo, sliding doors, disc-operating couplers — — — 13

9466 WANAMAKER RAILWAY LINES 1983, tuscan-painted plastic body with gold-painted door and gold lettering. This car commemorated the Ives special Wanamaker cars of the early 1920's. At that time, Ives produced specially lettered cars for John Wanamaker, then and now the pre-eminent department store of Philadelphia. The moving force behind this new commemorative car was Nicholas Ladd, a long-time train enthusiast and senior Wanamaker store manager. The Eagle logo is original Wanamaker art adapted by Arthur Bink. The Wanamaker Railway Lines logo was copied from the original lettering on an authentic Ives Wanamaker car. Note that the Lionel artist intentionally made the "M" look like an "N" in the script. It is not a factory error. Lionel produced 2,500 of these cars. Interested Wanamaker employees bought 1,400 of them and another 1,000 were sold over the counter at a special train fair held at Wanamaker's Philadelphia store in conjunction with the car's release. The remaining 100 cars were retained by the store. — — — 70

9468 UNION PACIFIC 1983, double door box car, red body, white lettering, die-cast trucks, disc-operating couplers, available only in No. 1361 Gold Coast Limited set — — — 40

9600 CHESSIE 1976, hi cube, dark blue body, yellow lettering and door
(A) Thin door stop 7 9 12 15

187

9700 BOX CARS

9700 BOX CARS

(B) Thick door stop 7 9 12 15

9601 I C 1976-77, hi cube, orange body, black lettering and door
5 7 10 12

9602 A T S F 1977, hi cube, red body, white lettering, 2 inch high emblem, silver door
(A) Complete markings 5 7 10 12
(B) All markings to right of door on both sides are missing — — — 350

9603 PENN CENTRAL 1976-77, hi cube, green body, white lettering, silver door
5 7 10 12

9604 NW 1976-77, hi cube, black body, white lettering, silver door
5 7 10 12

9605 NH 1976-77, hi cube, orange body, white lettering, black door
5 7 10 12

9606 UNION PACIFIC 1976-77, hi cube, yellow body, blue lettering, yellow door
(A) Lighter yellow 5 7 10 12
(B) Darker yellow 5 7 10 12

9607 SP 1976-77, hi cube, red body, gray stripe arrow, gray roof, white letters
5 8 11 13

9608 BURLINGTON NORTHERN 1977, hi cube, green body, white lettering
5 7 10 12

9610 FRISCO 1977, hi cube, yellow body, black lettering, available only in Rocky Mountain set
7 10 15 20

9611 TCA 1978, "TWENTY FOURTH NATIONAL CONVENTION BOSTON MA," "Home of the Flying Yankee," light blue sides, black roof and ends, one brakewheel, white doors, white clearance boards on car ends, Bettendorf trucks, disc couplers with tabs. Some of these cars were repainted into the 1018-1979 Mortgage Burning Ceremony Car. See entry 1018-1979 for details of this interesting story.
— — 25 30

9620 NHL WALES CONFERENCE 1980, white car with different team symbols on each side, disc-operating couplers, opening doors
— — 9 12

9621 NHL CAMPBELL CONFERENCE 1980, white car with different team symbols on each side, disc-operating couplers, opening doors
— — 9 12

9622 NBA WESTERN CONFERENCE 1980, white car with different team symbols on each side, disc-operating couplers, opening doors
— — 9 12

9623 NBA EASTERN CONFERENCE 1980, white car with different team symbols on each side, disc-operating couplers, opening doors
— — 9 12

9624 NATIONAL LEAGUE 1980, white car with different baseball team symbols on each side, disc-operating couplers, opening doors
— — 9 12

9625 AMERICAN LEAGUE 1980, white car with different baseball team symbols on each side, disc-operating couplers, opening doors
— — 9 12

9626 A T S F 1982-83, hi cube, red with white lettering and door, disc-operating couplers
— — 8 9

9627 UNION PACIFIC 1982-83, hi cube, yellow with red letering, white door, disc-operating couplers
— — 8 9

9628 BURLINGTON NORTHERN 1982-83, hi cube, green with white lettering and door, disc-operating couplers
— — 8 9

9629 C & O 1983, hi cube, blue with yellow lettering and logo, disc-operating couplers, metal wheels
— — — 10

MICKEY MOUSE SET

NOTE: The Mickey Mouse set consists of cars 9660-9672 plus an 8773 U36B engine, 9183 caboose and the limited edition 9672, 50th Anniversary car. Set price
— — — 675

9660 MICKEY MOUSE 1977-78, hi cube, white body, yellow roof and ends
5 7 10 13

9661 GOOFY 1977-78, hi cube, white body, red roof and ends
5 7 10 13

9662 DONALD DUCK 1977-78, hi cube, white body, green roof and ends
5 7 10 13

9663 DUMBO 1978, hi cube, white body, red roof and ends 5 7 11 13

9664 CINDERELLA 1978, hi cube, white body, pink roof and ends
5 7 11 13

9665 PETER PAN 1978, hi cube, white body, orange roof and ends
5 7 11 13

9666 PINOCCHIO 1978, hi cube, white body, blue roof and ends
20 25 30 37

9667 SNOW WHITE 1978, hi cube, white body, green roof and ends
40 45 50 65

9668 PLUTO 1978, hi cube, white body, brown roof and ends
20 30 40 50

9669 BAMBI 1978, hi cube 5 8 11 13

9670 ALICE IN WONDERLAND 1978, hi cube 5 7 11 13

9671 FANTASIA 1978, hi cube 5 8 11 13

9672 MICKEY MOUSE 50th ANNIVERSARY 1978, hi cube, limited edition
— — 105 125

9678 T T O S 1978, hi cube, convention car, white plastic body painted white, red ends and roofs, red doors, lettered "Hurrah for Hollywood," Bettendorf trucks, two disc couplers with tabs, cars come with TTOS decal; convention attendees received a special decal showing Chaplin with "78" on his derby
(A) Regular car — — 20 30
(B) With Chaplin decal — — 30 40

9700 SERIES BOX CARS

9700 SOUTHERN Type IX body except for (A), red painted red door, white lettering, Bettendorf trucks, Type I frame
(A) SOO red painted Type VI SOO red plastic body, metal door guides
— — 60 75
(B) Shiny red painted shiny red body 4 6 8 10
(C) Dark red painted dark red body, green dot added by dealer
4 6 8 10
(D) Same as (C) but no green dot 4 6 8 10

9700-1976 TCA Bicentennial Convention Car, 1976, unpainted white body, unpainted blue doors, red painted roof and ends, Bettendorf trucks. Brown, black, white and gold eagle electrocal and TCA logo to left of door, TCA Philadelphia convention data to right of door
— — — 45

9701 BALTIMORE & OHIO Double-door auto car with metal door guides, Bettendorf trucks
(A) Shiny black painted black body, flat black painted black doors, white lettering, Type I frame, 900 made 30 40 60 70
(B) Same as (A) but white rubber stamped LCCA CONVENTION CAR
— — 75 85
(C) Same as (A) but only one built date — — 65 75
(D) Black sides, silver roof painted on blue plastic, yellow painted yellow doors, yellow lettering, Type II frame, 12 made — — 400
(E) Black sides and silver roof painted on gray plastic body, light blue painted light blue doors, light blue lettering, Type II frame, preproduction sample NRS
(F) Silver painted gray plastic body, black painted black doors, black lettering, Type II frame 6 8 11 15
(G) Same as (F) but dark blue painted dark blue doors 6 8 11 15
(H) Same as (F) but Type I frame 6 8 11 15
(I) Same as (F) but medium blue painted medium blue doors
6 8 11 15
(J) Same as (F) but light blue painted light blue doors, Type I frame
6 8 11 15
(K-0) have contrasting color Lionel doors added outside of the factory
(K) Same as (F) but green painted green doors, Type I frame
6 8 11 15
(L) Same as (F) but orange painted orange doors 6 8 11 15
(M) Same as (F) but burnt-orange painted burnt-orange doors
6 8 11 15
(N) Same as (F) but silver painted gray doors, Type I frame
6 8 11 15
(O) Same as (F) but silver painted gray doors 6 8 11 15
(P) Deep blue painted deep blue plastic body, black painted black doors, yellow lettering, printed on only one side, Type II frame, Fuhrmann Collection NRS

9702 SOO White sides, black roof painted on white body, red painted red door, black lettering, Bettendorf trucks
(A) Type VIII body, Type I frame 3 5 7 10
(B) Type IX body, Type II frame 5 7 10 12

9703 C P RAIL Type IX body, black lettering, Bettendorf trucks
(A) Burnt-orange painted burnt-orange body, burnt-orange painted red doors, Type II frame 15 20 30 47
(B) Light burnt-orange painted medium red body, medium red doors painted red doors, Type I frame 15 20 30 47
(C) Dark green painted light green body, dark green painted light green doors, Type II frame, one of five preproduction samples, one side blank
— — 600 —

9704 NORFOLK & WESTERN Type IX body except (A), white lettering except (C), Bettendorf trucks
(A) Tuscan painted Type VII maroon body, tuscan painted maroon doors, Type I frame — — 95 120
(B) Tuscan painted tuscan body, tuscan painted tuscan doors, Type II frame
— 6 9 11
(C) Same as (B) but gray lettering — 6 9 11
(D) Same as (B) but Type I frame — 6 9 11
(E) Tuscan painted gray body, tuscan painted tuscan doors, Type I frame
— 6 8 10

9705 DENVER & RIO GRANDE Silver painted gray plastic doors except (A) and (B), black lettering except (A), (B) and (C), Bettendorf trucks
(A) Silver painted gray Type IX plastic body, red painted red doors, Type I frame, red lettering, 16 made — — 400 —
(B) Same as (A) but Type II frame — — 400 —
(C) Silver painted Type IX gray plastic body, orange lettering, Type II frame, ten made — — 500 —
(D) Dark orange painted Type VIII orange plastic body, Type I frame, deep stamped lettering — 35 50 66
(E) Light orange painted Type VIII orange plastic body, Type I frame
— 6 8 11
(F) Dark orange painted orange plastic body, Type I frame
— 6 8 11
(G) Dark orange unpainted orange body, silver painted gray doors, very deep stamped gloss black lettering, MPC logo, Bettendorf trucks, Type IX body, Type II frame, probably late production, La Voie Collection
— 6 8 11

9706 C & O Type VIII body (A), Type IX body (B-D), yellow lettering, Bettendorf trucks
(A) Black painted gray plastic, black painted black door, Type II frame, four preproduction samples known — — 700 —
(B) Blue painted blue plastic body, yellow painted yellow door, Type II frame
— — 400 —
(C) Same as (B) but Type I frame 5 7 8 10
(D) Same as (B) but blue painted gray plastic body 5 7 8 10

9707 MKT Stock car, metal door guides, red painted translucent plastic except (D), white lettering, Bettendorf trucks, 6356-19 frame
(A) Light yellow painted light yellow door, electrocal decoration
5 7 8 10
(B) Medium yellow painted medium yellow door, rubber stamped lettering
5 7 8 10
(C) Same as (B) but hot stamped lettering 5 7 8 10
(D) Dark red painted red plastic, medium yellow painted medium yellow doors NRS
(E) Flat red painted red body, unpainted yellow doors, dull white rubber stamped lettering, LaVoie Collection NRS

9708 US MAIL Type IX body, painted red plastic body except (J), white and black lettering, Bettendorf trucks, Type II frame, MPC logo on (A-E), no MPC logo on (F-J), painted red plastic door
(A) Dark red and light blue painted body, red painted door
5 7 8 10
(B) Same as (A) but red and light blue painted door 5 7 8 10
(C) Dark red and medium blue painted body, red and medium blue painted door 5 7 8 10
(D) Same as (C) but red and dark blue painted door 5 7 8 10
(E) Light red and dark blue painted body, red and dark blue painted doors, no MPC logo 5 7 8 10
(F) Dark red and light blue painted body, red and medium blue painted door
5 7 8 10
(G) Dark red and medium blue painted body, red and medium blue painted door 5 7 8 10
(H) Dark red and medium blue painted body, red and dark blue painted door
5 7 8 10
(I) Medium blue and dark red painted gray body, red painted door
— — — 400
(J) Gold overstamped Toy Fair '73 — — 115 135

9709 BAR 1973-74, Type VIII bodies: A-C; Type IX bodies: D-I; Bettendorf trucks, Type II frame
(A) Blue and dark red painted gray body, blue and red painted gray door, white lettering, printed one side only in white areas 35 45 50 60
(B) Same as (A) but white and black lettering, printed white and black on both sides 15 20 30 40
(C) Blue and dark red painted gray body, red painted red door, white and black lettering 30 45 60 70
(D) Blue and dark red painted gray body, blue and red painted gray doors, printing on one side only in white area 20 30 40 60
(E) Same as (D) but no printing on the white areas of either side
— — — 125
(F) Dark blue and medium red painted blue body, blue and red painted blue doors, white and black lettering 15 20 30 40
(G) Medium blue and light red painted medium blue body, dark blue and red painted red doors, white and black lettering 15 20 30 40
(H) Blue and light red painted blue body, blue and red painted gray doors, white and black painted lettering 20 35 40 50
(I) Same as (H) but number stamped on angle 30 45 60 70

9710 RUTLAND 1973-74, Type VIII bodies: A,B and C; Type IX bodies: D and G; yellow painted yellow doors, green and yellow lettering, Type II frame
(A) Medium yellow and green painted gray body, shifted shield
10 11 15 17
(B) Light yellow and green painted gray body, shifted shield
10 11 15 17
(C) Same as (B) but shield centered, "9710" not underscored
15 20 25 30
(D) Dark yellow and green painted gray body, shifted shield
10 15 17 20
(E) Medium yellow and light green painted green body, shifted shield, no "CAPY 100000" 15 18 25 28
(F) Light yellow and light green painted green body, shifted shield, "9200" on car end 10 18 25 28
(G) Dark yellow and green painted gray body, shifted shield
10 14 16 20

9711 SOUTHERN 1974, Type IX body, white lettering, Bettendorf trucks, Type II frame, "LIONEL" to the right of door, except (C)
(A) Tuscan painted tuscan body, tuscan painted white doors
6 8 10 14
(B) Same as (A) but tuscan painted tuscan doors 6 8 10 14
(C) Same as (A) but tuscan painted tuscan doors, "LIONEL" to the left of door 6 8 10 14
(D) Tuscan painted translucent body, reported but not verified NRS

9712 BALTIMORE & OHIO 1973-74, double door automobile car, metal door guides, blue painted blue body, yellow painted yellow door, yellow lettering, Bettendorf trucks, Type II frame 9 12 15 20

9713 C P RAIL 1973-74, Type IX body, green painted green doors, black lettering, Bettendorf trucks, Type II frame
(A) Green painted green body 5 7 9 11
(B) Light green painted green body 5 7 9 11
(C) Same as (A) but metallic gold overprinted, "SEASONS GREETINGS '74" — — 80 125
(D) Green painted clear body, reported but not verified NRS

9714 RIO GRANDE 1973-74, Type IX body, silver painted, Bettendorf trucks, Type II frame
(A) Silver painted gray body, red painted red doors, red lettering
3 5 9 11
(B) Same as (A) but silver painted opaque body 3 5 9 11
(C) Same as (A) but orange painted orange doors, orange lettering
— — — 295

9700 BOX CARS

GT (Grand Trunk Western)	9735	Chessie System C&O	9740	TaB	9744	CP Rail	9748	Frisco SL-SF Ship it on the Frisco!	9751
Milwaukee Road	9731	Rio Grande D&RGW	9737	Sprite	9742	Chessie C&O	9747	DT&I	9750
	9731	Central Vermont CV	9737	Minneapolis & St Louis M&STL	9742	Fanta	9745	Penn Central PC	9749

192

(D) Same as (A) but silver painted translucent doors, dark orange lettering
— — — 280

9715 CHESAPEAKE & OHIO 1973-74, Type IX body, Bettendorf trucks, Type II frame
(A) Black painted black body, yellow painted yellow door
5 7 9 11
(B) Same as (A) but yellow painted white door 5 7 9 11
(C) Black painted white body, light yellow painted white door
5 7 9 11
(D) Same as (C) but dark yellow painted white door 5 7 9 11

9716 PENN CENTRAL 1973-74, Type IX body, green painted green body and green door, Bettendorf trucks, Type II frame 5 7 9 11

9717 UNION PACIFIC 1973-74, Type IX body, black roof, yellow painted yellow door, black lettering, Bettendorf trucks, Type II frame
(A) Light yellow painted yellow body 5 7 9 11
(B) Medium yellow painted yellow body 5 7 9 11

9717 SOO 1983, operating car with plunger mechanism, door opens, worker moves toward door, tuscan car. Reissue of 3494-625 SOO from 1957. Reader comments on the differences and similarities of these cars would be appreciated. — — — 26

9718 CANADIAN NATIONAL 1973-74, Type IX body, white lettering, Bettendorf trucks, Type II frame
(A) Tuscan painted tuscan body, yellow painted yellow door
5 7 9 11
(B) Tuscan painted orange body, yellow painted translucent door
5 7 9 11
(C) Same as (B) but yellow painted yellow door 5 7 9 11
(D) Tuscan red painted tuscan red body, yellow painted yellow door NRS
(E) Gray painted tuscan body, yellow painted yellow door
— — — 100

9719 NEW HAVEN Double-door box car, orange painted orange body, black painted black door, Bettendorf trucks, Type II frame, coupon car
(A) Black and white lettering 10 12 17 25
(B) Black overprinted on white lettering NRS
(C) White overprinted on black lettering NRS

9720 ASSORTED CASE OF CARS NRS
9721 ASSORTED CASE OF CARS NRS
9722 Not used

9723 WESTERN PACIFIC 1974, Type IX plastic body, black lettering, Bettendorf trucks, Type II frame
(A) Unpainted orange plastic body and doors 10 14 20 25
(B) Same as (A) but gold overstamped "Toy Fair '74" 50 70 80 100
(C) Fanta orange painted orange body and orange doors
20 25 30 35
(D) Fanta orange painted orange body and white doors
20 25 30 35

9724 MISSOURI PACIFIC 1974, Type IX plastic body, black and white lettering, Bettendorf trucks, Type II frame, silver painted roof and side band
(A) Medium blue painted opaque-white body, yellow and silver painted yellow doors 18 25 30 35
(B) Same as (A) but medium blue painted gray body 18 25 30 35
(C) Dark blue painted gray body, yellow and silver painted yellow doors
15 20 25 30
(D) Dark blue painted navy body, yellow painted yellow doors
15 20 25 30

9725 M K T 1974-75, double-door cattle car, "The Katy SERVES THE SOUTHWEST," black painted black door, Bettendorf trucks, Type I frame
(A) Light yellow painted yellow body 4 5 6 8
(B) Medium yellow painted yellow body 4 5 6 8
(C) Medium-dark yellow painted yellow body 4 5 6 8
(D) Dark yellow painted yellow body 4 5 6 8

9726 ERIE LACKAWANNA 1978, Type IX body, blue painted blue doors, white lettering, Type III frame, Scale 0 die-cast sprung trucks, part of Service Station set
(A) Shiny blue painted blue body 7 9 12 15
(B) Lighter shiny blue painted blue body 7 9 12 15

9727 T.A.G. Uncatalogued, Type IX body, white lettered "TENNESSEE ALABAMA & GEORGIA" and "1973 LCC of A." Convention car, maroon painted body, Bettendorf trucks, Type II frame — — 140 170

9728 UNION PACIFIC Uncatalogued, stock car, yellow painted yellow body, silver painted roof and ends, unpainted yellow doors, red lettering, LCC of A 1978 Convention car, 6,000 made — — 28 35

9729 CP RAIL Type IX body, Bettendorf trucks, black, white and red painted black body, black painted black door, white lettering, Type III frame, from Great Plains set, some sets came with 9417 car identical except for number 10 20 25 29

9730 CP RAIL 1974-75, Type IX body, Bettendorf trucks, Type II frame, white lettered A-B, black lettered C - F

White Lettering
(A) Silver painted gray body, silver painted gray door 9 11 14 17
(B) Same as (A) except silver painted white body 9 11 14 17

Black Lettering
(C) Same as (A) except flat silver painted white body 11 14 20 25
(D) Same as (A) except silver painted opaque door 11 14 20 25
(E) Same as (A) 11 14 20 25
(F) Same as (A) except silver painted yellow door 11 14 20 25

9731 MILWAUKEE ROAD 1974-75, Type IX body, white lettering, red door, Bettendorf trucks, Type II frame
(A) Light red painted red body 4 5 7 9
(B) Medium red painted red body 4 5 7 9
(C) Silver painted red body NRS

9732 SOUTHERN PACIFIC 1979, black roof and silver sides on gray plastic Type IX body, black painted black door, black and orange lettering, Scale 0 sprung die-cast trucks, Type III frame, from Southern Pacific Limited set
— — 30 37

9733 AIRCO 1979, LCC of A National Convention car, a unique Lionel car in that inside there is a full sized white molded unpainted tank with an orange painted base. Blue tank lettering cannot be seen unless box car shell is removed from frame leaving only the tank. This is essentially two cars in one. The box car comes with solid dish wheels, 6,000 made NRS

9734 BAR Type IX body, red body, red doors, white lettering, Standard O trucks, from Quaker City Limited set of 1978 8 15 23 30

9735 GRAND TRUNK WESTERN 1974-75, Type IM body, white lettering, Bettendorf trucks, Type II frame
(A) Blue painted blue body, blue painted dark blue doors
4 5 6 8
(B) Same as (A) but blue painted opaque body 4 5 6 8
(C) Blue painted opaque body, blue painted white doors
4 5 6 8

9736 Not used

9737 CENTRAL VERMONT 1974-75, Type IX body, white lettering, Bettendorf trucks, Type II frame
(A) Tuscan painted tuscan body and tuscan doors 4 5 6 8
(B) Tuscan painted orange body and tuscan painted white doors
20 25 35 40
(C) Same as (B) but tuscan painted tuscan body 4 5 6 8
(D) Tuscan painted tuscan body, tuscan painted translucent doors, LaVoie Collection 4 5 6 8

9738 ILLINOIS TERMINAL 1982, Type IX body, yellow painted sides and blue painted roof, die-cast sprung trucks, disc-operating couplers, part of No. 1260 The Continental Limited set — — 30 40

9739 RIO GRANDE 1975, Type IX body, black lettering, Bettendorf trucks, Type II frame
(A) Dark yellow and silver painted yellow body, silver painted yellow doors, no stripe 60 100 140 160
(B) Light yellow and silver painted transparent white body, silver painted gray doors, no stripe 60 100 140 160
(C) Medium dark yellow and silver painted yellow body, same doors as (B), long stripe 4 5 6 8
(D) Dark yellow and silver painted yellow body, same doors as (B), long stripe 4 5 6 8
(E) Medium yellow and silver painted yellow body, same doors as (B), long stripe 4 5 6 8

9700 BOX CARS

9700 BOX CARS

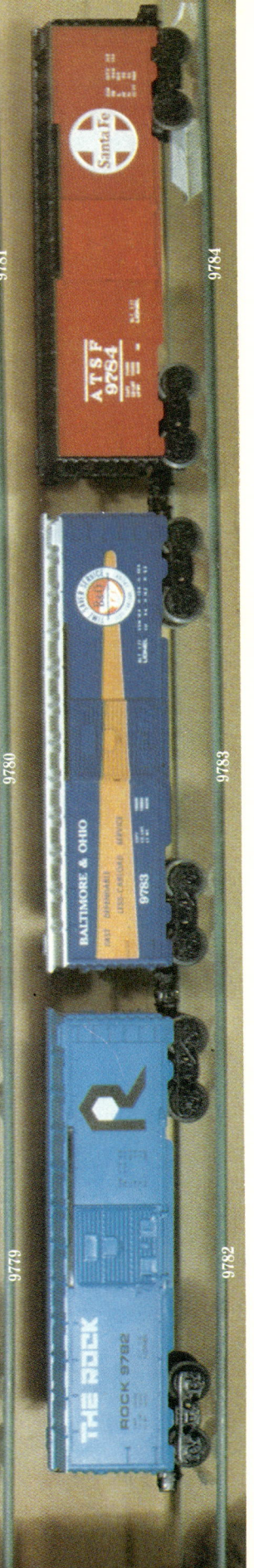

9770 NP
9771 NW
9772 Great Northern G N
9773
9774 The Southern Belle
9775 M&StL
9776 S.P.
9777 Virginian
9778 Seasons Greetings 1975
9779
9780 Johnny Cash
9781 Delaware & Hudson D&H 9781
9782 The Rock ROCK 9782
9783 Baltimore & Ohio 9783
9784 ATSF 9784 Santa Fe

(F) Light yellow and light silver painted yellow body, same doors as (B), long stripe **4 5 6 8**
(G) Same as (F) but silver painted yellow doors **4 5 6 8**
(H) Dark yellow and silver painted yellow body, same doors as (B), short stripe **4 5 6 8**
(I) Light yellow and silver painted opaque body, silver painted opaque doors, short stripe **4 5 6 8**
(J) Medium yellow and silver painted opaque body, silver painted opaque doors, long stripe **4 5 6 8**
(K) Same as (J) but silver painted gray doors **4 5 6 8**
(L) Light yellow and light silver painted opaque body, silver painted opaque doors, long stripe **4 5 6 8**
(M) Medium yellow and silver painted yellow body, silver painted translucent doors, long stripe, LaVoie Collection **4 5 6 8**
(N) Similar to (H), but special edition made for 1978 L.C.C.A. Convention, long stripe, "L.C.C.A./THE LION ROARS" and heat-stamped lion logo in black to right of door, Breslin Collection. Reports conflict concerning number of cars produced. One report indicates that Fundimensions made fewer than 100 of these cars and donated them to the L.C.C.A., Breslin comment. However, another report states that many more were eventually produced, Bohn comment. Readers are asked to help resolve this conflict. **NRS**

9740 CHESSIE 1974-75, Type IX body, yellow painted yellow doors, except D and E, blue lettering, Bettendorf trucks, Type II frame
(A) Dark yellow painted yellow body **4 5 6 8**
(B) Medium yellow painted yellow body **4 5 6 8**
(C) Light yellow painted yellow body **4 5 6 8**
(D) Light yellow painted yellow body, yellow painted white doors **4 5 6 8**
(E) Light yellow painted opaque body, same doors as (D) **4 5 6 8**

9741 Not used

9742 MINNEAPOLIS & ST LOUIS Type IX body, metallic gold lettering, Bettendorf trucks, Type II frame, coupon car
(A) Green painted green body and doors **9 11 14 20**
(B) Light green painted green body, green painted gray doors, metallic red overstamped "Seasons Greetings 1973" **40 60 80 95**
(C) Same as (B) but dark green painted green body **40 60 80 95**
(D) Green painted white body, green painted gray doors **9 11 14 20**
(E) Same as (D) but green painted white doors **9 11 14 20**

9743 SPRITE Type IX body, Bettendorf trucks, Type II frame, dark green lettering
(A) Light green painted light green body, green painted green door **7 9 12 15**
(B) Medium green painted dark green body, doors same as (A) **7 9 12 15**
(C) Light green painted white body, green painted white doors **7 9 12 15**
(D) Same as (C) but green painted green doors **7 9 12 15**
(E) Medium green painted white body, green painted white doors, KMT overstamping "75th Anniversary" **7 9 12 15**
(F) Medium green painted medium green body, medium green painted dark green doors **7 9 12 15**

9744 TAB Type IX body, white lettering, Bettendorf trucks, Type II frame
(A) Medium red-pink painted light red body, pink painted red doors **7 9 11 15**
(B) Dark red-pink painted dark red body, pink painted red doors **7 9 11 15**
(C) Medium red-pink painted white body, pink painted white doors **7 9 11 15**
(D) Light pink painted white body, pink painted red doors **7 9 11 15**
(E) Same as (D) but pink painted light red doors **7 9 11 15**
(F) Dark pink painted white body, pink painted white doors, KMT overstamping "75th Anniversary" **7 9 11 15**

9745 FANTA Type IX body, black lettering, Bettendorf trucks, Type II frame
(A) Light orange painted orange body, orange painted orange doors **7 9 11 15**
(B) Flat medium orange painted orange body, same doors as (A) **7 9 11 15**
(C) Shiny medium orange painted orange body, same doors as (A) **7 9 11 15**
(D) Same body as (C), orange painted white doors **7 9 11 15**
(E) Dark orange painted orange body, same doors as (A) **7 9 11 15**
(F) Light orange painted white body, same doors as (A) **7 9 11 15**
(G) Medium orange painted white body, orange painted white doors **7 9 11 15**
(H) Medium orange painted orange body, same doors as (A), KMT overstamping "75th Anniversary" **7 9 11 15**

9746 Not used

9747 CHESSIE SYSTEM 1975-76, double door auto car, blue painted blue doors, yellow lettering, Bettendorf trucks, Type II frame
(A) Flat blue painted blue body **5 7 10 14**
(B) Slightly darker, shiny blue painted blue body **5 7 10 14**

9748 CP RAIL 1975-76, Type IX body, white lettering, Bettendorf trucks, Type II frame, medium blue painted medium blue doors: A-G, medium blue painted white doors: H-N

A-G: Medium blue painted medium blue doors
(A) Dark blue painted dark blue body **4 5 7 9**
(B) Medium blue painted dark blue body **4 5 7 9**
(C) Medium light blue painted dark blue body **4 5 7 9**
(D) Medium light blue painted medium blue body **4 5 7 9**
(E) Dark light blue painted medium blue body **4 6 7 9**
(F) Medium dark blue painted medium blue body **4 6 7 9**
(G) Medium blue painted medium blue body **4 6 7 9**

H-N: Medium blue painted white doors
(H) Flat medium dark blue painted medium blue body **4 6 7 9**
(I) Medium dark blue painted medium blue body **4 6 7 9**
(J) Medium light blue painted medium blue body **4 6 7 9**
(K) Medium light blue painted white body **4 6 7 9**
(L) Medium dark blue painted white body **4 6 7 9**
(M) Lightest blue painted white body **4 6 7 9**
(N) Royal sides but lighter royal top on royal body **4 6 7 9**
(O) Royal painted royal body, royal painted royal doors **4 6 7 9**
(P) Royal painted medium blue body, royal painted white doors **4 6 7 9**
(Q) Royal painted sides and medium blue top on medium blue body, light blue painted white doors **4 6 7 9**
(R) Purple painted medium blue body, purple painted white doors **4 6 7 9**
(S) Royal painted light blue body, royal painted royal doors **4 6 7 9**

9749 PENN CENTRAL 1975-76, Type IX body, white and red lettering, Bettendorf trucks, Type II frame
(A) Green painted green body, green painted gray doors **4 6 7 9**
(B) Same as (A) but green painted jade doors **4 6 7 9**
(C) Same as (A) but green painted lime green doors **4 6 7 9**
(D) Slightly darker green painted green body, green painted gray doors **4 6 7 9**
(E) Lightest green painted white body, green painted white doors **4 6 7 9**
(F) Same as (A) but green painted green doors **4 6 7 9**

9750 D T & I 1975-76, Type IX body, yellow lettering, Bettendorf trucks, Type II frame, glossy green body except (E)
(A) Medium green painted dark green body, medium green painted dark green doors **4 5 6 8**
(B) Same as (A) but medium green painted clear doors **4 5 6 8**
(C) Medium green painted light green body, medium green painted dark green doors **4 5 6 8**
(D) Medium green painted white body, medium green painted dark green doors **4 5 6 8**
(E) Flat green painted light green body, flat green painted light green doors **4 5 6 8**
(F) Light green painted white body, medium green painted dark green doors **4 5 6 8**

9751 FRISCO 1975-76, Type IX body, white lettering, Bettendorf trucks, Type II frame, red painted red doors
(A) Flat red painted red body   4   6   8   10
(B) Shiny red painted red body   4   6   8   10

9752 LOUISVILLE & NASHVILLE 1975-76, Type IX body, yellow lettering, Bettendorf trucks, Type II frame
(A) Light blue painted royal blue body, medium blue painted royal blue doors   4   6   8   10
(B) Medium blue painted navy blue body, same doors as (A)
                                             4   6   8   10
(C) Light blue painted royal blue body, medium blue painted white doors
                                             4   6   8   10
(D) Medium blue painted navy blue body, same doors as (C)
                                             4   6   8   10

9753 MAINE CENTRAL 1975-76, Type IX body, green lettering, Bettendorf trucks, Type II frame
(A) Medium yellow painted yellow body, dark yellow painted yellow doors
                                             3   5   7   10
(B) Light yellow painted yellow body, light yellow painted white doors
                                             3   5   7   10
(C) Medium yellow painted yellow body, same doors as (B)
                                             3   5   7   10
(D) Darker yellow painted yellow body, medium yellow painted white doors
                                             3   5   7   10
(E) Light yellow painted white body, same doors as (D)
                                             3   5   7   10
(F) With NETCA imprint   —   —   —   15

9754 NEW YORK CENTRAL 1976-77, "Pacemaker FREIGHT SERVICE," Type IX body, white lettering, Bettendorf trucks, Type II frame, red painted red doors
(A) Light flat red painted red body   3   5   7   10
(B) Medium red painted red body   3   5   7   10
(C) Dark red painted red body   3   5   7   10
(D) With METCA imprint   —   —   —   15
(E) Same as (B), but Type III frame, LaVoie Collection   3   5   7   10

9755 UNION PACIFIC 1975-76, Type IX body, white lettering, Bettendorf trucks, Type II frame
(A) Tuscan painted brown body, tuscan painted brown doors
                                             6   8   12 15
(B) Tuscan painted white body, tuscan painted white doors
                                             6   8   12 15
(C) Tuscan painted brown body, tuscan painted white doors
                                             6   8   12 15

9757 CENTRAL of GEORGIA Type IX body, red lettering, Bettendorf trucks, Type II frame, tuscan car with large silver oval on side
(A) Tuscan painted brown body, silver painted gray doors, lightly speckled oval   10 15 20 25
(B) Same as (A) but medium speckled oval   10 15 20 25
(C) Same as (A) but shiny silver oval   10 15 20 25
(D) Same as (A) but silver painted clear doors, shiny silver oval
                                             10 15 20 25
(E) Same as (A) but silver painted yellow doors, shiny silver oval
                                             10 15 20 25
(F) Tuscan painted clear body, silver painted yellow doors, shiny silver oval
                                             10 15 20 25
(G) Tuscan painted brown body, silver painted gray doors, number misprinted   NRS

9758 ALASKA 1976-77, Type IX body, lettering usually yellow, Bettendorf trucks, Type II frame, blue car with yellow stripe
(A) Blue painted dark blue body, blue painted white doors
                                             5   7   9   12
(B) Same as (A) but blue painted blue doors 5   7   9   12
(C) Blue painted medium blue body, blue painted white doors
                                             5   7   9   12
(D) Blue painted white body, blue painted white doors 5   7   9   12
(E) Same as (D) but white lettering   5   7   9   12
(F) Same as (D) but white lettering, without "at your service"
                                             —   150 225 325
(G) Blue painted blue body, blue painted blue doors, white lettering
                                             —   —   —   325

9759 PAUL REVERE Type IX body, red painted white plastic car, blue or dark blue painted white plastic door, blue lettering, Bettendorf trucks, Type II frame   5   7   10 14

9760 LIBERTY BELL Type IX body, black painted white plastic body, red painted red plastic door, blue lettering, Bettendorf trucks, Type II frame
                                             5   7   10 14

9761 GEORGE WASHINGTON Type IX body, red painted white plastic car, blue painted white plastic door, blue lettering, Bettendorf trucks, Type II frame   5   7   10 14

9762 WELCOME TOY FAIR 1975, Uncatalogued, Type IX body, red and silver painted white plastic body, red painted red plastic door, metallic silver lettering, "9762" does not appear on car   —   —   55 85

9763 RIO GRANDE Stock car, orange painted orange plastic body, black painted black plastic door, black lettering, Bettendorf trucks, Type I frame, metal door guides
(A) Bright orange paint   3   4   6   10
(B) Dull orange paint   3   4   6   10

9764 GRAND TRUNK WESTERN Double-door box car, blue painted blue plastic body, blue painted dark blue door, white lettering, Bettendorf trucks, Type II or III frame, all rivet detail missing   6   8   10 14

9765 Not used

9766 Not used

9767 RAILBOX Type IX body, yellow painted yellow plastic body, black painted black plastic door, black lettering, Bettendorf trucks
(A) Light yellow paint, Type III frame   4   6   8   10
(B) Medium yellow paint, Type II frame   4   6   8   10
(C) Dark yellow paint, Type II frame   4   6   8   10

9768 BOSTON AND MAINE 1976-77, Type IX body, black and white lettering, Bettendorf trucks, black painted black doors
(A) Glossy blue painted gray body, Type II frame 4   5   6   8
(B) Flat blue painted gray body, Type III frame   4   5   6   8
(C) Same as (B), but Type III frame, LaVoie Collection 4   5   6   8

9769 B. & L. E. 1976-77, Type IX body, black and white lettering, Bettendorf trucks
(A) Flat orange painted orange body, orange painted white doors, Type II frame   4   5   6   8
(B) Shiny orange painted orange body, orange painted orange doors, Type III frame   4   5   6   8
(C) Shiny orange painted orange body, orange painted white doors, Type III frame   4   5   6   8
(D) Same as (C) but Type II frame   4   5   6   8

9770 NORTHERN PACIFIC 1976-77, Type IX body, orange painted orange doors, white and black lettering, Bettendorf trucks
(A) Glossy orange painted orange body, Type II frame 4   5   6   8
(B) Flat orange painted orange body, Type III frame   4   5   6   8
(C) Flat orange painted opaque-white body, Type III frame
                                             4   5   6   8

9771 NORFOLK AND WESTERN 1976-77, Type IX body, white lettering, Bettendorf trucks
(A) Blue painted blue body, blue painted blue doors, Type III frame   4   5   6   8
(B) Same as (A) but blue painted gray body   4   5   6   8
(C) Same as (A) but blue painted white doors, Type II frame
                                             4   5   6   8
(D) Same as (A) but stamped TCA Museum & National Headquarters   NRS

9772 GREAT NORTHERN Type IX body, green and orange painted green body, green and orange painted green door, yellow and black lettering, Bettendorf trucks, Type III frame, part of 1976 Empire State Express set
(A) With regular lettering   15 19 25 30
(B) Missing number and GN on one side. We wish to learn how many of this variety are in collector hands. Reader comments are invited.   NRS
(C) Same as (A), but completely missing GN logo on right. Black lettering and underscoring on left side is present, but has shifted downward so that the underscoring is through the yellow line, Breslin Collection. We wish to learn how many of this variety are in collector hands. Reader comments are invited.   NRS

9773 N Y C Double door stock car, black painted black doors, black lettering, Bettendorf trucks, Type I frame

197

9700 AND 9400 CARS

THE MICKEY MOUSE SET

(A) Light yellow painted yellow body   8   10   12   16
(B) Dark yellow painted yellow body   8   10   12   16

9774 THE SOUTHERN BELLE 1975, uncatalogued, Type IX body, orange sides and silver roof and ends painted on orange body, green painted white doors, green and black lettering, Bettendorf trucks, Type II frame, 1975 TCA National Convention car   —   —   40   50

9775 MINNEAPOLIS & ST. LOUIS Type IX body, uncatalogued, red painted red doors, white lettering, Type II frame, scale 0 sprung die-cast trucks, from Service Station set
(A) Light red painted red body   8   10   15   20
(B) Dark red painted red body   8   10   15   20

9776 S. P. Uncatalogued, Type IX body, black painted black doors, white and gold lettering, scale 0 sprung die-cast trucks, Type II frame, from Service Station set
(A) Black painted black body   10   12   17   25
(B) Black painted opaque-white body   NRS
(C) Same as (A) but double-stamped lettering and emblems   —   —   —   35

9777 VIRGINIAN 1976-77, Type IX body, yellow lettering, Bettendorf trucks
(A) Blue painted light blue body, dark blue painted dark blue doors, Type II frame   4   5   6   8
(B) Blue painted light blue body, light blue painted light blue doors, Type III frame   4   5   6   8
(C) Blue painted medium blue body, light blue painted light blue doors, Type III frame   4   5   6   8
(D) Blue painted light blue body, blue painted white doors, Type II frame   4   5   6   8

9778 SEASONS GREETINGS 1975 Uncatalogued, Type IX body, blue painted blue body, silver painted gray doors, silver lettering, Bettendorf trucks, Type II frame   —   100   150   180

9779 TCA 9700-1976 Uncatalogued, Type IX body, red roof and ends, white sides painted on white body, blue painted blue doors, Bettendorf trucks, Type II frame, 1976 TCA National Convention car. **Note:** "Philadelphia" misspelled on all cars   —   20   30   40

9780 JOHNNY CASH Uncatalogued, Type IX body, black roof, silver sides painted on gray body, black painted black doors, black lettering, Bettendorf trucks, Type III frame   —   25   30   40

9781 DELAWARE & HUDSON 1977-78, Type IX body, yellow painted yellow door, Bettendorf trucks, Type III frame
(A) Light yellow painted yellow body, blue lettering   4   6   8   10
(B) Medium yellow painted yellow body, dark blue lettering   4   6   8   10

9782 THE ROCK 1977-78, Type IX body, white and black lettering, Bettendorf trucks, Type III frame
(A) Blue painted gray body, blue painted gray doors   4   6   8   10
(B) Blue painted light blue body, blue painted blue doors   4   6   8   10

9783 BALTIMORE & OHIO 1977-78, Type IX body, blue sides and ends, silver roof painted on blue body, blue painted blue doors, white and blue lettering, Bettendorf trucks, Type III frame, "Time Saver Service"   4   6   8   10

9784 A T S F 1977-78, Type IX body, red painted red body and red doors, white lettering, Bettendorf trucks, Type III frame, black roof   4   6   8   10

9785 CONRAIL 1977-79, Type IX body, white lettering, Bettendorf trucks, Type III frame
(A) Blue painted blue body and doors   4   6   7   8
(B) Same as (A) but overprinted "TCA MUSEUM EXPRESS," Pinta observation   NRS

9786 CHICAGO AND NORTH WESTERN 1977-79, Type IX body, tuscan painted tuscan doors, white lettering, Bettendorf trucks, Type III frame
(A) Tuscan painted gray body   4   5   6   8
(B) Tuscan painted tuscan body, stamped "TCA MUSEUM EXPRESS"   NRS

9787 CENTRAL OF NEW JERSEY 1977-79, Type IX body, Brunswick green painted green body and doors, metallic gold lettering, Bettendorf trucks, Type III frame   4   5   6   8

9788 LEHIGH VALLEY 1977-79, Type IX body, cream painted cream body and doors, black lettering, Bettendorf trucks, Type III frame
(A) Decal on door   4   5   6   8
(B) No decal on door   4   5   6   8

9789 PICKENS Type IX body, blue painted blue body and doors, white lettering, Bettendorf trucks, Type III frame, from Rocky Mountain set   10   15   24   30

9801-9809: STANDARD "O" SERIES

9801 BALTIMORE & OHIO 1975, box car, gray mold, silver body
(A) Light blue stripe   7   11   15   18
(B) Dark blue stripe   7   11   15   18
(C) Same as (B), except B & O decal is misplaced on one side only, Klaassen Collection   NRS

9802 MILLER HIGH LIFE 1975, reefer, white mold, red lettering
(A) White mold, red lettering   7   9   11   13
(B) Gray plastic body, red doors and lettering, "BLT 1-73," red plastic snap-on walkway, die-cast sprung trucks, disc-operating couplers, the "2" in 9802 is slightly higher than "980," five known to exist, Fuhrmann Collection   —   —   700   —

9803 JOHNSON'S WAX 1975, box car, red mold, black and white lettering
(A) Painted red, white and dark blue   7   9   11   13
(B) Painted red, white, light blue   7   9   11   13

9805 GRAND TRUNK 1975, reefer, gray mold, silver paint, black lettering   8   10   12   16

9806 ROCK ISLAND 1975, box car, red mold, tuscan paint, white lettering   12   15   18   30

9807 STROH'S BEER 1975-76, reefer, red mold, red paint, gold and white lettering   10   12   15   20

9808 UNION PACIFIC 1975-76, box car
(A) White mold, painted dark yellow, yellow door mold painted light yellow   17   25   40   50
(B) Light yellow mold painted dark yellow, yellow door mold painted light yellow   17   25   40   50

9809 CLARK 1975-76, reefer, red mold, blue lettering
(A) Medium red paint   7   9   11   13
(B) Dark red paint   7   9   11   13

9811 PACIFIC FRUIT EXPRESS 1980, yellow painted yellow plastic body, tuscan painted tuscan plastic roof, yellow painted yellow plastic doors, gold diamond FARR Series 2 logo, red, white and blue UP shield, blue SP logo, part of Famous American Railroad Series 2, available as separate sale only   —   —   14   17

9812 ARM & HAMMER 1980, billboard reefer, yellow sides, tuscan roof and ends, disc-operating couplers   —   —   9   12

9813 RUFFLES 1980, billboard reefer, turquoise roof and ends, Bettendorf Trucks, red and blue electrocal
(A) White sides   —   —   9   12
(B) Light blue sides, Samson Collection   NRS

9814 PERRIER Water Billboard reefer, 1980, dark Brunswick green sides, light yellow ends and roof, Bettendorf trucks. "PERRIER" electrocal to right of door, mountain spring electrocal to left of door shows a Perrier bottle bubbling from beneath the earth.
(A) As described above   —   —   14   17
(B) Perrier bottle missing from mountain spring electrocal, McCabe Collection. We do not know how rare this variety is. Reader comments requested.   NRS

9816 BRACHS 1980, billboard reefer, white sides, brown roof and ends, disc-operating couplers   —   —   9   12

9817 BAZOOKA 1980, billboard reefer, white sides, red roof and ends, disc-operating couplers   —   —   9   12

9818 WESTERN MARYLAND reefer, 1980, orange-red sides, Standard "O" sprung die-cast trucks. Part of 1070 Royal Limited Set.
(A) Black roof, ends and lettering   —   —   15   20
(B) Brown roof, ends and lettering, Griggs Collection   NRS

9819 WESTERN FRUIT EXPRESS 1981, reefer, yellow sides and ends, Great Northern goat logo, FARR Series 3 logo, disc-operating couplers, part of Famous American Railroad Series 3, available as separate sale only   —   —   10   13

9825 SCHAEFER 1976-77, reefer, white body, red lettering and roof, Standard "O" Series　　　　　　　　　　　　　10　13　15　20

9826 P & LE 1976-77, reefer, white lettering, Standard "O" Series
(A) Flat green, first run, 500 manufactured　　12　17　25　35
(B) Shiny green　　　　　　　　　　　　　　　7　10　15　20

9827 ARTHUR TREACHER'S SEAFOOD 1982, reefer, yellow sides, green roof and ends, part of Favorite Food series, available only as separate sale, disc-operating couplers. The Advance Catalogue's 9827 number does not match earlier set numbers (7509, 7510, 7511) and the number is expected to change　　　　　　　　　　　　　　　　　　— 　— 　10　14

9829 BONANZA 1982, reefer, white sides, red roof and ends, red lettering, part of Favorite Food series, available only as separate sale, disc-operating couplers, see 9827 for background　　— 　— 　10　14

9830 TACO BELL 1982, reefer, white sides, tuscan roof and ends, part of Favorite Food series, see 9827 for background, tuscan lettering, disc-operating couplers, available only as separate sale　— 　— 　10　14

9831 PEPSI COLA 1982, reefer, white sides, blue ends and roof, disc-operating couplers　　　　　　　　　　　　　— 　— 　10　14

9832 CHERRIOS 1982, reefer, yellow body, black lettering, disc-operating couplers　　　　　　　　　　　　　　— 　— 　10　14

9833 VLASIC 1982, reefer, white sides, yellow roof and ends, black lettering, disc-operating couplers　　　　　　　　— 　— 　10　14

9834 SOUTHERN COMFORT 1983, billboard reefer, disc-operating couplers, opening doors　　　　　　　　　— 　— 　— 　15

9835 JIM BEAN 1983, billboard reefer, white sides, red roof and ends, disc-operating couplers, opening door　　— 　— 　— 　15

9836 OLD GRANDDAD 1983, billboard reefer, disc-operating couplers, opening doors　　　　　　　　　　　— 　— 　— 　15

9837 WILD TURKEY 1983, billboard reefer, disc-operating couplers, opening doors　　　　　　　　　　　　— 　— 　— 　15

9849 LIONEL 1983, bright orange refrigerator car with orange doors and blue roof, very large circular old-fashioned "LIONEL" logo in red, white and blue to the right of the door. Lionel "lion" electrocal to the left of the door. The number to the immediate right of the lion is "5718" not "9849". This car and others in this series may have been prompted by the unauthorized repainting and sale of Lionel rolling stock in similar fashion by a small New England firm. Disc-operating couplers, Bettendorf trucks. LaVoie comment
　　　　　　　　　　　　　　　　　　— 　— 　— 　25

9850 BUDWEISER
(A) Type I body, light red roof, white body and door, red and black lettering　　　　　　　　　　　　　　　　　7　9　11　14
(B) Same as 9850 (A) except medium red roof　　7　9　11　14
(C) Same as 9850(A) except Type I body with dark red roof
　　　　　　　　　　　　　　　　　　　　　7　9　11　14
(D) Same as 9850(A) but LARGE period after BEER CAR 9　11　15　20

9851 SCHLITZ
(A) Type I body, shiny brown roof, white body and door, brown lettering
　　　　　　　　　　　　　　　　　　　　　4　5　6　8
(B) Same as 9851(A) except Type II body with dull brown roof
　　　　　　　　　　　　　　　　　　　　　4　5　6　8

REEFER BODY TYPES
by Donald J. Mitarotonda

Type I
Two metal door guides
Two metal bars running underneath frame, secured in center by one Phillips head screw
Trucks secured to metal
Doors, underneath the ladders on each side of the body, are wider than the ladders
Roof has three ice hatches, third ice hatch in one corner

Type II
Same as Type I, except
Doors underneath the ladders are the same width as the ladders
Roof has two ice hatches in opposing corners

Type III
Two plastic door guides
No metal bars underneath frame
Trucks secured to the frame with a plastic pin
Doors underneath the ladders are the same width as the ladders
Roof has two ice hatches in opposing corners

9852 MILLER
(A) Type I body, shiny brown roof, white body and door, black lettering
　　　　　　　　　　　　　　　　　　　　　4　5　6　8
(B) Same as 9852(A) except Type II body with dull brown roof
　　　　　　　　　　　　　　　　　　　　　4　5　6　8

9853 CRACKER JACK
(A) Type I body, brown roof, light caramel body, dark caramel door, red and black lettering, with border around Cracker Jack　15　20　25　35
(B) Same as 9853(A) except medium caramel body and door
　　　　　　　　　　　　　　　　　　　　15　20　25　35
(C) Same as 9853 (B) except no border　　50　70　80　95
(D) Type I body, brown roof, white body and door, red and black lettering, with border, rare　　　　　　　　　　　　　　　　NRS
(E) Same as 9853 (D) without border　　5　7　10　14
(F) Same as 9853 (E) but red roof　　　5　7　10　14

9854 BABY RUTH
(A) Type I body, red roof, white body and door, red and blue lettering
　　　　　　　　　　　　　　　　　　　　　4　5　6　7
(B) Same as 9854 (A) except no "R"　　4　5　6　7
(C) Same as 9854 (B) except Type II body　4　5　6　7

9855 SWIFT
(A) Type I body, black roof, silver body and door, black lettering, "BLT 1-73"
　　　　　　　　　　　　　　　　　　　　　4　5　6　7
(B) Same as 9855 (A) except "BLT 1-7"　10　15　20　30

9856 OLD MILWAUKEE Type II body, gold roof, red body and door, white and black lettering　　　　　　　　　　　5　7　9　11

9858 BUTTERFINGER
(A) Type I body, flat blue roof, orange body and door, white and black lettering　　　　　　　　　　　　　　　　　4　5　6　7
(B) Same as 9858 (A) except blue gloss roof　4　5　6　7

9859 PABST
(A) Type I body, medium blue roof, white body and door, blue and red lettering　　　　　　　　　　　　　　　　　4　5　6　7
(B) Same as 9859 (A) except Type II body　4　5　6　7

9860 GOLD MEDAL
(A) Type I body, bright orange roof, white body and door, black lettering
　　　　　　　　　　　　　　　　　　　　　4　5　6　7
(B) Same as 9860 (A) except dull dark orange　4　5　6　7

9861 TROPICANA
(A) Type II body, flat green roof, white body and door, green and orange lettering　　　　　　　　　　　　　　　　12　15　21　27
(B) Same as 9861(A) except Type III body, shiny green roof, opaque-white body and door　　　　　　　　　　　　　5　7　9　11
(C) Type III body, translucent white body and roof, green and orange lettering　　　　　　　　　　　　　　　　　5　7　9　11

9862 HAMMS Type II body, white roof, blue body and door, red and white lettering　　　　　　　　　　　　　　7　9　11　14

9863 REA
(A) Type II body, green roof, green body and door, gold lettering, no electrocals (rubber stamped)　　　　　　　　　12　15　18　20
(B) Same as 9863(A) except with electrocals　10　12　16　18
(C) Same as 9863(B) light green roof, with electrocals (gray mold)
　　　　　　　　　　　　　　　　　　　10　12　16　18
(D) Same as 9863(C) except Type III body and green roof　10　12　16　18

9864 TCA 1974 Convention Car, 9800-series reefer construction, Type II body with metal door guides and Channel, Bettendorf trucks. White body with medium royal blue roof, ends and doors, black, red and blue Seattle's World's Fair Space Needle Tower logo at left of door; "1954-1974" in red and TCA logo in black above large blue "20" at right of door　　NRS

9866 COORS
(A) Type III body, brown roof, white body and doors, black and dark yellow lettering, no "R"　　　　　　　　　　　　6　8　10　12
(B) Same as 9866(A) except has low "R"　　7　9　13　15

9800 CARS

202

(C) Same as 9866(A) except high "R" 5 7 10 13
(D) Same as 9866(B) low "R" touching "S" 20 30 40 52

9867 HERSHEY'S Type III body, silver roof, chocolate brown body and door, silver lettering 7 9 12 14

9869 SANTA FE Type III body, brown roof, white body, brown door, black lettering, sprung metal trucks 12 17 25 33

9870 OLD DUTCH CLEANSER Type III body, red roof, yellow body, red door, white and black lettering 4 6 7 8

9871 CARLING BLACK LABEL Type III body, black roof, red body and door, white, gold and black lettering 5 7 8 10

9872 PACIFIC FRUIT EXPRESS Type III body, silver roof, orange body and door, black and white lettering 5 7 8 10

9873 RALSTON PURINA 1978-79, Type III reefer, blue plastic ends and roof painted blue, white plastic sides painted white, elaborate Ralston-Purina electrocal in red, white and blue on car side states "Car used 1945-64," Bettendorf trucks, disc couplers — 6 9 11

9874 LITE 1978-79, (Miller Lite), Type III reefer, blue plastic roof painted blue, white plastic sides painted white, white doors painted gold, blue electrocals, dark blue "LITE," Bettendorf trucks, two disc couplers — 6 9 11

9875 A & P 1979, Type III reefer, brown painted roof, mustard painted sides, red A & P electrocal — 6 9 11

9876 CENTRAL VERMONT 1978, Type III reefer, black plastic roof painted black, gray sides painted silver, green lettering, silver door, standard O trucks, disc couplers with tabs, from Milwaukee Special set — — 15 20

9877 GERBER 1979, Type III reefer, black painted roof, blue painted sides, famous baby shown on electrocal, white lettering — 6 9 11

9878 GOOD AND PLENTY 1979, Type III reefer, pinkish-purple painted roof, white painted sides, Good and Plenty box electrocal 3 6 9 11

9879 HILL BROS 1979, Type III reefer, yellow painted roof, red painted sides, coffee can electrocal — 6 9 12

9880 SANTA FE 1979, Type III reefer, tuscan painted roof, orange painted sides, from Famous American Railroad series — 15 20 23

9881 RATH PACKING 1979, billboard reefer, yellow sides, tuscan roof, Rath logo, die-cast sprung trucks, disc-operating couplers, available only as part of No. 1970 Southern Pacific Limited set — — 18 22

9882 N Y R B 1979, (New York Central reefer), Type III reefer, tuscan painted roof, orange painted sides, sprung die-cast trucks, from Quaker City Limited set — 15 20 23

9883 NABISCO 1979, Type III reefer, blue painted roof, gray painted sides, Oreo cookie package electrocal — 8 12 14

9884 FRITOS 1982, billboard reefer, yellow sides, red roof and ends, Fritos logo electrocal, disc-operating couplers — — 9 12

9885 LIPTON 100 TEA BAGS 1982 billboard reefer, deep red and gold sides, dark brown roof and ends, disc-operating couplers — — 9 12

9886 MOUNDS 1982, billboard reefer, white sides, red roof and ends, disc-operating couplers, Mounds package electrocal — — 9 12

9887 FRUIT GROWERS 1983, billboard reefer, yellow sides, dark green roof and ends, die-cast Standard O sprung trucks, disc-operating couplers, FARR Series 4, car sold separately, Caponi comment — — — 20

9888 GREEN BAY & WESTERN 1983, billboard reefer, gray sides, red roof and ends, die-cast Standard O sprung trucks, disc-operating couplers, only sold as part of No. 1361 Gold Coast Limited set. Catalogue showed car with white sides. Caponi comment — — — 20

9780 JOHNNY CASH

9853 CRACKER JACK

9850 SERIES REEFERS

9850

9851

9852

9853

9854

9855

9856

9858

9859

9860

9861

9862

9863

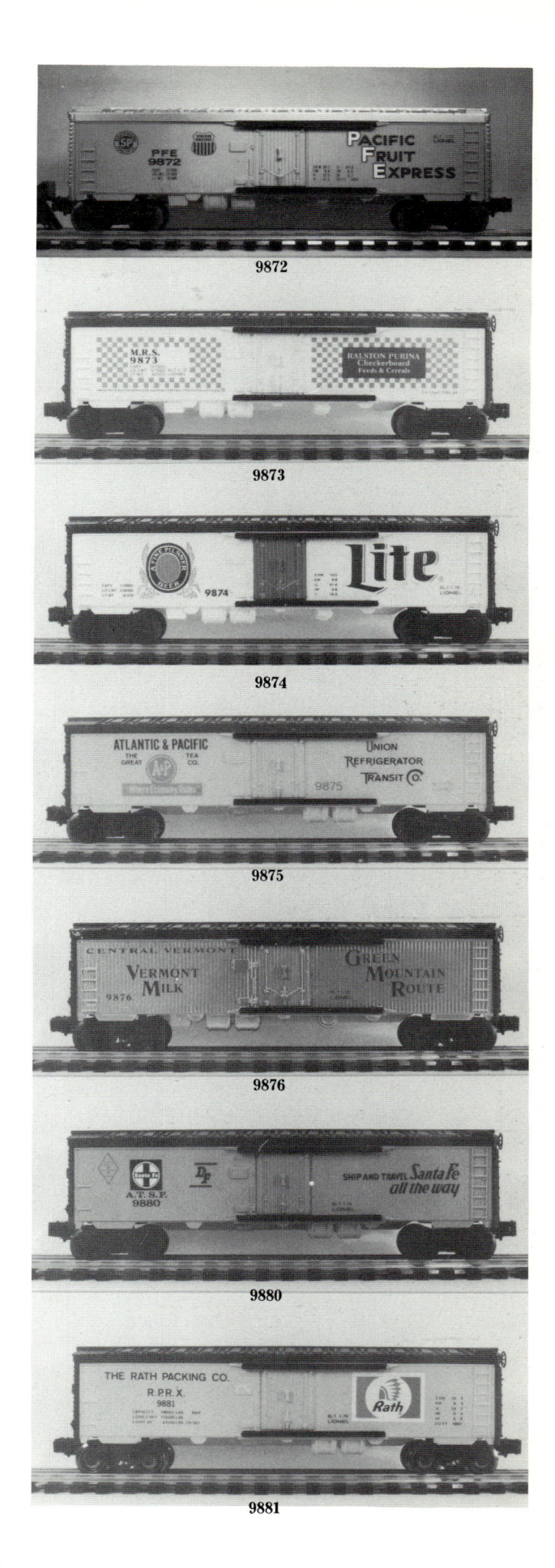

9866

9867

9869

9870

9871

9872

9873

9874

9875

9876

9880

9881

205

7508
ILLINOIS CENTRAL
9160
CN
9161
PENNSYLVANIA
9162
ATSF 9163
9163
CANADIAN PACIFIC
9165
C&O 9167
Chessie System
9167
UNION PACIFIC
9168
VIRGINIAN
9175
SPIRIT OF 1776
BANGOR and AROOSTOOK
9176
9180
THE ROCK
9180
9181
9181
NW
9182
9182
MICKEY MOUSE
EXPRESS
9183
9183
GT
GTW 9185
GTW 9185
CONRAIL
9186
9186
Main Street of the Northwest
9270
9270
SOUTHERN 9287
9287
LEHIGH VALLEY
9288
9288
CNW
9289
9289

Chapter XVIII
FUNDIMENSIONS CABOOSES

S P Caboose Types

Types I through IV are described in Chapter V, Lionel Cabooses.

To the best of our knowledge, Fundimensions did not reuse (Lionel) molds I through IV and began its production with a new model (Type V).

Type V
1. Two rivets on side bottom corners
2. No window frames on front and back cupola windows
3. Plain plastic handrail stanchions on cupola roof
4. Slightly larger door knobs
5. Plainer plastic handrail stanchions by front and rear doors
6. Steps not built into car mold
7. Horizontal window bars
8. Missing short vertical row of rivets on body under cupola between cupola windows, no rivets on ledge over side windows

Type VI
1. Two rivets on side bottom corners
2. No window frames on front and back cupola windows
3. Plain plastic handrail stanchions on cupola
4. Slightly larger door knobs
5. Plainer handrail stanchions by front and rear doors
6. Steps not built into car mold
7. Horizontal window bars
8. Missing short vertical row of rivets on body under cupola
9. Wood-grained catwalk and hatches

Type VII
1. Two and a half rivets on side bottom corners
2. No window frames on front and back cupola windows
3. Plain plastic handrail stanchions on cupola
4. Small door knobs
5. Plainer handrail stanchions by front and rear doors
6. Steps not built into car mold
7. Horizontal window bars
8. Missing short vertical row of rivets on body under cupola
9. No wood-grained catwalk

S P End Types

Type I Smooth walkway surface
Type II Rough walkway surface

N5C Caboose Types

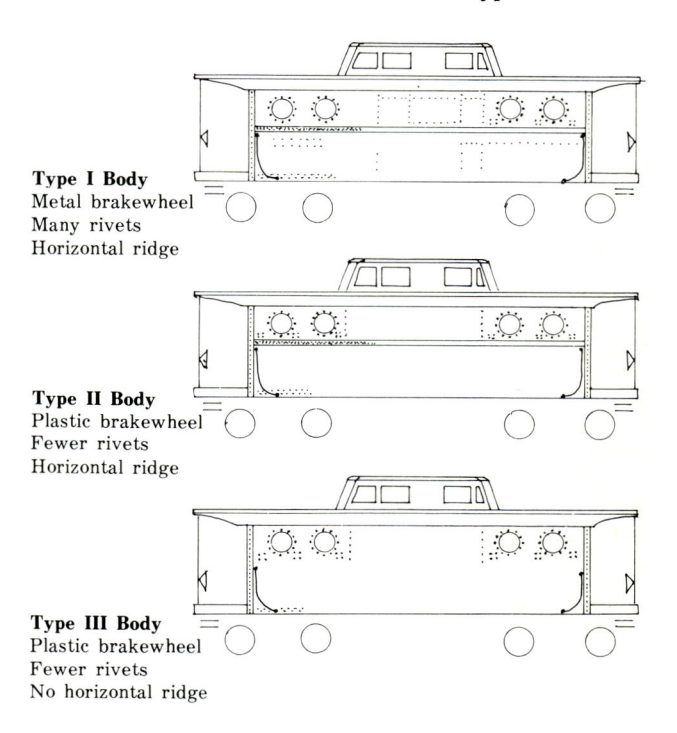

Type I Body
Metal brakewheel
Many rivets
Horizontal ridge

Type II Body
Plastic brakewheel
Fewer rivets
Horizontal ridge

Type III Body
Plastic brakewheel
Fewer rivets
No horizontal ridge

                        Gd. V.G. Exc. Mt.

1776 N & W 1976, N5C Type II, white sides, red roof, gold lettering
(A) Flat red roof   9 12 15 20
(B) Shiny, darker red roof   9 12 15 20

6401 VGN Bay Window, yellow sides with broad blue stripe through center, including bay, yellow and blue safety striping along lower side, "VGN" logo with yellow letters inside circular blue field surrounded by yellow and blue rings, blue, heat-stamped, sans-serif lettering "BLT 1-81/LIONEL" in two lines at one end and "6401" at other end, Bettendorf trucks with disc couplers, Brewer Collection. Catalogued on page 22 of the small 1981 catalogue. Matches 8950 Virginian Fairbanks - Morse. Also a good match for 8659 Virginian rectifier electric and Virginian SD-18 pair, 8071-72. — — 15 20

6420 READING 1981-82, Work Caboose, dark yellow shanty on flat car with dark green base, available only as part of Reading Yard King freight set #1154 — — 10 15

6421 COWEN 1982, Bay Window, gold and dark tuscan with picture of Cowen, lettered "JOSHUA LIONEL COWEN" and "BLT 1-81 LIONEL," issued as a limited edition in the "Spring Collector Series" — — 18 26

6422 DULUTH MISSABE 1981-82, Bay Window, tuscan with yellow stripe, illuminated — — 15 20

6426 READING 1982, Maintenance Caboose, yellow flat car, green cab, yellow diamond, reverse color scheme from Yard King set caboose
— — 7 10

6432 UNION PACIFIC 1981, S.P. Type, part of No. 1151 U.P. Thunder Freight — — 3 4

6433 CANADIAN PACIFIC 1981, Bay Window, gray with maroon roof and lettering, die-cast sprung trucks, illuminated, part of No. 1158 Maple Leaf Limited set — — 30 40

6438 GREAT NORTHERN 1981, Bay Window, tuscan and dark green, illuminated, GN goat logo,(FARR) series 3 logo, from Famous American Railroads Series 3, only sold separately — — 15 20

6441 ALASKA 1982, Bay Window, shown with metal trucks but expected with plastic trucks — — 15 20

6449 WENDY'S 1981-82, N5C, red with yellow roof, part of Favorite Food Series, sold separately only — — 20 25

6506 L.A.S.E.R. 1981-82, Security Car with gun, black base, chrome-finished cab, blue cab lettering, part of No. 1150 L.A.S.E.R. Train set
— — 15 20

6900 N & W 1982, Extended Vision Caboose, red sides, white lettering, standard 0 trucks, disc-operating couplers, part of No. 1260 Continental Limited set, shown as "7301" in 1982 catalogue illustration   **NRS**

7508 LIONEL 1975-76, N5C Type II, silver sides, 75th ANNIVERSARY SPECIAL, "BLT 1-75,"lights, enclosed windows, broad red stripe runs halfway across body.   7 11 15 18

7600 FRISCO 1975-76, N5C Type II, red, white and blue sides, lights, enclosed windows, Spirit of '76 Series
(A) Flat red roof   6 8 20 24
(B) Shiny red roof   6 8 20 24

7606 FRISCO 1974, N5C Type II; red, white and blue sides, red roof, "BLT 1-74," lights, enclosed windows, Spirit of '76   5 8 12 15

9021 SANTA FE 1970-74, Work Caboose, black frame with yellow lettering, caboose converts into "wood" deck flat car
(A) Medium red cab, light red tool box, "9201" on frame, Timken trucks, plastic wheels, one manumatic coupler, one fixed coupler
3 5 7 9
(B) Same as (A) but light red cab, two manumatic couplers
3 5 7 9
(C) Dark shiny cab and tool box, Bettendorf trucks, one operating coupler, one fixed coupler, "9021" not on frame   3 5 7 9
(D) Same as (A) but orange cab   6 9 12 18

9025 D T & I 1971-74, Work Caboose, black frame with white lettering, orange cab with black lettering, dark red tool box, metal wheels, magnetic coupler in front, fixed rear coupler   3 5 6 8

9027 SOO 1975, Work Caboose, black frame with white lettering, red cab with white lettering, dark red tool box, plastic wheels, one manumatic coupler in front, caboose converts into flat car with stakes   3 5 6 8

9057 C P RAIL 1978-79, SP Type VII, yellow plastic painted white and black, Type II ends, Bettendorf trucks, one manumatic coupler, one dummy; stack, from Great Plains Express set, no lights   5 7 9 11

9058 LIONEL LINES 1978-79, SP Type VII, orange unpainted plastic; black lettering, Type II ends, Bettendorf trucks, plastic wheels, manumatic couplers, unlighted   1 2 3 4

9059 LIONEL LINES 1978, SP Type   1 2 3 4

9060 NICKEL PLATE 1970-71 SP Type VI or VII, maroon or brown body, white lettering, MPC logo, Type I ends, tuscan or black frame
(A) Type VI, maroon body   3 5 6 8
(B) Type VII, maroon body   3 5 6 8
(C) Type VII, brown body   3 5 6 8

9061 A T S F 1970-71, 78, SP Type V or VII, red body, yellow lettering
(A) SP Type V, MPC logo, Timken trucks, Type I end   2 3 4 6
(B) SP Type VII, Bettendorf trucks, one manumatic coupler, Type II ends, metal wheels   2 3 4 6

9062 PC 1970-71, SP Type V or VII, green body, white lettering, Type I ends
(A) SP Type V, MPC logo   2 3 5 9
(B) SP Type VII, MPC logo   2 3 5 9
(C) SP Type VII, no MPC logo   2 3 5 9

9063 GT 1970, SP Type V or VI, light orange or maroon body, white lettering, Timken trucks, MPC logo, Type I ends
(A) SP Type V, orange body   5 7 10 20
(B) SP Type V, dark orange body   4 6 9 19
(C) SP Type VI, maroon body, Canadian release   5 7 10 13

9064 C & O 1971, Type VI or VII, yellow body, red stripe, blue lettering, Type I ends, MPC logo
(A) SP Type VI, light yellow body, light red stripe, light blue lettering
2 3 5 7
(B) SP Type VI, medium light yellow, red stripe, blue lettering
2 3 5 7
(C) SP Type VI, medium yellow, red stripe, blue lettering
2 3 5 7
(D) SP Type VII, medium light yellow, red stripe, blue lettering
2 3 5 7

9065 C N 1971-72, SP Type VI, maroon with white lettering, Type I ends, MPC logo, Canadian release   5 7 8 10

9066 SOUTHERN SP Type IV, red body, white lettering, Type I end, no MPC logo   2 3 6 9

9067 KICKAPOO VALLEY & NORTHERN 1972, Bobber, black frame, four wheels, gold lettering
(A) Red body   1 2 3 5
(B) Yellow body   1 2 3 5
(C) Green body   1 2 3 5

9068 READING 1973-75, Bobber, green body, yellow lettering, black frame
1 2 3 4

9069 JERSEY CENTRAL 1973-74, SP Type VII, brown body, white lettering, Type I ends   1 3 5 8

9070 ROCK ISLAND 1973-74, SP Type VII, gray with black and gray lettering; Type I ends   3 5 6 9

9071 A T & S F 1974-75, Bobber, red body, white lettering, black frame, uncatalogued, Sears Set 79C9715C   2 3 4 7

9073 COKE 1973, SP Type VII, red body, white lettering, Type I ends, no MPC logo
(A) Light red body   3 5 7 8
(B) Medium red body   3 5 7 8
(C) Dark flat red body   3 5 7 8

9075 ROCK ISLAND SP Type VII, red body, white lettering, Type 1 ends, no MPC logo   3 4 5 6

9076 WE THE PEOPLE SP Type VII, white and red sides, blue roof, white and blue lettering, American flag, Type I ends, no MPC logo
4 7 9 11

9077 RIO GRANDE 1977-79, 81, SP Type VII, orange body, black lettering, Type II ends, no MPC logo   3 4 5 6

9078 ROCK ISLAND 1977, 79, Bobber, red body, white lettering, black frame   1 2 3 5

9079 A T S F 1979, details needed   NRS

9080 WABASH 1977, SP Type VII, red body, black roof, white lettering, Type II ends, no MPC logo   5 7 10 11

9085 A T S F 1980-81, Work Caboose, plastic trucks and wheels, one operating disc-coupler, one fixed coupler   1 2 3 4

9160 IC 1971, N5C Type II except for (B)
(A) Darker flat orange sides and roof, black lettering, white "ic," Bettendorf trucks, one operating coupler   10 15 18 21
(B) Flat light orange sides and roof, black lettering, white "ic," Timken trucks, pre-1970 wheels, operating couplers, Type I body
12 17 23 28
(C) Darker flat orange sides and roof, black lettering, white "ic," black circle   10 15 17 20
(D) Darker flat orange sides and roof, yellow "ic"   10 15 17 20
(E) Orange and white sides, white roof, black lettering, white "ic," white areas added by Glen Uhl   NRS
(F) Flat light orange roof, orange sides, black lettering, white "ic," Bettendorf trucks, one disc coupler, one fixed coupler   10 15 17 20

9160 IC 1975, ITT Cable Hydrospace; ITT sticker obscures all but IC emblem on side, one coupler. Type N5C II body, see 8030 (C) in diesel chapter, valued with set

9161 CANADIAN NATIONAL 1971, N5C Type II, orange body, white lettering, black roof, lights, "BLT 1-72" body, white lettering, black roof, lights, "BLT 1-72"   5 7 9 11

9162 PENNSYLVANIA 1972-76, N5C Type II, tuscan, white lettering, lights
(A) Green markers   6 8 11 15
(B) Red markers   6 8 11 15

9163 A T S F 1973-76, N5C Type II, red with white lettering, lights, blue Santa Fe herald   3 5 7 9

9165 CANADIAN PACIFIC 1973, N5C Type II, red with white lettering, lights, came in C.P. Service Station Special   7 11 15 17

9166 RIO GRANDE 1974, SP Type VII, silver roof and stripes, black lettering, no MPC logo, lights, stack, enclosed windows, Type I ends
(A) Light yellow sides   4 6 8 10
(B) Medium yellow sides   4 6 8 10

9167 CHESSIE 1974-76, N5C Type II, light yellow sides, silver roof, orange stripe, blue lettering   4 6 8 10

9174
9177
9184
9188
X9259
9268
9269
9323
9271
9272
9273
9274
9316

9168 UNION PACIFIC 1975-76, N5C Type II, yellow sides, red or green lettering, black roof, lights, enclosed windows
(A) Red lettering   3   5   7   9
(B) Green heat-stamped lettering   —   —   — 335

9169 MILWAUKEE ROAD 1975, SP Type VII, brown sides, black roof, red lettering, lights, enclosed windows, Type I ends   6   8   11   15

9170 N & W 1976, listed under 1776

9171 MISSOURI PACIFIC 1975-77, SP Type, red sides and roof, white lettering, lights, stack, enclosed windows, Type I ends
(A) SP Type VI   3   5   7   9
(B) SP Type VII   3   5   7   9

9172 PC 1975-77, SP Type VII, black sides and roof, white lettering, lights, stack, enclosed windows, Type I ends   5   6   8   10

9173 JERSEY CENTRAL 1975-77, SP Type VI or VII, red sides and roof, white lettering, lights, stack, enclosed windows, Type I ends
(A) SP Type VI   3   5   7   9
(B) SP Type VII   3   5   7   9

9174 P & E (New York Central) 1976, Bay Window, green sides, black roof, white lettering, Bettendorf trucks from Empire State Express
                                                              15   22   30   44

9175 VIRGINIAN 1975-77, N5C Type II, blue sides, yellow roof, yellow lettering, lights, enclosed windows   5   7   9   11

9176 B A R 1976, N5C Type II, red, white and blue with red roof, lights, enclosed windows, 1976 Bicentennial Issue, came with 8665 engine
                                                               7   10   15   17

9177 NORTHERN PACIFIC 1976, Bay Window, silver roof, green and dark or medium yellow sides, black lettering, metal trucks, Service Station Special
(A) Dark yellow sides   9   15   20   25
(B) Medium yellow sides   9   15   20   25

9178 ILLINOIS CENTRAL GULF SP Type VII, light or dark orange, silver roof, black lettering, white "IC," Type II ends
(A) Light orange   5   9   11   18
(B) Dark orange   5   9   11   18

9179 CHESSIE 1979, Bobber, yellow body, blue lettering, black frame, four plastic wheels   1   2   3   4

9180 ROCK 1977-78, N5C, blue, black and white sides, white roof, lights, enclosed windows
(A) Type II   3   5   7   9
(B) Type III, Rohlfing Collection   3   5   7   9

9181 BOSTON & MAINE 1977, N5C blue, black and white body, lights, enclosed windows
(A) Type II   3   5   7   9
(B) Type III, Rohlfing Collection   3   5   7   9

9182 N & W 1977-80, N5C, black body, white lettering, lights, enclosed windows
(A) Type II   3   5   7   9
(B) Type III, Rohlfing Collection   3   5   7   9

9183 MICKEY MOUSE 1977-78, N5C, white sides, red/orange roof, Mickey and lettering decal yellow, black, red and blue; Bettendorf trucks, one operating coupler   9   12   15   20

9184 ERIE 1977-78, Bay Window, red and white lettering, two operating couplers   5   8   11   14

9185 GT 1977, N5C, gray plastic painted blue, orange ends, white lettering, red marker lights, Bettendorf trucks, one tab coupler, lights
                                                               4   5   6   8

9186 CONRAIL 1977-78, N5C, gray plastic painted blue, black roof, white lettering, red marker lights, Bettendorf trucks, one tab coupler, lights
                                                               4   5   6   8

9187 GULF MOBILE & OHIO 1977-78, SP Type, gray plastic painted red, black roof, white lettering, Type II ends, lights, metal wheels, Bettendorf trucks, one tab operating coupler   7   11   13   15

9188 GREAT NORTHERN 1977, Bay Window, blue and white sides, black roof, white letters, two operating couplers, lights, from Rocky Mountain Special set   13   15   25   35

9231 READING 1979, Bay Window, green and yellow sides, yellow lettering, green roof, metal wheels, part of Quaker City Limited set
                                                                   15   23   28

9259X SOUTHERN 1977, Bay Window, LCCA Convention car red and white, Kruelle Collection, 4,500 made   —   —   35   40

9268 NORTHERN PACIFIC Bay Window, black and gold sides, yellow hash marks, red lettering, gold ends and roofs, die-cast Timken passenger trucks
                                                               —   —   15   20

9269 MILWAUKEE ROAD 1978, Bay Window, orange and black, red logo, die-cast trucks   —   20   25   30

9270 NORTHERN PACIFIC N5C, orange body, white letters
                                                               4   7   9   11

9271 M & St. L 1978-79, Bay Window, maroon and white sides, blue roof, white lettering, lights, two operating couplers, die-cast trucks
                                                              10   13   17   20

9272 NEW HAVEN 1978-80, Bay Window, dark red, white and black lettering, lights, two operating couplers   6   8   10   12

9273 SOUTHERN 1978, Bay Window, green and white body, gold stripes
                                                              10   13   15   20

9274 SANTA FE 1979, Bay Window, black roof, red sides, white letters, two operating couplers, reportedly only 3,000 made   20   30   40   50

9275 SANTA FE 1978, Bay Window; we do not know if this was manufactured   NRS

9276 T & P 1980 SP Type blue with white lettering catalogued but not made   Not Manufactured

9287 SOUTHERN 1978, N5C, gray plastic painted red, red roof, white lettering, red markers, Bettendorf trucks, one tab coupler, lights
                                                               4   5   6   8

9288 LEHIGH VALLEY 1978, 80, N5C, gray plastic painted red, yellow roof, yellow lettering, red markers, Bettendorf trucks, one tab coupler, lights   4   5   6   8

9289 C N W 1978, 80, N5C gray plastic body painted yellow, Brunswick green roof, black lettering, red marker lights, Bettendorf trucks, one tab coupler, lights
(A) As described above   4   5   6   8
(B) Same as (A), except two disc couplers, Dunn Collection
                                                               4   5   6   8

9309 T P W 1980-81, Bay Window (Toledo, Peoria & Western); red with silver roof and white lettering, from No. 1072 Cross Country Express
                                                               —   —   13   15

9316 SOUTHERN PACIFIC 1979, Bay Window, silver with black roof, illuminated, disc-operating coupler, die-cast sprung trucks, from Southern Pacific Limited set, No. 1970   —   —   22   29

9317 A T S F 1979, Bay Window, blue with yellow lettering, operating couplers, lights, matches A T S F SD-18 engine   9   12   15   18

9323 A T S F 1979, Bay Window, tuscan, white lettering, operating couplers, metal wheels, lights, from (FARR) Series I, available as separate sale only
                                                              10   15   22   30

9326 BURLINGTON NORTHERN 1979-80, Bay Window, green painted body, white lettering, lights   —   9   12   18

9328 WM CHESSIE SYSTEM 1980, Bay Window, yellow with silver roof, from No. 1070 Royal Limited set   —   —   17   25

9341 ATLANTIC COAST LINE 1979-82, SP Type, red with white lettering, glow-in-the-dark windows, Timken trucks, from No. 1960 Midnight Flyer set
                                                                              6   8

9346 WABASH 1979, SP Type, dark red sides, white lettering, black roof, from No. 1962 Wabash Cannonball and No. 1991 Wabash Deluxe Express, Young Collection   —   —   6   8

9057

9058

9060

9061

9063

9064

9065

9066

9069

9070

9073

9075

9076

9077

9080

9166

9169

9171

9172

9173

9178

9187

9346 NY NH & H 1980-81, SP Type, white sides, black roof and ends; "New York, New Haven and Hartford" in black script, came with No. 1050 New Englander set   —   —   —   8

9355 D & H 1980, Bay Window, blue and white with yellow stripe, (Delaware & Hudson), illuminated, matches 8050 - 8051 D H U36C diesels   —   —   14   16

9357 SMOKEY MOUNTAIN LINE 1979 Bobber, one-piece plastic cab and roof, one-piece black unpainted plastic frame, two black unpainted plastic end railing units, plastic wheels on metal axles, fixed plastic coupler fastened to frame by metal screw (for a total of 3 metal parts), body and frame highly detailed, frame underside lettered "LIONEL MPC 9067-10"; came with No. 1965 Smokey Mountain Line set
(A) Unpainted green plastic body, black heat-stamped lettering "SML," logo between windows   1   2   3   4
(B) Red plastic body, white lettering shown in catalogue, verification requested   **NRS**

9361 C N W 1980, Bay Window, yellow sides, black roof, illuminated, disc-operating couplers   —   —   13   16

9368 UNION PACIFIC 1980, Bay Window, yellow with red roof and lettering, FARR 2 series, only sold separately   —   —   15   17

9372 SEABOARD 1980, Bay Window, tuscan with black roof, from No. 1071 Mid Atlantic Limited set   —   —   22   25

9380 NY NH & H 1980, SP-Type, from No. 1050 New Englander set, verification requested

9381 CHESSIE 1980, SP-Type, yellow sides and end, silver roof, blue lettering, from No. 1052 Chesapeake Flyer set   —   —   6   8

9382 FLORIDA EAST COAST 1980, Bay Window, red and yellow with white stripe, illuminated, matches 8064 and 8065 GP-9 diesels   —   —   14   16

9387 BURLINGTON 1981, Bay Window, red sides, white lettering, illuminated, die-cast sprung trucks, disc-operating couplers, from No. 1160 Great Lakes Limited set   —   —   25   30

9068

9071

9176

8078

9021

9025

9027

Chapter XIX
FUNDIMENSIONS TANK CARS

Fundimensions adopted the 6315 chemical tank car (the platform, single tank car) as its preferred style. It modified the 6315 tank by replacing the brakewheel on a standing post with a low brakewheel on the frame. Fundimensions created two types of platform, single dome cars:

Type 1 Lettering on the ends above the railing

Type 2 No lettering on the car ends

9153 Chevron comes with both Type 1 and 2 ends. Starting with 9154 Borden, circa 1975, only Type 2 ends are found.

	Gd.	V.G.	Exc.	Mt.

6300 CORN PRODUCTS 1981, yellow three domes, from 1154 READING YARD KING set — — 14 16

6301 GULF 1981-82, single dome, white with orange "Gulf" — — 14 16

6302 QUAKER STATE 1981-82, three domes — — 15 18

6304 GREAT NORTHERN 1981, green platform, single dome, white lettering, FARR Series 3 logo, disc-operating couplers, from Famous American Railroads Series 3, only available as separate sale — — 12 13

6305 BRITISH COLUMBIA 1981, green platform, single dome, white lettering, die-cast sprung trucks, disc-operating couplers, from No. 1158 Maple Leaf Limited set — — 25 30

6306 SOUTHERN 1983, single dome silver tanks, black lettering, gold FARR4 series emblem, die-cast trucks, disc operating coupler, separate sale item — — — 22

6308 ALASKA 1982, blue single dome, disc-operating couplers, small frame — — 5 7

6310 SHELL 1983, two dome yellow tanks red lettering, black stamped steel frame, disc operating couplers, separate sale item, Caponi comment — — — 8

6315 - 1972 See page 135.

6357 FRISCO 1983, single dome black tank, white lettering yellow tank cover, die-cast Standard 0 trucks, disc operating couplers. Only available as part of No. 1361 Gold Coast Limited set. — — — 30

9036 MOBILGAS 1978-80, single dome, small frame, 7 7/16 inches long, white plastic tank painted white with red lettering, black ends, one brakewheel, Bettendorf trucks, one disc coupler with tab, one fixed coupler, metal wheels 1 2 3 5

9039 MOBILGAS 1978, 80, red single dome plastic tank painted red, black ends, white lettering, black frame, one brakewheel, Bettendorf trucks, metal wheels, one disc coupler with tab, one fixed coupler 1 2 3 5

9050 SUNOCO 1970-71
(A) Yellow-orange body, blue lettering, Timken trucks, one operating coupler, one fixed coupler, MPC logo, medium orange-yellow background in Sunoco logo 4 5 7 9
(B) Medium yellow body, blue lettering, Bettendorf trucks, one operating coupler, one fixed coupler, MPC logo, medium orange-yellow background in Sunoco logo 4 5 7 9
(C) Same as (B) but dark yellow body 4 5 7 9
(D) Same as (B) but light yellow body, light orange-yellow background in Sunoco logo 4 5 7 9
(E) Same as (B) except green lettering NRS

9051 FIRESTONE 1974-75, short car, Bettendorf trucks, one operating coupler, one fixed coupler, no MPC logo
(A) Unpainted shiny white body, light blue lettering 3 4 5 7
(B) Painted flat white body, blue lettering 3 4 6 8

9138 SUNOCO 1978, three dome black tank, white lettering, Sunoco decal, "BLT 1-78," black plastic frame, black brakewheel, standard 0 trucks, disc couplers with tabs, part of Minneapolis Service Station set 10 15 18 25

9147 TEXACO 1977, long car, platform, single dome, chrome and black body, red and black lettering, Bettendorf trucks, two operating couplers, no MPC logo 5 7 10 12

9148 DUPONT 1977-79, 81, long car, three domes, cream, yellow and green body, green lettering, red logo, Bettendorf trucks, no MPC logo, operating couplers 4 6 8 10

9150 GULF 1971, long car, platform, single dome, white body, Bettendorf trucks, operating couplers, MPC logo
(A) Black and orange lettering 8 12 15 22
(B) Black and dark orange lettering, Piker Collection 8 12 15 22

9151 SHELL 1972, long car, platform, single dome, yellow body, yellow ends, red lettering, Bettendorf trucks, operating couplers, MPC logo 4 5 6 8

9152 SHELL 1973-74, long car, platform, single dome, yellow body, black ends, red lettering, Bettendorf trucks, operating couplers, no MPC logo
(A) Light yellow body 6 7 9 12
(B) Medium yellow body 6 7 9 12

9153 CHEVRON 1974-76, long car, platform, single dome, silver and blue body, blue lettering, Bettendorf trucks, operating couplers, no MPC logo
(A) Light blue and red decals 5 6 8 10
(B) Dark blue and orange decals 5 7 8 10

9154 BORDEN 1975-76, long car, platform, single dome, chrome and black body, black lettering, Bettendorf trucks, operating couplers, no MPC logo 5 6 8 10

9155 MONSANTO 1977, LCCA Convention car — — 40 55

9156 MOBILGAS 1976-77, long car, single dome, red and blue lettering, Bettendorf trucks, operating couplers 5 7 9 11

9159 SUNOCO Long car, platform, single dome, chrome and blue body, blue lettering, Bettendorf trucks, operating couplers, no MPC logo, available only in sets 10 15 20 25

9189 GULF Long car, platform, single dome, chrome and black body, blue lettering, Bettendorf trucks, operating coupler, no MPC logo, available only in sets 10 14 17 22

9250 WATERPOXY 1971, long car, three domes, white body, blue and green lettering, MPC logo
(A) Metal trucks, two old-type brakewheel stands 7 10 12 15
(B) Bettendorf trucks, two operating couplers, one plastic brakewheel 6 7 9 11

9277 CITIES SERVICE 1977, single dome, green body and dome, metal ladder and platform around dome, black plastic frame, one brakewheel, handrails run nearly completely around tank, die-cast sprung trucks, disc couplers with tabs 6 10 13 16

9278 LIFESAVERS 1978-79, platform, single dome, extraordinarily bright pressure sensitive decal showing five flavors, tank and dome car chrome-plated, metal walk and ladders, metal handrails run nearly completely around car, one brakewheel, Bettendorf trucks, disc couplers 8 10 12 15

9279 MAGNOLIA 1978-79, three domes, white plastic body painted white, black ends, black lower third of tank, shiny metal handrails, black metal ladders, black plastic frame, Bettendorf trucks, disc couplers with tabs 5 6 7 9

9313 GULF 1979, three domes, black plastic painted shiny black, shiny metal handrail, black metal ladders, disc couplers, one brakewheel, die-cast sprung trucks, part of Southern Pacific Limited set — — 15 20

FUNDIMENSIONS TANK CARS

9321 A.T.S.F. 1979, platform, single dome, silver painted body, metal walkway, black metal ladders, dull metal handrail almost all the way around, black plastic frame, Bettendorf trucks, disc couplers with tabs, black and white Santa Fe decal, FARR Series 1 logo 6 8 10 14

9324 TOOTSIE ROLL 1979, 81-82, single dome, white ends, brown center tank section, white lettering, Bettendorf trucks, disc couplers 6 8 10 15

9327 BAKELITE 1980, white three domes, red lettering, red and white, UNION CARBIDE logo, disc-operating couplers — — 12 14

9331 UNION 76 1979, single dome, die-cast sprung trucks, from No. 1071 Quaker City Limited set — — 16 18

9334 HUMBLE 1979, single dome, silver painted tank, red and blue lettering, Bettendorf trucks, disc couplers 6 8 9 11

9344 CITGO 1980, white, three domes, blue lettering, red and blue CITGO logo, die-cast sprung trucks, disc-operating couplers, from No. 1070 The Royal Limited — — 16 18

9347 NIAGARA FALLS 1979, TTOS National Convention car — — 35 40

9353 CRYSTAL 1980, red, three domes, white lettering, disc-operating couplers — — 11 13

9354 PENNZOIL 1981, chrome-finished, single dome, disc-operating couplers, yellow and black logo — — 10 12

9367 UNION PACIFIC 1980, single dome, disc-operating couplers, FARR Series 2 logo, available only as separate sale — — 12 14

9369 SINCLAIR 1980, green single dome, die-cast sprung trucks, from No. 1071 Mid Atlantic set — — 15 20

9373 GETTY 1980-81, white single dome, orange logo, disc-operating couplers, from No. 1072 Cross Country Express set — — 8 10

9386 PURE OIL 1981, white single dome, die-cast sprung trucks, disc-operating couplers, from No. 1160 Great Lakes Limited set — — 15 20

Chapter XX
FUNDIMENSION VAT CARS

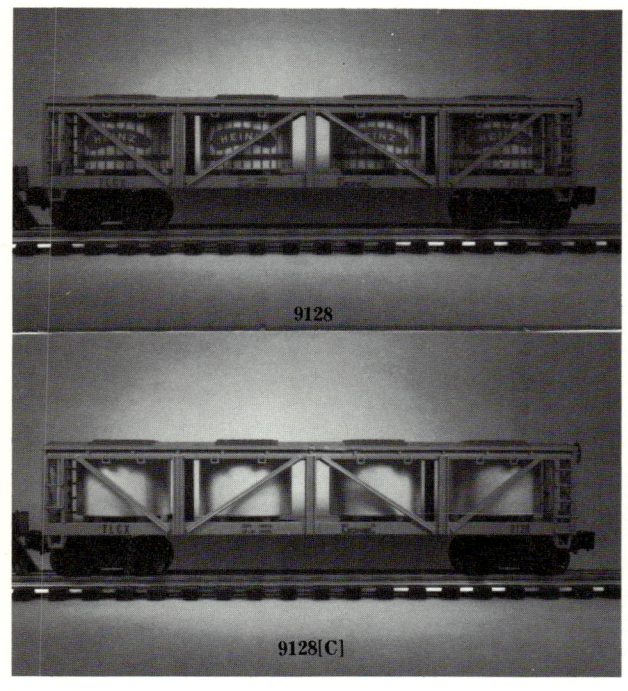

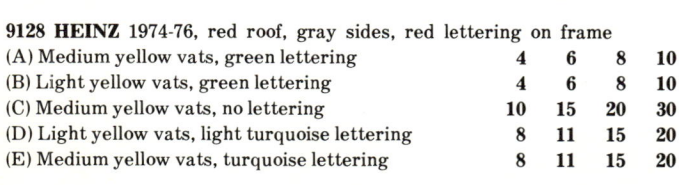

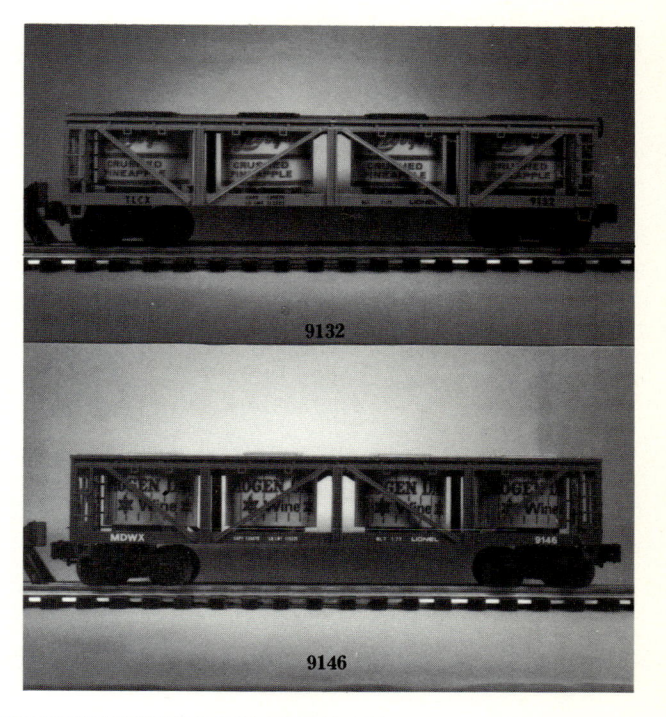

9128 HEINZ 1974-76, red roof, gray sides, red lettering on frame
(A) Medium yellow vats, green lettering 4 6 8 10
(B) Light yellow vats, green lettering 4 6 8 10
(C) Medium yellow vats, no lettering 10 15 20 30
(D) Light yellow vats, light turquoise lettering 8 11 15 20
(E) Medium yellow vats, turquoise lettering 8 11 15 20

9132 LIBBY'S CRUSHED PINEAPPLE 1975-77, green roof, gray sides, yellow vats, red and brown lettering on vats, green lettering on frame 4 6 8 10

9146 MOGEN DAVID 1977-79, silver roof, blue sides, tan vats, blue vat lettering, white frame lettering 4 6 8 10

9193 BUDWEISER 1983, silver roof, red sides, red and silver vats, red vat lettering, operating disc couplers, separate sale item that has sold well. Caponi comment — — — 11

217

Chapter XXI
FUNDIMENSIONS OPERATING CARS

                       Gd. V.G. Exc. Mt.

6201 See Gondolas, Chapter XX

7900 See Box Cars, Chapter XVII

7901 See Box Cars, Chapter XVII

8868 AMTRAK See Chapter XIII, Diesels

8869 AMTRAK See Chapter XIII, Diesels

8870 AMTRAK See Chapter XIII, Diesels

8871 AMTRAK See Chapter XIII, Diesels

9217 See Chapter XVII, Box Cars

9218 See Chapter XVII, Box Cars

9300 P C 1970-73, dump mechanism, green body, white lettering, MPC logo, Bettendorf trucks, two disc couplers
(A) With helium tank	5	7	9	11
(B) With log	4	6	8	10

9301 See Box Cars, Chapter XVII

9302 L & N 1973-74, searchlight, brown body, mold 6511-2, Bettendorf trucks with disc couplers, gray superstructure with mold 6812-5. Yellow lettering on flat car base. Superstructure embossed "TRACK MAINTENANCE" and has two shovels, wire, control panel and oxygen tanks molded in as part of mold 6812-5. The searchlight is not a part of the superstructure as such, but it is fastened to the superstructure by a circular metal fastener and is not intended to be removed. Griggs Collection
(A) MPC logo	5	7	10	12
(B) No MPC logo	4	5	7	9
(C) All white lettering	–	–	33	53

9303 UNION PACIFIC 1974, 79, log dump, yellow body, red lettering, Bettendorf trucks, one disc coupler, one fixed coupler   4   5   6   8

9304 C & O 1974, coal dump, blue and yellow lettering, Bettendorf trucks, one disc coupler, one fixed coupler
(A) White "coal" from raw plastic pellets	4	5	7	9
(B) Black "coal"	4	5	7	9

9307 See Chapter XX, Gondolas

9308 See Chapter XVII, Box Cars

9310 A.T.S.F. 1978-79, 81-82, log dump, red body, yellow lettering, "BLT 1-78," Bettendorf trucks, disc coupler with tab, fixed coupler, operating disc on underside, when center pulled down load dumps three dowels about six inches long, 5/8 inch diameter   5   7   9   13

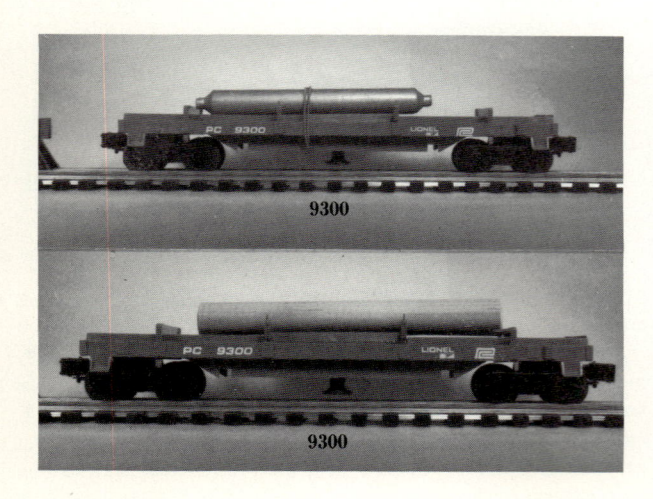

218

9311 U P 1978-82, yellow coal dump with black coal, Bettendorf trucks, one disc coupler, one fixed coupler, when operating disc pulled down load dumps   **5   7   9   13**

9312 C R 1978-82, searchlight, blue body, white lettering, mold "No. 6511-2," gray or orange plastic superstructure, mold "No. 3520-12," with box embossed "Track Maintenance" and tools, wire, control panel, oxygen tanks and searchlight unit

(A) Unpainted gray superstructure, plastic rivet holding trucks, Nordby observation   **5   6   8   13**

(B) Orange assembly, metal rivet holding trucks, Rohlfing and Nordby observation. The view that this car is scarce has been questioned in recent reports. We would appreciate further reader comments concerning the scarcity of this car. Bryan Smith observation   —   —   **40   55**

CRANES

6508 CANADIAN PACIFIC 1981, tuscan base and boom with white letters, gray cab with maroon lettering, part of No. 1158 Maple Leaf Limited set   —   —   —   **40**

6510 UNION PACIFIC 1982, yellow cab with silver roof, gray plastic base, red "UNION PACIFIC" lettering, tall stack, notched boom at high end, six-wheel passenger trucks. Weisblum Collection   —   —   —   **40**

6670 LIONEL 1981, red flat with yellow derrick, from No. 1154 Reading Yard King set (Listed as 9378 in Fundimensions listing)   —   —   —   **20**

9329 CHESSIE SYSTEM 1980, blue base, yellow cab with silver roof, six wheel trucks, came with No. 1070 The Royal Limited   —   —   —   **30**

9332 READING 1979, green base, yellow cab, green roof, yellow boom, from Quaker City Limited set   —   —   **20   30**

9348 SANTA FE 1979, blue with yellow lettering, Standard "O" trucks   —   —   **30   36**

9398 PENNSYLVANIA 1983, coal dump, tuscan frame and bin, gold lettering, rubber stamped Keystone, mechanism activated by special track, disc operating couplers, with coal bin, sold separately   —   —   —   **14**

Chapter XXII
FUNDIMENSIONS PASSENGER CARS

	Gd.	V.G.	Exc.	Mt.

577 NORFOLK & WESTERN See 9562

578 NORFOLK & WESTERN See 9563

579 NORFOLK & WESTERN See 9564

580 NORFOLK & WESTERN See 9565

581 NORFOLK & WESTERN See 9566

0511 TCA ST. LOUIS Convention baggage car, 1981, Brunswick green body with black roof, "THE GATEWAY TO THE WEST/ST. LOUIS" in rubber stamped gold lettering, gold stripes above and below windows run the length of the car, "0511" on box only, "1981" at both ends of car, white TCA logo, six-wheel die-cast passenger trucks — — — 60

1973 TCA BICENTENNIAL SPECIAL Red, white and blue, set of three cars: 1973; 1974; 1975 — — 125 135
1973 only — — 40 45

1974 TCA BICENTENNIAL SPECIAL Matches 1973 — — 40 45

1975 TCA BICENTENNIAL SPECIAL Matches 1973 — — 40 45

6403 AMTRAK 1976-77, Vista Dome, aluminum with red and blue window stripes 6 9 12 16

6404 AMTRAK Matches 6403, Pullman 6 9 12 16

6405 AMTRAK Matches 6403, Pullman 6 9 15 20

6406 AMTRAK Matches 6403, Observation 10 13 15 20

6410 AMTRAK Matches 6403, Pullman 5 7 12 16

6411 AMTRAK Matches 6403, Pullman 5 7 12 16

6412 AMTRAK Matches 6403, Vista Dome 5 7 12 16

7200 QUICKSILVER 1982, Pullman, blue and silver, lighted, part of No. 1253 Quicksilver Express — — 20 24

7201 QUICKSILVER 1982, Vista Dome, matches 7200 — — 20 24

7202 QUICKSILVER 1982, Observation, matches 7200 — — 20 24

7203 NORFOLK AND WESTERN 1983, dining car, matches 9562, 9563, etc. — — — 175

7204 SOUTHERN PACIFIC 1983, dining car, matches 9594. See 9594 for background — — — 150

7205 TCA DENVER Convention combine car, 1982, matches 0511, "7205" on box only, gold-lettered "THE ROCKY MOUNTAIN ROUTE/UNITED STATES MAIL/RAILWAY POST OFFICE/DENVER" — — — 60

7206 TCA LOUISVILLE Convention Pullman car, 1983, matches 0511, "7206" on box only, gold-lettered "GREAT LAKES LIMITED/LOUISVILLE" — — — 60

7207 NEW YORK CENTRAL 1983, extruded aluminum dining car, "TWENTIETH CENTURY LIMITED," matches 9594 and other New York Central passenger cars — — — 110

7208 PENNSYLVANIA 1983, dining car, "JOHN HANCOCK," matches Pennsylvania "Congressional Limited" passenger cars — — — 115

7211 SOUTHERN PACIFIC 1983, Vista-dome car, "Daylight," matches Southern Pacific Daylight passenger cars — — — 175

7215 BALTIMORE AND OHIO 1983, blue sides, gray roof, white lettering, General style coach, part of No. 1351 Baltimore & Ohio set with 7216 and 7217 — — — 17

7217 BALTIMORE AND OHIO 1983, baggage, matches 7215 — — — 17

8868 AMTRAK See Chapter XIII

8869 AMTRAK See Chapter XIII

8870 AMTRAK See Chapter XIII

8871 AMTRAK See Chapter XIII

9500 MILWAUKEE ROAD 1973, Pullman, "CITY OF MILWAUKEE," flat orange, flat maroon roof, lights, roof fastened with tabs through floor 10 15 22 25

9501 MILWAUKEE ROAD Pullman, "CITY OF ABERDEEN"
(A) Flat orange, flat maroon paint 10 15 22 25
(B) Shiny orange and shiny maroon paint 10 15 22 25

9502 MILWAUKEE ROAD Matches 9500, Observation, "PRESIDENT WASHINGTON" 12 18 25 30

9503 MILWAUKEE ROAD Matches 9500, Pullman, "CITY OF CHICAGO" 7 10 15 22

9504 MILWAUKEE ROAD 1974, Pullman, "CITY OF TACOMA," flat orange, flat maroon roof, lights
(A) Roof fastened with tabs through floor 7 11 15 20
(B) Roof fastened through windows 7 11 15 20

9505 MILWAUKEE ROAD 1974, Pullman "CITY OF SEATTLE," flat orange, flat maroon roof, lights
(A) Tabs through floor hold roof 7 11 15 20
(B) Tabs through windows 7 11 15 20

9506 MILWAUKEE ROAD 1974, Baggage combine, "U.S. MAIL," flat orange sides, flat maroon roof 5 7 10 14

9507 PENNSYLVANIA 1974, Pullman, "CITY OF MANHATTAN," tuscan with black roof, gold lettering, lighted, one center rail pickup roller, ground pickup contacts on other truck, fully detailed undercarriage 10 15 22 30

9508 PENNSYLVANIA "CITY OF PHILADELPHIA," Pullman, matches 9507 10 15 22 30

9509 PENNSYLVANIA Observation, "PRESIDENT ADAMS," matches 9507 10 15 22 30

9510 PENNSYLVANIA 1974, Baggage-mail-coach combine, matches 9507, lights, "UNITED STATES MAIL RAILWAY POST OFFICE" in gold heat-stamped letters 10 15 20 25

9511 MILWAUKEE ROAD 1973, Pullman, "CITY OF MINNEAPOLIS," special coupon car, lights 15 25 30 35

9512 SUMMERDALE JUNCTION 1974, special for TTOS, yellow with maroon roof, lights — — 30 35

9513 PENNSYLVANIA 1975, Pullman, "PENN SQUARE," lights, matches 9507 10 15 20 25

9514 PENNSYLVANIA 1975, Pullman, "TIMES SQUARE," lights, matches 9507 10 15 20 25

9515 PENNSYLVANIA 1975, Pullman, "WASHINGTON CIRCLE," matches 9507, lights 10 15 20 25

9516 BALTIMORE & OHIO 1976, Pullman, "MOUNTAIN TOP," matches 9517 10 15 22 30

9517 BALTIMORE & OHIO 1975, Coach, "CAPITAL CITY," blue, gray windows, yellow stripes, gray roof, lights 20 25 30 40

9518 BALTIMORE & OHIO 1975, Observation, "NATIONAL VIEW," lights, matches 9517 20 25 30 40

9519 BALTIMORE & OHIO 1975, Baggage combine, "UNITED STATES MAIL," lights, matches 9517 20 25 30 40

9520 TOY TRAIN OPERATION SOCIETY 1975, special for National Convention, matches 9512
(A) No decal — — 30 45
(B) With Phoenix decal for convention attendees — — 31 46

9521 PENNSYLVANIA 1975, double-door Baggage, tuscan with black roof, lights 20 30 45 60

9522 MILWAUKEE ROAD 1975, double-door Baggage, flat orange, flat maroon roof, lights 20 30 45 60

THE BLUE COMET

9536 BARNARD
9537 HALLEY
9538 FAYE
9539 WESTPHAL
9540 TEMPEL

SOUTHERN CRESCENT LIMITED

9530 HARRIS
9531 PICKENS
9532 BEAUREGARD
9533 JACKSON
9534 LEE

9523 BALTIMORE & OHIO 1975, double-door Baggage, "AMERICAN RAILWAY EXPRESS," lights, matches 9517   15   20   25   35

9524 BALTIMORE & OHIO 1976, Pullman, "MARGARET CORBIN," lights, matches 9517   10   15   20   25

9525 BALTIMORE & OHIO 1976, Pullman, "EMERALD BROOK," matches 9517   10   15   20   25

9526 TOY TRAIN OPERATING SOCIETY 1976, matches 9512, special for National Convention
(A) No Utah decal   —   —   30   35
(B) With Utah decal for convention attendees   —   —   31   36

9527 MILWAUKEE 1976, "ROOSEVELT," campaign observation, red, white, and blue bunting on car sides, small flag on rear platform   10   12   15   20

9528 PENNSYLVANIA 1976, "TRUMAN," campaign observation, lights, matches 9507   10   12   15   20

9529 BALTIMORE & OHIO 1976, "EISENHOWER," campaign observation, matches 9507   10   12   15   20

9530 SOUTHERN 1978, Baggage, "JOEL CHANDLER HARRIS"   10   15   20   25

9531 SOUTHERN 1978, Combination, "ANDREW PICKENS"   10   15   20   25

9532 SOUTHERN 1978, Pullman, "P. G. T. BEAUREGARD"   10   15   20   25

9533 SOUTHERN 1978, Pullman, "STONEWALL JACKSON"   10   15   20   25

9534 SOUTHERN 1978, Observation, "ROBERT E. LEE"   10   15   20   25

9535 TOY TRAIN OPERATING SOCIETY 1977, matches 9512, special for National Convention
(A) No Ohio decal   —   —   31   35
(B) With Ohio decal for convention attendees   —   —   31   36

BLUE COMET SERIES, 1978

9536 THE BLUE COMET 1978, Baggage, "BARNARD," blue unpainted plastic sides, dark blue roof, cream stripe through windows, gold lettering, gold stripes above and below windows, illuminated, six-wheel trucks, full detailed undercarriage, two disc couplers, glazed windows   10   12   15   20

9537 THE BLUE COMET 1978, Combination, "HALLEY," matches 9536   10   12   15   20

9538 THE BLUE COMET 1978, Pullman, "FAYE," matches 9536   10   12   15   20

9539 THE BLUE COMET 1978, Pullman, "WESTPHAL," matches 9536   10   12   15   20

9540 THE BLUE COMET 1978, Observation, "TEMPEL," matches 9536   10   12   15   20

9541 SANTA FE 1980, 82, Baggage, "RAILWAY EXPRESS AGENCY," part of No. 1053, The James Gang set   —   —   15   20

9544 TCA CHICAGO Convention Pullman car, 1980, matches 0511, "9544" on box only, gold-lettered "LAND OF LINCOLN/CHICAGO"   —   —   —   60

9551 W&A 1860-type Baggage for General set   —   15   20   25

9552 W&A 1860-type Coach for General set   —   15   20   25

THE ALTON LIMITED [Includes Loco and Tender]

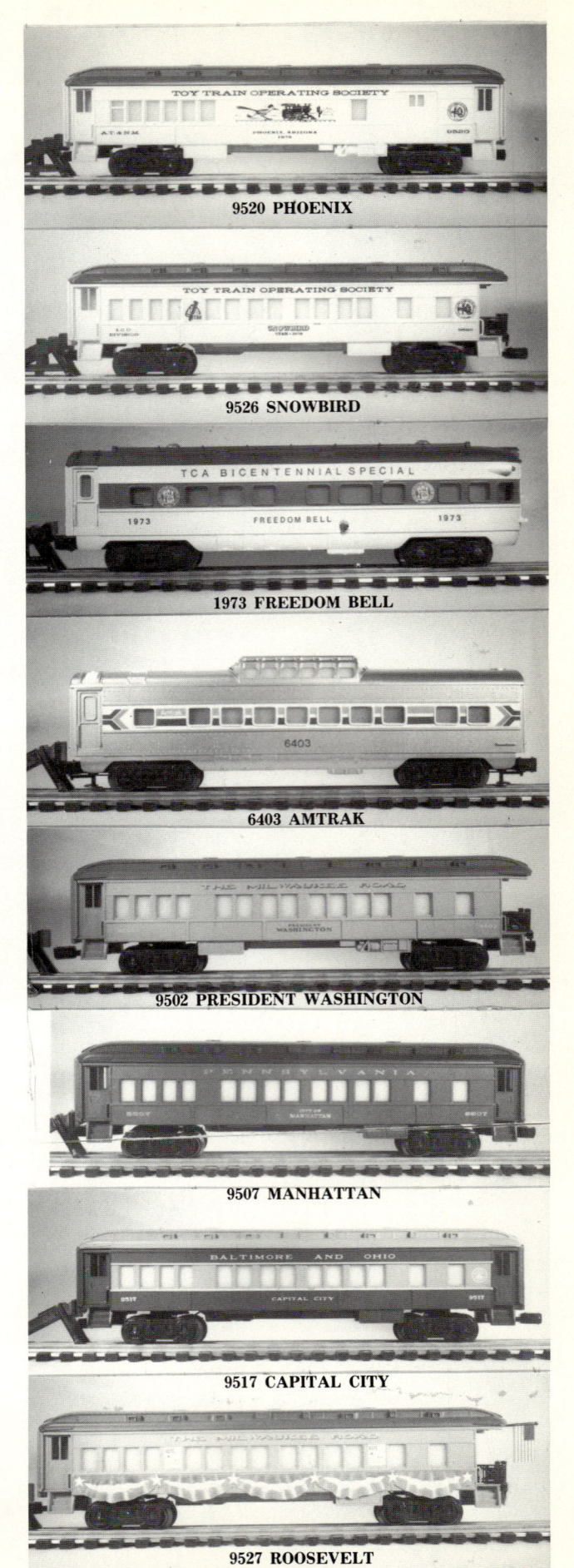

9520 PHOENIX

9526 SNOWBIRD

1973 FREEDOM BELL

6403 AMTRAK

9502 PRESIDENT WASHINGTON

9507 MANHATTAN

9517 CAPITAL CITY

9527 ROOSEVELT

9512 SUMMERDALE JUNCTION

222

9554 ALTON LIMITED 1981, Baggage, "ARMSTRONG"
— — 20 25

9555 ALTON LIMITED 1981, Combine, "MISSOURI" — — 20 25

9556 ALTON LIMITED 1981, Coach, "WILSON" — — 20 25

9557 ALTON LIMITED 1981, Coach "WEBSTER GROVES"
— — 20 25

9558 ALTON LIMITED 1981, Observation, "CHICAGO" — — 20 25

9559 ROCK ISLAND 1981 Combo, 1860s style car, illuminated, disc-operating couplers, matches 9560 and 9561 and goes with 8004 loco; all only available as separate sale — — 20 25

9560 ROCK ISLAND 1981 Coach, matches 9559 — — 20 25

9561 ROCK ISLAND 1981 Coach, matches 9559 — — 20 25

THE POWHATAN ARROW [Includes Loco, Tender and 9588 Vista Dome]

9562 NORFOLK AND WESTERN 1981 Baggage, "577" and in script "The Powhatan Arrow," first painted extruded aluminum passenger car made by Lionel, with black roof, maroon sides, gold striping and lettering; catalogue number is stamped on the boxes, not the cars — — 50 60

[9563] NORFOLK AND WESTERN 1981, Combine, "578," matches 9562
— — 50 60

[9564] NORFOLK AND WESTERN 1981, Coach, "579," matches 9562
— — 50 60

[9565] NORFOLK AND WESTERN 1981, Coach, "580", matches 9562
— — 50 60

[9566] NORFOLK AND WESTERN 1981, Observation, "581," matches 9562
— — 50 60

[9567] NORFOLK AND WESTERN 1981, Vista Dome, matches 9562
— — 65 75

9569 PENNSYLVANIA 1981, Combination, "PAUL REVERE," matches 9571 — — 65 75

9570 PENNSYLVANIA 1979, "RAILWAY EXPRESS AGENCY," small door baggage, mirror polished aluminum, plastic ends, same trucks as original Lionel baggage cars but with fast angle wheels — 40 50 60

9571 PENNSYLVANIA 1979, "WILLIAM PENN," Pullman, mirror polished aluminum, iridescent maroon stripes; spring loaded lamp receptacle, rerun of 1950's 2543, but 2543 had flat flnished aluminum, brown, flatter stripes, 252 crossing gate light unit with sliding shoe or rivet end contact
— 40 50 60

9572 PENNSYLVANIA 1979, "MOLLY PITCHER," Pullman, matches 9571 — 40 50 60

9573 PENNSYLVANIA 1979, "BETSY ROSS," Vista Dome, matches 9571
— 40 50 60

9574 PENNSYLVANIA 1979, "ALEXANDER HAMILTON," Observation, matches 9571, "Lionel Limited" on back door inside of protective gate
— 40 50 60

9575 PENNSYLVANIA 1979, Pullman, "THOMAS A. EDISON," aluminum passenger car, matches 9571 — — 75 85

TEXAS ZEPHYR (Includes 8054, 8055 and 8062 Engines and 9588 Vista Dome)

9576 BURLINGTON 1980, extruded aluminum Baggage, "SILVER POUCH," die-cast trucks, disc-operating couplers, 16" long, for 0 Gauge track, only available for separate sale — — 45 55

9577 BURLINGTON 1980, Coach, "SILVER HALTER," matches 9576
— — 45 55

9578 BURLINGTON 1980, Coach, "SILVER GLADIOLA," matches 9576
— — 45 55

9579 BURLINGTON 1980, Vista Dome, "SILVER KETTLE," matches 9576
— — — 46

9580 BURLINGTON 1980, Observation, "SILVER VERANDA," matches 9576 — — 45 55

CHESSIE STEAM SPECIAL [Includes 8003 Loco and Tender]

9581 CHESSIE 1980, Baggage, yellow sides, gray roof, blue ends and lettering, vermilion stripe on sides — — 20 25

9582 CHESSIE 1980, Combine, matches 9581 — — 20 25

9583 CHESSIE 1980, Coach, matches 9581 — — 20 25

9584 CHESSIE 1980, Coach, matches 9581 — — 20 25

9585 CHESSIE 1980, Observation, matches 9581 — — 20 25

9588 BURLINGTON 1980, Vista Dome, "SILVER DOME," matches 9576
— — 65 75

SOUTHERN PACIFIC DAYLIGHT

9589 SOUTHERN PACIFIC 1982, extruded aluminum Baggage with distinctive red, orange, white and black "daylight" colors; part of Spring Collector Series; includes four matching cars and a matching pair of F-3 diesels (8260 and 8262), all sold separately — — 50 60

9589 SOUTHERN PACIFIC 1982-83, part of Spring Collector Series for 1982 with four matching cars and a matching pair of F-3 diesels (8260 and 8262). In the 1983 Collector Series Catalogue the set was offered again. Then in the 1983 Fall Collector Series, the 7211 Vista Dome was added. Also in 1983 a 7204 Dining Car and a 8261 Diesel B unit were offered. The three later cars were apparently intentionally made in quantities lower than market demand causing a dramatic short term price appreciation. It will be most interesting to see if the price differentials hold. — — — 75

9590 SOUTHERN PACIFIC 1982-83, Combo, matches 9589
— 50 60 75

9591 SOUTHERN PACIFIC 1982-83, Pullman, matches 9589
— 50 60 75

9592 SOUTHERN PACIFIC 1982-83, Pullman, matches 9589
— 50 60 75

9593 SOUTHERN PACIFIC 1982-83, Observation, matches 9589
— 50 60 75

9594 NEW YORK CENTRAL 1983, double door, extruded aluminum baggage, painted gray and white, sold as a separate item, with matching diesels 8370, 8371, 8372, and matching cars 9595, 9596, 9597, 9598, and 7207, die-cast trucks, operating couplers — — — 80

9595 NEW YORK CENTRAL 1983, extruded aluminum combine, illuminated, matches 9594 — — — 80

9596 NEW YORK CENTRAL 1983, extruded aluminum coach, "WAYNE COUNTRY PULLMAN," illuminated, matches 9594 — — — 80

9596 NEW YORK CENTRAL 1983, extruded aluminum coach, illuminated, "HUDSON RIVER" and "PULLMAN," matches 9594 — — — 80

9598 NEW YORK CENTRAL 1983, extruded aluminum, observation, "MANHATTAN ISLAND" and "PULLMAN," illuminated, matches 9594
— — — 80

FUNDIMENSIONS CONGRESSIONAL PASSENGER CARS

9570 RAILWAY EXPRESS

9571 WILLIAM PENN

9573 BETSY ROSS

9572 MOLLIE PITCHER

9574 ALEXANDER HAMILTON

Chapter XXIII
FUNDIMENSIONS AUTO CARRIERS

9123

Gd. V.G. Exc. Mt.

1973 TCA Convention auto carrier, 1973, black body, Bettendorf trucks. TCA logo in gold on one letter board, "NATIONAL CONVENTION/DEARBORN, MICH./1973" in gold on second letter board, same side. All lettering deep heat-stamped. Gold "TRAILER TRAIN" reporting marks on flatcar side **NRS**

9123 CHESAPEAKE & OHIO 1974, two or three-tier body, either one or two boards lettered, Bettendorf trucks, operating couplers
(A) Three-tier black body, yellow lettering, upper board on each side lettered "C & O," Johnson Collection 5 7 10 12
(B) Same as (A) but C & O markings on both upper and lower boards on each side 7 9 11 14
(C) Three-tier blue body, yellow lettering, one board lettered 4 6 8 10
(D) Three-tier blue body, yellow lettering, two boards lettered 6 8 10 12
(E) Three-tier yellow body, blue lettering, "BLT 1-73," only upper board lettered, only 10 in existence, Fuhrmann Collection — — 400 —
(F) TCA 1973, Dearborn, Michigan, National Convention car, came in 9123 Lionel box but 9123 does not appear on the car's side, black with gold lettering — — 25 30
(G) Two-tier blue plastic body, no road name, white lettering, "BLT 1-73" and "9123," only 6 made, Fuhrmann Collection — — 600 —
(H) Two-tier black plastic body, yellow lettering, "C & O FOR PROGRESS" on boards, "TRAILER TRAIN RTTX 9123" and "BLT 1-73" on frame, Bettendorf trucks, metal wheels, disc-operating couplers, not catalogued, came in factory sealed No. 1386 Rock Island Express set in lieu of the 9125 blue N & W two-tier auto carrier shown on the box and in the 1973-74 catalogues, Johnson Collection **NRS**

9125 NORFOLK & WESTERN 1974, two-tier blue or black body, white lettering, single board lettered, Bettendorf trucks, operating couplers, sold only in sets
(A) Blue body, lettered with road name, number and built date, "TRAILER TRAIN" 8 11 15 25
(B) Black body, Wilson Collection 8 15 20 40

9126 CHESAPEAKE & OHIO 1973-74, three-tier body, either one or two boards lettered, Bettendorf trucks, operating couplers
(A) Yellow body, blue lettering, one board lettered 2 4 6 8
(B) Light yellow body, light blue lettering, two boards lettered 3 6 9 12
(C) Same as (B) but one board lettered 2 4 6 8

9129 NORFOLK & WESTERN 1975, brown body, white lettering, single board stamped, Bettendorf trucks, two operating couplers 2 4 8 9

9139 PENN CENTRAL 1977, green body, white lettering, single board stamped, Bettendorf trucks, two operating couplers 2 4 8 9

9145 ILLINOIS CENTRAL GULF 1977, orange body, black lettering, single board stamped, Bettendorf trucks, two operating couplers 2 4 8 9

9216 GREAT NORTHERN 1978, blue plastic, white lettering, from Milwaukee Special set, black car stops on each level, standard 0 trucks, disc-operating couplers with tabs 4 8 10 12

9125

9126

9129

9139

9145

9281 A.T.S.F. 1978-79, two-level carrier in red plastic, white lettering, white and red Santa Fe electrocal on upper boards on both sides, lower boards blank, "BLT 1-78," black vehicle stops on ends, Bettendorf trucks, disc-operating couplers with tabs 2 5 7 9

9351 PENNSYLVANIA 1980, three-tier tuscan body, gold lettering with old-style red and gold keystone insignia on upper board, blank lower board — 5 7 10

225

Chapter XXIV
FUNDIMENSIONS FLAT CARS

                              Gd. V.G. Exc. Mt.

6500 LIONEL 1982, depressed center die-cast flat   NRS

6504 L.A.S.E.R. 1981-82, helicopter on black flat, similar to Lionel 3419, from No. 1150 L.A.S.E.R. set   — — 12 15

6505 L.A.S.E.R. 1981-82, satellite tracking car, similar to Lionel 3540, from No. 1150 L.A.S.E.R. set   — — 12 15

6506 L.A.S.E.R. 1981-82, security car, see Chapter XVIII, Cabooses   — — 12 15

6507 L.A.S.E.R. 1981-82, A.L.C.M. cruise missile on blue flat car, from No. 1150 L.A.S.E.R. set   — — 12 15

6509 LIONEL 1981, depressed center die-cast flat with four trucks, disc-operating couplers   — — 30 35

6561 Unlettered, 1983, olive drab flat with cruise missile, fixed couplers. From No. 1355 Commando Assault Train; decals furnished with set, Caponi comment   — — — 10

6562 Unlettered, 1983, olive drab flat with crates and barrels, fixed couplers. From No. 1355 Commando Assault Train; decals furnished with set, Caponi comment   — — — 10

6564 Unlettered, 1983, olive drab flat with two tanks, fixed couplers. From No. 1355 Commando Assault Train; decals furnished with set, Caponi comment   — — — 10

6670 DERRICK See Operating Cars, Chapter XX.

9014 TRAILER TRAIN 1978, yellow body, black lettering and stakes, plastic trucks and wheels, manumatic couplers, from No. 1864 Santa Fe Double Diesel set   — — 3 4

9019 FLAT CAR, 1978, a base that came with either a superstructure for a box or crane car, work caboose, or log loader, as part of No. 1862 Logging Empire or No. 1860 Timberline set   — — 1 2

9020 UNION PACIFIC 1970-77, plastic wheels, one manumatic coupler, one fixed coupler
(A) Medium yellow body, black lettering   2 3 4 5
(B) Light yellow body, light blue lettering   2 3 4 5
(C) Dark yellow body, dark blue lettering   2 3 4 5
(D) Medium yellow body, blue lettering   2 3 4 5
(E) Medium light yellow body, blue lettering   2 3 4 5
(F) Medium yellow body, blue lettering, wood-grained floor   2 3 4 5
(G) Medium light yellow body, blue lettering, wood-grained floor   2 3 4 5
(H) Unpainted tuscan plastic, heat-stamped, yellow lettered, "CAPY 100000 LD LMT 121800 LT WT 47200 UP 9020 UNION PACIFIC BLT 1-70," wood-grained floor, 16 stakes, Timken trucks, one fixed, one disc-operating coupler, Wolf Collection   NRS

9022 A.T. & S.F. 1971, 78, yellow lettering, metal wheels, one operating coupler, one fixed coupler, bulkheads, logs
(A) Red body, wood-grained floor   3 4 5 7
(B) Red body, plain floor   3 4 5 7
(C) Black body   3 4 5 8

9023 MKT 1974, 78, black body, white lettering, metal wheels, one operating coupler, one fixed coupler, bulkheads, logs   1 2 3 4

9024 CHESAPEAKE & OHIO 1974, yellow body, blue lettering, plastic wheels, fixed couplers   1 2 3 4

9025 D T I 1978, probably yellow body, black lettering and stakes, reportedly came with No. 1964 Santa Fe Double Diesel as an optional insert, verification requested   NRS

9026 REPUBLIC STEEL 1975-77, 80, blue body, white lettering, plastic wheels, one manumatic coupler, one fixed coupler, wood-grained floor   1 2 3 4

9120 NORTHERN PACIFIC Green body, white lettering, white vans with black lettering, one operating coupler, one fixed coupler, wheel stops
(A) Timken trucks, MPC builder's plates, no side slip bars 4 5 6 8
(B) Bettendorf trucks, no MPC builder's plates, with side slip bars   4 5 6 8

9121 L & N 1974, 1976, 78-79, with yellow dozer and scraper kit, Bettendorf trucks
(A) Brown body, white lettering, Kaiser Collection 4 5 7 9
(B) Maroon body, white lettering   4 5 7 9

9122 NORTHERN PACIFIC Vans with black lettering, Bettendorf trucks, disc couplers
(A) Green body, white lettering and white vans, Bettendorf trucks, disc couplers   5 7 12 15
(B) Tuscan body, white lettering, gray vans   4 5 6 8

9124 P L E Green unpainted plastic body, lettered "PC PENN CENTRAL BLT 1-73 CAPY 14000 LD LMT 136700 LT WT 63300," comes with three logs, two black plastic ribs, mold number "6424-11" on underside, arch bar trucks, one operating coupler with plastic semi-disc for manual operation (known as manumatic coupler), one fixed coupler, Cunningham and Ristau Collections   — 2 3 4

9133 BURLINGTON NORTHERN 1976, 80, green body, white lettering, Bettendorf trucks, disc couplers
(A) No load   4 5 6 8
(B) Two Burlington Northern trailers, 1980   — — 7 9

9149 C P RAIL Red body, white lettering, silver, white, and black van with white letters, Bettendorf trucks, disc couplers   5 7 9 11

9157 C & O 1976-78, 81, blue body, yellow lettering, P & H yellow crane kit, Bettendorf trucks, disc couplers   5   9 11

9158 PENN CENTRAL 1976-77; 80, green body, white lettering, steam shovel kit, Bettendorf trucks, disc couplers   5 7 9 11

9212 LCCA 1976, Atlanta, flat with vans, originally stamped only on one side, LCCA offered to restamp them for members and many were restamped, 3500 mfgd.
(A) One side stamped   — — 20 25
(B) Two sides stamped   — — 25 30

9222 L & N 1983, tuscan flat car with two "L & N" trailers, disc operating couplers.   — — — 13

9232 ALLIS CHALMERS 1980, gray atomic reactor load, orange base, blue lettering, rerun of No.6510 from 1958-61   — — 20 25

9233 TRANSFORMER 1980, tuscan painted depressed center die-cast flat with red transformer with white insulators, lettered "LIONEL TRANS - FORMER CAR," four trucks with 16 wheels, part of No. 1071 MID ATLANTIC LIMITED set   — — 35 40

9234 RADIOACTIVE WASTE 1980, red flat with white lettered "LIONEL," two rails run car length, two removable energy containers with flashing red lights   — — 25 30

9282 GREAT NORTHERN 1978, 81-82, orange body, green lettering, black plastic brakewheel easily broken, green vans with elaborate GN decal, trailer undersides marked "LIONEL" with "MPC 1000" without letters "MPC", van with hole for tractor and tractor lift   5 7 9 13

9285 IC GULF Black body, white lettering, silver vans with black lettering, Bettendorf trucks, disc couplers, in sets only   8 10 15 20

9306 ATSF 1980, brown base and fence, two horses, part of No. 1053, The James Gang Set   — — 9 13

NOTE: 9325 is used on several different cars.

9325 NW 1980-81, part of uncatalogued No. 1157 Wabash Cannonball set and No. 9196 Rolling Stock Assortment. Black plastic body, 8 1/2" long, with heat-stamped white letters on side: "BLT 1-79 N & W 9325 NORFOLK

9020

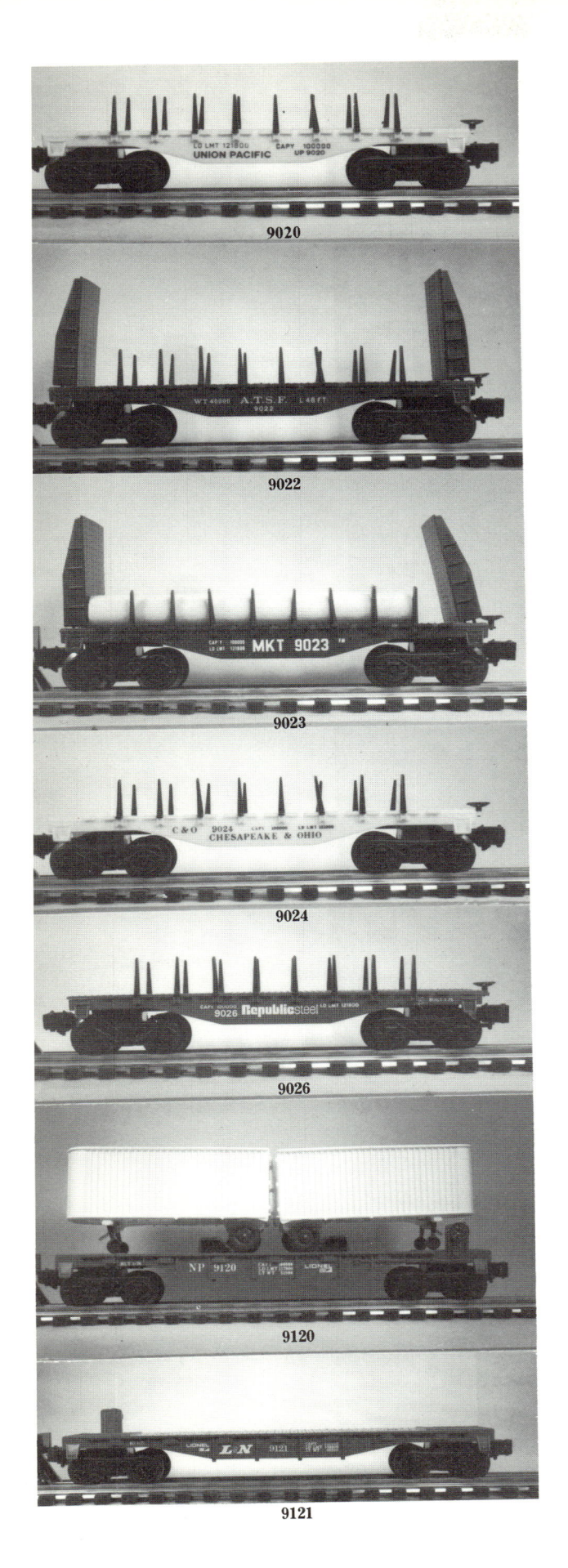

9022

9023

9024

9026

9120

9121

9122

9133

9149

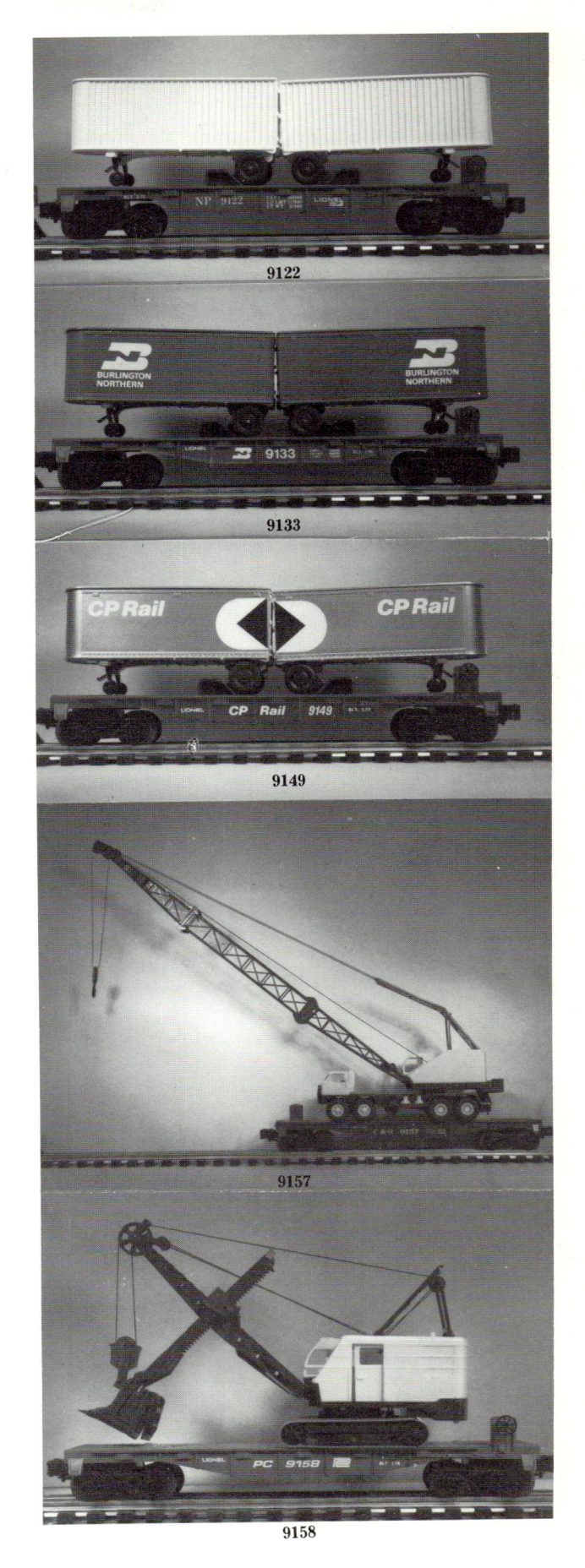

9157

9158

227

AND WESTERN LIONEL." Simulated wood grain floor, partial floor cutout about 9/16" in diameter, plastic brakewheel, two-rung tan plastic fencing around floor perimeter, with three plastic pieces offset to clear brakewheel on end, Bettendorf trucks, plastic wheels, one operating and one dummy coupler. Bottom stamped "9325-T-5A LIONEL MT. CLEMENS MICH. 48045." Came in box with ends marked "LIONEL 027 GAUGE FLAT CAR WITH FENCES 6-9325." Barry Smith Collection — 1 2 3

9325 NW flat car with cab and boom, 1978-79, red plastic flat car with yellow plastic cab and boom, "NW" in white. Unassembled; purchaser snaps car together. Bettendorf trucks, two dummy couplers. Car came in box numbered 9364, but number on car is 9325. This number also used on companion dump car. Catalogued with "dump car and crane car assortment" in 1978-79
— 1 2 3

9325 DUMP CAR came with "dump car and crane car assortment" in 1978-79, details needed.

9333 SOUTHERN PACIFIC TOFC flat car, 1980, tuscan body, Bettendorf trucks, white lettering, one brakewheel, two white vans with black wheel and black "SOUTHERN PACIFIC" lettering on sides with red-outlined large "S" and "P", Griggs Collection — — 8 12

9352 TRAILER TRAIN 1980, black flat car with two yellow Chicago & North Western vans, lettered "FALCON SERVICE" — — 8 10

9379 LIONEL flat car with derrick, catalogued in 1980 as part of Texas and Pacific diesel set, but never made **Not Manufactured**

9383 UNION PACIFIC 1980, piggyback, part of FARR Series 2, available for separate sale only — — 20 25

9389 RADIOACTIVE WASTE 1981, two rails run car length, two removable energy containers with flashing red lights — — 14 18

9553 W & RR 1978-79, brown base and fence, gold lettering, six horses, operating disc couplers, metal wheels, available separately, matches General loco and coaches — — 15 20

9823 A. T. & S. F. 1976, tuscan body, white lettering, sprung die-cast trucks; two sets of tan plastic crates — 15 20 25

9031

9032

9033

9055

9131

9136

9140

9141

9142

9143

9144

9283

9284

9315

Chapter XXV

FUNDIMENSIONS GONDOLAS

Gd. V.G. Exc. Mt.

6200 F.E.C. 1981, orange body, yellow numbers and letters, three silver-finished plastic canisters, part of No. 1154 Reading Yard King set
— — 8 10

6201 UNION PACIFIC 1982, security guard chases hobo around crates, (uses belt drive from axle) — — 9 13

6201 UNION PACIFIC 1983, yellow body, tan crates, red lettering, animated car with vibrator motor; railroad cop chases hobo around crates
— — — 15

6202 WESTERN MARYLAND 1982, black with white lettering, black plastic coal load, standard 0 trucks, disc-operating couplers, part of No. 1260 Continental Limited set **NRS**

6205 CANADIAN PACIFIC 1983, tuscan with white lettering, CP electrocal, die-cast trucks, disc operating couplers, two gray canisters, available as separate sale item — — — 16

6206 C & I M 1983, red with white lettering, two gray atomic energy type canisters without lights and lettering, disc operating couplers, part of No. 1354 Northern Freight Fixer set — — — 8

6207 SOUTHERN 1983, black with white lettering, two red canisters, part of No. 1353 Southern Streak set — — 3 4

6208 B & O 1983, black body, yellow "B & O" and "6208" at left of car, yellow Chessie cat at center, and yellow "Chessie System" at right. Reporting marks along lower girders, disc operating couplers, standard O die cast sprung trucks. Designed to be added to the 1980 Royal Limited set, LaVoie comment — — — 20

9017 WABASH 1978, 80-81, red with white lettering, three canisters
— — — 4

9030 KICKAPOO 1972, 79, black base
(A) Green top 2 3 5 7
(B) Red top 1 2 3 4
(C) Yellow top 2 3 4 6

9031 NICKEL PLATE 1974, 79, 83, brown body, white lettering, Bettendorf trucks, fixed couplers 1974, 79, operating couplers, 1983. We do not know if the 1983 version has small or large brakewheel. The 1983 version came as part of No. 1253 Heavy Iron set.
(A) Large brake wheel 2 3 5 7
(B) Small brake wheel 2 3 5 7

9032 SOUTHERN PACIFIC 1975, 78, red body, white lettering, Bettendorf trucks, fixed couplers
(A) Light red body, small brakewheel 1 2 3 4
(B) Dark red body, small brakewheel 1 2 3 4
(C) Medium red body, large brakewheel 1 2 3 4

9033 PENN CENTRAL 1977, 79, 81, 82, light green body, white lettering, Bettendorf trucks, fixed couplers, small brakewheel 1 2 3 4

9055 REPUBLIC STEEL 1977-81, yellow body, dark blue lettering, one fixed coupler, one manumatic coupler, plastic Bettendorf trucks, plastic wheels 1 2 3 4

9131 RIO GRANDE 1974, orange body, black lettering, Bettendorf trucks, one disc coupler, one fixed coupler, no MPC logo
(A) Light orange body 1 2 3 4
(B) Medium orange body 1 2 3 4
(C) Darker orange body 1 2 3 4

9136 REPUBLIC STEEL 1976-79, blue body, white lettering, Bettendorf trucks, one manumatic coupler, one fixed coupler, plastic wheels, MPC logo
(A) Lighter blue 1 2 3 4
(B) Medium blue 1 2 3 4
(C) Darker blue 1 2 3 4

(D) Darker blue, MPC logo dropped 1 2 3 4

9140 BURLINGTON 1970-71, 80-81, green body, white lettering, one manumatic coupler, one fixed coupler, plastic wheels
(A) Light green body, Timken trucks, flat surface brakewheel, MPC logo, 1970 1 2 3 4
(B) Medium light green body, Bettendorf trucks, no MPC logo, 1971
1 2 3 4
(C) Medium dark green body, Bettendorf trucks, no MPC logo, 1971
1 2 3 4
(D) Dark green body, Bettendorf trucks, no MPC logo, 1971
1 2 4 5

9141 BURLINGTON NORTHERN 1971, green body, white lettering, Bettendorf trucks, one manumatic coupler, one fixed coupler, metal wheels, MPC logo, flat surface brakewheel
(A) Light green body 1 2 3 4
(B) Medium green body 1 2 3 4
(C) Dark green body 1 2 3 4
(D) Tuscan body — — 95 115

9142 REPUBLIC STEEL 1971 green body, white lettering, Bettendorf trucks, one manumatic coupler, one fixed coupler, plastic wheels, MPC logo
(A) Dark green body 1 2 3 4
(B) Medium green body, whirly brakewheel, Rohlfing Collection
1 2 3 4
(C) Medium green body, flat brakewheel, stamped "LCCA", Rohlfing Collection **NRS**

9143 CANADIAN NATIONAL 1973, maroon body, white lettering, Bettendorf trucks, one manumatic coupler, one fixed coupler, metal wheels, MPC logo, sold primarily in Canada 4 6 9 12

9144 RIO GRANDE 1974, black body, yellow lettering, Bettendorf trucks, two disc couplers, metal wheels, no MPC logo 1 2 4 5

9283 UNION PACIFIC 1977, yellow body, red lettering, Bettendorf trucks, disc-couplers, metal wheels, no MPC logo 2 5 8 10

9284 SANTA FE 1977-78, red and yellow body, yellow and red lettering, Bettendorf trucks, disc couplers, metal wheels, no MPC logo
2 5 8 11

9290 UNION PACIFIC 1983, operating barrel car, man "unloads" barrel, vibrator mechanism, five or six wooden barrels, plastic unloading bin, black with yellow lettering. Die-cast trucks, disc operating couplers. Reissue of 3562 type car from 1954-58 although with new road name. Only availble as part of No. 1361 Gold Coast Limited set — — — 60

9307 ERIE 1979-83, red with white lettering, gray crate load, animated car with vibrator motor, railroad cop chases hobo around crates
(A) Partially painted hobo — — 33 40
(B) Completely painted hobo, Mellan Collection. Other observations show differences in the cop and hobo figures, such as elaborate hand-painting on either or both figures which may be factory production. Further reader comments are invited **NRS**
(C) Same as (A), but lettering and numbering completely absent from one side of car, probable factory error, Moss Collection **NRS**

9315 SOUTHERN PACIFIC 1979, brown plastic body painted brown, white lettering, "BLT 1-79," Southern Pacific decal with white letters on black background, built-in small brakewheel, part of Southern Pacific Special set, standard 0 trucks, disc couplers with tabs 8 10 15 20

9336 CP RAIL 1979, red plastic car, 9 9/16" long, white lettering, brakewheels embossed in car ends, black and white logo appears at end opposite brakewheel, sprung die-cast trucks, disc-operating couplers with small tabs, no apparent mold designation on car, from No. 1971 Quaker City Limited set, Miller observation — — 10 15

9340 ILLINOIS CENTRAL GULF 1979-81, orange with black lettering, yellow canisters, plastic wheels, Bettendorf trucks — — 3 5

1954 LET'S PLAN THE FINEST LIONEL LAYOUT IN TOWN 16 pages including covers. 10 7/8" wide x 8 1/4" high, front cover shows dad and son with Lackawanna Train Master, Seaboard NW-Z and 736 steamer; front cover and interior pages printed in black and red ink on white paper. Salamone Collection 2 3 5 9

1955

ADVANCE CATALOGUE
(A) 11 1/4" x 7 3/4", 20 black and white pages, lightweight coated stock
5 10 15 20
(B) 11 1/4" x 7 3/4", 20 pages including covers, orange and black ink on white stock featuring magnetraction. Salamone Collection
5 10 25 40

A SPECIAL DEALER'S CATALOGUE showing set compositions and components, cars, track, etc. White with black and white halftones of 1955 sets on gloss paper, 27 pages printed one side only, shows 27 sets (rare - 3 in existence in Chicago area). Zydlo Collection **NRS**

CATALOGUE 11 1/4" x 7 5/8", 44 pages, full color, coated stock, cover illustration in white with five trains and six happy faces 3 6 9 12

ELLIOTT ROWLAND CATALOGUE Usually imprinted with store advertising
(A) 8 3/8" x 11 1/8", yellow covers with "Lionel Trains by (Store Name)," pages 5 and 14 are yellow, pulp paper; cover illustration shows father leaning against easy chair while grandfather operates the trains and children look on .50 1.00 2.00 3.00
(B) Same as (A), but color cover with blue background .50 1.00 2.00 3.00
(C) 8 3/8" x 11 1/8", color covers, pulp paper, cover illustration shows family looking at Lionel layout through store window .50 1.00 2.00 3.00

HOW TO OPERATE LIONEL TRAINS AND ACCESSORIES Includes Service Station listing, 8 1/2" x 5 1/2", 64 pages in black and white, plus brown and white wrap around cover, Form 926-55 .25 .50 1.00 2.00

ACCESSORY CATALOGUE 11 1/4" x 7 3/4", front cover printed in black and orange ink on white stock, inside pages printed in black ink on white stock, 20 pages including covers. This is the same as Advance Catalogue (B) except for title and ink. Salamone Collection 2 5 12 20

TEMPLATES FOR LIONEL "027" LAYOUTS Form 1061 Rev 11-55 upper left corner. Peel off track templates (reusble if used on surface such as porcelain, linoleum, etc.) 8 1/2" x 11" .50 1.00 2.00 3.00

1956

ADVANCE CATALOGUE 11" x 8", 48 pages, black and white, red cover with "Order Now!" 5 10 15 20

CATALOGUE 11 1/4" x 7 5/8", 40 pages, full color, coated stock, cover illustration shows PRR and NH Electric, Lionel Lines steam loco, 3530, 3360, and 3927
(A) "Remember: Lionel Train Sets Start as Low as $19.95...." in white block on back cover 3 5 7 10
(B) No lettering in white block on back cover 3 5 7 10

ACCESSORY CATALOGUE 11" x 8", 24 pages, red and black on pulp paper
1 2 3 4

HOW TO CLEAN AND LUBRICATE... 5" x 4", 12 pages, black and white, coated stock .10 .25 .35 .50

HOW TO OPERATE LIONEL TRAINS AND ACCESSORIES
(A) Includes Service Station listings, 8 1/2" x 5 1/4", 64 pages, black and white, red and blue wrap around cover, form 925-56. Graham Collection
.25 .50 1.00 2.00
(B) Pale yellow and dark blue cover, drawing of dad and son playing trains, 64 pages copyrighted inside front cover of 1950, came with advertising sheet, "Send for Billboards" (25 cents) one side and send for "Romance of Model Railroading Book" on other side, copyrighted 1956, contains individual items only. Weber Collection **NRS**

1956 ELLIOTT ROWLAND CATALOGUE 247 pages including covers, 8 1/4" wide x 11" high, front covers, in full color, shows mom, dad, and two children looking in a store window at a Lionel layout, catalogue shows retail prices. Rowland was authorized by Lionel to print and distribute these inexpensive catalogues depicting the Lionel line. Salamone Collection
2 3 4 6

1957

ADVANCE CATALOGUE 11" x 8 1/4", 54 pages, red and black covers, black and white coated stock 5 10 15 20

AND NOW H10 - BY LIONEL 10 3/4" x 7 5/8", "For the Discriminating Hobbyist...," supplement to Advance Catalogue, four-page color folder, may have been distributed separately and/or in consumer catalogue in addition to Advance Catalogue .25 .50 1.00 2.00

COLLECTOR CARDS .10 .25 .35 .50
Boston And Maine — M-K-T
Virginian — Norfolk & Western
Seaboard — Rio Grande
Canadian Pacific — Baltimore and Ohio
Rock Island — Pennsylvania
Southern — Great Northern
New Haven — General
Northern — Milwaukee
Santa Fe — Wabash
Western Pacific — Union Pacific
Alaskan — Burlington

SALES SHEET: VITAL SMALL PARTS FOR LIONEL TRAINS, SUPER "O" TRACK FOR LIONEL TRAINS 19 3/4" x 14", black and white. Graham Collection .50 1.00 2.00 3.00

CATALOGUE 11 1/4" x 7 1/2", 52 pages, full color, coated stock, cover has "New Super 'O' Track" 1 2 3 7

ACCESSORY CATALOGUE With Service Station Directory for 1957-1958, 10" x 7 1/2", 32 pages, red and black covers, black and white pulp paper
.25 .50 1.00 2.00

HOW TO OPERATE LIONEL TRAINS AND ACCESSORIES 8 1/2" x 5 1/2", 64 black and white pages plus red and black wrap-around cover, pulp paper .25 .50 1.00 2.00

BANNER: HO BY LIONEL THE LEADER IN MODEL RAILROADING 21 3/16" x 6 1/2", yellow paper printed with black and red ink. Graham Collection .50 1.00 2.00 3.00

POSTER: LIONEL TRAINS AND ACCESSORIES COME IN AND GET YOUR NEW FREE CATALOGUE 28" x 12", full color, six engines with 2379 and 746 in center. Graham Collection 1 2 3 5

BANNER: COME IN AND GET YOUR BIG NEW LIONEL CATALOGUE 10 1/4" x 4 1/4", red and black ink on white paper. Graham Collection
.25 .50 .75 1.00

1958

ADVANCE CATALOGUE 10 7/8" x 8 1/4", 64 pages, red and black cover, NH and M & StL trains passing missile launching sight, black and white, H0 scale section has burgundy marker with gold stamped "H0"
5 10 15 20

CATALOGUE 11 1/4" x 7 5/8", 56 pages, cover like Advance Catalogue but in full color on coated stock 2 4 6 8

ACCESSORY CATALOGUE With Service Station Directory, 11 1/8" x 8", 32 pages, red and black cover, black and white, pulp paper. Title "Lionel 1958 Accessory Catalog" contains individual items only. Cover picture is similar to regular catalogue, inside front cover copyrighted 1958. Weber Collection .50 1.00 2.00 3.00

ADVANCE HO CATALOGUE 10 7/8" x 8 1/8", 8 pages, black and white, cover has red background and illustration of H0 display, rear cover shows dealer displays "For Your H0 Department" .50 1.00 2.00 3.00

HO CATALOGUE
(A) 8 3/8" x 10 7/8", 6 page fold-out, full color, coated stock
.50 1.00 2.00 3.00
(B) 8 1/4" x 11 1/4", 8 pages, full color, coated stock .50 1.00 2.00 3.00

1959

ADVANCE CATALOGUE 8 1/2" x 10 7/8", 44 pages, full color, black and white, fold-out pages, coated stock, cover lettered "Lionel 1959," illustration shows 1872 General and 44 missile launcher 3 7 12 18

CATALOGUE 11" x 8 1/2", 56 pages, full color, coated stock, cover illustration shows 736, 1872 General and 44 U.S. Army 3 5 9 12

ACCESSORY CATALOGUE 11" high x 8" wide, red and black front cover with 1872 and 44 locos, black ink only on pulp interior pages, 36 pages. Schreiner Collection .75 1.50 2.00 3.00

1960

ADVANCE CATALOGUE 8 1/2" x 11", 60 pages, color cover, black and white, red and white back cover with promotional slogan, coated stock, cover illustration shows father and son viewing twin railroad layout
3   5   7   12

CATALOGUE 11" x 8 3/8", 56 pages, full color, coated stock, cover illustration shows family viewing close-up section of twin railroad layout
3   5   9   12

ACCESSORY CATALOGUE With Service Station listing, 8 5/8" x 11", 40 pages, color cover, black and white pulp paper   1   2   3   4

HOW TO OPERATE LIONEL TRAINS AND ACCESSORIES
(A) 8 1/2" x 5 3/8", 64 black and white pages on coated stock, heavy paper wrap around cover in black and white with red background, Form 926-60
1   2   3   4

(B) Cover shows black and white photo of N & W Y6b, left and rear side with orangish red right half with black and white lettering, 62 pages, copyrighted 1960 inside rear cover. Smith and Weber Collections
1   2   3   4

CATALOGUE POSTER 10 1/4" x 4 1/4", one-side, coated stock, apparently intended for store window
(A) "Come in and get your Big New Lionel Catalog," red and black letters on white background   1   2   4   6
(B) Same as (A), but black and white letters on red background
1   2   4   6

GET SET FOR ACTION.... Promotional flier, 22 1/4" x 27 1/2" folded to 11 1/8" x 7 1/8", two sides, red and black on heavy white stock
1   2   4   6

PLEDGE POSTER 9 1/4" x 11 3/4", black and white, green border, "We pledge to all Lionel Customers....," small tear-off section at bottom reads, "Mr. Dealer: Display this message prominently"   .50 1.00 2.00 3.00

PROMOTIONAL POSTER 22" x 8 1/2", one side, coated stock, black and white, "Lionel Trains and Accessories" in red letters   1   2   4   6

CONTEST POSTER 22" x 8 1/2", one-side, coated stock, black and white on red background, "Hey Kids! Big Lionel Contest..."   1   2   4   6

CONTEST INSTRUCTIONS 11" x 8 3/8", 4-page folder, color cover similar to catalogue cover, black and white interior, coated stock
.50 1.00 2.00 3.00

UNION PACIFIC RAILROAD, A BRIEF HISTORY 5 3/16" wide x 8 7/8" high, printed April 1946, 16th printing, March 1960, 16 pages, coated stock. Railroads buffs will find in this brief history of the Union Pacific Railroad a wealth of information. Lionel is indebted to the Union Pacific Railroad for providing this material. Smith Collection   .50 .75 1.00 2.00

LIONEL TRACK LAYOUTS FOR "027", SUPER "O" AND H0 GAUGES, START BUILDING YOURS TODAY! 8 3/8" x 11", 4 pages, not numbered
(A) Price 10 cents on front, page 2 has "1-115" on lower right, heavy white paper black and gray. "Address inquiries to: Lionel Service, Dept 74-E, Hoffman Place, Hillside, NJ 07205" on back page. Smith Collection
.25 .50 .75 1.00

(B) Similiar to (A) but no price, no number, coated paper stock. On bottom last 3 pages concerning inquires, "simply write to: Engineer Bill c/o The Lionel Corp., 15 East 26th St., New York, 10 NY." Smith Collection
.25 .50 .75 1.00

HO CATALOGUE 8 1/2" x 10 7/8", 12 pages, full color, coated stock, cover reads, "Operating Cars - 1960's Most Exciting H0 News"   1   2   3   4

HOW TO OPERATE LIONEL HO TRAINS 8 1/2" x 5 1/2", 24 pages plus red and black covers   .50 1.00 2.00 3.00

1961

ADVANCE CATALOGUE 8 1/2" x 11", 76 pages, John Bruce Medaris on cover, color cover, black and white coated stock   3   5   7   10

SALES TIPS 8 1/2" x 11", 4-page folder, John Bruce Medaris on cover, black and white coated stock, sales tips for dealers   .50 1.00 2.00 3.00

CATALOGUE
(A) 8 1/2" x 11", 56 pages, layout and science sets on cover, red and black covers, inside black and white pulp paper, "Honorary Stockholder" on rear cover   .50 1.00 2.00 3.00
(B) 8 1/2" x 11", 72 pages, cover same as (A), but catalogue differs, full color coated stock, HO raceways on rear cover   1   2   4   6

JOIN WITH LIONEL Dealer flier, 25 7/8" x 22", order form for custom ad mats (used for store windows and advertisements), one-side, black and white   .50 1.00 2.00 3.00

LIONEL-PORTER SCIENCECRAFT CATALOGUE
(A) 8 1/2" x 11", 8 pages, red and black, coated stock, "The Lionel Corporation, Hagerstown, Maryland"   .50 1.00 2.00 3.00
(B) 8 1/2" x 11", 8 pages, red and black ink on white coated stock, "The Lionel Corporation, Hagerstown, Maryland." This catalogue was initially dated as 1961 based on associated materials. However, a price sheet supplied by I. D. Smith states, "Net billing prices to you are guaranteed against voluntary . . . decline during 1962." This could indicate a 1961-62 catalogue since schools would be one of the principal purchasers of this equipment and school years span the calendar year. Further comments requested. Smith Collection   .50 1.00 2.00 3.00

VITAL SMALL PARTS FOR LIONEL TRAINS sales sheet, 8 1/2" x 11", folded, unfolds to 17" x 11", printed one side, block ink on heavy paper, Lock-ons, Sayer O track parts, 0 and 0-27 track pens and adapter pens, contractors, controllers actuators, No. 2524, 11-61, Printed in U.S. of America, lower left. Smith Collection   .50 1.00 2.00 3.00

1962

CATALOGUE 8 1/2" x 11", 100 pages, cover lettered "Lionel 1962"
1   2   4   6

ADVANCE CATALOGUE "Lionel Trains and Accessories - The Leader in Model RR 1962," 64 pages, 4 color cover, black and white inside, includes displays and H.O., 8 1/2" x 11" vertical. Zydlo Collection   NRS

ACCESSORY CATALOGUE 8 3/8" x 10 7/8", 62 pages, full color cover, first 2 and last 2 pages are coated stock, rest is black and white pulp. Ocilka Collection   NRS

ACCESSORY CATALOGUE 8 3/8" x 10 7/8", 40 pages, red and black cover, black and white, pulp paper   1   2   3   4

LIONEL-SPEAR-TRIANG ADVANCE CATALOGUE 8 3/8" x 11", 56 pages, color coated stock, top cover illustration shows science lab, bottom illustration shows phonographs, rear cover features "Scalextric" racing
1   2   4   6

LIONEL-SPEAR CATALOGUE 8 3/8" x 11", 56 pages, color coated stock, cover lettered "Lionel-Spear '62"   1   2   3   4

1963

CATALOGUE 8 3/8" x 10 7/8", 56 pages, color cover, red and black interior coated stock   1   2   4   6

ADVANCE CATALOGUE "Lionel 1963," 8 1/2" x 11", 80 pages, yellow, black and white cover, interior black and white, includes trains, Lionel-Porter, and racing sets, etc. Smith and Zydlo Collections   NRS

ACCESSORY CATALOGUE With Service Station listing, 8 3/8" x 10 7/8", 40 pages, blue and black cover, interior black and white pulp paper
.50 1.00 2.00 3.00

SCIENCE CATALOGUE 8 3/8" x 10 7/8", 32 pages, red and black two-tone pulp paper, cover lettered "Lionel 1963 Science Catalog"   1   2   3   4

1964

CATALOGUE 8 3/8" x 10 7/8", 24 pages, black and blue
(A) Pulp paper, page 13 lists 6402 flat car at $2.50   1   2   4   5
(B) Same as (A), but 6402 is incorrectly listed at $3.95   1   2   4   5
(C) Same as (A), but coated stock   1   2   5   7
(D) Same as (B), but coated stock   1   2   5   7

LIONEL RACEWAYS CATALOGUE 8 1/2" x 11", 12 pages, green and black coated stock, cover lettered "Lionel Raceways and Accessories for 1964"   .50 1.00 2.00 3.00

HELIOS 21 Remote Control Space Craft, 8 1/2" x 11", 4-page folder, red and black with black and white photos, cover lettered "Hey! Hey Helios 21 is Here," Advance for dealers   .50 1.00 2.00 3.00

PROJECT X CATALOGUE 22 7/8" x 11", tri-fold, red and black with silver, Lyter-N-Air remote control space ships, Advance for dealers
.50 1.00 2.00 3.00

LIONEL "U-DRIVE" BOAT, 8 1/2" x 11", 2 pages. This versatile boat can be used in a backyard, local pond or small lake. Stekoll Collection
.50 1.00 2.00 3.00

LIONEL COMBINES SIGHT WITH SOUND Phono-Vision, 8 1/2" x 11", 4 pages, two color printing, front cover shows boy and girl with record player with slide projector lens on right side and image shown on inside of record player case, believed to be 1964 (Verification of date requested) Stekoll Collection
.50 1.00 2.00 3.00

1965

CATALOGUE 8 1/2" x 10 7/8", 40 pages, multi-color printing and backgrounds

(A) Pulp paper	1	2	4	5
(B) Coated stock	1	2	5	7
(C) Same as (A) 6119 and 6401 (errata)	1	2	4	5
(D) Same as (B) 6119 and 6401 (errata)	1	2	5	7

HOW TO OPERATE LIONEL TRAINS 8 1/2" x 11", 32 pages, black and white plus yellow wrap around cover, uncoated paper   .50 1.00 2.00 3.00

LIONEL-PORTER SCIENCE SETS CATALOGUE 8 3/8" x 10 7/8", 8 pages, two-tone brown and black, coated stock, 8 items illustrated on cover
.25 .50 .75 1.00

LIONEL-SPEAR CATALOGUE 8 1/2" x 11 1/8", 4-page folder, two-tone brown and black coated stock, cover lettered "Lionel-Spear 1964"
.25 .50 .75 1.00

PHONO-VISION CATALOGUE 8 1/2" x 11", 4-page folder, two-tone yellow and black coated stock, cover lettered "Lionel Combines Sight with Sound! Phono-Vision"   .25 .50 .75 1.00

1966

CATALOGUE 10 7/8" x 8 3/8", 40 pages, full color coated stock, cover illustration shows father and son watching trains rush by
(A) Set illustrations on pages 8 and 10   .50 1.00 2.00 3.00
(B) No illustrations as in (A)   .50 1.00 2.00 3.00

WELCOME TO THE WONDERFUL WORLD OF LIONEL Trains, raceways, phonographs, science sets, 8 1/2" x 21 3/4" folded to 3 1/2" x 8 1/2", black and white with orange and blue trim, No. 1-117. Dixon Collection **NRS**

1967

CATALOGUE NOT ISSUED

1968

TRAINS AND ACCESSORIES CATALOGUES 8 1/2" x 11", 8 pages, folds out to 34" x 11", full color coated stock   1 2 3 5

HAGERSTOWN SET 11" x 8 1/2", two sided, blue on white coated stock, shows 11600 set on one side with "Lionel '68," track and accessories on the other with "The Lionel Toy Corporation - Hagerstown, Maryland 27140"
(A) Original   .50 1.00 2.00 3.00
(B) Reproduction by Greenberg Publishing Co.   — — — .50

1969

CATALOGUE
(A) 11" x 8 1/2", 8 pages, full color coated stock   1 2 3 5
(B) 11 1/8" x 8 1/2", 8 pages, similiar to (A), but printed on brown and white coated stock, pages not numbered   1 2 3 5

DATE UNKNOWN

Help us date this material

THE LIONEL PARTS STORY 8 1/2" x 11", 4 pages, heavy paper, black ink. 3 pictures on each page, shows "The Permanent Staff," Lennie Dean, Parts Supervisior, Emma Alvino, Lorraine Ciasullo, John Farley, Alex Charron, and Al Visicaro

Chapter XXVII
LIONEL BILLBOARDS
by I.D.Smith

Introduction

This list is organized from the Lionel Catalogues starting in 1950. Numbers have been used instead of letters for each change as it appears. There were many repeats in the years following initial listing.

Second step was to take my collection, fill in better description where not clear from the catalogues and verify dates where shown on uncut billboard poster set(s).

Third I used slides of Alan T. Weaver's collection following the same steps. Mr. Weaver's slides show a number of billboard posters designated "Outdoor Adv." and "Indoor Adv." where "Standard" showed in the early '50's. These have NOT been included as they appear NOT to be Lionel. If "Standard" shows on billboard, it is noted by "STD". Otherwise, it was not shown.

For each year(s) I have listed the page number of the catalogues where the no. 310 Billboard is listed; number of plastic frames; number of billboard or posters noted in catalogue as set for that year. Following this, if there were possible billboards shown in the catalogue, I have listed those pages on which it appears. Obvious advertisements on particular set or train features printed inside green billboard frame picture are not included.

No. 310 BILLBOARD 1950-1968 unpainted green plastic frame with cardboard advertisements.

Beginning in 1950, Lionel offered a billboard assortment, the No. 310. The assortment usually consisted of five green unpainted plastic frames with an uncut sheet of different billboards. In 1950, ten different billboards were offered. Later this was reduced to 8,7,6 and in the later years to 5 different billboards.

The billboards made through 1956 include the words "Standard" in white letters with black background. Thereafter "Standard" was dropped from the sign. Many different billboard advertisements were offered. It appears that there were partial annual changes in the billboards as shown each year in the Lionel catalogues starting in the '50's. In later years changes in billboards show up on other catalogue pages. The dating of these billboards has been based on the Lionel catalogues and uncut dated billboard sheets. It may be that our readers have reliable source information that will contradict or supplement these billboard dates. Readers' comments are welcomed as this is our first listing of these signs. (It is very important to note date that appears on uncut billboard sheets which will aid in establishing and verifying other billboard set dates).

In describing these signs the exact words and spelling including upper and lower case letters as appear on the sign are noted. Additional descriptive words have been added to aid in the description.

As additional information it is noted that in the August l, 1959 numerical parts list part No. 310-3, frame was listed. However, in the 1968 listing part No. 310-2 billboard had been added and also was shown in the 1970 MPC Lionel parts listing. It has not been determined if the number 310-2 covered an uncut sheet of the specified number of various individual billboards.

This listing does not include any of the small size 40 or Raceway Game Lionel Billboards. Many of those were reduced sizes of the No. 310 billboards.

1950 Page 41,(5 frames,Billboards)
1 LIONEL MAGNE-TRACTION GIVES YOU MORE SPEED, MORE PULL, MORE CLIMB, MORE CONTROL (1950 red and silver Santa Fe with part of second diesel unit, blond haired boy)
2 AMERICA'S BIG THREE; GRAND CANYON, NIAGARA FALLS, SILVER SPRINGS, American flag design in red, white and blue (Std)
3 Baby Ruth, another CURTISS Candy slice and serve (candy, sliced, falling into dish) (Std)
4 Get a DUPONT ANTI-FREEZE, ZEREX ZERONE $3.50-1.25 (Std)
5 Enjoy Chewing Wrigleys SPEARMINT GUM with light green background (man with hat placing piece of gum to his mouth) (Std)
6 Wow! FORD V-8 (bear with tree) (Std)
7 GREAT CARS SINCE 1902 NEW Nash...RAMBLER (ad shows old car and current model) (Std)
8 YOUR PLYMOUTH DEALER INVITES YOU TO DRIVE THE NEW PLYMOUTH 1950 blue car, red background (Std)
9 Snowy-Soft with "FLUFF" NORTHERN TISSUE (ad shows dog and boy on red sled) (Std)
Sources: Sykes Collection 2, 3, 4, 5, 6, 7, 8, Smith Collection 2, 3, Weaver Collection, uncut billboard sheets dated 1950; 2, 5, 6, 7 and 3, 4, 8, 9 Weaver Collection 5, 9, 2, 3, 4, 6, 8, 7

1951, Page 31 (5 frames, show 10 billboards)
3 See 1950 catalogue
4 See 1950 catalogue
10 Same as 1950 catalogue but price now $3.75 and $1.50 (Std)
11 Level best on the roughest roads, NEW PLYMOUTH (Green Plymouth; man, woman and dog in car) (Std)
12 Compare...and you'll know they're better; Heinz Soups (bowl of tomato soup with can of Heinz Tomato Soup) (Std)
13 Made for once-a-week shopping. The new FRIGIDAIRE, SEE YOUR FRIGIDAIRE DEALER (open refrigerator in center of yellow background) (Std)
14 Safe Traveling, THE GENERAL TIRE, SEE YOUR GENERAL TIRE DEALER (shows tire on right, squaw and papoose on left) (Std)
15 I'm a television cameraman... and in my home we have hollicrafters. (shows TV on right, man on left) (Std)
2 See 1950 catalogue
16 WOW! ITS A "LIONEL" (shows blond haired boy on floor with steam engine, dog, part of passenger car, automatic gateman).
17 Enjoy Wrigley's Spearmint Gum daily-chewing aids teeth, breath, digestion (shows pack of gum lower right of billboard) (Std)
18 Keeps your car on the go-ATLANTIC (shows waterway with city in background, red and white Atlantic sign) (Std). This billboard does not appear in the 1951 catalogue but Weaver Collection ties this billboard to 1951.
Sources: Smith Collection, 10, 11, 12, 13, 14, 15, 17, 18; Weaver Collection, uncut billboard sheets dated 1951; 11, 12, 15, 17 and 2, 3, 10, 13, 14, 18; Weaver Collection 5, 12, 17, 15, 13, 10, 11, 18, 14.

1952 Page 33 (5 frames, 8 billboards)
19 HEINZ OVEN-BAKED BEANS (shows blond haired boy holding a plate of beans on left and can on right) (Std)
20 You mean you haven't seen FLORIDA'S SILVER SPRINGS! (shows baby's face on left) (Std)
21 WRIGLEY'S SPEARMINT for real chewing enjoyment (shows pack of gum) (Std)
22 SUNSWEET good to feel-good! (lady in two piece white sunsuit on beach. Box of Sunsweet Prunes on right) (Std)
23 HIGH-TEST at regular gas price BLUE SUNOCO ANTI-KNOCK PERFORMANCE! (shows man on left winking, red arrow Sunoco sign) (Std)
3 See 1950 catalogue
24 Shelves roll out... All the way! CYCLA-MATIC FRIGIDAIRE Automatic Defrosting! SEE YOUR FRIGIDAIRE DEALER (shows refrigerator on left and closer view of roll out shelves on right) (Std)
25 Straight to the Point...TOP QUALITY, SEE YOUR GENERAL TIRE DEALER, THE GENERAL TIRE (shows tire on right, dog on left) (Std)
26 VOTE FOR VALUE Plymouth (shows red X by word Plymouth, Plymouth car on right side of billboard) (Std)
10 See 1951 catalogue
Sources: Smith Collection, 19, 23, 25; Weaver Collection uncut billboard sheets dated 1952; 19, 21, 22, 26, and 3, 10, 20, 23, 24, 25; Weaver Collection 21, 24, 19, 22, 26, 25, 23, 20;

1953, Page 33, (5 frames, 10 billboards) (also page 21)
27 Travel refreshed. DRINK Coca-Cola IN BOTTLES (shows train engineer drinking a bottle of Coca-Cola, portion of steam locomotive to right) (Std).
28 NO SHIFTING! NEW PLYMOUTH HY-DRIVE (shows new Plymouth blue convertible) (Std).
10 See 1951 catalogue
29 WRIGLEY'S SPEARMINT CHEWING GUM (shows earth in background with infinite packs of gum coming from earth. Planet Saturn also shows in background) (Std)
30 Save at Sunoco, Tires and Batteries (shows Kelly tire on left, Sunoco battery center, SUNOCO yellow sign with red arrow pointing to the left) (Std)
11 See 1952 catalogue
31 Relax now! at FLORIDA'S SILVER SPRINGS (shows lady in two piece red swim suit on beach) (Std)
32 Cycle-matic FRIGIDAIRE Food Freezer-Refrigerator YEARS AHEAD (shows open refrigerator on left) (Std)
19 See 1952 catalogue. This billboard does not show in 1953 catalogue but Weaver Collection ties this billboard to 1953.
33 (See page 21) LIONEL "O" GAUGE plus LIONEL MAGNE-TRACTION, MORE PULL, MORE SPEED, MORE POWER
34 RED MAGIC, HEINZ Ketchup (shows bottle of Heinz Tomato Ketchup, a hamburger with pickles on a plate) (Std) This billboard does not show in 1953 catalogue but Weaver Collection ties this billboard to 1953.
Sources: Smith Collection 27, 28, 29, 31, 32, 34; Weaver Collection uncut billboard sheets dated 1953; 27, 28, 29, 34 and 27, 28, 29, 19; Weaver Collection, 31, 32, 29, 27, 34, 28, 30, 31.

1953 Accessories Catalogue, page 12 (lists 5 frames and 10 lithographed billboards)

1954 Page 40 (5 frames, 8 billboards)
35 Only LIONEL has MAGNE-TRACTION, MORE SPEED-MORE POWER-MORE CLIMB (shows boy on left) (Std)
Note: Description of 8 firms represented on page 40 indicates this was NOT a billboard
36 Change now for LONG Mileage (shows service station man on right holding in his hand on left side of billboard a can of Sunoco Dynalube Motor Oil) (Std)
37 GET a DUPONT ANTI-FREEZE ZEREX-ZERONE $2.95/$1.50. (Std)
38 BRECK Beautiful Hair THREE BRECK SHAMPOOS (shows woman and hair trademark in center and bottles of shampoo left side) (Std)
39 NEW DEPARTURE, Safety Brake, STEER WITH YOUR HANDS STOP WITH YOUR FEET (shows brake on right, boy riding red bike on left) (Std)
40 It's Still Clean, FRAM-OIL-AIR-FUEL-WATER FILTERS, FOR NEAREST DEALER CALL WESTERN UNION OPERATOR 25 (shows service man looking at clean oil on oil dip stick, filter on right, yellow background) (Std)
41 Campbell's SOUPS MMM, GOOD! (shows can of Campbell's Tomato Soup on right, Campbell's Chef on left, yellow background) (Std)
42 WRIGLEY'S SPEARMINT GUM, (ad is full size face of gum package). (Set of 6 uncut billboards Smith Collection dated 1955 shows this billboard to have man driving car. On bottom "Chew—freshen your taste" on billboard) (Std) Weaver Collection of uncut billboards shows same as Smith Collection except dated 1954.
43 Coolest drink under the sun LIPTON ICED TEA (shows tall glass of iced tea on left, man sitting on grass holding glass of iced tea and leaning against push lawn mower. Box of Lipton Tea pictured in lower right corner) (Std)
Sources: Smith Collection 41, 42, 43, 40, 36, 37; Weaver Collection uncut billboard sheets dated 1954, 38, 39, 40, 41, 42, 43, 37, 36; Weaver Collection 43, 41.

1954 Distributor's Advertising Promotions Catalogue page 14 shows 8 billboards. Those shown are the same as shown in the 1952 catalogue which are 10, 19, 20, 21, 22, 23, 25, 26.

1954 Accessories Catalogue page 8 lists set of 5 frames and 8 billboards.

1955 Page 38 (5 frames, 7 billboards) (shown or listed, see page 19 for pictures)

35 See 1954 catalogue
44 SNOW CROP PEAS (shows package of frozen peas with peas spilling out left end. Bear on right) (Std)
45 LOG CABIN SYRUP (shows bottle and famous "Log Cabin Tin" of Syrup)
46 Makes the Cakes! LOG CABIN SYRUP (shows picture of sausage, forks, pitcher of syrup, pancakes with butter. Bottle and tin of syrup lower right) (Std)
47 FRAM FILTERS (shows red filter on right) CLEAN OIL MONTHLY CHANGE OIL AND FILTER NOW, FOR NEAREST DEALER CALL WESTERN UNION OPERATOR 25 (Std)
48 KOOL AID (shows package of Kool-Aid with glass on package)
49 DUPONT ANTI-FREEZE ZEREX-ZERONE (does NOT show prices in catalogue. However set of the same uncut billboards from Smith and Weaver Collections shows $3.25/$1.60) (Std)
42 See 1954 catalogue
50 Kool-Aid, .05 package makes two quarts (shows package of Kool-Aid lower left. Pitcher of Kool-Aid with happy face being drawn by finger) (Std)
Sources: Smith and Weaver Collections uncut billboard sheet dated 1955; 44, 46, 47, 49, 42, 50; Weaver Collection 46, 44, 48, 47, 49.

1956 Page 34 (5 frames, 6 posters) (also see page 13 and 23)
35 See 1954 catalogue
42 See 1955 and 1954 catalogues
50 See 1955 catalogue
49 See 1955 catalogue
47 See 1955 catalogue
45 See 1955 catalogue
44 See 1955 catalogue

1957 Page 48 (5 frames, 5 posters) (also see page 4, 5, 8, 15, 24, 32)
51 NAVY, Graduates chose your field (shows young man with diploma on left and 5 Navy insignia over NAVY)
52 WRIGLEY'S SPEARMINT CHEWING GUM, pure, wholesome, inexpensive (shows man with hat reaching way out with right arm showing pack of gum)
53 NABISCO, the original SHREDDED WHEAT (shows boy holding box of Shredded Wheat)
54 AIREX-REELS-RODS-LINE-LURES
55 LIONEL TRAINS (red letters) with MAGNE-TRACTION (shows lion with engineer's cap on left on page 48)
Sources: Smith Collection 55; Weaver Collection 51,52,53,55

1958 Page 39 (5 frames, 5 posters) (see page 21,37,38,40)
56 Train and gain new nuclear NAVY (shows nuclear sub, two white hat sailors, officer and missile)
57 CHEVROLET OK USED CARS AND TRUCKS (shows CHEVROLET emblem and red "OK" in yellow background in green circle)
58 "Change-um oil filter...car run heap better". Purolator (shows new American Indian driving car)
59 WRIGLEY'S JUICY FRUIT CHEWING GUM DIFFERENT, DELICIOUS (shows pack of Juicy Fruit gum in yellow wrapper. Leaf with picture of a woman's face superimposed on leaf)
60 (Description needed)
Sources: Weaver Collection 56, 59, 58.

1959 Page 35 (5 frames, 5 posters) (see page 34)
70 JOIN THE NAVY (white letters blue background)
71 (Description needed)
72 (Description needed)
73 (Description needed)
74 (Description needed)

1959 Advance Catalogue, page 25 (5 frames, 5 posters) (see page 31)
56 See 1958 catalogue
59 See 1958 catalogue
55 See 1957 catalogue
75 AIREX-REELS-RODS-LINES-LURES (shows reel on left, man in water reaching out with net to catch hooked fish jumping out of water)
76 TWICE AS POPULAR, CHEVROLET OK USED CARS AND TRUCKS (shows 3 children's faces and "OK" symbol in yellow circle at lower right and left with Chevrolet emblem)
51 See 1957 catalogue

52 See 1957 catalogue
Sources: Weaver Collection, 75, 76

1960 Page 39 (5 frames and billboards) (see page 29,13,30)
70 See 1959 catalogue
77 EAGER BEAVER SERVICE all the way (shows gasoline pump on left and City Service emblem on right. Beaver reading road map center left).
78 GOOD TRAINING FOR GETTING AHEAD, Underwood PORTABLE TYPEWRITERS (shows portable typewriter on right side, boy with first prize cup on left).
79 SPACE AGE TRAINING NAVY (shows planet earth in background with navy jet in center and red rocket).
80 (Description needed)
81 (Description needed)
Sources: Smith Collection 77, 79; Weaver Collection 78, 79, 77

1960 Advance Catalogue page 32 (5 frames, 5 posters) (see page 42, 45)
79 See 1960 catalogue
78 See 1960 catalogue
59 See 1958 catalogue
55 See 1957 catalogue
Page 42
58 See 1959 catalogue
56 See 1959 catalogue
59 See 1958 catalogue
82 AIREX-REELS-RODS-LINES-LURES (shows man in stream fishing near rocks about to net hooked fish)
76 See 1959 Advance Catalogue
Sources: Smith and Weaver Collection 82

1960 Accessory Catalogue (page 13 shows name as 1960 Advance Catalogue)
1961 Page 58 (5 frames, 5 posters) (see page 23, 29, 30, 32, 39)
83 BIG GALLON, BIG Mileage Performance (shows a gas pump as the "I" in BIG. Cities Service emblem upper right)
84 Hot Diggety! Swift Premium FRANKS. (shows a frank on fork, cheese on frank)
85 NAVY Diploma—Stay in school (shows American flag on staff in center)
87 FINISH LINE (shows black and white checkered flag with 2 cars racing).
Sources: Weaver Collection 83, 84, 85, 86

1961 Advance Catalogue (see page 53, billboards shown are the same as shown in the 1960 Accessory Catalogue and the 1960 Advance Catalogue)
1962 Page 50 (5 frames, 5 posters) Billboards pictured are the same as shown in the 1961 Adavnce Catalogue. (see page 10, 13, 22, 24, 25)
88 AMERICA'S FIRST, FINEST, FAVORITE (shows can of Van Camps Pork and Beans on left. Ladle of beans on right)
89 Get close to America by car! BIG GALLON, Quality alone makes it BIG! (shows City Service emblem on right, part of car center bottom. Big Gallon in red)
85 See 1961 catalogue
90 (Description needed)
91 (Description needed)
Sources: Weaver Collection 88, 89

1962 Trains and Accessories Catalogue 63 pages, (page 41 billboards shown are the same as shown in the 1961 catalogue)
1963 Page 33 (5 frames, 5 posters) (see page 18, 19)
92 LIONEL PORTER (shows Microcraft Student Microscope)
93 LIONEL Spear (shows Mickey Mouse phonograph)
85 See 1961 catalogue
86 See 1961 catalogue
87 See 1961 catalogue
1963 Accessory Catalogue, 40 pages (page 13) (5 frames, 5 posters)
94 Serve with Pride, GO NAVY
95 MODEL RACING LIONEL (shows two race cars)
96 LIONEL PORTER (shows young man performing chemical tests)
86 See 1961 catalogue
87 See 1961 catalogue
1963 Advance Catalogue (Lionel 1963 on cover, cover yellow, black and white, 80 unnumbered pages) (page 10, billboards shown are the same as 1963 accessory catalogue)
1964 Page 14 (5 frames, 5 posters) Billboards shown are the same as shown in the 1961 catalogue and the 1962 Trains and Accessory Catalogue.
1965 Page 15 (set of billboards with 5 frames) Billboards shown are as shown in 1964 catalogue.
1966 Page 15 (Set of billboards with 5 frames) Billboards shown are as shown in 1964 catalogue.
1967 Catalogue not issued.
1968 (Inside of back page) (Set of billboards with 5 frames) Billboards shown are as shown in 1964 catalogue.
(LAST YEAR LISTED)

The following billboards have been observed, but have yet to be dated.
A LIONEL Construction Kits (shows boy with wrecker truck built from kit) (Std)
B FORD (in reverse) (shows man, boy and dog looking through window with FORD on window) (Std)
C FRESH Kellogg's CORN FLAKES (shows box of Corn Flakes on right, bowl with bananas on left) (Std)
D He'll only chase a Nash (shows black dog on right, two girls on left) (Std)
E Your nose knows, your best buy in tissues! (shows box of Kleenex Tissues on right. Girl pointing to her nose on left) (Std)
F Curtis Baby Ruth (red letters on large Baby Ruth candy bar—Background white. No green billboard outline, may be printing error)
G TARGET RANGE, Red, white, blue target, yellow background. Comes with cardboard stand and instructions attached. On part of stand "Test your aim with Lionel's exciting missile launchers. There is a wide variety to choose from".
Sources: Smith Collection G; Weaver Collection A, B, C, D, E, F, G.

H Blister Pack B310, Billboard set of five plastic frames. Top frame shows poster "Buy U.S. Savings Bonds" (shows package of savings bonds, Series E, color light purple) Lionel with red and blue arrow design on pack like 1966 catalogue. Weaver Collection

I Billboard: "Education is for the birds (the birds who want to get ahead). To get a good job get a good education." Light purple, Weaver Collection.

J Billboard: Horse cartoon-horse with collar—speaking "Get a Dodge". Light purple, Weaver Collection.

Appendix
NEW YORK CENTRAL GONDOLAS
by Richard Vagner

The New York Central Gondolas — 1949-1969

In 1949 the Lionel Corporation introduced a new longer gondola which carried the New York Central markings in every year it was made. The new car was 10 3/8" long and had a very realistic appearance. The detailing included rivets, steps, brakewheels, brakewheel chains and good interior detailing. The car was included in the majority of the better freight sets produced during the remaining twenty one years of Lionel's history. During the production run of this car thirteen different number/color combinations were produced which are all relatively easy to find. In addition a large number of visual variations were produced including herald position, number of lines of weight data, presence or absence of built date, brakewheels and steps. Finally there were variations in truck types. Other changes include die modifications, coupler changes, truck connections, color differences, frame changes and various combinations of the above. Using only the visual variations which can be seen with the car sitting on the shelf, about thirty different combinations can be found and if the manufacturing changes are included, over fifty different variations can be found.

If a matrix is constructed using the year in which various changes were made on one axis and each number/color combination produced on the other axis, these gondolas can be dated to certain time spans. The matrix can be used to insure the correct gondola is in a set for a given year; it can tell the year a set was manufactured as a result of manufacturing changes and if the car has been altered. These production changes can also be used to date other Lionel cars to definite time periods.

Most of the information as to when certain rolling stock was produced comes from the Lionel catalogues. There are some gondolas not shown in the catalogues in certain years which show manufacturing details clearly dating them to years in which production is not indicated in the catalogue. There are gondolas shown in the catalogues in colors in which they have never been found. Any gondola can be compared with the matrix and placed into a time frame depending on the known dates of various manufacturing changes.

The NYC gondolas introduced in 1949 are 10 3/8" from coupler centers or 9 5/8" outside body length. (In prototype practice, railroad cars are measured from coupler center to coupler center, rather than coupler end to coupler end, as the former measurement will actually provide accurate information on train length because it compensates for overlapping within the couplers.) There are five distinct mold variations which separate the cars into distinct time frames. The first was body mold Type Ia. This was only found in the black 6462 gondola which was produced in 1949. On the floor, inside the gondola, in the center panel, were three round marks. The center mark was the result of injecting the plastic into the mold and was either raised or depressed. The other two marks were from round plugs on a diagonal in the same panel.

The next was body mold Type Ib. Type Ib is identified by the addition of another round plug in the panel to the right of the center panel. To find the right hand side of the gondola, examine the four rectangular holes holding the metal tabs which hold the frame to the body. On the floor inside the car on the left side of one pair of these holes will be found three rivets on the edge of the hole. This goes to the right. To identify a Type Ib mold look in the panel to the right of the center panel for the round plug. This is only found on the black and tuscan red 6462 gondolas produced in early 1950.

The next was body mold Type "Ic" which first appeared in mid-1950. Type "Ic" is identified by the addition of another round plug in the panel to the left of the center panel. This Type "Ic" mold is found on the black and tuscan red 6462s and the 6002 black gondola with Scout trucks. This mold continued into 1953 in the tuscan red and black 6462 gondolas.

Next is body mold Type IIa, beginning in 1954. This was a completely new mold, and the machine, with its dual dies, produced two cars at one time. On the floor of the car were now four round plug marks in panels 1, 5, 9 and 13. Under the body hidden by the metal frame was a part identification number. It is a 6462-2 and underneath it is a 1 or 2 indicating which of the two molds the car was formed in. This body mold is used on the light red painted, red plastic, black, green and pink 6462s, the grey, red and black 6562s and the red 6342 culvert gondola. This mold was used from 1954 to 1958.

The final mold Type IIb, was introduced in 1959. This mold is changed to eliminate the metal frame and allow the trucks to be riveted directly to the gondola floor. This body mold is used on the black 6062, the blue and red 6162, the yellow 6162 Alaska gondola and the 6342 red culvert gondola produced from 1966 to 1969. The Type IIb mold was used from 1959 to 1969. The mold numbers 6462-2/1 or 6462-2/2 are readily visible since the frame was eliminated. It appears that equal numbers of both mold 1 and 2 are found.

The black 6462 is the only gondola found in the first four mold types: Types Ia, Ib, Ic and IIa. The tuscan red 6462 gondola is found only in mold Type Ib and Ic. The painted red and red unpainted plastic 6462 is found only in mold Type IIa. The red 6342 is the only gondola found in both mold Types IIa and IIb. The green and pink 6462s and the grey, red and black 6562s are only found in mold Type IIa. The 6062 and 6162s are only found in mold Type IIb.

The next major distinguishing feature is the position of the the N in NYC and the style of lettering used for the herald. From 1949 to 1955 the N is found in the second panel. From 1956 to 1969 the N is found in the third panel. The lettering style changes from the early serif to the later block type.

The black 6462 and black 6002 are only found with the N in the second panel. The tuscan red 6462 is found only with the N in the second panel. The light red cars are found with the N in the second or third panel and the red unpainted plastic are only found with the N in the third panel. The green 6462s are found with the N in the second or third panel. The pink 6462, the gray, red and black 6562s, the red 6342 and the 6062 and 6162s are all found with the N in the third panel.

The third major distinguishing feature is the type of car truck. There are two major types of trucks with two variations of each type. From 1949 to 1958 the 10 3/8" gondolas had metal trucks with die-cast sides. From 1949 to 1951 these trucks were the staple-end variation and from 1952 to 1958 they were the bar-end variation. From 1959 all 10 3/8" gondolas were manufactured with plastic Timken trucks. From 1959 to 1961 these had a metal knuckle pin on the operating trucks and from 1962 to 1969 the knuckle pin was part of the plastic knuckle.

If the bar graph is examined it will be seen that the 1949 black 6462 is the only 1949 car and the only car found in mold Ia. In 1950 the black 6462 was made with both molds Ib and Ic. Then, in 1952, the trucks were changed from staple-end to bar-end while the body was still in mold Ic. In 1954 the black 6462 was found in body mold Type IIa with bar-end trucks. We consequently have five variations with only three manufacturing changes.

The tuscan red 6462 is slightly different from the black in that although all tuscan red bodies seem to have been painted during 1950, they were assembled as needed into at least 1952. Thus the tuscan red is found in body molds Ib and Ic in both staple-end and bar-end trucks.

The green and light red painted 6462s started in 1954 and are only found in body mold Type IIa. In 1954 and 1955 these cars have the N in the second panel and in 1956 the N is found in the third panel.

During 1956 the red 6462 changed again to a self colored red plastic. It seems to have been made in this red plastic into 1958.

There are other variations in the 1950 black and tuscan red 6462s including the presence or absence of steps and the brakewheels. The early 1950 black and tuscan red 6462s had both steps and brakewheels. The 6002, produced later in 1950, did not have steps and had no hole in the body for the brakewheels. The steps had been part of the metal frame and used much more metal as part of the frame, since the steps protrude out and require a

241

substantially larger piece of metal to be stamped for the frame. Assuming that Lionel made 500,000 gondolas and each gondola frame required an extra half inch of steel, a considerable amount of money was involved over the production run. Thus, early 1950 black and tuscan red gondolas have steps and Type Ib and Ic molds. Later 1950 and 1951 black and tuscan red gondolas have brakewheels but no steps because the frame die had been changed when the 6002 was made. During 1951 the brakewheels were eliminated from the black 6462. Some time later in 1951 the "built date" was dropped from this car. The tuscan red 6462 retained its brakewheel and "built date" into 1952 and probably 1953.(1)

Thus, the black 6462 shows several other variations. First, one other variation in the black 6462 needs to be mentioned. Sometime during 1950 the third line of weight data found on the 1949 and early 1950 models was eliminated. The three lines of weight data are found on mold Types Ia and Ib and on cars with brakewheels, steps and the built date. The black 6462 from 1950 has two more variations with the two lines of weights being found with and without steps. All 1951 cars came with staple-end trucks and are found with and without the built date and with and without brakewheels.

There are eight recognizable variations in the black 6462 which can readily be found. If two other criteria are added the number of variations increases again. The 1950 black plastic car had the beginning of a die break visible in the floor of the car. This die break can be traced through the black plastic 6002, with the Scout trucks, into the 1951 and 1952 cars, until finally, in 1953, the end posts of the car deform and the die was abandoned. The die break is progressive through the other production changes. However the die break is not found in the tuscan red 6462s which confirms these bodies were produced in 1950 and assembled into 1952. The other source of variations were the mold colors. Clear, blue, gray, green, brown, pink and black mold colors have been reported. The 1954 black 6462s have been reported in pink and black molds. Other mold colors are possible and the number of possible combinations using the existing breakdowns based on other criteria is not known.

Coupler variations are another means of classifying years of production. The 1949 black 6462 has the Type IV mechanical coupler which has no hole in the activator flap and has the flared end of the rivet showing. In 1950 the hole in the activator flap appears and during the late 1950 production of the 6002 the end of the rivet appears as round. There is no other change until 1955 when the tab coupler was introduced. During 1957 the tab coupler was phased out and the cars produced during this time may or may not have tab couplers. Dating based on coupler type is not highly reliable since couplers broke and were changed.(2)

During 1956 a number of new gondolas were introduced with different loads. From 1949 through 1956, the 6462 gondolas probably came with a load of six wooden barrels. The 6002 Scout seems to have been produced without any load. In 1956 the 6562 red and gray gondolas came with a load of four round plastic LCL canisters. A new special gondola, the red plastic 6342, was introduced with the 342 culvert loader which carried a load of seven metal culverts on a sloping metal ramp.

In 1957 another 6562 in black was introduced and the pink 6462 came as part of the Girl's Train. Both carried a load of four canisters. The 6342 was continued with the 342 culvert loader. One significant 1957 change was in the method used to fasten the trucks to the metal frame. Previously a metal pin was swaged to the truck and a metal horseshoe clip fitted to the pin to retain the truck. In 1957 Lionel went to a sheet metal clip made from spring steel to hold the truck to the frame. This creates a variation in the 6342 gondola. It seems the cars that came with the early 342 culvert loader use the early style pin and the cars which came with the later 345 unloader came with the sheet metal clip. During the overlap of these two accessories during 1958 the 342 may have come with a 6342 using either method of truck fastening.

During 1958 there is some uncertainty as to what gondolas were produced. A red 6562 is stated to have been produced while there is some evidence a red plastic 6462 was made also. Information relative to this is needed. The 6342 continued and the pink 6462 was available as leftovers from the previous year.

A new gondola was produced in 1959 when the Type IIa mold was modified to eliminate the metal frame and allow the trucks to be fastened directly to the frame. The final two numbers in the series were introduced. The 6062 was catalogued in red but was probably only produced in the black in which it has been found. The load for the 6062 gondola at the start of production was probably two wire reels. If this load was continued throughout the production run confirmation would be appreciated. The yellow 6162 Alaska was part of the Alaska set of that year. While it is the only 10 3/8" which does not carry the NYC herald, it does belong in this series. The 6162 Alaska seems to have come with a load of four white canisters. These are reports of 6162 Alaska gondolas with four dark blue cannisters. Confirmation of canister color would be appreciated. These cars have the new plastic Timken trucks which appeared earlier on many cheaper cars. Technically, these are not Timken trucks as Timken did not make trucks but only bearings. Actually these are A.A.R. trucks with Timken bearings. See Greenberg's Repair and Operating Manual, page 660. These trucks have the coupler cast in plastic as part of the truck. The early plastic trucks before 1962 have a metal knuckle pin which in 1962 was changed to plastic which was part of the knuckle.

In 1961 the last regular production run number/color combination was introduced. This 6162 was catalogued in red or black but it was actually produced as a blue. This blue 6162 continued until the end of the Lionel production in 1969. The blue 6162 comes in a number of color variations and with "built dates" and without "built dates". The colors range from very light blue to dark blue. This car was produced with the same features as the black 6062 which was also produced this year. It had a load of four cannisters in red or white and possibly other colors.

In 1962 the final changes were made which produced the last variations in this series. This is the change to the late plastic trucks. The plastic knuckle pin has already been mentioned. The trucks were modified so the axles are visible from the bottom and the dummy couplers are mounted on Arch bar trucks from the General rolling stock of 1959-62. One significant visual variation created with this change is the dropping of the built date.

In 1966 a 6342 culvert gondola was introduced without the metal frame under the car. It is the same as the 6162 except for the metal ramp for the culverts and the different color and number. It ran until 1969 along with the blue 6162.

One other gondola was made in 1969 or 1970 using leftover culvert gondola bodies. It was a red 6162 boxed as 6162-110. It came without a load and had the 3/16" hole in the center of the floor for the rivet which held the ramp in the 6342. It is not known if this car was made by Lionel or MPC.

Two other 6462s are known from single examples and there are unconfirmed reports of other variations. An orange 6462 is known which has the N in the 3rd panel and bar-end trucks and a yellow-cream color gondola similar to the 6464-515 Katy box car from the Girl's Set! This car was the IIa mold with bar-end trucks and the N is in the third panel.

We would be most appreciative of your comments, additions and corrections to this essay.

---

(1) We assume that these were painted at one time because of the unusually high color consistency and that all variations are found in both Ib and Ic molds.

(2) Coupler dating is much more reliable when the car is obtained from the original purchaser, as the principal source of confusion would be repairs. However, in the case of goods obtained at collector meets, less reliance should be placed on coupler dating.

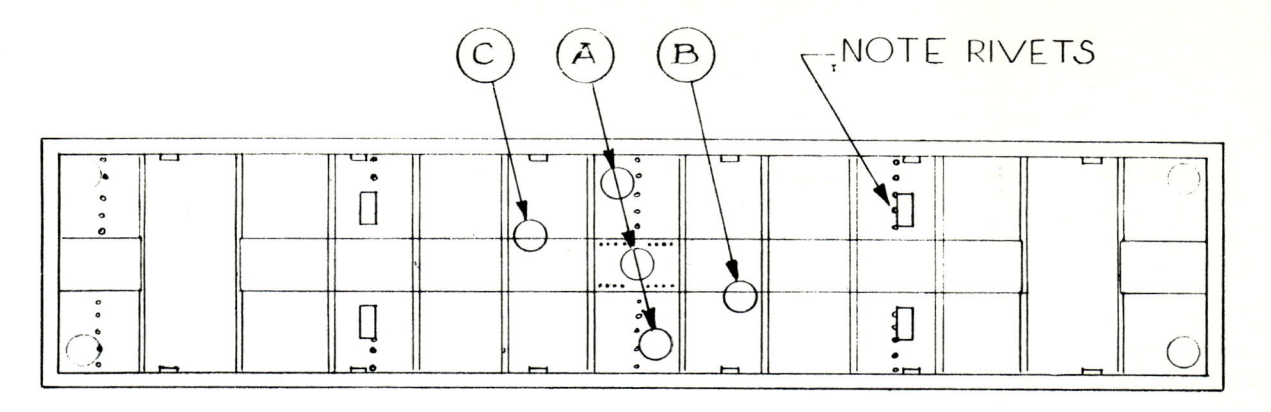

Type I molds.
Ia: center only (three a's plus b)
Ib: center plus right (three a's plus b)
Ic: all (three a's, b, c)

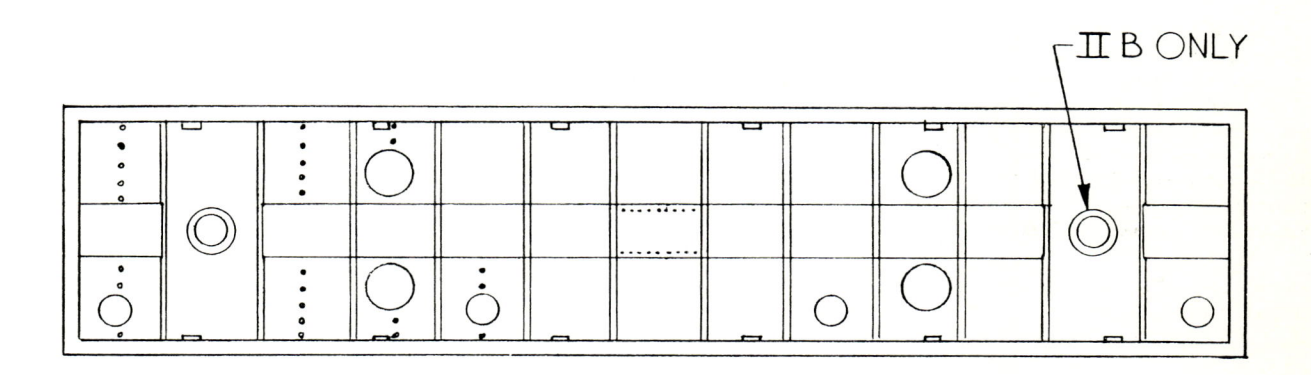

Type IIa: plastic molded clips hold frame
Type IIb: metal frame not used, trucks riveted directly to body

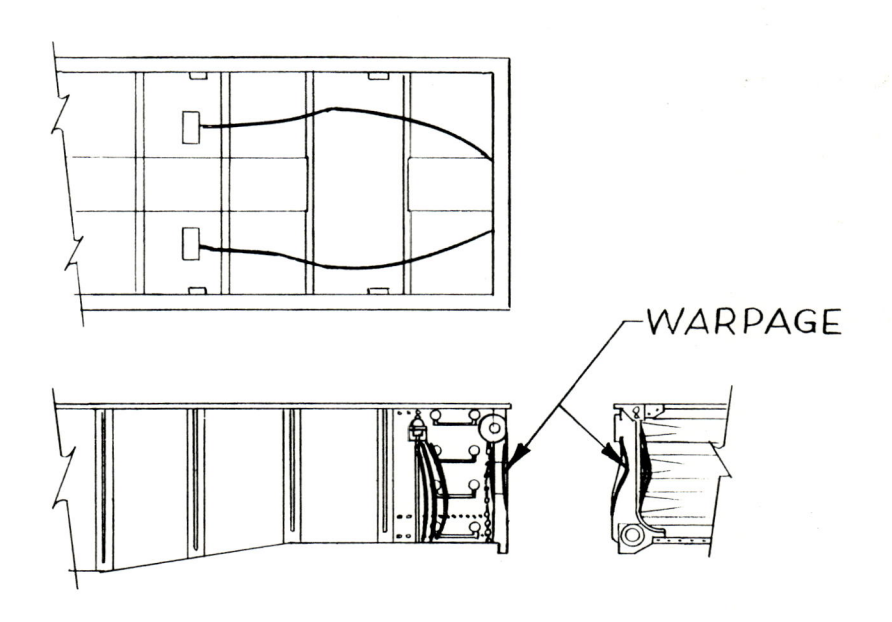

Drawings by Trip Riley

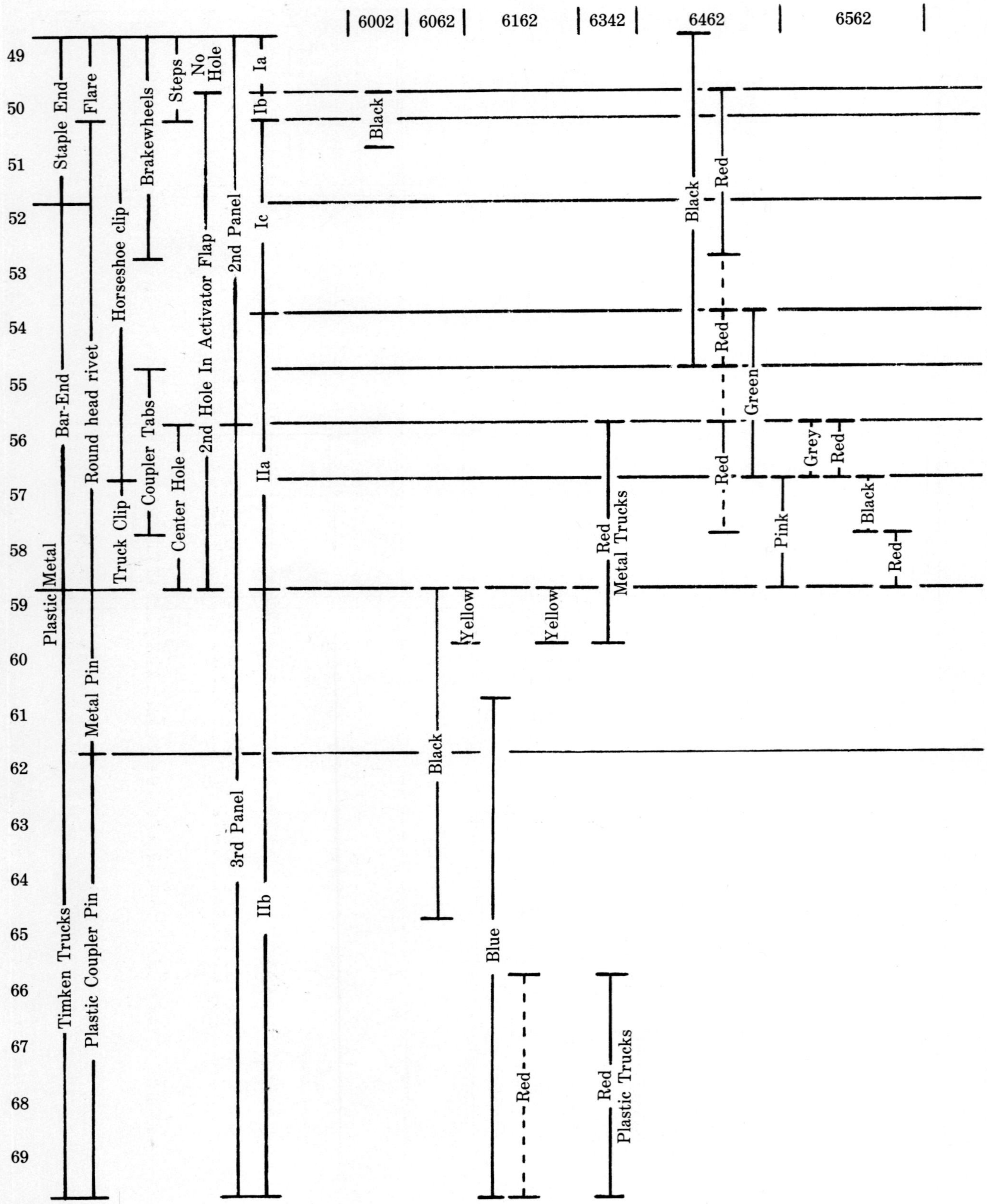
6002
6062
6162
6342
6462
6562
49
50
51
52
53
54
55
56
57
58
59
60
61
62
63
64
65
66
67
68
69
Staple End
Bar-End
Flare
Round head rivet
Horseshoe clip
Truck Clip
Brakewheels
Coupler Tabs
Steps
Center Hole
No Hole
2nd Hole In Activator Flap
2nd Panel
3rd Panel
Ia
Ib
Ic
IIa
IIb
Plastic
Metal
Metal Pin
Plastic Coupler Pin
Timken Trucks
Black
Yellow
Yellow
Blue
Red
Red
Metal Trucks
Red
Plastic Trucks
Black
Red
Red
Green
Red
Pink
Grey
Red
Black
Red

INDEX
by Dr. W. Jeffery Miller

ITEM	PAGE	ITEM	PAGE	ITEM	PAGE	ITEM	PAGE	ITEM	PAGE	ITEM	PAGE	ITEM	PAGE	ITEM	PAGE
3	161	88	53	213	55	356	59	682	39	1013-17	63	2018	47	2321	13
011-11	50	90	53	214	55	362	59	685	39	1013-42	63	2020	47	2322	13
011-43	50	91	53	215	8	364	59	686	39	1015	68	2023	13	2324	168
020	50	92	53	216	8	364C	59	703	39	1016	68	2024	13	2328	13
020X	50	93	53	216A	8	365	59	703-10	61	1018	63	2025	47	2329	16
022	50	97	53	216B	8	375	59	725	39	1018-1/2	63	2026	47	2330	16
022-500	50	100	53	217	9	390C	59	726	39	1018-1979	177	2028	13	2331	16
025	50	109	53	218	9	394	59	726RR	39	1019	63	2029	48	2332	16
026	50	110	53	218	9	395	59	736	39	1020	63	2029W	48	2333	16
027C-1	50	111	53	219	9	397	59	746	39	1021	63	2031	13	2334	16
30	50	111-100	53	220	9	400	59	760	61	1022	63	2032	13	2337	16
31	50	112	53	221	33	404	59	773	39	1023	63	2033	13	2338	16
31-7	50	112LH/RH	53	221	9	410	59	783	161	1024	63	2034	48	2339	16
31-15	50	112-125	53	222	9	413	59	909	61	1025	63	2035	48	2340	16
31-45	50	112-150	53	223	9	415	59	919	61	1026	68	2036	48	2341	16
32	50	114	53	224	33	419	59	920	61	1032	68	2037	48	2343	16
32-10	50	115	53	224	9	443	59	920-2	61	1033	68	2037-500	48	2343C	16
32-20	50	118	53	225	9	445	59	920-5	61	1034	68	2041	13	2344	16
32-25	50	119	53	226	9	448	59	920-8	61	1037	68	2046	48	2344C	16
32-30	50	120	53	227	9	450	59	925	61	1041	68	2055	48	2345	16
32-32	50	121	53	228	9	452	59	926	61	1042	68	2056	48	2346	21
32-33	50	123	53	229	9	455	59	926-5	61	1043	68	2065	48	2347	21
32-34	50	123-60	53	230	9	456	59	927	61	1044	68	2110	166	2348	21
32-45	50	125	53	231	9	460	59	928	61	1045	63	2111	166	2349	21
32-55	50	128	53	232	9	460P	61	943	61	1047	63	2122	166	2350	21
33	50	130	53	233	33	461	61	950	61	1050	43	2125	166	2351	21
34	50	131	53	235	33	462	61	951	61	1053	68	2126	166	2352	21
35	50	132	53	236	33	464	61	952	61	1055	13	2127	166	2353	21
36	50	133	52	237	33	465	61	953	61	1060	43	2128	166	2354	21
37	50	137	53	238	33	470	61	954	61	1061	43	2129	166	2354C	21
38	50	138	53	239	33	480-25	61	955	61	1062	43	2133	166	2355	21
39	50	140	53	240	33	480-32	61	956	61	1063	68	2140	166	2356	21
39-25	50	142	53	241	33	494	61	957	61	1065	13	2145	166	2356C	21
40	50	142-125	53	242	33	497	61	958	61	1066	12	2151	166	2357	94
40-25	50	142-150	53	243	33	520	9	959	61	1073	68	2151	166	2358	21
40-50	50	142BH/LH	53	244	33	577	220	960	61	1101	68	2154	166	2359	21
40-25	50	145	53	245	33	578	220	961	61	1101	43	2156	166	2360	21
40-50	50	145C	53	246	33	579	220	962	61	1110	45	2162	166	2360-25	21
41	7	147	53	247	35	580	220	963	61	1120	45	2163	166	2363	21
41	50	148	53	248	35	581	220	964	61	1121	63	2170	166	2365	21
42	50	150	53	249	35	600	9	965	61	1122	63	2171	166	2367	27
42	7	151	55	250	35	601	12	966	61	1122E	63	2175	166	2368	27
43	50	152	55	251	35	602	12	967	61	1122LH/RH	63	2180	166	2373	27
44	7	153	55	252	57	610	12	968	63	1122-234	63	2181	166	2378	27
44-80	50	154	55	253	57	611	161	969	63	1122-500	63	2195	166	2379	27
45	7	155	55	256	57	611	12	970	63	1130	45	2199	166	2383	27
45	50	156	53	257	55	613	12	971	63	1203	13	2214	166	2383C	27
45-N	50	157	55	260	57	614	12	972	63	1615	45	2240	13	2400	127
48	50	160	55	262	57	616	12	973	63	1625	45	2242	13	2401	127
50	7	161	55	264	57	617	12	974	63	1640-100	63	2243	13	2402	127
51	7	163	55	282	57	621	12	980	63	1654	45	2243C	13	2404	127
52	7	164	55	282R	57	622	12	981	63	1655	45	2245	13	2405	127
53	7	167	55	299	57	623	12	982	63	1656	45	2256	166	2406	127
54	7	175	55	308	57	624	12	983	63	1665	45	2257	94	2408	127
55	7	175-50	55	309	57	625	12	984	63	1666	45	2280	166	2409	127
55-150	50	182	55	310	57	626	12	985	63	1776	137	2282	166	2410	127
56	7	192	55	313-82	57	627	12	986	63	1776	207	2290	166	2411	106
56X	50	193	55	313-121	57	628	12	987	63	1862	47	2300	166	2412	127
57	8	195	55	314	57	629	12	988	63	1865	127	2301	166	2414	127
58	8	195-75	55	315	57	633	12	0000	7	1866	127	2302	166	2416	127
58X	50	196	55	316	57	634	12	0511	220	1872	47	2305	166	2419	96
59	8	197	55	317	57	634	137	0512	177	1875	127	2306	166	2420	96
60	8	199	55	321	57	635	12	0780	177	1875W	127	2308	166	2421	127
61	50	202	8	332	57	637	35	1001	43	1876	127	2309	166	2422	127
62	50	204	8	334	57	638-2361	71	1002	117	1877	106	2310	168	2423	127
64	50	205	8	342	57	645	12	1004	71	1882	47	2311	168	2429	127
65	8	206	55	345	57	646	35	1005	134	1885	127	2312	168	2430	127
68	8	207	55	346	57	659	161	1007	94	1887	106	2313	168	2431	127
69	8	208	8	347	57	665	35	1008	63	1973	220	2314	168	2432	127
70	53	209	55	348	57	670	35	1008-50	63	1973	223	2315	168	2434	127
71	53	209	8	350	57	671	35	1010	68	1974	220	2316	168	2435	127
75	53	210	8	350-50	59	671RR	35	1011	68	1975	220	2317	168	2436	127
76	53	211	8	352	59	675	35	1012	68	1976	140	2319	168	2440	127
89	53	213	8	353	59	681	39	1013	63	2016	47	2320	168	2441	127

245

ITEM	PAGE	ITEM	PAGE	ITEM	PAGE	ITEM	PAGE	ITEM	PAGE	ITEM	PAGE	ITEM	PAGE	ITEM	PAGE
2442	127	2901	168	3562-50	117	5710	177	6142-75	118	6410	220	6462-125	121	6511	113
2443	127	2905	168	3562-75	117	5711	177	6142-100	118	6411	220	6462-500	121	6512	113
2444	127	2909	168	3619	73	5713	177	6142-150	120	6411	112	6463	135	6517	102
2445	127	2927	168	3620	104	5714	177	6142-175	120	6412	220	6464	92	6517-1966	102
2446	127	2951	168	3650	104	5715	177	6149	68	6413	112	6464-1	80	6518	113
2452	117	2952	168	3656	73	5716	177	6151	109	6414	112	6464-25	80	6519	113
2454	71	2953	168	3662-1	73	5717	177	6157	100	6415	135	6464-50	82	6420	104
X2454	71	X2954	71	3665	73	5718	177	6162	120	6416	112	6464-75	82	6530	91
2457	96	2955	134	3666	73	5900	168	6162-60	120	6417	101	6464-000	91	6536	126
2458X	71	2956	124	3672	73	6002	118	6167	100	6417-3	101	6464-100	82	6544	113
2460	103	2957	96	3672-79	68	6004	76	6167-25	100	6417-25	101	6464-124	82	6555	135
2461	106	2960	168	3820	109	X6004	76	6167-50	100	6417-50	101	6464-150	82	6556	91
2465	134	3100	161	3830	109	6007	96	6167-85	100	6417-51	101	6464-175	83	6557	102
2472	96	3309	106	3854	76	6012	118	6167-100	100	6418	68	6464-200	83	6560	103
2481	127	3330	106	3927	27	6014	76	6167-125	100	6418	112	6464-225	83	6560-25	103
2482	127	3330-100	63	3927-50	68	X6014	76	6167-150	100	6418	112	6464-250	83	6561	113
2483	127	3349	106	3927-75	68	6015	135	6175	109	6419	101	6464-250	91	6561	226
2494	168	3356	71	4060	168	6017	96	6176	124	6419-57	101	6464-275	83	6562	121
2521	127	3356-150	63	4090	168	6017-50	98	6200	230	6420	101	6464-300	83	6562	226
2522	127	3359-55	124	4150	168	6017-100	98	6201	230	6420	207	6464-325	86	6564	226
2523	127	3360	27	4250	168	6017-185	98	6202	230	6421	207	6464-350	86	6572	91
2530	127	3361-55	106	4357	96	6017-200	98	6205	230	6422	207	6464-375	86	6630	113
2531	129	3362	106	4452	118	6017-225	98	6206	230	6424	112	6464-375	91	6636	126
2532	129	3364	106	4454	76	6017-235	98	6207	230	6425	135	6464-400	86	6640	118
2533	129	3366	71	4457	96	6019	68	6208	230	6425	207	6464-425	86	6646	92
2534	129	3366-100	63	4460	103	6024	76	6219	100	6426	207	6464-450	87	6650	113
2541	129	3370	71	4651	168	6025	135	6220	27	6427-3	101	6464-450	91	6650-80	68
2542	129	3376	71	4671	48	6027	98	6233	226	6427-60	102	6464-475	87	6651	113
2543	129	3386	71	4681	48	6029	68	6250	27	6427-102	102	6464-475	91	6657	102
2544	129	3409	106	4810	27	6032	118	6257	100	6427-500	102	46464-500	87	6660	113
2550	27	3410	107	4935	140	X6034	76	6257X	101	6428	77	6464-510	87	6670	226
2551	129	3413	107	5012	168	6035	135	6257-25	101	6429	102	6464-515	87	6672	91
2552	129	3419	107	5013	171	6037	98	6257-50	101	6430	112	6464-525	87	6736	126
2553	129	3424	71	5014	171	6042	118	6257-100	101	6431	112	6464-525	91	6800	113
2554	129	3424-100	63	5017	171	6042-125	118	6262	109	6432	207	6464-650	90	6801	113
2555	134	3428	72	5018	171	6044	76	6264	109	6433	207	6464-650	91	6802	113
2559	27	3429	107	5019	171	6045	135	6300	215	6434	77	6464-700	90	6803	113
2560	103	3434	72	5020	171	6047	100	6301	215	6436	125	6464-700	91	6804	113
2561	129	3435	72	5021	171	6050	76	6302	215	6436-1	125	6464-725	90	6805	113
2562	129	3444	117	5022	171	6057	100	6304	215	6436-25	125	6464-735	91	6806	113
2563	129	3451	107	5023	171	6057-50	100	6305	215	6436-57	125	6464-825	90	6807	115
2625	129	3454	72	5027	171	6058	100	6306	215	6436-100	125	6464-900	90	6808	115
2627	129	3456	124	5030	171	6059-50	100	6308	215	6436-110	125	6464-900	91	6809	115
2628	129	3459	124	5033	171	6059-60	100	6310	215	6436-1969	125	6464-1965	90	6810	115
2630	129	3460	107	5038	171	6062	118	6311	109	6437-25	102	6464-1970	91	6812	115
2631	129	3461	107	5041	171	6062-50	118	6315A	135	6438	207	6464-1970	177	6814	102
2671	48	3462	72	5042	171	6067	100	6315B	135	6440	129	6464-1971	91	6815	115
2709	168	3462P	63	5090	171	6076	124	6315C	135	6440	112	6465A	135	6816-100	68
2710	168	3464	72	5113	171	6100	172	6315-1972	135	6441	129	6465B	135	6818	115
2714	168	3464X	72	5121	171	6101	172	6342	120	6441	207	6465C	135	6819	115
2717	168	3469	124	5122	171	6102	172	6343	109	6442	129	6465D	135	6820	115
2718	168	3470	107	5125	171	6103	172	6346-56	125	6443	129	6467	112	6821	115
2719	168	3472	72	5132	171	6104	172	6352-1	76	6445	77	6468-1	91	6822	104
2720	168	3474	72	5133	171	6105	172	6356-1	77	6446-1	125	6468-25	91	6823	115
2721	168	3482	72	5149	171	6106	172	6357	101	6446-25	125	6469	112	6824	102
2722	168	3484	72	5159	68	6107	172	6357	215	6446-54	126	6470	91	6825	115
2755	134	3484-25	72	5159-50	68	6109	172	6357-25	101	6447	102	6472	91	6826	115
X2758	71	3494-1	73	5193	171	6110	48	6261	109	6448	77	6473	91	6827	115
2784	168	3494-150	73	5500	171	6110	172	6362-55	109	6449	207	6475	136	6827-100	68
2785	168	3494-273	75	5510	171	6111	109	6376	77	6452	120	6476	126	6828	115
2786	168	3494-550	73	5543	171	6111	172	6401	109	6454A	77	6477	113	6828-100	68
2787	168	3494-625	73	5545	171	6112	118	6401	207	6454B	77	6480	91	6830	115
2788	168	3509	107	5551	171	6112-135	118	6401-50	109	6454C	77	6500	113	6844	115
2789	168	3510	107	5572	171	6113	172	6402	109	6454D	77	6500	226	6900	207
2790	168	3512	109	5700	177	6114	172	6402-50	109	6454E	20	6501	113	7200	220
2791	168	3519	109	5701	177	6115	172	6403	220	6454F	77	6502-50	113	7201	220
2792	168	3520	103	5702	177	6119	100	6404	220	6456	126	6504	226	7202	220
2793	168	3530	68	5703	177	6119-25	100	6404	109	6457	102	6505	226	7203	220
2796	168	3535	109	5704	177	6119-100	100	6405	220	6460	103	6506	207	7204	220
2797	168	3540	109	5705	177	6120	100	6405	112	6460-25	103	6506	226	7205	220
2855	134	3545	109	5706	177	6121	109	6406	112	6461	112	6507	226	7206	220
2856	124	3559	124	5707	177	6130	100	6406	220	6462	120	6508	219	7207	220
2857	96	3562-1	117	5708	177	6142	118	6407	112	6462-25	121	6509	226	7208	220
2900	168	3562-25	117	5709	177	6142-50	118	6409-25	112	6462-75	121	6510	219	7211	220

ITEM	PAGE	ITEM	PAGE	ITEM	PAGE	ITEM	PAGE	ITEM	PAGE	ITEM	PAGE	ITEM	PAGE	ITEM	PAGE
7215	220	8008	161	8266	144	8557	146	8803	164	9047	182	9161	208	9277	215
7217	220	8010	140	8268	144	8558	146	8850	150	9048	182	9162	208	9278	215
7301	177	8020	140	8269	144	8559	146	8851	150	9050	215	9163	208	9279	215
7302	177	8021	140	8300	162	8560	146	8852	150	9051	215	9165	208	9280	186
7304	177	8022	140	8302	162	8561	146	8854	150	9052	182	9166	208	9281	225
7500	140	8025	140	8303	162	8562	146	8855	150	9053	182	9167	208	9282	226
7501	177	8030	140	8304	162	8563	146	8857	150	9054	182	9168	210	9283	230
7502	177	8031	140	8305	162	8564	146	8858	150	9055	230	9169	210	9284	230
7503	177	8040	161	8306	162	8565	146	8859	150	9057	208	9170	210	9285	226
7504	177	8041	161	8307	162	8566	146	8860	150	9058	208	9171	210	9286	174
7505	177	8042	161	8309	162	8567	146	8861	150	9059	208	9172	210	9287	210
7506	177	8045	161	8310	162	8568	146	8862	150	9060	208	9173	210	9288	210
7507	177	8050	140	8311	164	8569	146	8864	150	9061	208	9174	210	9289	210
7508	207	8051	140	8313	164	8570	146	8866	150	9062	208	9175	210	9290	230
7509	177	8054	140	8314	164	8571	146	8867	152	9063	208	9177	210	9300	218
7510	177	8055	140	8350	144	8572	148	8868	152	9064	208	9178	210	9301	186
7511	177	8056	140	8351	144	8573	148	8869	152	9065	208	9179	210	9302	218
7515	177	8067	140	8352	144	8575	148	8870	152	9066	208	9180	210	9304	218
7517	177	8059	140	8353	144	8576	148	8871	152	9067	208	9181	210	9304	174
7518	177	8060	140	8354	144	8600	164	8872	152	9068	208	9182	210	9305	186
7600	208	8061	140	8355	144	8601	164	8873	152	9069	208	9183	210	9306	174
7601	177	8062	140	8356	144	8602	164	8900	164	9070	208	9184	210	9306	226
7602	178	8063	140	8357	144	8603	164	8902	164	9071	208	9185	210	9307	230
7603	178	8064	140	8358	144	8650	148	8903	164	9073	208	9186	210	9308	186
7604	178	8065	140	8359	144	8651	148	8904	164	9075	208	9187	210	9309	210
7605	178	8066	140	8360	144	8653	148	8905	164	9076	208	9188	210	9310	218
7606	178	8067	140	8361	144	8654	148	8950	152	9077	208	9189	215	9311	174
7606	208	8068	140	8362	144	8655	148	8953	152	9078	208	9193	217	9311	219
7607	178	8071	140	8363	144	8656	148	8955	152	9079	172	9195	168	9312	219
7608	178	8072	140	8364	144	8657	148	8956	152	9079	208	9200	182	9313	215
7609	180	8100	161	8365	144	8658	148	8957	152	9080	208	9201	182	9315	230
7610	180	8101	161	8366	144	8659	148	8958	152	9085	208	9202	182	9316	210
7611	180	8102	161	8367	144	8660	148	8960	152	9090	182	9203	182	9317	210
7612	180	8104	161	8368	144	8661	148	8961	152	9110	172	9204	182	9319	186
7613	180	8111	140	8369	144	8664	148	8962	152	9111	172	9205	183	9320	186
7700	180	8140	162	8370	144	8665	148	8970	152	9112	172	9206	183	9321	217
7701	180	8141	162	8371	144	8666	148	8971	152	9113	172	9207A	183	9322	174
7702	180	8142	162	8372	144	8667	148	9010	172	9114	172	9207B	183	9323	210
7703	180	8150	140	8374	144	8668	148	9011	172	9115	172	9208	183	9324	217
7704	180	8151	140	8375	144	8669	148	9012	172	9116	172	9209	183	9325	226
7705	180	8152	140	8376	144	8670	148	9013	172	9117	172	9210	183	9326	210
7706	180	8153	140	8377	144	8701	164	9014	226	9118	172	9211	183	9327	217
7708	180	8154	140	8379	146	8402	164	9015	172	9119	172	9212	183	9328	210
7709	180	8155	140	8380	146	8703	164	9016	172	9120	226	9213	183	9329	219
7710	180	8156	141	8406	164	8750	148	9017	230	9121	226	9214	183	9330	174
7711	180	8157	141	8452	146	8751	148	9018	172	9122	226	9215	183	9331	217
7712	180	8158	141	8453	146	8753	148	9019	226	9130	172	9216	225	9332	219
7800	180	8159	141	8454	146	8754	148	9020	226	9131	230	9217	183	9333	174
7801	180	8160	141	8455	146	8755	148	9021	208	9134	172	9218	183	9333	228
7802	180	8161	141	8460	146	8756	148	9022	226	9135	174	9219	186	9334	217
7803	180	8162	141	8463	146	8757	148	9023	226	9136	230	9220	186	9336	230
7806	180	8163	141	8464	146	8758	148	9024	226	9138	215	9221	186	9339	186
7807	180	8164	141	8465	146	8759	148	9025	208	9139	225	9222	226	9340	230
7808	180	8190	168	8466	146	8760	148	9025	226	9140	230	9230	186	9341	210
7809	180	8200	162	8467	146	8761	148	9026	226	9141	230	9231	210	9344	217
7810	180	8203	162	8468	146	8762	148	9027	208	9142	230	9232	226	9346	210
7811	182	8206	162	8469	146	8763	148	9028	172	9143	230	9234	226	9347	217
7812-1977	182	8209	162	8470	146	8764	148	9030	230	9144	230	9250	215	9348	219
7813	182	8210	162	8471	146	8765	148	9031	230	9145	225	9259X	210	9349	186
7814	182	8212	162	8473	146	8766	150	9032	230	9146	217	9260	174	9351	225
7815	182	8213	162	8474	146	8767	150	9033	230	9147	215	9261	174	9352	228
7900	182	8214	162	8475	146	8768	150	9034	172	9148	215	9262	174	9353	217
7901	182	8250	141	8477	146	8770	150	9035	182	9149	226	9264	174	9354	217
7902	182	8252	141	8500	164	8771	150	9036	215	9150	215	9266	174	9355	213
7903	182	8253	141	8502	164	8772	150	9037	182	9151	215	9267	174	9357	213
7904	182	8254	141	8506	164	8773	150	9038	172	9152	215	9268	210	9358	174
7909	182	8255	141	8510	164	8774	150	9039	215	9153	215	9269	210	9359	186
8001	161	8258	141	8550	164	8775	150	9040	182	9154	215	9270	210	9360	186
8002	161	8260	141	8551	146	8776	150	9041	182	9155	215	9271	210	9361	186
8003	161	8261	141	8552	146	8777	150	9042	182	9156	215	9272	210	9362	186
8004	161	8262	141	8553	146	8778	150	9043	182	9157	218	9273	210	9365	186
8005	161	8263	141	8554	146	8779	150	9044	182	9158	226	9274	210	9366	174
8006	161	8264	144	8555	146	8800	164	9045	182	9159	215	9275	210	9367	217
8007	161	8265	144	8556	146	8801	164	9046	182	9160	208	9276	174	9368	213

ITEM	PAGE	ITEM	PAGE	ITEM	PAGE	ITEM	PAGE	ITEM	PAGE	ITEM	PAGE
9369	217	9464	187	9579	223	9721	193	9809	200	OC-51	68
9370	231	9465	187	9580	223	9722	193	9811	200	OS	68
9371	174	9466	187	9581	223	9723	193	9812	200	RW	68
9373	213	9468	187	9582	223	9724	193	9812	200	SP	68
9373	217	9500	220	9583	223	9725	193	9813	200	SW	68
9374	174	9501	220	9584	223	9726	193	9814	200	TW	68
9376	186	9502	220	9585	223	9727	193	9816	200	VW	68
9379	231	9503	220	9588	223	9728	193	9817	200	ZW	68
9380	213	9504	220	9589	223	9729	193	9818	200		
9381	213	9505	220	9590	223	9730	193	9819	200		
9382	213	9506	220	9591	223	9731	193	9820	231		
9383	228	9507	220	9592	223	9732	193	9821	231		
9384	174	9508	220	9593	223	9734	193	9822	231		
9385	231	9509	220	9594	223	9735	193	9823	228		
9386	217	9510	220	9595	223	9737	193	9824	231		
9387	213	9511	220	9596	223	9738	193	9825	201		
9388	186	9512	220	9598	223	9739	193	9826	201		
9389	228	9513	220	9600	187	9740	196	9827	201		
9398	219	9514	220	9601	190	9741	196	9829	201		
9400	186	9515	220	9602	190	9742	196	9830	201		
9401	186	9516	220	9603	190	9743	196	9831	201		
9402	186	9517	220	9604	190	9744	196	9832	201		
9403	186	9518	220	9605	190	9745	196	9833	201		
9404	186	9519	220	9606	190	9746	196	9834	201		
9405	186	9520	220	9607	190	9747	196	9835	201		
9406	186	9521	220	9608	190	9745	196	9836	201		
9407	186	9522	220	9610	190	9747	196	9837	201		
9408	186	9523	222	9611	190	9748	196	9849	201		
9411	186	9524	222	9620	190	9749	196	9850	201		
9412	186	9525	222	9621	190	9750	196	9851	201		
9413	186	9526	222	9622	190	9751	197	9852	201		
9414	186	9527	222	9623	190	9752	197	9853	201		
9415	186	9528	222	9624	190	9753	197	9854	201		
9416	186	9529	222	9625	190	9754	197	9855	201		
9417	186	9530	222	9626	190	9755	197	9856	201		
9418	186	9531	222	9627	190	9757	197	9858	201		
9419	186	9532	222	9628	190	9758	197	9859	201		
9420	186	9533	222	9629	190	9759	197	9860	201		
9421	186	9534	222	9660	190	9760	197	9861	201		
9422	186	9535	222	9661	190	9761	197	9862	201		
9423	187	9536	222	9662	190	9762	197	9863	201		
9424	187	9537	222	9663	190	9763	197	9864	201		
9425	187	9538	222	9664	190	9764	197	9866	201		
9426	187	9539	222	9665	190	9765	197	9867	203		
9427	187	9540	222	9666	190	9766	197	9869	203		
9428	187	9541	222	9667	190	9767	197	9870	203		
9429	187	9544	222	9668	190	9768	197	9871	203		
9430	187	9551	222	9669	190	9769	197	9872	203		
9431	187	9552	222	9670	190	9770	197	9873	203		
9432	187	9553	228	9671	190	9771	197	9874	203		
9433	187	9554	223	9672	190	9772	197	9875	203		
9434	187	9555	223	9678	190	9773	197	9876	203		
9436	187	9556	223	9700	190	9774	200	9877	203		
9437	187	9557	223	9700-1976	190	9775	200	9878	203		
9438	187	9558	223	9701	190	9776	200	9879	203		
9439	187	9559	223	9702	191	9777	200	9880	203		
9440	187	9560	223	9703	191	9778	200	9881	203		
9441	187	9561	223	9704	191	9779	200	9882	203		
9442	187	9562	223	9705	191	9780	200	9883	203		
9443	187	9563	223	9706	191	9781	200	9884	203		
9444	187	9564	223	9707	191	9782	200	9885	203		
9445	187	9565	223	9708	191	9783	200	9886	203		
9447	187	9566	223	9709	191	9784	200	9887	203		
9448	187	9567	223	9710	191	9785	200	9888	203		
9449	187	9569	223	9711	191	9786	200				
9450	187	9570	223	9712	191	9787	200	A	68		
9451	187	9571	223	9713	191	9788	200	Q	68		
9452	187	9572	223	9714	191	9789	200	R	68		
9453	187	9573	223	9715	193	9801	200	V	68		
9454	187	9574	223	9716	193	9802	200	Z	68		
9455	187	9575	223	9717	193	9803	200	JC-1	171		
9461	187	9576	223	9718	193	9805	200	KW	68		
9462	187	9577	223	9719	193	9807	200	OC	68		
9463	187	9578	223	9720	193	9808	200	OC-18	68		